SURVEY
OF
SOCIAL
SCIENCE

SURVEY
OF
SOCIAL
SCIENCE

SOCIOLOGY SERIES

Volume 2
443-902

Culture and Technology—Homelessness

Edited by
FRANK N. MAGILL

Consulting Editor

HÉCTOR L. DELGADO
UNIVERSITY OF ARIZONA

SALEM PRESS

Pasadena, California   Englewood Cliffs, New Jersey

∞ The paper used in these volumes conforms to the
American National Standard for Permanence of Paper for
Printed Library Materials, Z39.48-1984.

Library of Congress Cataloging-in-Publication Data
Survey of social science. Sociology series / [edited by]
Frank N. Magill; consulting editor, Héctor L. Delgado.
    v. cm.
    Includes bibliographical references and index.
    1. Sociology—Encyclopedias.   I. Magill, Frank
Northen, 1907-   . II. Delgado, Héctor L., 1949-   .
HM17.S86   1994   94-31770
301'.03—dc20   CIP
ISBN 0-89356-739-6 (set)
ISBN 0-89356-741-8 (volume 2)

PRINTED IN THE UNITED STATES OF AMERICA

CONTENTS

SOCIOLOGY

SURVEY
OF
SOCIAL
SCIENCE

CULTURE AND TECHNOLOGY

Type of sociology: Culture
Field of study: Components of culture

Technology is the use or application of organized knowledge to achieve practical solutions to problems such as turning resources into the material goods and services that a society needs. Technology, a part of material culture, is an important component of culture.

Principal terms

CONTEXTUALISM: a view of the complex relationship between science, technology, and society in which social and political forces are seen as determining the design of technology

CULTURE LAG: the difference between the rates of change in material and nonmaterial culture

INFORMATION SOCIETY: a technologically developed society in which the primary activity of a majority of the labor force involves information production, processing, and distribution

TECHNOCRACY: the predominance of technological elites in the policy making process of a society

TECHNOLOGICAL DETERMINISM: a view that technology is an autonomous system not subject to human control

TECHNOPHOBIA: the fear of new technology

Overview

Culture may be defined as the complex patterns of living developed by humans and passed down through the generations. A society is composed of people who have a distinctive culture—a way of life characterized not only by norms, customs, habits, beliefs, and language but also by material artifacts. Everything that people learn is culture. Culture consists of both material and nonmaterial components. One important part of culture pertains to the various materials and objects that people learn to use for practical purposes—the culture's technology.

Sociologist William Ogburn points out that sociology's interest in technology takes two major forms. First, sociology wants to understand the conditions that produce technology and promote its uses by the society. Second, sociologists study the effects of such uses on the society.

Ogburn explains that new inventions, when made available to consumers, not only change their habits and customs directly but also produce a chain of derivative effects. The invention of the automobile, for example, caused most people to ride in automobiles rather than in horse-drawn vehicles or railway cars. The change in people's traveling habits caused a reduction in the number of railway workers and horse-buggy makers. These were the first derivative effects. The loss of railroad passengers led to a series of secondary derivative effects, such as the reorganization of railroads, modernization of equipment, and abandonment of short-haul tracks. The impact of invention continues through a chain of derivatives. For example, a diminished demand for horses led to the planting of more wheat and corn, producing more food for humans. The automobile also freed young men and women from direct parental observation by making it possible for them to work at great distances from their homes, and it transformed the traditional family by undermining the authority of the father.

Ogburn suggested that the rate of invention in a society is a function of the size of the existing culture base. He also believed that material and nonmaterial culture change in different ways. While change in material culture may be judged by consensual standards of efficiency and utility, nonmaterial culture does not lend itself to such objective evaluation. For example, a new model of airplane can be judged by such standards as its ability to fly higher and faster and to carry more payload at a lower cost, but a painting by an artist or a form of government cannot be judged by objective standards.

Ogburn also believes that material culture tends to change faster than nonmaterial culture. While technology changed at a breathtaking pace during the twentieth century, the changes and adjustments necessary in government, the economy, education, and religion in order to keep pace with the technology have been much slower in coming. Ogburn labels this difference in rates of change in material and nonmaterial culture "culture lag."

Some sociologists do not agree with Ogburn and reject the premise that change in material culture comes before change in nonmaterial culture. They contend that technology stems from the existing knowledge base of the society and that knowledge and science belong to the realm of nonmaterial culture. Hence, the relationship between the two is reciprocal. Some also point to the fact that historically there have been many instances where change in the material culture has been resisted by entrenched interests, while rapid change has occurred in nonmaterial culture.

Scholars of technology fall into different categories because of the relative emphasis they place on either the positive or negative qualities of technology. Some also emphasize the deterministic nature of technology. For example, many optimistic scholars, such as Melvin Kranzburg, a historian of technology, believe that technology-based modern, urban-industrial societies offer vastly more freedom than traditional rural societies; they offer greater choice of occupations, lifestyles, friends, and activities. Technology has cut the work week in half and has satisfied many basic human wants and needs.

Others point out that technology offers a mixed bag of benefits and risks and argue that the task of technologists and policymakers is to manage the risks. Just as some technologies poison the environment, others reduce pollution; some displace workers, but others create jobs that provide outlets for more creativity; some have undesirable consequences, but these often can be solved through other technologies.

Optimistic views of technology are often subjected to criticism as being unrealistic, naïve, and romantic. Ian Barbour, in his *Ethics in an Age of Technology* (1993), summarizes the critical arguments. The optimists, critics say, do not pay adequate attention to environmental costs and human risks; even when pollution control technologies are used to alleviate the problems of industrial pollution, they often fail to address the unexpected, delayed, or indirect consequences of certain agents such as carcinogens that may not appear for decades. Many examples exist of dangerous consequences that were either not anticipated or ignored at the time of the development and use of new technologies. Increased death rates among workers exposed to asbestos, toxic wastes contaminating ground water long after disposal, the hole in the ozone layer caused by release of chlorofluorocarbons (CFCs), massive deforestation, soil erosion, and global warming caused by the use of fossil fuels provide a few dramatic examples of society's lapses in risk assessment.

Other arguments focus on the multifaceted problems of technology use ranging from alienation from nature and loss of delicate ecological balance to the concentration of economic and political power in a few hands and among a few nations. Wealthy nations use a disproportionate share of the world's wealth and resources. Their high level of consumption is not sustainable in the long run even for these few nations, let alone the prospects for the poor nations tempted to imitate the consumption behavior of the affluent. Moreover, the elite in poor nations often develop the same consumption habits as those in the developed nations, exacerbating the problems of inequality in income and unsustainable consumption patterns.

Other problems include large-scale technologies that give rise to capital-intensive production practices as opposed to labor-intensive strategies. This poses particular problems in areas afflicted by a high unemployment rate. Large-scale systems also tend to be vulnerable to error, accident, and sabotage. The Three-Mile Island nuclear accident (1979) and the Chernobyl nuclear disaster (1986) provide two examples of the disastrous consequences of the breakdown of a large-scale system.

Technology also tends to create technocracy—rule by technocrats or technological elites. Harvard University economist John Kenneth Galbraith, in his book *The Industrial State* (1967), explains the rise of technocracy in modern Western society, often referred to as the postindustrial or information society. Galbraith argued that during the agrarian age, landowners controlled the economy; in the industrial age, the capitalists controlled the economy. During the postindustrial age, however, technical experts (managers and technicians), rather than owners of corporations, control the economy. This change has important implications for society's system of social stratification. The demands of modern technology require a corporation to perform sophisticated and complex planning tasks, a job possible only if technical experts control the management of a corporation.

Those who see technology as a threat to human fulfillment emphasize certain characteristics of technology. For example, they suggest that modern technology causes not only excessive standardization of products but also uniformity and homogeneity of culture because of the obliteration of regional and individual differences. In order to achieve certain narrowly defined criteria of efficiency, too much emphasis is placed on specialization, fragmentation, rational organization, and quantitative goals rather than human needs and desires. In a technological system, humans become cogs in a machine, and work often leads to dehumanization and a sense of meaninglessness and powerlessness among workers.

In summary, some scholars adopt a linear view of technology which suggests that science leads to the development of technology that is useful and beneficial to the consumer. The needs, demands, and preference of the consumer in the marketplace cause the adoption of the technology, based on rational criteria. Others adopt a view that has come to be known as technological determinism. There are different notions of the degrees and types of determinism, but essentially this viewpoint sees technology as an autonomous system with its own logic that is not subject to human control. In other words, humans create tools, but tools ultimately control the humans. A third view, labeled contextualism, recognizes a complex relationship among science, technology, and society. In this view, social and political forces influence and determine the design of technology and the ways it is put to use. Technologies are not neutral because they are intimately connected with social goals.

Applications

Technology is fundamental to the survival of humankind. In common usage, the term "technology" usually denotes nineteenth and twentieth century developments such as railroads, airplanes, television, computer systems, and advanced medical technology. To a sociologist, however, technology refers to that part of any culture that centers on the practical use of knowledge. Technology utilizes innovative methods, tools, and skills to improve human productivity and biological potential and simply to make life easier. Humans have been making tools—first of stone, then of metal— since prehistoric times.

From a technological standpoint, human history may be divided into three time periods: the agricultural age (from about 8000 B.C.E. to 1750 C.E.) the industrial age (1750 to 1950), and the information (or postindustrial) age, beginning about 1950. It should be noted that these time ranges refer to developed countries such as the United States, Japan, and many European countries; there are societies elsewhere that are still essentially agricultural or industrial. During the agricultural age, people engaged in farming, growing food, and using muscle power to do jobs such as pumping water and plowing fields. During the industrial age, people used machines to replace muscle power; many worked in factories powered by steam and electricity. The current age has been called the information age because a majority of workers are employed in information-related activities rather than in industrial production.

How the specific needs of people in different cultures have been satisfied has varied, depending on the level of technology available, the form of societal organization, and the prevailing cultural values. The facts that technology has evolved and that the human race has thrived imply that technology has managed to satisfy basic human needs for food, shelter, clothing, defense, transportation, communication, and health.

Material culture grows in two ways: through invention of new traits within a culture or through diffusion of new traits from outside the culture. Both historical records and prehistoric findings indicate that the rate of technological change was quite slow in the beginning but has moved at an increasingly rapid rate. It took a million years to go from using stone tools to using bronze, for example, but only about five thousand years to move from bronze tools to machines. During the 1700's, inventions occurred more rapidly. Many of these inventions were various types of machines run by steam engines. This mechanization led to the Industrial Revolution, in which steam power completely changed methods of producing and transporting goods. The invention of the telegraph and telephone made long-distance communication quick and easy. The inventions and technological developments during the Industrial Revolution laid the foundations for the modern age, in which technological changes are taking place at an exponential rate; changes are occurring so fast that many people have barely enough time to master a technology before it becomes obsolete. The need to use increasingly sophisticated technology, combined with the fear of it, has given currency to such terms as "technophobia"and "technostress" in modern information societies.

Context

The concept of culture emphasizes social heritage as distinct from biological inheritance. Technology, as a part of social heritage, is an important component of culture. Social scientists have offered many definitions of culture, but a few basic ideas are common to these definitions.

Culture is symbolic. Material objects do not have meanings other than those meanings assigned to them by humans. One theory holds that culture lies in the symbolic meaning of objects. Some social scientists see technology as the determinant cause of social change. The study of culture, therefore, must include study of technological advancement. Culture is also transmissible. In the contemporary world, technology is transferred fairly easily from one culture to another because of the extensive communication systems available. Since the global system is composed of interdependent national systems, there is a need for the sharing of finite resources and the transfer of technology. Another trait of culture is that it is learned. An individual's attitude toward technology depends on the prevailing attitudes in the broader social environment, consisting of the educational system, the media, the religious institutions, and the political and economic systems. The concept of cultural lag, however, suggests that human beings are slow to respond intellectually to changes in their physical world. Culture not only reflects but also conditions the physical aspect of human existence. Just as technology causes social change, technological change presupposes cultural acceptance. Because technology itself is an important part of culture, it influences other components.

The implications of the accelerating pace of technology for a culture and how it changes the society and culture have been a subject of discussion and debate among social scientists for decades. Technological advance has been much greater in the past hundred years than in the previous two thousand or more. Each technological advance changes a society. Just as a new technology provides a culture with new capabilities and new opportunities, it also makes certain conventional values, lifestyles, and production techniques obsolete. Traditional social institutions that provide stability in family life, religious attitudes, educational programs, and recreation activities have all been affected by technology. Traditionally, a family—regarded as a fundamental unit of society—served not only as an agent of protection of its members and socialization of its children but also as a producer of goods. In the past, a family worked together to create the economic, moral, and religious cohesion that a society needed for its stability and order. Technology and industrialization eroded the traditional family structure both by separating work from the residence and by causing economic diversification within the family.

Various labor-saving devices in the home freed women to seek employment and recreation outside, thereby freeing them from economic dependence on men and causing a major readjustment of relations within the family. The technology of contraception, by separating sex from procreation, has changed a basic and traditional function of the family, the ordering of sexual relations. This has had profound implications for family structures, traditional norms of morality, and gender relations in society. The family structure now serves primarily as a consumer rather than a producer of goods, and it is based on a notion of companionship rather than on the recognition of the patriarchal rule-making role of the father. Social scientists have been concerned with these kinds of issues as well as with related issues such as the impact of technology on politics, religion, and education.

Bibliography

Allen, Francis, et al. *Technology and Social Change*. New York: Appleton-Century-Crofts, 1957. This is an important book, though it is somewhat dated. The authors provide an excellent, authoritative discussion on the impact of science and technology on society.

Barbour, Ian. *Ethics in an Age of Technology*. New York: HarperCollins, 1993. Barbour examines the prevailing views on technology and analyzes important social values, such as justice, participatory freedom, and economic development. An insightful book on technology and values.

Ellul, Jacques. *The Technological Bluff*. Translated by Geoffrey W. Bramily. Grand Rapids, Mich.: W. B. Eerdmans, 1990. A French philosopher and social thinker, Ellul is a major conceptualist of technology and what it really means in the modern world. Other influential books by Ellul include *The Technological Society* (1964) and *Technological System* (1977).

Hacker, Michael, and Robert Barden. *Technology in Your World*. 2d ed. Albany, N.Y.: Delmar, 1992. The authors explain, in simple terms, what technology is and discuss various technological processes related to communication, manufacturing, construction, biotechnology, and transportation systems. A basic book that introduces students to the study of technology.

Markert, Linda Rae. *Contemporary Technology: Innovations, Issues, and Perspectives*. South Holland, Ill.: Goodheart-Willcox, 1989. The author introduces college students to the pervasive nature of technological innovations. She discusses developments and breakthroughs in various disciplines, such as genetic engineering and artificial intelligence. She also addresses sociological viewpoints regarding such issues as the effective use of technology and the stability of social institutions.

Mesthene, Emmanuel. *Technological Change: Its Impact on Man and Society*. Cambridge, Mass.: Harvard University Press, 1970. This book presents studies conducted at the Harvard University Program on Technology and Society. Mesthene discusses, among other things, how technological change impinges on society and how technology leads to value change. He also examines the impact of technology on economic and political organization.

Pytlik, Edward, Donald Lunda, and David Johnson. *Technology, Change, and Society*. Rev. ed. Worcester, Mass.: Davis, 1985. The authors discuss the human meaning of social and technological change. They cover a wide variety of subjects ranging from changes in the family brought about by technology to futurology. They also provide case studies of societies at various levels of technological development.

Mazharul Haque

Cross-References

Culture: Material and Expressive Culture, 430; Culture and Language, 436; High Culture versus Popular Culture, 870; Leisure, 1075; Social Change: Sources of Change, 1786; Technology and Social Change, 2043.

DAY CARE AND THE FAMILY

Type of sociology: Major social institutions
Field of study: The family

Day care, the care provided for young children while parents are working, has become an integral part of life for millions of American families. Ensuring quality care and determining the effects of day care on children are among the major concerns of parents and of people within the child care community.

Principal terms
ADULT-CENTERED CARE: day care that is based on what is best (sometimes simply what is easiest) for the adults providing the care
CHILD-CENTERED CARE: day care that is centered on what is best for the children whose care is being provided
CUSTODIAL CARE: child care that emphasizes attention to primary care needs such as safety and food and excludes or minimizes educational activities
DEVELOPMENTALLY APPROPRIATE: refers to goals, activities, and equipment that meet the intellectual, social, and emotional levels of each child in a center or facility
HEAD START: a federally funded program that provides advantages such as day care and preschool instruction to disadvantaged children

Overview

Day care is an umbrella term used to describe nonparental care during the day for children too young to provide for their own primary needs and safety. When day care for children becomes necessary, a family has two main choices: in-own-home care or out-of-the-home care. As is implied in the name, in in-own-home care, someone comes into the home to stay with the children. A distinction can be drawn between in-own-home day care and babysitting in that day care is provided for the time the parents are at work, whereas babysitting applies to the times parents are engaged in other activities, such as shopping or entertainment.

In-own-home care is the most favored choice, especially by parents of infants; however, the use of in-own-home care is shrinking. In 1991, 28 percent of children receiving care were cared for in their own homes, compared with approximately 70 percent in 1965. The providers of in-own-home care may be relatives or nonrelatives. Care provided by a relative is preferred by the parents of infants.

Out-of-the-home care includes family day care homes and day care centers. Family day care homes provide care in the caregiver's home. The provider of care in a family day care home may care for her (or his, although most day care workers are women) own children plus four to five other children. In some states, family day care homes are regulated by state licensing procedures, and the number of children other than relatives that can be cared for is limited.

Advantages of family day care include the smaller number of children being given care, more individual attention, and a more open and direct relationship between parent and caregiver. In addition, family day care is more likely to be conveniently located and is usually more economical. There are also disadvantages to family day care. While some family day care providers are specially educated and trained, most are not; also, the atmosphere is more likely to be adult centered, accountability is minimal, and arrangements may be tenuous. More family day care providers, especially those not involved with a training network, identify their purpose as custodial care, and any instruction given the child is informal and may take place while the caregiver is performing primary care functions. Family day care homes are the first out-of-the-home care choice of families with infants and toddlers. The supply of family day care homes, including regulated ones, appears to be growing with the need.

Day care centers are a group approach to child care. They vary in sponsorship or ownership, clientele, location and facilities, and program emphasis. Both nonprofit and for-profit centers exist in the United States. There is day care sponsored by nonprofit organizations; these are usually church-sponsored and community-sponsored centers. Government centers such as the Head Start centers and research centers found at universities with child development studies are also included in the nonprofit group. Day care centers operated by for-profit organizations include chain and independent centers and centers located on or near the premises of a large corporation to provide a service for the company's employees.

Day care centers do not all serve the same clientele. Some day care centers cater to a specific age group—for example, restricting enrollment to infants or to pre-schoolers—while other centers are designed to care for more than one age group and include after-school care for school-age children. In addition, location and facilities of centers vary depending on the resources of the sponsor. The types of facilities range from centers in old church basements to facilities in modern corporate buildings.

Program emphasis also differs according to the underlying philosophy of the center. Some centers exist for custodial purposes only; they provide for the primary care and entertainment needs of the children and give minimal attention to guiding children toward developmentally appropriate activities. Conversely, other centers believe that they should care for the children plus provide programs that will enrich each child's experiences at his or her own level.

Sharon L. Kagan of Yale University, in a 1991 study, describes differences in the two types of centers. Nonprofit centers typically have fewer staff members per number of children than for-profit centers do. Yet she reports that quality was generally found to be higher at nonprofit centers. These two characteristics are related to the finances of the centers. Nonprofit centers are often subsidized by the sponsoring organization (a church, synagogue, or United Way agency, for example), thus allowing them to have lower tuition fees. On the other hand, for-profit centers, while they may accept children who receive federal help, must meet all expenses—including the maintaining of quality—from the profits generated by the consumers of their day care.

Kagan suggests that day care in the United States is heading toward an economically segregated child care system. Children from low socioeconomic backgrounds (who are likely to be in government-subsidized programs) and children from very high socioeconomic environments (whose parents can afford the best for-profit care available) are receiving the highest quality care. Children from the middle socioeconomic strata are most often found in the for-profit centers of lower quality, thus receiving poorer care.

Day care centers have advantages and disadvantages. Their continued presence and availability is a strong advantage; in addition, they are more likely than day care homes to have child-centered environments. The staff is more likely to be trained, and the physical facilities and equipment are generally better than those of family day care homes. On the other hand, center care may be inconveniently located, is typically less flexible concerning arrival and departure times, does not provide special care for the ill child, and usually is more expensive.

According to child development specialist Edward F. Zigler and family policy issues consultant Mary E. Lang in their book *Child Care Choices: Balancing the Needs of Children, Families, and Society* (1991), use of a day care center is the most popular form of child care for children ages three to five. Centers are favored primarily for the educational experiences they can provide.

Applications

Approximately 20 percent of American mothers spend their days as full-time homemakers and mothers, with the remaining mothers working full- or part-time. Three out of four mothers with children of the age to need day care are in the workforce. Moreover, a significant number of single fathers are in the labor force. Day care, therefore, is a reality for millions of American children. The quality of the care received by their children is a major parental concern. All parents want their children to have the highest quality care possible, but the quality of care varies widely. Most states regulate child care through a licensing program that is intended to establish minimum quality standards for care.

Quality standards, as defined by child care professionals, usually address health and safety; physical space; materials, equipment, and activities; care providers, including their education, experience, and stability; and amount of parent-teacher interaction. The standards for health and safety include guidelines for medicine, what to do with ill children, accidents, fire drills, and cleanliness of the facilities, caregivers, and children. These standards also address nutrition and food supply for the children.

Children of all ages are affected by their physical environment. Ideally, child care facilities should provide outside play areas as well as indoor environments. Additionally, the psychological aspects of the center are tremendously important. Child care consultant Jim Greenman notes that one can determine whether a center has a positive environment by asking oneself certain questions: "How does it feel to live and work here all day, day after day?, What do we do here?, and What should we accomplish?"

Materials and equipment should be in good repair, and the supply should be large enough to encourage individual and group play. Toys should be kept clean and germ-free. Activities in higher quality centers are based on sound curriculum planning. When materials, equipment, and activities are sufficient and developmentally appropriate, the center is contributing to a high level of care.

The importance of the education, training, and experience of the caregivers has been proved in repeated studies. Linda J. Waite, Arleen Leibowitz, and Christina Witsberger of the RAND Corporation summarized research on day care in 1991. They report that when a caregiver is trained, benefits to the children include an increase in children's verbal interaction, less restriction on children's activities, less punishment, and safer environments.

In addition to education, previous experience working with children is beneficial. Child care specialist Alison Clarke-Stewart notes that providers with fewer than two or three years of experience are more likely to "go along" with the children rather than initiating new activities; conversely, caregivers with considerable experience appear to become more adult centered or more controlling, strict, and less stimulating.

Another quality characteristic related to staff is the length of time a caregiver remains on the job. Experts agree that consistency in caregivers is important to children. Clarke-Stewart reports that a high turnover of staff is related to an overall rating of poorer quality. The converse of this is not necessarily true, however; that is, one cannot assume that because caregivers have been at one center for an extended period, they are providing a high quality of care. Stability of child care workers allows children a chance to develop secure relationships. Moreover, it is an indication of the center's respect for its staff. The reality, however, is that there is high turnover among child care staff. One study concluded that 41 percent of child care workers quit during any given year. A major cause of the high turnover is the low wages paid to child care workers. The amount of interaction that occurs between parent and caregiver is also a contributing factor to the high quality of care.

Context

The need for day care is the result of a number of societal factors. The Industrial Revolution of the eighteenth and nineteenth centuries took people out of their homes and away from their villages and farms to work in urban factories. Some form of child care outside the home, in fact, has existed from the 1800's; the first day care "nurseries" were directly related to the employment of women in urban areas. The dramatic increase in day care after the 1970's had to do with societal changes that produced an increase of women in the workforce. The women's movement was a driving force in urging women to pursue careers, and economic pressures pushed women into the workforce as it became harder for families to meet their needs on one person's paycheck. Moreover, as the divorce rate grew, increasing numbers of single parents, both mothers and fathers, needed to work full-time and provide care for their children.

Research on child care is a relatively new phenomenon, but many aspects of it have been examined. Because American society has traditionally assumed that care provided by parents is superior to other forms of care, the effects of a child's spending many hours away from home is one such aspect. Alison Clarke-Stewart compared her own and others' research on day care and child development in a 1991 article. She reports that care in centers has a positive effect on social skills, resulting in children who are more self-confident, independent, and cooperative with adults and peers. When they enter school, they are more likely to be goal-oriented and to exhibit leadership qualities. Differences in intellectual development were also observed. Clarke-Stewart notes that these differences are not long-lasting, however, lasting for approximately two years.

There is also evidence to the contrary, some of it centering on the amount of time an infant spends away from the mother. One study found that infants with more than twenty hours of nonmaternal care per week exhibit less secure attachments to the mother and have a higher chance of displaying emotional or disciplinary problems in later childhood.

Clarke-Stewart notes some pitfalls concerning research on day care. First, one cannot assume that day care centers studied accurately represent a large number of centers. Second, it is difficult to control studies in this area, so it is nearly impossible to prove cause and effect relationships between day care and behavior. Third, the instruments used to assess children's characteristics are imprecise.

Bibliography

Berry, Mary Frances. *The Politics of Parenthood: Child Care, Women's Rights, and the Myth of the Good Mother*. New York: Viking Press, 1993. Provides comprehensive information on the history of parenthood and covers social and political issues related to the care of children. An index is included.

Clarke-Stewart, Alison. *Daycare*. Rev. ed. Cambridge, Mass.: Harvard University Press, 1993. A major work that synthesizes a broad range of research available on child care. A suggested reading list and an index are included.

Greenman, Jim. *Caring Spaces, Learning Places: Children's Environments that Work*. Redmond, Wash.: Child Care Information Exchange, 1988. Practical approach to managing the environments of child care for optimum utility and benefit to the children. Poetry and photographs are interspersed within the text.

Kagan, Sharon L. "Examining Profit and Nonprofit Child Care: An Odyssey of Quality and the Auspices." *Journal of Social Issues* 47, no. 2 (1991): 87-104. A literature review and synthesis of research available that compares characteristics of quality in profit and nonprofit child care.

Lusk, Diane, and Bruce McPherson. *Nothing but the Best: Making Day Care Work for You and Your Child*. New York: Quill, 1992. A practical layperson's guide to using child day care on a regular basis. A day care information and referral list and index are included.

Waite, Linda J., Arleen Leibowitz, and Christina Witsberger. "What Parents Pay For: Child Care Characteristics, Quality, and Costs." *Journal of Social Issues* 47, no. 2 (1991): 33-48. Original research on what constitutes quality care, including findings on the value of training for day care workers.

Wingert, Pat, and Barbara Kantrowitz. "The Day Care Generation." In *Annual Editions: Human Development*, edited by Larry Fenson and Judith Fenson. Guilford, Conn.: Dushkin, 1993. This article was originally published in a special edition of *Newsweek*. It looks at the debate over the long-term effects of day care and includes a checklist of questions to ask when searching for child care.

Zigler, Edward F., and Mary E. Lang. *Child Care Choices: Balancing the Needs of Children, Families, and Society*. New York: Free Press, 1991. A detailed and comprehensive description and analysis of day care. Zigler and Lang view child care from a systems perspective. Author and subject indexes are included.

Diane Teel Miller

Cross-References

DECRIMINALIZATION

Type of sociology: Deviance and social control
Fields of study: Controlling deviance; Social implications of deviance

Decriminalization refers to changing criminal law so that certain behaviors, particularly those behaviors to which all adult parties involved have consented, are no longer criminal. This is a controversial concept, for it is based on the idea that, with respect to these behaviors, criminal laws add to social problems and increase deviance rather than control it.

Principal terms

CONSENSUAL CRIME: illegal behavior to which all parties involved have consented; the term is preferred to "victimless crime" by some researchers

CRIMINALIZATION: the process of converting specific behaviors into criminal behaviors through the passing of criminal laws

LEGALIZATION: making legal that which was against the law; another word for decriminalization, but one that can also apply to regulatory and civil law

MORAL LEGISLATION: laws that exist to control behavior regarded as immoral even though it causes no provable injury

OVERCRIMINALIZATION: the creation of too many laws (and therefore of too many crimes) or of laws that are unjustifiable or unenforceable

PUBLIC ORDER CRIMINALITY: a widely used term for victimless criminality that also includes disorderly conduct, harassment, and trespassing

VICTIMLESS CRIME: behavior in violation of criminal law in which there is no injured party or victim in the traditional sense of one who would complain to the police if it were feasible

Overview

Criminalization refers to making an activity a crime by passing a law against it; all industrialized countries have laws that make certain activities crimes. Overcriminalization occurs when a society passes laws that are frivolous or unenforceable or passes so many laws that they become contradictory, dated, or simply frivolous. It results in what criminologists Norval Morris and Gordon Hawkins have called an "overreach of the law"—attempts to control more behavior than law could or should control. Many argue that overcriminalization is counterproductive and results in increased social problems. Decriminalization, the elimination of laws seen as unwise or unnecessary, may be viewed as the opposite of overcriminalization.

Legal philosopher Herbert L. Packer developed a seven-point theory of criminal law, taught in law schools, which argues that a situation must involve a clear and direct injury or harm, whether physical or not, for a law against it to be justified. In his 1968 book, *The Limits of the Control Sanction*, Packer listed conditions that should be considered before the law is used to try to control behavior. He maintained that when these conditions are not met in existing laws, the resulting crimes should be "decriminalized"—that is, the laws that make the behaviors legally defined crimes should be modified or dropped.

Sociologist Edwin M. Schur, in *Crimes Without Victims* (1965), claimed that there is a category of crimes in which there are no victims or injured parties, and he listed reasons for decriminalizing these crimes. In the controversy that followed, various other terms for "victimless crimes" were created, including consensual crimes, folk crimes, moral crimes, and the most ambiguous, public order crimes. The category "vice," used by law enforcement, is too narrow, but it does include most of the major activities identified with victimless crimes: drug use, gambling, homosexuality, pornography, and prostitution. Schur included abortion, which in 1965 was generally a crime, further fueling controversy over the meaning of "victimless."

Most of the arguments for decriminalization, as developed by Schur and others, are not crime-specific, something that is often overlooked by those who favor legalizing marijuana but not heroin, or who favor legalizing homosexual acts but not prostitution. It should also be clearly understood that although broad categories such as "drugs" and "prostitution" are often used for convenience, the arguments for decriminalization are not intended to apply to cases involving coercion, children (as they are too immature to consent in full knowledge of what they are doing), or obvious intrusions on other people's privacy. Thus, the decriminalization arguments do not promote legalization of child pornography or statutory rape. It cannot be assumed that because someone is for decriminalizing victimless crime they approve of the prohibited behavior; however, those in favor of the laws do tend to disapprove of the behavior strongly. Decriminalization is not a liberal versus conservative issue. Many conservatives, such as commentator William F. Buckley and economist Milton Friedman, have advocated decriminalization of drug laws. Ralph Salerno, a leading police expert on the daily workings of organized crime, has lectured on the need for decriminalization as the only way to control organized crime. Many liberals favor decriminalization of some behaviors, such as homosexual acts, but oppose decriminalization of others, such as drug use.

The arguments for decriminalization can be broken into two large categories: moral and pragmatic. The moral argument was advanced in 1859 by philosopher John Stuart Mill in *On Liberty*, in which he stated that everyone has a right to individual liberty; as long as there is no infringement on other people's liberties, no one has the right to try to force people to do (or not do) anything, no matter how wrong, immoral, dangerous, or self-destructive their behavior. This is a stance that the American Civil Liberties Union (ACLU) supports. The adherents to this moral philosophy are often identified as "libertarians." Those who oppose decriminalization, on the other hand, believe that a consensus regarding moral issues is possible and is an important aspect of society; for this reason, they are sometimes called "moralists." Lord Devlin, opposing the sentiment for decriminalization in the 1960's, stated that society cannot ignore the morality of the individual, for without it society dies. Virginia Swigert maintained in 1984 that a legally enforced morality is a necessary cost of human association. To them and many others, it is self-evident that the danger to society from legalized vice is sufficient to result in an injury to every individual; the very act of legalization constitutes a moral defeat for society. The counterargument of the libertarians is that imposing what they see as a private morality on others is itself destructive to a free society.

A number of pragmatic arguments have been put forward for decriminalization. A few of them follow. Victimless crimes are not enforceable, it is argued, for there are no complainants; moreover, there is common, widespread victimless crime behavior and a high demand for illegal services such as drugs and prostitutes. The inability to enforce these laws leads to lack of public respect for the law, which increases crime and problems with enforcement. The effort to enforce the law wastes resources in the form of money, time, and personnel. By treating people as criminals who might otherwise be law abiding, society further isolates and stigmatizes them; they then associate with other criminals, and so secondary crime is created. The difficulty in enforcing the law leads to police brutality and corruption. For example, police who enforce drug laws may take bribes from organized crime, extort money from dealers, use drugs themselves, buy and sell drugs for profit or to reward informants, and perform illegal searches and seizures. Reliance on criminal laws abridges the use of social services and civil laws that could be used to reduce some of the deviant behavior, or in the case of addiction, reduce the medical problem.

Those who are against decriminalization have generally denied the validity of these arguments. They have pointed out that most burglaries, larcenies, and robberies are not solved either but that no one says that the laws against these crimes should be abolished simply because they are hard to enforce. They argue that better enforcement and harsher penalities are needed. Despite the evidence that very little of the victimless crime that occurs results in arrests, some maintain that the laws are a deterrent and argue that without the laws there would be more victimless crime behavior. They also note that where gambling has been legalized, powerful lobbies and the states themselves have encouraged gambling through heavy advertising. The same could therefore be expected if drugs were legalized, it has been argued, for the large pharmaceutical companies already have one of the most powerful lobbies in the nation.

Applications

In the 1960's, Schur, Packer, Morris and Hawkins, criminologist Jerome Skolnick, political scientist Stanley Kadish, philosopher Herbert Bedeau, and other intellectuals debated victimless crime, thereby fueling a ragged movement toward decriminalization. Although various decriminalization arguments became well known, however, they have never been used by policy-making groups to try to decriminalize all offenses to which they apply. In crime-specific areas, proponents and decision makers often do not take into account all the decriminalization arguments and counterarguments. This inconsistency has contributed to a continuation of a confused pattern of changing law.

There are a number of factors that make decriminalization a confusing issue. One is the fact that the concept of decriminalization has been applied inconsistently from state to state and from issue to issue. Another is that the results of decriminalization (as well as of the effects of laws themselves) are difficult to measure; establishing a cause-and-effect relationship between decriminalization and an increase or decrease in behavior, for example, is problematic. The Supreme Court has also handed down decisions that have affected decriminalization in conflicting ways.

A guideline known as the Model Penal Code, developed in 1962, has been used in reforming the criminal laws in more than thirty states. It has engendered acceptance of or debate concerning its provisions for eliminating laws against adultery, fornication, lewd cohabitation, seduction, and private acts of consensual homosexualty, as well as laws that discriminate against juveniles by making promiscuity an offense (a law used to incarcerate girls, but not boys). Several high-level commissions have recommended decriminalization of various offenses, recommendations which have generally been ignored for political reasons. Several commissions have recommended the decriminalization of marijuana, for example. During the Nixon Administration, a federal commission recommended the decriminalization of pornography.

States and localities have followed policies that have taken them both toward and away from decriminalization. A number of states and municipalities have struck down laws criminalizing homosexual acts or discriminating against homosexuals. In 1992, however, Colorado voters passed an amendment to the state constitution forbidding gay rights legislation. In the 1980's and 1990's, many states legalized many forms of gambling while (frequently contradicting their own reasoning) forbidding others. Nevada allows counties to decriminalize prostitution except in Las Vegas, where illegal prostitution thrives. "Blue laws" governing the sale of alcoholic beverages remain in existence in a checkered pattern, often on the books but unenforced.

The pattern of changing laws is most confused and inconsistent in the area of drugs. In Texas in the 1970's, two men in different cases were sentenced to life imprisonment for possession of less than one cigarette's worth of marijuana. At the same time in Ann Arbor, Michigan, simple possession resulted in a five-dollar fine, payable by mail. Eleven states reduced or eliminated penalties for simple possession of marijuana, and Alaska went so far as to allow citizens to grow marijuana for their own use. The Controlled Substances Act has undergone many revisions, establishing different penalties for different drugs. From 1965 to 1990 there were sixteen major changes in federal efforts to control drug use; except for the 1966 Narcotic Addict Rehabilitation Act, they were all punitive in nature. In the 1990's, Alaska rescinded its law permitting the growing of marijuana for home use.

Although social science studies can provide certain information regarding laws and criminality, it is doubtful whether such studies can provide a basis for objective decision making regarding decriminalization. Moral arguments for and against it are not amenable to scientific appraisal. Even the pragmatic arguments do not lend themselves to the tight logic of laboratory experimentation, so the scientific evidence is piecemeal and tentative. A central question is whether decriminalization increases the behavior categorized as victimless crime. Proponents of decriminalization point out that Prohibition did not curtail drinking but did lead to widespread organized crime and corruption. Opponents note that alcohol consumption declined by 30 percent to 50 percent during Prohibition and that organized crime simply found other areas to exploit when it ended. Criminologists William Blount and Herbert Kaplan performed research investigating complaints by horse and greyhound track executives that Florida's new lottery in the 1980's was hurting their profits. They found that despite the popularity of the lottery, other legal gambling business had not declined. Moreover, the illegal lottery in Tampa remained robust. Gambling had simply increased. Opponents point out that a documented percentage of users of certain drugs and of gamblers become compulsive and irrational and argue that any increase in users will result in an increase in these "addicts" to their and society's detriment.

Context

Edwin Schur and other sociologists of deviance have considered decriminalization primarily in the context of labeling theory, in which people are singled out by society and labeled as deviant. The criminal law and the criminal justice process are powerful tools for labeling behavior and people deviant. The people subject to this labeling are, in theory, prone to seeing themselves as deviant and criminal as a result. This stigma leads to their increasingly behaving as deviants and criminals. Edwin Lemert called for "judicious nonintervention," particularly with juveniles, to try to minimize these labeling effects. Schur, in *Radical Nonintervention* (1971), built on Lemert's work and advocated decriminalization of some offenses, among other techniques for minimizing labeling effects.

Most people believe that laws are created because society as a whole is against the behavior being criminalized. This consensus model of law making is no doubt true with respect to crimes such as murder. Sociologists who are conflict theorists, however, regard the law as a product of special interest groups. This conflict model seems to be in evidence in the confused patterns of change regarding victimless crime laws.

Proponents of decriminalization paint a picture of immense social problems existing because of the victimless crime laws. Organized crime, for example, is regarded as almost entirely the product of these laws. The criminalization of a large class of people who would otherwise be ordinary citizens, some with problems for which they might otherwise be successfully treated if they wished, is seen as a disaster for them and for society. The waste of criminal justice resources is regarded as being matched only by the corruption and brutality of police that is unintentionally engendered by these laws. Statements of these problems by proponents of decriminalization may be exaggerated, but the problems themselves are nevertheless real. Provocative, if overstated, arguments on both sides of the issue have helped focus attention on a number of significant social problems.

Sociological research that might reveal whatever objective support there is for decriminalization was only initiated in the 1960's. Large-scale research in this area is badly needed. Until there is a more substantial body of objective evidence, the confusion and the controversy over the effects of decriminalization of victimless crime laws cannot be resolved.

Bibliography

Geis, Gil. *Not the Law's Business.* New York: Schocken Books, 1979. This readable and well-written book by a distinguished criminologist makes a strong case for decriminalization.

Mill, John Stuart. *On Liberty and Other Essays.* New York: Oxford University Press, 1991. Originally published in 1859, this famous essay was required reading in many college courses long before the decriminalization controversy. Mill defines the libertarians' argument.

Packer, Herbert L. *The Limits of the Control Sanction.* Stanford, Calif.: Stanford University Press, 1968. This influential work argues for using law as a control of last resort and then only if it appears workable. Packer expressly made the case for decriminalization in cases of overcriminalization.

Schur, Edwin M. *Crimes Without Victims.* Englewood Cliffs, N.J.: Prentice-Hall, 1965. This paperback is the classic work on victimless crimes and the need for decriminalization.

Schur, Edwin M., and Herbert Bedeau, eds. *Victimless Crime: Two Sides of a Controversy.* Englewood Cliffs, N.J.: Prentice-Hall, 1974. An early and thoughtful treatment of the arguments on both sides of the decriminalization controversy.

Hill Harper

Cross-References

Crime: Analysis and Overview, 373; The Criminal Justice System, 380; Deviance: Analysis and Overview, 525; Labeling and Deviance, 1049; Organized Crime, 1322; Victimless Crime, 2150.

DEINDUSTRIALIZATION IN THE UNITED STATES

Type of sociology: Major social institutions
Field of study: The economy

Once the preeminent industrial nation in the world, the United States has become part of a global economy and imports more manufactured goods than it exports. The resulting displacement of American workers from high-paying manufacturing jobs has serious consequences for families and communities but may herald the beginning of a robust, knowledge-based, service economy.

Principal terms

ALIENATION: the perception by an individual or group of holding an unacceptable position in the social structure

BUSINESS CYCLE: the general trend in free market economies for periods of growth to be followed by periods of recession, including temporary increases in unemployment

CAPITAL MOBILITY: the ability of investors to recover funds invested in one enterprise and reinvest them freely in another

CYCLIC UNEMPLOYMENT: temporary unemployment caused by recession, with many workers expecting eventual reemployment in the same location and industry

DEINDUSTRIALIZATION: the closing of industrial facilities in one country or region as a result of the movement of capital to other countries or regions, or to nonindustrial investments

DISPLACEMENT: loss of employment caused by the disappearance of jobs of one type, possibly compensated by job creation in another sector of the economy

SOCIAL INTEGRATION: the extent to which the members of a society identify with that society, share its values, and accept its structure

STRUCTURAL UNEMPLOYMENT: unemployment caused by a change in structure of the economy, with most workers not expecting eventual reemployment in the same location and industry

Overview

The economy of the United States has undergone several major transitions throughout its history. Initially an agrarian nation, the United States became an increasingly industrialized one as agricultural productivity increased through mechanization and improved crop management, freeing workers for industrial production, while vast resources of hydroelectric, coal, and oil power fueled a rapidly growing industrial base. World War II marked a major turning point in the American economy. Under wartime pressures, agricultural production increased by several times, while automation was introduced on a large scale in heavy industry and large defense contracts spurred the growth and integration of the largest industrial corporations. At the same time, the industrial production capacity of the other belligerent nations suffered wartime damage or lost workers who were called to military service. As the industries of other nations recovered to a competitive level in the postwar world, and as American companies turned to less developed nations for cheap labor, investment in manufacturing facilities in the United States diminished, with plants being closed and industrial workers being displaced. Since 1950, the United States has become increasingly an importer of finished or partially finished industrial goods.

From an economic standpoint, deindustrialization occurs in a country when the amount of capital invested in industrial production—that is, the money spent for plants and production machinery—decreases, at least relative to investment in other sectors of the economy in that country. Three causes of deindustrialization are generally recognized: foreign competition, reducing the number of buyers of American industrial goods; the opening of production facilities by American companies in foreign countries, usually to secure lower-wage labor; and the movement of capital to nonindustrial sectors of the economy. Deindustrialization results in structural unemployment, but economists do not necessarily agree on how much of the total unemployment at any given time is structural unemployment caused by deindustrialization, how much is structural unemployment caused by reinvestment in different geographic areas of the United States, and how much is cyclical unemployment caused by the business cycle.

For economists and political leaders, the major question raised by deindustrialization is whether the economy of the United States has the capacity to absorb the workers displaced by the closing of industrial plants. Although there is general agreement that deindustrialization has not directly been the major cause of unemployment in the United States, employment in the manufacturing sector has generally been associated with wages higher than those of the agricultural sector or the service sector, and the loss of income by industrial workers has a potentially large effect on service workers in the communities in which they live. The stance of classical economics—that the "invisible hand" of market forces will eventually establish wages, prices, and levels of employment that are optimal for a society—suggests that new businesses and career fields will be available for workers who have been displaced by deindustrialization. Opponents of restrictions on plant closings and capital movement across national borders frequently cite the late Harvard University economist Joseph Schumpeter, who argued that the "creative destruction" of inefficient firms was necessary to permit the reallocation of resources to more efficient producers, who would hire and make better use of the former workers of the inefficient producers. Based on a careful analysis of employment data between 1973 and 1980, however, economist Barry Bluestein found that during the 1970's, substantial deindustrialization had occurred in such major industries as those that produced tires, household appliances, motor vehicles, textiles and clothing, electrical distribution equipment, consumer electronics, and chemicals, and that the economy generally failed to provide comparable jobs in other sectors for the skilled and highly paid workers who had been displaced from their jobs.

Many economists and social scientists consider deindustrialization to be a natural part of a major economic transition to a knowledge-based, service-based economy. The term "postindustrial society" was coined by Harvard economist Daniel Bell to describe an economy based on the accumulation and transmission of information. Bell argued that the transition from an economy based on the extraction of resources in nature (such as agriculture and farming) to one based on the production of material goods by industry is naturally followed by one in which the applications of knowledge to the control and improvement of production and distribution hold central importance. The production of goods for use in the United States could then occur anywhere in the world, with the production system having been designed and being monitored by the appropriate specialists. According to Bell, this transition is occurring first in the United States but will also eventually occur in Western Europe and Japan. Opponents of deindustrialization maintain that the postindustrial information-based society envisioned by Bell will relegate too many people, including many workers in the information industry, to an economic underclass with low income and little employment security.

Applications

The notion of well-paid industrial workers, union members with a high level of job security, had become a fixture in American popular culture by the middle of the twentieth century. In the automobile, steel, and other major industries, it was not uncommon for a man, his sons, and later his grandsons and granddaughters to plan on career-long employment with the same employer. Manufacturing work offered some of the best economic prospects available to citizens without postsecondary education.

Unemployment caused by the plant closings that occur during deindustrialization has serious social costs. Increases in unemployment have been correlated with an increase in premature deaths as a result of heart disease and other causes, with increases in crime and mental illness, and with increases in divorce and family problems. The mental health effects are generally more pronounced for older, less skilled, and less educated workers.

For workers, families, unions, and communities affected by a plant closing, economic freedom and social status are reduced. Workers can count on unemployment insurance and, usually, severance pay to meet economic needs for a number of weeks but must frequently choose among relocation, retraining, and working at much lower pay. Spouses and older children might start working or take on additional work to supplement the family income, or the unemployed worker might become dependent on more distant family members for support. Unions are threatened by a loss in membership base at the same time that they may be negotiating wage concessions or transfers for other members. Communities will feel the effects of the loss in income of the displaced workers. Merchants and service providers will see a drop in their income as industrial workers economize. The tax base may decrease significantly, forcing dismissals of teachers, police officers, and other employees of local government. Understandably, the likelihood of a plant closing often triggers substantial community action.

Of particular interest to sociologists is the effect of structural unemployment resulting from a plant closing on social integration; that is, the extent to which the newly unemployed person and his or her family feel that they are a part of the community, accept its class structure, and seek to advance within it. Unemployment usually results in a loss of social standing and often a decrease in social interaction. In comparative studies of displaced and employed workers in one Indiana community, researchers found that displaced workers were far less likely to express confidence in high-status professionals, such as physicians, lawyers, or governmental officials, than were employed workers; that they felt far more isolated from the community; and that they were more likely to believe in the need for radical social change. Workers displaced by plant closings were also found to be far more likely than employed workers to have a "worker consciousness," an awareness of belonging to a separate group within society that has common interests and is subject to the effects of social and economic forces.

The possibility of preventing or discouraging plant closures by legislation, at the state or federal level, is supported by some economic analysts and opposed by others. A number of laws have been proposed at federal and state levels to discourage plant closings and to protect workers from some of the consequences of structural unemployment. Usually, the proposed legislation requires employers to provide advance warning, up to a year in some cases, of a planned closing, to increase the amount of severance pay, and to extend eligibility for health insurance. Some proposals would require the operators of a closed plant to pay restitution to the affected community. Opponents of such legislation point out that each of the provided remedies adds to the cost, and thus the risk, of operating an industrial plant and might actually encourage the flight of production facilities from the United States. The majority of such proposed laws have not been enacted, but the Trade Adjustment Act and the Job Training Partnership Act of 1982 include severance and retraining benefits for workers who lose their jobs as a result of foreign competition.

A number of activist groups have formed to monitor plant closings and to marshal public opinion against them. Once a planned closing is identified, they may act to publicize the foreign operations of the corporation and the pay and working conditions of workers in these "offshore" operations. They frequently draw attention to the high salaries of the corporate executives of the company who are planning a plant closing and organize boycotts of the company's products and those of others with a financial stake in the company. In several instances, large corporations have changed plans to close a facility in response to pressure generated by such groups.

On a more cooperative level, employees have in some instances used pension funds to purchase the plant that would otherwise have closed or have negotiated for job retraining and relocation. Communities that provide tax exemptions to recruit industrial plants have begun to negotiate in advance the recovery of tax dollars if the plant closes within a preset time.

Context

The United States emerged from World War II as the greatest economic and industrial power on Earth. Economists estimate that three-quarters of the world's invested capital and two-thirds of its industrial capacity were concentrated in the United States at that time. This position resulted both from the wartime growth of industrial production in the United States and from the decimation of populations and industry in Europe, the Soviet Union, and Japan caused by the conflict. As other nations recovered, they became competitive with the United States. Thus, although the United States produced 46 percent of the world's crude steel and 82 percent of its passenger cars in 1950, twenty-five years later it produced only 16 percent of the steel and 27 percent of the automobiles. By 1980, the productivities of factories in Canada, Western Europe, and Japan often exceeded those of their U.S. counterparts. American corporations began to invest in and merge with foreign producers, neglecting to improve their own plants and technology. American corporations became multinational in scope, with production facilities and markets located in many countries.

As the wages of American workers increased and laws required greater employer expenditures to protect the health and safety of workers, American manufacturers increasingly looked to less economically developed regions of the United States and then to the poorer nations of the world as sources of labor at lower wages. Over the period 1969 to 1976, New York State lost more than 400,000 industrial jobs, while Texas gained more than 300,000. Multinational corporations increasingly turned to globally integrated manufacturing, in which workers in the United States and other technologically advanced countries performed more highly skilled manufacturing tasks, while workers in the so-called Third World provided more labor-intensive inputs to the final product. The electronic products industry provides an excellent example of this process, since the manufacturing process of electronic devices has easily identifiable high-technology and labor-intensive components. Precision components could be manufactured in the United States and then shipped to assembly sites where wages were low. The "offshoring" of the labor-intensive part of production was facilitated by provisions of the United States tax code which allowed import duties to be paid only on the foreign labor cost in such cases. Imports of electronic products increased nearly twentyfold between 1966 and 1975, and U.S. electronics manufacturers had set up 680 manufacturing plants outside the United States, 193 of them in Mexico, by 1977.

The advent of the electronic computer, communications satellites, and fiber-optic technology has contributed greatly to the globalization of industry by providing the technological basis for the control and coordination of the production and distribution of goods. It has also created numerous new career fields and professions, including the new managerial class required by operations on a global scale. Initially, the majority of workers in the information industry received only modest wages, below the level that characterized traditional industry; they were generally not unionized and had limited employment security. Whether an information-based postindustrial society can provide the same economic benefits to the same number of workers as traditional industry did in its day remains likely to divide economic thinkers for some time.

Bibliography

Bell, Daniel. *The Coming of Post-Industrial Society.* New York: Basic Books, 1973. This influential book was one of the first to express the view that industrial production could and should be displaced as the core of the United States economy by the production of knowledge and the management of information.

Bluestone, Barry. "Is Deindustrialization a Myth?" *Annals of the American Academy of Political and Social Science* 475 (September, 1984): 39-51. This scholarly but very readable article looks closely at the shifts in employment in different sectors of industry and regions of the country. The author affirms the reality of deindustrialization by identifying key industries and geographic regions in which the number of jobs lost over a decade is not at all balanced by a growth of comparable jobs that could absorb the displaced workers.

Cohen, Stephen S., and John Zysman. *Manufacturing Matters.* New York: Basic Books, 1987. The authors argue strongly, supporting their contention with economic data, that deindustrialization in the United States has adverse effects on the standard of living and economic competitiveness which cannot be compensated for by growth in the service sector.

Dickson, Tony, and David Judge. *The Politics of Industrial Closure.* Houndmills, England: Macmillan, 1987. Includes essays on plant closings in Britain, which provide an instructive basis for comparison with studies focused on the United States.

Gordus, Jeanne P., Paul Jarley, and Louis A. Ferman. *Plant Closings and Economic Dislocation.* Kalamazoo, Mich.: Upjohn Institute for Employment Research, 1981. A detailed study of the causes of plant closings and the adjustments made to closings by displaced workers and their communities. A good source of information on the economic and health consequences of plant closings.

Haas, Gilda. *Plant Closures: Myths, Realities, and Responses.* Boston: South End Press, 1985. This brief book is written from the standpoint of an activist concerned with preventing plant closings through community action and new legislation. It describes the human impact of some specific plant closings in poignant detail.

McKenzie, Richard B. *Fugitive Industry.* Cambridge, Mass.: Ballinger, 1984. The author is a leading exponent of noninterference with plant closings, recommending instead aggressive but realistic efforts by labor unions and communities to ensure the vitality of the industries on which they depend. This work includes a considerable amount of data on employment in regions affected by deindustrialization.

Perrucci, Carolyn C., et al. *Plant Closings: International Context and Social Costs.* New York: De Gruyter, 1988. An excellent overview of the causes of plant closings in the United States and their economic and social effects, with an emphasis on the need for governmental action to ameliorate the negative effects.

Donald R. Franceschetti

Cross-References

DEINSTITUTIONALIZATION OF MENTAL PATIENTS

Type of sociology: Major social institutions
Field of study: Medicine

Deinstitutionalization is the name given to the change in mental health policy that led to the moving of thousands of patients living in state mental hospitals to community-based residences. People with mental disorders were no longer to be treated in enclosed state mental hospitals but rather treated in outpatient clinics and community hospitals.

Principal terms

CHRONIC MENTAL DISORDER: a mental disorder that is severe and of extended duration
CHRONIC MENTAL PATIENT: an individual with a chronic mental disorder who is, has been, or might have been but for deinstitutionalization on the rolls of a state hospital
COMMUNITY MENTAL HEALTH CLINICS: clinics that were established under the Community Mental Health Acts of 1963 and 1965
MENTAL DISABILITY: impairment in one of more important areas of functioning in daily living
MENTAL DISORDER: an updating of the term mental illness which is used in the diagnostic manual of the American Psychiatric Association
STATE MENTAL HOSPITALS: large state institutions built during the late nineteenth and early twentieth centuries, most often in remote rural settings, for the institutional care of mental disorder

Overview

According to Ernest Gruenberg, the term "deinstitutionalization" originated in 1975 with Bertram Brown, at that time the director of the National Institute of Mental Health. Brown defined deinstitutionalization as consisting of three parts: the release to the community of patients from psychiatric hospitals who were prepared for community living; the prevention of unnecessary hospital placement; and the development of treatment services in the community for persons with severe mental disorder. Thus, his definition covers the release of patients from state mental hospitals, the diversion of patients away from the hospital to outpatient services, and the development of community services. Ann Braden Johnson, in *Out of Bedlam: The Truth About Deinstitutionalization* (1990), however, attributes the term to John Maurice Grimes, a physician, who in the 1930's surveyed six hundred state hospitals and documented their deplorable conditions. He proposed "de-institutionalization," by which he meant the discharge of all suitable patients to after-care clinics in the community.

Beginning in the 1960's in the United States, deinstitutionalization represented a shift in the type of facility at which treatment was provided for people with severe mental disorders. The shift to the community for treatment was supported by reports of scandalously poor treatment provided to persons with chronic mental disorders at state mental hospitals; the ideology of the community mental health movement, which stated that chronic disorder could be avoided by primary prevention and early treatment in the community for those with acute conditions; the development of drugs to treat mental disorder; and federal legislation that provided funds for alternative care in other institutions or in the community. This change in where care was provided led to the discharge of hundreds of thousands of individuals from state hospitals and prevented the hospitalization of countless others.

The populations that were most affected by deinstitutionalization were those individuals who had developed chronic mental conditions. In a community study described in *Psychiatric Disorders in America: The Epidemiologic Catchment Area Study* (1991), by Lee N. Robins and Darrel A. Regier, a sample of twenty thousand people was tested to form the basis for understanding how many people have specified mental disorders in the United States. In general, one can say that about 20 percent of the population has some current mental disorder; this includes conditions at all levels of severity and duration. The lifetime rate for more serious disorders that may have chronic forms has been estimated at about 1 or 1.5 percent of the population.

There is special concern for those with severe and chronic mental disorders because this group of people is likely to need long-term treatment and supervision. It was this group of patients who filled state hospitals until after 1955. At that time, there were close to 560,000 resident patients in state and county mental hospitals in the United States. By 1986, the number had been reduced to 110,743.

With so many people leaving the mental hospitals or no longer being kept there, it is natural to ask where these people went and what happened to them. In December of 1980, the Steering Committee on the Chronically Mentally Ill issued *Toward a National Plan for the Chronically Mentally Ill*. In it they provide the following approximations of how many community-dwelling persons with chronic mental disabilities there were and where they were located. Some 300,000 to 400,000 lived in boarding homes, 150,000 to 170,000 lived with their families, about 110,000 were hospitalized for short periods in community hospitals, and an unknown number of others were living in transient hotels and/or on the street. In addition, about 900,000 were still in institutions (750,000 were in nursing homes, and 150,000 were in longer-term mental hospitals).

Applications

Deinstitutionalization began because many people were concerned about the poor conditions of care that long-term mental patients received. Many experts are now concerned about the large number of homeless persons with mental disabilities living in American communities. It has been estimated that about one-third of homeless people have a severe mental disorder. Unlike many of the homeless, people with mental disabilities are eligible for some social welfare benefits, including Supplemental Security Income (SSI), a federal program that provides poor people with disabilities who cannot work with a basic minimal monthly income to provide for their needs; Medicaid, a federal-state program to cover medical care costs; and food stamps, to supplement dietary needs. The person with a mental disability may not be aware of these programs or may not be willing to become involved with the welfare system.

By definition, people with mental disabilities may not be able to manage their affairs or always make decisions that would most protect their own interests. They may also refuse to continue to take medications because of unpleasant side effects. Yet without the medication their conditions may grow worse. In addition, homeless, poor, and uninsured chronic patients tend to be abandoned by the community mental health clinics that were presumably built as a community alternative to institutionalization. The Community Mental Health Centers (CMHC) Act of 1963 provided for the construction of community mental health centers that would meet the needs of community residents who were unable to pay for care at existing private clinics and hospitals. Legislation to provide staffing for these clinics was enacted in 1965. Unfortunately, the CMHC legislation also stated that a state could exempt a clinic from the requirement to provide free services for the indigent if it were not financially feasible for the facility to do so. The state hospitals and their outpatient clinics continued to be used by indigent chronic patients until the development of Community Support Programs (CSPs) by the federal government (through the National Institute of Mental Health). Some chronic patients are being reached by these newer community support programs. There are not enough of these programs to meet the need, however; in addition these are voluntary programs, and some individuals may be too disturbed to use them effectively.

Often, chronic patients do not stay out of the hospital completely. Frequently people with a chronic mental disability, without adequate supportive care and without medication, become deteriorated enough to necessitate rehospitalization. They are held a short time, improve in the hospital, and are then released, only to begin the cycle again.

A remarkable aspect of deinstitutionalization, according to Gruenberg, is that as a historical event it did not really happen: Rather, institutionalization actually increased during the 1960's and 1970's. The figures clearly show that there was an increase in the numbers of people in institutions if one counts both mental hospitals and nursing homes. In 1960 there were 469,717 in nursing homes and 543,412 in state mental hospitals for a total of 1,013,129. In 1980 there were 1,426,371 in nursing homes and 132,164 in state hospitals for a total of 1,558,535. This shifting of populations from one type of institution to another came about primarily as a result of the development of Medicaid. State hospitals could send their patients to nursing homes and have the cost paid largely by federal dollars. This was done under the guise of moving older adults closer to family and community, but it too frequently resulted in patients being placed in far less agreeable accommodations that were more restrictive than the hospitals the patients had left. Moreover, younger patients (in their forties or fifties) who are sent to nursing homes appear to do poorly; research indicates that they deteriorate rapidly there. In addition, the costs of nursing home care have risen dramatically. Nursing homes appear to be a very expensive and inadequate alternative to state hospital care.

The ideal of moving mental health services to the community has been problematic in that most people object to the positioning of service centers in their neighborhoods. Little has been done to alleviate the stigma of mental disorder. People generally fear a person with unusual and unpredictable behavior and see that person as a threat. They do not want such individuals living in, or even being provided with services in, their neighborhoods. Therefore, services are often located in deteriorated neighborhoods where the residents are too overwhelmed by their own problems to organize opposition effectively. These are areas of high crime rates and substandard housing, where the vulnerable chronic mental patient becomes an easy target for theft and assault.

Context

The roots of deinstitutionalization go back to a number of events at the beginning of the twentieth century, when there was a growing feeling that the state hospitals were not operating as it was first believed they would. The state hospitals were developed in the middle to late nineteenth century as a humane response to the plight of persons with mental disorders. These persons previously had been the responsibility of local governments or family units. They often were kept in locked rooms or basements or in almshouses (a catch-all residential provision for all economic dependents). Some were auctioned off to the lowest bidder, who would be paid by the local government to provide care. Against this history the early state hospitals, modeled after the small private hospitals that were reputed to be quite successful, were optimistically developed to provide care and, it was hoped, to cure those with mental disorders. Rather than being cured and returned to their families and communities, however, large numbers of patients with severe mental disorders developed chronic conditions and remained in hospitals as custodial patients. This changed these institutions from curative treatment centers (their original purpose) to places for long-term custodial care. Their ever-increasing numbers of patients strained state budgets, and care became minimal.

The problems of the state hospitals were brought to public notice during and after World War II by conscientious objectors who had been sent to state hospitals to perform alternative service. They were shocked to discover the neglect, squalor, and lack of care that prevailed in the hospitals. They formed the National Mental Health Foundation and publicized the condition of the hospitals. Their efforts attracted the attention of Albert Deutsch, a journalist, who wrote articles about the terrible conditions of the state hospitals that were later published in *The Shame of the States* (1948). In 1946, a former state hospital nurse, Mary Jane Ward, published the widely acclaimed book *The Snake Pit*, which was subsequently made into a motion picture. These exposés and others attracted much public attention.

Many mental health professionals believed that the lack of active psychotherapeutic care and prolonged residence in the poorly run custodial state hospitals were related to the development of a secondary disorder characterized by passivity, dependency, and dulled emotional expression. (It is now thought that these are long-term symptoms characteristic of schizophrenia, a mental disorder that frequently develops a chronic form.) Another factor that many have thought to be at the heart of deinstitutionalization was the development of psychotropic medication (drugs that have a special action on the mind) in the 1950's and 1960's. These medications were found to be quite helpful in regulating the behavior of patients on the hospital wards. After only limited testing for long-term use, the drugs were hailed as an answer to the problem of long-term chronic mental disorder. Thirty years of experience, however, has shown that while these drugs may control some symptoms, such as agitation and confusion, they do not help to cure the underlying disorder. It has also been learned that these drugs have long-term nonreversible side effects.

Unfortunately, policy makers in the United States failed to learn from the British experience with deinstitutionalization that occurred somewhat earlier. In the early 1960's, evidence accumulated that the release of patients from the hospitals was having distressing effects on families and that halfway houses were being overfilled with patients who lacked the capacity for independent living.

It would appear in retrospect that much of the rationale behind the deinstitutionalization movement does not hold up under scrutiny. The motivation of reducing the financial burdens of care has not been satisfied either; the burden has merely been shifted to different programs that are paid for at a different level of government. It remains undisputed, however, that the hospitals were in deplorable condition and that many individuals had been deprived of basic civil rights through involuntary hospitalization. Many patients were not provided with therapeutic care or helped to resume community living.

Bibliography

Bachrach, Leona L., ed. *Deinstitutionalization*. San Francisco: Jossey-Bass, 1983. Although this is an edited book, it is more than a loose collection of articles. The contributions were planned to cover the topic well. The book includes discussion of the history, demographics, and laws related to deinstitutionalization as well as principles of rehabilitation; ends with a description of community support systems and a look to the future. Each chapter has an extensive literature review. The book has an index.

Bloom, Bernard L. *Community Mental Health: A General Introduction*. Monterey, Calif.: Brooks/Cole, 1977. A general introduction to community mental health and the ideology and movement behind deinstitutionalization. It was the belief in the validity of the community as the treatment arena of choice that put much professional and public support behind deinstitutionalization. The book also contains a retort to the rather scathing reporting of Chu and Trotter (see following entry). Includes a subject and author index and an extensive bibliography.

Chu, Franklin, and Sharland Trotter. *The Madness Establishment: Ralph Nader's Study Group Report on the National Institute of Mental Health*. New York: Grossman,

1974. The authors present an investigation of the policies that surrounded deinstitutionalization and the Community Mental Health movement. They point out that deinstitutionalization was begun based on concern for mental patients and an untested belief that treatment in community settings was a viable alternative. When the idea was implemented, however, politics, competing interests of some of those involved, and fiscal limitations ensured failure.

Group for the Advancement of Psychiatry. *The Chronic Mental Patient in the Community.* New York: Author, 1978. This short booklet provides a quite readable and concise history of the care of the most seriously and chronically disabled mental patients. It then looks at the results of deinstitutionalization. Basic terms are all clearly defined. Each of the chapters contains a list of references. References include quotes from a collection of "Dear Abby" letters that help to make the text open and readable.

Gruenberg, Ernest. "The Deinstitutionalization Movement." In *Public Mental Health: Perspectives and Prospects,* edited by Morton O. Wagenfeld, Paul V. Lemkau, and Blair Justice. Beverly Hills, Calif.: Sage Publications, 1982. This chapter gives an excellent brief history of the deinstitutionalization movement and its results. The author defends the state hospitals, saying that they were treating and releasing patients but were becoming filled with patients with chronic conditions, for whom there was no known treatment. Responsibility for the large numbers of chronic patients left limited resources for the treatment of patients with acute disorders for whom known treatments may have been effective.

Johnson, Ann Braden. *Out of Bedlam: The Truth About Deinstitutionalization.* New York: Basic Books, 1990. A clear discussion of deinstitutionalization and some of the issues and problems that surround it, from the historical context to issues of homelessness, the use of jails to house those with disabilities, and consideration of the mental health bureaucracy. The book has very extensive chapter notes and is indexed.

Joint Commission on Mental Illness and Health. *Action for Mental Health.* New York: Basic Books, 1961. This is the now classic report of the commission that was established by Congress in 1955 to survey resources and make recommendations for combating mental disorder in the United States. It proposed, among other things, development of community treatment alternatives to the state hospital, converting the large state hospitals into centers for the care of chronic diseases, and development of after-care, intermediate care, and rehabilitation services. Contains appendices that include the Mental Health Study Act of 1955, footnotes, references, and an index.

Mechanic, David. *Mental Health and Social Policy.* 3d ed. Englewood Cliffs, N.J.: Prentice-Hall, 1989. The book puts deinstitutionalization in context. It discusses mental health policy in general and in one chapter, "The Development of Mental Health Policy in the United States," addresses the history preceding deinstitutionalization and the events in policy development into the Reagan years. It has a subject and author index and an extensive bibliography.

United States National Advisory Mental Health Council. *Caring for People with Severe Mental Disorders: A National Plan of Research to Improve Services.* Washington, D.C.: Superintendent of Documents, U.S. Government Printing Office, 1991. This document examines the nature of the problem of major chronic mental disorders. It contains a section on the service systems that provide mental health care. It states that after thirty-five years of deinstitutionalization it is time to ask again what the proper mix of federal, state, and local funding for mental health services should be and whether there could be better cooperation among all service providers.

Joan Hashimi

Cross-References

Health and Society, 852; Homelessness, 897; Labeling and Deviance, 1049; The Medical Profession and the Medicalization of Society, 1159; Medical Sociology, 1166; Medical versus Social Models of Illness, 1172; The Medicalization of Deviance, 1178.

DELINQUENCY PREVENTION AND TREATMENT

Type of sociology: Deviance and social control
Field of study: Controlling deviance

Delinquency prevention and treatment involve efforts directed toward controlling or arresting the deviant behavior of juveniles. These efforts include the development of theories that seek to explain the causes and advance remedies for delinquent behavior as well as the assessment and evaluation of policies and programs that have been established to prevent or control delinquency.

Principal terms

AGING-OUT: the process in which most juveniles desist from delinquent behavior as they grow older; also known as the desistance phenomenon

DELINQUENCY: behaviors for which a juvenile can be formally sanctioned; collectively, these behaviors include status offenses and those behaviors prohibited under criminal law

DIVERSION: a mechanism by which juveniles are either formally or informally kept from formal juvenile court processing

DIVERSION PROGRAMS: programs designed to provide juveniles who have been diverted from formal court processing with various types of services and delinquency interventions

PARENS PATRIAE: the doctrine which allows the state to usurp parental rights on behalf of the best interests of the child

STATUS OFFENSE: a behavior which has been deemed inappropriate and codified as illegal only for those under the age of majority; examples include truancy, curfew violation, and smoking cigarettes

Overview

Three perspectives or sets of ideas have dominated the thinking and practices directed at the treatment and prevention of delinquency in the United States. These are the punishment, treatment, and noninterventionist ideologies. The ideologies differ in their fundamental assumptions and prescriptions, and each has had a distinct influence on policy. The punishment ideology is the oldest and may be the most persistent.

Eighteenth century philosophers Cesare Beccaria and Jeremy Bentham were instrumental in establishing the rationale for punishment as the means to control delinquency as well as other types of deviant behavior. These philosophers reasoned that humans are rational beings and that all behavior is the result of a mental calculus based on the pain-gain principle. This means that humans weigh the gains and the pains before acting; if the perceived gain of a behavior outweighs the perceived pain, then action will result. In other words, delinquent behavior is a chosen activity among juveniles who perceive the gains of that behavior to be greater than the pains. This concept is often referred to as "choice theory"; choice theory and its prescriptions for the control of deviance compose the ideology known as the classical school of criminology.

The classical school philosophers held that deterrence and punishment are the most effective means of controlling delinquent and other types of deviant behavior. In the ideal sense, the threat of punishment for delinquent behavior should deter juveniles from choosing deviant behavior in the first place. That is, the perceived pains of a delinquent action (punishment) should outweigh the gains. For those who are not deterred by the threat or fear of punishment, punishment should be sure, swift, and in proportion to the deviant action. Under classical school thought, this should not only effectively deter those punished from re-offending but also deter others by using punished offenders as examples of the consequences of delinquent activity. The three major propositions of the classical school are choice, deterrence, and punishment. Each of these is challenged by the treatment perspective.

The treatment ideology is rooted in the positivist school of criminology. Having emerged during the nineteenth century, the positivist school holds that human behavior is not simply the result of individuals making choices based on the pain-gain principle; rather, human behavior is determined, or at least conditioned, by forces that supersede purely rational choice. Thus delinquency is not a result of choosing deviant behavior but the manifestation of some underlying deviant disorder or dysfunction.

The factor or factors that have been implicated as responsible for delinquent behavior according to positivism have varied widely. Physicians and psychologists have emphasized individual predispositions and attempted to identify physiological or psychological anomalies, while sociologists have concentrated on socialization or learning processes and the broader, social structural influences, such as poverty, disorganized neighborhoods, and lack of opportunity. The fundamental assumption that factors other than simple free will are responsible for delinquency leads to the positivist school's remedy for delinquency, treatment.

Under the treatment ideology, punishing delinquents is viewed as ineffective and even potentially harmful. Instead, the factors which are responsible for delinquency need to be identified and "treated." On the individual level, this could involve psychotherapy, counseling, job training, remedial education, or other services directed toward "fixing" or rehabilitating the delinquent. On the broader social level, treatment can take the form of social programs, with efforts directed at neighborhood organization, increased employment opportunities, and enhanced public education. These social programs are directed toward changing a dysfunctional social structure or environment and are generally geared toward preventing delinquency rather than rehabilitating known delinquents. While punishment is believed to be counterproductive from the treatment perspective, from the noninterventionist perspective, punishment, individually based treatments, and official juvenile court processing are all viewed as detrimental for the great majority of delinquents.

Proponents of nonintervention recognize that almost all juveniles engage in behaviors for which they could be adjudicated delinquent and that furthermore, the vast majority of delinquency involves minor infractions or status offenses. It is also recognized that most juveniles "age-out," or desist from deviant behavior as they grow older. Thus, under the noninterventionist ideology, the most effective means to control or prevent delinquency is to impose controls which are the least intrusive so that the natural and spontaneous "aging-out" process can occur.

Under the noninterventionist ideology, formal court processing should be restricted to the most serious juvenile offenders who pose a real threat to the safety of the community. For the majority of offenders, a warning or reprimand is sufficient. This prescription is founded on the labeling theory proposition, which holds that formal processing may initiate a self-fulfilling prophecy mechanism in which juveniles who are labeled or treated as delinquents ultimately define themselves as such and ultimately adjust their behavior to be consistent with their delinquent self-concepts. Consequently, instead of extinguishing delinquent behavior, involvement with juvenile court perpetuates and intensifies delinquency. Treatment is also suspect from a noninterventionist position. Treatments such as psychotherapy and individual counseling can increase a juvenile's exposure to control agencies, exposure that may continue indefinitely. These treatments may also result in the escalation of delinquency with the imposition of negative labels or "diagnoses."

The noninterventionist ideology has had some impact on the thinking and practices involving the treatment and prevention of delinquency; nevertheless, the treatment and punishment ideologies have had considerably more influence. The persistent assumption among juvenile justice professionals as well as the general public is that juveniles who break the law need more, be it punishment or treatment, than a "slap on the wrist."

Applications

Sociologists seek to identify the social, political, and economic forces in the United States that have influenced the definition and explanation of delinquency over time and seek to understand how these larger processes have shaped the agendas and policies for delinquency prevention and control. Historically, these changing philosophies have been marked by, first, urbanization and child saving; second, the juvenile court movement and treatment; third, deinstitutionalization and noninterventionism; and finally, crime control and punishment. Prior to the reforms of the nineteenth century, there were no separate courts or penal institutions for juveniles. Those under the age of majority were subject to trial in the criminal courts, adult sanctions, and incarceration in adult facilities. In the mid-1800's, special treatment for juveniles was advocated and initiated by a group of reformers known as the "child savers."

The typical child saver was a white, Protestant woman who had moved, during the period of rapid industrialization and urbanization, from a rural area to an urban one. The child savers were shocked by the disorganization, crime, and (as they perceived it) general vice of the city. Having a strong sense of the "Protestant work ethic," these reformers were appalled at the various self-indulgent amenities the city offered, and to which children were exposed, such as intoxicants and amusement parks. It was the idleness and poverty of children, however, which provided the most grist for the child saver's mill.

The child savers believed that if the work ethic and good American values were instilled into children, primarily poor immigrant children, they would grow up to be productive members of society. It was reasoned that poor immigrant parents were ill prepared or lacked the capacity to accomplish this task because of their poverty and their unfamiliarity with American culture. The solution was to remove children from their homes and rear them in institutions where they would be nurtured and socialized into the American way of life and would be saved from lives of crime and destitution. Houses of refuge and reform schools proliferated during this period. Children were placed in these institutions under legislation which allowed authorities to usurp parental rights to custody. This trend marked the transfer of the general control of children from parents to the state and a movement from adult punishment for the criminal behavior of children toward rehabilitation or treatment.

The early juvenile institutions have been described as austere warehouses for juveniles. Sanitation and the physical care of children were poor, and discipline was harsh; whippings and long periods of solitary confinement were common. The juvenile court movement at the end of the nineteenth century was largely influenced by the child saving movement; it was an attempt to reform the recognized failings associated with it. The rapid establishment of juvenile courts in the United States formalized the commitment to the *parens patriae* philosophy. The courts were established not to punish but to treat children. For court advocates, it was believed that children, with the paternal arm of the juvenile court authority around them, could be rehabilitated through community treatment. Emphasis was placed on probation services in which juveniles would be provided with services while remaining in the community and, ideally, with their families. Yet regardless of these goals, and despite other community-wide efforts to prevent delinquency that were implemented in the first half of the twentieth century, the pattern of institutionalization of status offenders as well as those who violated criminal law continued almost unabated. It was not until the 1970's that a concerted effort to remove large numbers of children from institutions was launched.

The noninterventionist movement emerged in the late 1960's with the call for removing youth, particularly status offenders, from juvenile institutions and for diverting the bulk of both status and minor property offenders from formal processing in the juvenile justice system. Noninterventionism was buttressed by federal policy recommendations such as the Juvenile Justice and Delinquency Prevention Act of 1974, which, with federal funding incentives, encouraged states to deinstitutionalize status offenders. In addition, other federal initiatives were directed at facilitating the diversion of nonserious offenders.

The noninterventionist movement was relatively short-lived. While policy making and funding was being directed toward status and minor property offenders, the relatively small category of serious chronic offenders was being ignored. Concurrently, the number of juvenile offenses continued to climb. This, coupled with publicity surrounding some research that concluded that treatment did not work, gave the general public the impression that the juvenile justice system was too soft on offenders. Thus, by the late 1970's, the general public was ready for yet another reform in juvenile justice—a "get-tough" approach that supporting politicians have found to be an expedient route into office since the early 1980's.

Part and parcel of the "get-tough" approach to juvenile justice is punishment, which is seen as the most effective and efficient means to control and prevent juvenile delinquency. Many state legislatures during this time increased the length and severity of sanctions for juveniles, lowered the age of eligibility or otherwise made it easier for juveniles to be transferred and tried in adult criminal courts, and supported new control mechanisms or punitive programs for juveniles such as electronic monitoring and "boot camps." The official policy of William P. Barr, U.S. Attorney General under the Bush Administration, included the recommendation of institutionalization for juveniles who were first-time minor property offenders. This proposal for delinquency intervention through institutionalization is reminiscent of the child saving movement, but the stated goal is quite different: For the child savers it was treatment and rehabilitation, but for the "get-tough" advocates, it is control and punishment.

Context

The prevention and treatment of delinquency crosscut an array of disciplines, such as psychology, sociology, criminal justice, and medicine, and they are grounded in numerous social and political entities, including social service agencies, legislative bodies, law enforcement, and the judiciary. In general, sociologists must always be aware of the broader historical, social, and political processes as well as the vested interests of the actors, groups, and organizations which have a bearing on their specific topic of study or research.

Research and academic interests in the area of delinquency prevention and treatment vary widely among sociologists. Those who formulate and test causal theories of delinquency are motivated, or at least obliged, to relate the policy implications of their work. For other sociologists, engaged in the evaluation of current and historical policies and practices, delinquency treatment and prevention is the primary research objective.

The first sociologists to study crime and delinquency in the United States were affiliated with the University of Chicago. "Chicago school" sociologists Clifford Shaw and Henry McKay were among these early scholars. Their extensive study of delinquency in Chicago, from which their classic theory of the origins of delinquency was derived, provided the impetus for the highly regarded Chicago Area Project as well as similar prevention programs that were implemented in other cities.

A comprehensive social theory regarding the cause of delinquency formulated by sociologists Richard Cloward and Lloyd Ohlin was based largely on the work of two other sociologists, Robert Merton and Albert Cohen. Cloward and Ohlin's differential opportunity theory was influential in the development of rigorous delinquency prevention strategies of the 1960's, such as the federally funded War on Poverty programs and New York City's Mobilization for Youth project.

Labeling theory, largely developed and refined by sociologists Howard Becker and Edwin Lemert, was the foundation for a new perspective on delinquency prevention and treatment and was responsible for a radical reform in policy and programs in juvenile justice. The federal mandates for the deinstitutionalization and diversion of juveniles in the 1970's were based on labeling theory. Following the implementation of these reforms, research by sociologists has revealed how these policies and programs, in practice, have had the unintended and potentially harmful consequence of "widening the net" of social control and thereby intensifying, rather than minimizing, intrusion of and exposure to corrective agencies.

Since the early 1980's, sociologists have been engaged in research and analysis of the re-emergence of the punishment ideology. These efforts have provided insight, for example, into the effectiveness and success of deterrence strategies as well as the implications of more punitive sanctions for juveniles. For many decades, sociologists have revealed that efforts directed at the treatment and prevention of delinquency are often not based on what is actually known about the nature of delinquency and mechanisms to control it. Interventions are often developed without a theoretical basis and administered by unqualified personnel. The continued obligation of sociologists will be to evaluate and assess scientifically the methods used to prevent and treat delinquency under the ever-fluctuating ideologies of society.

Bibliography

Bernard, Thomas J. *The Cycle of Juvenile Justice*. New York: Oxford University Press, 1992. Highly recommended for undergraduates and others interested in juvenile justice and its history. Reveals the cyclical nature of juvenile justice—that is, its fluctuations between leniency and punitive controls, with neither approach addressing what is really necessary for the treatment and prevention of delinquency. Well referenced; includes an index.

Empey, LaMar T., ed. *Juvenile Justice: The Progressive Legacy and Current Reforms*. Charlottesville: University Press of Virginia, 1979. An interesting compilation of essays illustrating the divergent perspectives on delinquency and prescriptions for control. Addresses the history and ideals of the early juvenile court, the status as of the late 1970's, and recommendations for reform. Perhaps dated in some respects, but the historical analyses are not obsolete; many of the issues addressed are still being debated. No index or bibliography; references are limited.

Lundman, Richard J. *Prevention and Control of Juvenile Delinquency*. 2d ed. New York: Oxford University Press, 1993. A well-organized overview of delinquency prevention and control efforts. An exposé of fads in juvenile treatment and prevention and a good summary of evaluative research. Contains straightforward recommendations for future policy and programs. Includes a select bibliography and an index.

McGarrell, Edmund F. *Juvenile Correctional Reform: Two Decades of Policy and Procedural Change*. Albany: State University of New York Press, 1988. Examines trends in juvenile justice. A good analysis of the social and political influences on and organizational needs of the juvenile justice system. Focus of the book is on reform, and it provides a unique perspective to understanding the juvenile justice system using insights from organizational sociology and the sociology of deviance and social control. Includes an index and bibliography.

Schwartz, Ira M. *(In)Justice for Juveniles: Rethinking the Best Interests of the Child.* Lexington, Mass.: Lexington Books, 1989. A frank discussion written by a sociologist and former administrator of the federal Office of Juvenile Justice and Delinquency Prevention. The facts and myths of juvenile crime and control are emphasized as well as the failing of efforts to prevent and treat delinquency. Focus is on the rights of children and the abuses of treatment and punishment in public and private institutions. Well referenced; includes an index.

Douglas L. Kuck

Cross-References

Anomie and Deviance, 100; Conflict Perspectives on Deviance, 334; Crime: Analysis and Overview, 373; The Criminal Justice System, 380; Juvenile Delinquency: Analysis and Overview, 1036; Female Juvenile Delinquency, 1043; Labeling and Deviance, 1049; Parenthood and Child-Rearing Practices, 1336; Prison and Recidivism, 1519; Socialization: The Family, 1880.

DEMOCRACY AND DEMOCRATIC GOVERNMENTS

Type of sociology: Major social institutions
Field of study: Politics and the state

Democracy is a political system characterized by direct or indirect rule by the people. There are different models of democratic government, but the liberal conception as found in Western Europe and North America has emerged as the dominant view of democracy since the end of the Cold War era.

Principal terms

DEMOCRATIC CONSOLIDATION: the process of institutionalizing newly democratic regimes

DEMOCRATIZATION: the process of moving from an authoritarian to a democratic system

DIRECT DEMOCRACY: a form of government based on popular participation, majority rule, and political equality

ELITISM: the belief that in any society a small number of people—an "elite"—rule the rest

PEOPLE'S DEMOCRACY: the Marxist-Leninist model of democracy in which the communist party governs in the interest of the working class

PLURALISM: a theory of democracy that believes in multiple, competing elites determining public policy through bargaining and compromise

REPRESENTATIVE DEMOCRACY: a system of representative government based on free elections and limits on state activity

SINGLE-PARTY DEMOCRACY: a model of democracy found in the Third World in which the ruling party acts in the interest of the entire population and opposition parties are constitutionally banned

Overview

Democracy is a set of ideals and a form of government in which the people rule directly or indirectly. The term "democracy" is derived from the ancient Greek words *demos* (people) and *kratos* (rule), which combined simply mean rule or government of the people. Until the late eighteenth and nineteenth centuries, however, democracy did not achieve prominence, and only in the twentieth century did it become a value with considerable legitimacy. In the twentieth century, democracy became popular because of the growing faith in the abilities of the common man and woman. Unlike ideologies such as communism and fascism, however, democracy lacks conceptual precision. The meaning and inherent features of democracy continue to be the subject of debate.

Democracy is a dynamic entity that has been given many different definitions. It has become one of the most elastic political concepts in use since World War II. Because democracy is a principle of legitimacy, political regimes of all kinds have claimed to be democracies. A wide range of political systems inspired by diverse ideological orientations—socialist, communist, and one-party states—have claimed to be democratic. Nondemocratic political systems have often used the term by adding adjectives such as "people's," "soviet," "guided," "basic," and "one-party" to the word "democracy." As a result, there are a number of definitions and competing theories or models of democracy.

The classical meaning of democracy, based on the use of the term in ancient Greek city-states, especially Athens, is the rule by the majority (who were poor) through direct democratic participation or by the rotation of governing offices among the citizens. Democracy was conceived as a system of government by the people themselves in which the citizens met periodically to elect state officials by lot and to enact laws. Though Athenian democracy excluded a vast majority of the population from political life—slaves, women, and foreigners—it conceived of the concept in terms of direct popular government, popular sovereignty, popular power, and popular participation. From the ancient Greeks to eighteenth century philosophers such as Jean-Jacques Rousseau, democratic government has been identified with direct popular participation. Since popular participation was understood in terms of unrestrained mob rule, democracy was considered an undesirable form of government.

In the twentieth century, however, democracy has become a positive term that is synonymous with some kind of representative system. Since modern nation-states are much larger entities than were the small Greek city-states (Athens had an estimated population of fifty thousand), direct democracy is considered an impractical form of government. Contemporary political analysts seem to agree about the procedural and normative worth of democracy as a way of organizing political relations.

The most commonly used definition of democracy is that of Joseph Schumpeter in *Capitalism, Socialism, and Democracy* (1950): "The democratic method is that institutional arrangement for arriving at political decisions in which individuals acquire the power to decide by means of a comparative struggle for people's vote." This definition of democracy is rather narrow because it focuses on the procedure and mechanism for choosing political leaders at election time and nothing more. While accepting certain aspects of Schumpeter's definition, Larry Diamond, Juan Linz, and Seymour Martin Lipset have defined political democracy more broadly in *Democracy in Developing Countries: Asia* (1988) as

> A system of government that meets three essential conditions: meaningful and *extensive* competition among individual and organized groups (especially political parties) for all effective positions of government power, at regular intervals and excluding the use of force; a highly inclusive level of *political participation* in the selection of leaders and policies, at least through regular and fair elections, such that no major (adult) social group is excluded; and a level of civil and *political liberties*—freedom of expression, freedom of press, freedom to form organizations—sufficient to ensure the integrity of political competition and participation.

Applying these three criteria of competition, participation, and political liberties, one finds that democracy is more prevalent in 1994 than ever before and that the number of democratic governments has reached an all-time high. Since the mid-1970's, there has been a genuine move from authoritarian government to a full or partial form of democratic government in many parts of the world, and the end of the Cold War in 1989 gave further impetus to the process of democratization. At the end of 1991, about half of the world's independent states (eighty-nine) were democratic—twice the number of twenty years earlier—and the number of democratic and semidemocratic governments (such as Russia, Malaysia, and Thailand) has since been growing. Two years later, there were more than 110 states (out of a total of about 180 sovereign independent states) committed to certain basic democratic principles, such as open, multiparty, secret-ballot elections with universal franchise.

Applications

Democracy as an ideal and a method of governance has been applied in three competing political systems: liberal democracy in the industrialized West, "people's democracy" in the communist political systems, and one-party democracy in most of the Third World. While there are important differences between them, each claims its model of democracy to be superior, or at least appropriate to its own historical and socioeconomic conditions.

The history of the development of democratic theory and its practice in the West is intertwined with that of liberal ideology (as put forth in the writings of philosophers such as Thomas Hobbes, John Locke, Rousseau, James Madison, and Thomas Jefferson) and its economic expression—capitalism (articulated in the works of Adam Smith, especially *The Wealth of Nations* [1776], and utilitarian philosophers such as John Stuart Mill, Jeremy Bentham, and T. H. Green). At the core of liberal democracy lie the four cardinal principles developed by Locke: equality; individual rights and freedoms, including the right to own property; government based upon consent of the governed; and limitations on the state.

When applied to a system of government, liberal democracy emphasizes the following principles: political equality—that all adult citizens have the same opportunity, at least in theory, to participate in the political decision-making process; popular sovereignty—that the ultimate power to make political decisions is vested in all the people rather than in some of them (as in case of an oligarchy), or one of them (as in case of a monarchy or dictatorship); political consultation—that through some institutional machinery the public officials must learn and act upon the public policy preference of the people; and majority rule and minority rights—that decisions should ultimately be made by popular majorities but that the rights of minorities must be respected.

The idea of citizen involvement in political decision making through elected representatives is the most fundamental characteristic of liberal democracy and distinguishes it from other types of democracies. Until the nineteenth century, severe restrictions on citizenship had been imposed based on criteria such as age, sex, literacy, property, social status, race, and religion. In contemporary liberal democratic states, all native-born or naturalized adults enjoy citizenship and legal equality. The groups that had earlier been excluded—the working class, women, and racial and religious minorities—have now been enfranchised and given political equality.

Two distinct approaches to citizen involvement in a democracy have been taken by social scientists: pluralism and elitism. The pluralist theorists—Robert Dahl, Arthur Bentley, and David Truman—believe that individuals exert influence not as voters but as members of organized interest groups such as business or trade associations, trade unions, professional associations, and community groups. These interest groups dominate modern democratic societies, in which government acts essentially as a broker to facilitate compromise among them. Democracy, in this view, is premised on diversity of interests and the dispersion of power.

The theorists of democratic elitism (Robert Michels, Giovanni Sartori, and C. Wright Mills), however, believe that elites, not masses, govern in all societies, including liberal democratic societies. Taking their cue from Italian political sociologists Vilfredo Pareto and Gaetano Mosca, elitist theorists reject the pluralist view and argue that the ability of all interest groups to exert influence is not the same in a liberal democracy. Since financial, professional, and economic resources are distributed unequally in any society, a relatively small group ends up actually controlling the government as well as industry, the professions, and major interest groups. In this view, democracy allows competition among rival elites. Schumpeter, for example, argued that in a democracy people actually choose which elite will rule them.

The concept of "people's democracy" was the prevailing version of the democratic ideal followed by the communist countries until the late 1980's. It differs radically from liberal democracy because, following the Marxian notion of class and class oppression in a capitalist society, the communists advocate the establishment of a genuine, or "social," democracy by overthrowing the bourgeois democratic state, which they view as an instrument of the oppression of the working class (proletariat), or common people. This view is similar to the Greek democratic idea of rule by and in the interest of the common people. The emphasis of the communists, however, is on economic, not political, equality. Their version of democracy is based on the Marxist-Leninist principles that were practiced in the former Soviet Union and Eastern European states until the late 1980's and that still provide the ideological basis for the governments in China, Cuba, North Korea, and Vietnam.

In a people's democracy, the Communist Party enjoys a monopoly of power and guides both government and society. According to Vladimir Ilich Lenin, the Communist Party is the vanguard of the proletariat and conforms to the principle of democratic centralism—freedom of discussion, with centralized control and responsibility. In practice, however, freedom of discussion has been denied by most communist leaders—notably, Joseph Stalin in the Soviet Union, Mao Zedong in China, and Fidel Castro in Cuba. The communist regimes have invariably turned into authoritarian states. After the collapse of communism in the former Soviet Union and Eastern Europe and the adoption of an open competitive political system, however, the concept of people's democracy has been discredited. Yet the most populous country in the world—China—remains committed to the Leninist principle of Communist Party dictatorship. China's Communist Party maintained control over government and society by violently suppressing the democracy movement at Tiananmen Square in Beijing in June, 1989. The Chinese communist leaders, especially their paramount leader Deng Xiaoping, find Western liberal democratic ideas to be unacceptable and they insist on the need for China to continue with a "people's democratic dictatorship."

A third conception of democracy, different from both liberal and people's democracy, has been formulated by developing nations. In the wake of decolonization in Asia and Africa in the 1950's and 1960's, the newly independent states experimented with some form of liberal democratic (mostly parliamentary) government, but the new democracies in the Third World did not last very long, and they gave way to one-party government or military dictatorship. Many Third World leaders quickly recognized that neither the liberal model, which puts emphasis on political competition and open discussion, nor people's democracy, which works in the interest of the proletariat, was appropriate for them. Since most Third World societies emphasize cooperation and social harmony, they conceived of democracy in terms of a one-party system based on their own culture and tradition. In this conception of democracy, government would work for the overriding common purpose of the society—Rousseau's "general will"— through modernization and national economic development instead of serving certain interest groups and associations.

The experience of single-party democracy, however, suggests that the governments in those countries became highly corrupt and authoritarian mainly because of the absence of an open competitive political system. Instead of serving the people, one-party states often served the interest of the rulers and a small number of individuals in power. The people, therefore, demanded an end to the one-party rule and establishment of an open and competitive political system. In sub-Saharan Africa, for example, the masses have demanded a "second independence," this time from indigenous repressive rulers; they are convinced that their material improvement will come only when they gain power through political participation. Liberal democratic ideas thus have gained ground in the Third World, especially since the end of the Cold War. In the 1990's, the single-party democracies have given way to multiparty systems, political freedom and openness, and popularly elected and constitutional civilian governments. Francis Fukuyama, in *The End of History and the Last Man* (1992), has declared that, because of these historical developments of the late 1980's and early 1990's, the worldwide triumph of liberal democracy is imminent.

Context

Prior to World War I, only four democracies had extended suffrage to women— Australia, Finland, New Zealand, and Norway—but there has been an unprecedented movement toward liberal democracy since then, especially since the mid-1970's. Samuel Huntington, in *The Third Wave: Democratization in the Late Twentieth Century* (1991), presents data on transitions to democracy in the "third wave" of democratization that began in 1974 and continued in the 1990's. He finds that thirty countries made transitions to democracy between 1974 and 1990, which brought the total of free and democratic countries to seventy-five by 1991 compared to twenty-nine during the "first wave" of democratization (1820's to 1926) and thirty-six in the "second wave" (1943 to 1962).

A third wave of democratization, which started in Southern Europe (Greece, Portugal, and Spain) in the mid-1970's and moved to Latin America (Argentina, Uruguay, Peru, Ecuador, Brazil, Paraguay, and Chile) and Central America (Honduras, El Salvador, Nicaragua, Guatemala, and Mexico) in the 1980's, reached Eastern Europe and the former Soviet Union by the late 1980's and early 1990's. In Asia, it includes countries such as Papua New Guinea, Thailand, Pakistan, Bangladesh, the Philippines, South Korea, Taiwan, Mongolia, and Nepal. In Africa since 1989, there has been a general move from authoritarian rule to establishing a multiparty system and free elections. This is a significant development for sub-Saharan Africa, which had only four countries (Botswana, the Gambia, Mauritius, and Senegal) with a reasonable record of democratic rule between 1965 and 1987 and had experienced more than eighty successful and countless unsuccessful military coups during the same period.

The transition from authoritarian to democratic rule in the ex-Second World and in many parts of the Third World is indeed historical. Huntington has identified five factors that contributed to the occurrence and timing of the third-wave transitions to democracy. First, the authoritarian regimes lacked legitimacy in a world where democratic values were widely accepted. Second, the middle class in many countries has expanded as a result of the unprecedented economic growth of the 1950's and 1960's. Sociologist Seymour Lipset has also argued that there is a strong empirical correlation between economic development and democracy. Third, the role of the Catholic church shifted, especially in Latin America, from defender of the status quo to opponent of authoritarianism. The church advocacy of the doctrine of liberation theology is strongly antiauthoritarian in nature. (Approximately three-quarters of the countries that became democratic between 1974 and 1989 were predominantly Catholic.) Fourth, the European Community, the United States, and the former Soviet Union all contributed to the democratic transition—for example, the *glasnost* and *perestroika* reforms of the late 1980's, initiated by the former Soviet leader Mikhail Gorbachev. Finally, the demonstration, or "herd," effect of transitions stimulated democratization in other countries.

A sixth factor could be added to Huntington's list: the communication revolution of the 1970's and 1980's, which has made the world a global village. In the age of satellite communication, fax machines, and the global reach of CNN and MTV, authoritarian rulers cannot conceal the comparative success of the open political systems and free market economies of the Western industrialized nations in meeting basic human needs. They also cannot control the thought processes of their citizens as they could a generation ago. Therefore, people's aspirations for freedom and democracy all over the world could no longer be suppressed, especially after the end of the Cold War in 1989.

The phenomenon of democratic consolidation—whether and how the new democratic regimes can become institutionalized—has received attention from social scientists in the wake of the global resurgence of democracy in the 1990's. In 1992-1993, events in Haiti, Peru, Nigeria, Venezuela, Guatemala, and the ex-Yugoslavia have indicated that Fukuyama's prediction of the imminence of global transition to liberal democracy is fallacious. Emerging democracies are facing various challenges to democratic consolidation.

First, the absence of a democratic political culture has complicated the process of democratic institution-building in many countries. Second, lack of experience in multiparty politics poses a threat to stability, as witnessed in the December, 1993, Russian parliamentary elections. Third, introduction of a free-market economy in new democracies, which has resulted in poverty for a large number of people and increased social inequality, poses a threat to democracy, especially in ex-communist countries where the victims of economic reform have begun to long for the economic security of the old system. Fourth, the military, which played a central role in Latin American and African politics, continues to occupy an important position within the political elite in those societies and threatens the stability of new democratic regimes.

In spite of these challenges, democracy has made great progress throughout the world in the 1980's and 1990's, and a reversal toward authoritarianism in newly democratic states seems less likely, though its possibility cannot be ruled out. Social scientists are divided on the future of democracy. While optimists such as Fukuyama predict that liberal democracy will triumph, pessimists like Huntington argue that the global democratic revolution will not last forever and that there might be a new surge of authoritarianism. The trend in the early 1990's nevertheless indicates that more countries will move in the direction of a free, open, competitive, and democratic political system, notwithstanding the difficulties experienced by countries such as Haiti, Nigeria, and Peru. Experts predict that even China will allow some degree of political competition when a younger generation assumes leadership following the death of Deng Xiaoping, and will gradually move toward democracy. The durability of new democracies, however, will depend to a large extent on their economic performances.

Bibliography

Diamond, Larry, and Marc F. Plattner, eds. *Capitalism, Socialism, and Democracy Revisited*. Baltimore: The Johns Hopkins University Press, 1993. This volume is a reexamination of Joseph Schumpeter's classic study *Capitalism, Socialism, and Democracy* (first published in 1942) and its thesis regarding the relationship between political democracy and alternative economic systems.

_____ . *The Global Resurgence of Democracy*. Baltimore: The Johns Hopkins University Press, 1993. This volume contains more than two dozen essays by leading American and international scholars in the field. Part 1 deals with theoretical aspects of the global democratic resurgence since the mid-1970's; parts 2 and 3 deal with problems of democratic institutionalization and political corruption and democracy, respectively; and part 4 addresses the global democratic prospects. All of the essays are of high quality and are accessible to nonexperts.

Fukuyama, Francis. *The End of History and the Last Man*. New York: Free Press, 1992. In this provocative book, Fukuyama argues that after the collapse of communism in the Soviet Union and Eastern Europe there is no viable alternative to Western-style liberal democracy. The author therefore predicts the end of history.

Held, David. *Models of Democracy*. Stanford, Calif.: Stanford University Press, 1987. An excellent analysis of the classical and contemporary models of democracy. It also examines central problems of democratic theory and practice.

Huntington, Samuel P. *The Third Wave: Democratization in the Late Twentieth Century*. Norman: University of Oklahoma Press, 1991. A theoretical and empirical study of the "third wave" of transitions of about thirty countries from authoritarian to democratic political systems between 1974 and 1990. (The first and second waves of democratic transitions took place in 1828-1926 and 1943-1962, respectively.) Huntington provides an explanation of the political, economic, social, and cultural roots of the democratic process.

Lipset, Seymour Martin. *Political Man: The Social Bases of Politics*. Baltimore: The Johns Hopkins University Press, 1981. Through an analysis of an enormous amount of empirical data, Lipset in this classic study explores the conditions necessary for democracy; the relationship between political participation and voting behavior; and the support for pro- and antidemocratic movements and values.

Mainwaring, Scott, Guillermo O'Donnell, and J. Samuel Valenzuela, eds. *Issues in Democratic Consolidation: The New South American Democracies in Comparative Perspective*. Notre Dame, Ind.: University of Notre Dame Press, 1992. The eight essays in this volume, written by leading scholars in the field, provide perceptive analyses of the complex processes related to the transitions from authoritarian to civil rule in Latin America.

O'Donnell, Guillermo, Philippe Schmitter, and Lawrence Whitehead, eds. *Transitions from Authoritarian Rule: Comparative Perspectives*. Baltimore: The Johns Hopkins University Press, 1986. The essays contained in this volume deal with transitions from authoritarian to democratic regime in Spain, Portugal, and several Latin American countries in the late 1970's and early 1980's.

Schumpeter, Joseph. *Capitalism, Socialism, and Democracy*. 3d ed. New York: Harper & Row, 1950. A classic study of the three political systems and the nature of political systems that mix parts of each.

Vanhanen, Tatu. *The Process of Democratization: A Comparative Study of 147 States, 1980-88*. New York: Crane Russak, 1990. Through an application of the Darwinian theory of natural selection to the study of political systems, this comparative study explains variations of political systems and democratization in 147 states.

Sunil K. Sahu

Cross-References

Authoritarian and Totalitarian Governments, 153; Bureaucracies, 172; Legitimacy and Authority, 1055; The Nation-State, 1282; Party Politics in the United States, 1343; Political Action Committees and Special Interest Groups, 1387; Power: The Pluralistic Model, 1484; Revolutions, 1641; Socialism and Communism, 1873.

DEMOGRAPHIC FACTORS AND SOCIAL CHANGE

Type of sociology: Social change
Field of study: Sources of social change

Demographic factors refer both to a human population's static characteristics, such as age and sex compositions, and to its dynamic characteristic, such as birth, death, migration, and growth rates. These factors both contribute to and respond to various dimensions of social change.

> *Principal terms*
> CARRYING CAPACITY: the maximum population that a given society can support, given a set of resource and ecological conditions
> COMPOSITION: the proportion of a population composed of individuals possessing select characteristics; for example, a population's age composition indicates whether most of its members are old or young
> DEMOGRAPHY: the study of population
> POPULATION: a group of individuals or objects that share one or more common characteristics
> RATE: the number of events occurring in a time period divided by the population at risk of experiencing the event
> SECULARIZATION: the dispersal of an autonomous, individualistic outlook on life
> SOCIOCULTURAL SYSTEM: a term nearly synonymous with the term "human society," except that it emphasizes the interdependence of a society's components
> SUBPOPULATION: a term that refers to a subset of the total population that shares one or more distinguishing characteristics, such as age

Overview

Human sociocultural systems, or societies, consist of a number of interdependent components. A societal component both reflects the attributes of the other components of society and produces changes in them. One component is population, the group of people living within a society. The study of human populations is the domain of demography; accordingly, the characteristics of a population are often referred to as demographic factors. Demographic factors are sometimes divided into two groups: static factors and dynamic factors.

Static factors are the characteristics of a population that may be observed from a "snapshot" depicting a population at one particular moment. A population's composition, distribution, and size are among its static attributes. Population size, the most straightforward demographic factor, simply refers to the number of people living in the geographic area occupied or possessed by a given society. This basic factor performs a vital role in terms of social change; it has a major impact on a society's economic productivity, organizational complexity, and rate of technological innovation. For example, compared with their smaller counterparts, societies possessing relatively large populations are generally characterized by relatively high levels of productivity, complex governments and patterns of social interactions, and high rates of technological innovation. Changes in other components of society also affect population size. Demographers contend that the biophysical environment in which a society is situated, together with that society's technological capabilities to extract, produce, and distribute subsistence resources defines an upper limit on the size of a society's population, a limit often referred to as the society's "carrying capacity." Thus, societies that are characterized by a more productive level of technology and a more egalitarian pattern of resource distribution generally are capable of supporting larger populations than are those societies with less productive technologies and more marked inequality.

The distribution and composition factors refer to the relative size of select segments of a given society's population. Like the overall population size, these factors both contribute to and reflect other social change. The factor of population distribution, for example, addresses the issue of the proportion of a population living in one geographic area as opposed to the proportion living in another. A common distribution metric is the proportion of a society's population that resides in urban areas. On the one hand, populations characterized by a heavily urban distribution reflect previous social changes, perhaps most notably the presence of an economic surplus that freed some members of the population from the land-intensive task of agricultural production and industrialization, a much less land-intensive mode of production. On the other hand, heavily urban populations often lead to a variety of social changes, including the development of large, complex public service organizations such as police and fire-fighting forces; health care facilities; transportation systems; and water, sewer, and power utilities.

Dynamic factors refer to the changes that occur in the static factors during a given time period. Thus, as the static factors pertain to a population's size, the dynamic factors pertain to changes in a population's size. Demographers specify three possible sources of this change: fertility, mortality, and migration. These factors make up the so-called demographic equation, wherein a change in the size of a population between two points in time is attributed to births minus deaths plus in-migrants minus out-migrants. Population growth occurs when this summation is a positive figure, and population decline is experienced when the sum of deaths and out-migrants is greater than the sum of births and in-migrants.

Demographic research on the so-called demographic transition provides several good examples of the interdependence of the dynamic factors with other societal components. The demographic transition refers to a basic pattern of dramatic reductions in mortality rates and fertility rates that have occurred in many of the wealthier societies of the world. Such social changes as improvements in living standards and advancements in medical technology appear to have led to the substantial reductions in mortality rates. Until matched by a decline in fertility rates, reductions of mortality rates sometimes yield population growth that approaches some societies' carrying capacities. Although demographers have not yet determined all the sources of the fertility decline that complete the demographic transition, they have identified a variety of social changes that appear to have contributed to the decline, notably industrialization, improvements in living conditions, and secularization. Changes in fertility rates also have been identified as stimuli for social change. Reductions in fertility rates have been attributed to postponements in the average age at first marriage, increased female participation in the labor force, and a reduction in gender inequality. Overall, a population is generally larger after the demographic transition than before it, and, as noted above, the larger size leads to a variety of social changes involving the level of societal complexity, the roles of a number of social institutions (including the family), and the population's age structure.

Applications

Several good examples of the relationships between demographic factors and social change surface in comparisons of the earliest type of human societies, hunting and gathering societies, with later types. Hunting and gathering societies were characterized by a very rudimentary mode of subsistence technology which generally limited their populations to fewer than fifty people. The small size of these societies was often associated with a low level of societal complexity and with the central role of the family in social organization. For example, there was very little occupational specialization in hunting and gathering societies; by and large, the men hunted and the women gathered. This lack of differentiation carried over into the political and economic spheres, as these societies were generally marked by very little inequality. Typically, the populations of these societies were fairly homogeneous, and most members were related to one another. Indeed kinship—that is, the family—formed the basis of and outlined the structure of social organization. Sociologists Gerhard Lenski, Jean Lenski, and Patrick Nolan, for example, point out that in most hunting and gathering societies, "kin groups perform[ed] many of the functions that are performed by schools, business firms, governmental agencies, and other specialized organizations in larger, more advanced and more differentiated societies."

Compared with hunting and gathering societies, horticultural, agrarian, and industrial societies possess much more productive subsistence technologies and, as a result, possess much larger populations, ranging from several hundred members to several million members. The greater population sizes give rise to more heterogeneous population compositions and, in turn, increase societal complexity and reduce the parallelism between the society and the family that is found in hunting and gathering societies. The larger populations also contribute to reductions in the roles and functions performed by the family. In many of these societies, for example, one finds well-developed political, religious, and economic institutions that transcend the bounds of a single family, as well as economic, occupational, and other social relationships that rival the family for primacy in terms of organizing social interaction and relationships.

It bears emphasizing that the previously noted differences in societal complexity, population composition, and the role and functions of the family are at least the partial result of differences in population size. One might consider as an analogy some of the differences between a small family dinner and a large family reunion. The population of a small family dinner may consist of parents and their children, and the conversation and other interactions would likely be relaxed and informal, with the relationships between members being apparent to all. In contrast, the populations of family reunions may consist of several hundred people who do not regularly interact. As a result, interactions between members are often less relaxed and more formal, requiring name tags, seating charts, scheduled activities, and sometimes even a hired, outside planner. In short, a larger population yields greater complexity and more formal interactions. In a similar manner, the growth of the populations of human societies also spawns considerable social change.

Perhaps a more immediate example of the relationship between demographic factors and social change involves changes in the age composition of the United States' population since the nineteenth century. The median age of this population increased from about sixteen years in 1800 to more than thirty-two years in 1989. Thus, this population has grown older. Population aging is a result of the reductions in both mortality and fertility rates that compose the demographic transition. Decreased mortality rates make a population's age composition older by extending life. Decreased fertility rates contribute to the aging of a population by reducing the number of young people born into it and thus reducing the proportion of the population that is young.

The American population's aging also entails a demographic phenomenon that has become known as "graying." Graying refers to an increase in the proportion of the population aged sixty-five years or greater. John Weeks, a demographer and sociologist at San Diego State University, reports that the number of Americans aged sixty-five years and over increased from about three million in 1900 to thirty-one million in 1990. This aspect of the changing age composition of the United States population has produced profound social changes. For example, the growing elderly population was a major impetus for the passage of the Social Security Act in 1935. By providing a means for retirement, this legislation was intended to remove the burgeoning elderly subpopulation from the competition for the all-too-scarce jobs of the Depression era.

The graying of America has also left its mark on the economic dimension of society. On the one hand, the growth of the elderly subpopulation may be viewed as an economic asset. It has led to the development or expansion of numerous thriving industries that cater to the needs and desires of the sizable elderly subpopulation, a significant proportion of which receives income from pensions. These industries include health care, residential assistance, travel, and social clubs, to name but a few. On the other hand, a number of possible economic detriments of the graying of the United States' population have surfaced. For example, as the average length of life continues to be extended and as the proportion of the population that is elderly and retired or semiretired continues to grow, the United States' pay-as-you-go system of Social Security may be placed in jeopardy. In any event, the social changes associated with the graying of the U.S. population are likely to continue and expand as the large baby boom cohort moves into retirement.

Context

The existence of a relationship between demographic factors and social change has been acknowledged for centuries, and the characteristics of the relationship have been the subject of debate for almost as long. One of the most famous perspectives on the relationship between demographic factors and other social characteristics was that espoused by Thomas Malthus in his 1798 work *An Essay on the Principle of Population*. Malthus, writing in response to utopian social philosophers who contended that continuing technological advance would be able to support an infinitely large human population, argued that populations had the capacity to grow more rapidly than the support of subsistence resources. Hence, Malthus contended that unchecked population growth inevitably resulted in poverty, and that poverty could only be avoided through reducing fertility and, as a result, slowing the growth of a population's demand for subsistence resources. Many of the fundamental tenets of Malthus' theory remain popular and are reflected in the work of neo-Malthusians such as Stanford University biologist Paul Ehrlich, who argues that much of the world's misery and poverty could be reduced by the widespread adoption of low-fertility practices. Indeed, in 1990, the poorest societies of the world were generally among those with the fastest growing populations.

Malthus' basic position has been and continues to be met with considerable opposition, however; among Malthus' most notable critics were nineteenth century social philosophers Karl Marx and Friedrich Engels. Marx and Engels argued that the poverty described by Malthus was not attributable to the existence of too many people relative to the supply of resources but rather to inefficient, unjust systems of resource production and distribution. Devotees of this position persist, but attempts to apply it have met with, at best, limited success. The fact that the Marx-inspired Chinese government had to implement a coercive policy allowing only one child per family, for example, suggests that even large-scale social reorganization is not sufficient to meet the consumptive demands of a population experiencing unlimited growth.

Another very important but less controversial sociological perspective on the relationship between demographic factors and social change was proposed by Émile Durkheim. In 1893, Durkheim undertook a comparative approach and argued that increased population size produces greater societal complexity, in particular greater occupational specialization—a greater division of labor. Durkheim contended that "the division of labor varies in direct ratio with the volume and density of societies, and, if it progresses in a continuous manner in the course of social development, it is because societies become regularly denser and more voluminous." Durkheim's classic position is generally accepted and has been widely applied to the study of such phenomena as the complexity of large business organizations.

Bibliography

Ehrlich, Paul, and Anne H. Ehrlich. *The Population Explosion*. New York: Simon & Schuster, 1990. This book is an update of Paul Ehrlich's popular 1968 book, *The Population Bomb*. Like its predecessor, this book addresses the problems that may arise from the continued growth of the human population in conjunction with environmental degradation. It also assesses the social and environmental changes that resulted from the rapid population growth experienced since the publication of the earlier work.

Haupt, Arthur, and Thomas T. Kane. *The Population Reference Bureau's Population Handbook*. 3d ed. Washington, D.C.: Population Reference Bureau, 1991. This is an excellent, inexpensive, and invaluable resource for anyone interested in demography. It provides clear explanations and examples of demographic concepts and metrics, as well as information on various sources of demographic information.

Lenski, Gerhard, Jean Lenski, and Patrick Nolan. *Human Societies*. 6th ed. New York: McGraw-Hill, 1991. A clear overview of the relationships among population and other societal characteristics during the process of social evolution is provided in this unique introductory textbook. Durkheim's proposed relationship between population size and societal complexity may easily be seen in the numerous examples.

Malthus, Thomas. *An Essay on the Principle of Population*. New York: Penguin Classics, 1985. Although written in 1798, this classic document is surprisingly easy and enjoyable to read. This publication includes the first edition of the Malthus essay, a summary of the essay penned by Malthus, and an enlightening introduction by Anthony Flew.

Preston, Samuel. "Children and the Elderly: Divergent Paths for America's Dependents." *Demography* 21 (November, 1982): 435-457. Preston's accessible, engaging essay discusses some of the implications of the graying of the American population. In particular, it focuses on the direct and indirect competition for public resources that occurs between the large and growing elderly subpopulation and the infant and child subpopulation.

Wattenberg, Ben. *The Birth Dearth*. New York: Pharos Books, 1987. In this provocative and controversial book, Wattenberg suggests that the low levels of fertility that have characterized the U.S. population since the 1970's may lead to numerous negative social changes. Included among these hypothesized changes are a decrease in personal happiness, increased turmoil within American society, and an overall decline in the international stature of the United States.

Weeks, John R. *Population: An Introduction to Concepts and Issues*. 5th ed. Belmont, Calif.: Wadsworth, 1992. Perhaps the most popular demography textbook, Weeks's work provides a well-rounded introduction to demography that is both detailed and accessible.

Arlen D. Carey

Cross-References

Demographic Transition Theory of Population Growth, 499; Demography, 506; The Environment and Social Change, 654; Immigration and Emigration, 921; Population Growth and Population Control, 1421; Social Change: Sources of Change, 1786; Technology and Social Change, 2043; Zero Population Growth, 2215.

DEMOGRAPHIC TRANSITION THEORY OF POPULATION GROWTH

Type of sociology: Population studies or demography

Demographic transition theory refers to an empirical description and explanation of the process through which population moves from a low growth stage through a rapid growth stage to a low and stable growth stage. This transition occurs because of changes in mortality and fertility interacting with changing socioeconomic conditions.

Principal terms

DIFFUSION: the geographic spread of ideas, technologies, or products

FERTILITY: the actual live birth performance of a population, often measured by the crude birthrate

MARITAL FERTILITY: the live birth performance of a married population

MORTALITY: the level of death characterizing a population, often measured by the crude death rate

POPULATION MOMENTUM: the tendency for past birthrates to propel future population growth until a full generation of persons has passed childbearing age

SOCIAL DEMOGRAPHY: the study of the social causes and consequences of population phenomena

THEORY OF DEMOGRAPHIC CHANGE AND RESPONSE: a perspective that views fertility behavior as a response to demographic changes

THEORY OF WEALTH FLOW: a perspective that views fertility behavior as a response to the direction of wealth flow between generations

TRANSITION: a temporal process involving sequential shifts from an old stage to a new one

Overview

The demographic transition refers to a historical process of population change. The three-stage transition begins with a pretransition period of slow population growth resulting from combined high levels of fertility (births) and mortality (deaths). The second phase is characterized by declining mortality rates with sustained population growth. In the third stage, fertility rates also decline, resulting in low fertility, low mortality, and a return to low population growth rates.

The world has experienced two major demographic transitions so far. The first started in the late 1700's in Europe and North America and was largely completed by the mid-1900's. The second transition gathered momentum about the time that the first transition was concluding, and it has been concentrated in the developing countries in Asia, Africa, and South America. This second transition continues to the present. There are important distinctions between the pace and quality of these two transitions.

Unprecedented high rates of world population growth and their implications for poverty, social change, and environmental degradation dramatize the importance of understanding demographic theories and the light that they shed on social change.

The first description of three demographic phases was published by American demographer Warren S. Thompson in 1992. Thompson described fertility and mortality patterns of different countries in the period between 1908 and 1927 by dividing the world populations into three groups (A, B, and C) reflecting trends in human population growth in accordance with their levels of mortality and fertility. Group A represented the most advanced countries, characterized by low levels of fertility and mortality. Group B comprised countries where mortality had declined while fertility and population growth rates were still high. Group C referred to the least demographically advanced nations, where neither mortality nor fertility were under control. While Thompson's study provides an empirical description of the three phases of population growth, the causal explanations for the changes were not discussed.

The term "demographic transition" first appeared in Frank W. Notestein's essay, "Population: The Long Run" (1945). Notestein divided population growth into three types: "incipient decline," "transitional growth," and "high growth potential" populations, which are equivalent to Thompson's A, B, and C populations, respectively. In this study and in his later work, Notestein sought to explain why the demographic transition occurs. His theory focuses on the interaction between mortality and fertility in relationship to social and economic development. Following Notestein's research, the classic demographic transition theory can be briefly summarized as follows.

In ancient societies, high mortality was prevalent because of political instability, poor living conditions, and rampant disease. High fertility rates were essential to avoid significant population declines. Because high mortality and fertility canceled each other out, population growth rates were very modest throughout the millennia preceding the 1700's. Social, economic, and technological development in centuries that followed affected mortality before it affected fertility. There were few, if any, social or cultural obstacles to reducing mortality or increasing longevity. In contrast, reducing fertility required significant changes in social norms that had supported high fertility for millennia. The lag in fertility decline accelerated population growth, a feature of the early period of demographic transition. As European nations developed further, states classic transition theory, further declines in mortality and fertility eventually resulted in sustained low levels of population growth.

In European history, the Industrial Revolution generated entirely new social and economic environments. With modernization, the traditional family economy was replaced by specialized production and the free market. Family-based production, which favored large family size, was undermined. Modernization also caused an increase in secular education to levels that altered popular perceptions and social aspirations. Because of urbanization, mobility and opportunities increased and stimulated an increase of nonfamilial activities and labor force participation for both men and women. Because of the changes in socioeconomic settings, the functional value of children decreased, and the cost of child-rearing increased. Women's new economic role became less compatible with childbearing. The need for having many children also lessened with better assurance of child survival. The use of birth control also led to fertility declines in the late 1800's in Europe.

The principle of the demographic transition theory is that fertility decline is mainly an adjustment process in response to changing social and economic conditions. Although classic demographic transition theory is based on deductive reasoning and has been modified in different ways, its principle has been widely influential and provides a central analytical framework for modern social demography.

Applications

Knowledge gained from viewing European population processes in the light of demographic transition theories provides one basis for understanding historical population changes and predicting future population changes in developing countries. Comparison of experiences within European countries, however, indicates that there were important differences in how economic and social development related to fertility decline. Developing countries present their own distinct social, economic, and technological circumstances. Nevertheless, transition theory remains very influential in formulating policy strategies for population planning in developing countries.

The European Fertility Decline Project, led by American demographer Ansley J. Coale, is probably the most thorough attempt at applying transition theory to empirical data on fertility change. Historical mortality and fertility records from seven hundred province-size administrative units of Europe were compared to study the process of mortality and fertility declines. The project found that the classic transition theory does not explain well the diversity of fertility decline among European populations. The theory fits Britain very well; there, fertility decline took place only when a high level of modernization was achieved. In France, however, both mortality and fertility declined almost at the same time, around the French Revolution, when social and economic development remained at a very low level.

The study indicated that the onset of fertility decline in European countries was extraordinarily concentrated in time and was clustered in regions with similar cultural features, such as religion and language, but not with similar social and economic settings. American demographer John Knodel suggested in 1977 that diffusion of the knowledge and skills of family limitation was a significant independent factor for fertility decline. Fertility decline was found to be the result of both adjustment and diffusion.

The pace and magnitude of demographic change in developing countries are unprecedented. Modern medicine, stable agricultural production, and urban transportation systems contributed to an extraordinarily rapid decline in mortality rates, while fertility remained at high levels. The consequence was a dramatic rise in world population, often described as a population explosion, in the second half of the twentieth century. Although fertility has declined in most developing countries since the 1970's, the growth of world population is not projected to stabilize for several decades. The 1993 annual world population growth rate of 1.63 percent, if unchanged, would lead to a doubling of population—to over 11 billion persons—by the year 2035. In high-growth, less-developed countries, population doubling is expected to occur by 2020.

For more than two decades, the question of the relationships between development and family planning has been vigorously debated. Classic demographic transition theories suggest that fertility will spontaneously decline as modernization occurs. Rapid population growth, seen in this light, is only a temporary phase that can be shortened by promoting economic development. Yet lessons from European fertility studies argue that fertility decline can precede significant modernization through introduction of family planning programs. Slowing the pace of population growth may in fact encourage social and economic development. These views were debated at the First World Population Conference in Bucharest, Romania, in 1974. In the conference, many developing countries reiterated that the best contraceptive is development and that development itself will bring about a fertility decline. In contrast, arguments from the developed countries gave a high priority to family planning and the need to halt explosive world population growth. Each perspective argues for different intervention priorities for developing countries.

While the official document of the World Population Conference, *The World Population Plan of Action* (1974), gives greater priority to social and economic development, many developing countries have realized that the effect of social and economic development upon fertility is not immediate and may even be delayed for many decades. Since the 1970's most developing countries have adopted family planning programs. Though birthrates have begun to decline substantially in many of these countries, the impact on population growth rates will not be fully realized for decades. Past high birth rates have resulted in large numbers of young adults of childbearing age, a phenomenon called population momentum.

Demographic transition theory has also been applied to studies of subpopulations, such as ethnic and economic strata within a society. These studies, often classified as social demography, emphasize the effect of socioeconomic, political, ecological, and cultural factors on demographic behavior. In demographic transition theory, individual fertility behavior is considered to be affected by social and economic factors, such as education, urban settings, and the role or social status of women. This model has been adapted, for example, to the general framework of *Determinants of Fertility in Developing Countries: A Summary of Knowledge*, edited by American demographers Rodolfo A. Bulatao and Ronald Lee in 1983. In papers contributed by many leading demographers, fertility decline is analyzed with respect to direct and indirect determinants of the shift from high to low fertility during the process of modernization.

Another example of the application of demographic transition theory is Ronald Rindfuss and James Sweet's *Postwar Fertility Trends and Differentials in the United States* (1977). The authors systematically examine fertility trends and differentiate among different social and economic subgroups in the United States since World War II. Although trends of fertility change are not significantly different, differentials in fertility levels have existed among different social and economic subgroups in the postwar United States. The social, economic, and political implications of differences in mortality, fertility, and growth rates among subpopulations in the United States are matters of considerable public debate.

Social demography, being propelled by statistical analysis, has developed rapidly since the 1950's. The rapid spread of computers for data analysis in the late 1960's has provided sustenance for empirical studies on the interrelationship between fertility behavior and socioeconomic variables. To an extent, any examination of the determinants of mortality and fertility is an extension of the classic demographic transition theory.

Context

By the end of World War II, fertility had declined to very low levels in most of northern and western Europe and North America. Classic demographic transition theory emerged to explain this transformation in scientific terms. Demographic transition was described by American demographer Warren S. Thompson in 1929, French demographer Adolphe Landry in 1934, and British demographer A. M. Carr-Saunders in 1936. It was American demographer Frank W. Notestein, however, who first provided a theoretical explanation for demographic transition in 1945.

Demographic transition theory has been widely accepted as a profound generalization of human population change in modern times. Virtually all modernized societies have low levels of mortality and fertility. High levels of fertility in developing countries appear to be declining as they move toward modernization. Yet classic demographic transition theory lacks the specificity needed to account for the diversity of human population development. Modification of classic transition theory has been conducted in different ways. For example, an adjunct theory, called the theory of demographic change and response, described by American demographer Kingsley Davis in 1963, and Australian demographer John Caldwell's 1976 theory of wealth flow shed new light on understanding fertility transition. In 1971, Wilbur Zelinsky extended transition theory to explain migration, urbanization, and human settlement patterns.

One of the most important studies of transition theory, the Princeton European Fertility Project, concluded that modernization is a sufficient, but not a necessary, condition for fertility decline and that cultural factors can have an independent effect on fertility decline. Necessary conditions for fertility decline were proposed by Ansley J. Coale in 1973. According to Coale, decline occurs when marital fertility decisions are a calculated choice, fertility control is perceived as socially and economically advantageous, and effective means of birth control are available.

Classic transition theory that is based on Western experience cannot be simply applied to developing countries that are currently undergoing a rapid population growth. The first major transition occurred over a period of two hundred years. Developing countries are growing too quickly, often doubling in population every twenty-five years, to allow for another two hundred years of high fertility levels. Most developing countries have adopted family planning programs since the 1970's in conjunction with programs for socioeconomic development. The experience of developing countries in the past two decades indicates that both development and family planning programs are supportive of fertility decline.

Demographic transition theory provides a basic analytical framework that integrates social and economic factors into population studies. Based on this framework, contemporary social demographers have developed numerous studies of socioeconomic determinants of reproductive behavior. The links between fertility and social and economic factors postulated in classic transition theory will continue to influence research and social policies in the future.

Bibliography

Beaver, Steven E. *Demographic Transition Theory Reinterpreted*. Lexington: Mass.: Lexington Books, 1975. Based on analysis of Latin American demographic transition since the end of World War II, this book provides empirical support for demographic transition theory. Classic sociological theory of social change and multivariate statistical data analysis are presented within the framework of classic transition theory. Recommended for students with some introductory level knowledge of sociological theory and methods.

Conference on the Princeton European Fertility Project. *The Decline of Fertility in Europe*. Edited by Ansley J. Coale and Susan Cotts Watkins. Princeton, N.J.: Princeton University Press, 1986. This book is a systematic summary of findings from the European Fertility Project. It provides empirical verification and theoretical modification of classic demographic transition theory as well as rich historical data on European fertility decline.

Notestein, Frank W. "Population: The Long Run." In *Food for the World*, edited by T. W. Schultz. Chicago: University of Chicago Press, 1945. This paper is seminal work on the demographic transition theory. It provides the most basic theoretical considerations of the factors driving the demographic transition.

Van de Walle, Étienne, and John Knodel. *Europe's Fertility Transition: New Evidence and Lessons for Today's Developing World*. Washington, D.C.: Population Reference Bureau, 1980. This short monograph describes findings of the European Fertility Decline Project. By showing the role of diffusion in Europe's historical demographic transitions, the authors challenged classic demographic transition theory with its emphasis on fertility as an adjustment process.

Weeks, John R. *Population: An Introduction to Concepts and Issues*. 5th ed. Belmont, Calif.: Wadsworth, 1992. This introductory textbook has thorough coverage of the field of demography. Discussions of the issues and debates surrounding demographic transition theory are well written; historical population growth and population policy are also well documented. Suggested readings at the end of each chapter and the glossary are very helpful.

Jiajian Chen
Jichuan Wang
James H. Fisher

Cross-References

Demographic Factors and Social Change, 492; Demography, 506; Fertility, Mortality, and the Crude Birthrate, 761; The Industrial Revolution and Mass Production, 946; Industrial Societies, 953; Malthusian Theory of Population Growth, 1113; Population Growth and Population Control, 1421; Population Size and Human Ecology, 1428; Zero Population Growth, 2215.

DEMOGRAPHY

Type of sociology: Population studies or demography

Demography is the study of the characteristics of human populations in relation to birth, death, and migration patterns; it encompasses both empirical data and causal relationships. The field also studies population characteristics such as age, sex, race, income, education, and religion.

Principal terms

AGE/SEX PYRAMID: a graphical construction of the age and sex distribution of a population at one time period

COHORT: a group of people who simultaneously share some common social events, with year of birth being one possible social characteristic

DEMOGRAPHIC TRANSITION: the concept that nations, as they move from underdeveloped to developed, go through three phases that ultimately stabilize the population at relatively low birth and death rates

DEPENDENCY RATIO: the ratio of people of dependent ages (age zero to fourteen and age sixty-five and older) to people of economically active ages (ages fifteen to sixty-four)

EXPECTATION OF LIFE: the average duration of life beyond any particular age (of persons who have attained that age), calculated from a life table

GROSS NATIONAL PRODUCT PER CAPITA: a common measure of average income in a nation, calculated by dividing the total value of goods and services produced by the total population size

Overview

Demography is the scientific study of the characteristics of a human population, both static (stable) and dynamic (changing). In the study of a human population, it is necessary to be aware of the components of growth, which are related to fertility, mortality, and net migration patterns in a society. The fertility patterns of a society refer to the number of children born. In his book *Population: An Introduction to Concepts and Issues* (5th ed., 1992), John R. Weeks demonstrates that fertility may have both a biological and social component. The biological component includes the ability of women and men to conceive children, while the social component includes such factors as the timing of marriage (for example, child marriages in India versus marriage at a later age in Ireland) and restrictions on sexual behavior.

The mortality component of population growth is related to the expectation of life for individuals in a social order. This average expectation is related to the death rates for the younger and older members of a society. Nations may be described either as underdeveloped or developed in relation to their gross national product (GNP) per capita, with underdeveloped nations having a relatively low GNP (for example, $1,000) and developed nations having a relatively high GNP ($15,000). In underdeveloped nations there is a high death rate for both the very young and very old, whereas in developed nations the death rate is low for the very young, and then increases steadily with age. In underdeveloped nations people die from both communicable diseases (such as malaria) and chronic diseases (such as heart disease, cancer, and stroke), whereas in developed nations people are more likely to die from chronic illnesses.

With regard to migration, one may differentiate between internal and international migration. Internal population shifts are most often related to changes in economic conditions in different geographic areas; the human population is likely to move internally from areas of low economic growth to areas of higher economic growth. In the United States since World War II there has been a general westward migration related to increased economic opportunity in Western states. Roderic Beaujot's book *Population Change in Canada: The Challenges of Policy Adaptation* (1991) illustrates these influences at work in Canada, with British Columbia, with its growing economy on the Pacific rim, experiencing the greatest rate of population growth. International economic factors are also very important in explaining migration trends among nations.

The shifts in population growth within societies over time may be explained by the process known as demographic transition. As nations begin the process of modernization, which involves a shift from an agrarian economy to an industrial economy, they experience high rates of both fertility and mortality. As they undergo economic transformation, however, they experience an initial fall in their mortality rates, with their fertility rates remaining high. This initial demographic shift causes a significant increase in population for these nations. In the case of European nations, international migration served as a safety valve for many nations when they underwent this process. Over time, industrializing nations experience a fall in their fertility rates because industrialization increases the economic costs of children while reducing their economic benefits. When the fertility and mortality rates are in balance, these nations experience stable population growth. Many underdeveloped nations of the world are undergoing the process of demographic transition. In his book *Preparing for the Twenty-first Century* (1993), Paul Kennedy demonstrates that these nations are in a disadvantaged economic position compared to the European nations that underwent this process earlier, so the transition will be more difficult for these nations.

There are a number of measures that can be employed to examine the changing components of a human population. One measure is a cohort—people who experience some common social event. All individuals are members of a birth cohort, but at times a generational cohort may be formed by certain historical events. One illustration of a generational cohort is all individuals who participated in the American Civil War.

Another useful tool for examining a human population is an age/sex pyramid, which gives a graphical representation of the number of people of a given age and sex in a society during a particular time period. The population pyramid coveys useful information about the demographic characteristics of a society. For example, underdeveloped nations have a pyramid with a large base, since they have a high rate of fertility. By contrast, the upper portion of the pyramid is larger in developed nations because of falling fertility and an increased expectation of life. If a society experiences a significant rise in fertility (as the United States did with the baby boom between 1945 and 1955) or mortality (as in the Soviet Union between 1941 and 1945), these demographic changes will influence its population pyramid.

Another useful population measure is the dependency ratio (DR), which determines the relative ratio of the dependent population (most often given as ages zero to fourteen and age sixty-five and older) to the economically active population fifteen to sixty-four. As developed nations undergo aging, they experience a rise in their aged DR; underdeveloped nations continue to have a high youth DR until they become modernized.

The scientific study of human population involves a determination of the factors that cause shifts in fertility, mortality, and net migration within a society. In his classic study *Principles of Demography* (1969), Donald J. Bogue illustrates how one can quantify the previous measures and employ them to examine the characteristics of human populations mathematically.

Applications

The knowledge obtained from demographic studies can be employed in a number of substantive areas. The first area is the field of aging. An understanding of demography allows gerontological researchers to study changes in the relative age composition of a human population and to determine the social consequences of these changes. A fall in fertility and mortality rates, as is occurring in developed nations, implies that there will be fewer younger people to provide care for the elderly and proportionally more older people in these societies. The process of demographic transition is also occurring in underdeveloped nations. For example, the significant fertility drop in China, the result of strict government policies, will have social implications for that country well into the twenty-first century. The increased aging of the human population in developed nations also means that the aged DR will increase, which will put more social pressure on public institutions, such as the United States' Social Security system.

A second area in which demographic principles may be applied is the strategic planning of business organizations. These economic organizations need to have demographic information on the sizes and locations of their markets. Market research techniques are employed to locate different socioeconomic groups within this market. Marketing work related to the beer brewing industry provides an example. Market researchers for this industry have determined that young males are their prime market, and the industry targets these individuals with extensive advertising on televised sporting events. A dynamic examination of demographic trends indicates a shrinking of this market (attributable partly to the aging of the American population), which has caused this industry to diversify and create new products such as nonalcoholic beer.

A third area in which demographic information is crucial involves governmental activities. In order to apportion elected officials in the House of Representatives, the United States government needs information on the changing geographical distribution of the American population. The federal government also needs demographic information to manage a series of entitlement programs, including Social Security and Medicare. For these entitlement programs it is necessary for the government to have information on the numeric size and longevity of the elderly population as well as on future population trends. Similarly, the Department of Veterans Affairs needs demographic information on veterans in the United States, especially the large World War II cohort.

Demographic information is also useful in the scientific study of deviant behavior. A number of studies have shown that younger males make up the group most likely to commit criminal acts. Robert A. Easterlin has developed a theory arguing that the relative size of a cohort will influence its members' propensity for deviant behavior. According to this theory, smaller age cohorts, such as the youth cohort in the 1940's and 1950's, had greater economic opportunities, were subject to fewer social pressures, and therefore were less likely to commit deviant acts. The opposite is true for large cohorts, such as the youth cohorts in the 1960's and 1970's, and members of these cohorts have a greater probability of becoming deviant.

Race and ethnic relations is another area in which demographic information is useful. In this area there is a need for information on the relative size of minority populations, their fertility and mortality patterns, and their geographic distribution within the nation in order to formulate government policy. It is also necessary to have information on their socioeconomic situations as well as on their health characteristics. Studies carried out by the U.S. Bureau of the Census indicate that nonwhites have approximately half the income of whites, they own approximately one-twelfth the property of whites, and their children have a significantly greater probability of being in poverty.

Demographic studies are important in the field of international relations. United Nations organizations collect information on the demographic characteristics of nations throughout the world, and they use this information to aid nations in family planning and the control of mortality within their population. Early studies of mortality in underdeveloped nations showed a high level of mortality among young people caused by infectious diseases, and the United Nations proceeded to develop programs to control these diseases (malaria control in southern India is one example).

Religious organizations and the mass media also use demographic information. Religious organizations require information on the relative number of their adherents, their geographic location, and the socioeconomic characteristics of this population. The mass media (television, radio, popular magazines, and newspapers) require information on the size of their potential market and the demographic characteristics of the population that consumes their products.

Context

Since ancient times, leaders and philosophers have been concerned with population issues. Usually these concerns involved the replacement of people lost through high mortality rates. Prior to the Middle Ages, societies encouraged high fertility levels among their populations. During the Middle Ages, under the influence of Christian doctrines, there was an attempt to limit fertility, but this view changed with the Renaissance.

Prior to the 1700's, societies did not possess accurate information on the composition of their populations. The Roman Empire, for example, did conduct periodic census enumerations, but they had limited scientific value since they were taken only for administrative purposes and included only citizens and adult males. In 1749 Sweden began the first modern census, and it was soon followed by Norway, Denmark, and the United States. With the growth of statistical procedures in the nineteenth century to analyze the census information, this information began to be useful to policy makers and social scientists. In addition to performing numerical counts, censuses began to ask questions about the age, occupation, literacy, and employment characteristics of the population being examined.

The first scientific examination of the social consequences of population changes may be found in Thomas Malthus' work *An Essay on the Principle of Population* (1798), which maintained that population growth was subject to a natural law. According to Malthus, population unchecked would grow at a geometric rate, while agricultural production would only grow at an arithmetic rate. In order to have social stability, he said, it was necessary to bring them into balance. He identified two types of checks that could do this. First, there were positive checks, which increased mortality; these included war, famine, and plague. Second, there were preventive checks, which limited human births; these included abortion and the delay of marriage.

In the nineteenth century, Marxian theory criticized the Malthusian perspective, arguing that, historically, each society develops a means of economic organization that determines both the level and consequences of population growth. Later in the nineteenth century, Émile Durkheim related population growth to societal specialization.

With the growth of more accurate quantitative data and more sophisticated statistical techniques in the twentieth century, demography developed as a scientific discipline. Better census data, as well as the introduction of survey data, allowed the further development of the field, with an ability to test scientific theories (such as the theory of demographic transition). The field was also able to provide precise information that could be employed in a number of other disciplines. The computer revolution, which began after World War II, has been instrumental in expanding knowledge in the field. Computers have allowed investigators to develop techniques to better understand the current population distribution in a society and make future projections concerning this population.

Bibliography

Beaujot, Roderic. *Population Change in Canada: The Challenges of Policy Adaptation*. Toronto, Ont.: McClelland & Stewart, 1991. Using Canadian society as its empirical base, this book presents an excellent discussion of basic demographic concepts and uses them to interpret population changes in Canada.

Bogue, Donald J. *Principles of Demography*. New York: John Wiley & Sons, 1969. A thorough and complete analysis of demographic principles, with a mathematical exposition of techniques for population projections. An outstanding and classic work in the field of demography.

Coale, Ansley J., and Edgar M. Hoover. *Population Growth and Economic Development in Low-Income Countries*. Princeton, N.J.: Princeton University Press, 1958. A classic discussion of the economic consequences of continued population growth for countries such as India and Mexico. The work demonstrates the need for family planning in underdeveloped nations.

Kennedy, Paul. *Preparing for the Twenty-first Century*. New York: Random House, 1993. A well-written essay from a Malthusian perspective on the social, economic, and political consequences of population changes in developed and underdeveloped nations.

Mason, William M., and Stephen E. Fienberg, eds. *Cohort Analysis in Social Research*. New York: Springer-Verlag, 1985. A set of readings by various scholars that defines and explores issues related to cohort analysis in the social sciences. The book has an excellent discussion of how scholars may de-aggregate age, period, and cohort effects when analyzing longitudinal data.

Menard, Scott W., and Elizabeth Moen. *Perspectives on Population: An Introduction to Concepts and Issues*. New York: Oxford University Press, 1987. A set of readings by population scholars that considers demographic issues in a number of disciplines. For example, the book considers how birth order influences social behavior.

Weeks, John R. *Population: An Introduction to Concepts and Issues*. 5th ed. Belmont, Calif.: Wadsworth, 1992. A good general introduction to the field of demography, with a broad discussion of the history of the discipline and the broad analytic elements in the field. Many illustrative figures are used, and each chapter emphasizes central demographic principles.

Zopf, Paul E., Jr. *Population: An Introduction to Social Demography*. Palo Alto, Calif.: Mayfield, 1984. A broad and illustrative introduction to the field of demography, with many useful illustrations of issues in the field (such as zero population growth). The book will be most useful for students who need to have an elementary understanding of basic demographic concepts.

Ira M. Wasserman

Cross-References

Demographic Factors and Social Change, 492; Demographic Transition Theory of Population Growth, 499; Infant Mortality, 978; Malthusian Theory of Population Growth, 1113; Population Growth and Population Control, 1421; Population Size and Human Ecology, 1428; Population Structure: Age and Sex Ratios, 1434; Zero Population Growth, 2215.

DEPRIVATION THEORY OF SOCIAL MOVEMENTS

Type of sociology: Collective behavior and social movements
Field of study: Sources of social change

Society is constantly changing, and some of its large-scale shifts occur in discernible patterns. Such social movements have multiple causes, and deprivation theory focuses on one element: a group's grievances about its lack of resources in comparison with others. This theory can be applied to movements as diverse as Polynesian cargo cults and the American race riots of the 1960's.

Principal terms

ACTUAL DEPRIVATION: a condition in which one social group actually has fewer goods than another group to the extent that it has inadequate resources for living

CARGO CULT: a religious and social movement that develops when an underdeveloped society's contact with technology's benefits (such as cargo dropped by aircraft) makes the inhabitants aware of their relative deprivation

MILLENARIAN MOVEMENT: a religious movement organized around the expectation of the end of the world

PERCEIVED RELATIVE DEPRIVATION: a condition in which one group perceives itself to possess fewer goods and resources than an adjacent social group, regardless of actual conditions

RELATIVE DEPRIVATION: a condition in which one group possesses fewer goods and resources than an adjacent social group, though not necessarily to the extent that it has inadequate resources

RESOURCE MOBILIZATION THEORY: an explanation for social movements that focuses on changes in the distribution of resources and opportunities for collective action

SOCIAL MOVEMENT: an emergent form of collective behavior, organized in patterns that lead to social change and reorganization

Overview

Human existence is characterized by both materiality and mentality. In other words, people not only possess objects that form their physical environment and resources such as the availability of goods but also have expectations about what they should possess. Society distributes both resources and expectations in unequal ways, and thus differences arise between the resources and expectations. Deprivation occurs when one social group does not have enough resources to sustain life adequately. Relative deprivation describes the condition that exists when a group lacks resources in comparison with another group. In many cases, relative deprivation describes a case in which a group's resources are lower than that group's expectations. In such cases, a group feels deprived (regardless of its actual level of resources within the larger society) when it wants more than it can have. Relative deprivation theory holds that the origins of social movements lie in such feelings of deprivation.

Relative deprivation, according to this theory, causes social movements by galvanizing the group's sense of itself against other social groups (those perceived to have greater amounts of the desired social resources), leading to the group's organization in an attempt to increase its own share of the resources. Relative deprivation may vary with the type of resource that is perceived to be inadequate. Though the deprivation is often most clearly seen when it is economic, there can also be deprivations of civil rights, social influence, choices of geographic location, religious freedom, or other less tangible resources. The sociologists Hans S. Park and T. David Mason, in "The Developmental Parameters of Relative Deprivation Theory" (1986), classify the types of resources that can be considered lacking in cases of deprivation. They did this according to psychologist Abraham Maslow's "hierarchy of needs," thus categorizing deprivations into those affecting survival needs, belongingness needs, leisure needs, and control needs. What is important is not the outsider's objective measure of the deprivation, but the group's own internal sense of lack.

Since resources and expectations can occur in a variety of configurations, there are a number of types of relative deprivation. In some cases, a group consistently increases in resources, causing its expectations to rise as well. If the expectations rise faster than the actual availability of resources, then there is an aspirational relative deprivation: The group aspires to more than it receives. Decremental relative deprivation describes the case in which a group's expectations remain constant but the actual level of resources decreases, creating a widening gap between stable expectations and declining resources.

No matter which pattern formed it, a relative deprivation of sufficient intensity produces a sense within a social group that it must act in order to correct the situation. The social group expects the availability of certain resources, and if there is a sufficient threat to the group's ability to obtain them, the group will organize itself in order to change the social distribution of goods. The organization can be formal, such as the creation of a new political party, or it can be informal, such as group riots and other forms of collective violence. Each social group responds to its specific relative deprivation in ways appropriate to the precise nature of its deprivation as well as to the context of its own particular history and traditions. In religious groups, for example, relative deprivation can result in the formation of messianic movements that attempt to restructure society in favor of the group's religious adherents.

The theory of relative deprivation operates primarily within the cognitive domain. People perceive that their possession of resources is less than what they believe to be ideal or less than what they consider just and fair. As such, it operates as a cognitive examination of the world, an evaluative comparison of one's own group's position in relation to other social groups. It thus implies an awareness, at least partially, of the world beyond one's own group. This can be at an international scale, or as localized as within neighborhoods. Furthermore, relative deprivation requires that the deprived group believe that its deprivation stems from unjust treatment by others. That is, the group believes that it has not earned the lack of resources, but rather that there exists a situation that it evaluates as wrong, requiring an appropriate means of redress.

Relative deprivation theory is not without its problems. Since every society distributes its resources unequally, all societies deprive some groups in certain ways. Thus, every society experiences the sort of deprivation that might give rise to collective action. The difficulty is in the prediction of the collective behavior and the specification of the sort of reaction produced by the deprivation, and no theory has proven very successful in providing such predictions. Relative deprivation theory is therefore more powerful as a commonsense explanation of social movements than as a predictor of such movements' rise, even though more carefully nuanced versions of the theory provide greater promise for their predictive ability.

Applications

Many sociologists have argued that perceived relative deprivation causes social movements. For example, the so-called "cargo cults" of the southern Pacific islands provide examples of cultural contact that ultimately resulted in social movements. These island societies had experienced almost no contact with the outside world until the mid-twentieth century, when they began to notice airplanes flying above. Occasionally an airplane would crash or would drop cargo onto an island. This created a shocking awareness: The world contained many more resources than these islanders had ever known. Individuals then debated the best ways for them to obtain these resources. Since they often believed the airplanes to be gods, many of them constructed religious arguments about how to attain more goods. The sudden advent of perceived relative deprivation destabilized the island societies, resulting in a variety of social movements that often toppled existing patterns of social organization.

Historical sociologist Yonina Talmon, in "Millenarian Movements" (1966), defined millenarian movements as "the quest for total, imminent, ultimate, this-worldly, collective salvation." Millenarian movements provide the extreme example of relative deprivation's drive toward redress, since they emphasize the complete triumph of the deprived group. Rather than providing one advantage (whether to correct a specific deprivation or to compensate for it in a different part of life), millenarian movements seek to gain every advantage in all parts of life. Some of the Polynesian cargo cults partook of this extremist collective behavior, seeking a total transformation of their society. Anthropologist Kenelm Burridge observes that in some cases this collective behavior resulted in a society's first integration into a connected political whole. Thus, the group spurred by relative deprivation engaged in a social movement that gained control of their entire society. For such groups, there is no cost too great for immediate action to change the condition of deprivation. This immediacy explains the dynamic power of relative deprivation to produce changes in society, since it radicalizes the motivations of social actors.

Efficacy is another feature of movements stemming from relative deprivation. Not only must a movement attempt to address the deprivation in an immediate fashion, but also it must produce results visible in the transformation of the society and the way that the society distributes its goods. Typically, relative deprivation first provides a chaotic jumble of potential solutions. Once one of the solutions appears to be effective, the social group unites behind it. The collective behavior of the social movement begins once people begin to coalesce behind a specific reaction to relative deprivation. Thus, any example of relative deprivation may produce not only competing ideas of how to solve the problem, but also competing social movements that attempt to create social change to redress the deprivation.

The race riots of the 1960's in the United States provide another example. Whereas many African Americans participated in social movements such as the nonviolent Civil Rights movement, others chose riot and rebellion as the path that seemed to be more effective in creating change. Relative deprivation results in social movements that attempt to redress the perceived inequities in realistic ways. During the 1960's, American society distributed its resources with great inequity between white and black Americans. This did not mean that every African American citizen experienced relative deprivation in the same way. Within this framework of racial inequity there were many different levels of perceived relative deprivation. Some African Americans, including those who had risen to positions of prominence within their own communities, experienced a system that offered them legitimate means for progress that would bring about an equality between resources and the expectations that were part of American culture. These people tended to foster social movements for civil rights, working within the system toward an equality. For others, there was a greater gulf between resources and expectations, and some of these people chose rioting as a means toward equalizing their own personal resources and their expectations of an increasing standard of living. Many African Americans during the 1960's participated in neither social movements nor riots; their own relative deprivation may have been very little, with their possessed resources being equal to their expectations. Though this inactive group may not have been either richer or poorer than the civil rights workers or the rioters, they expected life to treat them in approximately the way that it actually had done, so they had no motivation toward either peaceful or violent social movement.

Immediacy also functioned as a differentiating factor regarding the choice to riot or to work for civil rights. For those with adequate resources in the present, there was less need to redress deprivation in an immediate fashion. Some more impoverished individuals, however, chose a violent means to obtain sufficient goods to raise their standard of living in an immediate fashion. Both the Civil Rights movement and the anarchist rioting, according to deprivation theory, stemmed from the same social factors of relative deprivation, though they were experienced with slight differences in different parts of the community.

Context

Deprivation theories, in one form or another, have influenced sociology through most of its modern period. Surveys of the theory have traced similar notions in writers as diverse as Émile Durkheim, Karl Marx, Robert K. Merton, Alexis de Tocqueville, and Max Weber. Clearly, many sociologists have been persuaded by the simplicity and explanatory power of relative deprivation theory. Groups that experience the frustration of lack, especially lack in comparison to the possessions of others, become increasingly likely to react in strong ways, including a variety of social movements and even collective violence. The theory flourished during the 1960's and 1970's and attempted to explain the race riots and other social movements prevalent in the United States. Elsewhere in the world, especially in western Europe, relative deprivation theory has been fruitfully used to understand phenomena as diverse as the women's movement, student movements, environmental campaigns, and antiwar or peace movements. These types of group behavior, in which subsets of society struggle against their neighbors, have proved to be amenable to analysis using relative deprivation theory.

More recent theoretical works, however, have downplayed the applicability of relative deprivation theory. Specifically, many sociological theorists have argued that relative deprivation theory is a reductionistic explanation of social movements and that there are not simple cause-and-effect relationships between deprivation and specific types of social organization. Furthermore, relative deprivation theory lacks predictive power to distinguish between the several possible reactions to such deprivation. Though this theory is still very prevalent among sociologists, it is now more likely to be found in a modified form, usually combined with other theoretical perspectives.

By the early 1990's, theories about social movements had moved away from concepts of relative deprivation to emphasize resource mobilization. Resource mobilization theory emphasizes the importance of social networks and the prior availability of resources in determining the origin and development of social movements. Also important, this theory holds, is the presence and nature of motivations for participating in social movements and whether these incentives are individual or collective. Other theorists have focused on newer social movements, demonstrating that movements arising in the 1980's and 1990's tend to react against modernism. Such social movements also emphasize noneconomic resources, such as relationships and self-actualization. As theory about social movements continues to develop, one might anticipate more attention being given to the social construction of consensus and to the various mechanisms for diversity and disagreement within that consensus. Such theoretical advances will critique the problems particular to the postindustrial, postmodern, global society.

Bibliography

Crosby, Faye J. *Relative Deprivation and Working Women*. New York: Oxford University Press, 1982. Crosby summarizes relative deprivation theory and applies it to the growth in the number of working women in the United States since World War II. The book offers insight into a case where actual deprivation without perceived relative deprivation resulted in the lack of rapid social change.

Foss, Daniel A., and Ralph Larkin. *Beyond Revolution: A New Theory of Social*

Movements. South Hadley, Mass.: Bergin & Garvey, 1986. This book deals with both relative deprivation and resource mobilization as potential causes of social movements involving physical violence. Offers interesting insights into the interference of social movements with the normal processes of social reproduction and notes the ramifications for relative deprivation.

Gurney, Joan Neff, and Kathleen J. Tierney. "Relative Deprivation and Social Movements: A Critical Look at Twenty Years of Theory and Research." *Sociological Quarterly* 23 (Winter, 1982): 33-47. This article clearly traces the development of relative deprivation theory and then critiques its conceptual basis and empirical usefulness. Though the authors affirm relative deprivation theory as an improvement over most explanations of social movements, they argue that it is not sufficiently reliable to take a central role in studying them.

Gurr, Ted Robert. *Why Men Rebel.* Princeton, N.J.: Princeton University Press, 1970. Gurr offers a very readable explanation of relative deprivation theory. His specific focus is on riots and rebellions in modern capitalist societies. This may be the best summary of theoretical developments in relative deprivation during the boom in work in the field during the 1960's.

Klandermans, Bert. "New Social Movements and Resource Mobilization: The European and the American Approach." *International Journal of Mass Emergencies and Disasters* 4 (August, 1986): 13-37. Klandermans assesses the state of relative deprivation theory in comparison to the newer approaches of resource mobilization and new social movements. He provides helpful sketches of these newer approaches to the question of social movements and carefully relates them to the elements of relative deprivation theory.

Runciman, W. G. *Relative Deprivation and Social Justice: A Study of Attitudes to Social Inequality in Twentieth Century England.* Berkeley: University of California Press, 1966. Runciman's study provides one of the most developed discussions of relative deprivation theory's explanation of particular social conditions and collective behavior, focusing on perceptions and actualities of class inequities. One of this book's particular strengths is its extensive reporting of attitudinal surveys from England in 1962.

Thrupp, Sylvia L., ed. *Millennial Dreams in Action: Essays in Comparative Study.* The Hague: Mouton, 1962. These essays provide an overview of many millenarian movements and cargo cults throughout the world, and this book was influential in interdisciplinary circles. David F. Aberle's chapter on relative deprivation theory provides essential theoretical underpinnings not only for this volume but also for much subsequent discussion of the theory.

Turner, Ralph H., and Lewis M. Killian. *Collective Behavior.* 3d ed. Englewood Cliffs, N.J.: Prentice-Hall, 1987. This overview of the field of collective behavior offers a context for a discussion of relative deprivation, which the authors describe as grievances and connect with great helpfulness to a more general notion of ideology as a basis for social movements.

Worsley, Peter. *The Trumpet Shall Sound: A Study of "Cargo" Cults in Melanesia.*

2d ed. New York: Schocken Books, 1968. This readable study interprets the social movements of Polynesian island residents during initial twentieth century contact with more technologically advanced societies. Worsley offers a specific focus on the interplay of charisma, religion, and nationalism within these social movements.

Jon L. Berquist

Cross-References

Antiwar Movements, 121; The Civil Rights Movement, 265; Collective Behavior, 291; The Free Speech Movement, 767; The Gay Liberation Movement, 799; Revolutions, 1641; Social Movements, 1826; The Structural-Strain Theory of Social Movements, 1997; The Women's Movement, 2196.

DESCRIPTIVE STATISTICS

Type of sociology: Sociological research
Field of study: Data collection and analysis

Descriptive statistics are numerical indices that summarize and communicate basic characteristics of a distribution of scores.

Principal terms

CORRELATION COEFFICIENT: a measure of the degree to which two
variables are related

INFERENTIAL STATISTICS: descriptive indices computed with a sample
of scores that are used to infer the characteristics of a population;
also includes techniques for testing hypotheses

INTERQUARTILE RANGE: the span of scores in a distribution between
which lie 50 percent of the scores

MEAN: a measure of central tendency that is the sum of all the scores
divided by the number of scores

MEDIAN: the point in a distribution below which lie 50 percent of the
scores

MODE: the score in a distribution that occurs most frequently

POPULATION: a group of scores that exhausts the entire universe of
observations of interest

RANGE: the highest score minus the lowest score of a distribution

SAMPLE: a subset of scores from a population from which
characteristics of the population may be inferred

STANDARD DEVIATION: a measure of variability that reflects the average
amount of distance the scores of a distribution are from the mean

Overview

Descriptive statistics are numerical indices used to describe a distribution of scores. In its broadest sense, descriptive statistics includes tabulating data by categories (for example, how many single mothers applied for public aid in a given year, or what percentage of college students practice "safe sex"), as well as sophisticated measures that indicate important aspects of quantitative data.

When behavioral scientists collect data, they often obtain scores that are arranged as a distribution (that is, they are arranged in order of magnitude). The scores may represent such measures as marital satisfaction, family income, political attitudes, or performance on a midterm exam. Simply viewing a list of scores is rather uninformative. For example, if a student has recorded the number of hours spent studying each day during an eight-week period and she is asked how productive she has been, she could simply recite fifty-six numbers, each number representing the amount of time spent studying on a given day. Although much information is communicated, it is not in a form that is very useful to the listener. Descriptive statistics summarize important characteristics of the distribution. One example of a numerical index used to summarize a distribution is the average of all the scores. In the field of statistics, a distinction is made between descriptive and inferential statistics. The distinction is based on whether the scores are viewed by the researcher as representing a population or a sample.

A population and a sample differ, depending on the investigator's primary interest. If the investigator is only concerned with the group of people from which the scores are obtained, then those scores define a population. Parameters are statistical values that describe the distribution characteristics of a population. Summarizing students' test scores on an examination is a common example of the use of population parameters. If the investigator's interest in a group of scores goes beyond those persons providing the scores, however, then the distribution is considered a sample. A sample is used to generalize the results to a larger group of persons. Statistics are those numbers used to generalize the results of a sample to a population. Thus, researchers refer to population parameters and sample statistics. One reason the distinction between a population and a sample is important is that, when summarizing a specific characteristic of a distribution of scores, a different formula might be used, depending on whether the scores are viewed as a population or a sample. When a researcher uses a sample to infer the characteristics of a population, he or she is using inferential statistics. Inferential statistics also includes statistical techniques used to test scientific hypotheses.

Three of the numerous aspects of a distribution that may be summarized are measures of central tendency, measures of variability, and a measure of the degree to which two variables are related. When a score is obtained from each subject in a group, it is typically the case that the same score will occur in the distribution more than once. Using class performance on a midterm exam as an example, the possible scores might range from 0 to 50. A few students might receive a score of 47, a few might receive a score of 20, and a relatively large number of students might receive a score of 38. A table or a graph can be used to show the number of times each score in the distribution occurs. The pattern of scores reflects the shape of the distribution. Descriptive statistics are used to reflect aspects of the shape of the distribution of scores. One important characteristic of a distribution is where in the distribution scores tend to center, or bunch. Numerical indices that reflect where in the distribution scores concentrate are called measures of central tendency. These measures are intended to indicate the middle of the distribution. The average, or arithmetic mean, is one measure of central tendency.

Although conveying measures of central tendency is crucial to the description of a distribution, it is only part of the picture. Measures of central tendency do not provide information about the degree to which scores are spread out in a distribution. Returning to the example of scores on a midterm exam, most of the students received similar scores, with relatively few students obtaining scores far from the average. In this instance, the distribution shows a small amount of spread or variation in scores. If a distribution does not show a "tight" bunching of scores, there is a large amount of variability among the scores. Researchers use measures of variability to convey the degree to which scores in a distribution vary from one another.

Measures of central tendency and variability are two important ways of communicating characteristics of a distribution of scores. A third way in which a distribution can be described is by the use of an index called a correlation, which reflects the degree to which two variables are associated. In the midterm exam example, each student supplies one score. A correlation cannot be computed, since there is only one variable, performance on the exam. If the instructor also obtained a measure of each student's reported amount of anxiety when taking examinations (called test anxiety), however, each student is supplying a pair of scores, one score for test anxiety and one score on the midterm examination. A list of the pairs of scores is called a bivariate distribution ("bi" meaning two, "variate" meaning variable). A correlation can be computed that describes the degree to which test anxiety and exam performance are related or associated.

Applications

Three measures of central tendency are used most commonly: the mean, median, and mode. Each measure communicates a different aspect of centrality. The mean is computed by summing the scores of a distribution and dividing by the number of scores. The mean is the most popular measure of central tendency, particularly in the field of inferential statistics. When the mean is used purely to describe the center of a population of scores, a problem might arise. The mean is highly sensitive to extreme scores in a distribution. If there is a small number of scores, only one score far from the middle of the distribution can affect the mean in such a way that the mean will convey a misleading picture of the middle of the distribution. For example, ten people might be asked to report their annual income. Nine people report incomes between $20,000 and $30,000. Based on these nine people, the mean would be somewhere between $20,000 and $30,000 and would be an accurate measure of where "scores" tend to bunch. If, however, the tenth person in the distribution reports an annual income of $100,000, the mean will be some number much higher than the value computed for the first nine people. In this instance, the mean will offer a distorted picture of where in the distribution annual incomes are centered. If the size of the population is considerably larger than ten people, one extreme score will not have much of an effect on the mean. Several extreme scores will have an influence, however, and the same problem arises. When a distribution has many values that are either relatively high or low, the median is a better descriptive measure of central tendency.

The median is the point in the distribution below which lie 50 percent of the scores. The median is determined by the number of scores below (and above) the middle of the distribution rather than by the value of the scores. Using the example of annual income, including the person with an income of $100,000 in the distribution will have only a small influence on the median. Consequently, the median will be a good representation of the middle of a distribution even when there are extreme scores.

The mode is the least frequently used measure of central tendency. The mode is the score in the distribution that occurs most often; it is the most typical score. The disadvantage of the mode is that it is determined solely by one score (sometimes there are two scores that occur with the same frequency, in which case there are two modes).

Three of the numerous measures of variability are range, standard deviation, and correlation. The first represents the degree to which scores in a distribution are spread out. The range is the entire span of scores, computed by subtracting the lowest score from the highest score. In practice, researchers usually report not only the span of scores but also the highest and lowest scores. Returning again to the example of the midterm exam, every instructor looks at the highest and lowest score; every student, after finding his or her own score in the distribution, looks to identify the top and bottom scores. The range can provide a misleading view of the variability of a distribution. The range is based solely on two scores; moreover, by definition, it is determined only by two extreme scores. In a distribution in which scores are bunched closely around the middle of the distribution (and thus there is little variability among the scores), one extreme score can create the misimpression of considerable variability. For this reason, researchers often rely on a different measure of range, called the interquartile range. The interquartile range is the span of scores within which lie 50 percent of the distribution. Extreme scores have little influence on the interquartile range.

The most common measure of variability is the standard deviation. Every score in the distribution is included in the computation of this index of variability. The standard deviation is based on the relation of all the scores in the distribution to the mean. Every score in a distribution lies some distance from the mean (except those scores that are the same as the mean, in which case the distance is zero). The standard deviation is derived from the average distance of scores from the mean. Imagine a distribution in which all the scores are close together; that is, the scores are close to the mean. The average distance the scores are from the mean will be small. If the distribution is more spread out, there are many scores quite a distance from the mean. In this case, the average distance that scores are from the mean will be greater. Therefore, the standard deviation is an excellent measure for describing the amount of variation among the scores of a distribution. A normally distributed distribution is depicted by a "bell-shaped" curve. In a normal distribution, 68 percent of the scores fall between plus and minus one standard deviation from the mean. For example, intelligence quotient (IQ) scores are normally distributed with a mean of 100 and a standard deviation of 15. Hence, 68 percent of the population have IQs between 85 and 115.

A special case of using a number to describe a distribution is the use of a correlation. A correlation coefficient is a measure of the degree to which variables are associated. A correlation can range in value from +1 to -1. The higher the absolute value of the correlation, the more closely associated the two variables are. A correlation of zero means that the two variables are unrelated. A positive sign means that higher values of one variable are associated with higher values of the other variable. IQ and number of years in school, for example, are positively correlated. A negative correlation means that higher scores of one variable tend to correspond to lower scores on another variable. The correlation between grade point average and test anxiety is negative: Higher scores on a measure of test anxiety are associated with lower grade point averages. The use of correlation coefficients is very common in sociology. Examples of correlations that are of interest to sociologists are the relationships between socioeconomic status and certain types of crimes, between the amount of exposure to violence on television and behavioral aggression, and between men's attitudes toward women and the viewing of pornography that depicts the humiliation of females. There is one important caveat when interpreting the meaning of a correlation: The fact that two variables are associated does not necessarily mean that one variable is the cause of the other variable.

Context

The earliest use of statistics was descriptive and involved the tabulation and summary of data by means of tables and charts. The ancient Egyptians and Chinese used statistics to keep track of tax collections and government expenditures. They also maintained statistics on the availability of soldiers.

The study of statistics in the West began in the seventeenth century with the Englishman John Graunt. Graunt tabulated information on deaths and noted that the frequency of certain diseases, suicide, and accidents occurred with remarkable regularity from year to year. His work was crucial for the establishment of insurance companies. Graunt also found that there were more male than female births but that, because of the greater mortality rate among men (partly from occupational accidents and wars), by marriageable age the number of men and women was about equal.

The first part of the nineteenth century witnessed the emergence of a towering figure in the application of descriptive statistics—Lambert Adolphe Quételet. Quételet conducted extensive observations of social phenomena, most notably criminal behavior. He concluded that criminal behavior was a product of many broad, situational factors surrounding the offender. Because he related social problems to environmental factors, Quételet can be viewed as the first sociologist.

In 1900, only nine universities offered courses in the application of statistics to the study of human behavior. By the 1990's it was impossible for undergraduates to major in any of the social sciences without taking a course in statistics. Sociologists have relied heavily on the use of descriptive statistics; one of the best examples is the analysis of census data. As sociological research has matured, theoretical questions have become more complex, as have methods for data analysis. There has been an increasing interest in conducting research to identify causal relations among variables, an interest that tends to shift the focus of data analysis from descriptive to inferential statistics used in scientific hypothesis testing.

At least one social scientist, Jacob Cohen, cautions against an excessive focus on inferential statistics with the admonition "less is more." What Cohen means is that researchers should closely examine the descriptive summaries of data before embarking on a series of ambitious inferential statistical analyses. The choice is not between descriptive statistics or inferential statistics; rather, he argues, sociologists must use descriptive statistics along with inferential statistics. There is some indication that social scientists are beginning to afford descriptive statistics a more important role in modern research. In 1977, for example, John Tukey published a seven-hundred-page book on "simply" describing data.

Bibliography

Brown, Foster L., Jimmy R. Amos, and Oscar G. Mink. *Statistical Concepts: A Basic Program*. 2d ed. New York: Harper & Row, 1975. This is an excellent paperback that presents many topics in statistics in the form of "learning modules." The modules that cover measures of central tendency and variability are presented as a series of "frames" with three parts: a brief explanation of a concept, a question about the concept, and the correct answer. Readers will be able to master the basic concepts of descriptive statistics in one day.

Grimm, Laurence G. *Statistical Applications for the Behavioral Sciences*. New York: John Wiley & Sons, 1993. This textbook devotes about 150 pages to descriptive statistics. Chapters 3 and 4 are devoted exclusively to measures of central tendency and variability. Written for students who do not have a strong background in mathematics.

Jaccard, James, and Michael Becker. *Statistics for the Behavioral Sciences*. 2d ed. Belmont, Calif.: Wadsworth, 1990. Chapters 3 and 4 cover measures of central tendency and variability. Chapter 5 presents the topic of correlation as a descriptive technique for measuring the association between two variables. This textbook is written at an introductory level.

Phillips, John L., Jr. *How to Think about Statistics*. Rev. ed. New York: W. H. Freeman, 1992. The author presents numerous introductory topics in the field of statistics. The emphasis is on the conceptual basis of statistics rather than on calculation. The content is very easy to understand. This book does not treat descriptive statistics in the depth found in college textbooks used to teach an introduction to statistics, but it is an excellent source if one is not taking a course in statistics.

Walker, Helen M. *Studies in the History of Statistical Method*. Baltimore: Williams & Wilkins, 1929. Widely viewed as the finest book on the history of statistics. The history of probability theory, inferential statistics, and descriptive statistics is traced from the beginning of history. Many sections will be difficult for the beginning student, but sections involving formulas can be skipped without hindering one's appreciation of the roots of modern statistics.

Laurence G. Grimm

Cross-References

DEVIANCE: ANALYSIS AND OVERVIEW

Type of sociology: Deviance and social control
Fields of study: Forms of deviance; Social implications of deviance; Theories of
 deviance

Deviance refers to behaviors that are defined by those in power as violations of
societal norms. Some forms of deviance break codified law; other behaviors are
defined as deviant because of the negative reactions of others. Deviance and its
counterpart, social control, are present in all societies and are essential to the
existence and smooth functioning of societies.

Principal terms
> ELITE DEVIANCE: deviant behaviors with little risk to the perpetrator;
> some are specifically criminal, some are unethical, and some
> endanger public health, safety, or financial well-being
> HEGEMONY: the preponderance of influence and power held by a
> society's formal leadership; governments and major religions tend to
> be the most predominant hegemonic structures in societies
> IDEOLOGY: a system of beliefs and values; a dominant cultural ideology
> is assumed to exist and be reflected in laws and regulations; in
> actuality, many ideologies coexist in a society
> LABELING: the process of naming deviance and deviants; a label
> "sticks" when bestowed by those in power, often creating stigma and
> master status
> MASTER STATUS: a deviant label that, once applied, is very difficult to
> shed; the labels "convict" and "child molester" are two examples
> MORAL ENTREPRENEURS: persons who attempt to define behavior as
> deviant; some have official power, but many do not
> NORMS: the behavioral expectations of a group or society, based on
> values held to be fundamental; some become codified into laws
> POWER: the ability of a person or group to force its will on others even
> in the face of explicit (or implicit) opposition
> SECRET DEVIANCE: a classification for acts such as gambling,
> prostitution, homosexual behaviors, and individual drug use;
> participation in such activities is said to be voluntary and consensual
> SOCIAL CONTROL: attempts by the leaders of a society to regulate the
> behavior of citizens by specifying certain behaviors as deviant and
> establishing consequences for engaging in such behaviors

Overview

Most sociologists would probably agree on a basic description of deviance as
behavior that violates basic values and norms of society. Differences quickly arise,
however, when more probing questions are raised. One might ask, for example, whose

basic values are being violated—and who defined certain values as "basic." Who defines what behaviors are violations of these basic values? Why is it that only some people who violate certain norms and values are labeled "deviant"?

A principal objective of all societies is survival, and all societies believe that to ensure survival, order must be maintained. The maintenance of order is accomplished through the passage of laws and regulations, the purpose of which is to control the behaviors of the population so that individuals do not succumb to individualistic behaviors which would be destructive to the collectivity. Thus, in a democracy, through the ideology supported by elected officials and other leaders, laws are passed "for the greater good" that prescribe and proscribe behaviors in which citizens may and may not engage.

In sociological terms, proscribed behaviors are known as "deviant" behaviors and are defined in relation to what people in power have defined as the society's basic values. Assisting the leaders of societies in their definition of deviant behaviors are what sociologists call "moral entrepreneurs"—people and groups who want particular behavior defined as deviant because the behavior violates their own norms and values. Over time, society labels numerous behaviors as deviant, even behaviors that do no harm to others—that have no "victims." For example, secret deviance (such as extramarital affairs and same-sex sexual relations) and victimless crimes (gambling, excessive drinking) are behaviors that are engaged in voluntarily and consensually.

Until fairly late in the twentieth century, most definitions of deviance were focused on what could be called "one-to-one" deviance—that is, acts committed by one person (or by a small group) against a single other person (a victim). In the mid- to late twentieth century, attention began to focus on what might be called "one-to-many" types of deviance: so-called elite deviance and white-collar crimes (such as violations of environmental laws, financial system scams and embezzlement, medical and health improprieties, and computer crimes) in which the action of an individual has wide-ranging effects.

The counterpart to deviance is social control, the purpose of which is to regulate the behaviors of people in a society in order to maintain the relatively tranquil survival of social systems. Social control may be seen as both necessary and functional. Yet in order for there to be a need for control, there must be behaviors in which people engage which have been defined by those in power as not under control (as deviant). This raises an interesting question: Which came first, the deviance or the social control? Perhaps it does not matter which came first; both deviance and social control exist in all societies, and both appear to be necessary and functional for the continuance of societies. Social control is needed for stability; deviance, as a catalyst for social change. Deviance and social control exist in a dialectic relationship with each other; that is, each acts on the other to produce yet another version of each.

A related phenomenon which must be considered when dealing with deviance and social control is the identification and labeling of perpetrators of the so-called deviant behaviors. Throughout the history of sociology and the development of various theories of deviance, the subjects of the studies on which theories of deviance have been based have, to a great extent, been those segments of the population without power. These subjects were most frequently from the lower classes; they were often people who were incarcerated, in therapy, or in hospitals—all representing some type of "captive" population. Moreover, a significant part of these populations has been male and/or African American. Thus, social control techniques would also seem to have been rather specifically directed at selected segments of the population: perpetrators who were primarily male, lower class, and often African American.

Applications

Numerous policies, practices, and jobs in societies derive from the various explanations of deviance and social control. For example, theories that describe deviance from biological or psychological perspectives place the locus, but not the responsibility, of deviance within the individual. From these explanations, numerous treatments and therapies were devised to correct the deviance (as opposed to practices intended to punish the deviant). These treatments and therapies removed, to an extent, the responsibility for the deviant behavior from the individual engaging in the deviant acts: The cause of the behavior was, by definition, often viewed as being beyond the control of the individual.

For example, some theories identify hormonal imbalance as the cause (or at least one cause) of deviance; thus, to exercise social control of the deviance, hormone therapies were developed to be administered in treatment programs in hospitals and prisons. Other types of treatments involve various psychoanalytical and group therapies (including groups such as Alcoholics Anonymous and Narcotics Anonymous), which some people exhibiting deviant behavior are required to attend as part of their rehabilitation, sentencing, and/or parole conditions. These requirements in turn produce a need for a large number of positions for psychologists, psychiatrists, counselors, and so on.

Later theories (cultural transmission, subcultural, delinquency and opportunity, differential association, anomie, and social control theories) moved away from biology, psychology, and medicine as explanations and began addressing deviance in terms of social norms and community activities. These theories began to question the relationship between so-called deviant cultures and communities and the dominant culture. Social control theory, for example, posits that all people are "bonded" and attached to society (the larger, dominant society) and that this bonding and attachment produces social control. Weakening of the bonds results in deviance. Studies have shown, for example, that the ties between delinquent adolescent boys and their parents are significantly less strong than the parent-offspring ties of other boys of the same age. A central aspect of control theory is that everyone has the urge to deviate occasionally and that it is the attachment to others that holds such urges in check.

Differential association theory, on the other hand, is a type of cultural transmission theory; conceived by Edwin H. Sutherland, it was intended to describe how delinquents and criminals learn the motives and skills involved in rule-violating behavior. Differential association theory is based on the idea that, in the socialization process, people learn "definitions" both favorable to obeying laws and favorable to disobeying laws. According to Sutherland's "principle of differential association," people engage in criminal behavior when they have more definitions that support violating the law than they have definitions that go against violating the law. The strength of these various definitions is influenced by how early in life one is exposed to them and how long one is exposed to them.

According to these theories of deviance, the ways to regain social control and reestablish the social order are to "fix," or realign, local communities or nondominant cultures so that their values more resemble the values of the dominant and hegemonic culture and to provide alternative opportunities—particularly to delinquent male youth—in order to dissuade them from activities in delinquent subcultures. These theories tend to view deviant communities as existing separate from and outside the dominant social system and consequently see a need to reintegrate them into the dominant, hegemonic culture.

Like biological and psychological perspectives, theories addressing deviant cultures, social norms, and communities have resulted in various social programs and occupations. Activities such as scouting, the Big Brother/Big Sister programs, YMCAs and YWCAs, youth bureaus, job training programs, support groups of various kinds, educational opportunities, and sports programs are designed to address and change the values and activities of individuals in "disorganized" communities—and sometimes the values of entire local communities themselves. The objective of such programs is to make the nondominant communities more resemble the dominant culture so that the individuals residing in the nondominant communities will be exposed to nondeviant activities, and thus to values that more resemble those of the established dominant culture. Through these activities, an attempt is made to reintegrate individuals residing in so-called deviant cultures and communities, or exhibiting deviant social norms, with the dominant culture (with its presumably prosocial norms) and thus to establish or regain social control. Society as a whole can thereby continue to function smoothly, using the assumed values of the hegemonic culture as the benchmark.

These explanations of deviance focus primarily on acts of "one-on-one" deviance (or, in some cases, secret deviance) and either on the individual or on the individual's community as the locus of the cause of deviance. Little or no attention is given to how the individual and the individual's community form a part of the larger society or to the fact that power differentials exist across various communities within the larger social structure. Yet such an awareness is essential to understanding the problematic nature of defining "deviance" and understanding the resulting differences in the consequences of such behaviors.

In terms of elite deviance, history suggests that there has been only a limited effort at exerting social control over perpetrators of corporate, governmental, and white-collar deviance. In everyday life, the response to individuals engaging in these forms of deviance has been quite mild in comparison with societal reactions to perpetrators of "one-on-one" deviance. One may note, for example, the mild types of sentences and places of incarceration meted out to people involved in governmental abuses (such as those that occurred during the Watergate and Iran-Contra scandals) or financial improprieties, even those involving billions of dollars and defrauding thousands, even millions, of people. Relatively meager fines are also levied against corporations violating environmental laws. These social control reactions may be compared with the sentences meted out to burglars, armed robbers, and, particularly, some drug users. The latter types of deviance tend to receive much more vigorous responses than the former, especially considering the difference in the numbers of individuals victimized. In other words, applications of the definitions of deviance and the mechanisms of social control vary widely according to many factors; among them seem to be the initial explanation of the cause of the deviance, who or what the victim of the deviance was, and the status of the perpetrator.

Context

The first clearly recognized development of the notion of deviance and its counterpart, social control, can be traced to a work by Émile Durkheim, "The Normal and the Pathological," found in *Les Règles de la méthode sociologique* (1895; *The Rules of Sociological Method*, 1938), as well as to his foundational work on deviance, *Le Suicide: Étude de sociologie* (1897; *Suicide: A Study in Sociology*, 1951). Durkheim, as one of the founders of sociology, was extremely influential in the development of theories about deviance and social control.

Immense growth in the development of the areas of deviance and social control occurred in the United States in the first half of the twentieth century. After an early focus on biological, psychological, and social psychological explanations of deviance, sociologists identified certain factors—massive immigration, urbanization, and industrialization—which some scholars claimed produced social disorganization in urban areas. They argued that these phenomena caused an erosion of the social norms of the dominant society, thereby giving rise to deviance). In terms of social control, the most prominent programs dealt with community development, urban renewal, employment, educational opportunities, and sports opportunities; some programs were also developed to address unequal distribution of wealth and power, although it is debatable whether these last types of programs have accomplished much.

The 1970's saw the development of theories of deviance which recognized power and class as significant social facts—social facts which caused some sociologists to rethink and reformulate earlier theories of deviance and social control. This decade saw not only the growth of so-called critical, radical, and conflict theories of deviance but also the beginnings of a focus on secret deviance, on victimless crimes, and on elite, corporate, and white-collar deviance. Analytically, deviance is important as a concept—a tool to help explain human behavior. Social control is important as a concept that helps to explain the maintenance of a fundamental societal goal: smoothly functioning systems of social institutions and people living together. Deviance and social control are both important components in the dynamics and existence of social systems.

Throughout the history of humankind, definitions of deviance and social control have established hierarchies of people. There are, for example, the official labelers of what and who is deviant; the recipients of the label "deviant"; the makers of policy and writers of society's rules, regulations, and laws; and the recipients of programs, policies, and practices (social control mechanisms) designed to address the labeled deviant acts and behaviors and thus to restore smooth social functioning. Occasionally, at various times, people who resist the label "deviant" also serve as catalysts for social change, for revisions in the dominant, hegemonic definitions of what is considered deviant.

Bibliography

Becker, Howard S. *Outsiders: Studies in the Sociology of Deviance*. New York: Free Press, 1963. A very readable classic in the sociology of deviance. Becker raises critical issues and questions, such as whose rules determine what is defined as deviant, who does the labeling, and who gets labeled. Recognizes and discusses the issue of power vis-à-vis definition creation and label bestowing.

Conrad, Peter, and Joseph W. Schneider. *Deviance and Medicalization: From Badness to Sickness*. St. Louis: C. V. Mosby, 1980. This book deals very well with the history of deviance and classifications of deviance. Examines the sociocultural contexts in which deviance is defined and created, including the ways in which interested groups (moral entrepreneurs) affect definitions of deviance. The authors place special emphasis on the role of medicine in relation to deviance.

Durkheim, Émile. *Suicide: A Study in Sociology*. Translated by John A. Spaulding and George Simpson. Glencoe, Ill.: Free Press, 1951. First published in 1897, this is a classic in the writings about deviance, with both methodological and historical importance. Details the ways in which an act, defined as deviant and seen as singular and personal, is explained by macro facts of social structure.

Hills, Stuart L. *Demystifying Social Deviance*. New York: McGraw-Hill, 1980. A short book with easy to follow but thought-provoking content. Offers selective topics within which to explore the notion of deviance and presents challenges to status quo definitions thereof. A relativistic perspective.

Kelly, Delos H., comp. *Deviant Behavior: A Text-Reader in the Sociology of Deviance*. 2d ed. New York: St. Martin's Press, 1984. Good groupings of the classic theories of deviance. Includes a variety of readings, some dealing with subjects not generally considered in the layperson's conception of deviance (such as UFO cults, and women as criminals). Treats both individual-level and macro-level deviance and discusses both perpetrators and control agents (such as the courts and mental institutions).

Little, Craig B. *Deviance and Control: Theory, Research, and Social Policy*. Itasca, Ill.: F. E. Peacock, 1989. A useful book with examples of specific types of deviance and their related social control mechanisms (social policies). One of the few books to deal with heterosexual sexual deviance; includes a good chapter on elite deviance. Very helpful charts.

Rubington, Earl, and Martin S. Weinberg, comps. *Deviance: The Interactionist Perspective.* 5th ed. New York: Macmillan, 1987. A variety of readings organized into four sections, each preceded by a brief introduction. This work has a single theoretical approach, that of interactionism (the idea that meanings are created by people in their exchanges with one another). If a balanced approach to the study of deviance is desired, other books must be consulted as well.

M. F. Stuck

Cross-References

Conflict Perspectives on Deviance, 334; Crime: Analysis and Overview, 373; Cultural Transmission Theory of Deviance, 424; Delinquency Prevention and Treatment, 476; Deviance: Biological and Psychological Explanations, 532; Deviance: Functions and Dysfunctions, 540; Juvenile Delinquency: Analysis and Overview, 1036; Victimless Crime, 2150; White-Collar and Corporate Crime, 2179.

DEVIANCE: BIOLOGICAL AND PSYCHOLOGICAL EXPLANATIONS

Type of sociology: Deviance and social control
Field of study: Theories of deviance

Biological theories of deviance argue that deviance is a product of an inherited trait or condition that predisposes an individual to commit deviant acts. In contrast, psychological explanations of deviance stress the role the environment plays in shaping personality and behavior. Both perspectives have been widely used to explain the origins of crime and juvenile delinquency in American society.

Principal terms

ATAVISM: the reappearance of a trait associated with an earlier, ancestral form of an individual or species

AUTONOMIC NERVOUS SYSTEM: the portion of the central nervous system that regulates bodily activities associated with emotional states

CALIFORNIA PSYCHOLOGICAL INVENTORY (CPI): a psychological test used to measure personality characteristics considered important for social learning and living

ELECTROENCEPHALOGRAPH (EEG): an instrument used to measure and record brain waves from the cerebral cortex

EUGENICS: the study of genetics and selective breeding to alter and improve the composition of the human gene pool

MINNESOTA MULTIPHASIC PERSONALITY INVENTORY (MMPI): a psychological test used to diagnose and study psychopathology

PHRENOLOGY: the study of the contours of the human skull in the belief that personality and intelligence can be inferred from the shape of the head

PHYSIOGNOMY: the study of human facial features in the belief that personality and intelligence can be inferred from facial characteristics

XYY CHROMOSOME: an abnormal chromosome pattern in which males are born with an extra Y chromosome

Overview

Biological explanations of deviance date to the late 1800's and argue that deviance is a consequence of constitutional deficiencies that predispose individuals to engage in deviant behavior. Biological explanations of deviance typically have minimized the influence of social factors on behavior, but some variants do acknowledge that environment plays a role in shaping behavior and in creating opportunities for the commission of deviant acts.

One of the earliest biological theories of deviance is found in the works of the Italian physician Cesare Lombroso. In *L'uomo delinquente* (1875), Lombroso argued that many criminals commit crimes because they are atavists. Lombroso labeled criminals "Homo delinquens" and viewed them as "throwbacks" to an earlier form of humanity. Lombroso stressed what he called the "animalistic" quality of criminals and believed that crime is a natural consequence of their genetic inheritance. He argued that criminals share certain physical traits that distinguish them from noncriminals. Lombroso modified his theory several times. In later versions, he downplayed the role of atavism in the origins of crime and acknowledged that crime could be a consequence of many factors, including insanity and situational conditions such as poverty.

Views similar to Lombroso's were expressed by the American anthropologist Ernest Albert Hooton. In *The American Criminal: An Anthropological Study* (1939), Hooton claimed that criminals suffer from hereditary physical and mental inferiorities. Like Lombroso, Hooton argued that criminals exhibit differences in physical appearance that set them apart from noncriminals. In the 1940's, William Sheldon, an American psychologist, argued that body build is inherited and is associated with certain personality characteristics and temperaments that predispose individuals to commit deviant acts. Specifically, Sheldon argued that individuals with mesomorphic (muscular) physiques are more likely to engage in delinquency than individuals whose physiques are more endomorphic (soft and round) or ectomorphic (lean and fragile).

Biological theories of deviance became less popular in the mid-twentieth century. Most early biological theories of deviance were based on poorly conducted research that suffered from serious methodological problems. Subsequent research found little evidence to support the theories of Lombroso, Hooton, or Sheldon. Most theorists of the twentieth century attempted to explain deviance in terms of social factors such as poverty, inadequate socialization, poor home environments, and peer group influence.

Edward O. Wilson's *Sociobiology: The New Synthesis*, published in 1975, revived interest in biological explanations of human behavior. Wilson argued that an individual's personality and behavior are shaped by physical and environmental conditions and by an innate need to dominate others, thus ensuring transmission of genetic material from one generation to the next. While Wilson's work has been sharply criticized, biosocial theorists have drawn inspiration from Wilson's work and believe that biological, social, and environmental factors operate in consort to shape human behavior. Contemporary biosocial research attributes deviance to a combination of inherited differences in cognitive ability and temperament, inherited instinctual drives, and social learning. Modern biosocial research on deviance has focused on twin and adoption studies, chromosome abnormalities, brain dysfunctions and learning disabilities, and neurochemical and hormonal imbalances.

Twin studies examining the relationship between criminality and genetics have found that when twin A has a criminal conviction, identical twin B (a monozygotic twin) is significantly more likely than fraternal twin B (a dizygotic twin) to have one as well. Because identical twins are more similar genetically than fraternal twins, these findings have been interpreted as evidence of a genetic predisposition toward criminality.

A study of 14,427 adoptions in Denmark found that adopted children whose biological parents had criminal convictions were much more likely to have criminal convictions for property crimes than adopted children whose biological parents lacked criminal convictions. No similar pattern was found for violent offenses. Adopted children whose biological and adoptive parents had criminal convictions had the highest rates of subsequent criminal convictions, suggesting an interplay between genetic inheritance and environmental influence.

Studies in Denmark found that men with an XYY chromosome complement had higher criminal conviction rates than men with the more typical XY pattern. Evidence also shows that men with the XYY chromosome pattern exhibit differences in autonomic nervous system functioning. Other studies show that violent criminal offenders are more likely than the general population to have brain dysfunctions and neurological defects. These defects appear to be located in the frontal and temporal lobes of the brain and to affect self-control. Minimal brain dysfunction, an abnormality of the cerebral structure, has been tied to aggressiveness and antisocial behavior. Similarly, juveniles with both attention deficit disorder and minimal brain damage have higher rates of delinquency than other juveniles.

Violent delinquents exhibit relatively high rates of abnormal electroencephalograph (EEG) readings. Abnormal EEG readings have also been associated with hostile, nonconforming, and impulsive behavior in adults. Hans Eysenck argues that criminals suffer from abnormal autonomic nervous system function that reduces the fear response. Consequently, such individuals may engage in impulsive or risk-taking behavior to compensate for their higher stimulation threshold.

Some recent studies indicate that juvenile delinquency is associated with learning disabilities. For example, evidence shows that hyperactive children are six times more likely to be arrested as juveniles for unlawful acts than are nonhyperactive children, even when differences in socioeconomic status are taken into account. While the cause of learning disabilities is not clearly understood, research has linked learning disabilities to neurological dysfunction. From this view, learning disabilities result in poor academic performance, rejection, and stigmatization, which in turn lead to crime and delinquency.

Other studies have linked criminal behavior to changes in the neurochemistry of the brain. Individuals who are sensitive to certain substances (such as sugar, food additives, or phosphates), who are exposed to environmental toxins (such as lead, pesticides, or herbicides), or who abuse drugs may experience changes in brain chemistry when exposed to these substances. Changes in brain chemistry may alter behavior and, in a way not currently understood, predispose an individual to criminal acts. Similarly, evidence indicates that neuroendocrinology may play a role in regulating human aggression, but the role neuroendocrinology might play in crime and delinquency is as yet poorly understood.

Psychological theories of deviance are diverse, and have focused on such issues as mental deficiencies, personality development, psychodynamics (the psychoanalytical approach), cognitive and moral development, and learning (behaviorism and social learning theory). Some research shows an association between intelligence and crime and delinquency. Intelligence is difficult to define and measure, and many intelligence tests suffer from cultural biases that call into question the validity of their results. Nevertheless, several well-designed studies have found that juvenile delinquents have somewhat lower intelligence quotient (IQ) scores than nondelinquent juveniles when differences in socioeconomic backgrounds are controlled for. Some psychologists, however, believe low intelligence does not cause delinquency. Instead, trouble in school, failure to learn, and lack of motivation associated with differences in social class may result in lower IQ scores. Indeed, some psychologists argue that institutional responses to students' low IQ scores promote alienation and encourage delinquency.

Many psychologists have attempted to identify personality traits associated with crime and delinquency. For example, Samuel Yochelson and Stanton Samenow have identified fifty-two "errors of criminal thinking" that they believe form the personalities of criminal offenders. Errors of criminal thinking include chronic lying, unrelenting optimism, great energy, intense anger, manipulativeness, and an inflexible, high self-image. It should be noted, however, that Yochelson and Samenow's study group was not a representative sample of all criminal offenders and that they did not use a control group. Consequently, their study is seriously flawed and their results may not be valid.

Glenn Walters and Thomas White argue that habitual offenders suffer from "faulty, irrational thinking," and they have identified eight cognitive traits they believe are characteristic of habitual offenders: mollification (justification of criminal behavior in terms of external forces compelling the individual to behave in a certain way), cutoff (a reduction or elimination of feelings of fear and anxiety that makes it easier to commit criminal acts), entitlement (a view that the world exists for their benefit and pleasure), power orientation (a focus on power in interpersonal relationships), sentimentality (the use of emotions in a self-serving manner to reduce feelings of guilt over harm caused to others), superoptimism (confidence in their ability to commit crimes without being caught), cognitive indolence (a tendency to be easily bored and to avoid critical thinking), and discontinuity (an inability to carry out plans to their fruition). Walters and White's study sample was not representative of all criminal offenders, however, and therefore must be viewed with much caution.

Some psychologists believe crime to be linked with the inability to tolerate frustration. According to Edwin Megaree, frustration may lead to aggressive behavior, including violent crime, when there is an instigation to engage in aggressive behavior, when aggression has been learned as the preferred way to respond to a given situation, when learned inhibitions against aggressive behaviors are limited or weak, and when an individual's needs may be best met by aggressive behavior.

Research using the Minnesota Multiphasic Personality Inventory (MMPI) shows that juvenile delinquents tend to score higher on three scales of the MMPI (the psychopathic deviate scale, the schizophrenia scale, and the hypomania scale) than nondelinquents do. High scores on these scales are associated with conflict with authority, weak personal attachments, hyperactivity, low or unusual affect (emotion), and avoidance of interpersonal relationships. Similar work using the California Psychological Inventory (CPI) indicates that criminal behavior is associated with poor social adjustment and a weak value orientation.

The psychodynamic or psychoanalytic perspective is based on the work of Sigmund Freud. According to Freud, crime and delinquency are a consequence of an imbalance between the three dimensions of the subconscious mind: the id, the ego, and the superego. The id is the component of the subconscious mind that is self-serving, egocentric, and concerned with self-gratification. Conversely, the superego is the component of the mind that represents morality and conscience. The ego mediates between the contrasting needs of the id and superego, and attempts to fulfill the desires of the id within the boundaries of social conventions. If the id or superego overpowers the mediating force of the ego, crime, delinquency, and other forms of deviance may occur. For example, if the id overcomes the forces of the ego and superego, an individual may act on his or her impulsive and egocentric desires. Consequently, instead of getting a job and earning money to buy a car, an individual simply steals one. If the superego is overly dominant, an individual is overcome with feelings of guilt and may violate the law in order to get caught. For this person, subsequent punishment atones for perceived feelings of guilt.

Other psychoanalysts have linked crime and delinquency to early childhood trauma. Alfred Adler argued that crime stems from an inferiority complex in which individuals engage in criminal acts to gain a sense of power and control over others. August Aichorn argued that delinquency is a consequence of preexisting dispositions to engage in antisocial acts as well as societal stress experienced during childhood. Aichorn tied delinquency to impulsiveness, self-centeredness, and lack of guilt. Seymour Halleck stated that criminal activity gives feelings of power and control to individuals who otherwise feel powerless.

Cognitive and moral development theories focus on the role moral reasoning plays in shaping behavior. According to the Swiss psychologist Jean Piaget, moral reasoning is developmental and occurs in two stages. In the earliest stage of moral development, children believe that rules are rigid and absolute and obey rules out of fear of punishment. By the age of twelve or thirteen, children enter the second stage of moral development. They view rules as social conventions that are necessary for social order but which may be broken if some greater good is achieved by their violation. Obedience to rules is a consequence of adherence to moral principles. Drawing on Piaget's work, Lawrence Kohlberg identified six stages of moral development. Kohlberg found that criminals are disproportionately concentrated in stages one and two of moral development (obedience based on hedonism and fear of punishment), while Scott Henggler found that noncriminals are typically concentrated in stages three and four of moral development (obedience based on the desire to avoid social censure). Moral development theorists attribute crime and delinquency to low moral development.

Behaviorism, based on the works of Ivan Pavlov and B. F. Skinner, argues that criminality and delinquency are learned behaviors and are a consequence of classical and operant conditioning. Deviance occurs when deviant behavior is rewarding to the individual and results in a learned pattern of response. Behaviorists believe that deviant behavior can be eliminated by rewarding appropriate behavior and reducing rewards associated with undesirable behavior.

Social learning theory also asserts that deviant behavior is learned and argues that behavior is shaped by external reinforcement (such as money or status), vicarious reinforcement (observation of others' behaviors and subsequent consequences), and self-regulatory mechanisms (internalization of values that provide self-rewards or self-punishments). According to Hans Eysenck, the impact of conditioning on the individual is influenced by the autonomic nervous system. Eysenck argues that criminals and delinquents fail to learn appropriate stimuli and thus do not develop a conscience that discourages rule-violating or antisocial behavior.

Applications

While most biological and psychological explanations of deviance are theoretical in nature, several attempts have been made to employ them in the prevention and control of crime and delinquency. For example, Sheldon Glueck and Eleanor Glueck developed a formula to predict whether a juvenile is likely to engage in delinquent behavior. The Gluecks assigned numerical ratings to five factors that they believed would provide reliable predictors of delinquency: discipline by the father, supervision by the mother, affection of the father, affection of the mother, and family cohesion. The Gluecks attempted to predict the likelihood of future delinquency based on a total score generated by their measurement system. The Gluecks advocated the testing of juveniles and called for the establishment of early intervention programs to prevent delinquency. Subsequent research, however, has called into question the validity of many of the Gluecks' claims. Additionally, some critics argue that labeling a child as a potential delinquent may actually promote future acts of delinquency because of the subsequent stigmatization the label produces.

Drawing from their analysis of "criminal thinking," Samuel Yochelson and Stanton Samenow developed a therapeutic technique in which they confront criminal offenders, examine the offender's thoughts and behaviors, and force the offender to accept responsibility for his or her actions. Yochelson and Samenow claim that by eliminating "criminal thinking" they can reduce future occurrences of criminal behavior. Support for Yochelson and Samenow's technique is limited. In a study of 255 criminal offenders, only thirty completed therapy. Yochelson and Samenow claim that twenty of the thirty offenders who completed therapy showed some elimination of criminal thinking. Yochelson and Samenow do not provide precise criteria for measuring improvement, however, and their sample size is so small that it is not a representative sample of all criminal offenders. Consequently, it is impossible to assess accurately the usefulness of their approach in eliminating or reducing criminal behavior.

Context

Biological and psychological explanations of deviance are a product of the positivist tradition that began to emerge in mid-nineteenth century Europe. Positivism advocates the use of the scientific method to analyze and correct social problems and believes much of human behavior is shaped by forces beyond the individual's control.

Following the fall of the Roman Empire, the intellectual traditions of early Greek and Roman societies were replaced by a belief in fatalism and an adherence to religious dogma. Gradually the rational and critical spirit lost with the decline of the Roman Empire was rekindled in Europe. The emergence of this new critical spirit gave birth to the Enlightenment, a period marked not only by the rediscovery of lost knowledge but also by the relatively rapid discovery of new knowledge. During the Enlightenment, a new rational method, science, was used to examine the nature of the universe and the human condition.

In the 1800's, Charles Lyell and Charles Darwin presented scientific explanations of geological and biological change. With the growing acceptance of Lyell's and Darwin's work, the positivist perspective gradually spread to other disciplines. As early as the late 1700's and early 1800's, physiognomists and phrenologists attempted to explain human behavior and personality in terms of biological predispositions. Lombroso's early effort to explain criminal behavior as a consequence of atavism reflects a continuation of this newly emerging scientific worldview.

Similar themes are reflected in psychology. Early psychological theory attributed insanity to demonic possession. In *Physiology and Pathology of Mind* (1867), however, Henry Maudsley provided a physiological foundation for human behavior and argued that criminality is a product of inherited mental traits. In contrast, Gabriel Tarde linked criminality to learning and argued that crime is a product of imitation. Both perspectives attribute human behavior to natural processes that can be examined and understood by the scientific method.

Biological and psychological explanations of deviance have become firmly established scientific perspectives. While the popularity of each approach has waned and waxed over the decades, they remain important components in the attempt to understand crime and delinquency. As research methods became more sophisticated, the biological and psychological foundations of deviance have become better understood. Because of the complexity of human behavior, however, it is unlikely that a complete understanding of the origins of deviance will be developed.

Bibliography

Ellis, Lee. "Genetics and Criminal Behavior: Evidence Through the End of the 1970's." *Criminology* 20 (May, 1982): 43-66. Reviews results of four types of studies examining the relationship between biology and crime: family studies, twin studies, karyotype (chromosome) studies, and adoption studies. Ellis claims that karyotype and adoption studies provide the greatest promise for an understanding of the biological basis of crime.

Eysenck, Hans J., and Gisli H. Gudjonsson. *The Causes and Cures of Criminality.* New York: Plenum Press, 1989. A comprehensive summary of Eysenck's theory on the interplay of biological factors and social learning regarding criminal behavior.

Sarnoff, A. Mednick, Terrie E. Moffitt, and Susan A. Stack, eds. *The Causes of Crime: New Biological Approaches*. Cambridge, England: Cambridge University Press, 1987. An excellent collection of papers from the 1980's on research examining the biological basis of crime and delinquency.

Wilson, Edward O. *Sociobiology: The New Synthesis*. Cambridge, Mass.: Belknap Press of Harvard University Press, 1975. Outlines Wilson's controversial position on the biological foundation of human social behavior. Formed the basis for the revival of interest in biological explanations of crime. Somewhat technical and difficult to read for the nonspecialist.

Wilson, James Q., and Richard Herrnstein. *Crime and Human Nature*. New York: Simon & Schuster, 1985. An extremely influential and popular book that argues criminal behavior is a consequence of biological traits, decision making, and learning. Proposes reducing crime by strengthening the structure of the American family.

Charles Vincent Smedley

Cross-References

DEVIANCE: FUNCTIONS AND DYSFUNCTIONS

Type of sociology: Deviance and social control
Field of study: Forms of deviance

No society exists without deviant behavior. Deviance is both dysfunctional and functional. It is dysfunctional in that it undermines and impairs society's capacity to provide for the well-being and safety of its members and to maintain their trust. It is functional because it facilitates the process of learning the meaning of laws and rules, acts as a warning signal, unites groups, and promotes solidarity.

Principal terms

CRIME: behavior that violates laws prohibiting such behavior and may be punished; often poses a threat to personal well-being and safety

DEVIANCE: behavior that violates widely accepted rules of social conduct

DYSFUNCTION: an impairment or abnormality in normal functioning that has adverse effects upon social organization

FUNCTION: normal, characteristic, and proper actions of a social organization which promote the survival and well-being of the organization and its members

"HARD" DEVIANCE: deviant behavior that causes physical damage to the personal well-being, safety, and security of members of a society and their possessions; examples are violent crimes and suicide

"SOFT" DEVIANCE: deviant behavior that does not cause physical harm or damage to those affected; examples are mental disorders, prostitution, and illegal gambling

Overview

Deviance refers to behavior that violates widely accepted rules of social conduct and that has the potential to cause significant social disorganization. Such violations are viewed sufficiently negatively by society that formal sanctions and controls are directed at them. Such deviant behaviors include criminal acts and behaviors caused by mental disorders.

If a society is to survive, it must be able to guarantee the survival of its members and provide for stable and predictable economic relationships. Society and its citizens mutually recognize that economic and interpersonal relationships must be regulated. Deviant behavior undermines and impairs society's capacity to provide for its members' survival and stability. Additionally, the diversion of funds and resources necessary to deal with deviant behavior, as well as the personal tragedy and economic loss inflicted by this deviancy, only add to the potential social disorganization.

Albert K. Cohen (1966) discussed three other ways in which deviancy is dysfunctional and destructive of social organization. First, deviance can adversely affect the social system at vital points by depriving it of essential components and by impairing or destroying the functioning of the larger social unit. For example, Gilbert Geis argued that white collar and corporate crime, by its insidious nature, destroys confidence, depletes the integrity of commercial life and has the potential to cause devastation. Imagine, says Geis, what would happen if nuclear regulatory rules were violated or if toxic wastes were dumped into a city's water supply.

Second, deviance has the potential to destroy the willingness of society's members to continue to contribute to the well-being of society. If "idlers," "fakers," "chiselers," "sneaks," "deadbeats," and others of this ilk are perceived as being disproportionately rewarded without undergoing the sacrifice and effort of honest, hardworking citizens, willingness to play by the rules of loyalty, self-discipline, and morality may be undermined.

Third, and most destructive according to Cohen, is that deviant behavior may undermine trust in the social system. Individuals make an investment in society's future by committing their resources and forgoing some alternatives on the assumption that if one conducts oneself according to society's rules, others will also behave appropriately. Distrust undermines motivation, leading people to view their efforts as pointless, wasted, and foolish, and the future as uncertain and hazardous. Trust is an indispensable prerequisite for any viable social enterprise.

Émile Durkheim argued in 1938 that deviancy is an inevitable part of any society, that it is impossible for any society to exist utterly free of it, and that therefore deviancy is a normal integral, useful, and necessary part of any healthy society. Deviancy may be regrettable ("pain has likewise nothing desirable about it"), but it does have a positive purpose. Similarly, Kai T. Erikson (1986) took exception to the view that one of the characteristics of an appropriately designed society is that it prevents the occurrence of deviant behavior.

According to Durkheim and Erikson, deviant individuals provide a needed service to society. By permitting members of society to understand what is deviant, they can also allow them to know what is not deviant and thereby help them to live according to appropriate shared standards. Deviance threatens the collective conscience and produces punishment, and punishment facilitates social solidarity and cohesion. Deviancy promotes respect for beliefs, traditions, and collective practices, and it increases society's capacity to adapt to changing conditions and new life situations. Deviancy is a critical mechanism for producing successful social changes and maintaining the vitality of the social system. Other sociologists have also advanced this theme. Cohen listed seven positive contributions made by deviant behaviors:

1. Identification with and concern for the well-being of a group may lead to the violation of rules. For example, a military unit needs supplies in excess of its normal quota, and the procurement officer violates rules to obtain those supplies.

2. Deviancy provides a safety valve that makes it possible to satisfy illegitimate desires that, if suppressed in enough people, might lead to an attack on rules or social institutions by the disaffected. Prostitution, for example, takes some strain off the legitimate order without threatening the integrity of the family.

3. Pushing the limits of rules and laws allows one to learn what those rules and laws mean, thereby reducing ambiguity and allowing the group to reach a common understanding.

4. The deviant population can function as a built-in out-group that unites the dominant in-group in emotional solidarity.

5. Deviance provides a contrast effect that makes conformity special and prized behavior and a source of gratification. As Shakespeare stated, "a good deed shines brightest in a naughty world."

6. Deviance may serve as a warning signal of defects in and discontent with the social order that need to be identified, addressed, and corrected.

7. Deviance may unite the group and promote solidarity and the virtues of kindness and patience in the form of working on behalf of the deviant, to reclaim or protect him or her.

8. An eighth function of deviance can be added to this list. By definition, a deviant is an outcast from the dominant, conforming society. By identifying with the world of other and similar deviants, the individual becomes a member of an exclusive group. Paul A. Inciardi has observed that the fraternity of professional thieves provides them with friendship, understanding, sympathy, congeniality, security, recognition, and respect that can be obtained nowhere else.

Applications

Violent crime is what Nachman Ben-Yehuda (1985) refers to as "hard" deviance (sexual deviance, drug abuse, and mental illness are "soft" deviance). Examples of "hard" deviant behavior are assault, homicide, suicide, organized crime, burglary, rape, and other crimes of violence. Such behavior illustrates both the dysfunction and function of deviant behavior. In violent crime, severe mayhem, injury, or loss is inflicted upon a person or property. Such behavior poses a significant threat to the well-being, safety, and security of people and their possessions; therefore, such behavior is labeled deviant. In this regard, violent crime is clearly dysfunctional.

According to the Uniform Crime Reports, published by the Federal Bureau of Investigation, the rate of violent crime has increased nearly 20 percent from 1988 through 1992. For example, gun deaths, including suicides, exceeded 37,000 in 1992. This is a homicide rate of about 10 for every 100,000 Americans (versus five and less than one for Canada and Japan, respectively).

Although this dysfunctional characteristic of violent crime indirectly or directly touches all Americans, nowhere is it more apparent than in African American communities. Tom Morgenthau has observed that in many African American communities, an "oppositional culture" rules the streets and neighborhoods. Composed of "profoundly nihilistic" teenagers, this culture condones and romanticizes violence and believes in the law of the streets, the power of guns, bravado, and respect. One result of this situation has been a steady escalation of black-on-black violence. In 1992, the rate per 1,000 people for victims of violent crime was 50.4 for blacks and 29.9 for whites. For blacks under age twenty-four, the homicide rate per 100,000 people increased from 84 in 1980 to 159 in 1991 (but also decreased significantly for those age 25 and over). The homicide rates per 100,000 people vary from nearly six to nine times greater for blacks than for whites, depending on age group. According to Morgenthau, black "gangsta" teens "are terrorizing the inner city as ruthlessly as the KKK ever terrorized the South." The result of this violence has been that communities have been paralyzed by the fear of crime. Black children worry significantly more than white children do that a family member will become a victim of a violent crime, and feel significantly less safe than white children do from violent crime in their neighborhood after dark. According to Morgenthau, this "puerile and self-destructive" violence subverts the positive values that form the foundation of society: hope, work, love and civility, the belief in success through hard and honest work, and faith in a happy and productive future.

From dysfunction, however, comes function. The increase in violent crime has seemed to galvanize and unite disparate groups in America, joining them in a common effort to get tough on crime. An October, 1993, poll by the newspaper *USA Today* revealed that 80 percent of the sample favored hiring more police and paying higher taxes to pay for it; 82 percent favored making it more difficult to parole violent prisoners; 79 percent favored harsher prison sentences; 75 percent favored making it more difficult to post bail; and 64 percent favored stiffer gun control laws.

For many years, crime has been one of Washington's phoniest debates. Congress habitually expressed concern and dismay at the rise in violent crime but contributed only a paltry $750 million a year to communities to help fight crime (95 percent of violent crimes are the responsibility of state and local governments). Additionally, the National Rifle Association (NRA), one of the most powerful, wealthy, formidable, and well-connected lobbies has adamantly and effectively campaigned against any gun control or restriction laws.

Against this background of congressional inaction lie polls revealing that Americans are more frightened, frustrated, and outraged than ever about what they perceive as a rising tide of violence. Clearly, the compact between citizens and government in which citizens consent to be ruled in exchange for the provision of personal safety and well-being by the government is perceived by the citizenry as not being fulfilled. As a result of this concern, disparate groups have coalesced to exert pressure on Congress to do something, and this pressure seems to have been effective. On this issue, partisan divisions between Democrats and Republicans receded, and in late 1993, Congress passed a crime bill and a gun control bill that were departures from politics as usual.

Additionally, the African American community has come together and mobilized in an attempt to deal with black-on-black crime. For example, the Reverend Jesse Jackson organized a summit meeting in 1994 to discuss strategies for combatting crime. Also, African Americans increasingly seem to agree that they must confront the moral and social problems of inner city crimes in order to save the vast majority of ghetto youth.

Whether congressional actions and the efforts of the African American community will prove fruitful is open to doubt. The dysfunctional nature of violent crime has served the function of uniting an entire society to begin to honestly address and develop adaptive solutions to violent crime and the threat it poses to society.

Context

Deviancy is an integral and normal part of any society, and it serves various useful functions. It is impossible for any society to be free of deviance altogether. Therefore, the important consideration is how much deviance a society can afford to tolerate so that the functional and dysfunctional aspects of deviance remain in balance and society can survive and continue to provide for the well-being, safety, and security of its members.

Daniel Patrick Moynihan has argued that deviant behavior (he discusses crime, mental disorders, and family breakdown) has reached epidemic proportions in the United States. There is more deviance than can be tolerated. Dysfunction has gained dominance over function. Presumably helpless to arrest this explosion of deviancy, society has attempted to restore deviance to a manageable level by "defining deviancy down." That is, deviance has been redefined so that what was formerly considered to be deviant is now normal. Deviancy, once redefined, becomes manageable and tolerable. For example, violent crimes that previously would have stirred the nation's sensibilities (for example, the St. Valentine's Day Massacre in 1929) now routinely occur. They are treated in a routine manner or played down, evoke only moderate responses, and rapidly are forgotten. There is considerable evidence that the disintegration of the two-parent family can produce intellectual, physical, and emotional damage, but divorce is now represented as part of a normal family life cycle. To many observers it is not deviant or tragic but is a basis for "individual renewal and new beginnings." Similarly, it is said that the main problem of the large population of street people, many of whom are former patients of mental hospitals, is that they lack affordable housing.

Charles Krauthammer argued that deviancy has also been defined "up." That is, behaviors that were formerly considered normal or at worst ill-mannered are now considered to be deviant and even criminal.

Krauthammer views defining deviancy "down" and "up" as processes. The deviant is defined as normal, the normal is defined as deviant, a moral equivalence is achieved, and an ideological agenda is accomplished: "a bold new way to strip the life of the bourgeois West of its moral sheen." Additionally, defining deviancy "down" allows coping by denial, a pretense that deviancy has disappeared. Defining deviancy "up" is also denial, but through distraction. By being distracted from feelings of helplessness in coping with real deviancy, by focusing on innocuous behaviors, an illusion is created that deviancy is in fact being addressed.

Denial and illusion create more problems. First, they prevent identifying, confronting, and solving the real problem: the fact that the voluminous increase in real deviancy has tilted the balance between functional and dysfunctional aspects of deviance toward the latter. Second, denial and illusion desensitize society's sense of outrage. Moynihan cites Judge Edwin Torres' description of how violent crime has resulted in a relentless and unabated slaughter of innocent people—subway riders, cab drivers, babies, bodega owners—in virtually every kind of location. Torres says, "This numbness, this near narcoleptic state can diminish the human condition to the level of combat infantrymen, who, in protracted campaigns, can eat their battlefield rations seated on the bodies of the fallen, friend and foe alike. A society that loses its sense of outrage is doomed to extinction." It was noted earlier, however, that public outrage and concern have forced politicians to face and to begin to deal more honestly with crime. Perhaps this is a positive sign of a willingness to confront the real issues and to restore a healthy balance between the functional and dysfunctional aspects of deviance.

Bibliography

Ben-Yehuda, Nachman. *Deviance and Moral Boundaries.* Chicago: University of Chicago Press, 1985. Provides a good introduction to the sociology of deviance and to the seminal contributions of Émile Durkheim. The author also discusses deviance within the context of a modern and complex society and discusses "offbeat" forms of deviance such as the occult, deviant science, and witchcraft.

Cohen, Albert K. *Deviance and Control.* Englewood Cliffs, N.J.: Prentice-Hall, 1966. A brief but well-written and incisive analysis of deviant behavior. The book has an interesting discussion of the functional and dysfunctional aspects of deviancy.

Durkheim, Émile. *The Rules of Sociological Method.* 8th ed. Translated by Sarah A. Solovay and John H. Mueller. Chicago, Ill.: University of Chicago Press, 1938. A seminal text by one of the founding fathers of the sociology of deviance. Durkheim forcefully and persuasively argues that deviance is normal, that it is impossible for a society to exist without it, and that it serves useful functions. This theme is also discussed in Durkheim's *The Division of Labor in Society* (Free Press, 1964).

Erikson, Kai T. *Wayward Puritans.* New York: Macmillan, 1986. Another classic text on the sociology of deviance. The book is a study of crime rates in the Massachusetts Bay Colony. Erikson found that the amount of deviance remains constant over time, suggesting that society does not seek to wipe out deviance but rather tries to keep it within reasonable bounds.

Krauthammer, Charles. "Defining Deviancy Up." *The New Republic* 209 (November 22, 1993): 20-25. This article provides the other half to Daniel Patrick Moynihan's argument that the epidemic of deviancy in American society has become so great that society deals with it by defining it away. Krauthammer argues that there is a complementary social phenomenon that has taken large areas of previously normal behavior and made them abnormal.

Moynihan, Daniel Patrick. "Defining Deviancy Down." *American Scholar* 62 (Winter, 1993): 17-30. Moynihan convincingly argues that deviant behavior in America has reached epidemic proportions. In order to avoid being overwhelmed and to comprehend the situation, Americans have "defined deviance down"—that is, redefined to be normal what was formerly considered to be deviant. Moynihan uses criminality, family breakdown, and mental disorders to state his case.

Laurence Miller

Cross-References

Crime: Analysis and Overview, 373; Deviance: Analysis and Overview, 525; Deviance: Biological and Psychological Explanations, 532; Functionalism, 786; Juvenile Delinquency: Analysis and Overview, 1036; Labeling and Deviance, 1049; The Medicalization of Deviance, 1178; The Structural-Strain Theory of Deviance, 1990; Victimless Crime, 2150.

INDIVIDUAL DISCRIMINATION

Type of sociology: Racial and ethnic relations
Fields of study: Dimensions of inequality; Theories of prejudice and discrimination

In the late 1960's, studies of prejudice and discrimination began to take into account different types of discrimination, most notably individual versus institutional discrimination (often called institutional racism). Individual discrimination is what one might call the "traditional" view of discrimination: the denial of rights and opportunities to certain groups based on prejudice and stereotypes.

Principal terms
CIVIL RIGHTS: the civil capacity to contract, to own property, to make wills, to give evidence, and to sue and be sued
DISCRIMINATION: the denial of opportunities and rights to certain groups on the basis of race, sex, ethnicity, age, or disability
DOMINATION: a condition in which people are forced to live their lives according to the will of those more powerful than themselves
MINORITY GROUP: any group that does not receive the same rewards as other groups in the society, because of its members' physical or cultural characteristics
PREJUDICE: unfounded, overgeneralized, stereotyped thinking formed without a solid assessment of the facts
RACISM: advocacy of the superiority of one's own group, people, or nation on the basis of racial differences
SEXISM: cultural beliefs and social practices based on the superiority of one sex, usually the male

Overview

Discrimination can be simply defined as prejudice transformed into action. Thinking of a group of people in a certain way and then promoting practices or conditions that support that thinking is discrimination. One example of such thinking is the stereotypical idea that African Americans are not able to adapt to twentieth century society. This thinking leads to the acceptance of the idea that African Americans are uneducated, which supports the conception that all African American people are fit only for low-paying jobs. This mode of thinking ultimately dehumanizes all African Americans.

Discrimination is a learned behavior. The learning process that takes place is circular: Attitudes are passed from society to the individual and then back from the individual to the society. Discrimination can be either intentional and conscious or unintentional and unconscious, and it can be practiced by a single individual, a group of individuals, or by institutions.

Four forms of discrimination have been identified by sociologists. The first form is intentional individual discrimination, which is an isolated act of discrimination performed by an individual on the basis of personal prejudice. For example, a male personnel officer routinely passes over females for supervisory positions because he believes and consciously acts on the belief that "female supervisors mean trouble."

The second form is unintentional individual discrimination, which is an isolated act of discrimination performed unconsciously by an individual. For example, if the personnel officer in the previous form were unaware of why he was passing over females for supervisory position, he would be performing an act of unintentional individual discrimination.

The third form, intentional institutional discrimination, occurs when discrimination is based on the personal prejudices of the members of an institution. For example, the male personnel officer would pass over women for supervisory positions because "boys in the company do not like to take orders from women."

The fourth form, unintentional institutional discrimination, is discrimination that is part of the routine behavior of an institution that has unknowingly incorporated sexually or racially prejudicial practices into its operating procedures. For example, a construction company routinely avoids hiring women because of its stereotypical assumption that women are not capable of doing heavy construction work.

Recent discussions of discrimination have focused on unintentional institutional discrimination by suggesting different measures for correcting this form of discrimination in the workplace. Some people believe that this form of discrimination can be corrected only by affirmative action programs. Others believe that these programs are inherently unjust and counterproductive. They believe that workplace discrimination can be corrected through antidiscrimination laws.

Individuals have been discriminated against on the basis of race, sex, ethnicity, age, and disabilities. Discrimination against the members of any of these groups is morally wrong, because discrimination denies these people their rights, which in turn robs them of their individuality. Discrimination has a significant economic impact on different groups of people. The U.S. government has taken various measures to reduce discriminatory attitudes. Sociologists believe that people's attitudes can be changed only by government policies. Much of the discrimination that takes place is unintentional. Therefore, it is argued that there will be little organized resistance to government antidiscrimination policies.

From the economic perspective, three viewpoints can be identified regarding the relationship between discriminatory attitudes and discriminatory behavior. Robert Cherry, in his book *Discrimination: Its Economic Impact on Blacks, Women, and Jews* (1989), points out that conservatives argue that discriminatory behavior can be eliminated without changing discriminatory attitudes. They believe that the cost involved in engaging in discriminatory behavior is sufficient to discourage such behavior in the marketplace. According to this view, discriminatory attitudes will remain, and it is not the business of government to legislate people's attitudes. Government intervention has a harmful effect on the disadvantaged groups.

Those who take a radical position on this issue claim that changing people's attitudes cannot be accomplished without changing the perceptions held by those who believe they benefit from discriminatory behavior. Some radicals believe that white male workers benefit from discriminatory practices. Others believe that within labor markets that are divided on the basis of race or gender, white male workers are harmed by discrimination. That is why these radicals claim that it is possible to build a united movement of black and white working-class men and women. Radicals also believe that government intervention will not end discrimination. Discrimination is profitable for important interest groups, and past governments have justified and protected discriminatory policies. Only a mass movement that consistently pressures government to enforce antidiscrimination regulation can reform the system.

Advocates of the liberal viewpoint contend that few groups either benefit from or are significantly harmed by their discriminatory behavior. Only through appropriate policies can discriminatory behavior be changed. That is why liberals favor government programs that are intended to reduce discrimination. Antidiscriminatory policies will be accepted by the corporate community once their benefits are realized.

Applications

The application of antidiscrimination laws can be found in the following acts. The Age Discrimination Act of 1975, like Title VI of the Civil Rights Act of 1964, prohibits exclusion on the basis of age from federally financed programs. The Age Discrimination in Employment Act, as well as some state laws, protects against age discrimination in employment.

The Americans with Disabilities Act (ADA) of 1990 is an expansion of the Civil Rights Act of 1964. The ADA aims to end the segregation, minority status, and political powerlessness of people with disabilities. The goal of this act is to ensure the equal opportunity, full participation, independent living, and economic self-sufficiency of disabled individuals. People with disabilities, as a rule, must have equal access to goods, services, facilities, accommodation, and public transportation. The most important provision of the ADA is Title I, which is similar to Title VII, the employment discrimination section of the 1964 Civil Rights Act. Title I does not allow any barrier to employment and promotion in the workplace. It requires employers to provide "reasonable accommodation" to an "otherwise qualified" individual with a disability. An employer cannot, however, be asked to bear an "undue hardship" in accommodating an otherwise qualified person with a disability.

The Civil Rights Act of 1957 marked the end of an eighty-two-year period of congressional inactivity in the field of civil rights, but it accomplished very little. The act created the Civil Rights Commission but granted it only investigative and reporting powers. It also created a separate Civil Rights Division within the Department of Justice that would be headed by an additional assistant attorney general. The act made it unlawful to harass those exercising their voting rights in federal elections and provided for the initiation of federal proceedings against committed or potential violations.

The insignificance and ineffectiveness of the Civil Rights Act of 1957 put pressure on the next Congress to enact a more effective civil rights law. The Civil Rights

Commission established by the 1957 act added to the pressure by issuing a report documenting the abridgment of black voting rights in the South.

The Civil Rights Act of 1960 required state election officers to retain for twenty-two months records relating to voter registration and qualifications in elections of federal officials. Whenever the right to vote was violated on the basis of race, the court was authorized to declare individuals qualified to vote and to appoint federal voting referees to take evidence and to report to the court on the treatment of black voters.

The Civil Rights Act of 1964 led to many changes. President John F. Kennedy, prompted by southern resistance to desegregation orders and violent responses to peaceful civil rights protests, took an aggressive new attitude toward racial discrimination. For African Americans, the act was a major legislative victory and certainly the most far-reaching civil rights measure in American history.

The Civil Rights Act of 1964 consists of eleven titles. Titles I and VIII reinforce the voting rights provisions of the Civil Rights Acts of 1957 and 1960 and limit the use of literacy tests to measure voter qualifications. Titles III and IV authorize court actions by the attorney general to challenge segregated public facilities and schools. Title V amends provisions governing the Civil Rights Commission. Title IX authorizes the attorney general to intervene in Equal Protection cases. Title X establishes a Community Relations Service to assist communities in resolving discrimination disputes. Title XI deals with miscellaneous matters. Titles II, VI, and VII are the most important parts of the law. Title II forbids discrimination in public accommodations. Title VI forbids discrimination in federally assisted programs. Title VII forbids employment discrimination. In 1972, Congress extended Title VII's coverage to most government employees. Employers must accommodate an employee's religious practices if they are able to do so without undue hardship. Title II generated little litigation, but Title VII has generated a huge backlog of cases in the agency charged with Title VII's administration, the Equal Employment Opportunity Commission (EEOC).

Title VII of the 1964 act was amended to include sex discrimination in the hope that such an amendment would weaken the bill's chance for passage, but the bill passed with the additional ban that revolutionized the formal status of female workers. Title VII owes much of its practical importance to chief justice Warren E. Burger's opinion for the Court in *Griggs v. Duke Power Co.* (1971). The Griggs decision removed the requirement that discriminatory intent be an element of Title VII cases. This was a case in which the Duke Power Company instituted a policy in 1955 requiring a high school diploma for workers who were to take positions in any operations department. This requirement for the upper divisions was not instituted as a ploy to bar promotions for African Americans, since at the time they were already explicitly barred on racial grounds. Title VI is also an important antidiscrimination law. *In Regents of the University of California v. Bakke* (1978), it provided the setting for the Court's first important pronouncement on affirmative action programs. This was a case in which a white man named Bakke was denied admission to graduate school in favor of a black man who was accepted by the University of California even though his scores were not as high as Bakke's.

The Civil Rights Act of 1968 capped the modern legislative program against racial discrimination that included the Civil Rights Act of 1964 and the Voting Rights Act of 1965. Title VIII of the act, which constitutes the nation's first comprehensive Open Housing Law, prohibits discrimination in the sale, rental, financing, and advertising of housing, and in membership in real estate brokerage organizations. The 1968 act also contained criminal penalties intended to protect civil rights activity and comprehensive measures to protect the rights of American Indians.

Context

The history of official and private discrimination in American life includes such institutions and occurrences as slavery in the South, the Civil War, Reconstruction, segregation in the military, massive resistance to school desegregation, sit-ins, and struggles for the right to vote. These injustices have been changed through sustained government action, which often depended on the use of force.

Before the 1960's and 1970's, blatant racial discrimination was a fact of life for many minorities, especially African Americans. Most African Americans have lived on the lowest economic level of American society. They have been discriminated against in the areas of housing, education, employment, and union membership. Women have also been discriminated against in many ways. Sexual discrimination has been extensive in the economic realm, with women's earning power being much less than that of men. Even today, the earning gaps between men and women, on the one hand, and white men and minorities, on the other hand, are very wide.

The Civil Rights movement was not very aggressive when it began in the 1950's, but it became militant in the 1970's. In the 1950's, Supreme Court decisions and governmental actions undermined the legal structure of segregation. Between 1955 and 1965, the Civil Rights movement reached its peak. In the 1970's, the momentum of the movement continued, as additional legal, political, and judicial decisions were made that helped to move the United States closer to the goal of equal access and racial integration. The social and economic progress for blacks took place primarily in the 1960's and early 1970's, though there has been much resistance to that progress. Some occupational mobility also took place. For example, in 1960, 25 percent more white men than black men held white-collar jobs, and 41 percent more white women than black women. By 1983, there was a 14 percent difference for men and a 17 percent difference for women. There was also a gain in the years of schooling for African Americans. For example, the gap between blacks' and whites' average number of years of schooling decreased from three years in 1960 to less than six months today, but blacks with the same number of years of schooling as whites do not earn comparable incomes. This fact demonstrates that the national civil rights struggle has run an uneven course; though there have been court rulings and legislation outlawing all types of racial and gender discrimination, such forms of discrimination still exist.

There is no doubt that the civil rights movement is one of the most powerful movements to take place in modern times. The Civil Rights Act of 1964 has continued to redefine its roles and expand its goals in a way that has affected all areas of U.S.

social life. Changes for the better have been made. Perhaps, in a competitive market-place, discrimination will not totally disappear, but the term "civil rights" has taken on a new dimension. Originally, the term referred to the civil capacity to contract, to own property, to make wills, to give evidence, and to sue and be sued, but in the modern context it refers to the removal of limits on freedom of association.

Bibliography

Backhouse, Constance. *Petticoats and Prejudice: Women and Law in Nineteenth-Century Canada*. Toronto: Women's Press, 1991. A good book for general readers. Backhouse analyzes nineteenth century Canadian law in a way that is comprehensible to any reader.

Cherry, Robert D. *Discrimination: Its Economic Impact on Blacks, Women, and Jews*. Lexington, Mass.: Lexington Books, 1989. This book assesses theories of discrimination and their effectiveness in explaining the contemporary situations of blacks, women, and Jews. The language is jargon-free, and when technical terms are used, they are explained. Contains very helpful endnotes, references, and an index.

Feagin, Joseph, and Clairece B. Feagin. *Discrimination American Style: Institutional Racism and Sexism*. Englewood Cliffs, N.J.: Prentice-Hall, 1978. The authors integrate materials on racism and sexism in their discussion of the central theme of discrimination. This well-written book makes an important contribution to race relations research. The references following every chapter make the book very useful. Contains footnotes and an index.

Holmes, Fred R. *Prejudice and Discrimination: Can We Eliminate Them?* Englewood Cliffs, N.J.: Prentice-Hall, 1970. Although this book is dated, it gives a straightforward analysis of prejudice and discrimination, providing case studies and questions for discussion. Contains a bibliography.

Levin, Jack, and William Levin. *The Functions of Discrimination and Prejudice*. 2d ed. New York: Harper & Row, 1982. A good book that examines its subjects from the perspectives of sociology, political science, economics, and psychology. The message of this book is that majority-minority relations cannot be understood apart from the consequences of discrimination and prejudice. Contains extensive references and an index.

Saltman, Juliet. *A Fragile Movement: The Struggle for Neighborhood Stabilization*. New York: Greenwood Press, 1990. This book examines the neighborhood stabilization movement on the community level and the national level from the perspective of one who has been involved in the movement. Contains a bibliography and an index.

Urofsky, Melvin I. *A Conflict of Rights: The Supreme Court and Affirmative Action*. New York: Charles Scribner's Sons, 1991. This book gives a superb account of the case of *Johnson v. Transportation Agency, Santa Clara County, California* (1987). The writing is free of technical jargon and is suitable for the general public. Contains an index.

Van Dyke, Vernon. *The Human Rights, Ethnicity, and Discrimination*. Westport,

Conn.: Greenwood Press, 1985. This book, which is part of the Contributions to Ethnic Studies series, focuses on the problems that arise when people of different cultures and goals interact. Includes an interesting analysis of the Charter of the United Nations, which requires members to promote human rights "without distinction as to race, sex, language, or religion." Contains a bibliography and an index.

Krishna Mallick

Cross-References

Ageism and the Ideology of Ageism, 41; Discrimination Against Children and Adolescents, 225; Discrimination Against Gays, 806; Institutional Racism, 996; Prejudice and Discrimination: Merton's Paradigm, 1498; Prejudice and Stereotyping, 1505; Improving Race Relations, 1559; Race Relations: The Race-Class Debate, 1566; The Race Relations Cycle Theory of Assimilation, 1572; Racial and Ethnic Stratification, 1579; Racism as an Ideology, 1586.

CAUSES OF DIVORCE

Type of sociology: Major social institutions
Field of study: The family

Divorce has long been a subject of sociological concern. Understanding the causes of divorce is difficult, at least partly because they are tied into societal expectations of what constitutes a good marriage, and these expectations change over time. Problems in communication are often said to be the fundamental issue that underlies many divorces.

Principal terms

DEMOGRAPHIC FACTORS: factors (in this case, factors affecting divorce) that are aspects of the study of population, such as age, gender, and income level

EXTENDED FAMILY: the family grouping that includes, in addition to the nuclear family, relatives such as grandparents, aunts, uncles, and cousins

PERCEPTION: the account or view of reality that is constructed by the mind after it experiences outside stimuli and interprets them via past experience

REACTIVE: behavior that changes (reacts) as a result of being observed

SELF-REPORT: a type of study that involves gathering information on events and attitudes from the people involved

Overview

Attempting to understand the causes of divorce is challenging partly because of the necessarily subjective nature of much of the data involved and partly because a wide variety of reasons for divorce are cited by divorced individuals. Another complicating factor is that, because divorce is one possible outcome of marriage, it is impossible to view divorce without examining the institution of marriage as well. The institution of marriage is in a constant state of change. At any given time, individual marital satisfaction is based on current beliefs about what a "good marriage" is, and in most cases those beliefs are inextricably linked with the prevailing attitudes of the society at large. Each new generation of couples has different expectations about marriage; therefore, the issues perceived to be primary in causing divorce change. For example, contemporary surveys examining the causes of divorce find that middle-class women most frequently mention problems with the emotional aspects of marriage, such as home life, shared values, and open channels of communication. In the 1940's, such issues were not mentioned. Instead, women cited problems such as nonsupport, drinking, the husband's absence from the home (as in being "out with the boys"), and an imbalance of authority in the relationship. Since the 1940's (and most dramatically since the 1960's), there have been profound changes in women's roles in society, as women have demanded equality and have entered the workforce in greater numbers. It is not surprising, therefore, that women's expectations about marriage and their perceptions regarding the causes of divorce have also changed.

Sociologists have uncovered a number of important themes regarding the causes of divorce. In uncovering such information, social scientists have primarily taken one of two approaches, sometimes contrasted as "objective" and "subjective" methods. With the objective method, the emphasis is on the identification of facts, known as demographic factors (characteristics such as age, sex, and educational level), that allow prediction of those at a higher risk for divorce. It is important to realize that demographic studies do not provide direct information about the causes of divorce. For example, one strong demographic finding is that people who marry younger are more likely to get divorced. It has been found that women marry younger than men and that women who marry between the ages of fourteen and seventeen are twice as likely to divorce as those who marry at eighteen or nineteen; they are three times as likely to divorce as women who marry between twenty and twenty-four. The same trend was found true for men. Young age, however, cannot truly be called a "cause" of divorce. The more likely causes are related to a lack of readiness to participate cooperatively within a relationship. Although objective findings do not pinpoint the causes of divorce, they do permit identification of groups at higher risk. This, in turn, provides direction regarding which groups should be studied subjectively. Demographic studies have identified gender, education, income, and the presence and gender of children in the marriage as important predictors of divorce likelihood. Briefly, couples who marry in their middle twenties, have been graduated from college, have a stable and adequate source of income, and have male children in the home are the least likely to be divorced.

Subjective studies more directly examine the causes of divorce. They are termed "subjective" because they are based on self-report studies. In many cases, investigators simply ask those applying for a divorce to tell them what happened. This type of information is based on an individual's perceptions of what happened; therefore, it may not accurately reflect what really went on. On the other hand, as several humanistic sociologists have pointed out, what is most important in understanding human crisis is understanding the perceptions of those involved; reality must be considered, but it is secondary to the individual's perception of it. Much has been learned about the causes of divorce in research that is based on this philosophy.

In one study, hundreds of men and women were interviewed to determine what they believed had caused their divorce. The findings of this study were in general agreement with several others. They showed that communication problems were most often mentioned as the primary cause. The second and third most frequently cited reasons were basic unhappiness and incompatibility.

Several differences have been found between women's and men's perceptions of the causes of their divorce. Women believe that the most significant causes of divorce are related to the quality of their marital relationship. Husbands are sometimes perceived as not permitting them enough independence or authority within the relationship. This class of problems leads to basic unhappiness, feelings of incompatibility, and a breakdown of communication. Abuse is another cause of divorce cited frequently by women. This includes emotional and physical abuse, alcohol problems (spouse or self), and financial problems. Infidelity is the third most important category of complaint made by women. Other factors often mentioned are drug abuse problems in their spouse, in-law problems, a lack of help around the home and with the children, and religious differences.

Men also cite communication problems, basic unhappiness, and incompatibility as the most important reasons for divorce. Two other factors that are cited frequently, however, are drug abuse (by the men themselves) and liberal, independent attitudes of their wives. Sexual problems are perceived as a more important cause of divorce by men than women, as are in-law problems and religious differences. Men also mention emotional abuse and infidelity as reasons for divorce. In general, the results of contemporary subjective studies on the causes of divorce suggest that women more often cite reasons related to the relationship itself (communication, friendship, interest, love, and independence), while men tend to focus their explanation on causes outside the emotional relationship with their wife (financial problems, women's liberation, in-laws, and drug abuse).

Applications

A goal of sociology is to identify trends within society and then gather additional information in an attempt to understand these trends better. It is often hoped that the insights gained can be used to help reduce social problems. The objective and subjective methods are used together for this purpose. First, objective (demographic) studies are conducted to identify societal trends, such as the rising rate of divorce. Then subjective methods are used to discover the reasons for the general trend and to note how perceptions may differ among demographic groups. Such is the case with studies attempting to identify the primary causes of divorce and to explore how causes are perceived differently by men and women. This two-stage approach has been used to understand how divorce rates differ between the young and old, rich and poor, and various ethnic groups, and to explore how sources of marital satisfaction change as the family (and hence the couple's time together) grows.

Once acquired, information can be applied to give meaningful advice to those considering marriage. First, and most important, both sociological and psychological findings agree that a person is not ready to marry until he or she has established an identity. A person must be comfortable with himself or herself, have a general life plan, and have confidence that this plan is valuable and meaningful. Without identity, people's commitments are overly simplistic and shallow, and their abilities to share and regulate all important aspects of their life with a partner are lacking. The idea of identity is instrumental in explaining the demographic findings indicating a high rate of divorce in young people, people of lower educational accomplishment, and people with little money or social power. Perceptual findings related to a lack of communication (and the accompanying unhappiness and sense of incompatibility) can often be explained with reference to identity problems, as can infidelity issues. Finally, a lack of identity is strongly related to the presence of alcohol and drug abuse problems, as well as to physical and emotional abuse. People have a much better chance of a happy marriage if they wait until after completing their education, until after they have devised a meaningful life plan, and until after they have established an adequate source of income.

Sociological data also suggest that for a marriage to be successful the couple's attitudes toward gender roles within the relationship must be considered. In light of data indicating that women frequently cite restrictions in their independence and power within the relationship as the primary cause of divorce, males must learn to value their wives' independence and support them in the realization of their own life plans. Both partners must avoid imposing their own values too strongly when interpreting each other's goals. Note that in the United States the wife's role has traditionally been to take care of the husband and family while he pursues his dreams. This is no longer the case. If divorce rates are to be brought down in the United States, sociological data indicates, males must adjust their attitudes about the female's role within the marriage. Consequently, people considering marriage should thoroughly think about and discuss their prospective partner's ability to provide such freedom and unconditional support.

Sociological findings also suggest that it is important for a couple to consider the compatibility of their values toward children and toward extended family. Whether one wants children represents an important aspect of one's life plan, and a cause of divorce frequently cited by women is the lack of interest in and help with childrearing. A discussion of when and how many children one ultimately wants is well advised, as are the expectations regarding each partner's role in childrearing. Further, because divorce rates are higher when children are female as opposed to male, a serious discussion of the differential value the man places on a child's gender should also be part of the marriage plans. Another often overlooked aspect of marriage is that one not only marries a person but also marries into that person's family. Unwelcome interference from in-laws is often cited as the cause of a breakup, more frequently by males. A discussion of future in-laws and the character of the intended relationship between them and the couple, and the clear communication of boundaries to the prospective in-laws themselves, should precede the marriage.

Finally, data on marital satisfaction suggest that the issues which are perceived as important change with time and the growth of the family. Consequently, throughout the marriage both partners must remain aware that they are counting on each other for support, friendship, love, and interest in each other throughout the family life cycle. In short, they are depending on each other for the fulfillment of their needs and for the sensitivity to realize when these needs change.

Context

American culture places a high value on the family, and the tracking and interpretation of divorce rates has been occurring since the late 1800's. For example, in 1889,

C. D. Wright published *A Report on Marriage and Divorce in the United States: 1867 to 1886*, and in 1897, Walter F. Wilcox published *The Divorce Problem: A Study in Statistics*. Early studies focused on identifying predictor variables. The first major finding was that a large divorce differential existed among the three belts of the United States (east, central, and west). As inadequate subjective data were available, the attempt to interpret these results created a lively debate. Although this debate continues, more recent evidence suggests that when age at marriage is considered, there is no divorce differential between east and west.

Early research efforts provided the impetus for more work, and demographic studies flourished. By the 1920's and 1930's, factors such as race, religion, and residence (urban versus rural) were all cited as reasons for the geographical differences in divorce rates. During this time sociologists were becoming better at collecting data and making interpretative predictions. Methodological advances permitted sociologists to control for the reactive nature of their subjects more effectively, and advances in representative sampling procedure made predictions much more accurate. The demographic tracking of the divorce rate has demonstrated that divorce is a pervasive problem. Consequently, efforts to understand the causes of divorce intensified, and the use of the subjective method began to flourish.

In their classic 1969 paper "Marriage and the Construction of Reality," Peter L. Berger and Hansfried Kellner explain the importance of examining the perceptions of those involved with divorce, as these perceptions, regardless of their accuracy, must first be understood in order to understand the reasons for divorce. This idea began a movement that led to the acquisition of a large database on the perceived causes of divorce. It was soon discovered that when the data were broken down by demographic group (such as males-females, rich-poor), different themes emerged. This discovery in turn had important implications for understanding the causes of divorce and understanding how society influences expectations regarding marriage.

The sociological study of divorce has led to a good understanding of the groups at risk for divorce and of the subjective reasons cited by these groups for divorce. Although the knowledge base is sound, the problem is stubborn. To give only one example, many experts have pointed to the circular nature of the problems with identity formation that can lead to marital problems. People with a sound sense of identity tend to do well in intimate relationships; those without do not. Whether a person achieves satisfactory identity formation is significantly influenced by home life in childhood. In American society, both parents frequently must work; in addition, increasing numbers of children are reared by divorced parents. In both cases, it is difficult for the parent(s) to provide the experiences and guidance necessary for the child to begin the process of forming a sound identity. When these children grow into adolescence, then young adulthood, without establishing an identity, they may marry and then divorce, thus perpetuating the cycle.

Bibliography

Berger, Peter L., and Hansfried Kellner. "Marriage and the Construction of Reality."

In *Recent Sociology,* edited by Hans Peter Dreitzel. New York: Macmillan, 1969. This chapter is a classic in the study of causes of divorce. It served as an impetus to increase the subjective study of divorce through convincing the sociological community that perceptions, distorted though they may be, provide valuable information. The chapter is appropriate for both high school and college students.

Cahn, Dudley D. *Conflict in Intimate Relationships.* New York: Guilford Press, 1992. This book addresses common conflicts that arise within a marriage and provides suggestions regarding how to avoid and, when necessary, resolve such conflict. The book is appropriate for college and advanced high school students.

Erickson, Erik H. *Identity, Youth, and Crisis.* New York: W. W. Norton, 1968. Erik Erickson, a prominent sociocultural theorist, presents a description of the turbulent process of adolescent identity formation in this book. A discussion of how earlier development affects the formation of identity is also presented. The book is appropriate for college-level students.

Reisseman, Catherine Kohler. *Divorce Talk: Women and Men Make Sense of Personal Relationships.* New Brunswick, N.J.: Rutgers University Press, 1990. This book explores the subjective perceptions of couples going through divorce. An excellent source to gain insight into the varied reasons people decide to divorce as well as into the effects of culture on expectations regarding marriage. Appropriate for both high school and college students.

Rhyne, Darla. "Bases of Marital Satisfaction Among Men and Women." *Journal of Marriage and Family* 43 (November, 1981): 941-967. This article is an excellent example of combining objective and subjective methodology to obtain valuable insight into the reasons for divorce and marital dissatisfaction across the family life cycle. It is appropriate for college students and advanced high school students.

Thornes, B., and J. Collard. *Who Divorces?* London: Routledge & Kegan Paul, 1979. The book is an extensive description of results obtained through the objective study of the reasons for divorce. An excellent source to help one better understand the influences of culture on marriage, although the reader is cautioned that earlier assessment of divorce correlates were not always valid. The book is appropriate for both high school and college students.

Alan J. Beauchamp

Cross-References

Effects of Divorce, 560; Extramarital Sex, 727; The Family: Functionalist versus Conflict Theory Views, 739; Remarriage and "Reconstituted" Families, 1629; Romantic Love, 1661; Spouse Battering and Violence Against Women, 1959; Two-Career Families, 2077; Violence in the Family, 2157.

EFFECTS OF DIVORCE

Type of sociology: Major institutions
Field of study: The family

Sociological research on divorce and separation has permitted insight into why divorce rates are rising, how this trend may affect society, and how divorce affects both parents and children. Understanding the consequences of divorce-related issues for society and family has permitted the refinement of methods to reduce the negative impact of this event.

Principal terms

ADJUSTMENT TRAJECTORY: a shift in perception in which one's former spouse is viewed with hostility and mistrust instead of the former love and respect

DISPLACEMENT COMMUNICATION: a method of indirect communication using an object or fictional character to represent the actions or thoughts of the person with whom one is talking

EGO DEFENSE MECHANISMS: unconscious and irrational ways that people distort reality to reduce anxiety

ENMESHMENT: an excessively close relationship between parent and child in which adult needs and concerns are communicated; an overdependence on the child by the adult is apparent

SEPARATION DISTRESS: the anxiety and panic that accompany the realization that one's marital partner is no longer available

SOCIAL SUPPORT NETWORK: a web of social relationships that provide emotional support for individuals

Overview

Separation and divorce terminate the social and legal contract of marriage and result in the breakup of the family. For both children and adults, divorce can represent the end of emotional suffering, escape from an abusive environment, and renewed potential for personal growth. Yet the experience of divorce can also be devastating. Adults are likely to experience depression, insomnia, loneliness, decreased efficacy, poor personal health habits, and anger both toward themselves and toward their former spouse. For children the situation is a bit more complex, because age, gender, level of emotional and intellectual development, the presence of siblings, access to an extended family or strong social support network, and the quality of parental relations (both before and after the divorce) are all influential factors. Symptoms in children typically include anger and aggressive behavior, sadness, low self-esteem, depression, and impaired academic performance.

Much has been written about the rising divorce rate in the United States. The divorce rate in the United States is the highest in the world. An estimated 50 percent of first marriages and 60 percent of remarriages end in divorce. Some sociologists even fear that this trend may lead to the collapse of the family as an institution. Concern centers on the fear that families will fail to perform their traditional functions: the socialization of children and the provision for their intellectual, physical, and emotional development. For example, some experts suspect that the increased level of drug abuse and violent crime can be attributed to a lack of parenting, indirectly resulting from divorce.

The conclusions of several studies on the question of why people get divorced indicate that the primary reasons are infidelity, incompatibility, financial difficulties, and marrying too young. There are also social forces behind high levels of divorce. For example, marriage today generally is not designed to perpetuate property and status. As women have become more independent, marriage is no longer as economically necessary as it used to be. Further, divorce is no longer viewed as negatively by society as it once was, and in the United States, a premium has been placed on individualism and personal satisfaction. All these factors contribute to rising divorce rates. Robert Weiss, in his book *Going It Alone* (1976), describes a definite adult adjustment trajectory to divorce. He explains that women suffer on an economic level far more than men do, but that the process of psychological and social adjustment is about the same for both sexes. In general, the respect and liking the couple had for each other disappear some time before they separate. Mistrust and hostility take their place. Yet the emotional bond between the couple tends to continue. Hence, even though a couple may argue bitterly prior to the separation, they experience profound feelings of separation distress. That is, the inability to have the former partner available creates feelings of anxiety and panic. On the other hand, some people report feelings of extreme happiness, and still others fluctuate between these two states. After a while, distress or euphoria gives way to feelings of loneliness. People long for the security of the family world. Separation is not only from one's former spouse, but also frequently from entire social support networks. Friendships and in-law relations are inevitably altered, contributing to the individual's feelings of loneliness.

All children generally experience a marked period of emotional anxiety following the separation of their parents. In an extensive five-year study on the effects of divorce upon children, Judith S. Wallerstein and Joan B. Kelly, in their book *Surviving the Breakup: How Children and Parents Cope with Divorce* (1980), found that preschool-aged children were confused and frightened, tending to blame the divorce upon themselves. Older children were intellectually and emotionally better able to cope with the divorce. They could understand their parents' motives for the divorce but were quite angry and often worried about how the divorce would affect their future. At the end of the five-year follow-up, most children were reasonably well adjusted. Approximately one-third, however, continued to experience problems. Many suffered from depression, expressed feelings of loneliness, and displayed behavioral problems such as aggression, drug and alcohol abuse, truancy, and promiscuity. It was concluded that long-term adjustment levels depended highly on the manner in which both parents explained the divorce to their children and continued to maintain contact with, and involvement in, their children's lives.

Many psychologists are quick to point out that, if a divorce is handled properly, most children of divorced parents do not carry long-term emotional scars. About 30 percent of couples do not handle the divorce properly, but instead enlist their children as allies in a parental war. It is clearly these children who are most likely to suffer from long-term psychological difficulties. To illustrate, Judith Wallerstein and Sandra Blakeslee report in their book *Second Chances: Men, Women, and Children a Decade After Divorce* (1989) that although only 30 percent of all children are from divorced homes, they account for between 60 percent and 80 percent of the children in mental health treatment, in special education classes, or referred by teachers to school psychologists.

Applications

The knowledge gained from studying the divorce process can be applied to decrease the impact of this traumatic event. Friends, family members, and mental health professionals such as psychologists must pay attention to the individual as well as to the family context from which the person emerged. It must be made clear that the adjustment trajectory is normal and that feelings of intense anger, rejection, loneliness, depression, and anxiety are to be expected. The person is no longer receiving the level of love and support from family that he or she was previously. The person's world is suddenly unpredictable on many levels, and this can be frightening. If the individual is from a troubled background—one that has included violence, substance abuse, rejection, or mental disturbance—he or she may not have the wherewithal to cope with the divorce effectively.

In such cases, the separation distress is intense, and the person is often unable to understand or cope with this discomfort. This may lead to high levels of hostility, rejection of the children, and even violent and self-destructive behavior. In this situation, professional help should be obtained from a clinical psychologist or other professional specially trained in this area. If, on the other hand, the individual is from a well-adjusted background, efforts to get him or her involved with whatever social support network remains may be sufficient. Friends, parents, brothers and sisters, and peers are invaluable in helping a person cope with the stress of divorce, and they should let the individual talk through his or her feelings surrounding the divorce. If permitted, the individual will do this repeatedly. Although at times this is trying for the listener, it can be very helpful for the person undergoing a divorce. It helps the person integrate the experience of divorce and reorganize his or her life accordingly.

Divorced women face the additional issue of economic hardship far more frequently than men do, so special emphasis needs to be placed on helping them find an economically feasible and self-fulfilling career. This process often compounds a woman's guilt, as it requires her to decrease her involvement with the children when she feels they need her the most. Research indicates, however, that it is not the amount of time spent with children but the quality of the interactions that is important. Further, this can be a positive event, as it provides a chance for the children to become more independent and competent. For example, they could be required to take over some age-appropriate roles and chores within the household to help out. In general, when this approach is combined with an effective coparenting relationship, such children when they become adults are found to display equal or superior adjustment when compared with individuals from intact homes. Successful adjustment can also be aided by federal and local government agencies which can often provide avenues of valuable support for the struggling mother. For example, available training opportunities, child care services, and economic support can reduce stress on the mother.

Although the effects of divorce on adults are not to be minimized, they are more transient than those that children frequently experience. Helping children adjust to divorce is of utmost importance for their long-term happiness. In general, younger children need to be reassured that the divorce is not their fault, while older children need help to understand the real reasons for the divorce as well as any long-term consequences this may have on their future.

Regardless of age, all children need continued exposure to both parents. Hence, it is crucial that both partners agree on an effective coparenting relationship. Parents must not engage in open warfare in front of the children, as this puts children in a horrible dilemma. That is, they love and need both parents and want both parents to continue loving and nurturing them. Forcing children to choose between parents psychologically rips them apart. The custodial parent must also use special care not to enmesh the children in an adultlike relationship, or become overdependent on a child. Children also need predictability in their world, and this must be facilitated. For example, divorced parents should attempt to set schedules so children know where they are and when they will be home, should try to use consistent child care, and should keep the children in the same neighborhood and school if possible.

Children seldom directly display the distress they feel regarding the breakup; this is particularly true of younger children. Instead, one can often see the unconscious use of ego defense mechanisms. Ego defense mechanisms are ways that people distort reality to reduce stress. For example, a mother may use ego defense by describing her former spouse in rather unfavorable terms. In this way she reduces the impact of the rejection, as the guy was a "jerk" anyway. Children do this as well. For example, preschool-age children often show regression, or a return to an earlier stage of development. Regression in sleep habits, toilet training, language, motor achievements, and emotional independence all signal trouble. Older children may isolate their feelings, appearing rather detached and unemotional about the breakup. On the other hand, they may displace their anger onto others by fighting, resisting authority, skipping school, and so forth. With older children, direct and frank discussions are useful. With younger children, clear and developmentally appropriate discussion is necessary while hidden issues can be addressed with a technique called "displacement communication." Neil Kalter's book *Growing up with Divorce: Helping Your Child Avoid Immediate and Later Emotional Problems* (1990) provides several excellent examples of how to apply this approach.

Context

The study of divorce has been a concern of sociology for many years. The rising incidence of divorce has been of particular concern. Divorce rates have fluctuated in the United States at different periods. They rose following World War II, then dropped off before rising to much higher levels. The divorce rate rose steeply from the 1960's to the late 1970's and peaked in 1981. According to Andrew Cherrin's book *Marriage, Divorce, Re-Marriage* (1981), through the 1970's the proportion of separated or divorced mothers heading households with children under eighteen years of age rose by 86 percent.

Alex Thio's textbook *Sociology* (1992) describes several social factors that have contributed to high divorce rates in the United States. First, increased acceptance of divorce has played a role; in the U.S., there is virtually no stigma attached to divorce. Second, a variety of opportunities and experiences that were previously provided only within a marital relationship are available to single people, including divorced people. For example, single people can engage in sexual activity with little or no censure. Moreover, women regularly pursue educational and career goals and achieve financial independence. A third factor is an increased specialization of family function for providing love and affection. Providing love and affection is central to the family's mission in most societies, but in countries with lower divorce rates, families serve several other functions as well, such as the education and socialization of the children. Although previously the realm of the family, in the United States the school systems are now largely responsible for these tasks. Hence, when love and affection dwindle, partners are more likely to break up the "empty" marriage. Fourth, people have higher expectations about the quality of the marital relationship than is the case in some societies. In traditional societies, young people do not expect a romantic and passionate relationship with their spouses, especially if the marriage was arranged by their parents. In the United States, an intense love relationship is expected, particularly by those who marry at a young age. Because such expectations are difficult to fulfill, the chances for disillusionment are great. Fifth, an American emphasis on individualism is thought to play a role. In countries that place a great value on the rights of the individual, divorce rates are relatively high. An individualistic society values the rights and needs of the individual more highly than those of the family unit. Hence, if people decide that they want a divorce, they believe they have the right to get one.

Yet although divorce rates are high, this fact does not mean that American marriages are unhappier than those in other countries. Actually, Americans are the most "marrying" people in the world, and they show very high levels of marital satisfaction. Americans do not reject marriage as an institution; they reject unhappy marriage. Hence, if divorce can be handled in a mature manner, with child welfare in mind, there may be less reason for alarm concerning the future of the family as an institution than some sociologists believe.

Bibliography

Hetherington, E. M., M. Cox, and R. Cox. "The Aftermath of Divorce." In *Mother/ Child, Father/Child Relationships*, edited by Joseph H. Stevens, Jr., and Marilyn Mathews. Washington, D.C.: National Association for the Education of Young

Children, 1978. This chapter represents pioneering work that documents how divorce affects children. Reactions of children to the news of divorce and to its aftermath are vividly described. The chapter can be read by high school and college students.

Johnston, Janet R., and Linda E. G. Campbell. *Impasses of Divorce: The Dynamics and Resolution of Family Conflict.* New York: Free Press, 1988. The authors describe their project, focused on helping parents mediate differences in hostile divorce situations. Issues sustaining conflict and preventing the development of a coparenting relationship are discussed, and methods to achieve a resolution are presented. An excellent source for family counselors.

Kalter, Neil. *Growing up with Divorce: Helping Your Child Avoid Immediate and Later Emotional Problems.* New York: Free Press, 1990. Kalter presents comprehensive advice on the emotional pitfalls of divorce, warning signs of distress, and methods of preventing and alleviating distress in children from infancy through adolescence. He provides a useful chapter on communicating with children. The book can be understood by high school and college students.

Wallerstein, Judith S., and Sandra Blakeslee. *Second Chances: Men, Women, and Children a Decade After Divorce.* New York: Ticknor & Fields, 1989. This represents a follow-up to Wallerstein's original 1980 study. Wallerstein's work presents excellent data in the long-term effects of divorce on both parents and children and is therefore extremely valuable. This book is useful for those anticipating divorce, attempting to cope with divorce, or interested in long-term consequences of divorce.

Wallerstein, Judith S., and Joan B. Kelly. *Surviving the Breakup: How Children and Parents Cope with Divorce.* New York: Basic Books, 1980. The authors present the results of a five-year study investigating how parents and children adjust to divorce. They present data on how parents reacted to divorce and on how these parental reactions affected children's adjustment. They also report how children interpreted and reacted to the divorce and how these views solidified or changed over the period of the study.

Alan J. Beauchamp

Cross-References

Causes of Divorce, 554; The Family: Functionalist versus Conflict Theory Views, 739; The Family: Nontraditional Families, 746; The Feminization of Poverty, 754; Nuclear and Extended Families, 1303; Poverty: Women and Children, 1466; Socialization: The Family, 1880.

DRAMATURGY

Type of sociology: Socialization and social interaction
Field of study: Interactionist approach to social interaction

Dramaturgical analysis considers the individual engaged in social interaction to be an "actor" who can, and will, change his or her performance "roles" as situations demand. This social-psychological perspective is more a descriptive tool than a theoretical perspective. Dramaturgy's focus is on the examination and explanation of everyday life in relation to the creation and maintenance of the individual self.

Principal terms
> DEFINITION OF THE SITUATION: individuals' definition of a social interaction by means of explicit or implicit agreement
> EXPRESSIONS GIVEN: performance-centered verbal communication
> EXPRESSIONS GIVEN OFF: audience-centered perceptions of nonverbal performance cues such as clothing and props
> IMPRESSION MANAGEMENT: individuals' attempts to control the impressions that others have of them
> OFFSTAGE/ONSTAGE: private/public elements of performances
> PERFORMANCE: actions meant to influence others in some way
> ROLES: performances that control both the impressions of and definitions of a particular interaction

Overview

The dramaturgic approach to social interactions is based on an overarching metaphoric framework that sees the world of human experience as a "theater" in which individuals "stage" a variety of "performances." From this perspective, everyday life is a kind of ongoing drama, complete with rehearsals, staging, costumes, roles, and an audience. This is not to say that life is "imitated" or copied by drama; instead, theater and ordinary experience share significant organizational and ritual elements, such as body language and an interest in spatial arrangements, and communicate meaning through similar symbolic and formal languages, such as speech, music, and dance.

Theater and ordinary life are also connected by parallels between dramatic performance and the ways in which social behavior creates and maintains social order. As a matter of fact, the degrees of ritual and "theatricality" of a social experience are directly related to the level of tradition and flexibility permitted by the structure in which it takes place. Matters of self-consciousness, awareness of conventions and rules of performance, and flexibility of rules help define the differences between theatrical and social experiences. Drama, as an art form, is more likely to allow for or, in the case of avant-garde theater, encourage radical manipulation of conventions, while social experiences and conventions tend to enforce more conservative perspectives and behaviors.

What defines dramaturgic analysis and separates it from other sociological approaches is its interest in a detailed recording of the experiences of subjects as they are being lived. Dramaturgy is a situation-based examination of interactions which focuses on social behaviors and social hierarchies as the products of encounters between people and groups rather than as the frameworks for such encounters. For dramaturgists, society is not a fixed construct that simply requires description to be understood. Instead, dramaturgy is built on a revolutionary sense of social realities; emphasizing their constructed nature opens up an infinite universe of pluralistic, and possibly contradictory, ways to meet the challenges of ordinary social life.

Dramaturgic sociologists generally assume that individuals are aware of their active parts in the creation and presentation of themselves to others. This should not be understood to imply, however, that these presentations are either self-consciously manipulative or exploitative. Social interactions should be seen as positive attempts to fit the self into individualized understandings of specific situations. The self and the mind are products of shared understandings and communication, reflecting the opinions of others.

George Herbert Mead conceptualized the self as having two interdependent parts: the "I," which is the subjective, nonreflective, spontaneous part of the self, and the "me," a reflective, evaluative, objectified aspect. In addition, Mead believed that an individual's self-concept was dependent on, and reflective of, the opinions of others. The bottom line for the "actor," then, is that if the "audience" recognizes and accepts the self that has been presented, then the "performance" is "good." Dramaturgical investigators are concerned with how this complex web of theatrical (dramatic) relationships and procedures sustains social interactions and creates and maintains social life.

Social interaction, then, becomes a performance within a set of prescriptive rules. Individuals are expected to present and preserve a consistent public "face" and to help other members of the group to do the same. One need not always do this alone; social performances may be put on by teams, or "casts," of players, such as spouses entertaining guests at home or military personnel working under a supervising sergeant. In this context, the social world may be divided into public (front) and private (back) staging areas. Life is like theater in that everyone tries, to some degree or another, to control the reality that others see. Success in this manipulation may enhance one's freedom, power, or status. Onstage, performers define and maintain their public roles and selves; offstage, in private, they can relax a bit, and if they care to, remove their performance "masks" when they are with other "insiders."

Successful realization of one's social roles incorporates both practical and expressive elements. Performances are essential to a lucid, consistent, and knowable social reality. In this way, social performances simultaneously create and control the world. Situations do not, however, simply define themselves; social interactions are shaped by symbolic communications, which may take on lives of their own, transcending the individuals who create them and live in them. For example, organizations are often symbolically represented by architecture and can exist without any of their current members, who are, for the most part, invisible and easily replaced. Therefore, the world is filled with things that exist only in people's minds, which must constantly be enacted and reenacted to maintain their presence. Society is, in very real and important ways, a theater, and performances in it—symbolic communications and rituals—are critical to its survival.

Applications

Dramaturgical analysis provides a framework of theatrical metaphors for looking at social relationships and in doing so focuses on the underlying, shared, and often unspoken assumptions that function in social life. The best-known and perhaps most influential practitioner of dramaturgy is Erving Goffman. His book *The Presentation of Self in Everyday Life* (1959) examines the ways in which individuals manage their roles and the various selves they present in them. With close observations of social interactions in everyday life, such as informal street encounters, and in a variety of social settings, such as restaurants, Goffman adopts the terminology of the theater and uses the metaphors of dramatic performance to describe and organize the ways in which people operate in society. In *Asylums: Essays on the Social Situation of Mental Patients and Other Inmates* (1961), Goffman was most interested in the "backstage" behaviors of patients, nurses, and doctors. His analyses illustrate many similarities between daily behaviors and the performances of actors on a stage, such as playing as a member of a team, "breaking role," and audience complicity.

Dramaturgical analysis argues that life is lived episodically and situationally, and examines the instruments and acts of communication that people use to construct and interpret social experience. Situations are reduced to their component elements, and then the symbolic nature of the communications is examined. For example, in *Frame Analysis: An Essay on the Organization of Experience* (1974), Goffman studied the impact of the situation on interpersonal behaviors. He used the concept of "frame analysis" to isolate and concentrate on the elements of any situation which affect its meaning. Situations may be changed by "keying" one's actions to situations that have different "frames"—different definitions of image, theme, script, or plot. Goffman identified several major "frames," including deception, fantasy, ritual, analysis, and rehearsal.

Goffman's work, and dramaturgical analysis in general, shows how people live in the world today. Successful use of this method depends on detailed and accurate observation in the field. Although it is basically a behavioristic approach, dramaturgy actually simply begins with behavior and then goes much further. Observation and description lead to interest in not only what people do but also how they live, what variables and variations affect behavior, and what similarities in behavior might be discovered in dissimilar situations. Dramaturgy's particular strength as a sociological method is its relationship to the observer's own experiences as a member of the social scene, as opposed to the researcher's application of some abstract, theoretical approach to his or her data.

Examining interrelated rings of experience in society, starting with the self, moving outward to others, and then to institutions and organizations, allows the dramaturgical sociologist to illuminate issues and questions that seem so familiar as to be taken for granted. For example, looking at the different ways in which people perform the same roles can indicate the parameters of behaviors which are legitimated by society and what level of self-disclosure people find comfortable. Similarly, observing face-to-face interactions reveals the ways in which deviance and labeling function in both individual and group experiences, and might lead to significant insights about the processes of social control. Finally, investigation of how individuals interact to create and re-create social institutions could lead to an improved understanding of their origins and effects on people's lives.

Context

Dramaturgy, as a sociological concept, is historically rooted in the development of the American philosophy of pragmatism in the 1920's and 1930's. John Dewey and George Herbert Mead, preeminent proponents of this movement, were committed to strengthening the connections between the life of thought and the practicalities of daily life. For these philosophers, action was the only way to prove the correctness of an idea. The philosophical system they constructed had connections to the social sphere. Both men believed that meaning was socially constructed and that even individual self-consciousness depended on group communication and understanding. For Mead, role-playing was not simply a means of socialization, it was a central interactive channel for the emergence of individuality and identity, essential to the development of both the individual and social selves. Mead's uses of the concept of role, and the vocabulary of analysis which is its logical extension, are at once dramatic and metaphoric. Beginning his analysis at the level of personality, Mead stressed the symbolic and human-centered nature of roles. The relationship between role and personality, however, adds a level of complexity to any use of dramaturgical analysis, because of the various approaches one may take to understanding their relationship.

A number of sociologists have built on Mead's understanding of personality as a synthesis of personal elements and social roles. For example, C. Wright Mills's important work in his and Hans Gerth's *Character and Social Structure* (1953) focused on the issue of multiple social roles and their relationship to the social structure.

Thomas Luckmann and Peter Berger went a step further in their use of role-playing as an analytical tool, fusing George Herbert Mead's role theory with the institutional theories of Émile Durkheim and Max Weber. Berger and Luckmann emphasize the dramaturgical nature of these connections. As indicated by their arguments in *The Social Construction of Reality* (1967), Berger and Luckmann understood social roles and institutions to be inextricably connected in two major ways. First, the performance of a specific role represents one's particular place in an institution. Second, the role performed may describe or symbolize an entire network of institutional behaviors.

The social scientist Erving Goffman is most often associated with the development and application of dramaturgical analysis as part of social interaction theory. In his first book, *The Presentation of Self in Everyday Life*, Goffman focused on situational conditions that seemed to affect interaction, such as settings, the performers, the audience, and explicit and implicit rules of performance. In particular, he was interested in the ways in which interactions were maintained or, if disrupted, restarted. Goffman's work has consistently been concerned with episodic and repeated interactions rather than with interactions as evolving, sustained dramas.

Dramaturgy is, in fact, a subarea and may be a descriptive tool for sociologists interested in social interactions. Both theoretically and methodologically, dramaturgical analysis is concerned with the process of interaction, and the linguistic and symbolic components of self-construction and definition. As a theory of social and personal roles, dramaturgy emphasizes overt role-playing and the observable relationship between expectation and performance. Dramaturgy is also related to other social-psychological areas of research, such as ethnomethodology. Ethnomethodology goes beyond dramaturgy in its minute analysis of the ways in which people construct everyday reality. A principal finding has been that although people behave as though reality is unambiguous, solid, and reliable, the social world is actually subjective, changeable, and contradictory. The potentially revolutionary implications of this viewpoint are that social structures exist only because people believe they exist and that individuals or groups with enough assurance or power can challenge these assumptions.

Dramaturgy's future may depend on its ability to extend these insights into testable observations. Expansion of the dramaturgical perspective into new spheres of investigation, such as anthropology and political science, also holds promise. Although description is an essential part of the sociological enterprise, observation is not enough to generate the scientific theories and empirical explanations that are central to the social sciences. Dramaturgy's ability to develop and organize complete and sympathetic portrayals of social experience, however, permits this perspective to contribute essential understandings about the complexities of everyday life.

Bibliography

Berger, Peter L., and Thomas Luckmann. *The Social Construction of Reality*. New York: Doubleday, 1967. A basic, important investigation of the social context of human experience and understanding.

Brissett, Dennis, and Charles Edgley, eds. *Life as Theater: A Dramaturgical Sourcebook*. Chicago: Aldine, 1975. A well-conceived and well-executed compilation of essays that illuminate dramaturgical methods and interests.

Burke, Kenneth. *Dramatism and Development*. Barre, Mass.: Clark University Press, 1972. An especially useful introduction discusses the "dramatistic pentad" (act, scene, agent, agency, and purpose) in terms of motives and actions.

Goffman, Erving. *Asylums: Essays on the Social Situation of Mental Patients and Other Inmates*. Garden City, N.Y.: Anchor Books, 1961. Front- and backstage, labeling and deviance, and role performance are investigated in this examination of the drama and rituals of institutional life.

_____ . *The Presentation of Self in Everyday Life*. 1959. Reprint. Woodstock,

N.Y.: Overlook Press, 1973. The basic definition and applications of dramaturgical analysis are provided by the preeminent practitioner of the method.

Hare, A. Paul. *Social Interaction as Drama*. Newbury Park, Calif.: Sage Publications, 1985. The first half of this excellent small volume includes insights from playwrights and actors as part of its discussion of the dramaturgical perspective. The second half of the book uses these insights to analyze conflict and conflict resolutions.

Mead, George H. *Mind, Self, and Society from the Standpoint of a Social Behaviorist*. Chicago: University of Chicago Press, 1934. A basic statement of Mead's central ideas and arguments about roles, planning, and action.

Mills, C. Wright, and Hans Gerth. *Character and Social Structure*. New York: Harcourt, Brace, 1953. In this volume, Mills developed the concept of social structure to refer to the integration of psychic and social roles.

Perinbanayagam, R. S. *Signifying Acts: Structure and Meaning in Everyday Life*. South Carbondale: Southern Illinois University Press, 1985. This elegant study of symbolic interactionism as an outgrowth of the work of George Herbert Mead's work includes an excellent chapter on "Dramatic Acts."

Shechner, Richard, and Mady Shuman, eds. *Ritual, Play, and Performance: Readings in the Social Sciences/Theater*. New York: Seabury Press, 1976. An important and informative selection of readings focusing on philosophical, aesthetic, and methodological areas of convergence of aesthetics, sociology, and dramatism.

Jackie R. Donath

Cross-References

Cultural Norms and Sanctions, 411; Exchange in Social Interaction, 715; Interactionism, 1009; Microsociology, 1192; Organizations: Formal and Informal, 1316; Role Conflict and Role Strain, 1655; Significant and Generalized Others, 1748; Statuses and Roles, 1978; Symbolic Interaction, 2036.

DRUG USE AND ADDICTION

Type of sociology: Deviance and social control
Fields of study: Controlling deviance; Forms of deviance

Sociology is interested in both the causes and the effects of drug use and addiction. Many variables, both psychological and sociological, affect the use of drugs, so it is a complex problem. The current enforcement approach has, according to many experts, proved to be ineffective; alternative approaches such as legalization or emphasizing treatment and education programs have been proposed, but they also have problems of their own.

Principal terms
ABUSE: the use of a drug to the extent that the user becomes impaired in personal, social, and occupational functioning
ADDICTION: a condition that includes an overwhelming involvement with the use of a drug, compulsive drug-seeking behavior, and a high likelihood of relapse after discontinuation of the drug
DRUG: a psychoactive substance or chemical that alters a person's mood or behavior after being smoked, injected, drunk, inhaled, or swallowed in pill form
TOLERANCE: the requirement of increased amounts of a drug to produce the desired effect
WITHDRAWAL: the severe psychological and physiological discomfort or illness that occurs after the discontinuation of using certain drugs (notably heroin and cocaine)

Overview

Although not often acknowledged, the use of various types of drugs is a part of American culture. Some are illegal, but others, such as prescription tranquilizers, alcohol, and the nicotine contained in cigarettes, are legal. Although most people are able to regulate their use of drugs adequately, a significant number become abusive of, dependent upon, or addicted to drugs. This unavoidable fact has caused major problems for society. The use of drugs is a complex matter that is influenced by a number of variables. Dan Hurley and Howard Reback have summarized several of the more important ones.

One is that drug use is related to a cultural "zeitgeist," or mood of the times. Hurley and Reback note, for example, that lysergic acid diethylamide (LSD) was popular in the 1960's, marijuana in the mid-to-late 1960's, heroin from 1969 to 1971, cocaine in the late 1970's and 1980's, and synthetic methamphetamine in the 1990's. Drug use is also related to ethnicity. White and American Indian drug users generally use alcohol (and most drugs) more frequently and at an earlier age than do African American, Hispanic, or Asian American users; they have the highest rates of heavy alcohol use and the lowest abstention rates. Asians and blacks have the lowest use and highest abstinence rates for alcohol.

Gender is also a factor. Women use drugs at significantly lower rates than men across all ethnic groups, although white women show considerably higher rates of use and problem use than do minority women. Another influence is age. Younger persons across all ethnic groups use drugs at a higher rate than older people. Use rates generally vary inversely with age.

The degree of acculturation of a minority group has an effect on the rate of drug use by members of the group. The more assimilated Hispanics and Asian Americans are into the white culture, for example, the more frequently they use drugs. Another sociocultural influence is stress and related coping behaviors. Indicators of stress within society (such as unemployment, divorce, poverty, inadequate housing, and discrimination) are positively correlated with indices of alcohol use (consumption rates and cirrhosis death rates), with high rates associated with minority membership. Stress is more frequent and severe for minority groups, and drug use may be a way of coping and finding relief. Drug use also varies significantly from city to city and across different geographic regions.

A strong predictor of drug use among both youths and adults of minority groups is peer use. In situations where parents provide models for drug use or are the source for drugs, youths are more likely to use drugs. Parental permissiveness and parent-child conflicts correlate positively with use by youths across ethnic groups. Social class is another factor in drug use patterns. Drug use generally seems to start among a small upper-class elite; it then filters successively down to the middle class and lower classes. The upper classes are also the first to stop using a drug and go on to something else. One notable example of this has been patterns of cocaine use.

Drug use also varies according to individual characteristics. Drug use by youths across minority groups is associated with rejection of conventional values, negative attitudes about work, permissiveness for deviation, low school achievement, and poor compatibility with friends and family. Additionally, as Richard C. Stephens points out, the results that individuals desire from drugs determine which drugs will be popular. Different drugs produce different states of intoxication. Heroin highs, for example, are sexually orgasmic, whereas barbiturates produce a euphoric feeling similar to being drunk on alcohol. Hallucinogens, as the name implies, induce altered states that can include disorientation and hallucinations.

Drug use and misuse are common behaviors that pose significant dangers and costs to society. Alcohol (between 1974 and 1988, 50% to 96% of the American population used alcohol, depending on age group), nicotine (40 to 85 percent), marijuana (10 to 68 percent), and cocaine (3 to 28 percent) are the most commonly used drugs.

By far and away alcohol causes the great majority of drug-related problems and costs to society. About 10 percent of the adults in the United States (about fifteen million people) are alcoholics; they abuse or are dependent on alcohol. The estimated yearly cost has ranged from 86 to 136 billion dollars. It is estimated that three out of every one hundred deaths is attributable to alcohol-related causes. Alcohol is responsible for more than half of all fatal automobile accidents and increases the risk of other accidents (such as drowning, falling, and starting fires). About two-thirds of husbands who abuse their wives do so under the influence of alcohol. The positive correlation between the use of alcohol (as well as other drugs) and criminal acts is well established. In the early 1980's, more than three million people were arrested annually for drunkenness, drunk driving, and liquor law violations. Tobacco use, strongly motivated by addiction to the drug nicotine, poses another significant problem; the surgeon general has estimated that five million of today's children will die in later years of smoking-related illnesses at current rates of use.

Although cocaine and marijuana are used much less frequently than alcohol, they also cause significant problems. Street-level activity involving drugs has become increasingly violent as homicide rates have risen and neighborhoods have been terrorized. The cost to government of enforcing laws against illegal drugs diverts funds from other uses. The huge profits to be obtained from trafficking in illegal drugs has attracted organized crime, with its concomitant pollution of the legal economy and society through investment in legitimate business, corruption of politicians and law enforcement officials, and encouragement of disrespect for the law. The number of drug arrests has seriously overburdened the entire criminal justice system (the police, courts, and prisons).

Drugs are also a major health problem. Infants of heroin- or crack-addicted mothers are predisposed to developmental and intellectual disorders. Although cigarette smoking has fallen sharply, thousands of people each year still die from heart and respiratory illnesses and cancer. Deaths also occur from drug overdoses. The spreading of disease, notably hepatitis and acquired immune deficiency syndrome (AIDS), through the sharing of needles is another drug-related problem. Drug users and their partners constitute a fast-growing population of AIDS cases and are considered to be the main connection between AIDS and the population at large. In New York it is estimated that 60 percent of the estimated 200,000 intravenous (IV) drug users carry the virus that causes AIDS. Of the 9,288 reported AIDS patients infected through heterosexual contact in 1992, 42 percent were infected by IV drug users.

Applications

It is clear that drugs impose a significant cost and burden on American society. As researchers Michael R. Gottfredsen and Travis Hirschi have pointed out, the conditions for drug use are readily identifiable. There must be a drug that is both available and desirable, and there must be someone who uses that drug without sufficient restraint. Efforts at regulation can thus be addressed toward the drug itself and/or the user. The attractiveness of a drug can be reduced by increasing its cost, by reducing its quality, by increasing awareness of its negative effect on health, or by interfering with or regulating its production, sale, or distribution. Drug use can also be reduced by reducing the number of users; however, each of these strategies has problems.

A vigorous government and public campaign against cigarette smoking has significantly reduced cigarette sales in the United States. From about 650 billion cigarettes in the mid-1980's (37 percent of the population smoked), sales declined steeply to slightly under 500 billion by 1993 (less than 30 percent of the population smoked). With profit margins of 27 percent, however, five hundred billion cigarettes still generated huge profits for tobacco companies. Further, the antismoking campaign may have bottomed out in its effectiveness to reduce smoking further. A 5 percent increase in smoking occurred in 1993, and print advertisements for noncigarette products were again showing people smoking.

Furthermore, cigarette companies have reacted to the decline in sales by vigorously directing efforts to create other markets, in particular young adults, minorities, and citizens of foreign countries. Federal government reports revealed a 13 percent increase in smoking by African Americans and an increase among children as well; about one billion packs of cigarettes are sold to minors each year, and about three thousand teenagers start smoking each day. Overseas cigarette sales increased sharply from about fifty billion in 1985 to 200 billion in 1993.

The other major legal drug, alcohol, is more of a problem, and efforts to reduce consumption (through warnings on packaging labels, educational campaigns, restricted advertising, taxes, and stiffer legal penalties) have at best been only marginally successful. The total percentage of youths age twelve to seventeen who have ever used alcohol declined from 52 percent in 1974 to 42 percent in 1988, but that number increased or held steady in all other age groups (69 to 81 percent for young adults age eighteen to twenty-five; 65 to 81 percent for older adults age twenty-six to thirty-four; and 76 to 79 percent for adults age thirty-five and older).

Attempts to control illegal drugs are even more problematic. The strategy chosen by the administrations of Ronald Reagan and George Bush was to increase criminal penalties for the sale and use of drugs and to attempt to eradicate drugs (and the people associated with them) by means of a "war on drugs." About 70 percent of appropriated funds were to be used for enforcement and 30 percent for treatment programs. The Clinton Administration proposed that a larger portion of funds be spent on treatment, but the emphasis was still on enforcement.

Christina Jacqueline Johns argues that this policy of emphasizing enforcement over treatment, decriminalization, and education has produced or increased a number of social costs. Among these are corruption, reallocation of police resources, increased illegal profits, overloading of the criminal justice system, increases in violent crime and escalation of firepower from turf battles by drug sellers, increased state control and powers, and abridgment of constitutional protections. In addition, this type of policy labels as criminals a group of people who otherwise follow society's laws and whose only lawbreaking activity could be considered victimless or complaintless.

Worse, Johns argues, the enforcement-criminalization policy has failed. Increased efforts at enforcement in one neighborhood move drug activity to other neighborhoods. The arrest of dealers only results in others taking their place. Where stepped-up enforcement has reduced the supply of a drug (as, for example, was the case with marijuana in New York City in 1989), its price may increase such that other drugs (crack and other forms of cocaine) become relatively cheaper. Interdiction of drugs from foreign countries is extremely expensive. To the extent that it is successful, it may serve only to stimulate domestic production of a drug to make up for the shortfall, thereby driving out the less efficient importers and allowing increased control and higher profits for those remaining.

Alternative strategies include legalization or decriminalization, increased funding for treatment programs, and increased education about the negative effects of drug use. Advocates of legalization argue that legalizing drug use would decriminalize a victimless crime, remove organized crime from its involvement with illegal drugs, and help unclog the criminal justice system. In conjunction with legalization, drug users could be licensed, much as automobile drivers are licensed, thus allowing monitoring and regulation of drug use. Principal objections to legalization are that social damage follows drug misuse and that legalization would make this even more of a problem. Also, the government would be sanctioning behavior that many people view as immoral and wrong. As Supreme Court Justice Lewis D. Brandeis observed, the government teaches by its example. Individual therapy, detoxification programs, and therapeutic community approaches have been effective with some people; however, they are very expensive, most of the participants do not stay the course, and of those who do complete the programs, relapse is a significant problem.

Additionally, neither treatment programs nor legalization addresses the cause of drug use or adequately stresses prevention. Many experts argue that programs of education and persuasion directed at relevant target groups may offer the best hope. The antidrug organization Partnership for a Drug-Free America has claimed that millions of children, especially in inner cities, can and have been taught to stay away from drugs. E. R. Oetting has promoted a psychological-social-cultural model for programs designed to prevent deviant behaviors such as drug use. Oetting identifies several key factors. First, youth should be the major focus. Second, the primary socialization forces in a youth's life (family, school, peer clusters), if healthy and strong, can minimize deviant behavior. Third, prevention programs need to reduce risk factors and increase resilience in order to promote strong bonds between the youth and the primary socialization forces in order to communicate nondeviant behavior.

Context

David F. Musto points out that the United States has an extensive history in the use and abuse of drugs that dates far back into the nineteenth century. Yet when Americans believe that they are caught in the middle of a drug crisis or epidemic, history and the valuable lessons it provides tend to be forgotten or ignored. People believe that what is happening at the moment is a unique problem requiring unique solutions. For example, when cocaine reappeared in the 1970's, it was largely forgotten that the United States had already had a similar previous experience. When first introduced in the 1880's, cocaine was lauded and welcomed as an ideal tonic. After about ten years, however, questions about its effects arose. By 1900 it was considered to be the most dangerous of all drugs, and the lessons learned from the effects of its prolonged use led to cocaine's decline in popularity by the 1920's. Enforcement and interdiction policies proved to be ultimately minor and unimportant factors in cocaine's disappearance. What mattered most was shock and disillusionment brought about by the effects of the drug on people and their families. Advocates of the legalization of drugs need to remember that, prior to the Harrison Act of 1914, little or no legal control of drugs existed and that this unregulated drug use did not result in a happy equilibrium from an "open" drug economy. Rather, it led to a demand by certain sectors of the public for regulation.

Drug use has in fact been gradually declining since the late 1970's amid a wave of public concern and growing intolerance similar to that at the beginning of the twentieth century. Musto worries that the intensity of intolerance could cause problems as the goal increasingly becomes eradication of drugs, drug use, drug users, and drug suppliers. For example, America's original fear of cocaine was transferred to a fear of Southern blacks and was combined with whites' fears about violence during a period of racial tension. Christina Jacqueline Johns has also warned of the dangers posed by the enforcement tactics of a "war on drugs" that focuses on minority populations. She observes that drug panics have been historically used in the United States (notably against African Americans, Jews, Italians, and Chinese) as part of a broader war against minority populations in order to marginalize and oppress them further.

Another issue of concern to social scientists is the disease or medical model of drug use and addiction—that is, the view that drug use and addiction are physical, perhaps genetically linked, mental illnesses or diseases. In this view, drug users are sick or emotionally ill people who need to be treated. Both Howard Reback and Richard C. Stephens argue that such a view removes drug use and addiction from a consideration of environmental influences, when, in fact, drug use and addiction cannot be understood or dealt with independent of the influences of culture and society. For example, Stephens views heroin use socioculturally as a measure of involvement—a badge of membership in a close-knit society of street addicts. Heroin users, he argues, do not take heroin exclusively for the momentary high that it produces.

Bibliography

Johns, Christina Jacqueline. *Power, Ideology, and the War on Drugs: Nothing Succeeds Like Failure.* New York: Praeger, 1992. Johns is highly critical of the government's enforcement policies and its "war on drugs" as viable strategies for effectively dealing with drug problems. She makes a persuasive case in this well-written and very readable book backed up by supporting evidence. Johns favors legalization of drugs but presents an incomplete argument for it.

Musto, David F. *The American Disease: Origins of Narcotic Control.* Expanded ed. New York: Oxford University Press, 1987. This very readable and highly informative book discusses the history of drug use in the United States and efforts to regulate and control it. (The books by Johns and Kleinman discuss history cursorily; to understand current drug policy fully, one needs to understand its history.)

Ray, Oakley, and Charles Ksir. *Drugs, Society, and Human Behavior.* 6th ed. St. Louis: Mosby Year Book, 1993. This is a classic and standard textbook written by two authorities. The book's nineteen chapters deal with definitions of drug use, drug use as a social problem, history, physiological effects, the major drugs that are used and abused, and efforts at education, prevention, and treatment.

Stephens, Richard C. *The Street Addict Role: A Theory of Heroin Addiction.* Albany: State University of New York Press, 1991. Stephens presents a study focusing on contemporary American use of heroin, the hardest of the "hard" drugs. Stephens presents a compelling study of the daily life of the street addict. Treatment programs for heroin addicts are also discussed.

Trimble, Joseph E., Catherine S. Bolek, and Steve J. Niemcryk, eds. *Ethnic and Multicultural Drug Abuse: Perspectives on Current Research.* New York: Harrington Park Press, 1992. Presents a detailed discussion of sociocultural variables that affect drug use. The book focuses on ethnic minority groups, in particular African Americans, Asian Americans, American Indians, and Hispanics. The provision of effective treatment for these groups and federal involvement in research are also discussed.

Laurence Miller

Cross-References

Acquired Immune Deficiency Syndrome, 8; Decriminalization, 456; Deviance: Analysis and Overview, 525; Deviance: Biological and Psychological Explanations, 532; The Medical Profession and the Medicalization of Society, 1159; The Medicalization of Deviance, 1178; Victimless Crime, 2150.

EDUCATION: CONFLICT THEORY VIEWS

Type of sociology: Major social institutions
Field of study: Education

Conflict theory, or radical, approaches to the sociology of education analyze the role that education plays in producing and reproducing society's political, economic, and cultural inequities. Conflict theorists argue that education is characterized by a "hidden curriculum" whose purpose is to reproduce the norms, values, and beliefs of society's dominant class.

Principal terms

CLASS: the self-identification of a group of people who share political, economic, and cultural experiences as being different from and opposed to other groups

CULTURAL CAPITAL: linguistic and cultural sophistication inherited by individuals that is dependent on their particular class

CULTURE: the values, norms, and material goods created by members of a particular group

IDEOLOGY: an array of ideas actively expressing the way groups, both dominant and subordinate, view the appropriate functioning of society's political, economic, and cultural institutions and activities

INSTITUTIONS: relatively stable arrangements designed to promote efficiency in meeting societal goals

REPRODUCTION: the theoretical proposition that institutions within the capitalist social system reproduce class, gender, and racial inequities to benefit those in positions of power

SUBJECTIVITIES: conscious and unconscious dimensions of experience that inform student behavior

Overview

Two major sociological viewpoints have served as a basis for extensive studies of the institution of education. The functionalist approach looks at the ways education prepares individuals for participation in society so that society can continue to function effectively. Sociologists who study education from the conflict perspective, on the other hand, emphasize the idea that different groups or classes are in competition (conflict) with one another for society's resources and that education is a part of that process. Conflict theorists are also known as radical sociologists, essentially because their views represent a radical departure from the functionalist perspective that was dominant when conflict theory first became a significant sociological movement. Radical educational sociologists stress the role of schools in the reproduction of cultural capital, work skills, and the ideology of society's elite. Sociologist Henry Giroux has identified three predominant theoretical models used by radical sociologists to critique liberal and conservative theories: the economic-reproductive model, the cultural-reproductive model, and the hegemonic-state reproductive model. Theorists applying these models to the study of education ask how schools function in society and how schools influence the ideologies, subjectivities, and needs of students. They also examine the role of education in reproducing capitalist social relations and the role of the state in encouraging or discouraging reproduction within schools.

Initially, the most influential conflict analysis of education was advanced via the economic-reproductive model. Drawing on the theoretical influence of Karl Marx, theorists such as Samuel Bowles and Herbert Gintis proposed a correspondence between the values, norms, and skills taught in the classroom and the reproduction of attitudes toward work. This theoretical proposition has been referred to as the hidden curriculum. This concept suggests that students learn to identify their roles within the social system, especially their roles in the workplace, through daily interaction with the temporal, spatial, and ideological characteristics of the schools. More specifically, Bowles and Gintis hypothesized that those social relations characteristic of working class schools, with their emphasis on order, capitulation to the authority of the teacher, strict adherence to time, limited epistemological freedom, and architectural separation (separate rooms, offices, and recreational areas) are necessary for the continued reproduction of working class students into working class jobs. Thus, contrary to the liberal and conservative models of education, which stress individual growth and social mobility, the economic-reproductive model hypothesizes that students, depending on their class, race, and gender, are imbued with different skills, attitudes, and values primarily based on their experiences with the hidden curriculum. The product of these experiences is often leveled aspirations and the reproduction of social inequity rather than personal growth and social mobility.

The cultural-reproductive model attempts to identify the role and function of education and its association with culture, class, and domination. Most often associated with the work of sociologist Pierre Bourdieu and his colleague Jean-Claude Passeron, the cultural-reproductive model avoids attributing to education a purely functional role. That is, while Bourdieu and Passeron recognize the significance of education as an important institution in the reproduction of class, race, and gender inequality, they do not, as Bowles and Gintis did, suggest that schools are overtly determined by class relations. Their model of reproduction centers on the relatively autonomous way in which the school acts as a transmitter of dominant culture. The centerpiece of the cultural-reproduction model is the struggle over meaning within the realm of culture. Culture becomes, as Giroux says, "the mediating link between ruling-class interests and everyday life." Perhaps the most illuminating insight offered by the cultural-reproductive model concerns not how but what students learn or do not learn. Ruling class domination is reproduced by the school through the subtle transmission of ruling class culture.

To accomplish reproduction in this manner, the school is said to participate in the proliferation of cultural capital. By this term Bourdieu means linguistic styles and cultural competencies (such as style, taste, and wit) inherited by individuals as members of a specific class. Schools, it is argued, reproduce dominant cultural capital by legitimating certain forms of knowledge and styles of speech, art, and music—those characteristic of the class-based experiences of only some (dominant-class) students. The result is a simultaneous confirmation of the culture of the dominant class and disconfirmation of the cultures of other social classes. The act of neglecting or underrepresenting the culture and values of the working class and the poor marginalizes their social significance. Conversely, overrepresenting the interests of the dominant class through the dissemination of its cultural capital gives the appearance of inevitability and neutrality. That is, as the interest and values of the dominant class begin to define the dominant culture, they become culture.

Finally, Bourdieu suggests that students of different class origins are differentially socialized in ways that affect cognitive, physical, and emotional development. He attempts to identify the ways in which students participate in the reproduction of their own class position by internalizing cultural prescriptions for physical and emotional behavior (such as proper posture, manners, and voice tone).

The last of the three most prominent radical sociological analyses of education has been put forward by theorists who view the state (the nation-state) as an actor that is in part responsible for the continued reproduction of the social relations of production. That is, the state is, above all else, interested in the preservation of the capitalist mode of production. It is helpful, then, to identify the way the state exercises economic, ideological, and repressive control over schools to accomplish these ends. Through the use of state-established certification, the school curriculum has been weighted in favor of the natural sciences and has deemphasized "nonscientific" knowledge such as the arts or disciplines within the social sciences and humanities. Moreover, in keeping with the state's interest in preserving order, schools serve the function of keeping children and young adults off the streets. Finally, the state plays a crucial role in legitimating the separation of knowledge from power. By training and giving credentials to "academics," the state legitimates forms of knowledge (cultural capital) that prohibit the working classes from participating in decision making. In this scenario the state is participating in what sociologist Nicos Poulantzas has termed a mental-manual division.

Applications

Theoretical insights offered by conflict theory views of education have been applied to many prominent areas of sociological concern. They include, among others, the use of technical control, as embodied in teaching systems, and the perpetuation of racism.

One of the most creative and interesting applications of the reproductive theme in radical sociological analyses of education concerns the "de-skilling" of both teachers and students. Some conflict theory analysts contend that the correspondence between the interests of industry, the state, and schools (in the reproduction of capitalist social relations) has the effect of de-skilling the teaching profession. To be more specific, there are, as sociologist Michael Apple notes, industry-driven programs initiated in the school system to facilitate increased awareness of industry needs and interests.

Sponsoring organizations, identified in name by their self-evident concerns, have such names as "Chairs of Free Enterprise," the "Ryerson Plan," and "The Institute for Constructive Capitalism."

The primary focus in the radical sociological literature is on how material is taught—the organization and presentation of curricular material. The most prominent way in which the message of industry is transmitted to teachers and students is through prepackaged course materials often referred to as "systems." Systems were originally marketed during the Cold War era of the 1950's and 1960's as a way to make teaching "teacher-proof." Today, systems continue to be marketed in mathematics, reading, social studies, and science. Systems include sets of standardized material stating the objectives of each lesson, all material needed for teaching the lesson, specified teacher actions, tests, and descriptions of appropriate student responses.

Some sociologists argue that such teaching systems represent a form of technical control. That is, through the use of packaged material, all planning, coordinating, and assessing of student learning is under the control of a person or group of people beyond the classroom. The ramifications for teachers are that, over time, skills once needed to perform the "thought work" of teaching and to foster interaction between students and teachers may atrophy. Students, expecting to pass from the first level of a system to the second, are under the control of a distant, centralized force. If students do not adhere to the appropriate responses as mandated in the packaged system's material, they are judged (graded) critically. Finally, teachers may be more isolated from one another. Since they have decreasing input in their own work, the argument goes, there is less need to interact. It may also be, as it is in other occupations in which de-skilling has been observed, that teachers using systems take less interest in their work.

How systems work ideologically to fashion individuals who will function "appropriately" within a capitalist society is a complex yet significant concern. The educational criterion that determines the "good" pupil is his or her ability to accumulate certain technical skills (cultural capital). These skills are said to be technical in that they are measured using tests and are acquired in logical progression. That is, mastery over one set of ideas leads to the discovery of the next, and so on. What is important about this process is that it is individualized: Facts are "consumed" by students in a manner similar to the consumption of goods sold on the market. Since systems allow no room for responses other than those specified, possibilities for discussion of alternative outcomes are rare. Students educated in this manner become adults with a "rules orientation"—that is, they internalize the rules and goals of the organization as their own. This leads to a homogenization of the labor force. Conflict is minimized, since employees have adopted the rationality of the firm and the firm's directives.

One compelling insight stemming from the work of educational sociologists has been articulation of the significance of language in the reproduction of dominant culture within the schools. Educators, acting as agents of dominant cultural capital, promote the cultural superiority of standard English. Language or dialect that strays from the dominant form is marginalized and devalued. Many African Americans and people of Afro-Caribbean descent, for example, speak different forms of English than standard English; these forms have been given a variety of names, among them patois, Creole, and Black English.

Traditionally viewed by educators as debased forms of standard English and as lacking in the formal properties which encourage organized thought and expression, these variants are generally considered inferior to standard English. The ramifications for students speaking them are potentially devastating. Numerous studies have identified teacher biases in their evaluations of students speaking patois or Black English. In general they are viewed as lazy, illiterate, unintelligent, and educationally subnormal. In many cases these students are offered programs for the "verbally deprived," "culturally disadvantaged," or "culturally deprived." There is no evidence, however, to support the dominant cultural belief that Black English is inferior to "proper" English. Research on this topic has demonstrated that Black English is a complex linguistic system with its own internal logic and coherence. When educators fail to recognize the cultural significance of this language form for African American students, they are acting in a racist fashion. The stigmatization too often leads to disfranchisement of students of color.

Context

Debate over the role of education in society has been ongoing since the 1850's. Initial focuses of education included aiding in the assimilation of immigrants into "American" culture and creating sturdy individuals who would be able to locate their places within the growing industrial economy. By specifying appropriate American values and morals and by facilitating the acquisition of skills and behaviors needed in industry, it was believed that schools would preserve a uniquely American sense of community. Early curriculum theorists included Franklin Bobbitt, W. W. Charters, Edward L. Thorndike, Ross L. Finney (a sociologist), Charles C. Peters, and David Snedden. Speaking primarily to the concerns of the middle class, these theorists made the notion of community synonymous with homogeneity and consensus.

Traditional analyses of education, located within what has been called the "achievement tradition," have difficulty formulating connections between education and its political, economic, and ideological context. To respond to these theoretical shortcomings, radical sociologists specializing in education initiated rigorous theoretical investigation. Beginning in the late 1960's and continuing through the 1970's and 1980's, two theoretical schools emerged: the status attainment school and the hidden curriculum school. Following the work of sociologists Eric O. Wright, and Samuel Bowles and Herbert Gintis, status attainment research seeks to determine the balance between achieved and ascribed characteristics in determining future educational and occupational success.

The 1960's and 1970's gave voice to a pivotal theoretical breakthrough with the publication of sociologist Michael F. Young's edited collection *Knowledge and Control: New Directions for the Sociology of Education* (1971). Young, along with sociologists Basil Bernstein and Pierre Bourdieu, argued that the organization of knowledge, its transmission, and its interpretation are crucial determinants to understanding the reproduction of dominant ideology and class position. Since the initial theoretical breakthrough, applications of this approach can be seen in the work of sociologists Jean Anyon, Joel Taxel, Landon Beyer, Michael Apple, Lois Weis, and Linda Valli, among others; such applications are typically classified as studies of the hidden curriculum.

Bibliography

Apple, Michael. *Ideology and Curriculum.* 2d ed. New York: Routledge, 1990. Apple is considered to be among the theoretical forebears of the radical approach to the sociology of education. This book illustrates the intellectual strength and lucidity of quality sociological analysis. Examines the works of Marx, Bourdieu, Freire, Girioux, and others while presenting very abstract material in a clear and concise way.

_____ , ed. *Cultural and Economic Reproduction in Education.* London: Routledge & Kegan Paul, 1982. A collection of articles on topics related to applications of the radical sociological analysis of education. Topics include the arts, patriarchy, the state, and television.

Bourdieu, Pierre, and Jean-Claude Passeron. *Reproduction in Education, Society and Culture.* Translated by Richard Nice. London: Sage Publications, 1977. While challenging for novice readers, this book has been the cornerstone of the "cultural" approach to reproduction.

Bowles, Samuel, and Herbert Gintis. *Schooling in Capitalist America.* New York: Basic Books, 1976. Bowles and Gintis' book stands as a centerpiece in the literature on reproduction. This book serves as one of the first clearly articulated attacks against mainstream education from a Marxist theoretical perspective.

Freire, Paulo. *The Politics of Education.* Translated by Donaldo Macedo. South Hadley, Mass.: Bergin & Garvey, 1985. In this series of essays, Freire discusses his views on power, more precisely the power embedded in the process of education. He places equal emphasis on both what is taught and how it is taught.

Giroux, Henry. "Theories of Reproduction and Resistance in the New Sociology of Education: A Critical Analysis." *Harvard Educational Review* 53 (August, 1983): 257-293. Giroux serves as a valuable source for sifting through the complex and abstract theoretical analyses that characterize much of the radical approach to the sociology of education.

_____ . *Theory and Resistance in Education.* South Hadley, Mass.: Bergin & Garvey, 1983. The strength of Giroux's analysis lies in his insistence on the politicization of education. This book articulates his specific remedies for mainstream education informed by analyses of reproduction.

MacLeod, Jay. *Ain't No Makin' It.* Boulder, Colo.: Westview Press, 1987. MacLeod's book is an ethnography of two groups of young males, one mostly white and one mostly black, each living in the same subsidized housing unit. While not solely an analysis of education, the book discusses the ways in which class position is reproduced.

Walker, Stephen, and Len Barton, eds. *Gender, Class, and Education.* New York: International Publications Service, Falmer Press, 1983. This collection of essays presents a critical analysis of the differential treatment of women within the educational system. The essays are not directed exclusively at students, but also at teachers and administrators.

Robert C. Schehr

Cross-References

Conflict Theory, 340; Education: Functionalist Perspectives, 586; Education: Manifest and Latent Functions, 593; Educational Credentials and Social Mobility, 600; Educational Inequality: The Coleman Report, 607; Equal Educational Opportunity, 661; Higher Education: Community Colleges, 884; School Socialization, 1693; Social Stratification: Analysis and Overview, 1839; Standardized Testing and IQ Testing Controversies, 1966; Tracking and Inequality in Education, 2057.

EDUCATION: FUNCTIONALIST PERSPECTIVES

Type of sociology: Major social institutions
Field of study: Education

Functionalist perspectives on education focus on the school's responsibility in transmitting to youth beliefs, knowledge, skills, and values that are essential to adult participation in society. Functionalist theory helps clarify the role of schooling in enabling societies to maintain themselves culturally, economically, politically, and socially.

Principal terms

HIDDEN CURRICULUM: an educational system's implicit means of aiding youth in internalizing social norms and values

HUMAN CAPITAL THEORY: an assumption regarding interrelationships between schooling and working in which investment in the former results in higher paying or more prestigious jobs in the latter

MERITOCRACY: any society in which ability and effort are deemed more important than inherited privilege and status in the allocation of cultural, economic, political, and social position

REPRODUCTION: a process that is said to occur during schooling in which existing cultural, economic, political, and social norms and structures are perpetuated

SOCIAL STRATIFICATION: a phenomenon in which people are differentially ranked in hierarchic fashion according to their social positions; schooling overtly emphasizes achieved social position based on ability and performance rather than ascribed social position based on natal circumstances

SOCIALIZATION: the process of developing the knowledge, skills, and values essential to future adult role performance

STATUS ATTAINMENT: in education, a research tradition that seeks to clarify why students from different socioeconomic backgrounds differ in school achievement and in the duration of their investment in the schooling process

STRUCTURAL DIFFERENTIATION: the concept that as societies become more complex, systems (for example, schooling, or the educational system) become more distinct and specialized in function

Overview

The institution of education in modern society has been given much attention by sociologists. Two major theoretical frameworks within which social institutions are examined are the functionalist approach and the conflict theory approach. In general terms, functionalism looks at society as a system of interrelated parts, the relatively harmonious operation (functioning) of which is necessary for the society's survival. Conflict theorists, on the other hand, emphasize the idea that different groups or classes are in competition (conflict) for society's resources. Education has been examined extensively from both these viewpoints.

Functionalist perspectives on education focus on understanding how the component subsystems of higher education and school systems effectively transmit the cultural, economic, political, and social values of a society to youth. The purpose of schools, according to Émile Durkheim (1858-1917), a French pioneer in applying a sociological approach to the study of educational systems, "is to arouse and to develop in the child a certain number of physical, intellectual, and moral states which are demanded of him by both the political society as a whole and the special milieu for which he is specifically destined."

Theoretical perspectives on education descended from Durkheim's work have been given a number of names, including functionalist-reproductionism, structural-functionalism, consensus theory, and equilibrium theory. They proceed from the premise that schools, colleges, and universities are interdependent parts of total social systems. The vitality of the total society, much like the health of the total human organism, depends on how effectively these parts—education, the family, and the economy, for example—contribute to the well-being of the entire system. An overarching social aim is to achieve an equilibrium of functioning. This condition implies that there is an interdependence among the system's components that is based on a consensus (a recognition of shared values).

Functionalist perspectives in education particularly emphasize how schools, colleges, and universities contribute to the socialization of individuals within a meritocratic society in which occupational and social roles are determined by ability and effort rather than inheritance. Moreover, functionalists view this meritocratic society as dependent on the production of highly trained people to fill these roles, roles largely shaped by new rational knowledge originating in the research activities of colleges, think tanks (the Rand Corporation, for example), and universities. Schools function to provide basic cognitive and highly specialized skills essential for participation in this expert society. Within functionalist perspectives on schooling, human capital theorists view education as an economic investment in which benefits (increased earnings) outweigh costs (a delayed entry into the workforce). Functionalists assume that the expansion of education's socialization function optimally occurs in a democratic society committed to the realization of human objectives. Schools, colleges, and universities become, in the functionalist paradigm, pivotal agencies for the socialization of youth into what a key contributor to functionalist theory, Talcott Parsons, termed "the commitments and capacities which are essential prerequisites of their future role performance." Among the essential characteristics of an educated citizenry, in the functionalist view, are a sense of social justice and a commitment to use that sense of justice to resolve issues important to the quality of life within the society.

Functionalist research in education has an intricate agenda: Functionalists study the structural parts of educational systems as cultural and social organizations. Sociologists within this theoretical tradition examine how the achievement of certain societal goals occurs through the functioning of educational subsystems—for example, elementary schools. Functionalists, following a Durkheimian tradition, examine schools, colleges, and universities as training grounds for occupational and social roles, places where discipline and morality, the requisites for an ordered society are learned. Functionalist perspectives in education, developed in the 1950's and 1960's by sociologists such as Burton Clark, Robert Dreeben, and Talcott Parsons, highlight the functioning of the educational system, assuming that it is aimed at developing broad-based skills essential for functioning in an increasingly technological world.

Applications

Among the functions attributed to the institution of education are socialization and the allocation of roles that individuals will continue to play when they leave school. Parsons performed pioneering research on structural differentiation processes in educational systems, and his work provoked numerous studies of education's role in a meritocracy. The school's dual role as an agency for occupational and social role allocation, together with its involvement in the reproduction of social norms, is highlighted in the application of functionalist assumptions to research on the "paracurriculum" and status attainment.

Robert Dreeben's *On What Is Learned in School* (1968) revealed how the explicit objectives of the school's formal curriculum contribute to learning the social norms ("specific standards for behavior") of achievement, independence, specificity, and universalism. Other functionalist studies have examined how what is taught outside the formal curriculum, yet in school, results in learning social norms. This informal teaching was termed the "hidden curriculum" by Benson R. Snyder in a 1971 book of the same title. It is frequently called the "lived curriculum"; in Britain it is sometimes called the "paracurriculum" at the suggestion of David Hargreaves, who has argued that "hidden" is a misnomer. This concept of an informal or unofficial curriculum refers to the implicit demands made on students to adapt to what Philip W. Jackson referred to as the three Rs of "rules, regulations, and routines."

Functionalists assume that the curriculum and the paracurriculum exist side by side in delicate balance. Success of the schooling endeavor depends on the forging of consensus, constructed in the assimilation of formal rules, regulations, and routines informally transmitted through the paracurriculum. In this consensus, cooperation and obedience are norms that are as important to the schooling process as achievement and performance are.

Although the concept of the hidden curriculum or paracurriculum is not unique to functionalist perspectives on education, functionalists consider how the informal curricular accent on assertiveness, competitiveness, and punctuality aids academic success and, subsequently, the attainment of high socioeconomic status. Moreover, from the functionalist perspective, students' relative degrees of adoption of this informal curriculum are very important to their future socioeconomic status. A central question is whether (as functionalists aver) what is learned in school affects students' educational and occupational expectations independently of the socioeconomic status of the students' families. Do the school's formal and informal curricula indeed occupy a pivotal point in the transition from home to work? Research in a sociological subfield known as status attainment has provided evidence for the functionalist view of a meritocratic society and has generally answered "yes" to these questions.

Status attainment research has clarified why the duration of students' involvement in formal education and their school achievement differ for students from different socioeconomic backgrounds. The most well-known study in this area is the "Wisconsin Social-Psychological Model of Status Attainment," a longitudinal study of Wisconsin students and their career paths after being graduated from high school. Performed by William H. Sewall and Robert M. Hauser, the study was inaugurated in 1957; the first results were published in 1976 in Sewall and Hauser's *Schooling and Achievement in American Society*; later findings were published in 1982. They concluded that the family's class position does have an effect on status attainment, but only insofar as it affects the type of personal influences that family members have on the student; parent and teacher encouragement during adolescence are also important. Beyond that, however, family background was viewed as inconsequential. The single most important factor in status attainment was the level of the person's schooling.

In that research on educational and status attainment has discovered large differences in educational attainment among individuals from differing social backgrounds, it supports an assumption implicit in functionalist perspectives on education: that ability (as measured by standardized intelligence tests), mitigated by the amount of support for educational achievement a student receives from friends, family, and teachers, is the best predictor of educational attainment and grades. Findings have suggested that teachers base their encouragement on student ability and student grades rather than on student social status. Schools operate, functionalists assert, in an essentially meritocratic fashion. These findings are not universally accepted, however; it should be noted that other studies have suggested a number of ways that students' socioeconomic status affects both their scores on tests and the ways the students are perceived and treated by teachers.

Status attainment research has two notable weaknesses. Because this research depends for its reliability on large samples, and because its conclusions are predicated on those samples, it is difficult to apply status attainment generalizations uniformly to smaller groups—to African American students, for example. The meritocratic model of student attainment does not explain the achievement of black students as satisfactorily as it does that of white students. Black students, scoring lower on standardized tests of ability than white students, have higher educational attainment than white students with similar test scores. What factors other than the influence of friends, parents, and teachers on black student aspirations explain this outcome? School-sanctioned discrimination against black students is not clearly evident as an explanatory factor. In addition, status attainment research only maps the effects of social status on ability and aspirations and, in turn, their effects on achievement and attainment. It does not explain why social status has the effects that it seems to.

Context

Prior to the pioneering work of Émile Durkheim on the functions of education (essentially, he saw it as contributing to the maintenance of the social order), few educational sociologists had researched relationships between school and society at large. They did not study the relationship between schools and social stratification, for example, a topic that has been the focus of contemporary sociologists operating within the functionalist framework. Durkheim's contemporary Max Weber suggested that a school's chief activity was teaching "status cultures" rooted in student power, prestige, and wealth, but few sociologists seriously explored the effects of societal domination by bureaucratic and rational ("modernizing") structures on schools.

Talcott Parsons' work in the 1950's on the school class as an agency of socialization in American society and Robert Dreeben's 1968 study of the school as an institution of socialization with the task of developing "capacities necessary for appropriate conduct in social settings that make different kinds of demands on them" were in the forefront of functionalist perspectives on education. The functionalist view of education has not been without its critics. Critics have found fault with the functionalist accent on the contribution of schooling to the consensually smooth operation of society as well as with the priority given in functionalist perspectives to the maintenance of social equilibrium and order in general.

Critics have made a number of interrelated observations regarding weaknesses in the functionalist perspective as applied to education. Jean Floud and A. H. Halsey noted in 1958 that functionalism accentuates a status quo orientation in industrial societies, which, Floud and Halsey argued, actually experience constant and rapid social change. Colin Greer's *The Great School Legend* (1973) and Joel Springs' *Education and the Rise of the Corporate State* (1972) assume that educational expansion has not resulted in greater equality of opportunity. Progress, they suggest, has collapsed because of (in Jeanne H. Ballantine's words) "the number of divergent interests, ideologies and conflicting interest groups in society." These conflicts and divergences are related to an increasing factionalism over what functions are important in education. This disagreement can be at least partly attributed to the frequent shifts in what David Tyack, Michael W. Kirst, and Elisabeth Hansot term the "issue-attention cycle" in education. This cycle tends to move public attention swiftly from one facet of educational systems to others—from, say, an examination of the core curricula required of everyone to programs for the gifted and talented.

The primary contrasts with functionalist perspectives on the role of education in society are conflict perspectives and interactionist perspectives. With roots in the writings of Karl Marx and Max Weber, conflict theorists argue that schools mirror tensions existing in the larger society between dominant and subordinate groups in their contest for power. Martin Carnoy's *Education as Cultural Imperialism* (1974) and Randall Collins' *Conflict Sociology* (1975) highlight conflict perspectives in education.

Interactionist perspectives in the sociology of education emphasize the need to study individuals as they interact with one another. A "microcosmic" approach, the interactionist perspective focuses on interactions between members of various groups: peer, teacher-principal, and teacher-student interactions, for example. This approach was central to the development in Britain and France in the early 1970's of a "new" sociology of education. Two of its chief proponents were Basil Bernstein and Pierre Bourdieu. Both conflict and interactionist modes for studying relationships between schooling and social stratification were stimulated by critiques of earlier perspectives.

Bibliography

Ballantine, Jeanne H., ed. *Schools and Society: A Reader in Education and Sociology.* Palo Alto, Calif.: Mayfield, 1985. A useful compendium of readings on the theoretical perspectives of functionalism. Helpful chapter introductions to basic writings on functionalist perspectives authored by Burton R. Clark, Randall Collins, Robert Dreeben, Émile Durkheim, Philip W. Jackson, Talcott Parsons, and Max Weber are accompanied by notes on specific questions raised by each primary source included.

_____ . *The Sociology of Education: A Systematic Analysis.* Englewood Cliffs, N.J.: Prentice-Hall, 1983. Ballantine's very readable introduction to the sociology of education contains excellent discussions of functionalist perspectives toward the purposes of schooling and higher education, the "hidden curriculum," and social stratification. Contains helpful chapter summaries and footnotes but no separate bibliography.

Dreeben, Robert. *On What Is Learned in School.* Reading, Mass.: Addison-Wesley, 1968. A classic study of the school as an agency of socialization, *On What Is Learned in School* argues that schooling provides a vital functional linkage between children's kinship relations and adult public life. Accompanied by author and subject indexes, Dreeben's work includes useful end-of-chapter reference sections on functionalism and education.

Hurn, Christopher J. *The Limits and Possibilities of Schooling: An Introduction to the Sociology of Education.* 3d ed. Boston: Allyn & Bacon, 1993. Hurn's clearly written and very readable text contains informative discussions on the functional paradigm of schooling, human capital theory, weaknesses of the functional paradigm, equality of opportunity and schooling expansion issues, meritocratic issues of educational achievement, status attainment research, and tracking or ability grouping in schools. A helpful bibliography completes the volume. Highly recommended.

Pai, Young. *Cultural Foundations of Education.* Columbus, Ohio: Charles E. Merrill, 1990. Contains an excellent and succinct treatment of functionalist/reproductive theory as well as opposing ideological views of the schooling process, conflict and interactionist/interpretivist theories in particular. Pai discusses the "hidden curriculum" or "paracurriculum" appropriately. End-of-chapter references are annotated occasionally; the annotated entries are especially helpful.

Malcolm B. Campbell

Cross-References

Education: Conflict Theory Views, 579; Education: Manifest and Latent Functions, 593; Educational Credentials and Social Mobility, 600; Educational Inequality: The Coleman Report, 607; Equal Educational Opportunity, 661; Functionalism, 786; Higher Education: Colleges and Universities, 877; Higher Education: Community Colleges, 884; School Socialization, 1693; The Sociology of Education, 1939.

EDUCATION: MANIFEST AND LATENT FUNCTIONS

Type of sociology: Major social institutions
Field of study: Education

Education serves four main functions in preparing students for their roles in society. These manifest, or overt, functions are socialization; selection and placement; accumulation of knowledge and transmission of culture; and personal development. Education also serves latent, or covert, functions, which usually occur through informal processes in school.

Principal terms
CONFLICT THEORY: a perspective that sees conflict, stemming from unequal access to social resources, as endemic to society
FUNCTIONALISM: a theory that views institutions as consisting of interdependent systems that work together to provide needed societal functions
HIDDEN CURRICULUM: a term that describes the way students are socialized in school through the rules, routines, and regulations that define behavior
LATENT FUNCTIONS OF EDUCATION: the unstated, frequently unrecognized, functions that influence the preparation of students for their roles in adult society
MANIFEST FUNCTIONS OF EDUCATION: the explicitly stated goals of schools

Overview

The goal of education is to prepare students to become contributing members of society. This goal is attained through four important manifest, or overt, functions. These functions are socialization; selection and placement; accumulation of knowledge and transmission of culture; and personal and social development. They are stated, in more or less explicit terms, in the mission statement of most schools. Education also serves latent, or covert, functions. These functions typically are not explicitly stated and may not even be recognized by school personnel, students, or parents. They generally occur through informal and social processes in school.

The first manifest function of education is socialization. In order for society to function productively and to ensure social control, students must be socialized to play certain roles as adults in society. Among those roles are worker, spouse, parent, citizen, and friend. While the school is only one of the many agents that socialize children, it is a critical one. Its influence stems from the extensive time children spend in school and from the deliberate efforts schools make to prepare children for citizenship.

A number of questions arise with respect to how students should be socialized in school. For what roles should they be prepared? What kind of job training is appropriate? Whose values should students be taught in school? Two major perspectives on these issues are represented by the viewpoints of functionalism and conflict theory. Functionalists assume that society is a set of interdependent systems that work together to create stability and productivity. They believe that schools should prepare students to play socially approved roles in their personal and public lives in the existing social stratification system. Conflict theorists argue that the status quo orientation of functionalist theory ignores the conflicting ideologies, values, and interests of the "haves," who control power, wealth, and influence, and the "have-nots," whose goal is to acquire these privileges. They would have schools explain these conflicts and prepare students to live in a society in which conflict is endemic and change is expected. Educational policy and practice are dependent on how differences between these two perspectives are resolved.

A second manifest function of education is selection and placement. Modern societies are highly stratified according to wealth, influence, and occupational prestige. A function of education is to prepare students to occupy a position in this stratification system. Educational attainment is a major way of improving a person's social class. Schools can select students for specific positions in the labor market and prepare them to occupy those positions. Functionalists believe that the job market is necessarily stratified into jobs that require different levels of talent and skills. Consequently they argue for selecting and preparing students for unequal positions. This is done through stratified educational opportunities in schools. Conflict theorists refuse to accept the idea that inequality must be endemic in society and would have the educational system make greater efforts to lessen inequality by providing equal opportunities for all. The functionalist perspective dominates current educational policy, and much criticism of schools reflects dissatisfaction with the way students are being selected and prepared for their positions in the stratification system.

A third manifest function of education is the communication of information and the transmission of culture. The information that is taught in school is organized into a curriculum. The curriculum comprises both the subjects that are taught and the specific content of each course. Considerable uniformity exists in the elementary curricula of public and private schools. Greater variation is found at the middle and secondary levels. Some countries have a national curriculum that must be taught in all schools, and the United States is moving in that direction. In addition to a formal body of knowledge, schools pass on to students cultural values and norms. These govern both intellectual and social activities. Some dimensions of cultural transmission occur explicitly and formally, while others are part of the hidden curriculum.

The main questions that arise pertaining to the process of transmitting knowledge and culture to students are what information and knowledge students should be taught and who should make that determination. Functionalists claim that students should be given the information, values, and norms that will enable them to perform successfully in society as it currently exists. Conflict theorists state that schools currently perpetuate an unjust capitalist society by preparing students to be exploited by the system. Rather, they claim that schools should serve the needs of disadvantaged members of society and help to create greater social equality. These and other perspectives drive the ongoing debate about the content of the curriculum and the context of schooling.

The fourth manifest function of education is fostering the personal and social development of students. The public school system in the United States is founded on the common school ideal: the belief that schooling should prepare all students, regardless of background, to live as respectable and productive citizens. Schools have traditionally aimed to instill in students such virtues as honesty, respect, diligence, discipline, and charity and to train them to live responsibly in the community. Contemporary schools strive to achieve these same aims. Functionalist theorists view this effort as ensuring social order, while conflict theorists see it as an attempt to control and manipulate students. They raise concerns about authoritarian procedures, the violation of student rights, and unequal opportunities for personal and social growth and development.

The manifest functions of education operate through the curriculum, the stated rules and regulations that govern behavior, and the authority structure of the school. In contrast, the latent functions of education occur through an informal system. One of the predominant ways the informal system affects students is through the "hidden curriculum." This term refers to the set of informal opportunities and constraints that influence teachers and students. It operates through the values, norms, and expectations that characterize a school; through the roles, negotiations, and strategies that characterize interactions; and through the pedagogical practices, rules, and routines that govern instruction.

Applications

The socialization function of education requires that students be prepared for the roles they are to play in society. One issue of considerable concern is how students should be socialized to their gender roles. The role of women in the workplace and in society in general has changed dramatically. Schools are now being asked to provide equal opportunities so that both girls and boys can learn and participate fully in school activities.

While progress toward gender equality has been made, evidence exists that some teachers still treat girls and boys differently. For example, some teachers call on boys more frequently, engage in qualitatively different interactions with them, praise and reward their ideas more frequently, and direct them toward more mathematics and science instruction than girls. This persistent stereotyping of girls is an obstacle to their learning, and it diminishes their self-esteem. It has led to a renewed interest in same-sex schools in order to provide a more supportive environment for female students. One of the greatest challenges to contemporary educators is to rid schools of any practice that supports sexism, racism, or any other behavior that limits students because of their ascribed characteristics (characteristics with which they were born).

Selecting and preparing students for their future positions in society is a particularly difficult task. It demands accurate judgments about students' present and future abilities. A topic of intense debate is the practice of tracking students for instruction. Tracking involves grouping students who have similar academic ability together for instruction. Proponents of tracking argue that the practice facilitates learning by allowing teachers to gear instruction to the level of each student's ability. Critics claim that tracking creates unequal opportunities for students because lower-track students are exposed to a less challenging curriculum, have poor role models, and experience more disruptions in class and lower teacher expectations. Some research shows that assignment to a lower track has a negative influence on a student's educational achievement and attainment. The alternative to tracking is grouping students heterogeneously for instruction. A significant number of schools have made this change; they have had varying degrees of success.

Resolving the tracking issue requires an understanding of how exposure to an academic, general, or vocational curriculum and to courses of varying degrees of complexity affects a student's future job opportunities and career. If a strong positive relationship exists between course selection and future educational attainment, occupational prestige, and income, then some form of tracking would be indicated. If the relationship is weak, the benefits of the practice might not outweigh its negative impact on student motivation and self-confidence. Although a large body of research exists on tracking and its effects, few of these studies are of sufficiently long duration to shed light on the complex issue.

With respect to the transmission of knowledge and culture, a question arises about who determines the content of the curriculum. Functionalists state that a core curriculum exists that reflects society's consensus about what should be taught. Others disagree that a general consensus exists with respect to curriculum content. They argue that those who have power define the curriculum to benefit themselves at the expense of less powerful groups.

In practice, a number of factors affect the content of the curriculum. Educators at the national, state, district, and school levels play a role in determining the body of knowledge taught to students. There is fairly wide agreement about what topics should be covered in most courses. Disagreement arises, however, with respect to the content of less traditional courses and the interpretation of certain material. An example is the controversy over the adoption of the Rainbow Curriculum, which teaches respect for student diversity resulting from differences in background, custom, history, and lifestyle.

Beginning in the 1980's, the issue of multiculturalism has created considerable conflict on college campuses. Proponents of multiculturalism decry the predominance of the work of white male Western scholars in the curriculum. They argue that the literary and artistic contributions of women, nonwhite scholars, and those from other parts of the world are ignored. In an effort to redress this perceived injustice, they have pressured educators to include a far more diverse body of work in course curricula. They also have worked to add new courses to the curriculum that highlight the history, culture, and contributions of other racial and ethnic groups. Critics of this effort argue that adding new material to the curriculum necessarily requires deleting important, high-quality scholarship. The debate that occurs between these two groups is effecting a marked change in the course offerings and content of the curriculum.

Schools also promote the social and personal development of students. Teachers want their students to acquire habits of self-discipline, responsibility, industriousness, and integrity as well as a constellation of personal characteristics that ensure healthy social interactions in a productive environment. One of the mechanisms that schools use to influence student development and behavior is the reward system. This includes a set of incentives to motivate appropriate behavior and a set of punishments for failure to adhere to the rules and regulations of the school.

In most schools, rewards are given to students for outstanding performance in academic work, athletics, and other cocurricular and extracurricular activities. Some view this kind of reward structure as reflecting a functionalist perspective, under which the schools prepare students for their roles in contemporary capitalist society. They argue that awards should be distributed more equitably, providing opportunities for students who do not have outstanding talent to be recognized for effort and more modest accomplishments. The practice of tracking and the emphasis of competition in sports is believed to reflect the functionalist perspective. Efforts to "detrack" schools, to encourage cooperative learning among students, to provide rewards for group effort, and to recognize progress rather than achievement reveal changes in the way rewards are used to influence student behavior.

Similarly, the kinds of behaviors that are punished in school and the nature of the discipline depend on how educators interpret their responsibility to foster students' social and personal development. Schools mete out different kinds of punishments, including corporal punishment, verbal reprimands, additional assignments, denial of privileges, suspension from classes or other activities, and expulsion. Some educators question the utility of one or more of these punishments, suggesting that their primary result may be producing resentment in students and exacerbating negative attitudes and behaviors. Others argue that certain kinds of punishments and disciplinary procedures violate students' rights. Considerable progress has been made in the adoption of legislation that protects students' rights in school.

Finally, the latent functions of education are served by the informal system of the school. The formal structure of a school is an authoritarian one in which adults are the predominant power brokers. In the informal system of the school, however, students acquire power in various ways. A clear example is found in the way students negotiate with teachers for grades. Teachers generally have objective standards for student performance. Nevertheless, students can influence them to grade more favorably by rewarding teachers with compliance or, conversely, by sanctioning teachers through disruptive behavior.

In developing strategies to exercise power in school, students rely heavily on their peer groups. Students develop subcultures that have norms and values either consistent with or oppositional to school goals. A peer group can exert considerable influence on a student's attitudes, values, and behavior and can provide support for activities that challenge school authorities. In attempting to maintain control and discipline, teachers develop coping strategies of their own. Teacher strategies include providing rewards and punishments, adopting interactional styles such as befriending or distancing students, and manipulating students through distraction techniques, such as redirecting their attention and energies to acceptable school activities.

Context

Functionalism and conflict theory provide considerable insight into the way schools function in society. Functionalist explanations of schooling have a longer history than conflict theory; the foundations of functionalism were established by Émile Durkheim, whose writings on education suggested that schools should serve the four functions outlined in the "Overview." Durkheim viewed education as a means to prepare young people to participate fully in society. He argued that education creates social homogeneity by transmitting to students the knowledge, values, and skills requisite for harmonious living in society. A second prominent contributor to the functionalist perspective was Talcott Parsons. He argued that society is in a state of equilibrium and the responsibility of schools and other social institutions is to help maintain that equilibrium.

In reaction to functionalism, conflict theorists, including Karl Marx, Ralf Dahrendorf, and Samuel Bowles and Herbert Gintis, stressed the disequilibrium endemic to a social system built on inequalities. They criticized the functionalist perspective as perpetuating a capitalistic society that is built on class distinctions and the unequal distribution of wealth and resources. Conflict theory has focused attention on inequities associated with school practices and policies and has acted as an agent of school reform. Without necessarily rejecting the four functions of education, conflict theorists continue to raise questions about how the goals of education are attained and whether the processes that link student background and achievement to their career opportunities are just.

Both functionalist and conflict theories provide useful perspectives in examining the goals of education and in explaining the processes and practices that characterize contemporary schools. The insights and explanations these theories offer have led to a better understanding of the manifest functions of education as well as the latent functions, particularly the role of the "hidden curriculum" in the educative process.

Bibliography

Ballantine, Jeanne H. *The Sociology of Education.* Englewood Cliffs, N.J.: Prentice-Hall, 1983. This book examines issues in the sociology of education from an "open systems" approach. It outlines the theoretical perspectives in the field and applies them to relevant applied issues in education.

Dahrendorf, Ralf. *Class and Class Conflict in Industrial Society.* Stanford, Calif.: Stanford University Press, 1956. A classic exposition of conflict theory, this book discusses dominance and subordination in institutions and describes how their members respond to conflicting goals.

Durkheim, Émile. *Moral Education.* Edited by Everette K. Wilson. New York: Free

Press, 1961. In this seminal work, Durkheim applied sociological theory to educational issues, thus defining the field of sociology of education.

Lynch, Kathleen. *The Hidden Curriculum: Reproduction in Education, a Reappraisal.* London: Falmer Press, 1989. This book critiques reproduction theories and uses Irish data to demonstrate some of the limitations of these theories.

Mulkey, Lynn M. *Sociology of Education: Theoretical and Empirical Investigations.* Fort Worth, Tex.: Harcourt Brace Jovanovich College Publishers, 1993. One of the most theoretical sociological texts on education, this book provides a comprehensive application of theory to educational issues.

Parsons, Talcott. "The School Class as a Social System: Some of the Functions in American Society." *Harvard Educational Review* 29, no. 4 (1959): 297-318. Parsons is a renowned functionalist, and his views on education as presented here emphasize the relationship between the system of the school class and society at large.

Maureen T. Hallinan

Cross-References

Education: Conflict Theory Views, 579; Education: Functionalist Perspectives, 586; Educational Credentials and Social Mobility, 600; Educational Inequality: The Coleman Report, 607; Educational Vouchers and Tax Credits, 614; School Socialization, 1693; The Sociology of Education, 1939.

EDUCATIONAL CREDENTIALS AND SOCIAL MOBILITY

Type of sociology: Major social institutions
Field of study: Education

Social stratification in the United States, except at the highest and lowest levels, is linked to earnings and job prestige. Few if any skilled jobs or professions are open to those without entrance credentials, which are usually educational. Thus, upwardly mobile individuals can improve their social status through education leading to degrees, certificates, or diplomas.

Principal terms
CREDENTIALISM: a misfunction of educational credentialing in which only the degree is sought or required, not the competence that it should signify
DIPLOMA MILL: a college or university with low or nonexistent standards where degrees can be obtained with little or no academic achievement
EDUCATIONAL CREDENTIALS: degrees, diplomas, or certificates earned at an institution of higher education as qualifications for jobs
JOB PRESTIGE: a subjective rating of the importance and desirability of a job within a company
OCCUPATIONAL ATTAINMENT: the level of job, judged by prestige and salary, reached in one's working life
SOCIAL HIERARCHY: in this article, the stratification of social classes according to salary and job prestige

Overview

Certification of competence is an obvious necessity in a wide variety of occupations. Some such occupations come readily to mind: surgeon, for example, or lawyer, or airline pilot. Others are less obvious, such as recreation director or forester. In most cases where certification is required, it has come to be supplied by educational institutions, some of which are highly specialized. While this process generally produces the necessary skills, in some areas it has led to the development of a system called "credentialism," which has two aspects: first, that some employers demand degrees for jobs that do not really require them; and second, that some individuals earn degrees at undemanding schools, with minimal effort, and do no follow-up learning once in the job (and hence the social position) to which they aspire.

Educational credentialing and credentialism can best be understood in historical context, beginning at a time when no college-level training existed for professions other than medicine and the clergy. In the United States, the Civil War serves as a convenient dividing line between a rural and agricultural society and an increasingly urban and industrial one. At the end of the war, less than one-fifth of the country's inhabitants lived in towns with a population of eight thousand or more. More than half of the workforce was agricultural. Business and manufacturing operations were local and small and were typically run by a man who could handle orders and accounts, as well as supervise his few employees, by himself, and who often passed his enterprise down to a family member when he retired. If someone wanted to become a lawyer, he started as a clerk in a lawyer's office and studied there until he could pass the bar examinations. If he wanted to become a physician he might go to medical school, but in many areas he might simply begin practicing. Even in technical trades such as chemical manufacture, the company owner was likely to be the only person with knowledge of the processes involved. Colleges were of no help in training students for professions, since they offered impractical curricula centered on classical languages and mathematics; graduate schools were virtually nonexistent.

By the beginning of World War I, the situation had changed so completely that an American born in 1800 would not have recognized the world of a century later and could not have functioned in it. Because of national rail transportation and steam-propelled shipping vessels, product distribution had become national or even international, rather than local. Even businesses that were primarily retail distributors, such as Sears Roebuck, were large and complex enough to require employees of specialized talent such as accountants or market analysts. Industrialization had completely revolutionized manufacture. Steam power and, later, electric power made possible factories on a colossal scale, erected in cities that were no longer restricted to the waterpower sites of the eastern seaboard but could spring up anywhere that raw materials and cheap labor could be found. Cheap labor was abundant because of the waves of immigrants of the late nineteenth century, but the new corporations needed skilled and professional employees as well: engineers, chemists, geologists, mining engineers, skilled machinists, managers who knew more than simply shop practice, and so on.

This need for specialized talent and training created an entirely new social hierarchy. The United States was no longer a country of wealthy landowners, independent farmers, merchants, and workers. The rich now consisted mainly of successful businessmen and entrepreneurs, and the workers were mostly factory hands with jobs that gave very little sense of identity or future improvement. Between these extremes was an entirely new middle class with various levels of social position based on salary, job prestige, and consumer spending. Most of the occupations that defined these social positions were open only to those who could display the proper credentials.

More often than not, the credentials were academic, consisting of a degree in a specific major subject such as agriculture, mechanical engineering, or petroleum geology. The lessons of the Industrial Revolution had not been lost on the universities and colleges in the half-century since the Civil War. Classical languages had been largely displaced by modern languages; mathematics had moved away from intellectual exercises such as Euclidean geometry toward powerful tools such as differential equations and statistics; it was possible to major in specific sciences such as meteorology, electrical engineering, or psychology; graduate schools designed according to the German pattern offered advanced training at many universities. The Morrill Land

Grant Act of 1862, which gave government land as an endowment or investment to states that would establish colleges to promote "agriculture and the mechanical arts," was a powerful stimulus, and ultimately some sixty-nine land-grant colleges or universities were founded, serving as fertile training grounds for the new class of working professionals.

In some cases, credentials were provided by professional societies, in addition to or in place of academic certification. The latter half of the nineteenth century saw the formation of most of the important discipline-oriented societies—the American Medical Association, the American Library Association, the American Chemical Society, the American Society of Mechanical Engineers, and the American Institute of Architects, to name only a few—and while they were formed partly for the exchange of information through meetings and journals, they were also formed to protect their members (and their salaries) by enforcing standards of competence. A business or industrial professional certified by a school or a professional society was assured of a job with a reasonable reward in terms of both money and social prestige.

The absolute requirement of credentials lay in the future, but the groundwork had been laid. A short digression into the author's personal family history will suggest the time scale of this progression. My grandfather, born in 1878, had only a year of engineering school before he went to work for U.S. Steel in Gary, Indiana. While working there, he took out patents on mechanical improvements in rolling mill equipment, eventually moved to another company, and ended up supervising the construction of steel mills in various countries. My father, a high-school dropout, got a needed boost from the shortage of competent civilians in World War II and ended up as head of repair programs for a number of Navy missile launcher systems at ports around the world. His era was probably the last time when competence alone was enough. When I began my professional career in the 1950's, it became clear very quickly that for the more desirable jobs in the chemical industry, and certainly in academia, I needed a Ph.D. With that as my union card, I was free to pursue the career I wanted. This history demonstrates the advance of academic credentials from merely an enhancement to an absolute necessity in occupational and social attainment.

Applications

Within most large companies that carry on both manufacturing and research, a social hierarchy exists that is nonetheless clear for being implicit. The plant supervisor and the research director stand at the head of their separate operations. Below them are the plant managers and the laboratory researchers; below these are the plant engineers, skilled workers, and ordinary laborers. The prestige of these jobs is, obviously, in descending order, as are the salaries. The level of educational attainment is directly related to salary and job prestige in all but the top positions: The plant supervisor and his or her managers usually hold the terminal degree in business, the M.B.A.; the research director and most of the laboratory staff will have Ph.D.'s. Plant engineers will hold bachelor's degrees in various areas of engineering; the skilled workers may have had some course work or specific training outside the company but usually do not have degrees; and the laborers will be high school graduates.

The standard markers of social position are usually associated with these job positions: at the top, housing in good neighborhoods with good school systems, prestige automobiles, club membership, volunteer work, involvement in municipal government, and so forth.

Are these stratifications immutable? Not at all, and this is where the educational credentialing comes in. The United States is traditionally a country where parents expect their children to have a better life than they do, and laborers and skilled workers urge their offspring to go to the state university or at least the local community college and get some kind of degree. Even an associate degree opens some doors and can lead to a step up the social ladder. Social mobility can be downward, also, but downward mobility is often a matter of choice.

Academic credentials, then, can produce social mobility through job improvement. At its best, this process is of value both to companies and to individuals, for it leads to a system that is sometimes called "meritocracy," in which the persons best educated for jobs are slotted neatly into those positions. When it is at less than its best, a variety of ills can beset it. Already mentioned is the problem of "credentialism." The company side of this can be the result of lazy personnel practices; it is often easier to require a bachelor's degree than to do the depth interview and background check that would be needed truly to evaluate a job applicant. A degree, after all, indicates that an applicant has shown sufficient initiative and determination to get that far, as well as a desire to occupy a professional position. Very likely, the applicant will continue in his or her course after hiring. The other cause of credentialism on the company's side can be an unwillingness to train people to fill certain jobs. Engineers, for example, can be purchased, degree in hand, and go to work directly. This costs a little more in salaries but is cheaper than setting up an extensive training program. Practices such as these may cost business and industry some potentially good employees, but the ambitious ones will simply go and get themselves certified and be hired anyway.

One the side of the individual, however, credentialism can create serious abuses. If a degree is the prerequisite to a desired position, some persons will do anything they must to get that degree: academic cheating, choosing the minimum number of the easiest courses in a major subject, sometimes in schools of marginal quality. These practices show a contempt for education and, far more important to employers, fail to produce the competence that employers expect to obtain. At the extreme, they produce credentials that are hollow shells. When enough people believe desperately enough that they need a degree, someone will fill that need. This situation gives rise to the diploma mill, a mail-order college that in some cases will sell a degree with no course work attached. A few are on the level, offering genuine instruction and examination by mail, but academically naïve students cannot sort one kind from the other. Some state regulation exists to control diploma mills, but none exists at the federal level.

The remaining problem associated with credentialism is what the hiree does after landing the job. The learning implied by entrance credentials must be kept up to date, and only a few professions have formalized systems to require this. Airline pilots, for example, are required to pass both physical examinations and requalification tests, as well as a review flight, at regular intervals. Physicians, however, have mostly only the imperative to "keep up with the literature" to retain currency. This can be bolstered by continuing education sessions, which are required in some states, but the tone of many of these is given away by the fact that they are held in Florida or the Bahamas and are heavily attended by drug company representatives. Companies can ensure that their professional employees stay current through the standard performance review, but no effective standard method exists in unsupervised professions such as medicine, law, and academia. Fortunately, these are fields whose practitioners are usually above the mean in conscientiousness.

Context

The historical background and context of academic credentials, job prestige, and social mobility have already been sketched in as a means of explaining their interrelatedness. In recent years, however, the context has changed significantly enough to require further explication. Educational credentialing, which has played a valuable role in providing jobs as means of mobility, has suddenly become a problem. Specifically, too many people are educationally qualified for too few jobs.

At some point in the 1980's, the ratio of high school students who go on to college passed the 50 percent level; by the 1990's it had climbed to nearly two-thirds. Not all of these college entrants stayed on to earn bachelor's degrees, but the increasing number of degrees implied by these figures was coupled with the deteriorating performance of the economy, both nationally and internationally, to produce a glut of college-qualified job applicants. Companies downsized, merged, streamlined, retrenched, and reorganized, in many cases releasing existing degreed employees. Suddenly, new graduates who expected the money and prestige of professional jobs found themselves accepting work as fry cooks, taxi drivers, and clerks. This situation was not confined to those with undergraduate degrees. Many new Ph.D.'s found that there were no job openings at their level of education and took whatever jobs they could.

This is a totally new development in a system of meritocracy that, in spite of all its faults, has functioned reasonably well. It is not clear whether it will be reversed, but given the premises of the foregoing discussion, it is clear that if it is not reversed, the nearly automatic social mobility of the past will no longer be a part of the expectations of every American.

Bibliography

Arnstein, George. "Credentialism: Why We Have Diploma Mills." *Phi Delta Kappan* 63 (April, 1982): 550-552. A discussion with many anecdotes by a specialist in accreditation, licensing, and evaluation.

Blau, Peter M., and Otis Dudley Duncan. *The American Occupational Structure*. New York: John Wiley & Sons, 1967. Old, but a classic in the field. Chapters 4, "Ascribed and Achieved Status: Techniques of Measurement and Analysis," and 9, "Kinship and Careers," have a particular bearing on the material of this article.

Crystal, Stephen, Dennis Shea, and Shreeram Krishnaswami. "Educational Attainment, Occupational History, and Stratification: Determinants of Later-Life Economic Outcomes." *Journal of Gerontology* 47, no. 5 (September, 1992): S213-S221. Holds that income in retirement is related to education and job level, just as it is during the working years.

Fallows, James. "A Substitute for Merit: The Case Against Credentialism." *Current* 340 (March-April, 1986): 3-17. Describes more kinds of credentialism than are discussed here, with examples from many areas. Reprinted from *The Atlantic* 256 (December, 1985, pp. 49-63) and excerpted from *Human Capital* (1986).

Ishida, Hiroshi. *Social Mobility in Contemporary Japan: Educational Credentials, Class, and the Labour Market in a Cross-National Perspective*. Stanford, Calif.: Stanford University Press, 1992. A comparison of Japan, England, and the United States in the aspects indicated by the title; finds that family background is as important as education in Japan. Appendices contain useful tables of the numerically quantified levels of prestige of occupations in Japan and England.

Jeffries, Vincent, and H. Edward Ransford, comps. *Social Stratification: A Multiple Hierarchy Approach*. Boston: Allyn & Bacon, 1980. Useful background in a collection of essays by experts, some well-known, in the field. Chapter 4, "Class Stratification in the United States: Methods and Empirical Studies," is particularly applicable to this article.

Kaus, Mickey. "The Challenge to Merit: Having Both Merit and Equality." *Current* 346 (October, 1992): 4-9. Opens with a discussion of the Clinton Administration's approach to job skills and employment but moves to a theoretical discussion of job and social stratification. Reprinted from *The New Republic* (June 22, 1992, pp. 21-27).

Lichtenstein, Paul, Nancy L. Pedersen, and G. E. McClearn. "The Origins of Individual Differences in Occupational Status and Educational Level: A Study of Twins Reared Apart and Together." *Acta Sociologica* 35, no. 1 (1992): 13-31. "For both education and occupation, environmental effects were more important among women and genetic effects were more important among men" (abstract).

_____ . "Social Science and the Citizen: Costs and Benefits of Higher Education." (Editorial.) *Society* 30 (January-February, 1993): 2. Labor Department statistics on lack of jobs for graduates.

Tomlinson-Keasey, Carol, and Todd D. Little. "Predicting Educational Attainment, Occupational Achievement, Intellectual Skill, and Personal Adjustment Among Gifted Men and Women." *Journal of Educational Psychology* 82, no. 3 (1990): 442-455. Parental education and home environment were found to be significant predictive factors.

Robert M. Hawthorne, Jr.

Cross-References

Education: Conflict Theory Views, 579; Education: Functionalist Perspectives, 586; Education: Manifest and Latent Functions, 593; Equal Educational Opportunity, 661; Higher Education: Colleges and Universities, 877; Higher Education: Community Colleges, 884; Social Mobility: Analysis and Overview, 1812; Social Mobility: Intergenerational versus Intragenerational Mobility, 1819; Social Stratification: Analysis and Overview, 1839.

EDUCATIONAL INEQUALITY: THE COLEMAN REPORT

Type of sociology: Major social institutions
Field of study: Education

Educational inequality is the provision of unequal learning opportunities to students. Unequal opportunities may stem from differences in schools' resources, such as per-pupil expenditures, facilities, and equipment. They also may result from school differences in student body and teacher characteristics, in school climate, and in peer influences. The Coleman Report investigated this educational inequality.

Principal terms

ACADEMIC CLIMATE: the attitudes of teachers and students toward learning; a strong academic climate is characterized by positive attitudes toward academic achievement

FIRST COLEMAN REPORT: the landmark 1966 survey, entitled *Equality of Educational Opportunity*, which examined the lack of equality of educational opportunity for nonwhite students

SCHOOL RESOURCES: expenditures per pupil, school facilities and equipment, library books, laboratories, and curricular materials

SECOND COLEMAN REPORT: report entitled *Trends in School Segregation, 1968-73* that described the phenomenon of white flight that followed court-ordered school busing to attain racial integration in the schools

THIRD COLEMAN REPORT: an analysis of the "High School and Beyond" survey which concluded that students attending private schools attained higher academic performance than those enrolled in public schools

WHITE FLIGHT: the movement of white families from a school district to avoid having their children bused to distant schools as part of a desegregation program

Overview

In 1964, as part of the Civil Rights Act, a team of sociologists was appointed to study education in the United States in order to determine how educational inequality was contributing to the lower academic achievement of minority students. The findings, published in 1966, ultimately surprised even the researchers themselves, led by James S. Coleman. They demonstrated that family background is the strongest predictor of student achievement. Differences between schools do play a role, but a smaller one than had been expected. The racial composition of a school emerged as a key influence on student achievement. In order to appreciate the study's findings fully, it is necessary first to look at definitions of educational inequality.

The concept of educational inequality has taken on a number of meanings over the past few decades. Initially, educational inequality referred to the unequal allocation of resources to schools, such as per-pupil expenditures, school facilities and equipment, and teacher credentials. Efforts to eliminate this kind of inequality can be seen in the plans of some states to equalize the amount of money spent on each student within the state.

Another meaning of educational inequality emerged at the time of the Supreme Court ruling against segregated schools in 1954 in *Brown v. Board of Education.* Prior to this date, the assumption was that segregated schools could provide the same quality of education to all students. After the Supreme Court decision, however, the term "educational inequality" was used to characterize schools that differed in racial composition. The prevailing belief was that only desegregated schools could produce similar educational outcomes for black and white students.

Educational inequality also refers to the climate of a school, measured by teacher and student characteristics such as student attitudes and morale, teacher expectations, and academic orientation. The belief is that schools with a strong academic climate provide a better education than do schools with a less academic orientation. Educational inequality also describes unequal outcomes of schooling. Inequality is believed to be present if students with similar backgrounds and ability fail to attain the same levels of academic achievement. The disparities in achievement may be the result of differences in resources, of differential exposure to a supportive academic climate, or of other factors.

Finally, educational inequality characterizes the situation in which disadvantaged students fail to attain the same levels of academic achievement as their more advantaged peers. Here, the role of the school is seen as compensatory. Schools are expected to provide special programs for students who are educationally disadvantaged to compensate for their inadequacies.

The first three of these definitions of educational inequality have to do with inequality of inputs—resources, student background, and climate—while the last two pertain to school outputs, in particular to student achievement. The goal of the landmark study *Equality of Educational Opportunity* (1966), commonly referred to as the Coleman Report (sociologist James S. Coleman led the study), was to determine the extent of educational inequality in the American public school system. The Coleman study addressed both these sets of meanings of educational inequality. It documented school differences in resources and racial composition, and it compared student achievement across schools. The primary concern of the study, however, was the fourth meaning of educational inequality: The study primarily examined the determinants of differences in student academic achievement. Since most previous empirical research on schools had concentrated on school differences in input measures, the Coleman Report represented a significant shift. It initiated a tradition of research that examined school effects on student outcomes and informed a number of policy decisions aimed at producing greater educational equality.

Applications

The Coleman study was commissioned by President Lyndon Johnson and Congress in 1964 to study the availability of equal educational opportunities for individuals who differ by race, color, religion, or national origin in American public schools. The motivation for the study was the belief that African American and other minority students attended schools that were inferior to those attended by white students, thus accounting for the lower academic achievement of nonwhite students.

The researchers collected information from a stratified random sample of more than 645,000 students in grades 1, 3, 6, 9, and 12 in 3,000 elementary and 1,180 secondary schools in the United States. The respondents included American Indians, Mexican Americans, Puerto Ricans living in the United States, Asian Americans, blacks, and whites. The data were obtained from questionnaires administered to superintendents, principals, teachers, and students.

The first main set of analyses examined school differences in school inputs, believed to be an indicator of school quality. Traditional measures of school resources were used, including teachers' salaries, number of library books, teachers' and principals' educational levels, school facilities, special programs, and the curriculum. In addition, measures of principal and teacher attitudes toward the school and the students, and toward desegregation policies, were included, as were aggregate measures of the student body's social background, race, attitudes, and aspirations.

The results of these analyses showed only small differences in resources across schools attended by minorities and by whites. White students generally attended schools that had slightly greater resources than black students' schools. More important, the racial characteristics of the student bodies of schools attended by black and white students differed. Segregation was greatest in Southern elementary schools and least in Northern secondary schools. Black students tended to have weaker socioeconomic and educational backgrounds than white pupils, and the data indicated that the academic environment of the schools attended by blacks was inferior to that of schools attended by whites. The study also found that the characteristics of teachers differed between schools attended by black and white students. The greatest differences were that teacher attitudes and scores on a vocabulary test were higher in schools attended by white students.

The second set of analyses sought to determine whether schools differed in student achievement. Higher performance could be attributed to the schools themselves, to differences in the family backgrounds of the students attending the schools, or to differences in community influences, distinct from family background. Consequently, the Coleman Report examined the differential impact of each of these sets of factors on student achievement. No attempt was made to determine the effects of within-school factors on variation in student achievement; data on the individual experiences of students were not collected in the survey.

The data revealed significant differences across schools in the aggregate achievement of students based on standardized tests administered to students in the sample. The analyses showed that the single most important determinant of school differences in achievement was differences in family background across communities. Moreover, the influence of family background on achievement remained fairly constant from the beginning of elementary school through secondary school.

A small amount of the variation in student achievement scores was attributed to school characteristics. These were divided into three parts: school facilities, curriculum, and other resources; teacher characteristics; and student characteristics. Of these three sources of influence, student body characteristics were found to have the strongest effect on student achievement. The effects of teacher attributes were slightly weaker, while the effects of school resources were markedly less.

The student body characteristics in these analyses included the mean educational aspirations and backgrounds of the students and school racial composition. The results showed that when students' aspirations and backgrounds were considered, their achievement increased as the aspirations and backgrounds of their peers increased. Student body characteristics exerted a greater influence on achievement beginning at sixth grade and continuing through high school. Moreover, the lowest-achieving students, particularly African American and Hispanic students, were more affected by their educational environment than were whites and Asian Americans. Students from educationally deficient backgrounds appeared to be disadvantaged by educationally deprived school environments to a greater extent than did more privileged students.

Differences in teacher characteristics across schools had the second strongest effect on variation in student achievement. While the influence of teacher characteristics was quite small at the lower grades, it increased with grade level, reaching its maximum effect in twelfth grade. Teachers' verbal skills had their greatest influence on student achievement between grades three and six, while teacher educational level had the greatest effect in secondary school, especially for blacks and other minorities.

Only a small amount of variation in school achievement was explained by differences in school facilities, curriculum, and other resources. Schools with a higher per-pupil expenditure, stronger curriculum, and more laboratories and library books tended to have slightly higher student achievement than schools with fewer resources.

In addition to these three sets of school characteristics, the survey analyzed the effects of student attitudes on achievement. The variables included mean student interest in school and amount of reading outside school, mean self-concept as pertains to learning and success in school, and mean sense of control of the environment. Of all the factors studied in the survey, including family background and school resources, these attitudinal measures explained the greatest amount of school variation in achievement. Self-concept is a strong predictor of achievement for white and Asian American students, while sense of control over the environment is a strong predictor for African Americans and other minorities. These results indicate that efforts to help disadvantaged students change their conception of their environment might improve their achievement.

Analyses showed that student background has a far greater effect on student achievement than do school characteristics. Schools, however, do have a small influence. School differences in achievement can be attributed to differences in student body characteristics, teacher characteristics, and, to a small degree, school resources. These results suggest that schools are unlikely to attain the kind of educational equality that would require canceling out the vast differences in background that students bring to the school. A more realistic goal would be to create a school climate and program that has a strong independent effect on student achievement in order to avoid further handicapping students whose backgrounds predispose them to low achievement.

Context

One of the major contributions of the Coleman Report was the support it provided, in the late 1960's and early 1970's, for court arguments promoting the integration of the public schools. The findings of the group's research indicated that students are disadvantaged by attending schools at which the students have weak educational backgrounds and low educational aspirations. Since schools with majority black enrollment generally possess these characteristics, the data supported arguments for school desegregation. Supreme Court rulings required integrating schools even in segregated neighborhoods. This requirement led to the practice of busing students from various locations to schools in other locations to ensure racial desegregation in the schools.

An unintended consequence of busing policies for school integration was "white flight": the exit of white families from racially integrated school districts to avoid busing. City neighborhoods became more black as whites moved to the suburbs. Some white families that did not change residence withdrew their children from the public schools and enrolled them in private schools. These consequences of school desegregation policies were documented in a report by James Coleman and his colleagues, *Trends in School Segregation, 1968-73* (1975), which became known as the second Coleman Report.

Reactions to the second Coleman Report ranged from concern to outrage. Those who opposed busing used the report to support their arguments that busing policy aimed at attaining racial integration was a failure. Those who advocated busing as a means of establishing school desegregation and ensuring civil rights felt betrayed. The report effectively destroyed the tenuous compromises that many school districts and community activists had established in their efforts to balance and accommodate various interests while working to integrate public schools. In time, however, a number of positive outcomes stemmed from the turmoil created by the second Coleman Report. Busing policies remained in effect in many school districts, and they generally became less controversial over time. Moreover, many school districts established more creative plans to attain racially integrated schools, such as the highly popular magnet and alternative schools.

Following the second Coleman Report, a large, longitudinal survey called "High School and Beyond" (HSB) was initiated to provide data for the study of a variety of educational issues. Information was collected on more than 57,000 sophomores and seniors in more than 1,000 high schools in the United States. These students were followed at two-year intervals. In what became known as the third Coleman Report (*High School Achievement: Public, Catholic, and Private Schools Compared*, 1982), Coleman and his colleagues analyzed these data and compared the effects of public and private schools on student achievement. They found that students in Catholic and other private schools demonstrated higher achievement than those in public schools. Moreover, Catholic schools were more beneficial for minority and low-income students than for other student groups.

The completion of the second wave of data collection in 1982 permitted longitudinal analyses of the HSB data. Coleman and his colleagues analyzed the data, and their results provided additional support for their original conclusions. They attributed the higher achievement of private (and especially Catholic) school students to differences in the school experiences of students in these two sectors. Catholic school students spent more time doing homework, had lower absentee rates, and were more likely to be placed in academic programs than their public school peers.

As with the previous reports, the results of the third Coleman Report provoked controversy. A number of social scientists criticized the study on methodological grounds; educators in the public sector again felt betrayed. Nevertheless, despite the debate over the interpretations of the results, the study succeeded in identifying the mechanisms that promote school achievement and provided policy direction for both private and public schools. The most important of these is to establish programs that challenge students academically and that demand student effort and discipline.

The first Coleman Report represents a significant contribution to social science research and to national educational policy and practice through its analysis of the effects of schools on student achievement. It was a landmark study, strengthening the role of social science research in informing agendas for national policy and reform. Moreover, it changed the direction of research in the sociology of education and began an intensive investigation of the determinants and consequences of academic achievement. The second Coleman report is an excellent illustration of how social science research can be used to shape national policy and of the importance of continued interaction between research and policy. The third Coleman Report extends the research on school effects by focusing on public and private school differences in achievement. Few contemporary social scientists can be credited with a contribution equal in significance to these sociological studies of the effects of schools.

Bibliography

Ballantine, Jeanne H., ed. *Schools and Society*. 2d ed. Mountain View, Calif.: Mayfield, 1989. This reader in the sociology of education includes a number of chapters related to research on schools and their effects as well as on broader educational issues, practices, and policies.

Coleman, James S. *Equality and Achievement in Education*. Boulder, Colo.: Westview Press, 1990. This book presents an excellent summary of each of the three Coleman reports, with greatest attention paid to *Equality of Educational Opportunity*. It also elaborates on the various meanings of educational equality.

Coleman, James S., et al. *Equality of Educational Opportunity*. Washington D.C.: U.S. Government Printing Office, 1966. The original Coleman Report is presented in this volume. Its findings, that school resources are less important than other factors in influencing achievement, surprised even its authors.

Coleman, James S., Thomas Hoffer, and Sally Kilgore. *High School Achievement: Public, Catholic, and Private Schools Compared.* New York: Basic Books, 1982. Analysis of the "High School and Beyond" data comparing academic achievement in public and private schools provides the content of this book. The study is often referred to as the third Coleman Report.

Mosteller, Frederick, and Daniel P. Moynihan, eds. *On Equality of Educational Opportunity.* New York: Vintage, 1972. The papers in this book were originally delivered at Harvard University in a seminar discussing the findings of the Coleman Report. Written by prominent researchers and policy makers, they provide a fairly comprehensive discussion and critique of the report.

Maureen T. Hallinan

Cross-References

Affirmative Action, 21; Busing and Integration, 179; The Civil Rights Movement, 265; Education: Conflict Theory Views, 579; Education: Manifest and Latent Functions, 593; Educational Credentials and Social Mobility, 600; Equal Educational Opportunity, 661; School Desegregation, 1686; School Socialization, 1693; The Sociology of Education, 1939.

EDUCATIONAL VOUCHERS AND TAX CREDITS

Type of sociology: Major social institutions
Field of study: Education

Educational vouchers and tuition tax credits refer to educational policy options designed to promote a greater degree of parental choice with regard to the schooling of children. They involve ways of shifting financial resources to parents in the hope that this will increase the range and quality of educational choices available.

> *Principal terms*
> RESTRUCTURING: efforts to alter and improve patterns of school governance and practice
> SCHOOL CHOICE: an educational policy intended to increase alternatives in schooling and promote parental choice
> SCHOOL IMPROVEMENT: as used by proponents of school choice, the provision by schools of a better education because of the competition created by choice
> TUITION TAX CREDIT: a plan under which parents can deduct a certain amount of their children's private school tuition from their taxes
> VOUCHER: a certificate given to the parents of students indicating the amount of public money they are entitled to distribute to the schools they choose for their children to attend

Overview

Traditionally, control of American public education has been concentrated in the hands of local and state education authorities. Both vouchers and tuition tax credits represent ways to shift some control to parents of school-age children. These plans would enable parents to choose to spend a certain amount of public education funds (in a sense, "their share" of these funds) to send their children to private institutions instead of automatically having the money go into the public education system. Because these proposals represent far-reaching changes to a fundamental societal institution, they have engendered much controversy and debate.

The notion of providing to parents of school-age children a voucher—a certificate endorsing their choice of where to spend their children's share of public education funds—is not a new idea. Tuition tax credits, allowing parents to deduct a certain amount of their children's private school tuition from their taxes, have also been discussed for many years. Economist Milton Friedman suggested the idea of vouchers as early as 1955. At the time, the idea did not evoke much interest. Vouchers and tax tuition credits were discussed off and on during the next few decades, but it was not until the mid-1980's that the idea received major support, spearheaded by President Ronald Reagan's support for these proposals.

A vigorous debate emerged in the early 1990's, spurred by President George Bush's support of vouchers in his *America 2000* educational policy report. The debate centered on the role of parental decisions in the choice of what schools their children could attend (or could afford to attend) and on proposals to have that role transformed and magnified. Voucher and tax credit proposals often fall under the rubric of "school choice." There are numerous kinds of choice plans in the United States. Some involve both public and private schools, while other plans limit parental choice to options within public school systems. Hundreds of articles have been written on the topic of educational choice since it became the focus of controversy and national debate.

Although volumes have been written on the subject, evidence for the variety of claims and arguments that have been put forward is remarkably limited. Instead, there has been an abundance of speculation as to what various efforts to stimulate choice by vouchers and tax credits might mean. Predictions range from extremely dire to boldly optimistic. Some of the principal kinds of speculative claims for and against school choice were summarized by educational researcher John F. Witte in 1992. Among the arguments for school choice are predictions that choice would mean less bureaucracy, more school-level autonomy, more highly motivated teachers and principals, more involved parents, more innovative and diverse schools, higher student achievement, and reduced school expenses. Among the arguments opposing voucher and tax credit plans is speculation that they would cause increased inequalities among schools, increased segregation, fewer services for learning-disabled students and students with other disabilities, and reduced minimum standards; it is also argued that they would result in information about schools being more accessible to wealthier parents.

There is some slim evidence on which to base predictions regarding school choice plans. One kind of evidence involves findings on certain aspects of the performance of private schools as compared to public ones. An influential work written in support of far-ranging changes in the direction of allowing parents a choice of private school is the book *Politics, Markets, and America's Schools* (1990), by John E. Chubb and Terry M. Moe, and the authors rely on this kind of evidence. They argue that private schools are superior in student achievement and that creating a market system under which schools would have considerable independence would stimulate the public schools to make necessary improvements in order to compete.

Critics have countered that the findings regarding differential levels of success for public and private schools are negligible when placed in the perspective of the problems facing all schools. Albert Shanker and B. Rosenberg, for example, have argued that the difference in performance between public and private school students is minuscule. They concluded that all American students are doing comparatively poorly. Other points to consider are that most parochial and independent schools have entrance criteria, that a higher percentage of their students' parents are college graduates, and that their students tend to take more academic courses and come from more affluent families. Because these characteristics have also been found to be related to higher achievement among public school students, many question the validity of the claim that private schools' students perform at a much higher level.

Theoretically, in a far-reaching choice plan, public schools would improve because of the competition, but it is not clear how hard-pressed public schools will be able to improve the quality of education while they are losing funds as a result of students leaving to attend private (or other public) schools. The specific nature of anticipated improvements under such conditions of declining support has not been discussed by the choice proponents.

Many supporters also adhere to the illusory belief that with a voucher parents will be able to choose any private school they want. It is quite clear, however, that vouchers will not cover the tuition of many private schools. Also, it is not possible to predict what kinds of entrance requirements might be put into effect. Clearly, not all students wishing to attend the most desirable schools would be able to do so. The relatively small size of private schools, which has been argued to be an important factor in the educational achievements of private schools, would probably be maintained. Alexander W. Astin argues that this could increase the selectivity of the more elite schools, excluding the majority of students applying. Educational researchers D. R. Moore and S. Davenport, in a study of public school choice, argue that school choice will lead to greater stratification and inequalities between students. Others, such as educational historian R. Freeman Butts, point out that a central feature of the choice debate concerns the degree to which many have lost sight of the original purposes of public education. The essential purpose of public schooling, he says, was not to give parents ultimate power over their children's education, but to teach good citizenship and a sense of civic community.

Applications

Although the choice debate has raged for many years, actual examples were slow in coming. The first voucher plan to involve both public and private schools was begun as a pilot program in Milwaukee, Wisconsin, in 1989. After the program had been in existence for a year, it was found that even though 55,000 students qualified to apply for vouchers, only 600 did apply; eventually, only 400 slots were made available in private schools for students with vouchers. Given its recent initiation, the consequences of the Milwaukee plan were not yet clear in the early 1990's. Nevertheless, there were some interesting preliminary indications. The earliest results indicated that poor and minority students were not doing substantially better in the participating private schools. In addition, some commentators urged those examining the initial effects of the program to note that in the Milwaukee choice plan, the participating schools did not have to provide an education for students with special needs or disabilities.

One source for evidence concerning public school choice plans comes from a 1992 report by the Carnegie Foundation for the Advancement of Teaching. It indicates that extant choice plans do not improve student performance. This report also suggests that they mostly are used by better-educated and more affluent parents and that such plans do not, therefore, tend to succeed in addressing the problems (such as poverty and poor health) that plague the children most in need of increased assistance. This report also concluded that 62 percent of the public opposed financing private schools with the help of public money. One prominent example of public school choice is the Minnesota open transfer program, which allows students to attend any public school in the state. In this program, transfers have been found to take place primarily because of convenience and location rather than school quality.

A 1990 study of public school choice in four large cities (New York, Chicago, Philadelphia, and Boston) indicated that the system of allowing students to choose their schools increases stratification and sorting among students. The study reports that students from a variety of at-risk populations (including African American and Hispanic students, low-achieving students, those from low-income families, those with behavior and/or attendance problems, students with disabilities, and those with limited proficiency in the English language) have limited opportunities to attend the more popular schools and take part in the most popular programs.

The study also found that most applicants and their parents were confused about the high school admissions process. Poor, uneducated, and non-English speaking parents and students had the most difficult time understanding and taking advantage of the workings of the system. Admissions standards in reality were often different from the ones officially stated in advertisements. Schools had considerable freedom in deciding whom they wanted to admit, and these judgments were often very subjective. Typically, limited-English-proficiency students and those with disabilities were not admitted to the more academically selective schools. In fact, most students who applied to these schools were turned down. This study suggests a strong basis for many key criticisms of school choice programs, and it indicates how adverse effects for some categories of students might actually come about. It is also worth noting that this study concerned only choice among public schools and under plans that were likely to have been fairly closely supervised. It is reasonable to assume that such effects could be magnified in a less-regulated plan that included diverse private schools as well.

Another type of stratification that might take place was indicated by an examination of the public school interdistrict choice plan in Des Moines, Iowa. Interdistrict choice allows the multiracial urban school population to attend schools in surrounding suburban school districts. In Des Moines, major efforts have been made to support public education, and the schools rank among the relatively successful urban schools in the United States. Nevertheless, in the first two years of the program, white students who decided to leave the city's schools for suburban, virtually all-white, schools outnumbered black students choosing to do so by 402 to 11. While this evidence is thin and preliminary, it suggests a basis for speculation about the ways in which choice plans might exacerbate existing patterns of segregation and racial isolation in American schools.

As of the early 1990's, based on the limited experience of school choice plans in existence, there was virtually no evidence suggesting that substantial school improvement would take place because of the competition between schools created by the choice plans.

Context

A shift toward greater choice of schools and toward public support for private educational options would represent a significant policy change in American education. As an approach to school reform, vouchers and tuition tax credits are closely aligned to wider political currents in American society. They received an important boost by way of support given by the Reagan Administration. The Reagan Administration's educational policy was based on the argument that a voucher system would increase the competition between schools, raising educational standards and in turn helping the United States to respond to the pressures of international economic competition. President Bush later made the choice issue a key component of his educational policy document *America 2000*. According to President Bush's last proposal, students who did not come from wealthy homes would receive $1,000 scholarships to attend the school of their choice. This proposal included independent and parochial schools. In this plan, funds would be given directly to the parents in order to avoid the public school bureaucracy. The amount would not have covered the full tuition of many private schools, especially those serving an affluent clientele, but it would have provided a subsidy for those whose children were already attending private schools.

The Bush choice plan gained considerable support among members of the New Right and others who saw a "free-market" ideology and privatization of public education as providing a solution to the perceived problem of low-quality public schooling. The Catholic church has also lent considerable support to the idea of choice plans. Faced with declining enrollment in parochial schools, the church viewed the choice plan as a way to revitalize parochial schooling through an influx of new students and sources of funding.

In addition, support for school choice has come from many urban educators and parents, both black and white. Many urban educators see it as a way to enhance the educational prospects for at least some of the large number of inner city students now suffering from deficient forms of public education in overburdened, underfinanced schools. A sense of deep frustration, even hopelessness, about the conditions of urban education has led many educators to give up notions of public school improvement in city schools. Many urban parents, realizing that their children's future to a large extent depends on the schooling they will receive, also are inclined to look favorably on proposals that promise a better education for their children. Given the diverse interests aligned in support of voucher plans, as well as the depth of the concerns raised about them by diverse critics, the debate is likely to continue. Since it is impossible to conclude definitively how productive or destructive any plan is until it has been in effect for a length of time, the range of speculative claims and opinions that have emerged on this matter will probably continue to be the focus of discussion in the years ahead as struggles to initiate or limit forms of school choice ensue.

Bibliography

Astin, Alexander W. "Educational 'Choice': Its Appeal May Be Illusory." *Sociology of Education* 65 (October, 1992): 255-260. This is a strong and thoughtful argument against school choice. Astin argues that choice would make schools more selective and would increase the differences in the quality of education offered. This issue includes other articles on school choice, including the Coleman article (below).

Boyd, W. L., and H. J. Walberg, eds. *Choice in Education: Potential and Problems*. Berkeley, Calif.: McCutchan, 1990. This edited book contains some interesting reports of cases where school choice has been tried within public school systems. Controversial as well as beneficial aspects of choice plans are explored by the various authors.

Chubb, John E., and Terry M. Moe. *Politics, Markets, and America's Schools*. Washington, D.C.: Brookings Institution, 1990. The authors examine the organization of effective schools and the causes of high student achievement. They conclude that school choice would create competition among schools and would thus force schools to improve. Consequently, they argue that school choice would provide more effective schools and higher student achievement.

Coleman, James S. "Some Points on Choice in Education." *Sociology of Education* 65 (October, 1992): 260-262. This article is a response to Astin's article in the same issue. Coleman presents a strong argument for school choice.

Cookson, Peter W., Jr., ed. *The Choice Controversy*. Newbury Park, Calif.: Corwin Press, 1992. This edited book provides a thoughtful introduction to the choice debate. It covers a range of issues including the performance of private schools versus the performance of public schools and the fundamental issues involved in school choice. The introduction provides a good summary of the debate.

Conway, G. E. "School Choice: A Private School Perspective." *Phi Delta Kappan* 73 (March, 1992): 561-563. This article provides a view of school choice from the perspective of a headmaster of a private school. The merits of school choice initiatives are represented from this perspective.

Educational Policy 6 (June, 1992). A special issue of this journal that focuses on the school choice debate. Articles range from a summary of the claims made by both opponents and supporters of school choice to the underlying background issues. Also discussed are questions of where the school choice movement might take education.

Kane, Pearl Rock, ed. *Independent Schools, Independent Thinkers*. San Francisco: Jossey-Bass, 1992. This book deals in detail with the issue of independent schools, which are discussed in relation to school choice options. Provides an important perspective on the school choice issue.

Phi Delta Kappan 61 (October, 1979). This special issue provides easily accessible information about the family's right to choose the school their children attend, the value of having schools compete for students and funds, and an article on work comparing the performance of public and private schools.

Rethinking Schools 7 (Autumn, 1992). A special journal issue that includes articles written by practitioners including principals, union representatives, and teachers; brings a different perspective to the school choice debate. Experimental school choice plans from a number of cities and states, including Colorado, California, Baltimore, and Milwaukee, are discussed.

Gunilla Holm

Cross-References

Alternatives to Traditional Schooling, 86; Busing and Integration, 179; Education: Conflict Theory Views, 579; Education: Functionalist Perspectives, 586; Education: Manifest and Latent Functions, 593; Educational Inequality: The Coleman Report, 607; Equal Educational Opportunity, 661; School Desegregation, 1686; The Sociology of Education, 1939.

THE ELDERLY AND INSTITUTIONAL CARE

Type of sociology: Aging and ageism
Fields of study: The family; Socialization over the life cycle

Through voluntary or involuntary placement, institutional care facilities become the final home for a portion of the very old in American society. Placement constitutes an individual decision and life change; however, because of the increasing numbers of elderly in the population, care of the elderly who cannot care for themselves is also a social phenomenon and responsibility.

Principal terms
   GERONTOLOGIST: a person who specializes in studying the problems of aging and the elderly
   INSTITUTION: an establishment devoted to the care of a particular subpopulation; often a place of confinement
   MIDDLE-OLD: individuals aged seventy-five to eighty-four
   NURSING HOME: a residence equipped to care for the aged or infirm
   VERY OLD: individuals aged eighty-five and older
   YOUNG-OLD: individuals aged sixty-five to seventy-four

Overview

Maintaining independence by living alone or with a spouse is important to elderly people. A 1986 Louis Harris poll, as reported in the *Congressional Quarterly* (1989), showed that 86 percent of elderly people living alone prefer it to other possible living arrangements. Living alone is the most common form of residence for elderly people. According to the U.S. Bureau of the Census, more than 50 percent of persons sixty-five years of age and older live alone. As independence diminishes, however, because of poor physical or mental health, lack of finances to pay for medical or other care, or lack of social support, decisions about how best to care for the elderly individual have to be made.

A profile of the average nursing home resident is a white widow eighty-five or older with living children; this individual has a low income, some ambulatory problems, and some medical problems. The average stay is short, and there may be only 5 percent of the population in the nursing home at one time. The very old, however, have a 25 to 50 percent chance of being placed in a nursing home.

Institutional care may refer to mental institutions, but typically, in reference to the elderly population, the term is applied to nursing homes. Two common types of nursing homes are available in the United States: intermediate care facilities and skilled nursing facilities. Intermediate care nursing homes provide some everyday care activities and limited medical care. Residents are usually able to provide for their own personal care and are able to move about on their own, either walking alone (perhaps with the aid of a walker) or using a wheelchair. These institutions are responsible for the daily scheduling of meal and social activities; to a large extent the resident must follow the schedule, thereby losing some right to choice. According to George D. Pozgar, in *Long-Term Care and The Law: A Legal Guide for Health Care Professionals* (1992), intermediate care facilities may be eligible for Medicaid programs.

Skilled nursing homes provide twenty-four-hour holistic care; they meet primary self-care needs and provide both daily living activities and medical care. Residents in skilled nursing homes are generally under the continuing care of a physician. Individual decision making concerning meals, social events, and time for personal care is eliminated. Skilled nursing homes must meet minimum licensing standards for the state and federal governments. In addition, they are entitled to apply for Medicare and/or Medicaid funds.

The quality of care and life provided by nursing homes ranges from very poor to very good. In an effort to regulate quality of care, the federal government has required nursing homes to meet certain standards. These minimum standards address the areas of staffing, services, and physical plant. Maria K. Mitchel of the National League for Nursing reported in 1989 that almost 30 percent of nursing homes did not meet standards in the personal hygiene category and 42 percent did not meet regulations pertaining to food safety. The commitment to and the enforcement of the standards is a small measure of the quality of a particular home; however, authors Maurice I. May, Edvardas Kaminskas, Jack Kasten, and David Allan Levine, in *Managing Institutional Long-Term Care for the Elderly* (1991), argue that quality is more than simple conformance to standards:

> [Quality] must embody a strategy for (1) discovering what is truly important to the infirm elderly who are in the care of the institution, their families, and the community; and (2) effecting ongoing, incremental, systematic improvements in the delivery of services to these various constituencies.

The quality of life and care influences the adjustment period for the new resident. Helen L. Bee, a professor of adult development, suggests in *The Journey of Adulthood* (1987) that the stress associated with placement in a nursing home is reduced when the home is perceived as offering quality care. This is especially true when warmth and autonomy are considered part of that quality.

Reporting in "The Environment and Quality of Care in Long-Term Care Institutions" (1989), professor of nursing Jeanie Kayser-Jones found that more nursing home residents preferred open ward accommodations to private or semiprivate rooms. Advantages listed by the clients included feeling less lonely and isolated. They also believed that the company of more persons would cut down on the possibility of getting a roommate they did not like. In addition, life in an open ward was seen as more stimulating and as offering a source of friendships and support groups. Disadvantages of open wards included problems with sleeping and interpersonal problems that resulted when confused residents were placed with the mentally unimpaired.

Another major area of quality evaluation is the competence of the staff, in particular the nurses, and their relationship to the residents. Kayser-Jones suggests that the bond formed between resident and nurse is more important in quality control than any environmental factors. The residents agree with the professionals concerning staff: They listed staff as being the most important attribute of quality in the National Citizens' Coalition for Nursing Home reform study reported by Mathy Mezey in "Institutional Care: Caregivers and Quality" (1989). Pozgar has made a number of suggestions for the continued improvement of nursing home quality. These include providing a common room in instances where both spouses are residents of a nursing facility, finding alternatives to institutional care, protecting residents from abusive persons, establishing and enforcing safety standards, and implementing procedures to safeguard patient rights. Pozgar also suggests offering education and training programs, supporting research, and improving the image of nursing facilities.

Applications

Voluntary or involuntary placement in an institutional care facility is a step in the life of an elderly person that is commonly thought to be a move to the individual's last home. Institutional care appears to be the final choice for care for the elderly after all other options have been exhausted. Timothy H. Brubaker, editor of *Aging, Health, and Family: Long-Term Care* (1987), suggests that many families will provide support and practical care for relatives until the task becomes so extraordinary that the family cannot meet the demands.

According to gerontologist Stephen M. Golant, moving into a nursing home involves an admission of a complete loss of independence. Moreover, the perception that one is moving there until death is common. The decision to move to a nursing home is met with fear both by the elderly person and by the person's family, according to original research by Paula J. Biedenharn and Janice Bastlin Normoyle. They reported in 1991 that 60 percent of their sample were quite fearful and 16 percent were extremely fearful; only about one in four expressed no fear at the prospect of relocating to a nursing home. A prevailing general perception (one that, unfortunately, is sometimes justified) that nursing homes offer poor-quality care also adds to anxiety about admittance to a care facility. As long as an image persists of homes where too much time is spent on television viewing, where socialization is limited, and where personal needs go unattended, anxiety will continue. The finding that care in nursing homes is generally a last choice of the elderly and their families is an indication of the negative attitudes that often prevail. In his book *The Nursing Home Primer* (1989), Hanns G. Pieper reports that gerontologists believe that 25 percent of the nursing home population would not be there if other services or options were available.

For some of the elderly there comes a time when available services at home (sometimes with the help of community programs) can no longer meet their needs. Predictors of nursing home placement include advanced age, inability to perform personal care and daily household activities, absence of someone to care for the person at home, a shortage of money to pay for care at home, and poor physical and mental health. Advanced age increases the possibility that a person will live some of their years in a nursing home; advanced age also increases the incidence of the other predictors of nursing home placement. For example, the older a person becomes, the more likely he or she is to develop medical problems or even to outlive family members who might provide care.

Being able to stay in their own homes, even if someone else is needed to care for them, allows elderly people to retain some control over their own lives and thus some independence. The inability to care for oneself or to have that care provided is a major reason for nursing home placement for all ages. The 1985 National Nursing Home Survey (as reported by Pozgar) states that for those over eighty-five the most common reason for entering the nursing home is that personal and/or medical care needed by the elderly individual has advanced to the point where family members can no longer provide it. Inability to perform daily living tasks effectively is the next most common reason for placement. The absence of someone else in the elderly person's home who can provide the care without extra charge is the determining factor for more than 50 percent of the elderly over the age of eighty-five.

The financial resources of the elderly population are as varied as those of the general population. Thus the cost of care in the home prohibits some elderly people from remaining in their own homes. For the elderly poor, placement in a nursing home allows at least a portion of the cost to be paid with Medicare and/or Medicaid, although Medicaid typically pays less than 50 percent of the cost of care.

The 1985 National Nursing Home Survey indicated that specific medical reasons for entering a nursing home are higher for the ages before eighty-five. This is another indication that elderly people select other options when there is a choice. For all ages of the elderly population, the most common medical reason for admittance is stroke. Other medical reasons include heart or circulatory problems, hip fracture, cancer, and Alzheimer's disease.

Context

Institutional care, specifically as provided by nursing homes, evolved from the almshouses of the 1600's. The first nursing homes as they are thought of today emerged in the early 1900's and were operated by private foundations. They were able to operate through the donations of philanthropists. The Social Security Act of 1935 was instrumental in the creation of more homes. As more persons had the funds to pay for care, more homes were needed. As the ability to pay for care was enhanced, with the creation of Medicare and Medicaid, there was an increase in the development of for-profit nursing homes.

The need for nursing homes increases as the population of elderly increases. According to 1990 census figures, more than 12 percent of the U.S. population was sixty-five and older. That will have increased to 13 percent by the year 2000. By 2030 it is expected that persons over sixty-five years of age will be nearly 22 percent of the population. At the early 1990's rate of 5 percent of elderly adults residing in nursing homes, the need for space and professionals will increase significantly. It has been predicted by some that the need for institutional care will change from a serious problem to a crisis because of the projected increase in the size of the elderly population. Because the need for institutional care will not disappear, and because entering a nursing home is such a traumatic event for an elderly person, more study is needed concerning the meaning of long-term care to the elderly individual. Barbara K. Haight suggests, in "Update on Research in Long-Term Care: 1984-88" (1989), the following areas for study: environment, health promotion and clinical problems, disease prevention, staff and costs, patient and family, and nursing practices.

There is a trend to cut nursing home costs by using other community facilities. Some of these alternatives to nursing homes are shared housing, boarding homes, retirement centers, congregate housing, and residential housing. In *Housing for the Elderly in 2010: Projections and Policy Options* (1989), Harold M. Katsura, Raymond J. Struyk, and Sandra J. Newman explore housing policy alternatives. These include voucher programs for renters and home owners, mortgage or equity use, and vouchers for low-income and impaired elderly people. Since lack of income to pay for care in one's own home is one major push to institutional care, such initiatives may eventually be instrumental in helping elderly people to remain independent as long as possible.

Bibliography

Aging in America: The Federal Government's Role. Washington, D.C.: Congressional Quarterly, 1989. This paperback is a synthesis of information from Congress and research concerning the prevailing views of aging.

Bee, Helen L. *The Journey of Adulthood*. New York: Macmillan, 1987. This college text provides a holistic developmental approach to adulthood. Theories of adult change are included along with topical coverage on topics such as work, stress, sex roles, and death. Contains a glossary and bibliography.

Biedenharn, Paula J., and Janice Bastlin Normoyle. "Elderly Community Residents' Reactions to the Nursing Home: An Analysis of Nursing Home-Related Beliefs." *The Gerontologist* 31 (January, 1991): 107-115. Original thesis research first reported at the Forty-first Annual Scientific Meeting of the Gerontological Society of America, 1988.

Brubaker, Timothy H. "The Long-Term Care Triad: The Elderly, Their Families, and Bureaucracies." In *Aging, Health, and Family: Long-Term Care*, edited by Timothy H. Brubaker. Newbury Park, Calif.: Sage Publications, 1987. This is one essay in a thematic collection of works by experts in the field of gerontology. Information concerning issues related to family care, community-based care, and institutional care is provided throughout the collection.

Ferrini, Armeda F., with Rebecca L. Ferrini. *Health in the Later Years*. Dubuque, Iowa: Wm. C. Brown, 1989. The emphasis of this college text is on health issues of the elderly. It provides a basic yet comprehensive foundation for studying the elderly.

Golant, Stephen M. *Housing America's Elderly: Many Possibilities/Few Choices*. Newbury Park, Calif.: Sage Publications, 1992. An examination of the strengths and weaknesses of the housing options available to older Americans. Includes references and index.

Haight, Barbara K. "Update on Research in Long-Term Care: 1984-88." In *Indices of Quality in Long-Term Care: Research and Practice*. New York: National League for Nursing, 1989. A review of the late 1980's literature related to institutional care.

Katsura, Harold M., Raymond J. Struyk, and Sandra J. Newman. *Housing for the Elderly in 2010: Projections and Policy Options*. Washington, D.C.: Urban Institute Press, 1989. A technical report on housing initiatives for the elderly.

Kayser-Jones, Jeanie. "The Environment and Quality of Care in Long-Term Care Institutions." In *Indices of Quality in Long-Term Care: Research and Practice*. New York: National League for Nursing, 1989. A comprehensive look at factors in the environment that affect the quality of nursing homes. Research statistics are given and conclusions are drawn.

May, Maurice I., Edvardas Kaminskas, and Jack Kasten, with David Allan Levine. *Managing Institutional Long-Term Care for the Elderly*. Gaithersburg, Md.: Aspen, 1991. A practitioner's book that emphasizes effective operation of institutional care. Twenty appendices plus index.

Mezey, Mathy. "Institutional Care: Caregivers and Quality." In *Indices of Quality in Long-Term Care: Research and Practice*. New York: National League for Nursing, 1989. A review of research focusing on the relationship of the nurse to quality institutional care.

Mitchel, Maria K. "Long-Term Care." In *Indices of Quality in Long-Term Care: Research and Practice*. New York: National League for Nursing, 1989. This is the introduction to a collection of essays, all concerning research on the quality of care in nursing homes. The perspective is from the health field, with emphasis on nursing.

Pieper, Hanns G. *The Nursing Home Primer*. White Hall, Va.: Betterway, 1989. A personal help book for those faced with the decision to place a loved one in institutional care. A nursing home checklist is included.

Pozgar, George D. *Long-Term Care and the Law: A Legal Guide for Health Care Professionals*. Gaithersburg, Md.: Aspen, 1992. An introduction to long-term care plus a specific layperson's guide to the law and how it applies to institutional care. Appendices and index are included.

Soldo, Beth J., and Emily M. Agree. *America's Elderly*. Washington, D.C.: Population Reference Bureau, 1988. A compilation of demographic and statistical information related to the elderly. Includes charts and graphs.

Diane Teel Miller

Cross-References

Ageism and the Ideology of Ageism, 41; Aging and Retirement, 47; The Aging Process, 53; The Elderly and the Family, 627; The Graying of America, 846; Rites of Passage and Aging, 1648; Social Gerontology, 1799; Social Security and Issues of the Elderly, 1832.

THE ELDERLY AND THE FAMILY

Type of sociology: Aging and ageism

The societal roles of older people began to change significantly in the later part of twentieth century, including their roles within the family. Most older people wish to live an independent life while maintaining deep affective bonds with their children, grandchildren, and great-grandchildren.

Principal terms

CHRONOLOGICAL AGE: age as determined by years of life, or birthdays

FAMILY OF ORIGIN: the family into which one is born or by which one is adopted

FUNCTIONAL AGE: age as determined by ability to interact with one's social, psychological, and physical environment

LIFE CYCLE (LIFE COURSE): a stereotypical description of life according to typical occurrences at particular ages

PROCREATIVE FAMILY: the family in which one's own production of children occurs

ROLE: what one does and says to be part of a group; what a group needs to be said and done by the person performing the role in order for the group to survive and grow

SOCIALIZATION: the process through which one learns the culture of one's society or group and thereby becomes a full participant in it; adopting the roles necessary to be a member of a group

Overview

A person is considered "elderly" in one of two ways: chronologically, according to how many years that person has lived, or how many birthdays have passed; and functionally, depending on how that person sees himself or herself and depending on how others see that person. Although sixty-five is chronologically the age used by many to indicate passage into the "elderly" years, local, state, and federal laws actually use a vast range of chronological markers of old age. Functional definitions of old age generally incorporate notions of "later maturity" and "old age"; the former refers to that time when one has a sense of freedom from responsibility, a deeper sense of closeness with one's spouse, less physical energy than previously, and greater susceptibility to illness. Old age, in contrast, is that period when one is physically fragile and more susceptible to death. The following discussion uses functional definitions of "elderly" while recognizing that society has various chronological markers of old age.

"Family" is another essential concept that requires definition. An essential unit of every society, its actual composition and the relationships among its members vary from culture to culture. In North America, one can discern at least two major types of family: one's family of origin, that into which one is born or by which one is adopted;

and one's procreative family, that in which one's own procreative behavior occurs. The elderly will play different roles in each type of family, and the roles within each type will differ as they age. In the family of origin, there will come a time when the adult children will be caretakers of one or both parents, when one of the elderly "children" assumes the role of convener of the family after the parents are dead, and when all of the children are elderly. In the family of procreation, spousal roles will change, as will the relationships between adult children and their elderly living parents and between adult children and a widowed parent.

More than half the older population is married and living with a spouse in an independent household: 70 percent of older men and 36 percent of older women. All evidence indicates that the vast majority of these older couples are happy and satisfied with their marriages. As couples enter later maturity, however, they find that they must make adjustments to maintain the stability and happiness of their lives. Coping with the loss of a very old parent is often one such adjustment; living with adult children in their procreative family household is another.

One of the most important adjustments, and one that has a significant effect on family life, is changing status as part of the workforce. Blue-collar workers usually retire before reaching age sixty-five. In the final quarter of the twentieth century, the retiring population of blue-collar workers was still predominantly male. If the husband is retiring and the wife has not worked outside the home during the greater part of their lives together, the family shifts identity as the husband reenters the household on a twenty-four-hour basis, requiring the wife to adjust to a new presence in the house. During this time, both spouses must redefine their roles within the family, particularly male-female roles. Many studies indicate that male-females roles are not played with the same distinctions that were made during the working years in traditional "one-breadwinner" families. As men and women begin to share general household tasks more fluidly, men must adjust to their retirement years in such households. This transition to sharing seems to happen more easily in white-collar families than in blue-collar families, perhaps because the traditional roles are typically more distinct in the latter group, but also because white-collar workers often have more choice in determining age of retirement. Sometimes in traditional families, the wife has begun work outside the house after the children left home, also easing the transition. At times, wives take on a job at the point of their husbands' retirement or shortly afterward in order to "keep the peace" and allow time away from each other. Whether abrupt or gradual, the transition marked by change in work status of either or both spouses heralds a new point in the life cycle: The couple is on its own more than ever before, since both the procreative family and the family of origin have changed significantly or disappeared. In the end, the data show that most couples who have weathered this transition feel happier as a couple than they did in middle age.

Given this successful experience of couplehood, when one member dies a remarriage often ensues. Since there are twice as many women as men over the age of sixty-five, men find it easier to remarry, but almost everyone seeks couplehood in some manner. Those who follow the traditional expression of couplehood in marriage produce a new type of family which brings together two procreative families composed of the grown children of each spouse and their own families. In consequence, a new, larger extended family is formed. In some cases, couplehood is sought outside marriage for financial reasons: One or both older persons might lose certain financial benefits if they were to remarry. In such cases, the couple might live together without telling their older children and thus live among three separate "families": the procreative families formed with the former spouses and their own, new couplehood.

Couplehood is also found in deep friendships developed between groups of women and men. In such instances, groups of men and women who gather for recreation, religion, or voluntary work may form support networks whose significance deepens beyond the ostensible reason for the group. Each person in the group has, or develops, roles necessary for the other members' survival. One, for example, may perform household repairs; another may be skilled as a financial planner; and another may be the "listener" and counselor. Such a family may in some cases form stronger bonds than those found in the families of origin or procreation.

In North America, the relationship between older parents and their adult children is usually quite good; the evidence suggests that it is a misapprehension to think otherwise. Eighty percent of the elderly have living children; about 10 percent have children aged sixty-five or older. If proximity is defined in terms of travel time rather than absolute distance, 84 percent of the elderly are within one hour of their children. There appears to be quite a bit of interaction between the parents and their older children: More than half the older children have some contact with their parents in a given twenty-four-hour period. The contact seems to be along the lines of "checking in" or "checking up" on each other when both parents are alive and living together; this contact becomes more extensive when the parents are alone, single, or ill. Often the contact results in actual time spent together: Grandparents may arrange to baby-sit their grandchildren; adult children may help the elder parents with physically demanding chores. Thus the interdependence of the procreative family's early years is translated into new roles. Only a small minority of older children give no support to their parents, and the opposite also holds true.

While both elderly spouses remain alive and healthy, they overwhelmingly prefer to live independently of their procreative families. Widow(er)hood, however, imposes new challenges on the adult children and their own procreative families as the elderly person's family relationships take yet another turn. For the remaining elderly spouse, first of all, self-identity must adjust to the death of a loved one. The success of this transition largely depends on the extent to which the widow(er)'s self-image was part of, or independent from, the dead spouse. Along with this identity crisis is a shift in role in relation to children: The elderly person not only must redefine self but also must redefine self in relation to children. Typically, widows attempt to make it on their own; if they have developed a role outside wife and mother (for example, in a church or temple, in the community, or simply in a group of friends), they are more likely to be successful. Even most women who see themselves primarily as mothers retain their independence as long as their health allows; in many cases, they do not wish to burden their children unnecessarily, and often neither the elderly mother nor the adult children wish to disrupt the way in which the adult children are rearing the grandchildren. Finally, the high ratio of elderly women to men means that there are more widows living independently, making such an arrangement both socially accepted and necessary. Consequently, the challenge for the family of the widow is often to help her establish her independence. On the other hand, widowers, because of a favorable male-female ratio in their age range, tend to remarry.

One's family of origin remains a factor in old age. About 80 percent of older people have living siblings, and many continue or reestablish their relationships with their brothers and sisters. After adult children, brothers and sisters provide the older person with a sense of family and a permanent home when he or she becomes frail. Relationships established in youth with brothers, sisters, aunts, uncles, nephews, or nieces are often renewed—and improved—during the later years as such family members acknowledge their mortality and the importance of family ties.

Applications

More Americans are sixty-five years old or older than ever before in history. That trend will continue as the baby boomers (those born between 1946 and the mid-1960's) become the senior boomers and as medical research allows boomers and non-boomers to live longer, healthier lives. Family life is therefore changing radically as well, which, in turn, is changing American culture.

Two facts in particular highlight these changes: Families now include more grandparents than ever before, and they include more great-grandparents than ever before. These grandparents and great-grandparents are, for the most part, in later maturity. They are generally healthy. They often have a significant amount of disposable income. To understand the relationship between these family members is imperative for government leaders, policy makers, educators, health care providers, and businesspersons. The number of elderly, their amount of disposable income, the amount of leisure time they possess, and their relationships to other family members are all new. Those who can develop and engage in scientific research associated with how the older families relate will provide valuable information for the future.

Research on the lives of the elderly and their families flies in the face of popular myth: Sex continues into old age; older parents do not, as a rule, live with their adult children; older parents and adult children are, however, interdependent, benefiting from each other's proximity in terms of both physical and emotional support; and new marriages occur in old age, as people continue to redefine their identities, looking forward to other family involvements. As societal change continues to occur, the elderly seek appropriate education, both to become aware of these social changes and to use their new knowledge to participate in those changes for personal purposes. Finally, both families of origin and families of procreation expand beyond the immediate parent-child relationships and even grandparent/adult child/grandchild relationships to include great-grandparent/grandparent/adult child/young child relationships.

Context

The family as a social unit changed significantly during the latter half of the twentieth century—not only because of the growing elderly population but also because of changing values and social norms. Evidence of these changes can be found in higher divorce and remarriage rates in North American society, in a high remarriage rate in old age, and in a growing variety of familial roles played by a variety of persons in a variety of family-like social units founded upon both blood ties and friendship ties. Such changes have arisen not only through new social values but also through an influx of different cultures into North America, each adding its own traditions to the plate of familial options.

A large part of this evolution, as noted, is attributable to the growing number and variety of elders who compose American society. The once static image of the family as mother-father and children is now a kaleidoscope including single-parent families, divorced-remarried families, gay families, and friendship networks. All of these models are increasingly adding elderly members to their ranks, in family roles that run the gamut from grandparent to sibling to caregiver to expert.

The undeniable fact that the elderly population is on the rise has had a significant impact on the way that older persons are perceived in a culture that in the 1960's seemed to value youth above all. Money and research go where the people are. In the past, sociologists spent much time and money on trying to understand the young; as the population ages, sociologists are focusing increasingly on the elderly and their role in society. The roles of the elderly are increasingly becoming the concerns of both researchers and the policy makers who must build the necessary strategies for dealing with these roles.

In the past, when sociologists discussed the happy elderly couple or the relationship between older children and their parents, that discussion was based on a more stable society and the role played in it by an idealized, rigid model of "the family." Sociologists do not yet know the consequences on the elderly of the "kaleidoscopic family," but as more longitudinal data are gathered, researchers will develop better models of what happens in a family as a result of the individuals within it growing older. As the former students of a youth culture reach their own senior years, they are becoming open to new insights into aging and the family—not as a process of disintegration but as a time of discovery and growth.

Bibliography

Atchley, Robert. *Social Forces and Aging*. 5th ed. Belmont, Calif.: Wadsworth, 1988. Chapter 7 provides the results of Atchley's years of research into family and older persons.

Baca Zinn, Maxine, and D. Stanley Eitzen. *Diversity in Families*. 2d ed. New York: HarperCollins, 1990. Diverse governmental policies regarding families are reviewed to show their effects on stable family structure.

Cherlin, Andrew J., and Frank F. Furstenberg, Jr. *The New American Grandparent: A Place in the Family, a Life Apart*. New York: Basic Books, 1986. A summary of the research on grandparenting with suggestions on how those currently playing the grandparent role will affect the future.

Grambs, Jean Dresden. *Women over Forty: Visions and Realities.* New York: Springer, 1989. A significant majority of the elderly are women, and any description and consideration of the elderly must deal with this fact. This book does so with sensitivity, knowledge, and challenge.

Rossi, Alice S., and Peter H. Rossi. *Of Human Bonding: Parent-Child Relations Across the Life Course.* New York: Aldine de Gruyter, 1990. To understand the family, one must understand parenting. This book provides one with insights and information to help shape that understanding.

Troll, Lillian E., Sheila Miller, and Robert Atchley. *Families in Later Life.* Belmont, Calif.: Wadsworth, 1979. An excellent summary of the various models for research and dealing with the family in later life.

Nathan R. Kollar

Cross-References

Ageism and the Ideology of Ageism, 41; Aging and Retirement, 47; The Elderly and Institutional Care, 621; The Graying of America, 846; Rites of Passage and Aging, 1648; Social Security and Issues of the Elderly, 1832.

EMBOURGEOISEMENT AND PROLETARIANIZATION

Type of sociology: Social stratification
Field of study: Basic concepts of social stratification

Embourgeoisement refers to the process whereby nonbourgeois individuals and groups become bourgeois or come to identify with the capitalist class; proletarianization is the process through which previously nonworking class groups find themselves in a position similar to those of laborers. These concepts help explain social stratification and social change in industrial capitalist societies.

Principal terms
> BOURGEOISIE: the class of capitalists who own the means of production and distribution and who hire workers for wages or a salary
> CLASS: a group of people who share a common economic relationship, common cultural beliefs, and a common ideological viewpoint
> IDEOLOGY: a belief system about the world which usually reflects and supports the interests of one segment of society over those of others
> POWER: the authoritative allocation of scarce resources; the ability to make others do as one wishes
> PROLETARIAT: the class of wage earners who, of necessity, work for the capitalists
> SOCIAL STRATIFICATION: a system in which groups are ranked hierarchically; stratification by social class is one type of stratification

Overview

The concepts of the bourgeoisie and the proletariat, particularly as they fit into a conception of social stratification and class struggle, are based on the enormously influential nineteenth century writings of Karl Marx and Friedrich Engels. Not only Marxist economists and sociologists, however, but many others as well have written extensively about these concepts and about the processes of embourgeoisement and proletarianization.

Embourgeoisement and proletarianization are two sides of a process of social change which is continuously taking place within industrial societies. Embourgeoisement occurs when a group within society which had previously been at a level of consumption and power typical of average workers finds itself above the existing norm. Although this group seldom reaches the level of power and consumption enjoyed by the bourgeoisie, or capitalist class, they begin to identify with the upper class and reject association with the average laborer. This process of embourgeoisement typically takes place when a group finds itself able to become property owners, if only on a modest scale. For example, a worker who is able to save enough to purchase an apartment building may begin to identify with the landowning bourgeoisie rather than with other workers. Workers who, because of unusually high wages, have reached a level of economic income which allows them to become commercial property owners have been referred to as an "aristocracy of labor."

The process of embourgeoisement is, therefore, economic in origin but often largely ideological in result. That is, the economic advancement which causes embourgeoisement is rooted in reality, but the shift in ideology is typically more pronounced than is warranted by the actual enhancement of power. In extreme cases, the worker begins to identify with the capitalists without there being significant material advancement. Thus, one can speak of groups which are objectively proletarian, or working class, but which have a bourgeois mentality. While social class remains an empirically definable reality, embourgeoisement often results in a change in ideology regardless of actual material changes.

On the other hand, proletarianization takes place when previously independent, or middle-class, groups find themselves reduced to the level of consumption and power of average workers. That is, groups which had formerly been self-reliant and in control of their occupations are forced to work for others for wages and lose their autonomy. As noted by the eighteenth century economist Adam Smith, in *The Wealth of Nations* (1776), as capitalist societies develop, the number of independent producers and free professionals decreases, while the number of people working for others increases.

Proletarianization may result from the shift of individuals from self-reliant occupations, such as independent small farming, to proletarian occupations, such as factory work. It may also result from a loss of control within an occupation, as when previously independent craftspeople or professionals are forced to become wage workers or employees. A lawyer, for example, unable to maintain an independent practice, might be forced to join a law corporation at which his or her practice is decided by the owners, who determine both work norms and pay level. In other words, the lawyer may practice the same type of work but now be hired (and perhaps fired) by someone else. Such individuals have lost their earlier freedom of controlling their own work and have become workers. Farmers who own the land they work are their own "bosses," for example. If they lose their land, however, they must work for someone else who will determine wages, working conditions, and so on. Even if these now landless farmers are performing the same tasks as before, they have become proletarian. Likewise, a professional, such as a doctor or lawyer, who has to work for a corporation as an employee may be said to have been proletarianized even though his or her income remains significantly above average.

The study of embourgeoisement and proletarianization places considerable significance on the way various groups either gain, or think they have gained, upward mobility or suffer a loss of social status and economic power. Use of these concepts implies that social stratification in the modern world is neither fixed nor stagnant but rather is constantly changing as society itself changes. Further, both concepts imply that a change in economic status ultimately results in a change of ideology for the affected groups and individuals. Independent farmers, craftspeople, or professionals may have a relatively conservative ideological outlook, whereas the same persons will become more critical of society if they find themselves proletarianized. Likewise, those whose situation within any society improves to the point of commercial property ownership are likely to become more conservative, or "become bourgeois" in mentality.

Both embourgeoisement and proletarianization have taken place in the United States as well as the rest of the industrialized world during the twentieth century. Groups of workers who have raised their living standards, whether through trade union activity, unique skills, or labor shortages in their field, have often adopted the attitudes of the bourgeoisie or business class. On the other side, people in many once self-reliant occupations have found themselves forced to work for large corporations, with a resulting lack of control, power, and status. One indication of this change has been the growth of trade unionism in what were previously considered nonproletarian or white-collar occupations; for example, unions have formed among physicians and university professors. Another indication is that changing voting patterns have been observed among occupational groups.

Applications

The concepts of embourgeoisement and proletarianization have allowed scholars to understand nuances of mobility between social classes and changes in ideology while explaining apparently contradictory developments. Social classes, occupational groupings, and social stratification systems are continually in a state of flux. Accordingly, the ideological predispositions of groups are constantly changing. A group whose standard of living rises (although by other standards it remains part of the working class) may begin to readjust its view of the world. People in this group may begin to act as if they were capitalists, all empirical evidence to the contrary.

This effect is often reflected in voting behavior. Traditionally working-class or labor-oriented political parties sometimes find themselves losing support among highly paid workers who prefer to view themselves as "middle class." For example, many highly skilled and highly paid auto workers in Germany have increasingly abandoned the traditional labor party, the Social Democratic Party, and voted for the conservative Christian Democratic Union. Meanwhile, groups which have suffered a reduction in status and economic power may react to proletarianization by realigning themselves toward traditional parties of the left. For example, in Sweden, teachers make up a disproportional number of the voters who support the Left Party (the Swedish Communist Party). Likewise, in the United States, the Democratic Party, which since the 1930's has been seen as the party of labor, has seen its support reduced among those better-off workers who may be said to have been embourgeoised. On the other hand, the Republican Party has lost allegiance from some traditional bases of support where proletarianization has occurred.

In the light of such patterns, social stratification may be seen as an extremely complex field of sociological investigation. The scholar must take into consideration not only the current position of any group within the social structure but also whether this group has gained or lost in social status, economic power, and political power. A group gaining in social and economic status may consider itself to be part of the capitalist class even while a group of objectively higher status may feel itself becoming proletarian. Cultural considerations also play a role; whether one owns a suburban home or lives in an urban apartment, for example, may have more influence on perceived social status than actual position within the social hierarchy.

On the whole, the social stratification system of most societies remains quite stable. Despite drastic transformations in the technological basis of modern societies, the actual economic positions of social classes seems to change slowly if at all. As the nature of work is transformed by technological innovations, however, occupations and professions change rapidly, and even a relatively small change in social status or economic wealth has the possibility to affect a group's ideology. This occurs despite the fact that changes in social position which appear significant for the individual often seem negligible for the society as a whole. The concepts of embourgeoisement and proletarianization are important in understanding not only actual changes in social status but perceived transformations as well.

Thus, to understand why so many middle-class Italians support the Party of Democratic Socialism, one must take into consideration the proletarianization of hitherto white-collar professions and the increasing economic pressure put on small business by large corporations. At the same time, the children of manual, or blue-collar, workers who now have white-collar jobs sometimes tend toward identification with the dominant class even if their actual position in the social structure is little better than that of their parents. Some scholars have pointed to the differences in work cultures to explain this development, citing the relatively individualist nature of office work as opposed to the more clearly collective norms of a factory. Yet over time, even within this white-collar labor group the process of proletarianization continues as the relative autonomy and independence once allowed is replaced by a new type of industrial discipline. Indicators of change include increased workloads as well as such policies as time limits on telephone calls, the monitoring of computer stations, and a variety of time-work restrictions which in many ways resemble the old factory model.

With the decline in the relative importance of manufacturing labor in the West and the corresponding growth of the "service" sector, the process of proletarianization will continue to increase in significance. Therefore, any analysis of social stratification will have to consider the latest changes in the nature of the workforce and the nature of work itself in order to grasp the subtleties of any given society. The shift from collectively based work to more individualistic types of work will encourage embourgeoisement to occur among specific social groupings. These two processes need not be seen as mutually exclusive. For example, as a larger number of computer workers replaces manual labor within a society, computer workers will become increasingly proletarianized, yet many former manual laborers may be involved in a process of embourgeoisement if they secure higher status and higher paying jobs than they previously held. As computer technology develops, many previously highly skilled workers will find their skills obsolete and will have to fight (and retrain) to maintain their standard of living. Hence, they will increasingly resemble the classic model of the industrial worker, yet the individual nature of their work may cause bourgeois attitudes to linger, particularly among those who see a new niche as an improvement over previous work.

Context

The concepts of embourgeoisement and proletarianization are associated with, although they are not exclusive to, Marxist sociologists. Both ideas were generated from the work of Karl Marx and Friedrich Engels during the nineteenth century. In 1882, Engels, in a famous letter to Karl Kautsky, complained that English workers viewed politics "the same as the bourgeois." In his writings, Engels argued that the capitalists had raised the wages of sections of the working class to the point where these workers "became bourgeois" in their mentality. This line of reasoning was further developed by Vladimir Ilich Lenin, who maintained that part of the profits from overseas imperialism were used to grant notably better conditions and wages to a "labor aristocracy" that consequently "deserts to the bourgeoisie."

In the 1930's, Italian Marxist Antonio Gramsci argued that embourgeoisement is primarily ideological rather than economic. After World War II, American sociologist David L. Sallach argued that embourgeoisement results from the primacy of ideological institutions within capitalist society. Many sociologists have struggled with the apparent contradiction involved in groups that are clearly part of the working class yet maintain an ideological outlook more typical to those above them.

Marx first looked at the process of proletarianization to help understand how the European working class had developed from feudal society; later he used it to explain how the working class continued to change as the economy changed. For Marx, and for those who followed his theories, proletarianization resulted from two historically ongoing developments: the separation of workers from control of the means of production and their increasing dependence on the sale of their labor power. Basing their work on this theory, many scholars have sought to examine how loss of control has transformed previously self-reliant groups into wageworkers. Kautsky, for example, saw the process of proletarianization as an unending one which would ultimately result in societies with a tiny bourgeoisie and a massive working class. This oversimplification of Marx, and Kautsky's ignoring of the role of embourgeoisement, has been criticized repeatedly and disproved by empirical sociological research, which has shown matters to be far more nuanced.

In 1974, Harry Braverman, in his *Labor and Monopoly Capital: The Degradation of Work in the Twentieth Century*, argues that new technology has increased proletarianization and has further "de-skilled" large sections of the population who are taught only the minimum they need to know to do their tasks. In a similar vein, sociologist Charles Tilly contends that the vast majority of the world's population has become working class and that "proletarianization was arguably the most far-reaching change in the quality of everyday life to occur in the modern era." Even most scholars who take a less severe view admit that the ever-changing nature of work relations in modern society make proletarianization a worthwhile concept. Still, the association with

Marxism has led some sociologists to avoid utilization of either concept as too "value laden."

Bibliography

Braverman, Harry. *Labor and Monopoly Capital: The Degradation of Work in the Twentieth Century*. New York: Monthly Review Press, 1974. Winner of the C. Wright Mills prize for critical sociology, this book remains one of the best descriptions of work and the process of proletarianization. Drawing upon literature from both management and labor sources, the author brings his theoretical viewpoints alive with numerous concrete examples and an excellent use of statistics.

Cottrell, Allin. *Social Classes in Marxist Theory*. London: Routledge & Kegan Paul, 1984. An attempt to take Marx's theories and update them in the light of twentieth century research, this title makes difficult reading but contains a number of important insights. Particularly recommended to those who wish to read a discussion of how the Marxist theory of social class can be applied to Great Britain.

Hobsbawm, Eric. "Lenin and the 'Aristocracy of Labour.'" In *Revolutionaries*. New York: New American Library, 1975. An unusually clear and penetrating analysis of the theory of embourgeoisement, especially as it was developed by Lenin in the context of his study of imperialism. Casts light on the theory of the "labor aristocracy" while presenting various sides of the debate.

Lenin, V. I. *Imperialism, the Highest Stage of Capitalism*. New York: International Publishers, 1970. In this well-known, and often overrated, work, the hypothesis is advanced that colonialism allows capitalists to bribe a section of their labor force, who thereupon become bourgeois in ideology. Written during World War I, this work suggests important concepts of embourgeoisement but lacks the more reflective depth of much of Lenin's other work.

Levine, David, ed. *Proletarianization and Family History*. Orlando, Fla.: Academic Press, 1984. Containing worthwhile articles by a number of scholars, including American sociologist Charles Tilly and Canadian historian Bryan Palmer, this volume will prove particularly valuable to advanced students of proletarianization. As is the case in anthologies, the essays cover a range of related topics; in this case, they include the social implications of proletarianization and the birth of capitalism.

Marx, Karl, and Frederick Engels. *Selected Works*. London: Lawrence & Wishart, 1968. Containing many of these men's most important works, this volume will allow the reader to delve deeper into the Marxist roots of embourgeoisement and proletarianization while providing much thought-provoking detail. The writing style and dated historical references, particularly in Marx, can be difficult at first.

Miliband, Ralph. *Divided Societies: Class Struggle in Contemporary Capitalism*. New York: Oxford University Press, 1989. While arguing that modern society cannot be understood without looking at class conflict, Miliband discusses class relations and social mobility. Social stratification in the modern world is clearly and concretely detailed throughout. An important book for anyone who wishes to understand how embourgeoisement and proletarianization operate.

Sallach, David L. "Class Domination and Ideological Hegemony." *Sociological Quarterly* 15 (Winter, 1974): 38-50. Taking the theories of Gramsci and comparing them to empirical sociological studies, this article attempts to build a model for understanding why people develop certain ideologies or worldviews. Rejecting both primarily psychological and economic models, the author argues that there are "ideological institutions" which shape thought.

William A. Pelz

Cross-References

Alienation and Work, 80; Capitalism, 191; Class Consciousness and Class Conflict, 271; Conflict Theory, 340; Marxism, 1127; Social Mobility: Analysis and Overview, 1812; Social Stratification: Analysis and Overview, 1839; Social Stratification: Marxist Perspectives, 1852.

ENDEMIC AND EPIDEMIC DISEASES

Type of sociology: Major social institutions
Field of study: Medicine

The terms "endemic" and "epidemic" are both commonly used to describe the incidence, prevalence, and distribution of disease (and diseaselike conditions) in human populations. An endemic condition is one which traditionally appears in a population and maintains a relatively high and a stable rate of incidence over time; an epidemic is a condition with a sudden onset and a rapidly increasing rate of distribution.

Principal terms

BABY BOOM: the large birth cohort of people born between 1948 and the mid-1960's whose size has created changes in American society as the baby boomers have aged

DEMOGRAPHY: the scientific study of population characteristics, distribution, and changes

PANDEMIC: an epidemic of multinational or global proportions

POPULATION: a large group, or "cohort," of people with something in common, such as sharing a physical location, year of birth, nationality, language, or personality type

SOCIAL EPIDEMIOLOGY: the scientific study of the occurrence and spread of disease, defects, or diseaselike conditions

SOCIAL PROBLEM: a condition or issue in society that is seen as harmful to specific social groups such as gender, ethnic, racial, or class groups

Overview

Epidemic and endemic diseases and social problems have been of interest to public health scientists and social scientists since the inception of each discipline. Historically, the plagues of disease and crime needed to be described and explained rationally (and, it was hoped, prevented); currently, the widespread occurrence of violence in American society requires the attention of scientists interested in lessening the impact of this increasing epidemic. Sociological approaches are also used to help people understand the nonbiological factors involved in the distribution of disease.

Epidemic and endemic disease are important topics in sociology because they both reflect and influence significant behaviors in society. According to Robert N. Wilson, in *The Sociology of Health: An Introduction* (1970), the most prominent health problems in developed societies include "a variety of chronic and degenerative ills, complemented by derangements in man's relation to his human and manmade environment." Wilson notes that these health problems are "known to depend heavily on social and psychological events that encourage or deter the onset of illness." This statement asserts the need for a scientific study of disease distribution that incorporates sociological analyses, an approach that yields insights that would otherwise remain neglected. The term "epidemic" stems from a Greek word denoting "something that is upon the population." It is commonly defined as "an unusual occurrence of a disease." The terms "epidemic" and "endemic" both imply serious disease or disease-like conditions within populations. The distinction between endemic and epidemic disease patterns encompasses two issues: first, the social, environmental, medical, demographic, cultural, economic, and biological factors which influence or cause serious diseases or social problems; and second, the distribution of such diseases or conditions within populations.

Endemic disease occurs as a result of socioeconomic, political, environmental, genetic, and cultural patterns that induce and sustain the condition. Such conditions are influenced and sustained by the lifestyles of those who are adversely affected. Consequently, endemic disease is difficult to ameliorate and is therefore more chronic (long-lasting) in nature than epidemic disease. An example of an endemic disease is chronic heart failure in the United States; this category of disease has been among the leading causes of "early" death in the United States for decades. In comparisons with other cultures, the death rate associated with heart failure has been found to be much higher in the United States than in countries such as Japan or China. Since a number of behaviors associated with the incidence of this disease are ingrained in American culture (eating red meat, maintaining high-cholesterol diets, smoking, working or living in polluted environments, and living stressful lives), it is difficult to ameliorate such conditions in the American population as opposed to Japanese or Chinese populations—which, for example, consume far less red meat. Deaths resulting from gunshot wounds show a similar pattern of extensive and persistently high rates in the United States and significantly lower rates in most other nonwarring nations. Sociologists are also concerned with the disparities in the rates of violent crime victimization, disease-related deaths, and exposure to toxic wastes among groups with different income or ethnic characteristics.

Another example of an endemic condition in contemporary American society is death induced by the excessive consumption of alcohol. First, drinking alcoholic beverages is an accepted part of American social behavior; the behavior is actually encouraged by tradition, advertising, and the behavior of role models in the mass media. Consequently, alcoholism has become an endemic disease, and the trend in alcohol-related deaths has remained high. Between 1970 and 1990, the age-adjusted death rate for alcohol-induced causes has fluctuated between 6.8 deaths per 100,000 persons in the population (1987) and 8.4 per 100,000 (1980), a difference of less than 2 persons per 100,000. In 1979, the cause-specific death rate for alcoholism was 8.2; by 1990, the rate had decreased slightly to 7.2, a difference of only 1 death per 100,000 persons. A consistent pattern of illness such as this constitutes an endemic pattern in the distribution of a particular disease.

Epidemic disease has a rapid onset, spreads quickly in a population, and requires immediate investigation and specific interventions. The interventions necessary to address acute epidemics are based on targeted surveillance of the disease within the population. Interpretation of this data allows conclusions to be reached about the meaning and causes of the changes observed. Legionnaires' disease and acquired immune deficiency syndrome (AIDS) are examples of disease epidemics that meet each of the aforementioned conditions. AIDS was introduced into the United States population by a highly contagious virus which was not found in the United States before the 1970's and was not identified until the 1980's. The rapid onset of the disease places it into the category of an epidemic condition. AIDS-related diseases are now among the leading causes of death for young African Americans. At the same time, AIDS-related deaths among gay white adolescent males have declined significantly in the United States.

Sociologists are concerned with epidemic and endemic disease patterns because such rates are indicators of behavior, well-being, and diversity within society. AIDS, for example, has been associated with sexual and other behaviors: "unprotected" sex, prostitution, homosexuality and bisexuality, and intravenous drug use (the sharing of needles). Historically, diseases such as influenza (flu) have spread as a result of specialized behaviors within populations and between individuals. One of the largest known worldwide epidemics was the influenza crisis of 1918 and 1919. Epidemics such as this, which span entire countries, are called "pandemics." During one month— October, 1918—the flu epidemic reportedly killed 196,000 people in the United States, more than twice the number of people who died of AIDS in the first ten years of that epidemic. This widespread and suddenly appearing disease was one of the most prominent epidemics in the history of medicine, public health, and the science of epidemiology. Both epidemics mentioned (acquired immune deficiency syndrome and influenza) involved diseases that manifested themselves in a short period of time, spread very rapidly within the population, and made many people seriously or fatally ill.

Applications

Specific examples of endemic disease and associated social conditions include chronic heart disease, infant mortality among working class African Americans, and unwanted teenage pregnancy. Sociological research has helped medical researchers and policy makers to understand both chronic and acute patterns of disease and social phenomena. Knowledge of sociological factors such as social class, culture, and lifestyle characteristics can help to alleviate or curtail some illnesses and other serious social problems.

Many Americans view unwanted teenage pregnancy as a pressing social problem in American society, one which shows a decline in American morals. Upon closer examination, however, it appears that teenage pregnancy has always occurred in the United States. In previous times, such pregnancies were usually addressed within the social institution of the family. Young fathers and mothers were encouraged by their culture to marry their mates, voluntarily or at the behest of the expectant mother's family. Many other cases were handled through either the physical movement of the mother-to-be from her hometown, abortion, or adoption. These cultural reactions to adolescent pregnancy have changed over the years, resulting in an apparent epidemic of teenage pregnancies.

This perception was addressed by James F. Jekel and Lorraine V. Klerman in 1979. They continued a trend in medical sociology, demography, and public health which addressed nondiseases (such as social problems) with the disease model. Jekel and Klerman discussed adolescent childbearing as a social problem that appeared endemic in the population in the same way that a disease does. While many reporters and public officials have treated adolescent pregnancy as an epidemic, the authors suggested that the true situation more closely resembled an endemic pattern. The factors which led to the increased attention given to adolescent childbearing included the fact that what actually increased during the 1970's were the increased number of teens and the proportion of live births to teenaged mothers. During this period, the American workforce saw an increase of working adult women. These women, who had previously remained outside the workforce to bear children and care for their families, began to bear fewer children during the 1970's because of their economic need or desire to work outside the home. The increase in the percentage of infants born by teenage girls was accompanied by fewer births to women between the ages of twenty and thirty-five. At the same time, live births to girls under age eighteen increased from 14 to 20 percent of total live births. The point to consider is that the number of births to these youth remained relatively constant. Therefore, teenage childbearing was an endemic rather than epidemic pattern between the 1960's and the 1970's, according to Jekel and Klerman. The authors also pointed out that while the number of children born to adolescent mothers increased, this trend should have been anticipated, since the population of girls in their teens had increased as a result of the increased number of "baby boom" teenagers during this decade: "For example, between the 1960 and 1970 census periods the population of 10-14 year olds increased 24 percent and the population of 15-19 year olds increased 45 percent."

Teenage childbearing has been a long-term, chronic condition in the American population. The rate of births to teenage girls has remained fairly constant for decades. The National Center for Health Statistics reports that between 1976 and 1988, the number of infants born to teenage mothers increased by only 81,000; there were 478,000 such births in 1976 and 559,000 in 1988. It is estimated that another 500,000 abort their unwanted pregnancies each year.

Context

The topics of epidemic and endemic disease are significant within the field of sociology because the discipline is concerned with trends, conditions, and behavior patterns that occur within large social groups (populations, societies, nations, and ethnic or cultural groups). Sociology as a distinct social science began as concerned persons applied the techniques and concepts of "science" to social conditions and social change. Auguste Comte, a French engineer and social philosopher, coined the term "sociology" around 1822 to describe the emerging specialty that would allow industrialists and politicians to pinpoint sociological factors which influence social stability ("social statics") and social change ("social dynamics"). He raised the question of how humans can explain and predict social statics and social dynamics: What causes society to remain stable (unchanged), what makes society change, and what are the implications of such changes for society? Comte sought to explain and possibly to prevent social problems by applying the techniques of science to the problems of society.

Two major factors in rapid social change during the nineteenth century were the Industrial Revolution and the French Revolution (which began in 1789). Industrialization and the subsequent influx of masses of people into the new urban centers caused widespread social problems, including the development of a new class of persons from those who were once the rural poor. Class conflict resulted in the French Revolution and other social upheavals. The first sociologists concentrated upon such social problems of the day. The prevention of disease epidemics such as the bubonic plague were also of great concern. This disease met the conditions of the aforementioned definition of an epidemic (the rapid onset and spread of a severe health problem). The plague was influenced by the technological advances made possible by science and the Industrial Revolution. Scientists such as Comte began to apply scientific techniques to the problems faced by the rapidly growing societies of the nineteenth century. Once the causes of diseases (such as poor sanitation, urban crowding, and infestations of insects carried by rodents) could be determined, preventive or curative "public health" techniques could be implemented.

The spread of serious disease and social problems is of particular interest to sociologists who study demography. Sociologists who study the organization and behavior of the health care delivery system also concern themselves with illness.

In *The Social Transformation of American Medicine* (1982), a social history of the development of the American health care delivery system, Paul Starr discussed the emergence of hospitals and the public health system. In colonial America, families and physicians (usually poorly trained) preferred to treat the sick in their own homes. Government-supported "almshouses" and public hospitals were a last resort for the poor and those without family support. "In a number of cities, public hospitals evolved out of almshouses infirmaries," Starr notes, and charity hospitals developed as "a somewhat better alternative for the more respectable poor with curable illnesses." Persons with morally condemned illnesses, such as syphilis, were excluded along with those who had a low probability of recovery. Since the hospitals were also training centers for physicians, and since hospital reputations were influenced by death (mortality) rates, these exclusions were supported by the hospital staff. Before this period, hospitals in America were known as houses of death; places where the victims of epidemics and those with incurable illness were "warehoused" until their demise.

Much of the surveillance of epidemics is controlled by the public health bureaucracy that is a formal component of federal, state, and local governments. Health departments developed after the Civil War within county and state jurisdictions; according to Starr, "cholera and yellow fever epidemics and concern about squalid living conditions of the 'dangerous classes' had stimulated the organization of citizens' sanitary or hygiene associations to clean up the cities." Although epidemics stimulated public interest, the United States did not establish formal public health agencies as rapidly as European nations. The American Public Health Association was founded in 1872 in New York. The health department there introduced a system of laboratory diagnosis and an active program of public education; in most other areas of the United States, public health services were still underdeveloped. In 1912, the federally funded U.S. Public Health Service began to conduct research on long-term (chronic) and infectious disease. World War II gave impetus to research on medical problems associated with the war (such as battle wounds, sexually transmitted diseases, and malaria).

In the future, social science and public health research will be able to help society come to grips with, and possibly control, modern epidemics such as AIDS and other sexually transmitted diseases, some of which are resistant to antibiotics. Endemic conditions such as chronic heart failure, unwanted adolescent pregnancy, and alcohol dependency require behavioral changes and changes within the social institution of the health care delivery system. The study of endemic social conditions and disease will help guide policy makers, physicians, public health officials, and the public to prevent or control endemic disease through behavior modification, therapy, technology, or treatment.

Bibliography

Alderson, Michael. *An Introduction to Epidemiology*. London: Macmillan, 1976. Alderson's introductory text provides an overview of the field of epidemiology. Provides a number of examples of the use of statistics in the field. Emphasizes methodology, sometimes at the expense of providing basic information, so the reading is occasionally challenging.

Fee, Elizabeth, and Daniel M. Fox, eds. *AIDS: The Burdens of History*. Berkeley: University of California Press, 1988. Compares the AIDS epidemic with past epidemics, attempting to show how the lessons of the past can be applied in the present. The authors note that false assumptions and generalizations result from ignorance of historical analysis.

Jekel, James F., and Lorraine V. Klerman. "Adolescent Fertility: Epidemic or Endemic Problem?" *Studies in Family Planning* 10, no. 3 (1979): 107-109. An analysis of data on adolescent childbearing trends and the response of the mass media. The authors contend that media labeling of the problem as an epidemic misrepresents the reality of the situation.

Mechanic, David. *Medical Sociology*. 2d ed. New York: Free Press, 1978. A well-written and detailed overview of the subdiscipline of medical sociology. Covers the environment, social epidemiology, identification of disease, illness behaviors, and the health care delivery system. Well-suited to a college audience.

Starr, Paul. *The Social Transformation of American Medicine*. New York: Basic Books, 1982. A social history of the development of the health care delivery system in the

United States. Provides comprehensive coverage of the evolution of the modern system dominated by physicians, bureaucracies, and corporations.

Bruce H. Wade

Cross-References

Acquired Immune Deficiency Syndrome, 8; The Germ Theory of Medicine, 839; Health and Society, 852; Medical Sociology, 1166; The Institution of Medicine, 1185; Sexually Transmitted Diseases, 1742; Social Epidemiology, 1793.

THE ENVIRONMENT AND HEALTH

Type of sociology: Major social institutions
Field of study: Medicine

The status of human health, both individually and collectively, depends directly on environmental quality. Environmental parameters that affect human health include physical, biological, social, and psychological factors. A thorough integration of these factors is necessary for better ecological and public health management.

Principal terms
ECOSYSTEM: the systematic aggregate of organism forms and interdependent physical and biochemical processes
ENVIRONMENTAL HEALTH: an integral and functional characteristic of a stable and sustainable complex natural system external to the human organism
GEOPHYSIOLOGY: the collection of cyclic and dissipative processes that govern the movements and reserves of chemical elements on a global scale
PHYSICAL ENVIRONMENT: all nonliving components of the surroundings external to the perceptive human organism
PSYCHOSOCIAL ENVIRONMENT: all mental, cultural, and interpersonal surroundings in which humans dwell and function
PUBLIC HEALTH: the collective state of well-being of a human population
SOCIAL ECOLOGY: the interactions between geographically separate human societies and between all human individuals or societies and their physical-chemical, biological, and cultural environments

Overview

The world faces a real and worsening threat to human health from changes in the global physical and ecological environment. These environmental disruptions threaten not only humans but also myriad other species that are at the brink of extinction as a result of habitat displacement and chemical contamination of aquatic, terrestrial, and atmospheric ecosystems. Direct threats to human health include the incidence of skin and systemic cancers from radiation and chemical exposures, lung diseases, immune response deficiency, and psychosocial stress.

The link between the quality of environmental sanitation and human health has long been known, and this knowledge has been directly responsible for the gains in public health management and the benefits that led to the medical revolution in the twentieth century. Simple provision of clean, disinfected water for domestic uses and efficient disposal and treatment of urban solid and liquid wastes led to the decline in the incidence of many infectious diseases with vectors in the physical or biological environment. Although John Snow demonstrated in 1855 that certain communicable diseases in humans were traceable to contaminated public water supplies, it was not until the last quarter of the twentieth century that environmental health academics, the public, and government officials all began to realize that the industrial and agricultural revolutions represented new and profound sources of danger to human health. Chemical contamination and human influences on the environment have created a state of geophysiological malfunctions. In essence, the total environment is suffering from serious health problems that have a profound effect on human health and well-being.

In their book *Critical Condition: Human Health and the Environment* (1993), Eric Chivian and coauthors describe the impact of new and critical environmental problems on human health. Health-damaging influences in the environment include global warming from fossil-fuel burning, leading to increased concentration of carbon dioxide and other "greenhouse" gases in the atmosphere; toxic and radioactive chemical pollution from commercial manufacture industries and weapons production; the hole in the atmospheric ozone layer caused by the production and worldwide use of chlorofluorocarbons for refrigeration; and a reduction in ecosystem biodiversity caused by monocultural agriculture and large-scale deforestation.

All such environmental health problems can be traced to two factors. The first factor is the increased efficiency of industrial and agricultural productivity based on the technologically enhanced ability to derive and process resources obtained from the Earth and its global ecosystem. This factor plays a larger role in the Northern Hemisphere than in the Southern Hemisphere. Increasingly, however, the effects are spread throughout the world, because of the location of previously untapped raw materials in the Southern Hemisphere and because of improved communication processes that encourage global technology transfer. The second factor often cited as responsible for environmental health problems is the exponential growth of the human population. At the end of the twentieth century, there will be an estimated six billion human beings on earth, most occupying countries with extremely limited technological resources to provide food and health-care management. Such geographical distributions of technological know-how and human populations inevitably lead to extensive social problems for all countries. Poverty, malnutrition, severe infectious diseases, and continued environmental degradation continue to plague countries in the Southern Hemisphere, while countries in the Northern Hemisphere continue to suffer psychosocial stress from unabated immigration, and undergo painful debates on the economic and environmental sustainability of current levels of industrial productivity.

In their book *Environment and Society: The Enduring Conflict* (1994), Allan Schnaiberg and Kenneth Alan Gould addressed seven widely believed myths concerning social and environmental health. These myths include the beliefs that scientific and government authorities are indeed seeking solutions to environmental problems, that economic growth is compatible with environmental protection, that recycling is the solution to waste management, that the public sector truly understands and is concerned about the severity of environmental degradation, and that education and new technology can be used to improve the quality of environmental health.

The study of linkages between geophysiological, environmental, and human health is widely recognized for its importance to the maintenance of smooth-running social infrastructures. The increasing cost of health-care provision, health insurance, and environmental remediation programs has gained the attention of health-management organizations, government agencies, economists, and industrialists alike.

Applications

Knowledge gained from the study of the link between environment and human health is applied in many ways to reduce unnecessary morbidity and mortality. Among the many approaches is environmental legislation such as the National Environmental Policy Act of 1969, the Clean Air Act of 1970, the Clean Water Act of 1977, the Resource Conservation and Recovery Act of 1976, and the Comprehensive Environmental Response, Compensation, and Liability Act of 1980. The 1970's ushered in a stream of federal regulations aimed at providing environmental protection. In total, the legislations were designed to protect human health by protecting people from exposure to degraded and contaminated environments.

Another application of knowledge gained by studying the interaction between environmental quality and human health is visible in international agreements that limit environmental pollution. Such agreements recognize the fact that environmental contamination is not limited geographically by political or national boundaries. Environmental problems such as acid rain, ocean pollution, and the hole in the ozone layer may be caused by a specific country or group of countries, but the health effects will likely be felt worldwide. Therefore, international agreements on environmental protection, typically overseen by the United Nations Environment Program (UNEP) and other international agencies, foster good social integration of health values across national boundaries. An example of such voluntary international agreements on environmental health is the 1987 signing of the Montreal Protocol by forty-three countries. The protocol called for a 30 percent reduction in the production of chlorofluorocarbons (ozone-level depleting compounds) by 1999. Other examples are the UNEP-sponsored conferences on the environment held in 1972 in Stockholm, Sweden, and in 1992 in Rio de Janeiro, Brazil. The UNEP conferences address broad environmental and human health issues that affect people around the world. Multifaceted proposals often take into consideration the economic, social, and psychological as well as ecological factors that may facilitate solutions to environmentally linked human health and welfare problems.

The results of studies focusing on the link between environmental health and human health have implications for the social aspects of urban and regional planning. The phrase "environmental racism" has been used to describe the location of facilities for environmental management (for example, hazardous waste incinerators) in low-income neighborhoods or neighborhoods inhabited by racial groups not included in the decision-making process. This phenomenon has led in some cases to the organization of self-help neighborhood watch groups that operate under the umbrella of a "nimby" ("not in my backyard") philosophy, with tremendous social and behavioral implications. The protest against facilities perceived to be environmentally hazardous is often based on reports in the popular media of potential human health effects. The public is increasingly aware of connections between specific concentrations of certain toxic chemicals in their environment and the incidence of cancers and birth defects. As a result of extensive media coverage of such public health disasters as have occurred in Love Canal in Niagara Falls, New York, and the San Joaquin Valley in California, in which serious human health problems have been traced directly to protracted toxic chemical contamination of neighboring environmental ecosystems, the public has greater awareness of such ominous potential health threats. Certainly, the siting of new facilities such as nuclear power plants, low-level radioactive waste landfills, and similar "necessary" facilities has become tremendously difficult because of public perception of potential health problems.

As more is learned about the physical environment and its accompanying eco-systems, it becomes increasingly difficult to justify disturbing the environment solely for economic or technological gains. Many nongovernmental organizations and environmental-protection groups have organized around the issue of biodiversity protection and the shrinking size of the tropical rain forests. The driving force for these groups is usually the potential pharmaceutical benefit that may be derived from the many uncataloged plant, animal, and microbial species unique to these forests, many of which are threatened with extinction through loss of habitat. Many people see such environmental losses as having direct effects on human health because of the loss of potential remedies to ailments such as cancer and acquired immune deficiency syndrome (AIDS). Society certainly longs for cures to these human diseases, and if environmental protection is necessary for preserving potential curative agents, environmental protection will rank high in the priorities of many political and social institutions. Political institutions have begun paying serious attention to environmental issues, as evidenced by the campaign rhetoric in the 1988 and 1992 U.S. presidential elections.

Scientific analysis of environmental health and the implications for human well-being have led directly to the earmarking of a large fiscal budget for the restoration of damaged environments. It has been estimated that a minimum of $30 billion will be needed to remediate contaminated environments included on the prioritized list assembled by the U.S. Environmental Protection Agency (EPA). This huge amount of money is earmarked mainly for technical remediation. The cost of supporting social infrastructures, including litigation, insurance, and health care benefits, has not been fully estimated. In the first ten years of implementation of the U.S. "Superfund" legislation, about $10 billion was spent, with less than 5 percent of the designated sites completely remediated. Most of the money was spent on fault-finding administrative functions. Awareness of the human health implications of polluted environments has led to a flurry of research to find cheap and innovative technologies for detoxifying contaminated ecosystems and to develop improved models for testing the toxicity of chemicals to humans and to the ecosystem.

Psychosocial analysis of environmental contribution to human health is also applied to the design of health-restoring environments such as theme parks and resorts. As the built environment increasingly encroaches on the natural landscape, researchers are beginning to reevaluate the benefits of open spaces, wooded areas, and natural running waters on human psychological well-being. In essence, the application of studies of the environment and human health is not limited simply to the negative impacts that a contaminated environment might have on human health, but also focuses on the intrinsic value of pristine environments in maintaining both physical and psychosocial health in asymptomatic individuals.

Context

The study of the human health dimensions of global environmental change requires a multidisciplinary analytical and interpretive approach. Before the 1960's, sociologists interested in the environment and health operated primarily from the point of view of human response to natural disasters; however, changes in global environmental systems can hardly be defined as natural disasters, because the origins of such changes and the repercussions for human health can be placed squarely on deliberate industrial and economic developments. Because sociology involves the systematic investigation of the behavioral processes of individuals, groups, and institutions, solutions to the problems of environmental degradation and public health crises demand the attention of sociologists in collaboration with physical and natural scientists. Perhaps the first authoritative integration of sociological principles within the context of human dimensions in environmental change is to be found in *Global Environmental Change: Understanding the Human Dimensions* (1992), edited by Paul Stern, Oran Young, and Daniel Druckman. The book represents the collaborative effort of two important committees of the National Research Council, the Committee on the Human Dimensions of Global Change and the Commission on the Behavioral and Social Sciences and Education.

The integration of the social and natural sciences in response to health-related aspects of environmental change facilitates deep solutions to behavioral problems impacting consumer tastes and industrial production. If a large proportion of the blame for environmental degradation is attributed to industrial pollution, permanent solutions must reside in manipulating supply-and-demand cycles that provide incentives for industrial practices that exploit irreplaceable natural resources and generate unmanageable quantities of hazardous wastes. Sociologists must begin to propose and test theories for their utility in the design of a justifiable postindustrial social order.

Sociologists are involved with solutions involving public participation in disincentives, such as the so-called green tax on products that endanger environmental and human health systems. In addition, the international nature of environmental issues puts pressure on sociologists to understand multicultural dimensions of the behavioral modifications needed to tackle environmental and health care issues. For example, incentives concerning product recycling or pesticide application that work for a social community of industrialists and consumers in California may need to be redesigned for social groups responsible for deforestation in South America or for pesticide-induced fishing in sub-Saharan Africa.

In addition to the challenges posed to sociologists by the multicultural and institutional dimensions of environmental health issues, there are traditional academic directions involving social relationships and human health that are being expanded to include the impacts of environmental and health conditions. Because human beings live in an elaborate system of social relationships, it is important to consider the broader social ramifications of environmental health problems. Damage to the physical environment may seriously undermine the functioning of important social structures that contribute to mental health and well-being. In Southern California, for example, carpooling and even the postponement of social activities involving transportation are strongly encouraged by government authorities on days in which atmospheric smog is especially bad. People suffering from lung diseases are advised to stay home to prevent further aggravation of health situations by atmospheric chemical pollutants. Suburban children are prohibited from wading or swimming in toxic chemical contaminated streams on hot summer days. The effects of such environmentally induced restrictions on social relationships and social activities have only begun to be studied, but the rewards of intensifying such social-ecological investigations may be substantial.

Bibliography

Chivian, Eric, et al. *Critical Condition: Human Health and the Environment.* Cambridge, Mass.: MIT Press, 1993. Presents an authoritative accumulation of medical information on the effects of environmental degradation, population growth, and war on human health.

Hartig, Terry, Marlis Mang, and Gary W. Evans. "Restorative Effects of Natural Environment Experiences." *Environment and Behavior* 23 (January 1, 1991): 3-26. An important contribution from seminal researchers on the topic of restorative environments and psychological stress. A persuasive argument for environmental conservation not simply for its own sake but also for the invaluable and direct benefits to human health.

House, James S., Karl Landis, and Debra Umberson. "Social Relationships and Health." *Science* 241 (July 29, 1988): 540-545. The best source of concise information and references on how an individual's social relationships affect health. In the present context, environmental degradations may limit social interactions, which may in turn cause health problems independent of those attributable to the impacts of unhealthy environmental systems.

Kassiola, Joel Jay. *The Death of Industrial Civilization.* Albany: State University of New York Press, 1990. A valuable source of information on the sources of social transformation relevant to environmental effects of the Western industrial revolution. Also provides guidelines for building a postindustrial civilization social order.

Schnaiberg, Allan, and Kenneth Alan Gould. *Environment and Society: The Enduring Conflict.* New York: St. Martin's Press, 1994. The authors present a critical look at the popular myths, conjectures, and opinions on social-ecological aspects of environmental problems. They present alternative ideas to mainstream approaches for tackling environmental issues.

Stern, Paul C., Oran R. Young, and Daniel Druckman, eds. *Global Environmental Change: Understanding the Human Dimensions.* Washington, D.C.: National Academy Press, 1992. This excellent collection of chapters by experts in social and natural sciences emphasizes the human cause and sociological solutions to the problems of global environmental change. The final sections outline areas for new research and identify the types of data that will be needed for sociologically based solutions to global environmental change.

Stokols, Daniel. "Establishing and Maintaining Healthy Environments: Towards a Social Ecology of Health Promotion." *American Psychologist* 47 (January 1, 1992): 6-22. A detailed social-ecological perspective on the question of how to promote healthy environments within culturally diverse social and physical institutions. Of special interest to those pursuing the historical background of health promotion.

Switzer, Jacqueline Vaughn. *Environmental Politics: Domestic and Global Dimensions.* New York: St. Martin's Press, 1994. An important contribution to the political implications of social and natural investigations of global environmental change. Although health effects are addressed only superficially, the book discusses the political underpinnings of policy formulations that influence industrial practices and environmental protection.

O. A. Ogunseitan

Cross-References

Demographic Factors and Social Change, 492; Endemic and Epidemic Diseases, 640; The Environment and Social Change, 654; The Germ Theory of Medicine, 839; Health Care and Gender, 858; Medical versus Social Models of Illness, 1172; Social Change: Sources of Change, 1786; Social Epidemiology, 1793.

THE ENVIRONMENT AND SOCIAL CHANGE

Type of sociology: Social change
Field of study: Sources of social change

Social institutions coevolve with human perceptions of the natural environment. Attitudes and behaviors toward the environment have changed from reverence to indifference to control and finally to exploitation. These attitudes and behaviors accelerate technological innovations, thereby precipitating social change. Understanding the environmental stimuli for social change can help guide policy on sustainable development.

Principal terms

GLOBAL ENVIRONMENTAL CHANGE: measurable changes through time in the independent composition of and interactions between the planetary compartments of atmosphere, hydrosphere, geosphere, and biosphere

GLOBAL VILLAGE: a concept of the interconnectedness of human societies, under which social and environmental policies of one community may have far-reaching effects on distant communities

SOCIAL ECOLOGY: synecology, or the study of interactions between individuals or groups in a society, between spatially isolated societies, and between social systems and the natural environment .

SOCIOMETRICS: the quantitative analysis of social parameters indicative of social change

SUSTAINABLE SOCIETY: a social population in steady state with respect to population density, resource requirements, waste recycle, and quality of life

Overview

Social organization and policies reflect the extent of human knowledge and understanding of the physical, chemical, and biological environments. These environments are collectively referred to as nature, or the natural environment, although it is frequently argued that the distinction between the artificial (built) and the natural is invalid because humans are indeed part of nature. Sometimes social change in response to knowledge of nature can be subtle and prolonged. For example, the discovery that the earth is spherical and therefore finite, as opposed to flat with undefined boundaries, deeply influenced the formulation and implementation of socioeconomic policies during the establishment of capitalist and colonial-expansionist Western civilization. At other times, discoveries about nature can have dramatic, sudden, and irreversible consequences for society. The discovery of nuclear fission by theoretical physicists, for example, which eventually led to the design and use of atomic bombs, greatly influenced all social, political, and economic policies in the world during the latter half of the twentieth century.

The two examples given above also illustrate two different processes by which environmental perception influences social change. The first is through modifications in existing social policy, represented by the market economy and by the mobilization of social populations through official incentives, legal institutions, or personal inducements. The second process by which environmental knowledge influences social change is through technological innovations, as in the case of nuclear weapons or the discovery of large underground petrochemical reservoirs, which enabled the development of automobiles.

Social changes that occur through policy and cultural modifications frequently arise through knowledge of environmental systems that are initially presumed immutable (such as the knowledge that humans inhabit a spatially finite planet), uncontrollable environmental events (such as the knowledge of heredity and evolution through natural environmental selection), or, more commonly, knowledge that enables the prediction of events, such as storms. On the other hand, social changes that occur through technological innovations typically arise during periods of extreme confidence by human societies, expressed through scientific capabilities, that they can control and exploit the natural environment. The Industrial Revolution of the nineteenth century, with all its technical and social ramifications, is an example of the latter, whereas the political and economic revolution that preceded the Industrial Revolution in Western civilization can be attributed in part, through increased travel and earth circumnavigation, to the former.

By the late twentieth century, a new type of environmental knowledge had begun to accumulate rapidly and to influence social change. The new development has been called "environmental activism," the initiation of which is often credited to Rachel Carson because of her trailblazing book *Silent Spring* (1962). Since its publication, a social awareness of detrimental environmental consequences of the Industrial Revolution has grown steadily. The new social awareness of environmental degradation has led to restrictions on the use of many chemicals, to the formulation of new environmental policies and regulations by political institutions, and, in the United States, to the establishment of the highly visible Environmental Protection Agency (EPA). Clearly, political and cultural history has been influenced dramatically since the early 1960's.

Since the early 1970's, scientific data have been made public concerning the increase in the concentration of carbon dioxide in the atmosphere, attributable at least in part to the burning of fossil fuels such as coal, natural gas, and petroleum. This condition, it is theorized, will eventually lead to increased global temperatures (global warming) and ultimately to floods, changes in weather patterns, and the submergence of coastal cities worldwide. Scientific data have also been made public concerning the accumulation in the upper atmosphere of ozone-depleting chemicals such as chlorofluorocarbons used for refrigeration, air conditioning, and spray-can propellant. The depletion of the ozone layer will presumably have serious health consequences for all societies in the global village. Similarly, data have been made public about depletion of biological diversity through human-caused extinction of species, acidic rainfall, and toxic chemical residues in all sorts of natural environmental systems. In certain cases, whole communities of people have been evacuated from their homes because of chemical or radiation contamination of their environment.

All these events have cumulative, and sometimes unpredictable, impacts on the direction of social change. In the 1980's, the number of organizations and groups concerned about environmental issues increased significantly, and confrontational environmental activism increased. Activist movements with an environmental focus range from global organizations such as Greenpeace International to local groups simply trying to keep environmentally detrimental facilities from being built in their areas. Social scientists have begun quantitative analyses of the impacts and consequences of environmental change on the community, city, national, and international levels.

Applications

The development of hypotheses regarding the interaction between societies and their environment has given credence to social-ecological, or synecological, approaches to the study of human societies in relation to the natural environment. Such hypotheses also aid in the formulation of proposals to remedy dangerous trends such as increasing global population densities, environmental pollution, biodiversity depletion, and excessive societal dependence on finite resources such as fossil fuels. Predictive models can also be built around sociometric parameters (including individual or community attitudes toward resource recycling, birth control, and environmental education) to illuminate future social change. In particular, changes involving behavioral patterns and "convenience sacrifices," such as carpooling for fuel conservation, can be monitored.

Because of developments in communications technology, the concept of the global village has been reinforced. Satellites orbiting the earth make the detection and reporting of environmental disturbances such as rainforest fires, desertification, and ozone layer depletion a worldwide activity. Already, significant changes have occurred in the agricultural practices of people in South America, with attempts to circumvent the detection of slash-and-burn farming practices by satellite. The late twentieth century witnessed a rift between societies in developed countries of the Northern Hemisphere, who still have the largest appetite for environmental resources (and have the means to monitor environmental degradation), and societies in the less technologically developed countries of the Southern Hemisphere, where the majority of material resources and biological diversity are located. Relatively poor developing nations are being told by nations that have already industrialized that they should begin following strict environmental standards. These developing nations argue that the industrialized countries were able to develop their economies unfettered by expensive conservation and environmental controls and that they should be able to as well. In this controversy, the needs of social development, economic prosperity, and environmental conservation are in conflict. In 1992, this rift between rich and poor nations caused divisions at the first international conference on the environment, the United Nations Conference on Environment and Development (UNCED), held in Rio de Janeiro, Brazil. Mediating such disputes requires professionals aware of the principles of social ecology, with its growing understanding of the reciprocal interactions between the environment and social change.

Studies of the interaction between the environment and social change are also important in mediating the various conflicts that arise between environmental activists, industries, multinational corporations, and government agencies. These conflicts have generated considerable litigation and numerous campaigns. Each side often cites scientific data from different (or sometimes the same) sources to support their points of view. This state of affairs can be attributed not only to a lack of consensus in the scientific community but also to the premature level of research in modeling and interpreting the social consequences of changes in the physical and ecological environments that support human civilizations.

Many technological developments that affect the way people view the earth as a whole have come from space research performed by the National Aeronautics and Space Administration (NASA) and its European and Russian counterparts. For example, the startling images of the earth sent back from satellites, manned flights, and space probes have reinforced the concept of the global village and of the earth as a fragile planet. These images caught the popular imagination and have strong potential for causing changes in attitudes.

Interest has increased, for example, among the general population in international institutions such as the United Nations Environment Program (UNEP) that are able to tackle environmental problems on a global basis. Nongovernmental organizations (NGOs) working toward environmental goals have proliferated, and many seek an international mandate on the environment and the various problems attributable to an unsustainably high appetite for resources. They decry the lack of an adequate environmental ethic among the world's political and economic institutions. This pressure was integral in the convening of the 1992 United Nations environmental conference in Brazil.

Finally, knowledge of how the environment and forces of social change interact can be used (and, in fact, must be used) to integrate societal issues that have been separated through many years of customary practice. For example, the study of the economies of nations and the study of ecology have long been their own discrete fields; however, in the 1980's it was realized by many that these fields can no longer be so strictly compartmentalized. In the United States, President Bill Clinton tried to integrate these two compartments in 1993 by proposing a "green tax" on environmentally sensitive resources such as gasoline. Social responses to the green tax proposal have been divided. Numerous interpretations of the consequences of such taxation policies have been presented. The situation clearly illustrates the necessity for conducting social science research on environmental science issues related to public perception and cooperation with remedial social policies proposed by government agencies.

Context

Social scientists have long studied social change through the historical analysis of previous civilizations. The interdisciplinary nature of studies on society-environment interactions, however, necessitates a new scheme of research analysis. More sociologists are beginning to understand the concepts of planetary and environmental science, while planetary and environmental scientists are cultivating an appreciation for understanding the social implications of their findings.

Scientific theories, investigations, and discoveries always occur in a social context. Therefore, the types of questions asked by scientists investigating environmental phenomena reflect the prevalent sociological conditions and pressures at the time and place in which the researches are proposed and pursued. One of the most provocative theories in environmental science toward the close of the twentieth century is that referred to as the Gaia hypothesis, initially formulated by British chemist James Lovelock and supported by American microbiologist Lynn Margulis. The Gaia hypothesis, perhaps representing the ultimate hypothesis in environmental synthesis, proposes a metaphorical concept of the earth as an individual living entity with holistic qualities. The hypothesis suggests that the "behavior" of the whole planet cannot be easily explained by the independent investigation of the characteristics of the various components, including the geosphere, hydrosphere, atmosphere, biosphere, and the sociosphere. The earth environment is seen as a self-regulating and evolving system in which the only significant input-output couple is energy and other radiation from the cosmosphere (in particular, the sun). Because of the myriad feedback processes that characterize the self-regulating property of the earth, the Gaia hypothesis reinforces the global village concept and expands it to include the whole biosphere. The implications of the Gaia hypothesis for social change depend on its verification or refutation through scientific methods, but it is cited in arguments made by both environmental activists and capitalist entrepreneurs. Clearly, there have already been some social consequences of the holistic view of the earth environment.

Environmental sources of social change are best managed through collaborative efforts of social and natural scientists. Perhaps the first such collaboration occurred in 1970, at the International Joint Conference on Environment and Society in Transition, which took place in New York. The proceedings of that conference, edited by Peter Albertson and Margery Barnett and published as *Managing the Planet* (1972), defined the fundamental parameters involved in the social consequences of environmental change. It was apparent that a situation could develop under which sensitive dependence on initial conditions could make a reversal of social policies difficult, if not impossible. Environmental degradation could then be irreversible.

Following the 1970 conference, analytical approaches to monitoring social responses to global environmental change became popular. Such analytical approaches diverged from the initially important, but simplistic, warning cries sounded by socially conscious natural scientists. The emergency of sociological research dealing with environmental change ushered in a wave of recommended solutions, some of which called for implementation without much knowledge of their potential for success.

Several sociobiologists, including Edward O. Wilson and Paul Ehrlich, developed models based on well-studied populations of other species, and they proposed solutions involving social policy modifications, based on their models. Norman Myers, in his work during the 1980's and early 1990's, developed conceptual frameworks for integrating social research with rapidly evolving environmental change.

Clearly, two issues revolving around environment and social change require the immediate attention of sociologists researching this area. The first is the increasing population growth in developing countries, with its inevitable consequences for resource allocation and increased strain on the natural environment. Stemming the exponential growth rate of the earth's human population can only be achieved through interdisciplinary and international collaboration. The social ecologist occupies a central position in such collaborations. The second issue concerns decreasing the appetite of industrialized countries for nonreplenishable environmental resources such as fossil fuels and reducing the atmospheric emissions that result from their use. Again, the solutions will require interdisciplinary effort guided by the principles of social ecology.

Bibliography

Carson, Rachel. *Silent Spring*. Cambridge, Mass.: Riverside Press, 1962. This book is credited with initiating environmental consciousness in the social population and therefore of starting environmental activism. Still as relevant as it was when initially published.

Hardin, Garrett. *Filters Against Folly*. New York: Viking, 1985. One of the many fascinating books written by Hardin on human ecology in a social and environmental context. He presents three "filters against folly" in the new age of environmental consciousness: the numerate filter, the literate filter, and the ecolate filter.

Harvey, Brian, and John D. Hallett. *Environment and Society: An Introductory Analysis*. London: Macmillan, 1977. An excellent introductory text on environmental analysis and social design. The examples are dated but are still useful in coordinating social ecological research.

International Joint Conference on Environment and Society in Transition, New York, 1970. *Managing the Planet*. Edited by Peter Albertson and Margery Barnett. Englewood Cliffs, N.J.: Prentice-Hall, 1972. This is an excellent selection of articles from an international conference on environment and society that took place in New York in 1970. It is a dated, but valuable, introduction to the historical development of the involvement of sociologists in contemporary environmental issues.

Lovelock, James. *The Ages of Gaia: A Biography of Our Living Earth*. New York: W. W. Norton, 1988. An excellent introduction to the Gaia hypothesis and how the earth influences social changes, including established social institutions, the future, and religion.

Mannion, Antoinette M. *Global Environmental Change: A Natural and Cultural Environmental History*. New York: John Wiley & Sons, 1991. Presents a social history of environmental change and of how changes in social institutions have managed to buffer the effects of environmental variations. One of the first books to appear on this interdisciplinary subject.

Myers, Norman. *The Environmental Consequences for the European Community of Population Factors Worldwide and Within the Community*. Brussels, Belgium: European Commission, 1992. Wide in its geographical focus, this book identifies some of the key players in international consequences of global environmental change, in particular, those relating to population growth and diminishing environmental resources.

Stern, Paul C., Oran R. Young, and Daniel Druckman, eds. *Global Environmental Change: Understanding the Human Dimensions*. Washington, D.C.: National Academy Press, 1992. A very important book, written by authors picked by the National Research Council. Detailed presentation of various environmental topics with an interdisciplinary focus.

O. A. Ogunseitan

Cross-References

EQUAL EDUCATIONAL OPPORTUNITY

Type of sociology: Major social institutions
Field of study: Education

"Equal educational opportunity" refers to the right of everyone to receive an education. It cannot truly guarantee that everyone will receive an equal education or even a quality education. The primary struggle in education in the twentieth century can be characterized as a struggle for equal educational opportunity.

Principal terms

COMPENSATORY EDUCATION: educational programs and experiences designed to help overcome the economic disadvantages and the cultural dissimilarities students may bring to school

DE FACTO SEGREGATION: segregation, sometimes unintentional, that typically results from residential segregation

DE JURE SEGREGATION: mandated by law; historically referred to as "Jim Crow" segregation

DESEGREGATION: the elimination of laws or statutes restricting the rights of specific groups to housing and public facilities, especially schools

EQUALITY OF OPPORTUNITY: the condition under which everyone in a society has the same chance to enter any occupation or social class

IDEOLOGY: a complex system of beliefs that attempts to explain or justify an existing or potential social arrangement

Overview

Equality of opportunity has historically been one of the linchpins of American society. It is an ideology that implies that everyone is afforded the same opportunity to achieve social, political, and economic success. Sociologist Ian Robertson explains this situation through what he describes as life chances: Everyone has the same chance to secure the scarce resources in society which lead to wealth, power, and prestige. Equality of opportunity, ideally, should be applicable to everyone regardless of race, sex, or socioeconomic status. Accordingly, wealth, power, and prestige should be gained through initiative, effort, and ability. Factors other than initiative, effort, and ability often influence the likelihood of gaining a greater or lesser share of the scarce resources in society. One way to overcome such inequities is to equalize everyone's chances. Historically, the preferred way to equalize life chances is through equalizing educational opportunity.

Equal educational opportunity has come to be accepted as a precursor to equality of opportunity. It is viewed as a means of ensuring equal competition in the labor market. Some advantages that certain groups have cannot be eliminated, but inequities in educational opportunities generally can be eliminated. Education, as a result, has come to be viewed as the great equalizer in American society.

Americans have long believed that schools could solve most social problems. They were used to Americanize the immigrants during the latter part of the nineteenth century and the early part of the twentieth century. Schools were viewed as the most appropriate institution for fighting childhood diseases and combating the advantage that the Soviets had in aerospace technology during the 1950's. During the 1960's, schools were the point of entry into fighting the "War on Poverty." In the 1970's, schools were seen as instruments in solving the problem of unemployment. Schools, in the 1980's, were perceived as instruments to help the United States increase its competitiveness in global markets. Essentially, in each decade since World War II the schools have been expected to solve one or more social problems. Above all, schools have been expected to provide equal educational opportunity.

"Equal educational opportunity" has been assigned a variety of meanings by a number of educational scholars. It is complex; its meaning often shifts, depending on the context in which it is used. According to Charles A. Tesconi, Jr., and Emanuel Hurwitz, Jr., in their book *Education for Whom? The Question of Equal Educational Opportunity* (1974), "equal educational opportunity" does not describe a state of affairs but suggests what ought to be—what should be, or what is desirable. Joel Spring, in *American Education: An Introduction to Social and Political Aspects* (1989), contends that equal educational opportunity cannot be achieved. The best that can be offered is the opportunity to *an* education. Factors such as intellectual ability, social class, and property value within specific school districts all affect access to education and the quality of education received. Consequently, the argument persists that the only way to approximate equal educational opportunity is to equalize educational "input": Equalization in access, curricula, facilities, staff, administration, and management must be approximated across schools. Conversely, if some schools provide significantly less in terms of facilities, staff, or curricular offerings, students attending such schools do not receive equal educational opportunity. These issues have prompted litigation, by poor school districts in many areas of the United States, which challenges traditional methods of financing schools. The assumption is that equalizing funding will help foster greater equal educational opportunity.

A different approach emphasizes educational "output," which is at odds with educational "input." Proponents of this approach hold that equal educational opportunity must be measured by how well students demonstrate achievement in school. Such a position maintains that whatever mechanisms (resources, staffs, or facilities) are necessary to assist primarily lower-income and minority students to achieve should be utilized in the effort to equalize educational opportunity. There is a prescriptive function to the notion of educational output. Educational output arguably could be viewed as the approach upon which the compensatory programs and legislation of the 1960's and 1970's were premised, including the Vocational Education Act of 1963, the Civil Rights Act of 1964, the Economic Opportunity Act of 1964, the 1965 revision of the National Defense Education Act, the Elementary and Secondary Education Act of 1965, Public Law 93-380 of 1974, and Public Law 94-142 of 1975.

Applications

The concept of equal educational opportunity was the basis upon which African Americans, through the National Association for the Advancement of Colored People (NAACP), were able to argue successfully before the Supreme Court (*Brown v. Board of Education of Topeka, Kansas*, 1954) to end the system of segregated schools in the South. The Supreme Court concluded in this landmark decision that the "separate but equal" doctrine established in *Plessy v. Ferguson* (1896) was "inherently unequal" and therefore unacceptable. The Supreme Court affirmed that racially identifiable African American schools did not provide equal educational opportunity. Chief Justice Earl Warren argued in the unanimous opinion of the Supreme Court that to separate black children from white children solely on the basis of race not only was unconstitutional discrimination but could generate a feeling of inferiority as well—one that might affect the hearts and minds of black children in ways unlikely ever to be undone. While the implementation of the mandate to desegregate the public schools in the South was delayed (in some instances by more than sixteen years), de jure segregation was constitutionally ended with the *Brown* decision. Still, desegregation of the public schools was only the first step in the effort to achieve equal educational opportunity for all.

Segregated schools were viewed as responsible not only for the disparity in facilities, the lower level of curricular offerings, and the overall lower qualifications of school personnel which were characteristic of black schools but also for the disparities in academic achievement between black and white students. Such beliefs contributed to an already growing body of research suggesting that minority students were culturally disadvantaged, or culturally deprived. Investigation into the beliefs and causes of the lower academic achievement of minorities (especially on standardized and IQ tests) became known as "deficit theory" research and functioned as the driving force behind many of the compensatory education programs of the 1960's and 1970's.

Many of the strategies suggested for remedying low academic achievement by African Americans (and poor students in general) were premised on deficit theory. Deficit theory inferred that the child, the family, or the culture of the child (which was much more palatable) made that child socially and intellectually unprepared for success in school. Arthur K. Spears, in "Institutionalized Racism and the Education of Blacks" (in *Readings on Equal Education*, 1984), later suggested that deficit theory was, in practice, more damaging than helpful because it failed to focus attention on the structural problems in public education. Nevertheless, much of the educational and social policy during the 1960's and 1970's looked to deficit theory to help explain educational, social, economic, and even political inequality. Beginning in the 1960's, educational policy began to address the perceived deficiencies of specific populations through compensatory education and early intervention programs.

One of the principal components of the 1964 Civil Rights Act was a call for the investigation into the suspected racial inequalities in educational opportunities. Researchers led by James Coleman collected data from approximately sixty thousand teachers and approximately five hundred seventy thousand students. The research findings suggested that social class background accounted for the variation in black and white academic achievement. Given that a significantly greater proportion of African Americans come from lower-class backgrounds than do whites, this fact was proposed as the rationale for their lower academic achievement. Based on Coleman's research, many social scientists and educators began to suggest that it was not minorities themselves that were intellectually deficient, as some earlier scientists had argued, but that these groups suffered from "cultural deprivation." It was their homes, families, neighborhoods, and in general their culture that made them disadvantaged. The solution proffered by some social reformers was early intervention programs and compensatory education. Early intervention programs, it was argued, would give disadvantaged youth a "head start" in preparation to enter school. Such programs would provide the proper cultural exposure and the intellectual stimulation missing from the child's normal environment. Compensatory education would provide the remediation (of skills and knowledge) for students already in school.

The Coleman Report (*Equality of Educational Opportunity*, 1966), along with liberal advocates (in and out of education), had a tremendous impact on U.S. education policy. President Lyndon B. Johnson initiated one of the most comprehensive domestic campaigns in U.S. history to eradicate poverty. Referred to as the War on Poverty, it was proclaimed to end poverty and inequality by destroying the "cycle of poverty" that tended to entrap the poor, generation after generation. Poor housing, inadequate health care, poor diet, and inequality of educational opportunity were thought to contribute to the cycle of poverty. Education was, by far it was thought, the most critical component in the cycle. If a link in the cycle were ever to be broken, it would best be accomplished through education.

Most of the educational programs created as a result of the War on Poverty were unsuccessful. Some proponents argued that inadequate funding and mismanagement were the reasons the programs failed to live up to expectations. A number of opponents argued that the programs were ill-conceived and were doomed to failure because they could not change the home environment of the child. One program, however—Head Start—did prove to be somewhat successful and has continued to assist low-income, preelementary youth in preparation for school.

Context

Whenever the issue of equal educational opportunity is debated, it usually includes a discourse on the 1954 *Brown v. Board of Education* decision and the subsequent struggle for civil rights. The *Brown* decision looms as the most important litigation of the twentieth century involving the issue of equal educational opportunity. Yet, equal educational opportunity is not an issue born of the twentieth century. Some educational historians maintain that equal educational opportunity was the major impetus behind the "common school" movement of the nineteenth century. From approximately 1812 to the beginning of the Civil War in 1861, the issue of equal educational opportunity was viewed as a basic right by many Americans. A belief in the equality of all citizens suggested that education should be available to every citizen. Common-school advocates such as Horace Mann, Henry Barnard, and James Carter helped establish universal free public education through their support of the common-school movement.

Two important issues involving equal educational opportunity occurred prior to the turn of the century: the drive to Americanize the growing immigrant population and the historic decision in *Plessy v. Ferguson* of 1896. The Americanization effort was motivated not only by a fear of the immigrant population, of the foreign cultures they represented, and their presumably questionable loyalty to the United States; Americanization was also perceived as the most obvious route to equality and social integration. The Supreme Court decision in *Plessy v. Ferguson* had the impact of establishing social and educational policy throughout the South for the next fifty-eight years. It established the "separate but equal" doctrine that permitted de jure segregation in public facilities.

The 1954 *Brown* decision overturned *Plessy*. The Supreme Court concluded in *Brown* that the *Plessy* decision, when applied to education, denied equal educational opportunity to African American children. In overturning the "separate but equal" doctrine, the Supreme Court indicated that it was attempting to establish some measure of equal educational opportunity. To continue to allow the public schools in the South to operate "dual" education systems, solely on the basis of race, was judged a violation of the Constitution. Interestingly, the Constitution was not amended in any way to account for the different conclusions reached in *Plessy* (1896) and in *Brown* (1954). The social and political climates, along with the social disposition of the justices, in part, contributed to the discrepant decisions.

The social and political climates also contributed to the rate of desegregation in the South. From 1954 to 1968, the degree of desegregation throughout the South was negligible. The mandate to desegregate "with all deliberate speed" handed down by the Supreme Court (1955) was ignored in some states and outright rejected in some others. Many Southern school districts delayed and obstructed federal decrees to desegregate for more than ten years.

Prior to the passage of the 1964 Civil Rights Act and the enactment of the 1965 Elementary and Secondary Education Act (ESEA), the federal government actually had very little power to enforce integration of Southern schools. The use of federal troops to enforce desegregation (which occurred in Little Rock, Arkansas, in 1957) was not a strategy that could be repeated for all the defiant school districts throughout the South. The denial of federal funds (through Title I of the 1964 Civil Rights Act and the ESEA) provided the federal courts with the power to force resistant Southern school districts to desegregate. Nevertheless, the process of desegregation was a slow and painful one. It became even more problematic when busing was chosen as a primary strategy to help integrate Southern schools.

Busing became almost as controversial as desegregation. Tesconi and Hurwitz (1974) argue that "anti-busing was motivated by irrational, ignorant, and racist behaviors," since busing was the method by which approximately 40 percent of elementary schoolchildren would attend school, whether mandated or not. It should be noted that prior to the *Brown* decision, busing was used to maintain segregation. Black students were bused across school districts to all-black schools, and white students were bused across school districts to all-white schools.

School desegregation has not accomplished the degree of equal educational opportunity that was envisioned by the NAACP and the Supreme Court. It has had little effect upon the achievement of minority students. Some sociologists attribute this circumstance to the atmosphere of hostility and resentment in which it occurred. In fact, the schools in large urban areas are actually more segregated than ever. Urban schools have become more identifiable—increasingly along social class lines as well as racial lines. The phenomenon of "white flight" that was so prevalent during the early stages of desegregation can now legitimately be termed "middle-class flight," as families of all racial groups seek to distance themselves from low-achieving schools.

At the heart of equal educational opportunity is nondiscriminatory education. Consequently, the concept of equal educational opportunity has expanded beyond the struggles of racial minorities. Women have come to realize that practices in schooling have historically denied or restricted opportunities for women. Other segments of the population have begun to challenge the traditional view of equal educational opportunity. People with disabilities and those who speak English as a second language have begun to demand the implementation of structures that help enable them to secure greater equality. The courts have increasingly begun to litigate a variety of issues involving equal educational opportunity—not only those based on traditional arguments of equality but those involving national origin, gender, and self-imposed isolation for educational purposes (as in Afrocentric schools). Many sociologists believe that until a more pragmatic method is found, the struggle for equal educational opportunity will continue to occupy a prominent place in the larger struggle for equality of opportunity.

Bibliography

Barnett, Marqueritz R., ed. *Readings on Equal Education*. New York: AMS Press, 1984. Contains twenty-two chapters by various scholars that examine a number of critical issues such as equal education, desegregation and integration, education of the disadvantaged, and issues of political and public policy about how to improve educational equality.

Coleman, James S., et al. *Equality of Educational Opportunity*. Washington, D.C.: U.S. Government Printing Office, 1966. Usually called simply the Coleman Report, this presentation of the findings of a government-sponsored study had far-reaching ramifications regarding public opinion and government policy.

Ogbu, John U. "Class Stratification, Racial Stratification, and Schooling." In *Class, Race, and Gender in American Education*, edited by Lois Weis. Albany: State University of New York Press, 1988. The author provides insight into the issue of equal educational opportunity that is rarely discussed in other literature on the subject. He demonstrates the relationship between race and class stratification in schooling in America.

Sadker, Myra P., and David M. Sadker. *Teachers, Schools, and Society*. 2d ed. New York: McGraw-Hill, 1991. Chapter 14 details some of the barriers that minorities have encountered in attempting to achieve equal educational opportunity. It also takes a brief look at the more important legal decisions that have had an impact on equal educational opportunity.

Spring, Joel. *American Education: An Introduction to Social and Political Aspects*. 4th ed. New York: Longman, 1989. The author gives an excellent overview of the forces that affect equal educational opportunity, placing issues of gender, ethnicity, and race in the context of a continuing struggle for equal educational opportunity. Well-written and up-to-date.

Tesconi, Charles A., Jr., and Emanuel Hurwitz, Jr. *Education for Whom? The Question of Equal Educational Opportunity*. New York: Dodd, Mead, 1974. Provides an excellent description of the issues surrounding the equal educational opportunity question. The authors take a dialectical approach to the debate.

Charles C. Jackson

Cross-References

The Civil Rights Movement, 265; Education: Conflict Theory Views, 579; Education: Functionalist Perspectives, 586; Education: Manifest and Latent Functions, 593; Educational Inequality: The Coleman Report, 607; School Desegregation, 1686; School Socialization, 1693; Standardized Testing and IQ Testing Controversies, 1966; Tracking and Inequality in Education, 2057.

EQUALITY OF OPPORTUNITY

Type of sociology: Social stratification
Fields of study: Dimensions of inequality; Maintaining inequality

Equality of opportunity is a belief which is related to the maintenance of inequality. In other words, equality of opportunity is an ideology. This ideology ignores the fact that there are different opportunity structures for people who differ by class, race, and gender. Many other variables also create unequal opportunities.

Principal terms

CLASS: a stratum of people with similar economic resources; these resources determine the ability to buy what is needed for a quality existence

CULTURE OF POVERTY CONCEPT: an ideology which maintains that poverty is caused by defective values and attitudes of those who are poor; sociologists generally view this as a myth

IDEOLOGY: a belief which is maintained, not because empirical research supports it, but because it helps to rationalize the status quo

INTERGENERATIONAL MOBILITY: the vertical social mobility that is measured by comparing offspring with their parents; the comparison usually entails comparison of occupational status of parents at a given age with occupational status of their offspring when they reach approximately the same age

INTRAGENERATIONAL MOBILITY: the vertical social mobility that is measured by observing the same person across time; studies usually entail comparing occupational status at an early stage with status at a later stage

OPPORTUNITY STRUCTURE: group of social norms that allocate different opportunities to those in different social roles and different social strata

POWER: the ability to exert one's will legally against the will of others; it determines the ability to have what one wants by calling upon the police powers of the state

SOCIAL STRATIFICATION: social inequality, especially with respect to class, status, and power

STATUS: position in a social structure; this social standing determines one's ability to attain what one wants through influence or persuasion

Overview

The concept "equality of opportunity" is used to express both an ideal and an ideology. As an ideal, few people would disagree with equality of opportunity, particularly as long as its meaning is not precisely specified. People tend to think that, generally speaking, women, blacks, people with physical disabilities, and others should enjoy equality of opportunity.

When used as an ideology, however, the concept conveys the idea that people in fact do enjoy equality of opportunity. There is much disagreement about this. Those who assert that the United States has an equal opportunity society cite certain facts in support of their assertion: Slavery and the legal segregation of the Jim Crow era have ended; blacks, women, and other groups now have the right to vote; and civil rights laws now protect minority populations against discrimination in housing, education, employment, and other important spheres of life. Those who make this argument sometimes go further, asserting that any individual who is not successful in today's society has only himself or herself to blame, because there is equal opportunity for all: "America [by which they mean the United States] is an open society," they declare, "and people get pretty much what they deserve."

Social scientists who challenge the ideology of equality of opportunity question and demand explanations of such vague beliefs as "People get pretty much what they deserve." (How wide a range, for example, does "pretty much" include?) They ask what the poor, the paralyzed, and the victims of discrimination did to deserve their situations. It should be apparent that, as the saying goes, bad things do happen to good people. A father may be killed in military combat; a hard-working couple may give birth to a child who requires expensive medical care; a person may be disabled by an industrial or automobile accident; a middle-class housewife who thought she was economically secure may be rejected by a husband seeking a younger woman. It would be difficult to argue that all these people "get what they deserve." Many people have observed the severe curtailment of opportunity and the diminishment of class, status, and power that follow such adverse events, yet the societal belief in equal opportunity is so strong that it makes the causes of inequality difficult to see and change.

Most inequality of opportunity is difficult to see because it is caused by differences in opportunity structures. Opportunities are structured differently for men than for women, for whites compared with blacks, for the affluent compared with the poor, and for the able-bodied compared with those with disabilities. Many other variables also influence the structure of opportunities, including birth order (the first-born compared with latter-born children), degree of physical attractiveness, the sex ratio (the number of men per one hundred women), a generation's place in the population cycle (baby boomers versus baby busters), and whether the nation is at war or peace or is in economic recession or expansion at the time one finishes school.

The belief that equal opportunity exists for all, coupled with the belief that the United States has an open class system in which there is considerable upward and downward mobility, constitutes perhaps the greatest defense of that part of the status quo that is referred to as the stratification system. These beliefs logically lead to the conclusion that there is no need to change the way things are, and especially no need to change the way income, wealth, status, and power are distributed. If society wants to help the poor and those low in status, all it needs to do, according to this view, is to find ways to motivate them, ways to make "them" more like "us." The fault, according to this view, is not with the social structure, but with those who have failed to make use of it.

William Ryan, a professor of psychology at Boston College, critically examines the ideology of equality of opportunity in his book *Equality* (1981). What, he asks, is the meaning of Thomas Jefferson's "self-evident" truth that all men are created equal, and that they are endowed with the inalienable rights of life, liberty, and the pursuit of happiness? Ryan disagrees with the ideological answers to these questions. It is common to define the right to life to mean simply that no one should kill another person—everyone has a right to live. Ryan argues that the right means much more, that people have a right to "the means of sustaining life." The right to liberty means more than protection from unlawful imprisonment; it is the right to "be free from arbitrary and unreasonable compulsion and coercion." The right to pursue happiness means more than the right to acquire "command over resources"; it means that people "must have a certain stock of resources if they are to preserve their own rights to life and liberty." The conventional view is that "equality of opportunity" exists if individuals are not denied the good things of life because of birth-ascribed statuses such as skin color, sex, or nationality. Ryan argues that equality of opportunity means much more: It means equality of access to resources "sufficient to sustain life at a decent standard of humanity and to preserve liberty and freedom from compulsion." The sweeping nature of Ryan's view of equality of opportunity makes it a very controversial idea and one that is unlikely to be embraced by a majority of Americans.

Applications

Several kinds of evidence indicate that the belief that there is equal opportunity for all is an ideology rather than a valid empirical conclusion. One kind of evidence comes from studies of intergenerational mobility. Richard H. de Lone, a former policy analyst for the Carnegie Council, found that the most important determinants of what one achieves in life are race, class, and sex, and that about one in five men will surpass his father's level of achievement. De Lone presented his conclusions in *Small Futures: Children, Inequality, and the Limits of Liberal Reform* (1979). After reviewing the research, William Ryan concluded that between 20 and 33 percent of men will surpass their father's level of achievement.

The Panel Study on Income Dynamics (PSID) is a longitudinal study of 16,000 individuals who have been interviewed each year since 1967. It included a study of intragenerational economic mobility between 1971 and 1978, which found that 40 percent of those in the sample were in the same income quintile at the end of the study that they were in at the beginning, and 77 percent were in the same quintile or only one quintile removed. Only 6 percent of those who had started in the lowest quintile had moved to the highest quintile. Those in the lowest quintile in 1971 had incomes below $6,132, and those in the highest quintile had incomes over $18,500. In 1978, these incomes had increased $9,000 and $32,100, respectively. Income stability within such a narrow range of incomes is consistent with the conclusions of de Lone, Ryan, and others that class is more a birth-ascribed status than an achieved status. This in turn means that those born into lower classes do not have equal opportunity, compared with those born into higher classes. Stated positively, society provides more and better opportunities to those in higher classes. For example, the financial resources of one's family of origin are an important determinant of the neighborhood where one lives, which in turn is an important determinant of the quality of elementary and secondary education one receives (Jonathan Kozol examines these issues in his 1992 book *Savage Inequalities*). Education quality in turn is an important determinant of the quality of university to which one is admitted. The financial resources of the family of origin are a determinant of many other things, such as the quality of health care one receives. There is no equal opportunity to be successful for those in poor health, compared with those who are healthy.

Another kind of evidence comes from observing the consequences of diminishing the inequality of opportunity. Theodore Cross, an authority on minority economics and law, has provided substantial evidence that as inequality of opportunity is reduced, blacks have taken advantage of the new opportunities to increase their numbers in political offices, trade unions, and the professions, as well as in educational institutions as both students and teachers (*The Black Power Imperative*, 1984).

Another type of evidence comes from the Panel Study on Income Dynamics, mentioned previously. If there were equal opportunity, then one would expect to find character traits among the poor which would help to explain their poverty. For example, maybe the poor are poor because they will not defer gratification, because they will not plan ahead, or because they are not committed to education and hard work. "The difference between rich and poor," adherents of the equality-of-opportunity ideology might argue, "is that the rich plan for generations and the poor plan for Friday night." Many studies have found a correlation between scores on attitude scales and success—those with better scores (more positive attitudes) are more successful. These results are often interpreted as evidence that better attitudes cause success. Such a conclusion is not warranted, however, because correlations do not prove causal relationships. It could more strongly be argued that success causes people to have more positive attitudes and that failure causes people to develop more negative attitudes. The PSID resolved the issue by administering attitude scales at the beginning of the study, in 1967-1968, and then observing, as the years went by, whether the scores were predictive of subsequent success or failure. The attitudes that were measured by one of the PSID researchers, James Morgan, included commitment to the American work ethic, self-confidence, ambition, motivation, planning ahead, looking for better jobs, and holding high hopes for the future. Morgan concluded that scores on these attitude scales did not help predict subsequent economic fortune or misfortune.

Other PSID researchers measured achievement motivation, sense of personal efficacy, orientation toward the future, and other attitudes. In Greg J. Duncan's words (1984), "We find almost no evidence that initial attitudes affect subsequent economic success." Martha Hill, another PSID researcher, measured motivation, fear of failure, future expectations, and orientation toward the future. Her conclusion: "We found no significant effects of [attitudes] on families' economic outcomes." Thus, the evidence from the Panel Study on Income Dynamics does not support the culture of poverty myth that personal defects of the poor, in an equal opportunity society, cause their poverty.

Another type of evidence bearing on the question of equal opportunity comes from efforts to answer the question, "If poor attitudes do not cause poverty, what does?" Again, the PSID is helpful. The study found that the "temporarily poor" (poor less than two years) were a cross-section of the population, reduced to poverty by events such as the death of the primary breadwinner, divorce, disabling accidents and illnesses, and birth (by adding to income needs while frequently reducing income by taking the mother out of the labor force). The study also found that persistent welfare dependents (people who received more than half their income from welfare for eight years or more, two percent of this representative sample of families) were not different from the rest of the sample with respect to their attitudes, but were different with respect to two birth-ascribed statuses: race and sex. All this evidence suggests that inequality is a consequence of unequal opportunity structures for blacks, women, the poor, and others.

Context

The United States has always been viewed as a land of opportunity, and the concept that anyone can rise from "rags to riches" has been a powerful, central American belief. This ideology was reflected, for example, in the popular books of author and clergyman Horatio Alger in the nineteenth century. The idea received a revival in the 1960's when it was implicitly incorporated into the concept of the culture of poverty, a term first used by Oscar Lewis. The idea of there being a culture of poverty has been heatedly debated, with most sociologists discarding the concept. Nevertheless, the term, used loosely and seldom clearly defined, has entered popular discourse. According to William Ryan (1971), Lewis himself used the term somewhat carelessly, sometimes suggesting that it was the culture of poor people that made them poor. What Lewis referred to as a culture is an adaptation to poverty (not the cause of it) made by some of the poor (about one-fifth, in Lewis' estimation) whose experience with poverty was relatively long term. Lewis held the view that such poverty was caused by social structures and, according to Ryan, that "social changes of a structural nature are necessary to deal with the problem of poverty." Unfortunately, the phrase "culture of poverty" has since been used by many who argue that this "culture" is the cause of poverty.

For example, Edward Banfield, a professor of urban government at Harvard University, argued in *The Unheavenly City Revisited* (1974) that it was not inequality of opportunity, but a culture of poverty, that held the poor in poverty. For example, when discussing education he wrote:

> . . . no matter how able, dedicated, and hardworking the teachers, no matter how ample the facilities of the school or how well-designed its curriculum, no matter how free the

atmosphere of the school from racial or other prejudice, the performance of pupils at the lower end of the class-cultural scale will always fall short.

Myron Magnet, an editor of *Fortune* magazine and a fellow of the Manhattan Institute, reiterated this culture of poverty theme in *The Dream and the Nightmare: The Sixties' Legacy to the Underclass* (1993). Magnet put a new twist on the argument: According to him, the poor are incapacitated by liberals (and some conservatives) who teach the poor that they have been victimized. Sociologists who argue that the culture of poverty is ideological rather than scientific say that this type of argument is analogous to claiming that people stutter because someone has taught them the concept of stuttering or even that people drown because they were taught the concept of drowning (both of these arguments have in fact been made by cultural determinists).

Bibliography

Banfield, Edward C. *The Unheavenly City Revisited*. Boston: Little, Brown, 1974. This book is a revision and expansion of Banfield's 1970 book *The Unheavenly City*. Both books have been the subject of intense debate between Banfield (and others who think poverty is caused by the culture of poor people) and those who believe that the "culture of poverty" is merely an adaptation to structural poverty.

Cross, Theodore. *The Black Power Imperative: Racial Inequality and the Politics of Nonviolence*. New York: Faulkner, 1984. The graphics alone make this a valuable resource. Includes solid documentation of inequality of opportunity with respect to race, of the role of the government in creating inequality of opportunity, of improvement as this inequality diminished, and of the need for further government efforts to enhance the opportunity structure for African Americans.

Guttentag, Marcia, and Paul F. Secord. *Too Many Women?: The Sex Ratio Question*. Beverly Hills, Calif.: Sage Publications, 1983. Opportunity structures influenced by the availability of opposite-sex partners in turn affect sexual behaviors and mores, patterns of marriage and divorce, child rearing practices, and family stability.

Kozol, Jonathan. *Rachel and Her Children: Homeless Families in America*. New York: Crown, 1988. A powerful portrayal, based on interviews of the homeless, of the adverse events that can reduce ordinary people to the state of homelessness.

Ryan, William. *Blaming the Victim*. New York: Pantheon Books, 1971. A witty and factual rebuttal of victim-blaming myths pertaining to minority school achievement, minority families and illegitimacy, minority poverty, minority health care, slums, crime, and riots. Many of the percentages (for example, of black births that are illegitimate) are dated, but the arguments are as valid and refreshing today as when they were first published.

_____ . *Equality*. New York: Pantheon Books, 1981. An excellent analysis of the "fair play" ideology of inequality, and an effective challenge to the ideology of individualism. Includes critiques of institutionalized discrimination in education and of the ideology of equal opportunity.

Donald M. Hayes

Cross-References

Conflict Theory, 340; Educational Credentials and Social Mobility, 600; Educational Inequality: The Coleman Report, 607; Equal Educational Opportunity, 661; Gender Inequality: Analysis and Overview, 820; Internal Colonialism, 1015; Racial and Ethnic Stratification, 1579; Racism as an Ideology, 1586; Social Mobility: Analysis and Overview, 1812; Social Stratification: Analysis and Overview, 1839; Tracking and Inequality in Education, 2057.

ETHICS AND POLITICS IN SOCIAL RESEARCH

Type of sociology: Sociological research
Field of study: Basic concepts

Social research is influenced by standards of professional ethics and embedded within organizational and community political systems. Therefore, social research, ethics, and politics are closely linked.

Principal terms

CONFIDENTIAL INFORMATION: private information that is shared only with the understanding that it will not be disseminated

INFORMED CONSENT: a subject's consent to participate in research, based on appropriate knowledge of that research

PRIVACY: the condition in which information is presumed to belong to a particular individual or group rather than to an investigator or the larger public

RESEARCH ETHICS: the informal and formal codes of appropriate research conduct, developed by professional communities to promote human good and/or minimize harm

RESEARCH POLITICS: behavior designed to change interpersonal or group relationships, including the distribution of power, respect, and other values, but usually independent of research quality considerations

SOCIALLY SENSITIVE RESEARCH: studies with potentially negative social consequences for the participating subjects or others

Overview

Social psychologist Stanley Milgram sought to understand the obedience and acts of cruelty that characterized the Nazi era by conducting experiments that led volunteers to take actions that appeared to shock other people severely. Arthur Jensen, a psychologist, published a study of intelligence that reported significant interracial test differences that were apparently the results of genetic heritability. Sociologist Laud Humphreys assumed the role of a voyeur-lookout at park restrooms to study men who engaged in casual gay sex. Later, he traced some of the restroom participants and, in disguise, interviewed them.

These are but three of many socially sensitive studies in the social and behavioral sciences that raise such important ethical and political issues as the appropriateness of deception and the societal benefits and costs of research. It is difficult to know what is appropriate. A basic ethical guideline, it is often argued, is that research should not place people at risk of harm. Yet many questions remain. Which people? What harm? Should consent matter?

The people who should be considered in a discussion of these issues fall into three categories: investigators, subjects, and others. Virologist Robert Gallo reports new science guidelines that preclude investigators from risking their own health. Most ethical concern, however, has been focused on subjects. Indeed, a vast regulatory bureaucracy of human subject protection now exists. Little attention has been given to the effects of research on other people, however, such as relatives of subjects or colleagues of the investigator.

Harm is obviously multidimensional and varies in degree. Furthermore, in important ways it is subjective. Harm may be physical; in the social and behavioral sciences, however, it is more likely to be psychological. Some of Milgram's subjects in the obedience experiments reported experiencing extreme psychological discomfort. Some readers of Jensen's reports were greatly distressed. Humphreys' study of gay sex was risky because of the danger of disclosure. Yet it is not clear who should assess potential harm.

The routine procedure for protecting subjects from involuntary risk is to obtain their "informed consent." Often, consent consists of a signature on a document that incompletely describes research procedures and risks, but deception is necessary in order to conduct many studies. Milgram, for example, could not inform his subjects that his experimental setup was pretense. Indeed, the adequate disclosure, understanding, and voluntary agreement essential for true informed consent are rare. Sociologist Edward A. Shils takes an absolute position about a subject's rights based on the sacredness of individuality and therefore human autonomy. "The claim to enhance our stock of understanding," Shils argues, "is no justification for the infringement of an important right of the individual." The more common view is that the knowledge to be gained should counterbalance the risk, but does one person's gain counterbalance another's harm? Who decides (the investigator or subject or others) makes a difference.

Ethical and political issues arise at various stages of the research process. At the stage of conception and planning, the prospective topic of research may be responsive to or otherwise affected by community or organizational politics; possible results include political correctness or myth maintenance. People are sometimes brought onto or excluded from a research team only for political reasons. Politics may dictate where funding is sought or avoided, and to which investigators it is given. A broader issue, related to voluntary consent, involves targeting people as research subjects who are relatively powerless; for example, prisoners, the elderly, or illiterate villagers. A related question is whether to compensate subjects for their intellectual property.

The middle stage of research includes data collection. It often involves observing or questioning, for which informed consent is politically and ethically central. For some research, the source of consent may be community leaders and/or organizational officials rather than (or in addition to) individuals. In a study of Nigerian student politics, for example, consent was obtained from a government agency, campus officials, student leaders, and individual members of the student body. Of course, obtaining consent does not shift all responsibility to the subjects; the investigator still must adhere to ethical standards.

Informed consent minimizes deception. When relatively harmless, deception is usually tolerated. Philosopher Sissela Bok observes, however, that "any deceptive practice harms not only those lied to, but also liars and trust more generally." Deceptive practices raise several questions: Are there research alternatives to deception? If not, should the research be conducted? If the answer is yes, what degree of deception should be tolerated?

To minimize harm, a post-research debriefing (desensitizing) procedure is often recommended—and often helpful. The goal is to eliminate any negative impact on the subject—that is, to make sure that any harm is not long-lasting. For example, Milgram debriefed all the subjects who were involved in his obedience experiments.

The final stage of most research projects involves preparing and disseminating results. A crucial preparation issue is interpretation, which is often based on a presumption of cross-cultural understanding but requires diverse interpretive perspectives. Dissemination raises the issue of confidentiality. In the course of conducting research, the investigator may obtain information that, if made public, would constitute an invasion of the subject's privacy. The subjects of Humphreys' research presumably did not want their tearoom activities to be known to family members. Ethically, the subject should be empowered to make decisions about the disclosure of private information.

Although honoring confidentiality, investigators are expected to make public the research methods they have used and the knowledge gained. The reader should be provided with sufficient information to understand the results and to judge their soundness. The place of publication may raise various issues. For example, some investigators have been criticized for writing a popular report before work has been peer reviewed, and some gatekeeping editors have made political rather than substantive publication acceptance judgments. Among the possible consequences of publishing a report based upon deceptive research is the elimination of future research opportunities for others.

Applications

A number of well-publicized studies conducted in the United States after World War II have led to heightened ethical and political concerns within and beyond scientific communities. This article is concerned with three of them—those mentioned in the introductory paragraph.

In the early 1960's, Stanley Milgram conducted a series of experiments designed to explore to what extent people would, under the influence of an authority figure, engage in seemingly harmful behavior. He wanted to understand the genocide that occurred in Germany under the Nazis. The mass killings, Milgram observed in a 1963 article, could only have been carried out if large numbers of people had followed immoral orders. In Milgram's experiments, naïve volunteer subjects were asked by an authoritative "experimenter" to operate an "electric shock generator" using increasing voltage intensities (the switch labels ranged from "slight shock" to "danger" to, finally, "450 volts, XXX") in order to punish a "learner" whenever he made mistakes in a memory test. The purpose of the shocks was said to be the study of the effect of punishment on learning. The setup was pretense; no shocks were administered, and the "learner" was acting. Most volunteers, encouraged or instructed by the authoritative experimenter, progressed to the highest voltage switches. Following the experimental situation, each subject was debriefed.

The initial 1963 report caused a furor over the ethical issues: the deception used in the initial explanation of the study to the volunteers, the validity of any consent given in what for some was a visually coercive laboratory setting, and the considerable discomfort experienced by some subjects during the experiment (Milgram observed trembling, groaning, and even a violent seizure). Finally, there might have been some long-term negative impact on the volunteers, although follow-up studies suggest otherwise.

Beginning in the late 1960's, Arthur Jensen created a national stir by publishing a series of books and articles that pointed to systematic differences in the measured intelligence (IQ) of black and white Americans. Most visible was a 1969 article in the Harvard Educational Review. Especially controversial was his conclusion that biological factors were more important than environmental ones (such as nutrition) in determining individual and group differences in educationally relevant traits. Jensen also raised policy-relevant issues. For example, he wrote about the identified differences as educational and social "dynamite" and the likelihood of "dysgenic trends" in urban poverty areas.

Jensen's publications evoked sharp scientific debates and ideological exchanges; issues such as culturally biased tests, nutritional deprivation, and poor motivation were raised, and words such as "pollution," "barbaric," and "racism" were used. One researcher publicly charged that the 1969 article had fifty-three errors, but he refused to state what these were and later indicated that the number was made up. Demonstrations were organized against Jensen, and his professional lectures were disrupted in the United States and abroad. Jensen's family was threatened, requiring police protection. Such politicization obviously has a dramatic effect on other scholars' agendas and raises important issues. A theoretical issue is the multidimensionality of intelligence, and a methodological issue is the valid and reliable measurement of intelligence. Additionally, there is the issue of academic freedom and restraint in educational institutions embedded within the larger society. Jensen (1987) has written: "I make no apology for my choice of research topics. Should we not apply the tools of our science to such socially important issues as best we can?" Perhaps his question has scientific, ethical, and political answers.

Laud Humphreys, a married minister turned sociologist, completed his controversial research during the late 1960's as a doctoral dissertation at Washington University in St. Louis; it was published as *Tearoom Trade: Impersonal Sex in Public Places* (1970). The focus was gay involvement in illegal "impersonal sex." The methods employed in the study caused considerable controversy at the time; indeed, Humphreys and one sociology professor engaged in physical combat. At issue was deception; rather than identifying himself as a sociologist, Humphreys assumed first the role of a privacy-securing voyeur-lookout at men's public park toilets (called "tearooms") and later the role of a social health surveyor visiting the homes of some men who had participated in the sexual activities. As voyeur-lookout, he observed numerous sexual acts and associated behavior. Humphreys also recorded the automobile license plate numbers of many of the tearoom visitors; one year later, in a second research stage, he assumed a disguise to conduct interviews with fifty of the men. He found that many of them were married and lived otherwise normal lives.

Humphreys maintained the men's confidentiality by taking precautions to prevent leaks linking names with data. Later, he destroyed all identifying information. Nevertheless, deception had twice been used to invade the men's privacy. A journalist wrote critically about "peeping into what we thought were our most private and secret lives." Clearly, there was some risk that lives would be ruined by an accidental disclosure, and the information probably could have been subpoenaed.

Context

Many people within the behavioral and social scientific communities have, until recently, advocated a program of research that is value-free. Research priorities and methods, they argued, should be determined by "value neutral" scientific paradigms, but values, value conflicts, and politics are influential. "The sociology of sociology," sociologist Dan Chekki writes, "examines the significant role of sociocultural variables in the production and development of different types of knowledge about social phenomena."

Research ethics and politics are embedded in historical and social contexts. Until after World War II, there were relatively few explicit ethical standards. Investigators have, however, been guided by implicit professional and societal norms. Research ethics became a matter of intense public concern as a result of revelations about medical "scientific" experimentation in Nazi Germany that apparently had little chance of producing useful knowledge yet caused great bodily harm or death. Immersing captured people in ice water to find out how long they would live under such circumstances is merely one gruesome example of such experimentation.

A series of major yet controversial studies that were publicized or conducted in the United States after World War II led to heightened concern about the ethics of research. For example, in 1954, University of Chicago researchers funded by the Ford Foundation obtained court (but not jury) permission to place a hidden microphone in a jury room in Wichita, Kansas, to learn about jury deliberations. The resulting controversy led to a federal law barring such research. In the early 1960's, two Harvard University investigators gave mind-altering substances to students and other subjects. Both lost their jobs. At about the same time, Milgram was conducting his obedience experiments.

In the mid-1960's, two sensitive government-funded projects exploded politically. The 1965 Moynihan Report on African Americans, which focused on family structure, poverty, disadvantage, and policy, led to a national debate over its purpose, methods, and interpretations. Project Camelot was designed to study, predict, and influence social changes in developing countries. Domestic and international criticism led to its cancellation. Sociologist Irving Louis Horowitz asked: "What are the vital connections between science and policy, . . . between the myths of society and the facts of sociology, between objectivity and commitment?"

These and other research activities led to the establishment of human subjects review boards designed to achieve a balance between the quest for knowledge and risks to individuals or groups which is acceptable to social science professionals and the larger society.

There is, of course, a relationship between scientific and societal ethics and politics. Surveys conducted among American college students reveal that cheating and other forms of intellectual dishonesty are widespread on campuses, and the news from other segments of society, including business and government, suggests that the problem is ubiquitous. It may be that contemporary ethical rules are helpful to investigators who want to distance themselves from the practices of the larger society. Furthermore, the rules may serve as a buffer against anti-intellectualism within society.

The politics of research is obviously linked with larger issues within the political system. That clearly has been the case with studies of racial differences not based on environmental theories. Jensen, in 1987, referred to "academically tabooed questions," noting that "virtually a *de facto* moratorium on research" on this subject prevails. He correctly observed that favored research projects are "in tune with the prevailing sociopolitical wind." Historically, that has been the case with studies of fetal tissue, human cell cloning, interracial marriages, and other "incorrect" topics. Indeed, the ultimate research-ethics-politics linkage is that the social and behavioral "sciences" often reflect and reproduce the structure of community power.

Bibliography

Bok, Sissela. *Lying: Moral Choice in Public and Private Life.* New York: Pantheon Books, 1978. The author, a philosopher, examines such issues as truthfulness, deceit, trust, and the consequences of lying. In a chapter devoted to deception in the social sciences, she emphasizes alternative research approaches.

Chekki, Dan A. In preface to *The Political Economy of the Social Sciences*, by Frederick H. Gareau. New York: Garland, 1991. The entire book is devoted to the sociology of sociology, and it raises important ethical and political issues.

Diener, Edward, and Rick Crandall. *Ethics in Social and Behavioral Research.* Chicago: University of Chicago Press, 1978. A broad survey of ethical issues ranging from harm to participants to the accuracy of research reports.

Horowitz, Irving Louis, ed. *The Rise and Fall of Project Camelot.* Cambridge, Mass.: MIT Press, 1967. A collection of commentaries on the ethics and politics of a well-funded but soon-canceled government project.

Humphreys, Laud. *Tearoom Trade: Impersonal Sex in Public Places.* Chicago: Aldine, 1970. This book-length research report concludes with a postscript on ethics. The 1975 edition includes additional discussion of ethical issues.

Miller, Arthur G. *The Obedience Experiments: A Case Study of Controversy in Social*

Science. New York: Praeger, 1986. Stanley Milgram's controversial research led Miller to examine some of the ethical and methodological issues that it involved.

Modgil, Sohan, and Celia Modgil, eds. *Arthur Jensen: Consensus and Controversy.* Philadelphia: Falmer Press, 1987. Although this book is primarily devoted to such theoretical and methodological issues as learning, genetics, and test bias, it also addresses the ethics and politics of Jensen's research. See especially Jensen's "Differential Psychology: Towards Consensus."

Shils, Edward A. "Social Inquiry and the Autonomy of the Individual." In *The Human Meaning of the Social Sciences*, edited by Daniel Lerner. New York: Meridian Books, 1959. This is an early, powerful argument for honoring the individual's autonomy over the needs of social research. See also Shils's *The Intellectuals and the Powers and Other Essays* (Chicago: University of Chicago Press, 1972).

Sieber, Joan E., ed. *NIH Readings on the Protection of Human Subjects in Behavioral and Social Science Research.* Frederick, Md.: University Publications of America, 1984. Includes the conference proceedings and background papers for a 1983 conference sponsored by the National Institutes of Health's Office for Protection from Research Risks. Papers cover such topics as informed consent, privacy, and the fostering of integrity.

William John Hanna

Cross-References

ETHNIC ENCLAVES

Type of sociology: Racial and ethnic relations
Field of study: Patterns and consequences of contact

Ethnic enclaves are isolated communities, free from contact from the majority population, that are usually intended to maintain customs and traditions that are under attack by outsiders. Enclaves are usually created by groups that feel oppressed by outside forces.

Principal terms

ASSIMILATION: the absorption of a minority group into the majority, which leads to the minority's disappearance as a distinct group

ENCLAVE: a territory wholly within the boundaries of a larger territory

ETHNIC GROUP: individuals who share a common historical tradition based on language or religious characteristics

PLURALISM: the acceptance of group diversity and the preservation of ethnic differentiation within a larger society

PREJUDICE: an illogical opinion of another group or person based on real or imagined characteristics associated with the group

Overview

Ethnic enclaves are territories inhabited by a distinct group of people who are separated from the dominant population by differences in language, religion, social class, or culture and who are frequently subjected to prejudice and discrimination. An ethnic group has a shared history based on a sense of difference from others resulting from several factors, including a unique set of experiences (such as being enslaved or defeated in a war), skin color or other physical differences (such as height), or geography. The word "ethnic" comes from the Greek *ethnos*, meaning "tribe" or "race." It is frequently used to refer to any minority group speaking a different language, wearing a different style of clothes, or simply looking different from the majority. Before 1900, the terms "immigrant group," "foreign stock," and even "race" were used to express the same meaning, as in "Polish race." Differences based on ethnicity are not as permanent as those resulting from skin color; therefore assimilation into the dominant culture can be easier for ethnic groups than for some racial groups.

Enclaves are established for two major reasons. Some are found in nations and among groups where a distinct sense of injustice exists between peoples. This sense of discrimination prevents communication and results in isolation and a sense of inferiority within the minority group. The dominant group persecutes persons deemed inferior who then withdraw into isolated communities to protect themselves from attack. Enclaves can also be built because of a sense of ethnic superiority, or ethnocentrism. In this case, one group sees itself as being far superior to any others and deliberately separates itself from the rest of society. This self-imposed isolation results from the view that the way of life being lived by group members should not be contaminated by "inferior" outsiders.

Ethnic enclaves result from the failure of groups to accommodate, acculturate, or assimilate. Accommodation is a reduction of conflict among groups as they find ways of living with one another based on mutual respect for differences. Groups maintain their differences but agree to live with one another. In places where enclaves develop, only physical separation lessens conflict as groups continue to hate and discredit one another but geography keeps them apart. Acculturation, meaning taking over some of the attitudes and beliefs of the other group, fails to take place in these situations because contact between different peoples is rare, and they stick to their traditional values. Instead of becoming more alike, as would be true under the process of assimilation, the groups become more and more different. A common culture fails to develop, and frequently misunderstandings and miscommunication can lead to violent conflicts. It is as if each group lives in a different world, with memories, sentiments, feelings, and attitudes that are totally unknown to the other. The more divergent peoples are or become, the more difficult assimilation will be. This situation is evident among the peoples of southeastern Europe, especially in areas of the former Yugoslavia, such as Bosnia, Croatia, and Serbia. It is also true in African states such as Burundi, Nigeria, and the Union of South Africa.

Societies that are divided into enclaves are not the same as pluralist systems. In this type of arrangement, diversity exists and people are divided into many distinct cultures and subcultures, but generally there are also larger loyalties toward a government or a king or a flag that provide a common framework with which people can identify in times of crisis or trouble. People living in enclaves rarely share any loyalty beyond that of the group and turn against the dominant culture or rival ethnic group in periods of conflict. Because of past prejudice and discrimination, groups living in enclaves, whether self-imposed or involuntary (such as Jews in medieval Europe), feel totally outside the system and lack any sense of obligation to aid other groups. Generally, the greater the differences in class, skin color, religion, or language, the more sharply divided the society will be and the more likely the enclave spirit ("It's us against them, and we cannot let them into our homes or communities without destroying everything that is valuable to us") grows and spreads.

In a few situations, enclaves develop as a defense against attacks by physically or numerically superior outsiders. If the group did not retreat and separate from the dominant society, it would be annihilated. In this case, cutting off the community from contact with others serves the function of preserving traditions, customs, and beliefs. Most often, this is done by withdrawing into the wilderness beyond the reach of the persecutors. In the United States in the 1840's, members of the Church of Latter Day Saints (Mormons) adopted this strategy to save themselves from mob attacks in the East. Brigham Young, the successor to the group's founder Joseph Smith, deliberately chose to settle by the Great Salt Lake, then part of Mexico, because it seemed far enough away from the United States that no one would bother him. The Mormons lived in this isolated area free from contact with others well into the 1880's and preserved their distinct religious beliefs.

Applications

One example of establishing an ethnic enclave is found in the province of Quebec, Canada. Founded by French explorers in 1608, the region, known mainly for the wealth of its furs, remained in the hands of the King of France until 1763, when the British received it as a prize for winning the Seven Years' War (1756-1763). Trouble began almost immediately, because the French-speaking population refused to submit to British law and government. After more than ten years of conflict, the English parliament bowed to pressure and passed the Quebec Act in 1774. This bill gave the French population the right to speak their own language, practice their Roman Catholic religion, and be governed by their own local laws rather than those of England. Though they constituted more than 80 percent of the population of their own province, the French *patriotes* were a distinct minority in the whole of Canada.

Social class also divided the peoples of Quebec, since the French were mainly small farmers, while the English-speaking minority controlled the business community and were generally wealthier than the people they labeled "Canucks," a word signifying inferiority and backwardness. Violence broke out in 1837 during a terrible economic depression, when the French farmers tried to overthrow the English-dominated provincial government. The British army quickly repelled the rebels, however, and drove them into the countryside. An investigation by a royal commissioner appointed by the king concluded that dissatisfaction would continue because there were "two nations warring in the bosom of a single state." Neither group wanted to reach accommodation with the other, and as long as that was true, violence and disorder would continue.

By the 1860's, continuing French Canadian protests forced the government in London to grant the Quebecois the right to control their educational system, making French the primary language of instruction. Officially, the province became bilingual, though English was rarely heard outside government offices and banks. After the French gained control of their schools, they gradually withdrew from active participation in Canadian society. Involvement in national politics seemed to give consent to the right of English speakers to rule, and the French would have none of that. Therefore, they focused on local rights and the rejection of English culture. French nationalism grew in Quebec as the people became more isolated from the Canadian majority.

In 1963, extremists founded the Quebec Liberation Front, which adopted terrorist techniques of bombing and kidnapping to press its demands for an independent French-speaking republic. Five years later, a political party, the Parti Quebecois (PQ), ran on a platform calling for political separation and won almost 25 percent of the vote in its first campaign. By 1976, the PQ captured a majority of seats in the provincial legislature, and Réné Levesque, an advocate of independence, became premier. Bilingualism was dropped, and French became the official language of the province. In 1980, a majority of voters rejected a call for independence, but twelve years later they surprised many Canadians by accepting the very same proposal. Thus, after 230 years of living in an enclave created by differences in language, social class, culture, and religion, the French-speaking population of Quebec rejected assimilation and accommodation and chose separatism instead.

Another example of ethnic hostility that led to the creation of enclaves can be found in the Balkan mountains of southeastern Europe. Ethnic tensions have divided the peoples of the region into hostile camps for hundreds of years, and every few years the ancient hatreds break out into violence. The origins of the problems date back to the 500's with the invasion by Slavic-speaking clans from the north. These invaders, the South Slavs, drove the native populations of Greeks and Celts into the surrounding mountains, where they built homes and villages and remained isolated from their conquerors for hundreds of years. The Slavs, united by language and culture with the Russians and the Poles, divided into several subgroups in the Balkans, including Serbs, Croats, Macedonians, and Bulgarians. They lived in the valleys of the region and generally dominated the local economy.

Complications arose with the arrival of Eastern Orthodox (Byzantine) Christian missionaries in the 900's. Some Slavs converted to Christianity, but most retained their traditional religions. Then, in the 1300's, the Ottoman Turks invaded the region, bringing their Islamic faith with them. For a while, the unified Slavs held out, but in 1371 and 1389 they suffered bloody defeats in battle with the Muslims. The Turks gained control of Macedonia and smaller regions in the mountainous areas of modern-day Yugoslavia, Croatia, and Montenegro. In some areas, the Turks were greeted as liberators by peasant populations long exploited by their Serbian and Croatian landlords. Many Christians fled to the woods and unpopulated mountain passes to escape the Turkish armies. Roman Catholic missionaries had great success converting Croatians to the Western-style Christian faith, making the regional population even more diverse.

In the early 1600's, Serbian Christians rebelled against the Turks and, with the assistance of the Austrian Habsburg armies, defeated the Ottomans, but when the Muslims withdrew they left behind several enclaves of Islamic believers, especially in Bosnia. These Bosnian Muslims survived into the twentieth century by withdrawing into isolated villages and separating themselves from the dominant Christian population. The creation of modern Yugoslavia after World War I led to an unsuccessful attempt by the king of Serbia, Croatia, and Slovenia (as the nation was first called) to downplay ethnic and religious rivalries. Later, after World War II, the communist regime of Marshall Josip Broz Tito began a campaign stressing unity over division, but tensions remained high and outbreaks of ethnic violence were controlled only by a strong military presence in troubled areas. With the death of Tito and the collapse of the central government, ancient hostilities, exploited by ambitious leaders, led to violence again as dominant Eastern Orthodox Serb and Roman Catholic Croatian populations made war against the Muslims and sometimes against each other. The long separation into enclaves made all sides less willing to find peaceful solutions to their differences and less able to respect and understand one another.

Another area of the world that has been subjected to violence because of ethnic clashes is the African nation of Burundi (population 4,580,000). This former Belgian colony experienced bloody massacres three times since 1965 during fighting between the Hutu and Tutsi populations. The Hutu make up more than 85 percent of the population but for the last 500 years have been dominated by the Tutsi (or Watutsi), who compose only 12 percent; the remaining peoples are mainly Twa pygmies, who live in the rain forest beyond the reach of the others. The Tutsi invaded from the north in the 1400's and quickly won control of the tiny kingdom. Over time, the original Hutu became the slaves and serfs of the Tutsi, who controlled most of the land. The Tutsi raised cattle and controlled the economy as the physically smaller Hutu withdrew into village enclaves and were subjected to terror, torture, and slavery. Relations between the two groups were always hostile and unfriendly, and intermarriage was extremely rare.

After Burundi won its independence in 1965, the Hutu won a majority of seats in the new legislature, but Tutsi soldiers shot and killed thousands of Hutu leaders as they established a dictatorship. In 1972, a Hutu revolt led to the murders of 200,000 more of their people and the continuance of Tutsi domination. Twenty-one years later, at least 500,000 Hutu villagers died in yet another outbreak of bloody fighting. The campaign of terror reached into the remotest Hutu enclaves as women, children, babies, and anyone else deemed to be a Hutu was slaughtered in a gruesome outbreak of ethnic mass murder.

Context

The concept of ethnic identity and ethnic enclaves developed in the 1800's, though different words and phrases such as "immigrant group," "foreign stock," and "race" were used in place of "ethnic." The term "ethnic" was first used by social scientists in the 1920's to differentiate the supposedly less fervent attachments based on language and history in comparison to the supposedly more fundamental biological attachments based on racial inheritance. Many social scientists were interested in the question of how people of different linguistic and historical traditions would become part of modern, specifically American, society. Robert Park of the University of Chicago developed a theory of intergroup relations based on an inevitable process of contact, competition, accommodation, and, finally, full assimilation. As group members moved upward in the American class system, they would gradually lose their ethnic attachments and ultimately be accepted as true citizens. The more different groups were from the white, Anglo-Saxon, majority, however, the longer and more difficult the process would be (as in the case of American Indians and African Americans). Gunnar Myrdal, the great Swedish sociologist, supported this view in his classic 1944 *An American Dilemma*, a study of race relations in the United States. Mostly, Park's analysis of assimilation has been accepted by sociologists, though Milton Gordon, in *Assimilation in American Life* (1964), has pointed out that assimilation takes much longer than has been assumed and is frequently marred by conflict and disorder. Most sociologists and historians writing on the subject since then have agreed with Gordon and have detailed the difficulties experienced by various American ethnic groups. Most observers have agreed that retreating into enclaves is sometimes necessary for group survival but always makes cooperation between groups more difficult.

As anthropologists, sociologists, and historians have broadened the discussion of ethnicity and ethnic enclaves to include the entire human community, they have become increasingly aware of the strength of linguistic, religious, and cultural traditions. Unless a spirit of tolerance develops that allows for human diversity and accepts the idea of "live and let live," conflict and violence will increase in the future. Ethnic prejudice, based on feelings of superiority and the rightness of one's own group, is found among both "superior" and "inferior" populations. Those on top explain their position by the superiority of their culture, while frustrated persons on the bottom find a sense of security and significance in unifying against their masters and exploiters. In situations of growing disparity based on wealth, culture, and historical traditions, the establishment of more enclaves for protection and a concomitant increase in ethnic violence in the future can be expected.

Bibliography

Glazer, Nathan, and Daniel Patrick Moynihan. *Beyond the Melting Pot: The Negroes, Puerto Ricans, Jews, Italians, and Irish of New York City.* Cambridge, Mass.: MIT Press, 1963. The classic study of the long-term persistence of ethnic identities in the United States. The authors discuss the effects of ethnic isolation on education, politics, and intergroup relations. Contains an index but no bibliography.

Gordon, Milton M. *Assimilation in American Life.* New York: Oxford University Press, 1964. Outlines the factors involved in the difficult process of assimilation into American society, but the author's insights and analysis of the process in the United States can be used to understand any society. Has a useful but dated bibliography and an index.

Marger, Martin N. *Race and Ethnic Relations: American and Global Perspectives.* Belmont, Calif.: Wadsworth Press, 1985. A recent survey of ethnic problems from a worldwide perspective. Has an excellent bibliography.

Simpson, George E., and J. Milton Yinger. *Racial and Cultural Minorities: An Analysis of Prejudice and Discrimination.* 3d ed. New York: Harper & Row, 1965. A general textbook that covers problems in every area of the world. The chapters in this volume cover almost every aspect of racial and ethnic relations and discuss how to achieve more tolerance between differing individuals and groups. Has a useful bibliography.

Thernstrom, Stephan, ed. *Harvard Encyclopedia of American Ethnic Groups.* Cambridge, Mass.: The Belknap Press of Harvard University Press, 1980. A very useful compilation of brief essays concerning almost every group in America. Also has useful articles on assimilation, ethnocentrism, and other key concepts. This is the place to begin in any search for ethnic experience and cultural history.

Leslie V. Tischauser

Cross-References

Annihilation or Expulsion of Racial or Ethnic Groups, 92; Assimilation: The United States, 140; Conquest and Annexation of Racial or Ethnic Groups, 353; Cultural and Structural Assimilation, 405; Ethnicity and Ethnic Groups, 689; Institutional Racism, 996; Internal Colonialism, 1015; Minority and Majority Groups, 1219.

ETHNICITY AND ETHNIC GROUPS

Type of sociology: Racial and ethnic relations
Field of study: Basic concepts

Ethnicity refers to a sense of belonging and identification with a particular cultural heritage. Ethnic groups are socially defined on the basis of their cultural characteristics. Members of ethnic groups consider themselves, and are considered by others to be, part of a distinct culture or subculture. These concepts help explain the cultural diversity which can occur in a given society.

Principal terms

ASSIMILATION: a process by which members of subcultures and minorities acquire cultural characteristics of the dominant group

CULTURAL PLURALISM: a system where different ethnic and racial groups can coexist without losing their respective traits

CULTURE: the beliefs, values, behavior, and material objects shared by a particular people

DISCRIMINATION: treating various groups of people unequally

ETHNIC GROUP: a group that shares a cultural heritage and is viewed by itself and by others as distinctive

ETHNICITY: a shared cultural heritage

MINORITY GROUP: a group that occupies an inferior or subordinate position of power, prestige, and privilege

RACE: a group that is socially defined on the basis of physical characteristics

RACISM: the ideology contending that actual or alleged differences among different racial groups assert the superiority of one racial group

Overview

Despite the considerable amount of attention devoted to the subject, scholars have not reached a consensus on the precise meaning of ethnicity. Since ethnicity is such a complex concept, many scholars have chosen to identify ethnic groups as those groups characterized by some of the following fourteen features: common geographic origins; migratory status; race; language or dialect; religious faith or faiths; ties that transcend kinship, neighborhood, and community boundaries; shared traditions, values, and symbols; literature, folklore, and music; food preferences; settlement and employment patterns; special interests in regard to politics; institutions that specifically serve and maintain the group; an internal sense of distinctiveness; and an external perception of distinctiveness.

Sociologist Milton Yinger defines an ethnic group as one whose members are thought by themselves and others to have a common origin and who share a common culture which is transmitted through shared activities that reinforce the group's distinctiveness. The term ethnic group has been used by social scientists in two different ways. Some definitions of ethnic groups are broad and include both physical (racial) and cultural characteristics. Others are narrower and rely solely on cultural or nationality characteristics. Sociologist Joe R. Feagin emphasizes that ancestry, whether real or mythical, is a very important dimension of ethnic group identity.

Sociologist William Yancey and his associates argue that ethnic groups have been produced by structural conditions which are linked to the changing technology of production and transportation. Structural conditions including common occupational patterns, residential stability, concentration, and dependence on common institutions and services reinforce kinship and friendship networks. According to Yancey, common cultural heritage is not a prerequisite dimension of ethnicity. Ethnicity is a manifestation of the way populations are organized in terms of interaction patterns, institutions, values, attitudes, lifestyle, and consciousness of kind.

A new consciousness is emerging concerning the meaning of ethnicity. Ethnic groups are joining together into larger ethnic groupings. The adoption of a panethnic identity is common among Asians, American Indians, and Hispanics. Sociologist Felix Padilla writes about the development of a Latino collective identity among Mexican Americans and Puerto Ricans. Ethnicity and one's ethnic identity is becoming more of a matter of choice, especially for white Americans of European descent. Most people have multiple layers of ethnic identity because of generations of interethnic marriages; these layers can be added to or subtracted from one's current identity. Sociologists Richard Alba and Mary Waters acknowledge that people often know their ancestors are from a variety of ethnic groups but for one reason or another identify with only some of them (or none of them). Often people identify with those with whom they have the least connection.

Sociologist Robert Blauner, in his influential book *Black Lives, White Lives* (1989), addresses the confusion that is often produced in the American consciousness by the concepts of race and ethnicity. Blauner argues that the imagery of race tends to be more powerful than the imagery of ethnicity and therefore often overshadows it. The reason for this is that race—although generally viewed by scientists and social scientists as a social construct rather than a scientific reality—is associated with biological and scientific imagery, whereas ethnicity is associated with cultural imagery. Other important concepts, such as class and religion, are also overwhelmed by the powerful social meanings of race. The confounding of race and ethnicity is a daily occurrence in American society. Blauner holds that African Americans represent both a racial and an ethnic group and argues that when blacks assert their ethnicity, whites perceive it instead as an assertion of racial identity. He postulates that part of the American heritage of racism has been to deny the ethnicity or cultural heritage of African Americans.

Most theories used to explain ethnicity, ethnic behavior, and ethnic and racial relations have been concerned with the issues of migration, adaptation, exploitation, stratification, and conflict. These theories can be classified into two groups: order theories and power-conflict theories. Order theories emphasize the assimilation of ethnic groups in a society, whereas power-conflict theories address the issue of persisting inequality of power and resource distribution between majority and minority groups.

Sociologist Milton Gordon has described three images of assimilation: the melting pot, cultural pluralism, and Anglo-conformity. The most compelling of the three images, according to Gordon, is Anglo-conformity, according to which immigrant groups give up much of their cultural heritage for the dominant Anglo-Saxon core culture. This process has occurred for the majority of immigrant groups. Gordon's perspective fits well as an explanation for the majority of white Americans of European descent, but it does not fully explain the experiences of non-European immigrant groups such as Asians, Hispanics, and African Americans.

Power-conflict theories (caste, internal colonialism, Marxist, split labor market, and enclave theories) focus on involuntary immigration and/or colonial oppression. Power-conflict theorists have stressed the forced nature of cultural and economic adaptation, and they emphasize the role played by the processes of coercion, segregation, colonization, and institutionalized discrimination.

Applications

In his book *Ethnic America* (1981), economist Thomas Sowell argues that the experiences of white ethnic groups and racial minorities have been different in degree rather than in kind. Historian Ronald Takaki, however, in his book *From Different Shores* (1987), challenges Sowell's assumption. Takaki emphasizes the facts that only blacks were enslaved, only American Indians were placed on reservations, only Japanese Americans were placed in concentration camps, and only the Chinese were excluded from naturalized citizenship. To understand fully the experiences and histories of ethnic groups one must acknowledge the role of economic and governmental contexts within which particular ethnic groups have immigrated and adjusted. The time of immigration and the resources brought by the immigrants have affected not only their economic and political success but also their social class position in the United States.

In his book *Race and Ethnic Relations* (1994), sociologist Martin N. Marger describes the American ethnic hierarchy as consisting of three parts. The top third consists primarily of white Protestants from various ethnic backgrounds. The middle third consists of Catholics from various ethnic backgrounds, Jews, and many Asians. The bottom third consists of blacks, Hispanics, American Indians, and some Asians. The most important aspect of this ethnic hierarchy is the gap between those groups in the bottom third of the hierarchy and the other two segments.

The median income of African American families in 1990 was $21,423, which was 58 percent of that earned by white families ($36,915). Black families are three times more likely than white families to live in poverty. In 1990 one in four black families was in the middle class, and one in ten was affluent.

The median income of Asian (Chinese, Japanese, Filipino, Asian-Indian, Korean,

Vietnamese, and others) families in 1990 was $42,240, while the national average was $33,500. Part of the explanation of why Asian Americans have a much higher median family income is that 39 percent of them have completed four or more years of college, whereas only 21.4 percent of the entire U.S. population has completed four or more years of college. The poverty rate among Japanese Americans is half that for the United States as a whole, but the poverty rate for Chinese Americans, especially in China-towns, is much higher than other groups in the inner city.

The median income of Hispanic (Mexican, Puerto Rican, Cuban, and others) families in 1990 was $23,431. The median income of Cuban Americans was well above that of other Hispanics at $31,439. Mexican Americans earned $23,240, while Puerto Ricans were well below the median income at $18,008. According to the U.S. Bureau of the Census, in 1990 25 percent of Mexican Americans, 37.5 percent of Puerto Ricans, and 13.8 percent of Cuban Americans were living in poverty. The number of Hispanic households with at least $50,000 in annual income more than tripled between 1972 and 1988.

By the 1970's Jews had attained the highest income levels of all European ethnic groups in the United States, closely followed by Irish, German, Italian, and Polish Catholics. Most white Anglo-Saxon Protestants trailed these white ethnics in income and educational levels. According to sociologist Andrew Greeley, Irish Catholics are one of the most prosperous of the white ethnic groups, while Irish Protestants tend to be one of the least prosperous groups. Sociologist Douglas Massey, of the University of Chicago, has shown that African Americans are more segregated within cities, less likely to move out of cities, and much more likely to move to segregated suburbs when they do leave cities than Hispanics and Asians. Asians are the least segregated and the most suburbanized of the three groups.

Context

Sociology became an accepted part of American academia during the end of the nineteenth century and at the beginning of the twentieth century primarily through the efforts of Sociologist Robert Park and his colleagues at the University of Chicago. Sociologists Ernest Burgess, Louis Wirth, Harvey Zorbaugh, Frederick Thrasher, and others produced now-classic studies of the urbanization process in Chicago. The study of community coincided with and included the study of ethnicity. Urban sociology began with studies of immigrants. Chicago was then (and still is) one of the United States' most ethnically diverse cities, and the intellectual tradition of urban community studies has continued with works such as Ruth Horowitz's *Honor and the American Dream: Culture and Identity in a Chicano Community* (1983) and Mitchell Duneier's *Slim's Table: Race, Respectability, and Masculinity* (1992).

Sociologist Scott Greer indicates that some of the early thinking about ethnicity in American sociology was stimulated by the National Origins Quota Act of 1924, which temporarily restricted the immigration of certain groups, primarily southern and eastern Europeans. This act was instituted because of a belief that groups of non-Anglo-Saxon background were much more prone to criminal activity; they were assumed to be genetically inferior. This act was repealed in 1931. Another watershed act that later contributed to a heightened interest in ethnicity was the Immigration Act of 1965. This legislation opened the doors of the United States to many groups, primarily Asians and Hispanics, who had been discriminated against by earlier immigration policies. Also, the civil rights legislation of the 1960's and the aftermath of government regulations and programs such as affirmative action provided opportunities for debate, research, and analysis concerning the state of ethnicity.

In his book *Ethnicity in the United States* (1974), Andrew Greeley concludes that no ethnic "revival" was occurring in the late 1960's or early 1970's; rather, white ethnic groups simply felt less inhibited in talking about themselves and their cultural heritage. Greeley indicates the attention given to black cultural diversity in the 1960's and 1970's legitimized other kinds of cultural diversity. Richard Alba, in his book *Ethnic Identity* (1990), describes the transformation of ethnicity which has taken place in the United States. Around the time of World War II and soon thereafter, the expectation was that ethnic Americans would assimilate and their sense of ethnicity would gradually disappear. This assumption was known as the melting pot theory. During the 1950's, 1960's, and 1970's, however, sociologist Nathan Glazer and political scientist Daniel Patrick Moynihan (among others) questioned the viability of the melting pot theory. Glazer, Moynihan, and others suggested that the United States was leaning more in the direction of cultural pluralism.

In the 1980's and early 1990's, the debate about the melting pot versus cultural pluralism, according to Alba, no longer dominated discussions of ethnicity, especially concerning white European ethnic groups. Alba argues that ethnicity is not less embedded in the structure of American society but rather that ethnic distinctions are undergoing change. He believes that ethnic distinctions based on European ancestry are dissolving, while a new ethnic group is forming based on ancestry from anywhere on the European continent.

Bibliography

Alba, Richard D. *Ethnic Identity*. New Haven, Conn.: Yale University Press, 1990. This book strongly suggests that what the United States was experiencing in the 1970's and 1980's was not a revival of ethnicity but a rise in symbolic ethnicity. A new ethnic group called "European Americans" is emerging with its own myths, Alba suggests; he argues that ethnicity among non-Hispanic whites is in the midst of a fundamental transformation.

_____ , ed. *Ethnicity and Race in the U.S.A.* Boston: Routledge & Kegan Paul, 1985. A collection of studies by leading scholars of ethnicity and race. These studies were originally presented at a conference on ethnicity and race held at the State University of New York at Albany in 1984. Many of the studies are based on 1980 census data. Chapters are devoted to blacks, American Indians, Hispanics, Asian Americans, white ethnics, and "unhyphenated" whites.

Feagin, Joe R., and Clairece Booher Feagin. *Racial and Ethnic Relations*. 4th ed. Englewood Cliffs, N.J.: Prentice-Hall, 1993. A standard college textbook in its fourth edition. Several introductory chapters discuss key racial concepts and theoretical models relating to ethnic relations. Chapters are devoted to discussing specific racial and ethnic groups: English Americans, Irish Americans, Italian Americans, Jewish Americans, American Indians, African Americans, Mexican Americans, Puerto Rican and Cuban Americans, Japanese Americans, and Chinese, Filipino, Korean, and Vietnamese Americans.

Glazer, Nathan. *Ethnic Dilemmas 1964-1982*. Cambridge, Mass.: Harvard University Press, 1983. A collection of papers by Glazer analyzing issues of racial and ethnic conflict such as cultural pluralism, bilingualism, and the affirmative action debate. Glazer argues that the fight against discrimination chose the wrong solution. An important source.

Glazer, Nathan, and Daniel P. Moynihan. *Beyond the Melting Pot*. 2d ed. Cambridge, Mass.: MIT Press, 1970. A classic, controversial, and often-cited book that focuses on five ethnic groups (blacks, Puerto Ricans, Jews, Italians, and Irish) in New York City during the early 1960's with an update for the 1970's.

Maldonado, Lionel, and Joan Moore. *Urban Ethnicity in the United States*. Beverly Hills, Calif.: Sage Publications, 1985. A collection of ten articles that discuss the "new immigrants" (Hispanics and Asians). The book is organized into two sections. The first builds a context for the study of contemporary racial and ethnic issues in American cities, and the second investigates the reciprocal impact of new immigrants and institutions (education, economy, politics, and so on).

Padilla, Felix M. *Latino Ethnic Consciousness*. Notre Dame, Ind.: University of Notre Dame Press, 1985. This study examines the process of Latino/Hispanic ethnic group formation in Chicago. It identifies and explains the conditions that have enabled Mexican Americans and Puerto Ricans to adopt a new or collective Latino or Hispanic identity distinct and separate from the groups' individual ethnic identities. Highly recommended.

Takaki, Ronald, ed. *From Different Shores*. New York: Oxford University Press, 1987. A collection of essays on race and ethnicity by contemporary well-known neoconservative, liberal, and leftist scholars. Sections of the book are devoted to articles on ethnic and racial patterns, culture, class, gender, and prospects for the future. Highly recommended.

Thernstrom, Stephan, ed. *The Harvard Encyclopedia of American Ethnic Groups*. Cambridge, Mass.: The Belknap Press of Harvard University Press, 1980. Arguably the most important single source in print concerning ethnicity and ethnic groups. The encyclopedia contains 106 entries on specific ethnic groups from Acadians to Zoroastrians, twenty-nine thematic essays dealing with such issues as assimilation and pluralism, and eighty-seven maps. The specific group entries discuss origins, migration, arrival, settlement, economic life, social structure and organization, family, kinship, culture, religion, education, and politics. Highly recommended.

William L. Smith

Cross-References

Anti-Semitism, 114; Assimilation: The United States, 140; Cultural and Structural Assimilation, 405; Ethnic Enclaves, 682; Immigration to the United States, 928; Minority and Majority Groups, 1219; "Model" Minorities, 1233; Pluralism versus Assimilation, 1374; Race and Racial Groups, 1552; Racial and Ethnic Stratification, 1579.

ETHNOGRAPHY

Type of sociology: Sociological research
Field of study: Data collection and analysis

An ethnography is a description of a culture, a subculture, or a group of people with a distinctive lifestyle. It describes the people, their customs, the events in which they participate, and their conversations. It also describes the materials they use (food, clothing, shelter, and utensils) in everyday life and how they use them.

Principal terms
CULTURE: the patterns for thinking, feeling, behaving, and interpreting experience used by a group of people to organize their way of life
ETHNOGRAPHY: a descriptive study of a culture that includes information about what people of the culture do and say as well as about their values, beliefs, and customs
FIELD NOTES: a written account of the social behavior observed by a field researcher while studying a culture
FIELD RESEARCH: research in which an observer goes to a culture and either records observations of that culture or participates to some extent in the culture and makes observations based on that participation
QUALITATIVE RESEARCH: the collection and analysis of descriptive data, rather than numerical data, that depict the social behavior within a culture
SUBCULTURE: a group with ways of thinking, feeling, and behaving that differ from those of the dominant culture in some essential respects

Overview

The term "ethnography" refers both to a type of research and to the specific studies that such research ultimately produces. Sociological research is often considered to be divided into four major types: experiments, surveys, observation, and historical or archival research. The terms "observation" and "ethnography" are sometimes used synonymously. In this sense, although ethnography originally referred to the study of ethnic groups, it may refer to the observational study of a number of different types of societal subgroups.

An ethnography is a descriptive study of a culture, a subculture, an institution, or a group of people. A study of the Yanomamo, a group of Indians who live in Brazil and Venezuela, would be the study of a culture. The study of the Amish, an American religious group that lives without modern conveniences, would be a study of an American subculture. The study of an elementary school would be the study of an institution. The study of a peer group of neighborhood children, residents of a retirement community, or a group of cocktail waitresses would be an ethnography of a group of people.

An ethnography describes what people do. Depending on the nature of the group under study, it may include a wide range of human activities. It may include how people obtain food, clothing, shelter, and other basic necessities. For example, in the case of food, people might hunt animals, gather herbs and fruit, plant crops, or buy food from others. The study might also describe how a group distributes food once it is obtained. Other aspects of life that could be examined include kinship structure (how families are formed and how they interrelate), religious rituals and behavior, political systems and activities, and leisure activities. Many other aspects of daily life may be examined by an ethnography, including conversations and other social interactions and descriptions of objects used in everyday life. Finally, most ethnographic studies attempt to provide some interpretation of the meaning of the culture under study—the "whys" behind the behaviors observed.

One of the most famous and classic ethnographic books is Margaret Mead's *Coming of Age in Samoa* (1928). Mead described the life of Samoan adolescent females as they made the transition from childhood to being Samoan adults. She discussed how Samoan adolescent life for these females involved casual or free love experiences. By avoiding the sexual repression demanded of youth in many Western cultures, Mead reported, the Samoan females enjoyed easy, pleasant, and nontroubling adolescent years.

Ethnographies are usually intended to be as holistic as possible. In other words, they attempt to study as much of the culture or cultural group as is feasible rather than to focus on limited aspects of life. An ethnographic study of a community would focus, for example, on how the people make a living and on how their families operate, as well as on their religion, politics, and neighborhood groups—a full round of life.

The sociologists and anthropologists who undertake ethnographic studies are usually called "field workers" because they go to where their subjects live and study them in their natural environment. Ethnographic research is distinct from the approach of researchers pursuing experimental or survey research. Ethnographic research is qualitative rather than quantitative—that is, it is concerned with describing and interpreting rather than with asking questions and counting and classifying answers. It is also subjective. The ethnographic researcher has more latitude than other researchers do when it comes to planning a study and has more flexibility regarding changes in the study once it is under way. What behaviors are observed, how they are observed and recorded, and which ones are selected as being especially significant are all decisions made by the researcher.

This subjectivity can be seen as both a strength and a weakness of ethnographic research. The ability of the ethnographer to adapt and modify a study once it is under way is a strength of the approach, but it requires that the researcher be constantly vigilant and open to new perceptions and ideas. Both survey researchers and experimenters, on the other hand, approach the study of human behavior with a predetermined plan of action—a set of questions or an experimental design—that they bring to the subjects of their studies. Whereas various rules and guidelines are specified in texts and guidebooks, field researchers may pick and choose from any number of different observational approaches. A drawback to this is that it becomes far more difficult to draw comparisons between different ethnographic studies than it is to compare experimental or survey results. Observations are usually recorded in the form of field notes. Researchers write down the things people do and say, and they record what objects people use; they record where things happened and exactly who was present. The field notes are later combined and organized to form the basis for writing the ethnography.

Applications

A number of steps are involved in producing an ethnography. The first step in studying a cultural group is the selection of the culture or group to be studied. This decision is usually based on a combination of the interests, background, and resources of the researcher. Although a researcher may be interested in studying a cultural group in an isolated part of the world, for example, such a study might not be possible because of the researcher's limited time, funds, or knowledge of the group's language. Another crucial factor is the willingness or unwillingness of the group itself to be studied.

A second step is to decide on the role that the researcher will take during the study—how involved he or she will be in the activities of the group under study. A researcher may act either as a participant observer (either overt or covert) or a nonparticipant observer. Most researchers choose to become a limited participant observer: They observe a group while participating in it in limited ways that would be appropriate for a visitor to the group. Fewer researchers choose covert participant observation—becoming involved in the group's activities without revealing that they are studying the group. The advantage of this approach is that it avoids the possibility that people's behavior will change because they know they are being observed. The serious disadvantage is that it raises ethical questions. Covert observation can be seen as invading the privacy of those under study and as dishonest in that the researcher usually must mislead or lie to members of the group to conceal his or her identity. A third approach is nonparticipant observation, in which a researcher observes the group without becoming involved in the group's lives or activities at all. The drawback to this method is that the researcher, by maintaining distance, may miss aspects of the group's culture that would be apparent upon closer (participant) examination.

One of the unique features of ethnography is the methods of observation and data collection that are used. Techniques in this research approach are much less standardized than those in experimentation or survey research. Each ethnographer must choose from an array of possible fieldwork techniques in order to record, interpret, and understand the group's actions. Researchers may take notes and photographs and may make audio or video recordings of activities. To clarify actions, individual or group interviews can be used. Napoleon A. Chagnon, in his ethnography *Yanomamo: The Fierce People* (1983), a study of kinship and village life among an Indian group in Brazil and Venezuela, used photographs effectively to help develop elaborate kinship charts to identify relatives living in different villages. Individual life histories can be obtained, and personal documents such as birth records, religious books and records, and personal belongings and papers can be used as sources of information.

Most ethnographers use one or more "informants" in their research. An informant is a member of the culture being studied who has considerable insider knowledge of that culture. Informants can be helpful in acquiring access to certain persons or events in the culture that would otherwise be off-limits or unattainable for the researcher by himself or herself. Informants can suggest things for the researcher to focus on or explain things about the culture from an insider's perspective that the ethnographer is having difficulty understanding. Informants can provide information to the researcher about events and ceremonies, for example, that the researcher as an outsider or member of the opposite gender would not be permitted to observe (such as the birth of a child or a puberty ritual).

Observations are almost always recorded by the researcher in the form of field notes. Important observations should be recorded as quickly as possible while they are still fresh in the mind. The notes can later be rewritten, modified, or expanded based on further developments in the ethnographic investigation. Computers are being used increasingly in the recording of field notes; they enable ease of additions, revisions, and reorganization. It is important that researchers record conversations as well as actions; moreover, a crucial aspect of conversation is how the hearers attribute meaning to what is said. Behaviors must be related to one another to form a larger picture of what is occurring. In American culture, for example, a number of behaviors, such as arguing, fighting, changing one's place of residence, and hiring lawyers, are part of a larger event known as divorce. Any meeting of two or more people must be viewed as a social interaction, and roles and relationships must also be examined.

Once data collection is completed, the ethnography itself can be written. Recurrent or important themes from the field notes are developed into an overall presentation about the group. The ethnographer usually recounts key experiences and describes the techniques used during the observation and writing of the study.

Context

Ethnographic research, or field research, is one of the four major approaches or methodologies for obtaining information on human behavior. The other three methods are experiments, surveys, and the use of available or existing data (often archival or historical data). Of these four methods, ethnographic studies produce results that are most directly related to real-life events and activities, because they occur in the natural environment of the people under study. Ethnography also lends itself to openness, flexibility, and new discoveries. Researchers can freely change course to pursue emerging interests or ideas and to abandon themes that become unproductive. It is weak on control, however, the strong point of experiments, because the researcher as an observer cannot (and should not) shape events in the real world as an experimenter can manipulate variables.

Before World War II, ethnographic research was the most common and most influential form of sociological research in the United States. In the early twentieth century, leading sociologists at the University of Chicago, under the guidance of

Robert Park, conducted much ethnographic research based on communities and lifestyles in Chicago and around the country. Following World War II, many sociologists embraced survey research and its seemingly more scientific approach to examining human behavior. The widespread utilization of computers, beginning in the 1960's and increasing thereafter as computers became more sophisticated, furthered the trend toward survey research.

Other sociologists have remained firm in their commitment to ethnographic research, a qualitative rather than quantitative approach. They argue that the understanding of human behavior is most appropriately accomplished by observing people in their natural environments rather than by looking at behavior in a laboratory or by asking questions. They point out that the very nature of testing hypotheses or framing questions to be asked imposes the ideas and worldview of the people doing the testing or writing the questions. Computers have significantly affected sociologists' approach to survey research. Because they are able to analyze closed-end questions (questions with a limited number of precoded options as answers), they have made this type of survey very popular. Closed-end questions provide a restricted view of the respondents' opinions, however, because they make it impossible for them to elaborate on their answers or to go in different directions, as is possible with open-ended questions. Computers are also useful in ethnographic research, it should be noted, and their increasing use in this area may ultimately increase the popularity and prominence of ethnographic research in sociology.

Bibliography

Chagnon, Napoleon A. *Yanomamo: The Fierce People*. 3d ed. New York: Holt, Rinehart and Winston, 1983. Chagnon offers a thorough and entertaining explanation of how he conducted his ethnographic research among the Yanomamo, a large tribe of tropical forest Indians who live along the border between Brazil and Venezuela. He studied their kinship patterns, ways of making a living, and political alliances and warfare patterns.

Fetterman, David M. *Ethnography: Step by Step*. Newbury Park, Calif.: Sage Publications, 1989. The author explains how fieldwork is conducted. He covers cultural concepts and terms and discusses how to enter the culture or begin the study. Methods of observation, interviewing, note taking, and analysis of cultural data are presented in a step-by-step manner. Finally, suggestions on how to write the ethnography are detailed.

Hall, Larry, and Kimball Marshall. *Computing for Social Research*. Belmont, Calif.: Wadsworth, 1992. Chapters 7 and 8 of this book present ways of using computers to collect, analyze, and present ethnographic data. These chapters explain how to use computers to take field notes, how to organize and analyze field data with word processors and indexing programs, and how to use specialized field research programs.

Liebow, Elliott. *Tally's Corner*. Boston: Little, Brown, 1967. This book presents an empathetic study of the lives of African American streetcorner men in Washington,

D.C., in the 1960's. It explains how they see work and family relations with their wives, former wives, children, friends, and lovers.

Mead, Margaret. *Coming of Age in Samoa*. New York: W. Morrow, 1928. This early, classic ethnography describes the roles of adolescent girls in the Samoan culture. The most famous and influential descriptions are those of the casual nature of free love and the lack of adolescent turmoil among the Samoan teenage girls.

Spradley, James P. *Participant Observation*. New York: Holt, Rinehart and Winston, 1980. This basic book explains, in twelve steps, how to conduct ethnographic research. Spradley presents guidelines on how to select a cultural group to study, how to observe cultural events, how to take field notes, and how to analyze cultural data. Finally, guidelines are presented for writing the ethnography.

Spradley, James P., and Brenda J. Mann. *The Cocktail Waitress*. New York: John Wiley & Sons, 1975. The authors employ ethnographic research methods to study the role of cocktail waitresses in a college bar setting. The emphasis in this ethnography is on the meaning of work from the perspective of women who are employed in a world predominantly populated and dominated by men.

Larry D. Hall

Cross-References

Ethics and Politics in Social Research, 675; Qualitative Research, 1540; Sociological Research: Description, Exploration, and Explanation, 1920; Surveys, 2030; Triangulation, 2071; Unobtrusive Research, 2103.

ETHNOMETHODOLOGY

Type of sociology: Socialization and social interaction
Field of study: Interactionist approach to social interactions

Ethnomethodology investigates the methods of commonsensical reasoning that ordinary social actors use to recognize features of the social world and to produce and understand everyday social actions. This approach treats commonsensical reasoning as a fundamental topic of sociological analysis and challenges approaches to sociology that ignore the role of ordinary reason in social action.

Principal terms

ACCOUNTABILITY: the commonsensical recognizability of objects, events, persons, and descriptions of these within the framework of a set of shared understandings

BACKGROUND KNOWLEDGE: the body of shared but tacit and taken-for-granted knowledge of the social world that is employed in making sense of everyday events

DOCUMENTARY METHOD OF INTERPRETATION: the description of commonsensical reasoning as a dynamic process in which the actors' grasp of a situation depends on the mutual elaboration of particular objects of perception and the contexts in which those objects occur

ETHNOMETHODS: commonsensical reasoning about the social world that actors use to produce and recognize courses of action in their everyday activities; also called "members' methods"

INDEXICALITY: the property of objects, events, and descriptions through which their meaning is shaped by the context in which they occur

JUDGMENTAL DOPE: Harold Garfinkel's terms for models of social actors that treat their actions as the causal products of determinate rules

REFLEXIVITY: the property of the recognition of objects, events, and descriptions through which that recognition shapes the context of a situation

Overview

According to ethnomethodology's founder, sociologist Harold Garfinkel, social order is located, in the first place, in shared understanding among ordinary social actors (an "actor" being anyone performing an action). Shared understanding or, to use Garfinkel's phrase, "knowledge held in common" is the primordial basis for an orderly, social world. To Garfinkel, knowledge held in common depends on a set of shared practices by which actors produce and recognize social reality as meaningful. All major social institutions and interactions—including, for example, socialization, exchange, and even warfare—depend on shared understanding. While ethnomethodology is similar to other sociological perspectives in emphasizing shared understanding as the foundation for social order, it is distinctive in treating shared understanding as a practical accomplishment.

Shared understanding is an *accomplishment* in that it depends on the everyday activities of society's members. Through their actions, members constitute the social world as the ordered, coherent, and reasonable place that it is typically understood to be. Moreover, as Garfinkel describes the situation, there are "no time outs" from the achievement of social order; it is an "ongoing accomplishment."

The accomplishment of shared understanding is *practical* because it depends on a common set of procedures whereby social action is produced and recognized as meaningful. Because these practices are rarely the objects of social actors' conscious reflections, Garfinkel described them as "seen but unnoticed." Though unnoticed, this shared set of practices is not unimportant. Garfinkel insisted that the practices, as well as the background knowledge that informs them, constitute the primordial basis for social order. Focusing on the procedural character of commonsensical reasoning and practical action, Garfinkel showed how social actors produce and maintain their sense of an orderly and meaningful social world even when incongruous events challenge that understanding. Garfinkel referred to this orderly, but typically unacknowledged, set of practices as "ethnomethods" and sought to explain both their properties and their import for the constitution of ordinary social activities and situations.

A major constituent property of ethnomethods is the "documentary method of interpretation." Garfinkel derived the term from the work of sociologist Karl Mannheim and used it to refer to the process by which ordinary social actors make sense of situations. According to Garfinkel, actors understand individual objects of perception in terms of the context in which the objects appear, and, at the same time, they understand context on the basis of particular objects occurring within it. Thus, rather than being discrete entities, the meaning of an object and its context are mutually elaborative: Each informs the meaning of the other. The most basic implication of this insight is that neither particular objects nor contexts can be understood as fixed; both are actively constructed by social actors themselves.

Ethnomethodologists argue that every social action is reflexive and indexical, requiring the interpretive work of social actors to attribute meaning to it. On the basis of this interpretive work, social order is achieved as an "ongoing accomplishment." To exemplify this process, Garfinkel conducted an exercise in which subjects were told to ask yes/no questions of a person described to them as a psychological counselor. The counselor's "answers" were predetermined in a random pattern. Nevertheless, in the context of a "counseling session," subjects used their background knowledge to make sense of the counselor's responses as if they were answers to their questions.

Most of Garfinkel's studies focus on concrete, everyday actions and are designed to explore the ways in which they are produced and understood. Garfinkel used a series of "breaching experiments" in which the experimenters would disrupt the details of a commonplace situation to make it somehow incongruous with the subjects' commonsensical expectations.

For example, Garfinkel used the game of ticktacktoe. After allowing the subject to move first, the experimenter would intentionally make an invalid move, without acknowledging it. In response, subjects either "normalized" the situation—by treating the invalid move as a joke or by concluding that the game being played was something other than ticktacktoe—or they "demonized" the situation, usually by demanding that the experimenter acknowledge, correct, and sometimes even apologize for the invalid move. Garfinkel concluded that either sort of response depended on an intricate intertwining of cognitive and moral expectations that he termed "accountability."

Garfinkel found the breaching experiments useful because the incongruous situations forced attention on the mundane details of everyday activities (such as describing an experience or playing a simple game) that are normally taken-for-granted. Not all of his ethnomethodological investigations depended on instigated instances of incongruity. In some of his studies Garfinkel investigated naturally arising incongruities. Most famous, perhaps, is his study of "Agnes," who was reared as a boy but as an adult assumed the identity of a female. To "pass" as a woman, Agnes had to overcome her lack of appropriate female anatomy and biography. Based on her experiences, Agnes learned how commonsensical practices work to create the normally taken-for-granted understandings of gender as both moral and natural. As Garfinkel's study of Agnes demonstrated, ordinary beliefs about gender as something fixed once and for all rest upon an entire range of seen but unnoticed assumptions and actions based on those assumptions.

Ethnomethodology consistently stresses the procedural character of social action. On the basis of shared sets of practices, actors are able to construct their own lines of conduct as well as to interpret the actions of others. Thus, rather than being imposed externally, social order emerges as a product of actors' own courses of action.

Applications

Ethnomethodology contends that any social setting, from the everyday conversations of two friends to the work of astrophysicists in a laboratory, is appropriate subject matter for ethnomethodological study. Many ethnomethodological studies have influenced related research in fields such as anthropology, artificial intelligence, cognitive science, linguistics, and psychology. Within sociology, investigators have applied ethnomethodology to understand the use of organizationally produced statistics on deviance, the social organization of the natural sciences, and, in a branch of sociology known as "conversation analysis," the orderly properties of talk.

Statistics have played a central role in sociology at least since sociologist Émile Durkheim's *Le Suicide: Étude de sociologie* (1897; *Suicide: A Study in Sociology*, 1951). In this tradition, sociologists have used statistics, collected by official organizations and regarding the rates of social phenomena such as crime, joblessness, and suicide, to assess the incidence and significance of these phenomena and to advance explanations for them. Ethnomethodology challenges this way of working by questioning the relationship between statistics and the phenomena the statistics represent. In sociological works such as J. Maxwell Atkinson's *Discovering Suicide: Studies in* the *Social Organization of Sudden Death* (1978) and Aaron Cicourel's *The Social Organization of Juvenile Justice* (1976), ethnomethodology suggests that these organizationally generated statistics are themselves social accomplishments.

Both those studies introduced concerns about the definitions and procedures used by official institutions for identifying deviant acts. The studies call into question not only the reliability of the organizationally collected data but also, more fundamentally, the validity of the data. In showing that the definitions and procedures for identifying deviance are themselves social practices, embedded in bureaucratic organizations, ethnomethodology shows how rates of deviance themselves are constituted by the institutions created to measure them. Consequently, quantitative studies of social phenomena must take into account the social practices involved in collecting official statistics.

Ethnomethodology has also contributed to the sociological understanding of the methods of natural science. In research such as sociologist Michael Lynch's *Art and Artifact in Laboratory Science* (1985), ethnomethodology shows how social practices inform supposedly "objective" findings in scientific investigations. Lynch examined the social processes by which neuroscientists using electron microscopes discovered, recorded, and described the destruction and regrowth of axons in rats' brains. According to Lynch and other ethnomethodological studies of natural science, the scientists' social practices of investigation have as much influence on their findings as do the objects of their investigation. Thus, ethnomethodology informs sociology's understanding of the performance and findings of natural science.

Finally, the principles of ethnomethodology have contributed to the field of sociology known as "conversation analysis" (CA). The pioneering work of Harvey Sacks, in collaboration with fellow sociologists Emanuel Schegloff and Gail Jefferson, continues to be a major resource for sociologists as well as researchers in the fields of anthropology, applied linguistics, and social psychology. The naturally occurring details of talk in interaction constitute the data of conversation analysis. By investigating audiotaped and videotaped records of actual, naturally occurring interactions, conversation analysts have been able to describe the organizational principles of talk as a social phenomenon in its own right. The organizational principles thus described by conversation analysts are embodied in the participants' own actions and are observably displayed in their orientations to and interpretations of those actions.

Conversation analysis proceeds by analyzing turns to talk and how these turns are built into connected sequences of interaction. Talk is thus viewed as being at once interactionally and sequentially organized. Therefore, conversation analysts consistently ask: How is the talk under study being constructed by the participants? What is the talk responsive to? What is it being used to do? By posing such questions, practitioners of conversation analysis have succeeded in providing detailed analytic descriptions of the organization of conduct for a variety of social settings, ranging from everyday conversation to talk in institutional contexts such as courtrooms, television news interviews, and medical interactions. In each instance, conversation analysis exemplifies the fundamental ethnomethodological insight that social order is produced and recognized by the participants themselves in the course of locally situated actions.

Context

Ethnomethodology began in the 1950's as a result of Harold Garfinkel's discontent with conventional approaches to social action that treated social order as governed by rules. Garfinkel provided an exhaustive, yet appreciative, critique of his mentor, sociologist Talcott Parsons, and Parsons' theory as presented in *The Structure of Social Action* (1937). At the time Parsons was the dominant figure in American sociology, but Garfinkel's critique did much to dislodge Parsons from that position. Garfinkel's critique of Parsons was twofold.

First, Garfinkel objected to Parsons' treatment of social order as fundamentally an analytical problem. Parsons had provided a theoretical explanation of social order. In contrast, Garfinkel treated social order as a practical problem. Instead of creating a theory of social order, Garfinkel sought to show how people in their everyday lives "enacted the world" as orderly. Whereas Parsons' theoretical perspective emphasizes the knowledge of the social scientist as a theorist, Garfinkel's perspective recognizes the reasoning practices of the actors being studied.

Second, Garfinkel rejected Parsons' theoretical reliance on rules, or norms, as either the motivators of social action or the foundations of social order. In Parsons' theory, social order depends on a commonly shared set of norms, that, ideally, each member of society internalizes. Norms, in turn, define coherent sets of social roles and stable social institutions. According to Garfinkel, Parsons' treatment of norms turns social actors into "judgmental dopes," incapable of thinking reflectively about the situations of their actions or the rules that supposedly guide them. Thus, whereas Parsons treated norms as determinative of social action, Garfinkel treated norms as resources by which members recognize and make sense of social actions and the contexts in which they occur.

One important consequence of Garfinkel's shift in perspective is that he shunned Parsons' aim of creating a general theory that could provide causal explanations of social action. Garfinkel resisted organizing ethnomethodology's findings into a single, general theory, preferring instead to describe individual cases of social action as deserving of investigation in their own right.

In seeking to improve on Parsons' rule-based theory of social action, Garfinkel drew heavily on the work of sociologist and phenomenologist Alfred Schutz. Schutz described human commonsensical knowledge of the world as patchy and approximate; nevertheless, Schutz contended that this knowledge was adequate for all practical purposes. Garfinkel developed many of his ideas about commonsensical practices from Schutz's work, but he had the express aim of turning Schutz's observations about knowledge as an abstract entity into the research agenda for his investigation of "knowledge-in-use," as embedded in courses of social action.

Ethnomethodology will continue to play a robust role in sociology because of its unique position with respect to everyday social action and organization. Ethnomethodology's great contribution to social science is the study of the taken-for-granted aspects of ordinary social action as interesting in their own right. This focus emphasizes the importance of actors' processes of practical reasoning in constituting their courses of action. As ethnomethodological studies show, these shared but tacit reasoning practices provide the orderly basis for social action. Ethnomethodology's commitment to studying practical reason as embedded in courses of social action provides sociology with an omnipresent setting within which to study social order as it is produced and reproduced by a society's members.

Bibliography

Atkinson, J. Maxwell. *Discovering Suicide: Studies in the Social Organization of Sudden Death*. London: Macmillan, 1978. One of the definitive ethnomethodological studies of the relationship between statistics of deviance and the phenomena they represent. Focuses on suicide rates as socially constructed phenomena, depending on the definitions and practices of official investigators.

Atkinson, J. Maxwell, and John Heritage, eds. *Structures of Social Action*. Cambridge, England: Cambridge University Press, 1984. A collection of fifteen contributions to the field of conversation analysis. Includes sections about preference organization, topic organization, the relationship between talk and nonvocal activities, and aspects of response. Although the editors' introduction provides a useful overview of conversation analysis, this volume would probably work best as a supplement to a more introductory text on conversation analysis.

Cicourel, Aaron V. *The Social Organization of Juvenile Justice*. London: Heinemann, 1976. This book shows how the determination of juvenile delinquency, and hence the rates of it, depend on the commonsensical reasoning and background knowledge of policing agencies. The analysis that results is socially engaged, demonstrating how the resulting statistics about delinquency rationalize the injustices of the policing practices themselves.

Garfinkel, Harold. *Studies in Ethnomethodology*. Cambridge, England: Polity Press, 1967. The seminal work in ethnomethodology, this is a collection of Garfinkel's early essays, with topics ranging from how jurors in a court case reach their verdicts to the famous case study of "Agnes." These essays are challenging because of Garfinkel's unorthodox thinking and his difficult writing style; nevertheless, they are well worth the effort invested.

Heritage, John. *Garfinkel and Ethnomethodology*. Cambridge, England: Polity Press, 1984. The most complete, detailed, and accessible secondary treatment of ethnomethodology. Traces the field from the influences of Parsons and Schutz on Garfinkel through Garfinkel's *Studies in Ethnomethodology* to a survey of subsequent research by Garfinkel and others. Highly recommended.

Nofsinger, Robert. *Everyday Conversation*. Newbury Park, Calif.: Sage Publications, 1991. A relatively brief introduction to conversation analysis intended for university and college undergraduates. Nofsinger covers the basics of conversation analysis, from basic sequences of talk such as questions and answers to the "turn-taking system" of ordinary conversation, with special focus on how these affect interpersonal relationships.

Pollner, Melvin. *Mundane Reason: Reality in Everyday and Sociological Discourse.* Cambridge, England: Cambridge University Press, 1987. Explains how people sustain their belief in the objective reality of the world and events in it, especially when faced with competing, divergent accounts of those events. Pollner's study of conficting testimonies in traffic law courts is an elegant elaboration of Garfinkel's studies; also recommended because of Pollner's unusually lucid prose.

Sacks, Harvey. *Lectures on Conversation.* Edited by Gail Jefferson. 2 vols. Oxford, England: Blackwell, 1992. A mammoth compilation of Sacks's demanding lectures, delivered between 1964 and 1972. Sacks stands as one of ethnomethodology's greatest contributors, and his genius and sparkle are abundantly present in these transcribed lectures. Emanuel Schegloff's lengthy introductions to both volumes are comprehensive, accessible, and unconditionally recommended to readers finding their way through this vast, unique body of work.

Wieder, D. L. *Language and Social Reality.* The Hague: Mouton, 1974. An ethnographic description of life in a halfway house for narcotics offenders that demonstrates how actors use the "convict code" to make sense of social actions in an institutional setting. Wieder's study remains important because it shows how rules retain their character as sense-making resources even in situations of sustained social conflict.

Andrew L. Roth

Cross-References

Cultural Norms and Sanctions, 411; Culture and Language, 436; Dramaturgy, 566; Interactionism, 1009; Microsociology, 1192; Sociology Defined, 1932; The Sociology of Knowledge, 1946.

EUTHANASIA

Type of sociology: Major social institutions
Field of study: Medicine

Euthanasia refers to the taking of a life for merciful motives. In a society with advanced medical technology, euthanasia takes on added significance because the medical profession has the capability to prolong life almost indefinitely. There is a debate over whether physicians should be allowed to assist patients to die.

Principal terms

ACTIVE EUTHANASIA: the taking of a deliberate action, motivated by mercy, to end the life of another

COMPETENCY: the ability of a patient to make clear and responsible choices regarding his or her treatment; a patient must be considered competent for a refusal of treatment to be respected

DURABLE POWER OF ATTORNEY: a legal document that appoints another competent adult to make decisions on a person's own behalf should that individual become unable to make his or her wishes known

LIVING WILL: a document signed by a competent adult expressing the individual's wishes regarding potential treatment in the event that the individual ever becomes incompetent

PASSIVE EUTHANASIA: the withholding or withdrawing of "futile" treatment (treatment that may prolong a patient's life but that also prolongs suffering); in essence, letting a patient die

TERMINAL ILLNESS: an illness for which the prognosis is death

Overview

Medical technology has progressed to the extent that society has not developed the ethical framework necessary to guide its actions in many circumstances. Problems associated with organ donation, genetic testing, fetal tissue testing, and in-vitro fertilization are all examples of how technology has outstripped ethics. This is also the case regarding the treatment of terminally ill patients. Many people argue that medical technology can now prolong life past the point at which life can be considered worth living. For many terminally ill patients, such as those in the final stages of cancer, to prolong life is also to prolong suffering. This reality places physicians in an ethical dilemma in which their charge to prolong life conflicts with their promise to alleviate pain. In these cases, many ethicists and physicians believe that the preferable action is to eliminate the suffering by allowing or even assisting the patient to die.

Euthanasia is a Greek word that is translated to mean "easy death." In modern times, euthanasia—or mercy killing, as it is commonly called—has been used to refer to any action or inaction taken with the intent to hasten the death of terminally ill and suffering patients with the motive of protecting them from further suffering.

Euthanasia may take either of two basic forms: active or passive. Active euthanasia refers to taking a specific action to kill a patient, such as giving a patient a lethal dose of a morphine sulfate. Passive euthanasia involves the withholding of treatment that could prolong life. In the United States and virtually every other nation, passive euthanasia is the only legally acceptable strategy for hastening the death of a terminally ill patient. This usually involves withdrawing a respirator or other "extraordinary" measures that are keeping the patient alive.

The problem associated with passive euthanasia in the withdrawing of extraordinary treatments concerns the fact that there is no clear distinction between "ordinary" and "extraordinary" care in many cases of terminal disease. For example, if a terminal cancer patient suffers renal (kidney) failure, is renal dialysis considered ordinary or extraordinary care? Can a physician ethically withhold treatment for the kidney failure to save the patient from suffering a painful death from cancer? Likewise, if a dying burn patient develops an infection (severely burned patients are prone to infection because their skin has been burned away) or pneumonia, is it permissible to forgo administering antibiotics and allow the infection to overcome the patient? Many people believe that the physician is morally obligated to do everything possible to keep these patients alive. Others feel that mercy would allow the patient to die as quickly as possible.

Active euthanasia, a deliberate action to end the life of a dying patient, is considered legally equivalent to murder in the United States. Therefore, it is impossible to estimate how often it takes place; it is usually not reported. In contrast to the United States, The Netherlands has a program in which physicians may actively assist terminally ill patients to die. Physician-assisted active euthanasia occurs in that country between five thousand and ten thousand times annually. It is still officially illegal in The Netherlands, but physicians are not prosecuted if the patient has requested euthanasia and if the physician abides by strict guidelines set forth by the legal system and medical association.

Many physicians draw a moral distinction between active and passive euthanasia, preferring to allow a patient to die of his or her disease rather than from an overdose of painkiller. This is consistent with the Hippocratic Oath, which states that doctors must not do anything that could kill their patients but are allowed to withdraw futile treatments when a patient is in terminal condition. Philosopher James Rachels disagrees with this interpretation in his book *The End of Life: Euthanasia and Morality* (1986); he asserts that there is no real ethical difference between active and passive euthanasia. Rachels argues that the decision to hasten the patient's death, not the method chosen to do so, is the ethically crucial factor. Once the decision has been made to end the life of a patient, Rachels says, the most ethical approach is to carry out that decision in the least painful way available. This approach would represent a fundamental change in the way that American society deals with terminally ill patients and their families. Many patients in a persistent vegetative state are kept alive by a feeding tube that is surgically implanted in the stomach. Rachels suggests that the ethical option is to offer a lethal injection rather than disconnecting the feeding tube so that the patient dehydrates over a ten- to twenty-day period.

The medical profession is not alone in drawing a distinction between active and passive euthanasia. The American legal system certainly recognizes a difference; it allows passive euthanasia, while active euthanasia remains a punishable offense. A physician who knowingly takes an action to kill a patient is likely to face criminal charges for homicide. In contrast, passive euthanasia is more readily accepted and occurs more often because "competent" patients have the legal right to refuse treatment. When a competent individual refuses treatment, a physician is not legally obligated to keep the patient alive.

When active euthanasia has been performed, the verdicts in attempted prosecutions of those involved have been varied. In the case of *People of the State of New York v. Vincent A. Montemarano*, Vincent Montemarano was tried and found innocent of murder in a 1974 euthanasia case. In contrast, a man named Roswell Gilbert was tried and convicted of murder in the first degree for killing his terminally ill wife in Fort Lauderdale, Florida, in a 1985 case. This conviction resulted in a life sentence with twenty-five years before he was eligible for parole. (Soon after the trial, the governor of Florida commuted Gilbert's sentence.) The inconsistency in the legal treatment of euthanasia provides an excellent example of how society has yet to deal adequately with policies that affect terminally ill patients.

The illegality of active euthanasia is not the only factor deterring physicians from assisting terminally ill patients to die a less painful death. Many physicians argue that allowing doctors to assist patients to die would violate the deepest ethics of medicine and would destroy the role of the physician in society. Euthanasia, they say, is more than a matter of personal autonomy of patients. Instead, if physicians are licensed to kill, society's trust in the profession will be destroyed. Many argue that the time-honored role of healer will be replaced by one of executioner.

Applications

The euthanasia debate is far more than an abstract philosophical discussion on the role of the physician in society. It pervades actual medical practice and the lives of ordinary people on a daily basis. Because of the use of life-sustaining technology, a huge number of deaths that occur in the industrialized world are negotiated. That is, physicians and families are forced to discuss when the appropriate time would be to disconnect the machines and allow a patient to die.

Karen Quinlan was one such case. Quinlan was in a persistent vegetative state as a result of alcohol and drug abuse. When she was admitted to the emergency room, she was placed on a respirator that enabled her to breathe. In September of 1975, her physician refused her parents' request to turn off the respirator and allow her to die. Initially, the court ruled that the doctors would not be allowed to turn off the respirator. Upon appeal in 1976, the Supreme Court of New Jersey reversed the Superior Court's decision and allowed Quinlan's doctors to disconnect the respirator. Quinlan was soon taken off the respirator and began breathing on her own. She was transferred to a nursing home where she was to be allowed to expire naturally. Karen Quinlan died in

June of 1985 after ten years of coma.

The Missouri case of Nancy Cruzan is another example. At the age of twenty-five, Cruzan was involved in an automobile accident and suffered irreversible brain damage. All of her higher brain functions were destroyed, leaving only her brain stem, which allowed her bodily functions to continue. She was unable to eat or drink for herself. As a result, an artificial feeding tube was surgically implanted in her stomach, keeping her alive—at a cost of over one hundred thousand dollars per year. Convinced that their daughter would never recover, Cruzan's parents asked that her feeding tube be withdrawn. The Missouri Rehabilitation Center would not comply with their wishes, and the case went to the courts. After a protracted legal battle in which Cruzan's parents lost their case in the Missouri Supreme Court, the United States Supreme Court decided that artificial feeding constituted medical treatment which could legally be refused. Nancy Cruzan died twelve days after the feeding tube was removed, seven years after her accident.

Perhaps the most familiar and controversial name associated with the euthanasia debate is Jack Kevorkian, the retired pathologist who assisted several terminally ill patients in ending their own lives. Most of these, such as Janet Atkins, were patients suffering from Alzheimer's disease who felt abandoned by the medical profession. Kevorkian was willing to help Atkins end her life and assisted her in the use of his "suicide machine," which sedated her and automatically injected a lethal dose of narcotics through an intravenous drip.

Kevorkian was labeled "Doctor Death" by the media, suggesting that he was deviant in his views. In fact, however, a majority of the medical profession agrees with the concept of legalized euthanasia. The 1991 *Physician Management Survey* found that more than half of American physicians would practice euthanasia (in certain cases) if it were legalized. In addition, researcher Diana Crane found that approximately 59 percent of physicians in an anonymous specialty had taken actions that they knew would hasten the death of a patient. Therefore, while Kevorkian may have little support for his particular actions, which violate the law, the values on which he based his actions are common to many in the medical profession.

These attitudes are also found in the general public. Many surveys have found that 50 percent of Americans believe that people such as Janet Atkins, the Cruzans, and the Quinlans ought to be allowed to enlist the help of their doctors in easing the dying process.

Society is yet to decide who should make the decisions about terminally ill or vegetative patients. This is the question raised by the previous landmark cases and by public debate. Should a patient's moral autonomy be respected to the extent that the patient, if competent, makes all the decisions? Often, patients with protracted terminal illnesses suffer from feelings of guilt over the financial burden they are placing on their families. In addition, they suffer from the social isolation of being sick in a society that focuses on wellness. The debate here centers on whether the patient's emotional discomfort is sufficient reason for a doctor to assist the patient in the dying process. Moreover, in a hospital setting, patients often feel an extreme loss of control over their own lives. It is possible that these problems, rather than the pain caused by the illness, may drive a patient's decision. Sociologist Émile Durkheim suggested that this loss of personal control may prompt a person to commit suicide in order to regain a sense of control. Durkheim argued that it is the ultimate expression of "self-reliance" to terminate self. Is one final expression of personal autonomy an acceptable motivation to allow terminally ill patients to end their lives? Such questions raise the issue of whether the patient is being spared the physical pain that comes with disease or whether the patient and family are being spared the guilt, financial burden, social isolation, and loss of control that are part of being thrust into the role of patient. These concerns have prompted many hospitals to discuss "living wills" and "durable powers of attorney" upon admitting a patient. These procedures give each patient the opportunity to address these issues before a crisis occurs. These documents make it more likely that a patient's wishes will be carried out in the event that the patient becomes unable to articulate his or her wishes.

Context

Before the advent of life-sustaining technology, euthanasia was not an issue of great concern to the general population. In the late twentieth century, however, the public became concerned about its options in the case of terminal illness, since medical advances allowed physicians to prolong life for many years. The lack of coherent policy shows that the various groups in society have not achieved a sufficient degree of consensus to create a social ethic that will satisfy most of the members of society.

One important task of sociology is to examine the process by which the various interest groups in society develop the consensus necessary to develop a consistent social policy. Although increasingly pluralist, the United States remains essentially a religious (Christian) society. Religious groups are likely to play a major role in the euthanasia debate. If the abortion debate is used as a predictor, it is questionable whether a true consensus on these issues is possible in a heterogeneous society such as the United States.

Another important sociological issue is the role of the state in prohibiting competent terminally ill patients from ending their own lives. Many theorists believe that the state might actually benefit from legalized euthanasia. Because a substantial percentage of American health-care dollars is spent on patients in their last year of life, the state may actually satisfy an economic interest by pressuring dying patients to end their lives. Many ethicists and sociologists, especially those approaching euthanasia from a Marxian perspective, view legalized euthanasia with suspicion because of the present inequality of access to health care. Affluent people can afford their own health care, while the poor are forced to rely on the state to provide medical care for them. Legalized euthanasia could conceivably bring about a new kind of inequality in which some terminally ill patients would be pressured to end their lives prematurely simply because they are poor.

There are far more questions than answers in the debate over euthanasia, and the sociological analysis of euthanasia is as young as the technology that has fueled the debate. As the problem matures, the sociological analyses of euthanasia policy will undoubtedly become increasingly sophisticated.

Bibliography

Baird, Robert M., and Stuart E. Rosenbaum, eds. *Euthanasia: The Moral Issues.* Buffalo, N.Y.: Prometheus Books, 1989. This volume consists of a collection of articles on various ethical dilemmas associated with euthanasia. It is an excellent compilation of different approaches and opposing viewpoints.

Koop, C. Everett. *The Right to Live, the Right to Die.* Wheaton, Ill.: Tyndale House, 1976. Koop began addressing the problems associated with euthanasia early in the debate. This work outlines the basic ethical viewpoint from an anti-euthanasia perspective. A former surgeon general of the United States, Koop is a respected voice in the debate over euthanasia and life-sustaining treatment.

Munson, Ronald, ed. *Intervention and Reflection: Basic Issues in Medical Ethics.* 4th ed. Belmont, Calif.: Wadsworth, 1992. Written in textbook format, this book elaborates on a variety of ethical issues in medicine, including euthanasia. Munson includes excellent discussions of historical approaches to the development of medical ethics and relevant examples of cases in which these ethics have been applied.

Prioreschi, Plinio. *A History of Human Responses to Death.* Lewiston, N.Y.: Edwin Mellen Press, 1990. An excellent social history of the development of ethics regarding many issues dealing with death, including euthanasia. The author is somewhat opinionated and asserts his own ideological agenda, but the book remains a valuable resource.

Rachels, James. *The End of Life: Euthanasia and Morality.* New York: Oxford University Press, 1986. This is a philosophical treatise on the ethical views that could be utilized to justify active euthanasia. Rachels is among the leading proponents of the morality of active euthanasia, and he provides an excellent overview of the perspective supporting legalized euthanasia.

David P. Caddell

Cross-References

The Hippocratic Theory of Medicine, 890; Medical Sociology, 1166; The Institution of Medicine, 1185; Organ Transplantation, 1310; Suicide, 2017.

EXCHANGE IN SOCIAL INTERACTION

Type of sociology: Socialization and social interaction
Field of study: Patterns of social interaction

People seek relationships that provide maximum rewards at a minimum cost. For a relationship to succeed, participants must be able to exchange desirable rewards that exceed those available from other partners. Exchange perspectives provide insight into the workings of close relationships and elucidate why some partnerships prosper while others fail.

Principal terms

COMMUNAL RELATIONSHIP: a relationship in which participants reward each other without expecting anything in return

COMPARISON LEVEL: the quality of outcomes one believes that one deserves from a relationship

COMPARISON LEVEL FOR ALTERNATIVES: the quality of outcomes that one believes to be available in other accessible relationships

EQUITY: the fair allocation of outcomes that occur when each partner gains benefits from a relationship that are proportional to his or her contributions to it

EXCHANGE RELATIONSHIP: a relationship in which participants provide rewards with the expectation of receiving comparable benefits in return

INVESTMENTS: the material and psychological resources in a relationship that one would lose by ending the relationship

OUTCOME: the net result of an interaction; it is calculated as all rewards received minus all costs incurred

PRINCIPLE OF LEAST INTEREST: the idea that the partner who is least dependent on a relationship will have the most power within that relationship

Overview

Exchange is a basic concept in economics; beginning in the late 1950's, sociologists began to explore the ways the concept of exchange could be applied to all human interactions and relationships. Exchange theory (or social exchange theory) suggests that people are motivated by self-interest in their interactions with others. People interact with one another when it is to their advantage to do so. According to exchange theory, people are essentially "interpersonal accountants" in that they constantly assess the rewards and costs of interactions with others. Sociologists Peter M. Blau and George C. Homans published influential work on exchange theory in 1964 and 1974, respectively; each viewed a broad spectrum of social behaviors and explored the elements of exchange involved. As Blau stated, exchange is involved "in friendship and even in love"; neighbors, he noted, exchange favors, children exchange toys, acquaintances exchange courtesies, and politicians exchange concessions.

According to exchange theory, for people to enter into relationships, they must believe that the rewards they will receive will equal or exceed the costs involved. For a relationship to continue to be satisfactory to an individual, the rewards must continue to equal or exceed the costs. A couple must be able to "exchange"—that is, provide each other with—rewards that are adequate for each partner. Exchange theory also asserts that the outcomes people receive from their interactions depend not only on how they behave but also on the choices and actions of their partners. People who are engaged in interaction affect each other's outcomes, and they often need each other for interpersonal rewards they cannot obtain alone. When this occurs, interacting partners become interdependent—they influence each other in significant ways.

Exchange theory was applied to personal interactions and relationships by social psychologists John Thibaut and Harold Kelley in their 1959 work *The Social Psychology of Groups*. They developed and subsequently refined the most influential applications of the theory in this area. Thibaut and Kelley suggested that there are two major ways people evaluate their relationships. The first determines whether or not a person is happy. Any participant in an interaction has a personal comparison level (CL) based on his or her past experiences in relationships. When the outcomes a person is currently receiving exceed his or her CL, the person is getting more than expected and is satisfied. The bigger the margin by which one's outcomes surpass one's CL, the happier one becomes. Comparison levels are idiosyncratic, however, and vary considerably from person to person. Whenever a person's outcomes from a relationship fall below his or her CL, the person becomes unhappy, even if he or she is in a situation that most other people would find satisfactory. For example, a spoiled film star may have an unusually high CL and be dissatisfied with a wonderful partner who would bedazzle almost anyone else.

An exchange perspective argues that satisfaction is not the only component that makes relationships last. Whether or not they are currently happy, people also judge their relationships using a comparison level for alternatives (or CL_{alt}) to determine whether they could do even better with someone else. The CL_{alt} is the standard that determines how dependent on a particular relationship a person is. If people believe that they already enjoy the best relationships available to them, then they are dependent on those relationships and will not leave them. On the other hand, if new potential partners seem to offer better outcomes, people may leave their current relationships to pursue those new partners, even if they were happy in the relationships they had.

This process of distinguishing between satisfaction and dependency in relationships is one of exchange theory's most important insights. It offers an explanation of why people sometimes get lured away from satisfying relationships. Less obviously, this perspective also explains why people may remain in unhappy, broken, and even abusive relationships: Although they are miserable, they are still dependent on their current partners because they do not think they can do better anywhere else. Research studies show that most divorced people become dissatisfied with their marriages long before they ultimately decide to divorce; they do not actually end their marriages until they finally come to believe that they can obtain better outcomes outside the marriage than within it.

A decision to end a relationship is based not only on the desirability of the rewards available elsewhere but also on the losses one would incur by leaving. Social psychologist Caryl Rusbult developed the concept of "investments" to describe all the assets a person loses by leaving a given partner. Investments may be material and financial, such as furniture and cars, or psychological, such as admiration from others. Because it is costly to lose them, high investments lower the overall quality of a person's CL_{alt} and increase dependency on a current relationship. Rusbult showed that commitment to a relationship is positively related to high satisfaction and high investments and negatively related to the quality of one's alternatives. According to this view, a relationship that is contented, would be costly to leave, and seems better than its competitors is likely to be an enduring relationship.

It may be important to get outcomes from our interactions that are not only good but also fair. Equity theory suggests that people are most satisfied with relationships in which each partner receives rewards that are proportional to his or her contributions to the relationship. Equity occurs when one partner's outcomes, minus his or her contributions, are equal to the other partner's outcomes, minus his or her contributions. For example, a husband may be receiving outcomes that are much bigger than those of his wife, but as long as he is contributing more time and effort to maintaining the marriage, his better outcomes may be equitable and fair. If, however, he is getting more out of the marriage without putting more in, the relationship is inequitable. In that case, his wife is likely to feel exploited because she does not receive fair reward for all the work she does, and he is likely to feel guilty for exploiting her. Equity theory thus argues that inequity is distressing both to those who get too little and to those who get too much. For that reason, the most stable and satisfying relationships should be those in which partners are fairly rewarded, and that is what research shows. As social psychologist Mary Utne and her colleagues declared in the *Journal of Social and Personal Relationships* in 1984, "Despite the popular notion that 'true love is unselfish,' for both men and women, the best kind of love relationship seems to be one in which everyone feels that he or she is getting what they deserve."

Applications

The dispassionate, nonromantic approach of the exchange perspective provides powerful insights into the workings of close relationships. One of its simplest but most significant contributions is to remind people of the need to reward those with whom they interact. Most people can be very pleasant and polite when they wish to be, but people are often less thoughtful and more abrupt toward their intimate partners (for example, showing their anger and dispensing criticism) than with anyone else they know. Social psychologist Daniel Perlman found that young adults encountered an average of nine meaningful hassles or irritations from their lovers each week. Apparently, once people settle into a lasting relationship, they sometimes stop trying to reward their partners as much as they did when the relationship was developing. By stressing the idea that interaction continues only when partners exchange fair, satisfying rewards that are the best available, the exchange perspective demonstrates the need for intimates to continue to keep their partners' interests and well-being in mind.

Exchange concepts also explicate important subtleties in relationships. For example, because it is based on past experience, a person's CL is variable and subject to change. If people find rewarding partners who far exceed their expectations, they will be very happy, at least for a while. As they become accustomed to their excellent outcomes, however, their CLs will rise as they gradually come to expect such treatment. As a result, a satisfying relationship can become less fulfilling over time even though a partner is as rewarding as ever. Once people start to take for granted outcomes that once seemed special, satisfaction wanes.

When unhappiness sets in, an exchange perspective provides a useful framework for therapies that can help improve relationships. Distressed couples often slide into a pattern in which they actually exchange punishing behaviors. Criticism and complaints become common, and compliments and commendations decline. When they seek help, such couples may be put on an explicit schedule that requires them to do or say at least one nice thing for their partner each day. The frequency of such kindnesses is then slowly increased as more rewarding routines gradually replace the partners' antagonistic pattern of interaction.

Power in a relationship, the ability to influence a partner's behavior, is also related to processes of exchange. Within a couple, the partner with the higher CL_{alt} is less dependent on the relationship because he or she has better alternatives, and therefore less to lose, if the relationship ends. A husband with a low CL_{alt} may need his wife more than she needs him, and therefore, according to the principle of least interest, she will have more power than he does. Research tends to support the idea that the partner who is more involved in a relationship wins fewer arguments and directs fewer decisions.

Many areas of social interaction beyond that of intimate relationships can be examined from an exchange perspective, including entire social structures and the process of international relations. Homans hypothesized in 1974 that social order itself is a result of repeated interactions; these interactions are repeated because participants seek the same rewards again and again. He held that people rationally weigh past costs and benefits and, if a behavior is rewarding enough, they repeat it. In international relations, exchange theory can easily be applied to the efforts of diplomats as they constantly bargain to gain the greatest rewards for their own countries at the least cost.

The concept of reciprocity is closely related to exchange; reciprocity states that people expect to be treated well when they treat another person well. When a person receives a reward from another, the person is expected to—and usually feels obligated to—reward the other person in return. Reciprocity exists when rewards among people are in balance. Adherence to reciprocity is so strong that it is often termed a cultural norm—a value or rule that is widely agreed upon in a society. An interconnected web of rewards and implicit obligations for delivering future rewards is seen by some sociologists as a powerful force that helps hold together couples and entire societies.

Context

Applications of exchange concepts to the interactions of individuals were embodied in the original formulations of exchange theory proffered by Thibaut and Kelley in 1959 and by sociologists Homans in 1961 and Blau in 1964. All four theorists developed economic models of human social behavior that likened interactions to shopping behavior in the marketplace. Their perspectives gained ready acceptance and gradually became the primary focus of a variety of research studies during the 1970's.

Early investigative work proceeded along two fronts. Homans' explication of equity theory was obviously relevant to the workplace, involving relations between employees and management, and several studies focused on job satisfaction, pay, and performance. Equity ideas were specifically applied to close personal relationships by Elaine Walster Hatfield and William Walster, social psychologists who persuasively demonstrated the usefulness of the exchange approach.

Then, late in the 1970's, Kelley and Thibaut extended their exchange analysis of relationships in two books that codified different forms of interpersonal power and described how partners' outcomes could correspond or diverge. These fuller accounts of exchange theory prompted new research, and throughout the 1980's exchange concepts provided the foundation for a surge of studies of close relationships.

The perspective's portrayal of people as hedonistic interpersonal accountants did not sit well with everyone. For example, social psychologist Margaret Clark argued that exchange principles did not necessarily apply to close, intimate relationships. Clark believed that people explicitly monitored their outcomes only in exchange relationships—relatively superficial partnerships in which those who did favors expected similar favors in return. More intimate interactions were assumed to take place in communal relationships in which people cared enough for one another that favors were provided regardless of whether they were returned.

Some observers thus believe that close relationships and superficial relationships are governed by different processes. Exchange theorists counter that people are especially interested in satisfying their intimate partners (on whom they are especially likely to depend), so people will often appear more altruistic and generous in close relationships than in casual relationships. Further, people may sometimes seem unconcerned with their rewards and costs in happy relationships because they know they are doing well and there is simply no need to quantify their investments and outcomes.

Thus, exchange researchers aver that all human interactions are influenced by exchange considerations; people are assumed to remain in even their most intimate relationships only because their current outcomes encourage their commitment. The exchange perspective was a major foundation for research studies in the last third of the twentieth century that began, for the first time, the scientific exploration of human relationships.

Bibliography

Brehm, Sharon S. *Intimate Relationships.* 2d ed. New York: McGraw-Hill, 1992. A comprehensive textbook written for college courses that includes chapters on exchange and equity in relationships. An excellent source that compiles studies of interaction from sociology, psychology, and communication studies. Superb index. Dry but accessible reading for all audiences.

Burgess, Robert L., and Ted L. Huston, eds. *Social Exchange in Developing Relationships*. New York: Academic Press, 1979. A wonderful collection of chapters written by experts who describe applications of exchange concepts to the growth and decline of close relationships. Included are chapters on conflict, relationship dissolution, and equity and intimacy. A good place to start for any reader interested in further detail.

Kelley, Harold H. *Personal Relationships: Their Structures and Processes*. Hillsdale, N.J.: Lawrence Erlbaum, 1979. This is the last of Kelley's books on exchange, and it represents the state of the art in systematic analysis of the processes of interaction. Impressively demonstrates the usefulness of exchange theory and elaborates subtleties not elucidated elsewhere. For a college audience.

Kelley, Harold H., and John W. Thibaut. *Interpersonal Relations: A Theory of Interdependence*. New York: John Wiley & Sons, 1978. A thorough updating and elaboration of the authors' original formulation of exchange in close relationships. Explains concepts such as fate control and correspondence of outcomes in detail. It is intended for a college audience but will be fascinating to any reader who wishes to delve deeply into the mechanics of social interaction.

Sprecher, Susan. "Social Exchange Perspectives on the Dissolution of Close Relationships." In *Close Relationship Loss*, edited by Terri Orbuch. New York: Springer-Verlag, 1992. Sprecher nicely reviews the use of exchange concepts to explain the deterioration and failure of relationships. Describes existing research results using a fine bibliography. Accessible to most readers.

Thibaut, John W., and Harold H. Kelley. *The Social Psychology of Groups*. New York: John Wiley & Sons, 1959. This classic scholarly work is the original application of exchange precepts to the study of close relationships. It created the concepts of comparison level and comparison level for alternatives and is filled with enduring insights. Intended for an academic audience but accessible to lay readers.

Walster, Elaine, G. William Walster, and Ellen Berscheid. *Equity: Theory and Research*. Boston: Allyn & Bacon, 1978. A delightful book that thoroughly reviews studies of equity using friendly prose, illustrations, and cartoons. Establishes the importance of equity in the workplace, among friends and lovers, and in families.

Rowland Miller

Cross-References

Causes of Divorce, 554; Dramaturgy, 566; Interactionism, 1009; Microsociology, 1192; Romantic Love, 1161; Symbolic Interaction, 2036.

EXPERIMENTATION IN SOCIOLOGICAL RESEARCH

Type of sociology: Sociological research
Fields of study: Basic research concepts; Data collection and analysis

Experiments are a particular type of research study among the many types of research that sociologists do. Unlike other types of studies, experiments allow researchers to determine cause and effect relationships; they are, however, harder to do, and they may not adequately reflect the complexity of real-life settings.

Principal terms
> CONFOUND: an uncontrolled variable which affects the dependent variable, either causing what appears to be an effect of the independent variable or masking a real effect
>
> CONTROL VARIABLE: any variable other than the independent variable or the dependent variable that is controlled by the researcher to prevent it from becoming a confound
>
> DEPENDENT VARIABLE (DV): a variable which is observed in an experiment because it is thought to be dependent upon (affected by) changes in another variable (the independent variable, or IV)
>
> DIFFERENTIAL STUDY: a study in which the independent variable is a nonmanipulated, existing difference between groups; it is not a "true experiment"
>
> DOUBLE-BLIND TECHNIQUE: preventing biases by ensuring that neither subjects nor researcher knows who is in which condition of the independent variable until after data are collected
>
> ECOLOGICAL VALIDITY: the ability to generalize from the experimental context to real-world situations; also called external validity
>
> HYPOTHESIS: a model or educated guess about the cause and effect relationship between two or more variables
>
> INDEPENDENT VARIABLE (IV): a variable which is manipulated in an experiment because it is thought to cause change in another (dependent) variable
>
> LONGITUDINAL STUDY: a study in which the independent variable is the passage of time; it is not a "true experiment"
>
> TRUE EXPERIMENT: a study which manipulates an independent variable, observes its effects on a dependent variable, and controls confounds, thereby allowing the discovery of cause and effect relationships

Overview

There are many types of research in sociology; most are not actually experimental. Experiments are studies specifically designed to determine whether there is a cause and effect relationship between two or more phenomena. Other types of studies have other goals; for example, a survey is designed to provide descriptive information on a certain topic or group of people, and correlation studies are designed to find statistical relationships between things—such as events, attitudes, or behavior.

Results from surveys or correlational studies or, sometimes, ideas based simply on "common sense" often lead the researcher to a hypothesis (basically an educated guess) about how and why two or more phenomena are related. Since different people think of different hypotheses about the same sets of events or phenomena, experiments are used to test which hypothesis or hypotheses are correct and which are not.

To test a hypothesis, an experimenter must be able to do three things. First, the experimenter must be able to manipulate whatever phenomenon he or she thinks is the causal phenomenon; this phenomenon is called the independent variable (IV) of the experiment. Subsequent to manipulating the independent variable, the experimenter must measure the phenomenon thought to be the outcome or effect of the manipulation; this phenomenon is called the dependent variable (DV). All along, the experimenter must also control any other extraneous phenomena which might have effects on the dependent variable. If the experimenter does not control these extraneous variables, then any changes in the dependent variable that happen over the course of the experiment could be the result either of the changes the experimenter made in the independent variable or of the uncontrolled changes in the extraneous variable.

Most uncontrolled extraneous variables are irrelevant to the experiment and to its interpretation. For example, a change in tax law is probably not going to have any effect on attitudes toward the death penalty, so if an experimenter were in the middle of an experiment on attitudes toward the death penalty when such a change occurred, he or she could probably continue with no worries. On the other hand, if an extraneous variable is viewed as likely to have an effect on the dependent variable, then the experimenter should be able to control, or at least monitor, that variable.

There are basically two ways to control extraneous variables. First, the experimenter might be able to ensure that the variable literally does not vary through the course of the experiment. Since this is usually not possible, the experimenter can, instead, have a "control group": a group of subjects who go through the experiment in exactly the same way as the experimental group except that the independent variable is not varied for them. Both the control group and the experimental group will experience the effects of the extraneous variable(s), but only the experimental group will experience the effects of the independent variable. Thus, any difference between the two groups at the end of the experiment can be attributed solely to the effects of the independent variable.

For this approach to work, the experiment must be double-blind. That is, the subjects must be randomly assigned to the two groups in such a way that neither the subjects nor the experimenter knows who is in which group until after the data are collected. The double-blind technique prevents placebo effects (named after medical placebos, or sugar pills), which are effects caused not by the independent variable itself but by the processes and thoughts that are associated with receiving a treatment.

If an uncontrolled extraneous variable covaries with (changes in parallel with) the independent variable, it is called a confound. If a confound occurs, there will be more than one possible interpretation of an experiment's results. The goal of the experimenter, then, is to design an experiment which minimizes the number of confounds and thus minimizes the number of possible interpretations of the results. In many situations, however, it is not possible to control all the confounds; in these cases one cannot do a true experiment. Instead, the experimenter might be able to do a pre-experiment or a quasi-experiment.

In pre-experiments, the researcher is actually able to control very little. In fact, in the simplest pre-experiments, the experimenter may not even be able to manipulate the independent variable directly. For example, if the researcher has a hypothesis that natural disasters cause people to cooperate more than usual, he or she may collect data on cooperation and then wait for a natural disaster to occur somewhere; only then can data be collected to see if cooperation increased after the event. In this example the researcher cannot control the timing or place of the independent variable, and many things in addition to the occurrence of the disaster may distinguish the "before" data from the "after" data.

In a quasi-experiment, the researcher may be able to manipulate the independent variable but is unable to control one or more confounds; alternatively, the researcher may be able to control the confounds but is investigating an independent variable which cannot be directly manipulated. Examples of quasi-experiments include longitudinal studies, in which the independent variable is the passage of time (which cannot be directly manipulated by the experimenter), and differential studies, in which the independent variable is some pre-existing difference between groups being studied (such as age, ethnicity, or gender).

Applications

One way to view the applications of sociological experiments is through hypothetical situations in which research could be conducted and then used. Much sociological research has been performed that explores various aspects of education. For example, a superintendent of public schools might want to decide how best to teach elementary schoolchildren about the concepts of stereotypes and prejudice. The goal is to reduce their level of prejudice. Several options have been suggested by the school board, but the superintendent is unsure which approach would be most effective. Each of the options that have been presented to the superintendent is based on someone's hypothesis about what factors in real life affect children's levels of prejudice. Since the superintendent wants to know which one (or more) of the hypotheses is correct, a sociologist might be asked to perform an experiment to find out.

The sociologist needs to be able to do three things: manipulate the independent variable (IV) of the experiment, observe and measure the dependent variable (DV), and control other variables that might also influence the dependent variable. In this case, the IV is the set of different options that have been suggested as possible ways to reduce children's prejudice, and the DV is children's prejudice level. The experimenter must, therefore, manipulate a situation so that different children receive different options and then measure and compare what the levels of prejudice are after each of the different options. In order to control other possibly relevant factors, the experimenter must assign children to the different options randomly, must have a control group of children who go through the study without getting one of the options, and must remain "blind" about who is in which condition until after the data are collected. If the sociologist can do all this, the experiment will be a "true" experiment, and the superintendent would be able to tell which options to choose for the school district by picking the option that led to the lowest prejudice scores.

It might not, however, be possible for the sociologist to conduct a true experiment. For example, some parents might not want their children to receive one of the options, and they might specifically request which option they want for their children. Since it would be unethical to go against the parents' wishes for the sake of the experiment, the experimenter may have to give up the idea of assigning children randomly to the different options. Now the study is no longer a true experiment, because there is an uncontrolled variable which may be a confound. That is, style of parenting and other variables related to home life may now be different for the children assigned to the different options. If the children who get different options have different prejudice levels at the end of the study, it might indeed be because the different options had different effects, but it also might be that the different children had different prejudice levels because of something related to their home life.

Even if there are no ethical problems with conducting a true experiment, it may simply be impractical to do a true experiment. It may be practical only to assign different classrooms of students (rather than different individual children) randomly to different options. In this situation, although it is unlikely that parenting styles will be a confound, it is quite possible that the different teachers will be a confound. Maybe some teachers already have given lessons on stereotypes and prejudice or are better role models in the classroom. If those teachers' students scored lower on prejudice level after the experiment, it would not be possible to determine whether that result was because of the IV (the different options that were tested) or because of the different teachers.

In another example, an individual might be trying to decide whether to ask her state representative to vote for or against instituting the death penalty in her state. One of her friends says that having the death penalty as a punishment for murder will deter some crimes and thus save lives. Another, however, argues that it certainly will not. These two views represent two competing hypotheses—that the death penalty either will or will not serve as a deterrent to crime. Since this issue is important, and because it is impossible and unethical to perform an experiment involving randomly assigning some people to the death penalty, she might want to examine what happened in other states after they either implemented or abolished the death penalty.

Here, whether a state has the death penalty is the independent variable, and the number, or rate, of murders in the state is the dependent variable. Note that in this example, unlike in the previous example of the effects of various school options on children's prejudice level, the experimenter cannot even manipulate the independent variable, let alone control for other possible relevant factors. Thus, no matter what the individual finds, there will always be several possible interpretations. This situation illustrates why equally intelligent people continue to disagree on so many social issues: Without a true experiment, one cannot determine which hypotheses are correct and which are incorrect.

Context

Because most research in sociology does not consist of true experiments, and because the results therefore have multiple interpretations, many people are hesitant to apply sociological research to real-world problems. Yet despite the shortcomings involved, there is one aspect of nonexperimental, pre-experimental, and quasi-experimental research that makes it more useful than experimental research: its external validity, or ecological validity.

Because they are so controlled, true experiments rarely give an accurate picture of reality; they have low ecological validity. There is always a tradeoff between the experimenter's ability to control the conditions of the experiment and the likelihood that the experiment will actually replicate real-life circumstances. Real-life situations, especially social situations, are complex, and extraneous variables are not controlled in real life. Thus, research that has few controls, while being open to multiple interpretations, is often more likely to produce results that can be generalized to real-world settings.

In addition, even though sociologists are less able than researchers in some other fields to do controlled experiments, they are able to utilize a variety of methods and to draw conclusions from the convergence of evidence. This approach is called "triangulation," named after the method of measuring the exact position of distant objects by comparing results of measurements taken from several different observation sites. By combining the results of different studies and different kinds of studies on a particular topic, sociologists can increase their certainty in the correctness of a particular hypothesis without losing the ability to generalize from their research results to the real world.

When researchers (and policy makers) are confident enough that a particular hypothesis is correct, they may try to apply their conclusions to solve real-world problems by manipulating variables in real-world settings. The effectiveness of such application efforts can then be assessed using either program evaluation or meta-analysis techniques. Program evaluation involves the development of a set of studies that are designed collectively to determine whether a specific application effort did what it was supposed to do. For example, did a new social program for pregnant teenagers actually reduce their school drop-out rates? Did it reduce their rate of premature births? Did it reduce the likelihood that the mothers would become pregnant again within a three-year period? Meta-analysis, on the other hand, employs a single study to analyze the collective outcomes of a wide variety of application efforts which all attempted to do the same thing. For example, looked at collectively, does it appear that prisoner rehabilitation programs work better when they use reward or when they use punishment?

To the extent that program evaluations and meta-analyses suggest that social interventions are not working, additional research can be designed to test more complex or more finely tuned hypotheses. In this way, the results of experimentation can be applied to the real world, and the results of the real-world applications are incorporated into future experiments in an ongoing mutual-feedback interaction.

Bibliography

Babbie, Earl R. *Social Research for Consumers*. Belmont, Calif.: Wadsworth, 1982. This is a standard college social science methodology text. Besides addressing experimentation, it presents good discussion of differential designs, program evaluation, and ecological validity.

Campbell, Donald T., and Julian C. Stanley. *Experimental and Quasi-experimental Designs for Research*. Chicago: Rand McNally College Publishing, 1963. This classic text goes into the intricacies of the design and interpretation of both true and quasi-experiments. Although short, it is fairly technical and is intended for those who plan to do research.

Howard, George S. *Basic Research Methods in the Social Sciences*. Glenview, Ill.: Scott, Foresman, 1985. This 250-page textbook is one of dozens which present essentially the same material as the Campbell and Stanley classic mentioned above, but which are much more basic and user friendly. This one includes evaluation research and an appendix of excerpts from the Huck and Sandler book mentioned below.

Huck, Schuyler W., and Howard M. Sandler. *Rival Hypotheses: Alternative Interpretations of Data Based Conclusions*. New York: Harper & Row, 1979. This book consists of brief summaries of one hundred social science research studies that have one or more confounds. It is up to the reader to figure out the confound (and alternative interpretation) of each. Answers are provided at the end, along with an appendix summarizing the most common types of errors made in interpreting research results.

Sullivan, Thomas J. *Applied Sociology: Research and Critical Thinking*. New York: Macmillan, 1992. This college research methods text covers true experiments as well as other types of research designs. Each methodological approach is put in context, and there are many examples. Program evaluation is addressed, as are ethical issues.

Linda Mealey

Cross-References

EXTRAMARITAL SEX

Type of sociology: Major social institutions
Field of study: The family

Extramarital sex, or adultery, has occurred ever since marriage was institutionalized in ancient times, but it has only been since the 1950's that researchers have studied the prevalence and effects of extramarital sex scientifically. Although most societies generally disapprove of extramarital sex, specific attitudes vary among cultures and eras.

Principal terms
ADULTERY: a commonly used term for extramarital sex; the term has strongly negative connotations
CONSENSUAL ADULTERY: an extramarital affair that is engaged in openly with the knowledge and consent of one's spouse, although that spouse may not choose to engage in extramarital sex also
EXTRAMARITAL SEX: sexual relations between a married person and someone other than his or her spouse
NONCONSENSUAL ADULTERY: extramarital sex that is kept secret from one's spouse
OPEN MARRIAGE: a form of consensual adultery in which both spouses openly engage in extramarital sexual experiences while putting the marriage itself first
PROCREATION: having sex for the sake of producing children rather than for pleasure

Overview

Extramarital sex usually occurs without the knowledge or approval of the spouse. Such a secret relationship is referred to as nonconsensual adultery, an affair, infidelity, or even cheating. In consensual adultery, extramarital relationships are conducted with the knowledge and permission of the marital partner. The term "extramarital sex" is often used by social scientists because it is less judgmental in tone than the word "adultery," which carries a negative connotation. Some extramarital affairs last only for a brief period of time, whereas others last for years.

Most societies around the world today have rules against extramarital relationships for one or both spouses. In societies in which extramarital sex is permitted for both spouses, husbands are usually allowed more sexual freedom than wives. Social scientists believe that there is no society that allows extramarital sex for wives and not for husbands. Approximately half of all societies around the world that have been studied permit men to have extramarital partners; in other words, they do not have sanctions against it. Only 11 percent, however, provide the same opportunity to women. Despite prohibitions, extramarital sex among wives occurred anywhere from occasionally to universally in about 75 percent of the societies studied in one crosscultural sample of fifty-six of the world's societies. It was rare or absent in about 25 percent of them. Male extramarital sex occurred from occasionally to universally in 80 percent of a sample of fifty-five societies. It was rare or absent in 20 percent of them.

Even in societies that permit extramarital relationships, social customs or rules regulate them. For example, among the Aleut people of Alaska's Aleutian Islands, men may offer visitors the opportunity to have sex with their wives as a sign of hospitality. The Chukchee of Siberia, who often travel long distances from home, allow a married man to participate in sexual activity with his host's wife, with the understanding that he will do likewise when the host visits him.

Attempts to strengthen kinship bonds often determine extramarital sexual access to partners. Among the people who live on the Marshall Islands in the Pacific, a woman may have a sexual relationship with her sister's husband. Among the Comanches of North America, a man is permitted to have intercourse with his brother's wife upon the consent of the brother. Sometimes extramarital intercourse is confined to ceremonial occasions. The Fijians of Oceania, for example, participate in extramarital relationships only after the return of the men from battle.

Studies differ on the extent of extramarital intercourse they find. In comprehensive studies done by Alfred Kinsey in the 1940's and 1950's, it was found that about half of the men and a quarter of the women admitted to experiencing extramarital sexual intercourse at least once by the time they were forty years old. In a *Playboy* magazine survey of the 1970's, under the direction of psychologist Morton Hunt, male subjects reported extramarital sex ranging from 32 percent for the under-twenty-five age group to 47 percent for thirty-five to forty-four-year-old men. The *Playboy* survey found, as had Kinsey's, that less-well-educated males had affairs at earlier ages. There was one major difference in the under-twenty-five age group between the Kinsey and *Playboy* samples. Only 8 percent of Kinsey's under-twenty-five females, as compared with 24 percent of those in the *Playboy* sample, reported having affairs. If the figures are correct, they may indicate that the changes in sexual attitudes (sometimes called the "sexual revolution") that began in the early 1960's encouraged married women to become more sexually active outside marriage.

Some possible problems must be taken into account when considering the data of these studies. For one thing, the reports cannot be verified. For another, many researchers believe that a number of people are reluctant to admit having experienced extramarital sex; if this is true, the frequency of extramarital sex is probably underreported, especially when respondents are not ensured of anonymity. Although researchers agree that accurate figures on extramarital sex are difficult to obtain, in the 1980's researchers at the Kinsey Institute reviewed the findings of a number of surveys and estimated that overall, about 37 percent of husbands and 29 percent of wives in the United States have had extramarital affairs.

Most people in the United States still disapprove of extramarital sex and, when asked, say that sex should be confined to one's spouse. In fact, 80 to 98 percent of the

Playboy sample reported that they would object to their mates' engaging in affairs (many of those people become involved in extramarital sex themselves nevertheless).

Although it is fairly unusual, some couples engage in sexually "open marriages" in which both spouses have a positive attitude toward extramarital relationships and allow each other the freedom to participate in such relationships. In one study, couples who participated in open marriage reported greater satisfaction with their marital relationship. Sometimes couples in sexually open relationships agree on guidelines, including giving top priority to the marriage, a restriction of the intensity of the extramarital relationship, making an agreement to keep the spouse informed about the affair, and obtaining consent from the partner before engaging in an affair.

Applications

Affairs may be motivated by a number of factors. Among them is the desire for variety, excitement, and unique experiences. Sex in long-term relationships can become routine and predictable. Data suggest that men are more motivated by the desire for sexual variety than are women. People sometimes become dissatisfied with the sexual nature of the marriage—for example, the spouse may not be interested in sex or may be unwilling to engage in variations, such as oral sex. Many times wives look to extramarital sex if they experience some type of deficiency in the marriage, whether it is sexual, emotional, or economic. Women who feel trapped in marriage may not want to be divorced because they have children or may not want to be divorced until they have earned a college degree. They may turn to an affair as a way to keep the marriage going longer. Some people enter affairs as a way to express hostility toward a spouse or to retaliate for some injustice.

Some people in heterosexual marriages engage in extramarital homosexual affairs. These individuals are likely to be unfulfilled in marriage; some have been homosexual or bisexual all along. Others want to engage in exploration to determine their sexual orientation or have discovered that their sexual orientation has changed from heterosexual to homosexual or bisexual during the course of the marriage.

Another frequent motivation for intercourse outside marriage is the desire to have one's attractiveness reassured. In American society, sexual attractiveness is paired with youth. If an older partner has an affair, it may confirm that he or she is still sexually desirable. Older people may also try to rekindle the love and romance associated with youth by means of an affair.

Sometimes the sexual motive is less important than the desire for emotional closeness. In one study, some women who reported affairs said they were seeking someone they could talk to. Also, prolonged separation from a spouse might lead individuals whose partners are on military duty or away on business to become sexually involved with a person outside the marriage to avoid loneliness.

The discovery of infidelity can evoke a range of emotional responses. The spouse who finds out may be filled with anger, jealousy, and even shame. Partners who participate in sex with someone else risk hurting their mate emotionally. Extramarital sex is not only a breach of intimacy but also a matter of deceit. If infidelity is discovered, the betrayed partner may lose trust in the other person. Another reason an affair can hurt the partner is that the decisions involved in an affair are based on what the individual person wants as opposed to what the couple wants. In addition to causing guilt, distrust, and emotional pain, participation in one affair may make it easy to enter a pattern of having future affairs. In this case, the person would increasingly look outside the relationship to have his or her needs met.

Extramarital sex that is discovered may result in a termination of the primary relationship. Not all marriages, however, are destroyed when infidelity occurs. An extramarital affair may be a symptom of a failing marriage rather than a cause. The harm an affair does to a marriage may reflect the meaning of the affair to the married couple. If a person has an affair because the marriage is deeply troubled, the affair may be a factor that speeds its dissolution. The effects on the marriage may depend on the nature of the affair. It may be easier to understand that a spouse has engaged in one unplanned encounter than to accept an extended affair. In some cases, the discovery of infidelity stimulates the couple to work to improve their relationship. If the extramarital activity continues, however, it usually undermines the couple's efforts to restore their marriage.

A percentage of spouses who have an affair believe that it has positive consequences for them and for the marriage. In one study, the majority of women having affairs said they enjoyed sex more with their extramarital partners than with their husbands. They not only enjoyed satisfying sex but also experienced personal growth and self-discovery. One possible positive effect of a partner discovering an affair is that the partner may become more sensitive to the needs of the spouse who had been having the affair and more motivated to satisfy those needs. The partner may realize that if the spouse is not satisfied (emotionally or sexually) at home, he or she will go elsewhere. Individuals may also find the affair to be beneficial if both of the people engaged in the affair have the same goals. They may agree that they do not want to get divorces but instead want to make the most of the limited time they might have to share in order to express their feelings in a physical way. On the other hand, an affair might also give a person the courage to leave a bad marriage.

One researcher found that an extramarital sexual encounter is least likely to have negative consequences if the extramarital affair is viewed only as a short-term relationship, not as a potential replacement for the marriage; if the spouse can successfully keep the lover and spouse "compartmentalized," or separated in thought; if the spouse avoids disclosing information about the lover to the spouse; if the spouse limits contact with the lover; and if the spouse has extramarital sex for recreational purposes only.

Context

The ancient Hebrew people viewed sex in marriage as part of a command from God to be fruitful and multiply. They thought that the expression of sexual needs and desires helped strengthen marital bonds and in that way strengthened the family. Among the ancient Hebrews, a wife was considered the property of her husband. A wife could even be stoned to death for adultery. She might also have to share him with secondary wives and prostitutes. Men who committed adultery by having sexual relations with the wives of other men were considered to have violated the property rights of the other men, and though subject to penalties for violation of property rights, they would not be killed.

The Greeks, like the Hebrews, valued family life, but they did not attempt to strengthen family ties by limiting sexual contact to marriage, at least not male sexual contacts. Women had a low status in society. A husband could divorce his wife without cause and, in fact, was obligated to do so if she committed adultery. A wife, however, could only divorce her husband under extreme circumstances, which did not include adultery.

Early Christian views on sexuality were largely shaped by Paul and the men of the church at the end of the fourth century. Adultery was very common among the upper classes of Rome during this period. It was largely because of the sexual decadence of the Romans that the early Christians began to equate sexuality with sin. The early Christians, like the Hebrews, were determined to restrict sex to marriage. They saw carnal temptations as distractions from spiritual devotion to God.

Like the Hebrews before them, the Christians demanded virginity of brides. Having sex was only appropriate for the sake of procreation. Unhappiness with one's spouse might demonstrate sexual, and therefore sinful, restlessness. Dissolving a marriage might also jeopardize the tight social structure that supported the church. Throughout the following centuries, Christian leaders developed even more negative views of sexuality. Augustine associated sexual lust with the original sin of Adam and Eve. To Augustine, any sexual expression, even intercourse within marriage, was evil to a degree, but nonprocreative sexual activity was thought to be the most sinful of all.

The Kinsey studies of the 1940's and 1950's shocked Americans with their reports of extramarital sexual activity (Kinsey's *Sexual Behavior in the Human Male* was published in 1948). Until that time, adultery was hardly ever discussed openly; suddenly, not only was it being discussed but also the number of people that admitted having affairs (underreported though they may have been) was higher than most people imagined. After the advent of the sexual revolution of the 1960's, abetted by the wide availability of birth control pills and later by such protest slogans as "Make love, not war," and "Free love," people became more open about sex, including extramarital sex. Partly as a result of the women's movement, women stressed that they were just as interested in sex as men were.

Bibliography

Atwater, Lynn. *The Extramarital Connection: Sex, Intimacy, and Identity*. New York: Irvington, 1982. This book provides enlightening insights into the reasons behind the decisions that women make to become involved in extramarital relationships. Atwater describes the effects the affairs had on the marriages and on the self-concepts of the women.

Crooks, Robert, and Karla Baur. "Sexuality and the Adult Years." In *Our Sexuality*.

5th ed. Redwood City, Calif.: Benjamin/Cummings, 1993. This textbook chapter provides information on extramarital sex in the context of sexuality throughout one's lifespan. Overall, the book is one of the most popular for sexual behavior courses on college campuses across the nation.

Fisher, Helen E. *Anatomy of Love*. New York: W. W. Norton, 1992. Fisher uses anthropological data to provide insight into various aspects of love, sex, and marriage. She looks at adultery in forty-two different cultures.

Lawson, Annette. *Adultery: An Analysis of Love and Betrayal*. New York: Basic Books, 1988. A review of several different studies, some of which have examined how long after marrying men and women begin affairs. A comprehensive, well-rounded book on sexual affairs in general.

O'Neill, Nena, and George O'Neill. *Open Marriage: A New Life Style for Couples*. New York: Evans, 1972. The authors suggest that, for some couples, it is possible to integrate extramarital sex into a marriage, if both spouses have a positive attitude toward extramarital relationships and give each other the freedom to pursue them.

Yablonsky, Lewis. *The Extra-Sex Factor: Why Over Half of America's Married Men Play Around*. New York: Times Books, 1979. Yablonsky examines why men participate in extramarital relationships. The author found that twice as many men as women have extramarital intercourse for purposes of sex without emotional involvement.

Deborah McDonald Winters

Cross-References

Cultural Norms and Sanctions, 411; Causes of Divorce, 554; The Family: Functionalist versus Conflict Theory Views, 739; The Family: Nontraditional Families, 746; Types of Marriage, 1120; Prostitution, 1526; The Women's Movement, 2196.

FADS, FASHIONS, AND CRAZES

Type of sociology: Collective behavior and social movements
Fields of study: Cultural variation and change; Sources of social change

Fads, fashions, and crazes are minor social movements that occur for brief periods and appeal to certain cultural groups. Though minor, these collective movements provide sociologists with important clues to understanding more serious issues within cultures.

Principal terms
COLLECTIVE BEHAVIOR: shared interactivity among a group of people who respond spontaneously to particular stimuli
CRAZE: an activity so compelling to a group of people that they become obsessed with it
CROWD: a temporary group of individuals who come together for some particular activity, such as Christmas shopping, a sporting event, a movie, or a rock concert
FAD: a frivolous trait or activity that temporarily becomes popular within a peer group, only to disappear just as quickly
FASHION: more widespread, more structured, and more lasting than a fad, a fashion reflects a culture's interests or values in areas such as dress, decor, and lifestyle

Overview

Fads, fashions, and crazes are types of collective behavior—that is, the emotional, cognitive, and behavioral responses of individuals acting in concert toward particular objects or foci. Usually, the actions of such audiences, publics, or crowds are spontaneous, mercurial, and loosely structured. Common group attention may be focused temporarily on a rock star, a "must-have" pair of sneakers, or a political candidate because of polling results spread by the media.

Although fads, fashions, and crazes have the commonality of being part of collaborative behavior, each serves a different function. Fads are minor cultural movements of short, intense duration and are usually confined to particular age or social groups. Typically, something new or distinctive comes to the attention of status-conscious consumers or devotees who adopt it because of its novelty until it becomes commonplace and then readily discard it.

Mass producers and marketing and advertising specialists, aided by the media, annually promote fads in toys, homeware, entertainment, or shared group activities (such as telephone booth stuffing of college students, "streaking" naked through the streets, or wife-swapping). While some fads sweep the nation, others do not, depending upon the acceptance or rejection of the fad by particular groups.

Fashions are of longer duration than fads. They involve temporary standards of socially acceptable or desirable appearance and behavior. Sociologists have long studied the significance of fashion categories—such as verbal expressions, cuisines and dining places, vehicles, weapons, architecture, occupations, sports and entertainment, tourism, billboards and signs, health products, and even underwear—for what the fashions reveal about the values, interests, and attitudes of a particular culture and its age.

Fashions tend to demand conformity of their participants. Especially among younger people, there are internal and external pressures to adopt the "in" or "hot" fashions so as not to be regarded as different. These same fashions—whether cowboy boots worn on urban streets or designer purses—often become status symbols. Orrin Klapp, in *Collective Search for Identity* (1969), states that "fashion is most important for those who have something to prove about themselves—especially when they cannot prove it by other means."

Yet some individuals, especially within a subculture, do not wish to conform. Instead, they violate current styles by adopting extreme fashions, such as "body piercing," in which ears, nostrils, navels, and even nipples are pierced so that rings and jewelry may be attached. They might indulge in grotesque body tattooing to call attention to themselves. Klapp calls these "ego-screaming" fashions, because they are done for shock value or in attempts to set up counterfashion norms.

Crazes are fashions or fads that take on overwhelming importance to a group of people, with serious consequences. Individuals who are caught up in crazes—such as land speculation, state-run lotteries, playing the stock market—lavish much time, money, and energy on particular crazes. Fervently hoping that their dreams will be fulfilled, they rush headlong into the scheme with little thought of the consequences.

Crazes arise most often during unstable times when people are frustrated or have great longings. Such people often see publicized big winners getting rich from sweepstakes while they, the losers, are left on the sidelines. They may also wish to share in the camaraderie that goes along with the winner's lot.

Sociologists have pinpointed areas in which crazes seem to occur most often: economic and financial arenas, such as the stock markets and casino gambling; the political arena, especially the frenzied stampedes at political conventions; religious functions, particularly in reference to revivalism and behavior on festival days such as Mardi Gras; and mental and physical health functions, such as diet plans and therapy for personal problems such as rolfing and behavioral modification techniques.

The characteristics of all three types of collective behavior—fads, fashions, and crazes—overlap in terms of classification and function. Generally, however, the determining factors distinguishing them are duration, intensity, and the importance of the event, object, or occurrence that is involved.

Applications

Contemporary sociologists tend to agree that on the surface fads, fashions, and crazes may appear trivial by their nature. Yet, as Arthur Berger contends, they "are symptomatic of serious dislocations in American society and exist because people are struggling to reconcile their desire for a sense of individuality and distinctiveness with the pressures to conform exerted by society."

In addition to using fads, fashions, and crazes to illuminate the struggle between independence and conformity among unpredictable groups, sociologists believe that the transitory changes shown in these three areas act as barometers and forecast possible major shifts that might possibly destabilize social institutions. Moreover, shifts in fads, fashions, and crazes may become direct threats to higher authority and established leaders, because the movers and shakers of these phenomena often threaten the status quo.

In *Sociology: An Introduction* (1990), Alex Thio likens the general processes of fads, fashions, and crazes to those of epidemic diseases, consisting of five stages: In an initial phase, a long-shot idea is invented or created by a few individuals; the initial idea catches on, spreading rapidly on the wings of the mass media; the idea peaks as hordes of subscribers jump on the bandwagon and adopt the idea; with mass adoption, the idea loses its attractiveness among participants and resistance sets in as the idea becomes stale; and as fresher ideas come on the scene, only a few faithful subscribers continue to hold on to the idea.

Sociologists are hard-pressed to explain why fads catch on, but they do offer some theories. Whether the fad involves kiwi-bran muffins, gumball machines, or ouija boards, sociologists contend that novelty and surprise are essential. Moreover, appropriate timing and catching the mood of potential customers are necessary. Often, the mass media—as willing accomplices of merchandisers—ferret out extreme fads, providing a promotional springboard for the fads with willing readers and viewers who want to keep up with the "latest" developments. One final factor must also be present: People's values must not be violated if fads are to be adopted. For example, some people readily take to the raunchy language of radio "shock jock" talk personalities, while others do not. The same thing may be said of the smoking of banana skins.

Fashions operate differently from fads. Herbert Blumer, a leading fashion theorist, contends that whereas fads spring up and disappear suddenly, fashions are rooted in previous fashions, forming relationships and bonds with those coming before and after. In aristocratic societies, there is the "trickle-down effect," in which fashions set by upper classes or elites are later adopted by the lower and working classes. For example, Paris fashion-house designs, with limited editions, appeal to the moneyed elite; later, the same designs may appear in lower-priced retail stores; finally, they will appear in discount stores.

Yet in democratic societies, Blumer says, the reverse may occur, with fashions moving from subcultures upward. For example, the sneakers, pockmarked jeans, and $125 ragged-waif haircuts adopted by youngsters were later appropriated by paunchy middle-aged individuals who aped these youthful styles. Of course, the movements— "the trickle-down" or "the spurt from the bottom upward"—are tracked and promoted by the advertising industry.

Because fashion is based on continuity from previous fashions, theorizes Blumer, certain conditions are necessary for the appearance of a fashion, whether it be thigh-high hose, bodysuits, or King Tut designs. First, there must be a readiness to adopt the new fashion, through either pressure or desire for change on the part of a public. Second, competitive situations develop where alternative models or proposals of the new fashion appear. The market must be free and open for choice among the competing models. Prestige figures—such as fashion designers Bill Blass and Calvin Klein, fashion models, and entertainment figures—use or espouse the fashion, and the ever-present mass media whet the public's appetite for the fashion. Finally, the public decides to accept or reject the fashion, determining its extent and duration.

Likewise, crazes (fashions and fads that become all-consuming manias for special groups) arise and go through definite cycles or patterns. Neil Smelser's *Theory of Collective Behavior* (1963) charted the particular conditions and actions that must occur, whether the craze involves land speculation, crash dieting, stock market killings, or gambling.

Smelser contends that the first stage in the development of a craze is "structural conduciveness," in which favorable conditions must be in place, usually with participants living in unsettled conditions. For example, in gambling on horse races, the gamblers may spend much time at the race track, be in debt, see buddies win huge stakes at great odds, and/or have a psychological addiction to betting. The second condition is "strain," which involves the uncertainty and ambiguity of winning because of track conditions, the odds dependent on other gamblers' views of particular horses, the health of the horses, and even lucky omens. Then there are the "beliefs" of the gamblers, those fantasies and gut feelings that winning will surely occur this time. The next stage is that of "precipitating factors," in which insiders and touts may whisper about betting on a "sure thing" and in which the odds-makers seductively hold up the possibility of huge fortunes to be had. During the "mobilization" stage, the gamblers make their decisions, plunge in with their bets, and get a "high" while the horses race the oval. The final stage, "social control," is that in which the set rules of the racecourse officials, government regulations, and track etiquette govern the division of the purse. Winners collect their money, losers tear up their tickets, and the process starts all over again.

Context

In contemporary terms, fads, fashions, and crazes are generally accepted under the sociological category of "collective behavior," along with other types of collective behavior, such as panics, rumors, riots, mob behavior, meetings, published opinion polls, and mass delusions. Yet it was not always so.

At the turn of the century, fads, fashions, and crazes were studied for their harmful effects. For example, Thorstein Veblen, in his influential *The Theory of the Leisure Class* (1899), viewed fashionable appearance and behavior as forms of "conspicuous consumption," done primarily to show off one's own social status, economic standing, and ego. For Veblen and others of his times, fashion served no serious social purpose. The prevailing thought was that fads, fashions, and crazes were irrational phenomena that lacked systematic patterns and were trivial and insignificant subjects for study.

The pioneer collective behavior theorist Edward Ross (1916), however, did recognize the limited importance of these phenomena. He analyzed historical crazes such as the wild tulip mania that struck Holland in 1636-1637, the religious fervor of the Crusades, the financial boom-and-bust eras, and end-of-the-world prophecies. In addition, A. L. Kroeber (1919) applied eight statistical measurements to women's evening dresses over a seventy-five-year period, studying them in the belief that it is possible to chart the origins, growth, and decline of fashions.

The period from 1920 to 1950 saw an increased interest in studying the changing trends in popular entertainment, such as movies, radio, sports, and comic books. During the 1950's and 1960's, studies examined mass consumption, suburban lifestyles, and the effects of television. According to Herbert Gans's *Popular Culture and High Culture* (1977), by the late 1960's attention shifted to the "youth culture" and the melding of high culture with popular culture.

Contemporary researchers have increasingly recognized the importance of studying the roles played by fads, fashions, and crazes in analyzing crowd behavior. For example, Herbert Blumer believes that fashions in particular should not be on the periphery of research in the ever-changing modern cultures but should be at its very center. He says that fashion imposes order on the ebb and flow of social order, helping to break the stranglehold of past fashions and to prepare society for future shifts of values and attitudes. For these reasons, most introductory textbooks on sociology now include at least a section on fads, fashions, and crazes.

In addition to recognizing the increased importance of the roles played by fads, fashions, and crazes in "collective behavior," sociologists have called for more sophisticated research techniques, especially the multidisciplinary kind. For example, Arthur Berger's *Reading Matter: Multidisciplinary Perspectives on Material Culture* (1992) demonstrates how a more meaningful analysis of blue jeans may be achieved by utilizing the varying perspectives of historians, sociologists, anthropologists, psychologists, journalists, and travelers. The once-dismissed types of "collective behavior"—fads, fashions, and crazes—have come into their own as important areas of research.

Bibliography

Berger, Arthur A. *Reading Matter: Multidisciplinary Perspectives on Material Culture*. New Brunswick, N.J.: Transaction, 1992. Examines fashions and fads from multiple perspectives—semiotics, historical, anthropological, psychoanalytic, Marxist, and sociological. Using a lively style and current examples, Berger shows why multidisciplinary research is effective.

Blumer, Herbert. "Fashion: From Class Differentiation to Collective Selection." *The Sociological Quarterly* 10, no. 3 (Winter, 1969): 275-291. A highly readable defense of the significant role that fashion plays in sociological research. It also provides fascinating insights into how fashions are born, grow, and wither away.

Gans, Herbert J. *Popular Culture and High Culture: An Analysis and Evaluation of*

Taste. New York: Basic Books, 1977. Although the examples used are somewhat dated, Gans analyzes the conflict between popular culture and high culture and their place in society. Gans effectively makes a plea for cultural pluralism.

Hughes, Helen M. *Crowd and Mass Behavior*. Boston: Allyn & Bacon, 1972. Distinguished sociologists report on crowd behavior and social movements such as women's liberation, black power, the peace movement, and hero worship.

Klapp, Orrin E. *Collective Search for Identity*. New York: Holt, Rinehart and Winston, 1969. Examines fads, fashions, cults, mystiques, heroes, and so forth in terms of what they reveal about the problems of the identity crisis going on within the 1960's and how the culture continually redefined the social order.

Smelser, Neil J. *Theory of Collective Behavior*. New York: Free Press of Glencoe, 1963. Provides an excellent discussion of crazes in chapter 7, exploring how and why they develop. Smelser believes that collective behavior is rational, occurs on a regular basis, and may be studied systematically.

Thio, Alex. "Collective Behavior and Social Movements." In *Sociology: An Introduction*. 2d ed. New York: Harper & Row, 1989. Provides a concise overview of fads, fashions, and crazes, including lively examples of how these types of collective behavior operate in the marketplace.

Veblen, Thorstein. *The Theory of the Leisure Class*. New York: Viking Press, 1967. This classic, originally published in 1899, reflects the negative attitudes of the time toward fashions. Robert Lekachman's introduction explains how the *zeitgeist* (the temper of the times) colored Veblen's sociological views.

Richard Whitworth

Cross-References

Collective Behavior, 291; Cultural Norms and Sanctions, 411; Culture: Material and Expressive Culture, 430; High Culture versus Popular Culture, 870; Rumors and Urban Legends, 1667; Social Movements, 1826; Socialization: The Mass Media, 1887.

THE FAMILY: FUNCTIONALIST VERSUS CONFLICT THEORY VIEWS

Type of sociology: Major social institutions
Field of study: The family

Functionalist and conflict views are sociological theories that explain "how society operates on a day-to-day basis through its major institutions," one of which is the family. These two views provide a realistic picture of society. They help explain how a family can be seen in terms of harmony and stability on the one hand and in terms of conflict and change on the other.

> *Principal terms*
> DAY CARE: any type of arrangement that is used to provide care, super-vision, or education for children under age six when parents are at work
> DUAL-EARNER FAMILY: a family in which both parents are fully employed
> EXTENDED FAMILY: a household consisting of spouses, their children, and other relatives
> FAMILY DAY CARE: child care that is provided at a caregiver's home
> INSTITUTIONS: stable social patterns and relationships that result from the values, norms, roles, and statuses that govern activities that fulfill the needs of the society; for example, economic institutions help to organize the production and distribution of goods and services
> NUCLEAR FAMILY: a unit consisting of a husband, a wife, and their children

Overview

The family is the most basic institution in all societies. Defining the family is, however, becoming more difficult because of the changes that are taking place in societies, particularly in Western societies. Sociologist Ian Robertson defines the family as "a relatively permanent group of people related by ancestry, marriage, or adoption, who live together, form an economic unit, and take care of their young." This definition is being challenged by some sociologists who argue that family members are not always bound by "legal marriage" or "adoption." In order to make the definition of a family more flexible and contemporary, sociologists Mary Ann Lamanna and Agnes Riedmann, in their book *Marriages and Families: Making Choices and Facing the Change* (1991), define a family as "any sexually expressive or parent-child relationship in which people—usually related by ancestry, marriage, or adoption—(1) live together with commitment (2), form an economic unit and care for any young, and (3) find their identity as importantly attached to the group."

The study of the family involves several theories, but the functionalist and conflict theories are the two most fundamental. The functionalist view attempts to answer two questions: "What role does the family play in the maintenance of the society?" and "How does the society as a social system affect the family as an institution?" Functionalist theorists, therefore, are interested in the functions that are performed by the family, and there are several of them.

First, the family must regulate sexual behavior. The incest taboo, for example, is an almost universal rule that prohibits sex between close blood relatives. Societies, however, have different family structures and related norms concerning the number of spouses one may have at a time. These family structures include the nuclear family, which limits sexual activity to a married man and his wife only. By contrast, in polygamous families, sexual activity is not limited to one husband and one wife, because such families involve multiple spouses. Second, in order for the society to continue, its members must be replaced. The family, according to the functionalist view, is the most stable social institution and is therefore ideal for the performance of this function. Third, the family, through the process of socialization, nurtures and prepares children to be productive members of society. It equips them with the cultural values and skills necessary for the society to survive continuously. Fourth, family members receive their basic needs, such as emotional and physical care, from their families. In most societies, there are groups or organizations that take up the responsibility of caring for or protecting the members of the society under certain circumstances. The family, however, seems to be the most appropriate of them all, especially regarding daily living in an impersonal environment caused by rapid changes. Fifth, at birth, children inherit their race, ethnic identity, and social class from their families. This function is critical because it affects the life course of each individual. In some cases, one's future may be predicted on the basis of this one factor, especially when parenting styles, socioeconomic factors, and environmental conditions are taken into account.

Finally, families serve an economic function. Prior to the Industrial Revolution, every society's economic system was dependent upon each family, whose task was to produce and consume the goods that were needed, but significant changes have taken place since then. The production of food and other material goods, for example, is no longer the sole responsibility of the family. The family has become more of a consumption unit than a production unit.

In fact, the drastic changes that are related to economic production and consumption are a major concern of the conflict view. In his book *In Conflict and Order: Understanding Society* (1985), sociologist D. Stanley Eitzen wrote:

> The transfer of production out of the household altered family life in two important ways. First, families surrendered functions previously concentrated in the home and took more highly specialized functions. Second, family units became increasingly private, set apart from society by distinct boundaries.

The specialized functions that the family still performs are "those of procreation, consumption, and rearing of children."

Unlike the functionalist theorists, who emphasize stability and harmony among different parts of the family, conflict theorists stress the constant struggle that exists among individuals and interest groups. In marriage and family, the struggle involves such areas as unequal power between men and women, changing traditional gender roles, economic matters, and different interests, values, and goals.

Studies of families continue to show that husbands tend to have more power in decision making even though changes are taking place. Traditionally, husbands, as sole breadwinners, had absolute authority over other family members. Most of their power resulted from the society's emphasis on gender differentiation, which created inequality between men and women. For example, for a long time, women were required to stay home and rear children. The rising cost of living is now encouraging more women to work full time outside the home. Studies show, however, that the wives and mothers who are in the labor force are not necessarily forced to work; they work for various reasons of their own.

The wage gap between men and women shows that inequality still exists even though women's movements have been fighting for equal pay for equal work. For example, 1989 statistics show that women who held full-time jobs earned only 71 cents for every dollar earned by men. The proportion of married women who are in the labor force has been increasing since World War II. In 1940, only 14 percent of married women were in the labor force, but in 1989, as many as 58 percent of married women were in the labor force, and the number is increasing yearly.

Conflict theorists consider this significant change as one of the sources of conflict in the family, since working wives and mothers continue to do more work despite the fact that they are fully employed. Sociologist Arlie Hochschild calls the additional work they do at home a "second shift." The "second shift" practice is likely to put strain on the family. Sometimes it is seen as a source of frustration that may lead to child abuse. Conflict theorists list the problems of child abuse and spouse abuse as examples of power struggles within families.

Applications

The functionalist and conflict approaches to the study of the family show that the society affects the family and, in turn, the family affects the society's social policies. Furthermore, they show that despite attempts to maintain harmony and stability within families, conflict and change seem to be inevitable. According to the conflict theorists, changes are not necessarily always negative, because they also enhance progress. Some of the changes that have occurred within the family are the increased number of women in the labor force, the increased number of families headed by single females, and high divorce rates.

The increased number of mothers with young children in the labor force has created a great need for child day care services. The 1993 *Statistical Abstracts of the United States* analysis shows that more than nine million children under the age of five are in some type of day care facility. The awareness of this need for child day care services has led some women to establish family day care services in their homes. The home day care facility is the most preferred child care service because it provides the children with a family atmosphere. Some such facilities, however, may be unreliable or may not provide quality day care service. Day care centers tend to be large. Children in such facilities may not get the individual attention they need, but they do acquire some of the skills that prepare them for school.

Some people are opposed to the idea of child day care; their belief is that children should be cared for in their homes by their mothers. Others blame women or dual-earner families for the social problems facing young people, such as drugs, teenage pregnancy, and lower school performance. There are disagreements, however, concerning these allegations. Studies of the effects of maternal employment on children show no conclusive differences in development between children whose mothers are working outside the home and children whose mothers are homemakers.

The Family and Medical Leave Act that was passed by the U.S. Congress and signed into law by president Bill Clinton in 1993 is one example that shows the government's attempts to reevaluate past policies and meet the needs of working mothers. This legislation was passed only after much disagreement and many long debates among politicians, the business community, and families. This law requires companies with fifty or more employees to grant an unpaid leave of up to twelve weeks to employees who need time off for the purpose of taking care of a newborn baby or an adopted or seriously ill child. Many people, however, criticize the law because it does not help to solve the problem of day care. Critics of this law argue that most families in low-income brackets cannot afford to lose any of their income, which is already inadequate.

There is a consensus among researchers that the current high divorce rate creates economic crises among families and that women and children tend to suffer most. This knowledge also has compelled the government to respond in support of the families that are affected. The Family Support Act is one such effort. One of the provisions of this act is an automatic withholding of child support from a noncustodial parent's paycheck. The success of this act depends on the cooperation of the economic institutions that employ such parents. Some economic institutions already cooperate with parents through flexible scheduling of work hours. Such an arrangement helps to reduce the role conflict often experienced by parents of young children.

The functionalist view of the family has influenced social workers and therapists to acknowledge that the family is a social system. Therefore, in their work, therapists who counsel individuals with behavior problems such as alcoholism, eating disorders, and other addictions end up treating the whole family as a unit. The idea behind this approach is that some of these problems are rooted in the family. Consequently, the whole family is affected and is in need of help. Child abuse, for example, is done by parents while fulfilling the function of rearing their children. Because studies of families show a high rate of child abuse within families, all states have now established compulsory child-abuse reporting laws.

The conflict view of the family provides insight into other problems that are manifested in the family. The removal of the production function from the family, according to this view, isolated the family from the rest of the community. This isolation and privacy left the family vulnerable to various problems, including domestic violence and divorce. Because of this understanding there are now certain programs that help the abusive parents. One of them is called Parents Anonymous (PA). There is also Alcoholics Anonymous (AA) for those individuals who are addicted to alcohol. These programs provide some ways of helping families cope with the problems that affect them. Indirectly, these programs are an admission that these problems are not only individual problems but also family and societal problems. Sociologist C. Wright Mills considers such problems "public issues."

The conflict over family roles has begun to receive more attention. This has caused some men to realize the need to share housework and child care. In addition, society as a whole is showing increased support for the family.

Context

The changes that followed the Industrial Revolution caused many social problems, which encouraged social scientists to seek answers and solutions to those problems. Sociology as a discipline emerged during this era. Herbert Spencer, a classical sociologist, in his book *Principles of Sociology* (1876, 1882), presented social institutions such as family, politics, and religion as subjects to be studied by sociologists. He compared society to a living organism with interdependent parts that contribute to its maintenance and stability.

The roots of the functionalist approach can be traced back to Herbert Spencer and Émile Durkheim, the French sociologist, who argued that the various parts of society, such as social institutions, have functions that help to maintain the stability of the social system. Some contemporary sociologists, such as Talcott Parsons and Robert K. Merton, expanded this view to include not only functions but also the positive and negative consequences that are experienced when certain parts of the social system are disturbed. In his classic work *Social Theory and Social Structure* (1968), Merton refined the functionalist view of society by making an important distinction between two types of functions: the manifest and latent functions. Manifest functions of the family are expected or intended; latent functions are unintended consequences. Many families today are producing socially responsible children. Others are producing maladjusted children who become members of subcultural groups such as gangs. Certainly, this is an unintended or latent function of the family.

The conflict theory has its origin in the work of Karl Marx, a German classical theorist, and his associates. They considered the main source of social conflict to be the struggles between social classes, such as between those who controlled the means of production and distribution and those who were mere workers. Contemporary conflict theorists such as Lewis Coser and C. Wright Mills have refined conflict theory. These theorists view conflict as being applicable to many situations in which tension is inevitable. For example, there is tension that stems from interaction between groups (parents and children, husbands and wives, and employers and employees, to name a few). Contemporary conflict theorists are concerned with the issues of competing interests and the benefits that arise from special arrangements in society.

In the 1970's and 1980's, many sociologists took it upon themselves to study all facets of family life. Numerous problems that affected the family were researched widely. Sociologists Arlene Skolnick and Jerome H. Skolnick, in *Family in Transition* (7th ed., 1992), put together readings from the works of various sociologists. The important aspect of this book is that it dispels myths about "perfect," stable, harmonious families of the past. It gives a more realistic view of societies and families in the past and in the present. In his book *The Strong Family: Growing Wise in Family Life* (1991), Charles R. Swindoll uses examples from the Bible to show that even centuries ago there were families that were dysfunctional. The fact that such families exist does not mean, however, that the family as an institution is doomed. Such analyses of the family are incentives to continue to strive to create better and stronger families.

Bibliography

Coser, Lewis. *The Functions of Social Conflict*. Glencoe, Ill.: Free Press, 1956. This book examines the concept of conflict and shows that conflict is not necessarily bad. Although it is dated, this is a good book for students who are interested in the study of conflict.

Eitzen, D. Stanley. *In Conflict and Order: Understanding Society*. 3d ed. Boston: Allyn & Bacon, 1985. Eitzen discusses important issues that affect societies. In several chapters, the author presents sociological analyses of social institutions, including the family. Both the functionalist and conflict views are integrated in his discussion of the topics. The book is suitable for students in introductory sociology classes.

Lamanna, Mary Ann, and Agnes Riedmann. *Marriages and Families: Making Choices and Facing the Change*. 4th ed. Belmont, Calif.: Wadsworth, 1991. This is an introductory text on marriage and family. Its focus is on changes and the choices that people have to make, particularly when it comes to marriages. The authors discuss many family-related issues. Theories, research, case studies, and different views on each topic are presented, and pictures are included in each chapter. The bibliography and the appendix at the end are very useful.

Merton, Robert K. *Social Theory and Social Structure*. New York: Free Press, 1968. A classic work that systematically defines and analyzes contemporary structural-functionalism. It shows how the functionalist perspective is applicable to different situations.

Mills, C. Wright. "The Promise." In *Sociological Footprints*, compiled by Leonard Cargan and Jeanne H. Ballantine. 5th ed. Belmont, Calif.: Wadsworth, 1991. Mills makes a distinction between the personal problems that originate within a person and social problems that arise from the environment. This valuable article may help to change the attitudes of the general public concerning problems that stem from society and tend to trap individuals, who have no control over them.

Robertson, Ian. *Sociology*. 3d ed. New York: Worth, 1987. This introductory text systematically presents concepts, theoretical perspectives, and research methods in sociology. Provides valuable historical information about the origins of sociology and social institutions.

Rubin, Lillian B. *Worlds of Pain: Life in the Working-Class Family.* New York: Basic Books, 1976. Even though this book was published in the 1970's, its content is still relevant to today's working-class families. Rubin uses case studies to demonstrate how industrialization affected a large segment of society. The book illustrates some of the conflict theorists' views on the family by showing how economic factors affect people's lives. A valuable book for students of marriage, family, and social stratification.

Skolnick, Arlene, and Jerome H. Skolnick, eds. *Family in Transition.* 7th ed. New York: HarperCollins, 1992. This book, through a series of articles by various authors, shows the diversity of and the changes that are taking place in the family. Every article in this book is easy to read and understand.

Swindoll, Charles R. *The Strong Family: Growing Wise in Family Life.* Portland, Oreg.: Multnomah Press, 1991. A well-written book that presents an optimistic view of the family. Swindoll examines the past, present, and future of the family. His analysis of the problems facing the family includes examples of dysfunctional families found in the Bible. The book offers some guidelines for healthy families.

Rejoice D. Sithole

Cross-References

The Family: Nontraditional Families, 746; Types of Marriage, 1120; Nuclear and Extended Families, 1303; Parenthood and Child-Rearing Practices, 1336; Remarriage and "Reconstituted" Families, 1629; Residence Patterns, 1635; Socialization: The Family, 1880; Two-Career Families, 2077; Women in the Labor Force, 2185.

THE FAMILY: NONTRADITIONAL FAMILIES

Type of sociology: Major social institutions
Field of study: The family

Nontraditional families include alternatives that emerged during the late twentieth century and have radically affected marriage. Premarital sex and cohabitation came to be viewed as legitimate by many people as people struggled to find solutions to the difficult problems incurred in closed marriages or sought options when marriage was disallowed by law, as is the case for gay and lesbian partners.

Principal terms
CHILD-FREE MARRIAGE: a marriage in which the partners have decided to refrain from childbearing and/or childrearing
COHABITATION: an ongoing emotional and sexual relationship in which living quarters are shared
EGALITARIAN MARRIAGE: a marriage characterized by equal power-sharing, decision making, and role flexibility
FEMINISM: a movement whose goal is social, political, economic, and sexual equality of men and women
HOMOSEXUAL RELATIONSHIPS: same-sex sexual relationships; "gay" refers to male same-sex sexual relationships, and "lesbian" refers to female same-sex sexual relationships
MONOGAMY: a relationship of sexual exclusiveness
OPEN MARRIAGE: a marriage in which partners mutually agree to have open independent relationships with others
POLYGAMY: a relationship that includes sexual involvement with several partners
SEXUALLY OPEN MARRIAGE: a marriage in which partners mutually agree to include sexual involvement with other consenting adults
SINGLE-PARENT FAMILY: a family in which one parent cares for one or more children

Overview

The feminist movement of the 1970's and other social changes occurring at that time caused a reevaluation of traditional marriage and intimate relationships. The "personal became political," and issues of sexuality and control over one's intimate relationships contributed to considerable changes in concepts of what constituted "the family." As a consequence, many alternatives to traditional marriage emerged, including choosing to remain single; entering into cohabitation arrangements; and forming families of choice, single-parent families, open marriages, lesbian and gay families, and group marriages.

According to the U.S. Bureau of the Census, by 1990 as much as 24 percent of the population lived alone. Sociologists reported that a few of those making this choice considered themselves to be unhappy. One of the major factors that contributed to their happiness was having networks of intimate friends who became "families of choice" with whom they interacted frequently. These singles tended to focus on autonomy, egalitarian roles, and the social relationships they formed with others, and tended to remain economically and emotionally independent. Singles have more time to spend with their friends, and they tend to go out frequently and have fun. Few report their lives to be dull, and many believe that they are happier than married couples even though they may experience loneliness at times.

Many people who remain single, as well as some who are separated and divorced, enter into cohabitation relationships. There are many different types of cohabiting relationships across a broad age span, ranging from those that are temporary and casual to trial marriages, and including permanent alternatives to marriage in which couples live together in committed relationships either because they have rejected the legal formality of marriage or because they are not permitted to marry by law, as in the case of gay and lesbian couples.

Sociologists have found major differences between cohabiting couples and those who are married in terms of pooling money and expectations for spousal domestic financial support. Cohabiting couples in general expect both partners to work and do not expect to pool money. Some cohabiting couples may even maintain separate residences, yet researchers find that these people tend to be committed to their partners and to their relationships; it is only the idea of marriage to which they are not committed. The levels of satisfaction in cohabiting relationships are high sexually as well as in terms of closeness, love, and self-disclosure. Few saw problems in their relationships.

Another alternative to the "traditional family" is the child-free marriage. Child-free marriages as a lifestyle choice were not openly and honestly discussed to any great extent as a legitimate alternative to traditional marriage until the late 1960's. At that time, the National Organization for Non-Parents (NON) emerged as a support group for couples who had decided to remain childless. Many felt no need to become parents or even to participate in the lives of children. This group, according to sociologists, affirmed the ideology that parenthood was not for everyone and that those who chose not to become parents were not necessarily immature or selfish.

Since the 1970's, there has been an increase in single-parent families. It has only been since the 1990's, however, that there has been increasing acceptance of single-parent families. Prior research studies focused only on the negative aspects of this phenomenon, often referring to single-parent families as "broken homes" and "dysfunctional families." Children living in such arrangements were often labeled "emotionally damaged" and were frequently expected to exhibit delinquency, poor school performance, and psychological problems. Contemporary sociological studies have looked at both sides of the issues, and many researchers have turned up positive aspects of single parenting, no longer assuming that the only healthy family is a two-parent family headed by a father, with the mother performing the role of homemaker. Naomi Miller's 1992 book *Single Parents by Choice: A Growing Trend in Family Life* examines four different groups of single-parent families, including single women who have become biological mothers, single men and women who have adopted, divorced and only parents who are actively involved caretakers, and gay and lesbian parents.

Regardless of sexual orientation, most people want a close, loving relationship. Intimate relationships are important for providing love, satisfaction, and security, and few differences exist between homosexual couples and heterosexual couples. Most homosexual couples are committed to the idea of long-term, marriage-like relationships that are sexually exclusive and emotionally binding. Most gay males and lesbians in the 1990's form relationships not only for companionship, emotional commitment, and intimate communication but also for dependable sex. When in committed relationships, gays and lesbians who form families seldom take the roles of husband and wife; instead, they tend to form egalitarian relationships, sharing both decision making and household duties, and to describe themselves as "happily married" dual-income earners.

Despite the fact that most people choose to be married, many are choosing a different kind of marriage. The idea of "open marriage" has attracted considerable interest since Nena O'Neill and George O'Neill wrote *Open Marriage: A New Life Style for Couples* in 1972, describing marriages in which partners were committed to individual freedom and sought alternatives to traditional marriages. Many middle-class couples in the late 1960's were dissatisfied with traditional marriages and felt the need to grow in less restrictive relationships that granted freedom and equality.

Open marriage allowed people to maintain self-identity while satisfying the need for intimacy, trust, affection, affiliation, and validation of experiences without relying on exclusivity or dependency. It provided a new way to make the institution of marriage more contemporary and in line with other social changes that were taking place. Some couples sought sexually open marriages and mutually agreed that each partner could have openly acknowledged and independent sexual relationships with others. Couples who agreed to engage in open sexual relationships, however, generally did so by formulating rules to guide their behavior in order to make sex predictable as well as orderly. These rules required partners to place their primary relationships first and other relationships second. By the 1990's sociologists found that as many as one-fourth of married couples had an understanding that permitted extramarital relations. Many more couples, however, have extramarital sexual relationships without an agreed-upon understanding.

Some couples enter into group marriages or communes. These arrangements may consist of triads, two couples, or up to as many as six partners who tend to be committed to an intimate relationship in a cooperative, complicated living arrangement. Much time and energy in such an arrangement is spent on decision making related to the division of labor, sleeping arrangements, and child rearing. The number of people entering such an agreement is minuscule, and group marriages tend to be transient, typically lasting less than one year, and not even 10 percent last five years or more.

Applications

There has been a shift to more positive attitudes toward singleness, with more emphasis on individual freedom, independence, privacy, opportunities for greater education and career concentration, availability of sexual experiences, and exciting lifestyles. Some sociologists contend, however, that the values held by singles differ from those held by people who choose marriage, and that while most singles value intimacy and sharing life with a special person, those who remain voluntarily single may not value getting married and establishing families. They often find that family norms conflict with their desires for personal growth and individual development.

Single women are not accustomed to being supported by men and do not expect to derive social and economic status from them. Ehrenreich also noted that men often reported feeling oppressed by family breadwinner obligations and attempted to flee commitment. For those singles who are better educated and economically successful, the rewards of remaining single can be great; for those who are less economically successful, singleness may not be such a positive experience. Thus, satisfaction with singleness may often be affected by finances and by involvement in supportive social networks.

It is not unusual for singles to be involved in several different social networks whose members may or may not be involved with one another. For some single women, dealing with a shortage of available single men may be cause to enter into a quasi-polygamous relationship with someone who is married for purposes of emotional and sexual involvement. Most of the free time of single women, however, is spent with other single friends and families of choice. These larger networks of intimate friends and families of choice make single life exciting and fun while reducing the sense of loneliness.

While many people have remained single by choice, others have become single again because of divorce, desertion, or separation and have come to head families with children. The proportion of children in single-parent families who lived with a never-married parent increased from 7 percent in 1970 to more than 30 percent by 1990. Consequently, the proportion of children living with one parent doubled between 1970 and 1990, reaching more than 25 percent, with more than 15 million children under the age of eighteen living in single-parent households. About 90 percent of single-parent households are headed by a woman. The major disadvantage of being a single mother is the overwhelming financial burden. Single mothers find it hard to be the sole financial support for their children.

Female-headed families with children had incomes lower than those of male-headed households. They often lacked health insurance, and children under the age of eighteen living in female householder families experienced high poverty rates overall (53.4 percent). This rate was even higher for African American children (64.8 percent) and Hispanic children (68.5 percent). Researchers have concluded that it is the lack of male income that contributes to many of the problems of single-parent families, not the lack of a male presence in the home.

Single-parent families face various problems, among them a lack of adequate child care facilities, strain on the sole decision maker, conflicts between home and work responsibilities, and time problems. In spite of the problems, however, most single parents see themselves as being competent and caring and as having comfortable relationships with their children. Most would rather be single parents than be involved in dysfunctional two-parent families.

Consequently, it is important to look at both sides of the issue of single parenting and to realize that most single parents and their children are doing quite well. With increased social support in the form of better and more available child care and improved financial conditions, they would do even better.

An important option for some couples is the decision to remain child free. Several interest groups support the concept of child-free marriages, including population control advocates and feminists who believe that motherhood should be not an ascribed position for all women but an option. These groups believe that those making the decision to remain child free should be respected and should not incur negative consequences. They adamantly insist that coercion should not be used to persuade women to become mothers against their will.

Population control advocates support child-free marriages because of their belief that the earth's resources are limited and that care should be taken to reduce population. They stress individual responsibility to control population and support non-procreation as a choice, even in marriage, stressing that a lack of concern for population control could cause disastrous results globally, because of not only the depletion of scarce resources but also the pollution and food shortages.

The decision to live together outside the legal bounds of marriage became widespread and accepted by the 1990's, primarily because the overall societal climate regulating sexuality became more liberal. The criteria used to judge cohabiting sexual intercourse shifted, and love, not marriage, became the legitimizing test for acceptance. Because women became more in control of their reproductive biology as a result of technological advances, more people postponed marriage to pursue education and career-related goals and opted instead for cohabiting relationships.

Consequently, sociological research indicated that cohabitation may actually improve marriage, since people who marry later have fewer children and stay married longer. More than half of all people who marry admit to having cohabited before marriage. Thus, cohabitation does not appear to be a threat to marriage, and as many as 90 percent of college students who enter into cohabiting relationships plan to marry at some time.

Liberal sexual attitudes often manifest in sexually open marriages. Sociological researchers found that there were no significant differences in marital stability between sexually open and monogamous marriages. When marriages broke up, the reasons given were not related to extramarital sex. There also were no appreciable differences in terms of marital happiness or jealousy. Couples who are involved in sexually open marriages tend to be upper middle class and have above-average educations and incomes. Both men and women tend to have full-time careers and to be characterized as imaginative, risk taking, and self-assured, seeking enjoyment in a variety of sexual experiences while maintaining primary loyalty to their marriages. The idea of sexually open marriages continues to create much controversy in contemporary society, however, and such marriages are further complicated by the reality of AIDS.

In response to the AIDS epidemic in the gay community and other social changes, approximately 40 percent of gay men and more than 60 percent of lesbians were coupled by the 1990's. More than 1.6 million same-sex couples were living together, and 92,000 of those couples had children residing with them. Yet, despite the success in recent years of lesbian and gay rights advocates to focus society's attention on accepting gays and lesbians as whole persons committed to family responsibilities, marriages between same-sex partners remained illegal. Consequently, gay and lesbian couples were forced to remain in quasi-marriages that remained legally ambiguous. Even though some of these couples have sanctioned their relationships with religious marriage ceremonies, their relationships lack legal standing. Lesbian and gay male families are denied the legal and economic benefits accorded heterosexuals, including rights of inheritance, community property, and potential savings from tax returns. There is, however, a sociological trend to consider allowing the registration of "domestic partnerships" in an attempt to allocate some legal benefits.

Context

On September 3, 1969, the American Sociological Association issued a public declaration endorsing the rights of homosexuals and other sexual minorities. Prior to that time, few sociologists contributed to research on alternatives to traditional marriages despite the findings of the Kinsey reports on sexuality of men and women conduced in the 1950's, which indicated the existence of many alternatives to traditional norms. Parsonian functionalism permeated family sociology, and alternatives were viewed as social problems and labeled deviant. Single-parent families were referred to as "broken homes." People entering into gay and lesbian relationships were considered to be mentally ill and emotionally disturbed, as were women who choose careers instead of marriage and motherhood. Cohabitation was illegal in most states until the 1980's, and group marriages were considered subversive.

Consequently, with the emergence of the feminist movement and the gay rights movement, alternatives to traditional marriage moved out of the realm of deviance and social problems in sociology into the mainstream. Betty Friedan's book *The Feminine Mystique* (1963) questioned the traditional lifestyles of comfortable suburban couples, and the O'Neills challenged the norms of togetherness and the isolation of traditional couples. Thus, issues of sexuality choices outside the realm of tradition, including same-sex partnering, single parenting by choice, and cohabitation, moved to the forefront in family sociology by the 1990's. Many researchers now explore the positive aspects of mother-only families and even indicate that the emotional quality of single-parent families is not poorer than those two-parent father-headed families.

Among the positive reasons for couples to remain child free is the fact that to do so is particularly advantageous for dual-career and commuter marriages. Research has indicated that remaining child free failed to have a negative impact on most couples' relationships and instead enhanced self-fulfillment and contributed to marital satisfaction.

Bibliography

Beauvoir, Simone de. *The Second Sex.* Translated and edited by H. M. Parshley. New York: Alfred A. Knopf, 1993. In this comprehensive treatment of women's development and social relations from a feminist perspective, the concept of women as the other in relationship to men emerges. This work provided important background information that furthered feminist ideology in the areas of family sociology and gender studies.

Cuber, John, and Peggy B. Harroff. *Sex and the Significant Americans.* Baltimore: Penguin Books, 1972. This book predated the concept of open marriage but presented evidence of extramarital sex in many of the cases studied. It provides a typology of marriages—including vital, devitalized, passive congenial, conflict habituated, and total marriages—concluding that there is a wide variety of preferred styles of marriage.

Friedan, Betty. *The Feminine Mystique.* New York: Dell, 1977. The concept that housework expands to fit the time available emerged in this sociological analysis of the discrepancy between the reality of women's lives and the image to which they were trying to conform as young mothers, housewives, and career achievers in suburban America. This book stirred much debate after it was first published in 1963 and contributed to consciousness raising.

Fuss, Diana, ed. *Inside/Out: Lesbian Theories, Gay Theories.* New York: Routledge, 1991. This essay collection presents the idea that the binary structure of sexual orientation has been used to exclude and exteriorize homosexuals in the same way that patriarchal views have been used to exclude and exteriorize women. Especially recommended for interdisciplinary studies of gender and sexuality.

Miller, Naomi. *Single Parents by Choice: A Growing Trend in Family Life.* New York: Insight Books, 1992. This book examines four groups of single-parent families, including gay and lesbian parents, divorced parents actively involved in parenting, single men or women who have adopted, and single biological mothers. It provides an excellent overview of single parenting by choice but is too apologetic and constantly defers to the preference for traditional heterosexual two-parent families.

O'Neill, Nena, and George O'Neill. *Open Marriage: A New Life Style for Couples.* New York: M. Evans, 1972. In this handbook for marriage and its alternatives, an optimistic exploration of contemporary marriages and innovative lifestyles gives rise to much criticism of the unrealistic expectations, unreasonable ideals, and myths of traditional (closed) marriage.

Garlena A. Bauer

Cross-References

Extramarital Sex, 727; The Family: Functionalist versus Conflict Theory Views,

THE FEMINIZATION OF POVERTY

Type of sociology: Sex and gender
Field of study: Poverty

The term "feminization of poverty" refers to the tremendous change in the makeup of the population living in poverty that has occurred in the United States and in other industrial countries since the 1960's. Specific to the concept are the economic and social consequences of being female.

Principal terms
   FEMALE-HEADED FAMILIES: families headed by single-parent women because of divorce, separation, widowhood, or the birth of a child out of wedlock
   LABOR MARKET DISCRIMINATION: the differential compensation of groups and/or individuals for their labor when there is no corresponding difference in productivity
   POVERTY: an insufficiency of food, housing, clothing, medical care, and other items required to maintain a minimal standard of living
   PUBLIC ASSISTANCE: benefits received by individuals or families based on need; often referred to as welfare
   SOCIAL WELFARE POLICY: the actions (and inactions) of a government that affect the quality of life of its people

Overview

Diana Pearce introduced the concept of the feminization of poverty in her 1978 study "The Feminization of Poverty: Women, Work, and Welfare." Pearce examined the apparent contradiction between women's greater participation in the labor force and their increased indigence and dependence on public assistance in her analysis of the interrelationships between gender, work, and welfare. She argued that gender cannot be ignored in formulating social and economic policies related to poverty and welfare. Since Pearce's initial work, "feminization of poverty" has become a term under which social phenomena such as female-headed families, child support, gender-related employment discrimination, public assistance programs, and teenage pregnancy have been addressed.

Evidence of the feminization of poverty in the United States began to appear in the 1960's. In 1960, approximately 10 percent of all families with children were headed by women. At that time, less than one-fourth of the families living in poverty were headed by females. By the mid-1970's, the number of female-headed families had doubled, as had the proportion of families headed by women that lived in poverty. This tremendous growth continued throughout the 1980's, so that by 1991 more than one

in five (21 percent) families with children were headed by a woman. By this time women and their families were a clear majority of the American poor.

Two underlying social trends help explain the significant increase in the number of families headed by women. First, the divorce rate has increased. In 1960 there were 2.2 divorces and annulments for every 1,000 persons living in the United States. By 1975 that rate had more than doubled, reaching 4.8. Throughout the 1980's the divorce and annulment rate remained relatively stable at about 5.0 per 1,000 persons, with a high in 1981 of 5.3 and a rate of 4.7 in 1988.

The second reason offered for the increase in the number of female-headed families is the increase in the number of children born outside of marriage. In 1970 approximately 400,000 children were born out of wedlock in the United States. These children constituted 10.7 percent of all children born that year. In 1989 the number of children born outside of marriage had more than doubled to nearly 1.1 million. In 1989 more than one in four births (27.1 percent) were to unmarried mothers.

The rate of out of wedlock births varies considerably by race. Nineteen percent of the white children born in 1989 had unmarried mothers. That proportion was up from 6 percent in 1970. For the black children born in 1989, 64.5 percent of them were born to unwed mothers, up from 38 percent in 1970.

The relationship between heading a family as a single parent and having a higher likelihood of living in poverty stems from several factors. The foremost factor is simply that a married-couple family has two adults that can contribute to the economic resources and support of the family, while a single parent family must rely on one adult. In 1940 less than 15 percent of all married couple families had both adults in the labor force. By the late 1980's, however, the percentage of all married-couple families with both adults working had increased to 63. In other words, nearly two out of three married-couple families rely on both spouses for contributions to the household's income.

Women are further hampered in regard to their ability to support their families by the well-documented differences between the employment prospects for women and men. Women have made great strides in removing barriers to employment resulting from labor market discrimination. Specifically, the earnings gap between men and women is closing . In 1988 the median annual earnings of women working year round on a full-time basis had risen to 65 percent of their male counterparts. As recently as 1979 this figure was 60 percent. Nevertheless, whether this difference in earnings is the result of differences in employment opportunities or is caused by wage differences for comparable work, women have a harder time supporting a family through their earnings than do men.

Single parents trying to provide for their families through earnings are disadvantaged in another way when compared with two-parent families. A single parent often must coordinate work and child care without the help of another adult in the household. For single parents with low earnings potential, the cost and availability of reliable child care frequently impedes their ability to obtain employment.

Inability to obtain child support from the noncustodial parent (the parent with whom the child does not live) also is related to poverty for single mothers. Ten million women in 1989 were eligible for child support as a result of being divorced or separated or of having children outside of marriage. About one-half of these women had legal authorization (enforceable child support awards) that entitled them to child support payments. Of the approximately 5 million women legally entitled to receive child support payments, about one-half of them collected the full amount, about one-fourth received some money but not the full amount, and about one-fourth received nothing. In other words, only 37 percent of the 10 million women eligible for child support received some payments.

The amount that a noncustodial parent should be required to pay in child support is a value judgment. Studies indicate that the amount to be paid by a noncustodial parent as determined by state child support guideline formulae may be inadequate to meet the cost of rearing children under certain circumstances in certain states. Each of these factors—the possibility of not being able to establish a legal child support award, the possibility of receiving an award amount that is inadequate in helping to support a family, and the possibility of not being able to enforce the award to collect child support—works to increase the likelihood that a single parent will live in poverty.

Applications

The effects of the feminization of poverty are most apparent on the children growing up in single-parent families. Approximately 13 percent of all families in the United States live in poverty, while one-third of all families headed by a female householder with no husband present live in poverty. One in five children in the United States lives in poverty.

The Center for the Study of Social Policy, in the 1993 edition of its annual *Kids Count Data Book*, reported that in 1990 there were 1.7 million families started with the birth of a child. Forty-five percent of these families started at a disadvantage because of one or more of the following risk factors: The mother had not finished high school when she had her first baby; the mother and father of the baby were not married at the time of the child's birth; or the mother was a teenager when her first baby was born. Twenty-four percent of these new families had at least two disadvantages. Eleven percent had all three risk factors: They were families started by an unmarried teen mother who had not finished high school.

These factors place children in jeopardy of experiencing insurmountable disadvantages and hardships. For example, only 8 percent of the children between ages seven and twelve in 1988 who were born to a mother who did not have any of the risk factors listed above (the mother was a high school graduate over age nineteen and married to the child's father at the time of the child's birth) lived in poverty. If the mother had one of the three risk factors, the percentage increased to 26. Nearly half (48 percent) of the children born to a mother with two of the risk factors lived in poverty, while 79 percent of the children in this age group with mothers who had not been graduated from high school, who were under age twenty at the time of the birth of their first baby, and who were not married to the child's father at the time of the child's birth lived below the poverty level.

The Center for the Study of Social Policy also reported some of the consequences of teen motherhood as it relates to poverty. They found that a teenage mother is less likely to complete her education than a teenager who is not a mother. As a result, her job prospects are limited, and she is therefore more likely to be poor. Nearly half of all teen mothers are poor. More than three-fourths of unmarried teen mothers receive public assistance at some time during the first five years after having given birth.

As early as the time of birth, children growing up in poverty are at a disadvantage compared with nonpoor children. Poor mothers are more likely to have children that were exposed to drugs in the womb and to bear premature babies and babies with a low birth weight. These children are then at a greater risk of experiencing frequent and serious childhood health problems. For example, low birth weight babies are forty times more likely to die during the neonatal period (first month after birth) than normal babies.

The effects of poverty and teen motherhood manifest themselves in many more ways throughout childhood. Children of early child bearers are more likely to have developmental delays and behavioral problems. By high school, they are more likely to fail academically or become delinquent. Students from low-income families are three times more likely to drop out of school as those from more affluent homes. Children born into homes in which the mother has one or more of the risk factors discussed earlier are more likely to be ranked academically in the lower half of their class. Children who live in extremely poor families are at greater risk of being involved in criminal activity. Children in families in which violence and adult conflict are common, and in which a male authority figure is often absent, also are at a greater risk of criminal activity.

Social policy analyst Andrew W. Dobelstein, in his book *Social Welfare: Policy and Analysis* (1990), examines the problem of poverty in the female-headed families. Dobelstein reports that uncollected child support is one of the most pervasive social welfare problems. He estimated that in 1984 alone $26.6 billion in child support was owed and could have been paid by noncustodial fathers. Only $6.1 billion was actually paid, leaving $20.5 billion uncollected. Dobelstein goes on to propose that if that money were distributed equally, such a total would provide more than $600 per year to every child living in a female-headed single-parent family. If the money were given only to poor children living in mother-headed families, each child would receive $2,740. Dobelstein contends that such a distribution could virtually eliminate poverty among children.

The feminization of poverty is undeniably linked to increasing numbers of families headed by women. The impoverization of these families has been related to two factors. First, these mothers are often teenagers when their first child is born, and they often fail to complete their education. Lower educational attainment leads to fewer employment opportunities. Second, a child in a two-parent household often receives financial support from both parents. A child in a household headed by a single parent often does not receive financial support from his or her nonresidential parent.

Context

Poverty in the United States has been a social concern since before the revolutionary war. The early colonists adopted many aspects of the Elizabethan welfare system, first introduced in England in 1601. An important part of the Elizabethan poor law was the need to distinguish between the "deserving" poor and the "nondeserving" poor. The Great Depression changed American thought regarding poverty. The realization that poverty could strike so many people forced Americans to consider large-scale economic reform. The philosophy of President Franklin D. Roosevelt's New Deal, with government involvement in public welfare, was a shift from the philosophy of rugged individualism so popular in the early days of the country.

While the Great Depression changed the attitude of Americans toward poverty, the actual population of the families living in poverty began to shift dramatically in the 1960's. In 1960, families with a female householder and no husband present constituted less than one-fourth of all poor families; by the late 1980's, women and their families were a clear majority of the American poor.

Social policy scholars Gertrude Schaffner Goldberg and Eleanor Kremen, in their book *The Feminization of Poverty: Only in America?* (1990), conclude that "the feminization of poverty occurs whenever there are insufficient efforts to reduce poverty either through labor market or social welfare policies and where single motherhood is sufficiently widespread." The authors maintain that both these conditions have been met in the United States. They further find that the feminization of poverty is a cross-national issue. Across the seven countries they studied—the United States, Canada, Japan, France, Sweden, Russia, and Poland—they found single motherhood and divorce to be increasing in all the countries but Japan. With the sole exception of the United States, there are social programs common to the countries studied that include paid maternity leave, national health care, and family allowances.

If poverty among female-headed families is to be reduced in the future, specific problems must be addressed. Factors related to the attainment of economic self-sufficiency by these families include limited employment opportunities in segregated labor markets, difficulty in obtaining affordable child care to allow the pursuit of employment, and irregular and insufficient payment of child support by noncustodial parents. Without support for families facing these hurdles on their path toward economic independence, there is little reason to expect the feminization of poverty to stop increasing even in a growing economy.

Bibliography

Anderson, Elaine A., and Richard C. Hula. *The Reconstruction of Family Policy*. New York: Greenwood Press, 1991. This volume of essays approaches the problem of poverty in the United States within the broader context of failed family policy. The chapters that discuss poverty from a female perspective address specific problems such as child support, public assistance, and child care. Includes an extensive bibliography and subject index. Recommended for individuals interested in family issues as they relate to public policy.

Feinberg, Renee, and Kathleen E. Knox. *The Feminization of Poverty in the United States*. New York: Garland, 1990. Feinberg and Knox have included more than five hundred references published between 1978 and 1989 in this selected and annotated bibliography of issues related to women and poverty. Selection was based on the ability of the piece to inform the reader regarding the issue under examination and its availability to the target audience, undergraduate students using a medium-sized college library with access to a federal depository collection and interlibrary loan services. A useful reference for anyone interested in this area.

Goldberg, Gertrude Schaffner, and Eleanor Kremen, eds. *The Feminization of Poverty: Only in America?* New York: Greenwood Press, 1990. The feminization of poverty is analyzed across seven industrial countries: the United States, Canada, Japan, France, Sweden, Russia, and Poland. Each chapter follows a four-factor framework: labor market factors, labor market policies, social welfare benefits and government transfers, and demographic factors. Goldberg and Kremen's thorough cross-national examination of the multiple factors related to the feminization of poverty is a valuable contribution to the literature. Includes extensive bibliographies.

Rodgers, Harrell R., Jr. *Poor Women, Poor Families: The Economic Plight of America's Female-Headed Households*. Armonk, N.Y.: M. E. Sharpe, 1986. Examines the problem of increasing poverty among households headed by women. Rodgers first details the growth of poverty in female households. He then identifies its most obvious causes and consequences; assesses existing welfare, social, and private-sector programs; and concludes by offering both welfare and nonwelfare related solutions. This text is well-written and easy to read. Although statistics presented are becoming dated, the discussions of problems and potential solutions remain relevant.

Stadum, Beverly. *Poor Women and Their Families*. Albany: State University of New York Press, 1992. Provides a powerful documentation of the role of women in poor families during the first thirty years of the twentieth century. Often these poor families were headed by women because of death and divorce. At other times a woman had to take over because of the debilitation of a man from unemployment. The interactions of poor women with public assistance programs during this period are superbly linked with the experiences of mothers receiving assistance from the Aid to Families with Dependent Children (AFDC) program in the later twentieth century. Well suited for those interested in placing the feminization of poverty in a historical context.

Zopf, Paul E., Jr. *American Women in Poverty*. New York: Greenwood Press, 1989. Zopf approaches the problem of women in poverty from a social demography perspective, detailing how their poverty results from structural flaws in society rather than from character flaws as individuals. Both the social causes and the social consequences of women's poverty are considered. Includes an extensive bibliography.

Steven Garasky

Cross-References

Demographic Factors and Social Change, 492; Effects of Divorce, 560; Gender Inequality: Analysis and Overview, 820; Gender Inequality: Biological Determinist Views, 826; Gender Socialization, 833; Poverty: Analysis and Overview, 1453; The Culture of Poverty, 1460; Poverty: Women and Children, 1466; The Urban Underclass and the Rural Poor, 2122; Welfare and Workfare, 2172.

FERTILITY, MORTALITY, AND THE CRUDE BIRTHRATE

Type of sociology: Population studies or demography

Fertility refers to births that occur within a population, and mortality refers to deaths that occur within a population. The interplay between fertility and mortality is responsible for any change in the size of the world's population.

Principal terms

COMMUNICABLE DISEASES: diseases capable of being transmitted from person to person; also known as infectious diseases.

COMPONENTS OF POPULATION CHANGE: births, deaths, and migration which change a territory's population; for the world's population, migration is not a factor

DEVELOPED COUNTRY: a country characterized by a high standard of living and low fertility; usually refers to Europe, North America, Japan, Australia, New Zealand, and the former Soviet Union

DEVELOPING COUNTRY: a country characterized by a low standard of living; it usually also has high fertility

LIFE EXPECTANCY: the average number of additional years a person could be expected to live if current death rates were to continue indefinitely

POPULATION EXPLOSION: the rapid increase in the size of the world's population in the twentieth century resulting from a substantially higher fertility rate than mortality rate

Overview

The level of fertility varies substantially among countries, with a society's fertility rate dependent on biological and social factors. The biological factor is denoted by fecundity, which refers to the physiological ability of individuals or couples to have children. Although the maximum fecundity of a population is about fifteen children per woman, even in the world's highest fertility countries, the average rarely exceeds eight children per woman. The social environment in which people live also affects the number and spacing of children. In particular, there are four factors that significantly affect the fertility of a country: the proportions of women who are married, the percent of women using contraception, the proportion of women (or couples) who are unable to have children, and the level of abortion. These factors operate in every society, but the relative importance of each varies tremendously among countries. For example, in the United States a relatively high proportion of pregnancies end in abortion, whereas in Ireland relatively few do.

There are several ways to measure fertility, with the most cited measure being the crude birthrate. The crude birthrate is defined as the number of births in a year divided by the midyear population, and it is expressed as the number of births per 1,000 people.

The crude birthrate is often used as a measure of fertility because the data necessary to calculate this rate (the number of births and the total population for a territory) are easy to obtain. This measure, however, can be somewhat misleading, because it is based on the total population even though only women of certain ages can give birth.

The general fertility rate is a more refined fertility measure that focuses on women of childbearing age. The general fertility rate is defined as the number of births in a year divided by the midyear population of women ages fifteen to forty-four. The problem with using either the crude birthrate or the general fertility rate is that it is difficult to visualize what a given rate—"40" for example—actually means.

An often cited measure of fertility is the total fertility rate, which is the average number of children that would be born alive to a woman (or a group of women) during her lifetime if she passed through her childbearing years giving birth at the prevailing rate at each age. The fertility of different populations is usually compared with the total fertility rate, since this measure adjusts for the age and gender composition of the population. Further, it is easy to understand exactly what is measured by this fertility rate: the average number of children per woman.

Like fertility, there are several measures of mortality. The length of an individual's life may be measured by life span or longevity. Life span is almost entirely a biological phenomenon; it refers to the oldest age at which human beings can survive. It is a theoretical maximum based on the premise that humans have a genetic clock that eventually orders the body to "shut down" after a certain age. Maximum life span, like maximum fecundity, is rarely achieved. Longevity, which has both biological and social components, refers to the ability to remain alive from one year to the next; this measure reflects the real life conditions in a population.

The most frequently used measure of mortality is the crude death rate, which is defined as the number of people dying in a year divided by the midyear population. It is usually expressed as the number of deaths per 1,000 people. The crude death rate is strongly affected by the age composition of the population. The probability of dying is relatively high during the first year of life. It then declines during the next few years and remains extremely low until middle age, when it begins to increase, reaching extremely high levels among the very old.

A more refined measure of mortality is life expectancy. The life expectancy at birth is a good measure of mortality conditions in a country because it adjusts for age composition by using the prevailing death rates at each age to estimate the average number of years a person may expect to live. An often cited measure of mortality is the infant mortality rate, defined as the number of deaths to infants under one year of age per 1,000 live births in a given time. Throughout the world, the infant mortality rate is a fairly sensitive indicator of societal development, because as the standard of living goes up, so does the average level of health in a population. The health of babies typically improves earlier and faster than the health of people at other ages.

Although there are hundreds of ways to die, there are three major causes of death: chronic diseases, communicable diseases, and products of the social and economic environment. Differences in the causes of death and the death rates at certain ages can reveal much about a population's standard of living and health care. In developed countries, for example, most of the people who die are elderly, and they generally die from chronic diseases; an extremely small percentage of the population dies before reaching adulthood. In developing countries, on the other hand, a substantial proportion of deaths is from communicable diseases and preventable causes of death, such as diarrhea, that affect children at a disproportionate rate.

Applications

Fertility and mortality play a part in everyone's life. Most people think about how many children they want, the spacing of these births, and the age at which they will have their first child. All living individuals know that they will eventually die, and most people at one time in their life think about how many more years they may live and what the cause of their death may be.

The world's population changes through the interplay of births and deaths. In 1990, the world's crude birthrate was 27 people per 1,000 people, and the crude death rate was 10 per 1,000 people, thus adding 17 persons per 1,000 people. This translates into an annual growth rate of 1.7 percent, which means that (assuming no changes in the birthrate or death rate) in the year 2031 the world's population will have doubled from 5.2 billion to 10.4 billion. In 1990, there were 143 million births and 51 million deaths in the world, resulting in an additional 92 million people. The possible addition of 5 billion people in a relatively short time has many world leaders and scholars debating whether the earth has enough resources to accommodate 10 billion people.

In the United States, the prime childbearing years occur in the twenties, followed by the early thirties and the teenage years. Despite the attention given to reducing teenage pregnancies in the United States, the rate of childbirth among teenagers in 1990 was virtually identical to that in 1972. Among women of all ages, there has been a tremendous increase in the proportion of births occurring to unmarried women since 1960: By 1990, more than one out of every four births were to unmarried women. Births to teenage and nonmarried women have an immediate impact on society, since many of these women need assistance to support themselves and their children. There is also an affect on society at a later date, since children born to these women, on average, have a lower level of education, are more likely to live in poverty as both children and adults, and have an increased likelihood of giving birth while teenagers or while single. Policy makers need to use the available information to direct resources more effectively to reduce the level of teenage pregnancies among high-risk groups. If teenage mothers are provided with educational opportunities and job training assistance, these women may be able to secure jobs that can adequately support themselves and their children, thus reducing the risk that their children will grow up in poverty and give birth at a young age.

The number of children born in a given year has both immediate and long-term impacts on the consumption of resources and the use of services and facilities. Some services specialize in the needs of infants. As these infants become a few years older, they will enroll in school, thus using different services and facilities. As teenagers, they may be expected to spend substantial amounts of money on clothes and enter-tainment. Approximately eighteen years after birth, most people will be entering the work force, with a substantial minority continuing their education in college. Young adults will need appropriate housing when they leave their family home, and they will need larger housing when they start their own families. Different services and facilities will be needed as people enter middle age, and specialized services and facilities such as "meals on wheels," retirement homes, and nursing homes will be needed for those entering old age.

The infrastructure (including physical structure such as schools and hospitals) may have to make major changes to accommodate the births occurring at any given time. The increase in the number of births during the baby boom period (1946-1964) resulted in numerous communities having to build more schools so that they would have adequate facilities to accommodate the increasing number of children entering school. In the United States, scholars and politicians have already begun debating how the Social Security system will be able to meet the needs of the tremendous number of elderly expected in the years between 2015 and 2025, when the largest number of baby boomers reaches retirement age.

Although every individual will eventually die, the causes of death vary by age and by country. In 1990, the average life expectancy at birth was 74 years in developed countries and 62 years in developing countries. The difference in life expectancy is primarily attributable to the large number of deaths among children in developing countries. In developing countries, deaths in the first year of life may account for one-fourth of all deaths in a year, whereas in a developed country such as the United States, first-year deaths may account for only 3 percent of all deaths. If the number of deaths from diarrhea, respiratory infections, and communicable diseases was reduced the life expectancy in developing countries could be increased several years, since deaths from these illnesses are disproportionately high among children. This can be accomplished by better distribution of food, antibiotics, and immunizations to children in developing countries. In developed countries, chronic diseases may account for about three-fourths of all deaths. Because chronic diseases occur at a disproportionate rate among the elderly, it becomes increasingly more difficult to increase the life expectancy in developed countries. By allocating resources based on death rates from specific causes, however, and by incorporating information on the variations in illness from specific causes, it is possible for people in developed countries such as the United States to live healthier lives and even somewhat longer lives.

Context

For most of human history, the fate of a population—whether it grew, stagnated, or failed to survive—depended more on mortality than on fertility. In premodern society, mortality was extremely high, with a substantial proportion of births ending in infant or childhood deaths. It was common for women to have seven or eight children with only two or three of them surviving to adulthood. Throughout history, there has been enormous pressure on women to have children, since high fertility levels were necessary to ensure the survival of the next generation. As the twentieth century has progressed, family size has declined in developed countries. There is still tremendous pressure on women in developing countries to have children, however, especially sons, since children can help the family in many tasks. Further, the parents look upon their children as a source of security for their old age. The desire for sons cannot be overstated. In situations where food is scarce, baby girls may be starved so that the rest of the family can be adequately fed.

The average life expectancy in the world changed little from the beginning of time until the start of the twentieth century, when a person could expect to live an average of 30 years. By 1990, that average was 65 years. The unprecedented improvement in conquering premature mortality since 1900 reflects the accumulation of knowledge about how diseases spread and consequent changes in personal hygiene and public health practices. In particular, antibiotics, immunizations, and clean drinking water have drastically reduced childhood deaths caused by communicable diseases, although deaths from communicable diseases still claim millions of lives in less developed countries.

Throughout the world, the infant and childhood mortality rates have declined substantially since the early 1900's, resulting in an increasing proportion of children living to adulthood and being able to have children themselves. Fertility levels have declined at a much slower rate than mortality levels, resulting in the worldwide population explosion; in particular, the population has increased dramatically since World War II. Societal encouragement of high fertility often persists even after mortality declines, because it is taken for granted as part of a person's life. High fertility and low mortality resulted in the earth adding more than 90 million people in the year 1990; 85 percent of these people were born in developing countries. A continuation of high fertility will result in many developing countries needing additional resources, including food and clean drinking water, to ensure that their population has the basic necessities of life. World leaders can no longer avoid addressing the question of how long the earth can continue to accommodate an additional 90 million people or more each year before seeing reductions in the standard of living and substantial increases in the number of people dying from starvation.

Bibliography

Haupt, Arthur, and Thomas T. Kane. *The Population Reference Bureau's Population Handbook.* 3d ed. Washington, D.C.: Population Reference Bureau, 1991. An excellent desk reference on the basics of population that is often used by journalists in writing population-related stories. A glossary contains definitions of population terms. Includes a section on population information sources that is quite beneficial.

National Center for Health Statistics. *Vital Statistics of the United States: 1987.* 2 vols. Hyattsville, Md.: United States Government Printing Office, 1989. This two-volume set tabulates the births (volume 1) and deaths (volume 2) in the United States in 1987. Contains numerous tables. Births are categorized according to numerous characteristics, and deaths are tabulated by causes and sociodemographic variables.

Most tables refer to the nation and to states, but some data for cities are presented. Sample copies of birth and death certificates are included.

Palmore, James A., and Robert W. Gardner. *Measuring Mortality, Fertility, and Natural Increase: A Self-Teaching Guide to Elementary Measures*. Honolulu, Hawaii: East-West Center, 1983. A highly recommended book that provides a basic understanding of fertility and mortality. The focus is on the interpretation of fertility and mortality data. Examples and exercises are an integral part of this book. General audiences will find this source accessible and beneficial.

Pratt, William F., William D. Mosher, Christine A. Bachrach, and Marjorie C. Horn. *Understanding U.S. Fertility: Findings from the National Survey of Family Growth, Cycle III*. Washington D.C.: Population Reference Bureau, 1984. This 45-page bulletin presents an overview of the trends and group differentials in the fertility, family planning, and reproductive health of American women. The book is clearly written, and general audiences can gain much insight on fertility related behavior, despite the limited number of pages. The lengthy bibliography provides good sources for further reading.

Preston, Samuel H., ed. *The Effects of Infant and Child Mortality on Fertility*. New York: Academic Press, 1978. A series of essays on the impact that a child's death has on the parents' subsequent fertility. Past and present societies are examined, and data are included from countries in different parts of the world. A solid understanding of demography is needed to appreciate this book fully.

Weeks, John R. *Population: An Introduction to Concepts and Issues*. 3d ed. Belmont, Calif: Wadsworth, 1986. The basic components of demography are presented in an easy-to-understand fashion, with three chapters devoted to fertility and mortality. The interrelationship between population and contemporary social issues is addressed, so an appreciation can be gained of the impact that population factors have on society in general and everyday life.

Howard Wineberg

Cross-References

Demographic Transition Theory of Population Growth, 499; Demography, 506; Infant Mortality, 978; Malthusian Theory of Population Growth, 1113; Population Growth and Population Control, 1421; Population Size and Human Ecology, 1428; Zero Population Growth, 2215.

THE FREE SPEECH MOVEMENT

Type of sociology: Collective behavior and social movements
Field of study: Sources of social change

The free speech movement was a social movement that began on the campus of the University of California, Berkeley, in the fall of 1964. It began as a dispute over the university's ban on political activity in an area on the edge of the campus. This event marked the beginning of a period of student activism in the 1960's.

Principal terms

COHORT: a group of people who experience the same event at the same time; the concept is most often used to refer to a birth cohort, people who are born within the same time period

COLLECTIVE BEHAVIOR: an activity engaged in by a number of people who are oriented toward the same goal

FRESH CONTACT: a process in which young people experience, in the adult world, a disjuncture between the ideals they have been taught and the realities of society

GENERATIONAL CONSCIOUSNESS: the awareness of belonging to a particular age group and of common interests associated with that membership

SOCIAL MOVEMENT: an ongoing attempt by an organization to change society or some aspect of society

YOUTH MOVEMENT: a group composed of and led primarily by young adults for the purpose of influencing or changing some aspect of society

Overview

The free speech movement was founded in 1964 at the University of California, Berkeley, in response to a dispute over student political activity on the university campus, and especially in an area near the Sather Gate on Telegraph Avenue. In his book *The Beginning: Berkeley, 1964* (1970), Max Heirich described the general atmosphere on the campus as well as the sequence of events as they unfolded. The university had a ban against political activity on campus, yet students had set up tables supporting various political causes on the edge of the Berkeley campus. The tables were located in a small area; it was not clear who controlled the area, the university or the city of Berkeley. Students resisted the university's restrictions of political activity in this area, and as a result eight students were expelled. Student political activity continued, however, and student Jack Weinberg, who occupied the table representing the Congress of Racial Equality (CORE), was arrested. A crowd of several hundred students responded to the arrest by surrounding the patrol car for a period of thirty-two hours, refusing to let the car move. Throughout this time period, students and other participants used the patrol car as a makeshift platform from which to deliver impromptu speeches. A group of students also moved to Sproul Hall, the building that housed university administration offices, where they held a sit-in and took over the building. After negotiation among students, faculty, and administrators, an agreement was signed by university president Clark Kerr agreeing to deed the property in question to the city of Berkeley. This settlement ended the demonstration but did not settle the broader issue of free speech versus the prohibition of political activity on the university campus. Thus, the organization called the "free speech movement" was formed, with Mario Savio, a junior philosophy major who had emerged as a student leader during the crisis, as the president of the organization.Throughout the school year of 1964-1965 there was a series of demonstrations and arrests over the issue of free speech on campus that culminated in a campuswide student strike in the spring of 1965.

The free speech movement comprised a series of events that marked the beginning of a period of student activism in the United States and other parts of the world in the 1960's. During the 1960's, there were student movements in France, Italy, Germany, and England, all of which were related to issues about university life as well as broader political and social issues. (Even the very different Cultural Revolution in the People's Republic of China, which occurred in the late 1960's, was a social movement in which the rank-and-file was composed of significant numbers of young adults and students.) The free speech movement occurred in a social climate in which much public debate concerned issues of civil rights for blacks and, in the later part of the 1960's, dissent over the Vietnam War.

Conditions at major state universities were changing in the 1960's. The Berkeley president, Clark Kerr, had referred to a new era in public education in which large universities, which he called "multiversities," would educate large numbers of young adults and prepare them for activity in the private and public sectors of the economy. To some students, this was a disturbing trend in which education was being designed to fit the needs of the established social order rather than remaining dedicated to the free exchange of ideas and the pursuit of truth. Students also resented the impersonal atmosphere of the big university, with its large classes. There was often little contact with professors, who had absolute authority over what was learned. The 1960's was also a period in which the children of the baby boom were reaching young adulthood, and they were going to college in record numbers. As the Vietnam War escalated, greater numbers of young men were in college because it offered them deferment from the draft. This led to a further increase in the size of the student population and exacerbated the problems of crowding and feelings of anonymity experienced by college students in large public universities.

This feeling of discontent occurred during a historical period in which many students already had experience with political activism by virtue of their participation in the Civil Rights movement. Significant numbers of students had gone to the South in the early 1960's to work for such goals as voting rights and school desegregation;

they then returned to northern and western universities to conditions in which they perceived that their own rights were not being respected. These students also brought home with them practical skills learned from experience with civil disobedience, demonstrations, political activity, and negotiation. They applied these skills, learned under fire, to their new situations at the university.

Applications

The free speech movement is an example of a youth movement as described by social theorist Karl Mannheim in his essay "The Problem of Generations" (1928). Mannheim stated that there are periods in history during which particular cohorts reach adulthood with a unique perspective on the world in which they come of age. These young adults experience what is called "fresh contact," in which young adults who have been socialized to certain ideals perceive a disjunction between those ideals and the real world. According to this perspective, there are times in history in which some young adults have trouble reconciling the gap between ideals taught to them by adults and the practical realities that exist in the adult world. This perception often results in the development of a generational consciousness that the young have certain interests in common and that they should act to achieve these goals.

In many respects, the students at Berkeley experienced fresh contact. These students had been socialized to the ideals of freedom of speech and political participation, as well as an ideal that education should have the primary goal of the free exchange of ideas and knowledge. These ideals came into direct conflict with the reality of higher education as a "factory" to produce workers for the economy and to promote the existing power structure in society. As a result, large numbers of Berkeley students became involved in the collective behavior of demonstrations and sit-ins and in social movements such as the free speech movement to promote their ideals in the university. The free speech movement can be seen as an example of the way youth movements emerge in the context of particular social institutions and in society in general. With this knowledge, the roles of age and developmental issues in the mechanism of social change can be better understood. A number of questions can be examined in the light of such knowledge, such as the point at which youth movements occur and under what conditions they occur. These questions in turn provide insight into the nature of social change and the role of human agency in that change.

Youth movements are important in human history and have occurred around the world. During the 1960's there were significant student demonstrations in many countries, including Korea, France, Germany, and Czechoslovakia. The youths who participated in these wide-ranging movements, although they were not necessarily the leaders, played an important role by providing energy and commitment. In the United States, after the Berkeley movement led the way, there were a number of student movements at other universities, including the University of Michigan, the University of Colorado, and Columbia University. These movements helped to bring about changes in the relationship between a student and the university, including such changes as abandoning the doctrine of "in loco parentis," which stated that the university served as substitutes for the students' parents with much of the same authority and responsibility. This policy change led to the abandonment of such practices as curfews and to the introduction of coed dormitories. Students also gained more input into the educational process. As the result of pressure from student organizations, many universities implemented women's studies and minority studies programs. In many respects these programs changed the nature of university life for subsequent generations of students.

The free speech movement contributes insights into the effect of activism on the lives of individuals and how they are influenced by the experience. This allows a determination of the way participation in historical events (such as political activism) and particular historical periods affects the life course of individuals. Sociologists Jack Whalen and Richard Flacks, in *Beyond the Barricades: The Sixties Generation Grows Up* (1989), a study of student activists from Santa Barbara, California, discovered continuity in attitudes and values from their college days. Another study that looked at changes in attitudes over time, *Generations and Politics* (1986), by political scientists Kent Jennings and Richard Niemi, showed that the experience of activism has a direct effect on students' attitudes. Whalen and Flacks measured high school students' political attitudes before and after participation in college social movements and found that those who participated in activism had a much greater change in their views toward radicalism than those who did not.

Other social scientists, such as sociologist Lewis S. Feuer, in *The Conflict of Generations: The Character and Significance of Student Movements* (1969), have described student movements as examples of youthful rebellion and generational politics rather than as enduring commitments that will persist throughout life. Subsequent research of activists they move into middle age has shown that this is not the case. Rather than being only youths in rebellion, many activists were expressing the values of their parents. Sociologist Todd Gitlin, in *The Sixties: Years of Hope, Days of Rage* (1987), demonstrated that many activists, especially in the early stages of student activism, had parents who also expressed left-wing orientations. Many researchers have found that student activists remain different from others in their age group, even in middle age, in many areas of life, including further political activism, political identification and attitudes, occupation, and family life events.

Context

The free speech movement occurred in the general societal context of the 1960's, when social turmoil was occurring simultaneously in other important areas of American life. The Civil Rights movement that began in the 1940's and 1950's had become more widespread and successful by 1964. The Freedom Rides, for example, had occurred in the summer of 1961. College students participated alongside blacks in rides on interstate public bus lines through the South in an effort to desegregate southern bus terminals. Some of the students involved in the protests at Berkeley had been involved in the Civil Rights movement or at least were seriously concerned with its development. Student organizations such as Students for a Democratic Society

(SDS) and the Student Nonviolent Coordinating Committee (SNCC) were instrumental in the civil rights work of the period. The Vietnam War was soon to be a focus of turmoil and unrest on campus as well. This reached a critical point in 1970, when demonstrating students were killed by National Guard Troops on the campuses of Kent State University in Ohio and Jackson State University in Mississippi. Many of the students who were active in the anti-Vietnam War movement got their early experience working for civil rights.

Sociologists themselves were involved in the political activity of the time. Many of the students most involved in the free speech movement were social science and liberal arts majors. Sociology was a popular major at the time because it deals with many of the subjects that concerned students, such as ethnic and minority relations and structural inequality. Sociologist C. Wright Mills and his book *The Power Elite* (1956) were used by many students as a guide to understanding the nature of American political power.

The role that movements may play in the future is unclear and is probably impossible to predict. It is difficult to be sure when a sufficiently large group of students will reach another critical period of disjuncture between ideals and reality and therefore experience fresh contact. Some researchers have suggested that there is a cyclical nature to student movements, noting that they seem to occur about every thirty years.

Bibliography

Farber, Thomas. *Tales for the Son of My Unborn Child*. New York: E. P. Dutton, 1971. This is a relatively short book (211 pages) that is a personal account of the events of the free speech movement in 1964-1965 from the perspective of a student who attended the University of California, Berkeley.

Feuer, Lewis S. *The Conflict of Generations: The Character and Significance of Student Movements*. New York: Basic Books, 1969. Feuer provides an analysis of student movements in world history and gives considerable attention to the student movement at Berkeley. Even though somewhat dated, this book has made an important contribution to the debate over the nature of student movements.

Gitlin, Todd. *The Sixties: Years of Hope, Days of Rage*. New York: Bantam Books, 1987. This book analyzes the social environment of the 1960's and places the free speech movement within the greater context of that historical period. The author of this book was himself an active participant in movements of the 1960's and served as president of Students for a Democratic Society (SDS).

Heirich, Max. *The Beginning: Berkeley, 1964*. New York: Columbia University Press, 1970. This is a detailed account of the events associated with the free speech movement in Berkeley. It also provides context and sequence to facilitate understanding of the importance of the event, its meaning, and its consequences.

Whalen, Jack, and Richard Flacks. *Beyond the Barricades: The Sixties Generation Grows Up*. Philadelphia: Temple University Press, 1989. An interesting study of students from the University of California, Santa Barbara, who were arrested for their participation in the burning of the Bank of America. More than a decade after the event, the authors found considerable continuity in the values, beliefs, and political activity in the lives of the former student activists.

Charlotte Chorn Dunham

Cross-References

Academic Freedom and Free Speech in the School, 1; Antiwar Movements, 121; The Civil Rights Movement, 265; Collective Behavior, 291; Deprivation Theory of Social Movements, 512; The Gay Liberation Movement, 799; Social Movements, 1826; The Structural-Strain Theory of Social Movements, 1997; The Women's Movement, 2196.

THE FRUSTRATION-AGGRESSION THEORY OF RACISM AND SCAPEGOATING

Type of sociology: Racial and ethnic relations
Field of study: Theories of prejudice and discrimination

The frustration-aggression theory, introduced in the late 1930's, attempts to explain the cause of hostile aggressive behavior. It proposes that many people will turn to intentionally hurtful behavior if they are blocked ("frustrated") in pursuing their goals. If the actual blocking agents cannot be identified or attacked, aggression may be displaced onto innocent, relatively powerless groups.

Principal terms
DISPLACED AGGRESSION: aggression that is directed at an innocent victim (a scapegoat)
FRUSTRATION: a reaction that occurs when one's attainment of a goal is blocked
HOSTILE AGGRESSION: an action intended to hurt another person
HYDRAULIC MODEL: a comparison of the frustrations building in a person to steam pressure building in a boiler that will eventually explode as aggression
INSTRUMENTAL AGGRESSION: an action intended to gain something that, secondarily, hurts someone
PSYCHOANALYSIS: the label for both the personality theory devised by Sigmund Freud and the elaborate process of psychotherapy that it engendered
THEORY: a proposed explanatory framework used to try to make sense of observed evidence

Overview

From the beginning of recorded history, one can trace the theme that people often become aggressive when prevented from reaching some very basic goals—having food, feeling a reasonable degree of personal safety, having the chance to better themselves, and so on. Many people have been hurt because they were responsible for blocking the goals of others, thereby creating frustration. They have been victims of "instrumental aggression"—aggression that is primarily directed at attaining a goal rather than hurting another. Even more people, however, have been hurt as innocent victims of frustrated individuals purposely venting their rage on whatever nearby group or individual was easy to identify and was relatively powerless. This is known as "hostile aggression," and it is carried out to make the aggressor feel better.

The seeds of a modern frustration-aggression theory can be found in the writings of Sigmund Freud, the father of psychoanalysis. He stated that aggression is an inherent characteristic of people and that they often use "displacement," an ego defense mechanism, to redirect aggression from its appropriate target to a more easily available and safer one. Freud stated that much of what people do is motivated by "unconscious" forces. By unconscious, he meant forces of which people are largely unaware but that are nevertheless active in their minds. This concept of unconscious motivation is key to the process of scapegoating. If people realized consciously that they were blaming innocent individuals for their problems, rational thought would stop them from doing so. Unconscious direction of behavior, however, bypasses such rationality.

American theorists expanded on Freud's ideas about frustration and aggression. John Dollard and his colleagues authored the now classic *Frustration and Aggression* (1939), which proposed that frustration always leads to aggression and that aggression is always preceded by frustration. The basic proposal was ultimately too simplistic, but the book motivated many researchers to examine and challenge parts of it. Leonard Berkowitz, for example, provided support for the commonsense notions that aggression may be generated by circumstances other than frustration and that frustration may produce responses other than aggression. He also documented what he termed the "trigger effect," the ability of something in the environment to set off aggression under conditions of high frustration.

When the cause of frustration is something that cannot be attacked, such as poor economic conditions, or when the cause is too dangerous to attack (for example, a powerful dictator), innocent victims often become scapegoats of hostile "displaced aggression." For the displacement of aggression to be comforting to a frustrated individual, several conditions must be satisfied. First, since displacement is carried out as a substitute for aggression against the causes of frustration that cannot directly be attacked, a good scapegoat must be manageable target. Attacking a person, or a few people, is far more manageable than attacking the government or an environmental condition such as a drought.

Second, a satisfying scapegoat must be relatively harmless compared with other possible targets and with the real cause of the frustration. Third, a scapegoat must be readily identifiable and easy to locate. Often a group (such as an ethnic or religious group) is an easy source of such individual scapegoats. A group contains many victims, some of whom are almost always present when needed, and the fact that it may also be easily identified and used by others gives social support for displacing aggression. Others may target the scapegoat for different reasons, but such differences are immaterial. That people can agree on their hatred is sufficient. This fact illuminates the connections between frustration, aggression, and racial prejudice.

Historical precedent can greatly enhance the utility of a group used as a scapegoat. African Americans were the first institutionalized victims of racial prejudice in the United States. Very early in the nation's history, they became an ideal scapegoat group; because they were slaves, they were helpless to defend themselves against unjust blame, and because of their appearance, most were subject to easy identification.

Prejudice against many peoples can be explained by many of the factors that still contribute to prejudice against blacks. Immigrants have often been the targets of displaced aggression. Even those who speak English are, for a time, easily identifiable by accented speech, differences in preferred dress, and different customs. Those immigrants speaking different languages are easier to spot; those with different features and skin color easier still. Identifiability as a factor leading to scapegoating was used in a malicious, yet clever, way by Adolf Hitler in the 1930's and 1940's. Jewish citizens were no more identifiable in pre-World War II Germany than Jewish citizens are in the United States today, so Hitler demanded that they identify themselves and their businesses by symbols (for example, a yellow star) worn on clothing or the word "Jew" displayed on properties. Hitler and his advisers well understood scapegoating, and they used it to deflect aggression away from themselves and toward a common "enemy." Historically, many politicians in the United States have done the same in an equally vile way, using Chinese, African Americans, or Hispanics, for example, as easily identified targets for hatred. Communists, intellectuals, and homosexuals have also been targets, but they have had to be somehow specially identified. Such scapegoating still occurs, but it generally takes more subtle and covert forms than it did in the past.

Applications

Understanding how the frustration-aggression theory of racism and scapegoating explains these clearly undesirable phenomena can suggest some ways to reduce their incidence. Reduction rather than elimination should be emphasized, since there are compelling explanations for racism other than simple scapegoating, and scapegoating may result in targets other than races being hit. Sexism, ageism, and other forms of prejudice may also be supported through scapegoating.

If the sequence "Frustration often creates aggression, and under some circumstances this aggression will be displaced onto scapegoats" is essentially correct, then there are several steps within it at which intervention could be attempted. The first is, when feasible, to try to reduce frustration levels by helping people reach more of their basic goals. As attractive and logical as this option may seem, trying to intervene at this step is often nearly impossible. For example, widespread poor economic conditions, with the host of problems that come from unemployment and resulting poverty, are a source of frustration that is extremely resistant to behavioral scientists' efforts to change.

The "trigger effect" studied by Berkowitz offers another theoretical approach to minimizing frustration-based aggression. He demonstrated in the research laboratory a phenomenon often suspected to occur in real settings: pent-up frustrations exploding into aggression because of the presence of stimuli earlier associated with aggression. The presence of armed police or National Guard troops, for example, may suggest to an angry crowd that violence is expected and therefore may actually promote it. Using a variation of the trigger effect to avoid setting off aggression is occasionally possible. For example, bringing religious leaders known to abhor violence to the site of a feared riot may suggest restraint to the crowd. Unfortunately, this approach is risky for the leaders involved, and it may be counterproductive if their presence is misinterpreted. The thought, "Even they have deserted us!" may add to the frustration, becoming a trigger rather than a calming influence.

When its causes cannot be controlled and frustration has built to dangerous levels, it may be preferable to suggest targets for its displacement rather than to let some spontaneously emerge. National leaders began doing this long before behavioral scientists provided the frustration-aggression framework for the practice. The process can be based on selfish madness, as was Hitler's persecution of the Jews, or it can be based on altruistic rationality.

For example, if people living in a deteriorating section of a city can be turned away from destructive violence and toward a task such as driving drug dealers from their neighborhood, some frustration is relieved and some societal benefit is realized. Such redirection of the aggression generated by frustration is certainly less desirable than preventing the frustration to begin with, but it may be far better than not intervening. Expelling drug dealers may do little to remedy other ills of the area, but it is desirable in itself, and the venting of frustration may reduce the likelihood of more violent aggression.

Another use of the frustration-aggression theory to reduce scapegoating and racist behavior may seem unpleasant, but it sometimes seems an unavoidable last resort. Because a satisfying scapegoat must be relatively harmless to attack, making a prospective scapegoat realistically dangerous to attack may prevent aggression or may deflect the aggression elsewhere. The dangerousness most typically is provided by the force of law.

A theoretical explanation of aggressive behavior, including racism, that is in direct conflict to the frustration-based concept is worth considering when evaluating ways of trying to reduce undesirable behavior. The frustration-aggression approach postulates a powerful need to release emotions generated by frustration. The need cannot be denied, and the release can, at best, be directed to reduce its damage. Social learning theory, a conflicting approach, postulates simple learning bases for aggression, racism, and other social behaviors. A person learns by watching others perform actions and experience the consequences or by personally being rewarded or punished for actions. If a person sees others benefit from aggression or racism, that behavior is likely to be tried. If aggression or racism seems to benefit a person directly, it is likely to be repeated.

One difference between the frustration-aggression theory's approach to reducing aggression and racism and the social learning theory's approach is particularly important. Frustration-aggression theorists, going back as far as Aristotle's notion of "catharsis" (emotional release), insist that the energy generated by frustration must be vented; it cannot be "held in." Social learning theory postulates no generation of energy and, therefore, holds that there is nothing to vent. For the social learning theorist, there is only practice at aggressing. Even if the action is directed at a socially acceptable target (for example, a competitor in sports), aggressing remains a practice that may, if rewarded, increase aggressiveness in other settings.

Context

The frustration-aggression theory of racism and scapegoating is a social psychological contribution to sociology, one that focuses on experiences of individuals as bases for group behavior. It looks for circumstances that block individuals' goal attainments (frustrations) and for targets they use while seeking someone to blame (scapegoats). The theory explains some kinds of racism first at the individual level and then, under the right circumstances, at the group level as well.

The frustration-aggression theory of racism can be applied concurrently with other, basically different explanations of the phenomenon. For example, after they were freed from slavery, many African Americans became competitors for jobs. If a white man saw a black man hired for a job he sought, racism based on economic issues could begin. "I hate him because he got my job" could easily be expanded to "I hate them because they're all after our jobs." Protection against such risks could be demanded by a majority group of workers, and discrimination against a race could become institutionalized. Scapegoating could support the institutionalized discrimination, and vice versa.

The long-honored view that racism can be caused by the formation of negative attitudes (prejudices) that lead to limiting behavior (discrimination) is also compatible with the frustration-aggression theory. "Aggression," as the theory uses it, can be at any level—intellectual, emotional, or behavioral. A frustrated individual who uses blacks as a scapegoat may believe that they are inferior people, may hate them, and may discriminate against them at every opportunity. Such a person holds the prejudice that is often hypothesized to underlie racism and to facilitate scapegoating.

The view that stereotypes encourage racism and scapegoating is also compatible with the frustration-aggression theory. Often a group chosen as a scapegoat is far more variable than the frustrated individual recognizes. By accurate perception, a person would recognize that only some (if any) of the group members "deserve" the hostility directed at them. Widely held stereotypes simplify the process of scapegoating. If all blacks are lazy, for example, and all Jews are money-hungry, the frustrated individual can simply hate them all without giving the matter further thought.

Even the most individualistic theory about scapegoating and racism, that of the authoritarian personality, meshes well with the frustration-aggression theory. An authoritarian personality, as first characterized in the 1950's, is a personality type characterized by a number of qualities that fall only a bit short of ones needed for classification as mentally ill. The person designated "high authoritarian" by a score on the F-scale devised by T. W. Adorno and the other authors of *The Authoritarian Personality* (1950) displays several qualities—conventionalism, authoritarian aggression, superstition and stereotypy, and projectivity—that directly predispose him or her to scapegoating as well as most of the behaviors inherent in the several other theories of racism. High authoritarians have developed their personalities over a lifetime and are not likely to change spontaneously or to be changed by others' efforts. Because of their typically rigid behaviors, they face many frustrations and are especially likely to find reasons other than their own shortcomings for their problems. High authoritarians' aggressiveness under frustrating conditions is a prototype for the frustration-aggression hypothesis.

Bibliography

Adorno, T. W., et al. *The Authoritarian Personality*. New York: Harper, 1950. The original source of the concept of the authoritarian personality and of the F-scale devised to measure it, this book contains material essential to understanding the pre-Fascist personality that the authors believe contributed to the perpetration of many of the atrocities in Nazi Germany. Some ʿof the material is probably too specialized for the general reader to digest, but most of it can be read and understood by anyone who is willing to make the effort.

Bandura, Albert. "The Social Learning Perspective: Mechanisms of Aggression." In *Psychology of Crime and Criminal Justice*, edited by Hans Toch. New York: Holt, Rinehart and Winston, 1979. An alternative to the frustration-aggression theory, social learning theory is a more direct approach to explaining aggression and racism and to suggesting how they may be controlled. Bandura's writings, here and in many other sources, are probably the clearest exposition of the theory to be found.

Berkowitz, Leonard. "The Frustration-Aggression Hypothesis Revisited." In *Roots of Aggression: A Re-examination of the Frustration-Aggression Hypothesis*, edited by Leonard Berkowitz. New York: Atherton, 1969. This collection presents papers written to challenge and to refine the original (then thirty-year-old) formulation. The book serves as a good example of the self-correcting nature of science and provides a broader appraisal than did the original source of the complexities of the frustration-aggression relationship.

Dollard, John, et al. *Frustration and Aggression*. New Haven, Conn: Yale University Press, 1939. This classic source proposed an extreme, inevitable relationship between frustration and aggression that many later researchers have questioned. The ideas that frustration always leads to aggression and that aggression always is preceded by frustration are now conceded to be extreme, but the book can be credited with calling many other scientists' attention to the questions.

Lorenz, Konrad. *On Aggression*. Translated by Marjorie Kerr Wilson. Reprint. New York: Harcourt Brace Jovanovich, 1974. Lorenz's book, first published in English in 1963, is an excellent presentation of the argument that inherent aggression must be recognized as real and that society must provide ways for it to be released with as little harm as possible. This view is even more extreme in its consequences than the one that frustration always leads to aggression.

Montagu, Ashley. *The Nature of Human Aggression*. New York: Oxford University Press, 1976. In direct contrast to Lorenz, Montagu argues that people are capable of behaving in many ways, not only those that seem an extension of their animal ancestry. He sees no merit in arguments that aggression is unavoidable and basically beyond human control. Modern social science finds Montagu's hopeful view considerably more likely than its biologically based opposite.

Harry A. Tiemann, Jr.

Cross-References

The Authoritarian Personality Theory of Racism, 159; Institutional Racism, 996; Prejudice and Discrimination: Merton's Paradigm, 1498; Prejudice and Stereotyping, 1505; Improving Race Relations, 1559; Race Relations: The Race-Class Debate, 1566; Racial and Ethnic Stratification, 1579; Racism as an Ideology, 1586; Socialization and Reference Groups in Race Relations, 1900.

FUNCTIONAL ILLITERACY

Type of sociology: Major social institutions
Field of study: Education

Generally, functional illiteracy refers to an individual's inability to read and write at a level high enough to perform even simple tasks in society. Specifically, functional illiteracy refers to those adults who read between fourth-grade and eighth-grade levels.

Principal terms
ILLITERACY: the inability to read or write
LITERACY: the ability to read and write at a level satisfactory to the needs of a given society
MINORITIES: groups in a society that are disadvantaged because they have less access to society's resources and privileges than the dominant group has
SOCIETY: a large social group that meets its own needs and that maintains a system of social interaction and relations across generations
VOLUNTEERISM: a philosophy encouraging individuals to offer their services free of charge for a good cause

Overview

In its most general sense, illiteracy is the inability to read and write; included within this designation is functional illiteracy, usually viewed as comprising adults who cannot read above an eighth-grade level. The concept of illiteracy in the United States tends to evoke a number of stereotypes. Some people envision new immigrants without satisfactory English-speaking skills, some think of adults who joined the labor force without finishing school, and others think of minorities who have not had the educational opportunities that others have had. In truth, there is no "typical" illiterate American. All three of the groups mentioned account for a percentage of illiterate Americans, but none is in the majority. The largest number of illiterates are white, native-born Americans. According to Jonathan Kozol's book *Illiterate America* (1985), more than 16 percent of white adults are functionally illiterate.

The statistics for illiteracy in the United States are surprisingly, even shockingly, high. Estimates for the total number of illiterates range anywhere from twenty to eighty-four million Americans. This large range is attributable to the fact that there are various types of illiteracy, and some estimates include certain types but not others. The figure most often cited in the early 1990's was seventy-two million, almost 25 percent of the total population of the United States.

Of these seventy-two million individuals, twenty-seven million cannot read a passage from a fourth-grade level textbook. The United States ranks forty-ninth among the 128 members of the United Nations in literacy levels. Almost 25 percent of all American citizens cannot read a simple newspaper article. In a country in which reading is such a large part of everyday life, millions of people face serious complications daily as a result of their illiteracy. People must be able to read to fill out an application, order from a menu, find a number in a telephone book, or even drive a car safely. In other words, a significant number of Americans are missing out on the American way of life.

Most scholarly journals, as well as most literacy programs, recognize three forms of illiteracy: total illiteracy, functional illiteracy, and advanced illiteracy. Totally illiterate individuals cannot read beyond third- or fourth-grade levels. Persons in this group, if they can read at all, can interpret only simple signs, messages, or warnings. Total illiterates have the most difficult time coping in society.

The second group includes those adults labeled functional illiterates. This term has a double meaning. In the general sense, functional illiteracy refers to the inability to read, write, and/or comprehend materials at levels satisfactory enough to function successfully in society. In a more scientific nature, functional illiteracy refers to the specific group of adults who are capable of reading materials ranging between fourth- and eighth-grade levels. They can comprehend many elementary directions, labels, and some newspaper or magazine articles; however, they cannot read at a level high enough to function successfully in the complex society of the United States. Many functional illiterates are capable of reading at low levels but cannot follow instructions (especially those with many steps); therefore, their job opportunities are extremely limited.

The final group, advanced illiterates, consists of those adults who read above an eighth-grade level but who cannot comprehend the meanings of what they read. Many of the individuals in this category seek help in the hope of obtaining a high school diploma or other equivalences and certificates. These are the illiterate individuals who most often seek assistance, because it is much easier to improve an existing rudimentary skill than it is to go through the complete process of learning to read.

There is no "typical" illiterate, and there is no particular racial or ethnic group that is more likely to be illiterate. There are, however, three groups that tend to become illiterate more than others: high school dropouts, students who do not receive the special educational attention they need, and those children who grow up in a home in which illiteracy is accepted and passed from generation to generation.

In 1986 almost 14 percent of all American high school students quit for one reason or another. If young people have not acquired the necessary skills to read by the time they reach high school, they may see no point in attending. They may view high school as a waste of time, since they could be working. The jobs from which dropouts must choose, however, to fit their limited skills, are menial, and the situation will most likely not improve significantly as they age. The next category encompasses those who do not receive the special attention they need to learn to read. Being at a disadvantage from the start because of either poverty or interaction with a parent who does not encourage education, such children are left behind as soon as they begin school. It is crucial, especially in the elementary years, to give these children the extra attention needed to overcome their problem. If they are overlooked or ignored by a teacher or other literate adults, they may give up trying to learn.

A child growing up in a home in which one or both parents have very poor reading skills will be more likely to become illiterate and be more likely to drop out of high school. The parents most likely will not provide the support the child needs to continue. Furthermore, the importance of an education will not have been stressed in an illiterate home as it has been in a home in which parents can read and write. These parents most often have jobs requiring little education; therefore, reading well is not seen as a crucial skill.

Applications

Various type of programs exist to help combat illiteracy in the United States, yet these programs have not been able to defeat the problem. Only about 4 percent of those in need get the necessary help. A number of factors are involved in this failure to reduce illiteracy even though it is theoretically possible to do so. One problem is that funding (particularly federal funding) is inadequate; another is that many more volunteers are needed. Literacy programs are generally broken down into three main types: competency-based programs, volunteer programs, and community-based programs.

Competency-based programs are those designed for functional illiterates or those categorized in the advanced illiteracy stage. Because both of these groups can at least read at minimal levels, the success rate for the programs is relatively high. These are mostly individual programs. Teachers work at each student's pace, often instructing the student regarding specific skills needed to pass a certain test such as a high school equivalency or proficiency test. Government-funded programs (including those in the military) are most often of this type. Volunteer programs range from large national based campaigns to small local programs. National volunteer programs include such large groups as the Literacy Volunteers of America and reach thousands of individuals each year. Volunteer programs are usually geared toward total illiterates and can be very successful if enough funding and volunteers are available. The number of volunteers has decreased, however, as the women who once composed most of the volunteer force have moved into the workforce over the years. One way to fight illiteracy is to bring more volunteers into these centers.

Community-based programs are similar to competency-based programs, except that the main focus is on the individual community and its learning process. This approach may work better than other programs because of its concentration on a particular community. Individuals seeking help are usually tested to determine the class level into which they should be placed. The classes are mostly group-oriented, but individual attention is also available. The group may discuss the problems of being illiterate and discuss ways to cope with these difficulties while learning to read, thereby creating a group identity.

Even though there are many programs fighting the illiteracy problem, the problem persists. With an estimated seventy-two million illiterate people in the United States, the number one problem is inadequate funding to reach all those people. Federal education budgets have been cut significantly since the late 1970's as the federal government has tried to pass education expenses to the states. Since the 1980's, concern about reducing the federal deficit has further affected education budgets as it has all aspects of the federal budget. Schools and literacy programs, as well as public libraries, have suffered. Many groups, including Literacy Volunteers of America, are also cutting back their budgets. Frequently budget cuts hit hardest in areas that most desperately need libraries and literacy programs—lower-class and inner-city areas.

Corporate funding is also badly needed. Some corporations offer free reading classes to employees. Others pay the costs for employees to enroll in educational classes to acquire new skills. Still others, such as Pepsico, through its Pizza Hut division, have started their own campaigns. In 1986, Pizza Hut began a program called Book It, designed to get children in grades one through six interested in reading. The children promise to read a certain number of books in a given time frame in exchange for such rewards as class pizza parties.

In addition to federal and corporate funding, literacy programs could be helped by increased public support. The Ad Council dubbed 1987 the "Year of the Reader" and supplied the media with messages aimed a raising public awareness about the illiteracy problem. The council announced that between 21 and 30 percent more Americans became informed of the situation as a result of the media blitz. This was at most a partial victory, however; public awareness is one thing, but public involvement is quite another matter. Volunteerism has steadily declined after its peak in the 1960's. Literacy programs are primarily based on volunteers because of their minimal cost to the program. Most programs are understaffed and desperately need more people to provide time and help for those illiterate persons in their area.

Context

The concept of illiteracy as a widespread social problem developed in the twentieth century. Before the changes wrought by the Industrial Revolution, there was little reason for many people to need to read, as they lived in small villages or on farms. With industrialization and urbanization, which did not deeply affect the United States until the late nineteenth century, came the need for new job skills and an increasing need for education. The technological revolutions later in the twentieth century made the need for literacy even more crucial. Another central aspect to the modern view of literacy is the belief that, in a democracy, citizens must be politically educated and aware. An educated awareness of a country's politics and policies can exist only if its citizens can read. Although illiteracy statistics have been calculated for some time, it was not until the 1950's and 1960's that national literacy campaigns were created to combat this serious social problem.

Studies of illiteracy per se have tended to focus on adult illiterates, but it is important to emphasize the connection between children's educational problems and adult illiteracy. Studies of the institution of education have produced much data regarding inequality in education in the United States. Children with unequal access to quality education (and therefore without sufficient role models or the influence of peers from more advantaged backgrounds) are at high risk for becoming the adult illiterates of the future. Children with illiterate parents need strong external influences to teach them the importance of being able to read and write. Other areas regarding children learning to read that need further study are the effects of television (used so frequently as an "electronic babysitter") on learning and literacy, and the quality of the primers used to teach beginning readers. Children used to the exciting images and language (much of which they can understand) of television may be uninterested in the relatively dull language and static storylines of most beginning readers. Schools and teachers must select reading material for beginners with an eye for exciting and intriguing passages.

The rapid pace of technological change is making literacy increasingly important. Many experts have argued that the United States is well on the way to being a "postindustrial" society or an "information" society. In such a society, some say, knowledge is power. Knowledge cannot be attained without literacy, and the gap between the job possibilities for educated and uneducated people will undoubtedly widen even further. Moreover, in more practical terms, many people change jobs frequently in their lifetimes, and retraining is often necessary. Even individuals working in factories will need to learn new skills in order to operate technologically advanced, computerized machinery, and illiteracy can present an insurmountable obstacle to the learning of necessary new skills.

Bibliography

Curtis, Lynn R. *Literacy for Social Change*. Syracuse, N.Y.: New Readers Press, 1993. Although Curtis' book gathers much of its information from literacy programs from other countries, it introduces and discusses many innovative programs in use to combat illiteracy.

Hunter, Carman St. John, and David Harman. *Adult Illiteracy in the United States*. New York: McGraw-Hill, 1979. Full of statistics and facts, this book covers many facets of illiteracy, from defining the term to giving suggestions to combat it. Suited for the average reader. An in-depth bibliography with summaries of the works noted is included.

Kozol, Jonathan. *Illiterate America*. Garden City, N.Y.: Anchor Press, 1985. An excellent book on the subject of illiteracy. Kozol uses hard facts as well as personal stories to describe the illiteracy problem in the United States. He offers readers a clear, well-written analysis and offers solutions to the problem. An index is included.

_____ . *Prisoners of Silence*. New York: Continuum, 1980. This book is the predecessor to *Illiterate America* and is in many ways a smaller version than the latter. Includes a bibliography but no index; offers a lengthy list of names and addresses connected to the literacy cause.

Neilsen, Lorri. *Literacy and Living*. Portsmouth, N.H.: Heinemann, 1989. Taking an unusual approach, Neilsen explores the lives of literate adults to show the importance of being able to read and write in everyday life. As Neilsen follows these adults through their everyday routines, the reader begins to understand the tremendous importance of literacy.

Venezky, Richard, David Wagner, and Barrie Ciliberti. *Toward Defining Literacy.* Newark, Del.: International Reading Association, 1990. The main intent of this work is to define illiteracy and other related terms. Definitions are presented and disputed in a variety of articles. Some of the articles are technical.

Jana L. Wallace

Cross-References

Adult Education, 15; Compulsory and Mass Education, 309; Education: Conflict Theory Views, 579; Education: Manifest and Latent Functions, 593; Educational Inequality: The Coleman Report, 607; The Culture of Poverty, 1460; Unemployment and Poverty, 2083.

FUNCTIONALISM

Type of sociology: Origins and definitions of sociology
Field of study: Sociological perspectives and principles

Functionalism is a major theory in sociology for analyzing and understanding certain social relationships. This perspective attempts to explain why and how certain social structures work in society by ascertaining their function.

> *Principal terms*
> ANOMIE: a condition of confusion that exists in both the individual and society because of weak or absent social norms
> CONFLICT THEORY: a social theory that focuses on tension and strain as a natural state within the social system
> DYSFUNCTION: a negative consequence which may lead to disruption or breakdown of the social system
> LATENT FUNCTION: an unrecognized or unintended consequence
> MACROSOCIOLOGY: the level of sociological analysis that is concerned with large-scale social issues, institutions, and processes
> MANIFEST FUNCTION: the intended or obvious consequences
> MICROSOCIOLOGY: the level of sociological analysis concerned with small-scale group dynamics

Overview

The sociological agenda throughout much of the twentieth century has been empirically rooted, and this approach has generated an abundance of research facts and figures. Empirical information remains useless, however, unless its meaning is discerned; this is the purpose of a theory. It organizes a set of concepts in a meaningful way by explaining the relationship among them. Theories thus make the "facts" of social life understandable by explaining cause and effect relationships.

Functional theory is one of the central sociological perspectives that is concerned with explaining large-scale social structures and relationships. In other works, it is one of the principal approaches of macrosociology. Functionalists attempt to explain why certain conditions exist in society by trying to ascertain their purpose—their function. This type of approach is used extensively, even dominantly, in all the social sciences as well as in many of the natural sciences, biology in particular. In sociology, the functionalist approach—examining how things work to meet people's needs and to promote social consensus—is contrasted primarily with conflict theory, which emphasizes the struggle and strain among different groups within society.

Sociologists use the functionalist perspective (sometimes called structural functionalism) to explain why social institutions such as the family take on a certain form or structure within a given society. It is assumed that for something to exist it must have a purpose within the social system. The premise underlying this assumption is that if the social institution served to purpose in its existing state it would either change to accommodate new social conditions or would simply cease to exist.

This question of why certain institutions or patterns of relationships exist in society was formulated by the French social philosopher Auguste Comte (1798-1857), who has been called the founder of sociology. Comte developed the basic organic analogy that was extended and popularized by the British sociologist Herbert Spencer (1820-1903), who drew parallels to the theories of the naturalist Charles Darwin (1809-1882). Darwin theorized that, over time, biological species adapt and change to survive as environmental conditions change. Spencer related Darwin's thesis to societies. Spencer's theory states that all the parts of the social system, like the parts of the human body, have a fit or function and connect to the whole; if one part of the system changes, the change will influence other parts of the system to change. Thus, as the family begins to change because of social changes in the environment (for example, the shift from an agrarian society to an industrial society), so too must the other social institutions (political, educational, and religious) change, leading to a realignment of all the social institutions so they all "fit" the new social order.

The functionalist school of sociology has from its inception been concerned with how society adapts and changes. The classic evolutionary view sees changes occurring slowly, allowing for adaptation and realignment of the various interrelated social institutions. A society which changes too rapidly is likely to experience structural misalignment in which parts of the system do not fit snugly together, leading to confusion or anomie for the society's members. Theoretically at least, the component parts of the system will eventually mesh, and the expected harmonious interconnection of social institutions will again be achieved.

This classic evolutionary adaptation of social systems has never posed a problem for functionalists, since such change tends to occur without disrupting the existing social system. More cataclysmic, conflictive forms of change, however, have challenged functionalist explanations because they tend to lead to social disharmony. This problem was addressed in various forms by sociologists from Max Weber (1864-1920) and Émile Durkheim (1858-1917) to Talcott Parsons (1902-1979) and Robert K. Merton (b. 1910).

The concept of viewing even disruptive change as functional may be used as a simplistic though straightforward summation of latter-twentieth century functionalism. Change, whether internal (such as recessions or depressions) or external (war), causes strain, throwing the existing system into a state of disequilibrium. Prolonged strain cannot be endured without the society suffering considerable damage. The destructive impact of prolonged stress on the human body, both physical and mental, has been well documented, and functionalists extend the same premise to society. They see society moving to restore balance or harmony (the "natural" social condition). The restored system, however, may be markedly different from the old. In other words, social change is a natural evolutionary process, and while it may sometimes be painful, it helps the system adapt and adjust to new social conditions; it is therefore functional.

For Parsons, social strain was natural; strain is the painful adjustment which results from society's continued growth, inevitably making each successive social stage more complex than earlier ones. This increased complexity causes tension. Merton took into consideration the idea that not everything which happens in society leads to equilibrium; indeed, Merton points out that certain changes, while beneficial for some, may be dysfunctional for others. Nevertheless, he maintains that these dysfunctions may be beneficial if one distinguishes between manifest functions, which are stated or intended, and latent functions, which are unintended or hidden. Competition provides an excellent example of Merton's thesis. Economic competition is often lopsided, with clear winners and losers, but competition also leads to benefits for the consumer, who gets improved products at reduced cost (latent function). In the process the winner, by building the "better mousetrap," reaps rewards in enhanced profits (manifest function). Yet from the competitive loser's vantage point, competition is seen as dysfunctional, since they did not benefit.

Applications

Functionalism primarily deals with large social units and attempts to understand how these units are interrelated. Functionalists work from a premise that these units strive to maintain a balance: order, equilibrium, homeostasis. As such, the social institution is connected to society and adapts to changes in the social environment. Two examples may be utilized to illustrate this connection. The first traces the normal evolutionary processes of adaption in the social institution of sports; the second examines the more disruptive but functional place of revolutions.

In the preindustrial, agrarian society of the early nineteenth century, sports fit the social environment: fishing, hunting, boating, cockfighting, foot racing, and other activities rooted to the land and water dominated. As the social environment began to change in the mid-nineteenth century, people moved from rural areas and adopted an urban, industrial way of life. Cities had a larger population base from which to draw, so arena and stadium sporting events replaced local sporting activities, giving rise to soccer, football, baseball, and boxing. Spectator sports replaced participatory sports, because industrialization required specialization and people no longer had either the time or talent to devote to sports; however, they did have more disposable income and could pay to see sporting events that had formerly been participatory and free.

As the twentieth century progressed, technological changes prompted adaption in sports. Radio and then television made stadium crowds unnecessary, either to generate income or to reach sports fans. Broadcasting made sports a mass event, no longer confined to particular cities and soon reaching tens of millions of listeners and viewers. Football, as well as most major sports, has been altered by the media; for example, time outs have increased to allow time for television advertising. The game time has thus been substantially extended. Other sports that have traditionally garnered only a small audience, such as tennis and golf, have received more coverage and risen in prestige, and more amateurs have become interested in the games. In addition, sporting forms which have previously not existed have been developed for television. One example in the late 1980's was a program called *American Gladiators*, in which athletes competed in a staged series of tests of strength and endurance in an atmosphere that was part carnival, part game show.

Sports, then, has changed; it has evolved as social conditions (notably urbanization and technology) have changed, and changes in sports have largely taken place without major disruption in other interrelated parts of the social system. The racial integration of sports has proceeded at a pace that reflects racial integration in other social institutions, such as education, politics, and the military, all of which took their first major strides toward integration during the 1950's. Similarly, the entrance of women into sports, as well as the increased attention paid to women's sports in the 1980's and 1990's, paralleled the general social movement of women as they entered the American workforce and political arena in increasing numbers during this period.

Changes in macropolitics are sometimes less harmonious. Revolutions are extraordinarily disruptive. They typically result in major upheavals and radical changes in all existing institutional arrangements. The American Revolution occurred in 1776; the French in 1789; the Russian in 1917. Germany underwent major political shifts between 1880 and 1910, though not marked by the same degree of violence. In other words, many of the major Western powers experienced radical political reform over a relatively short historical period, moving from monarchy systems to predominantly parliamentary forms of government. Such political "facts" require interpretation. Classic organic functionalism cannot explain this widespread social upheaval because the evolutionary process was not allowed to take its "natural" course. More contemporary forms of functionalism (Parsons, Merton) help in understanding the functional aspect of disruptive change.

The old monarchy systems were rooted in the feudal period, and they were once beneficial. Under the feudal system, the nobility protected the outlying agrarian populace from marauding bands. The peasant paid for this protection by providing the nobility with food and other services. Over time, the monarchy system decayed and became corrupt, providing fewer services for the populace. Ultimately, this resulted in forced change. The revolutions of the eighteenth and nineteenth century that swept Western Europe and North America were the result of corrupt, unresponsive systems of government (those of George III, Louis XVI, and Czar Nicholas in England, France, and Russia, respectively). Disruptive as these periods of strife were, they were necessary (functional) in moving the society from an agrarian monarchy system of government to an industrial and parliamentary one.

The industrial age requires adaptation and change, and entrenched parties in power (such as monarchies) are notoriously resistant to change. Parliamentary systems are thus more functional in the modern age. Great Britain, were the parliamentary system first arose in the aftermath of the English Civil War of the mid-seventeenth century, was the first nation to industrialize and became an early economic world leader. More recently, Japan's powerful monarchy was replaced by a parliamentary system after World War II, and Japan has since taken its place among the world's economic giants. Those countries which have lagged industrially have been totalitarian, most notably the Communist governments of China and the former Soviet Union. These governments struggled with the transition to industrialization because changing one aspect of their world, the economic-industrial stratum, requires change in other areas, especially the political. To function in the modern world they have been forced to make concessions; while change has led to major internal strife, such tension is necessary for countries to enter the industrial age.

Context

Functionalist explanations have been used for millennia by a diverse group of philosophers and scientists and have been used by sociologists to explain social conditions since Auguste Comte first coined the term "sociology." This theoretical heritage does not in itself ensure its continued dominance, but it is at the very least a strong indicator of its general historical importance. A number of important sociological perspectives have been developed in the twentieth century, but in a way they are all descendants of the functionalist view—all represent attempts to come to terms with what either functionalists or their critics have seen as weaknesses in functionalist theory. Conflict theory, which came into prominence in the late 1960's and the 1970's, is the most notable example. Moreover, functionalism itself has changed and adapted markedly since its initial formulation by Comte and Spencer.

Particularly since the 1960's, sociological theory has been moved forward significantly by the debate among those espousing various viewpoints; a central debate has been between functionalists and conflict theorists. The historical criticism of functionalism by theorists outside the functionalist tradition is that the theory is too one-sided: It assumes that simply because something exists it must have a function. This assumption has been criticized as being tautological. In the 1960's and 1970's, Marxist theorists also criticized functionalist views as being overly conservative and argued that they tended to be used to support the societal status quo. The criticism that functionalism is one-sided cannot truly be refuted, but it should be pointed out that other sociological perspectives can also be found to possess the same trait. Conflict theory, for example, tends to stress tension, struggle, and social strain to the exclusion of seeing any consensus or harmony in society; if society were as fractious as conflict theory sometimes suggests, it could be argued, peaceful and evolutionary change in society's institutions could hardly take place—as it certainly sometimes does.

It is perhaps most useful to view functionalist and conflict theories not as mutually exclusive but as pointing out each other's weaknesses. Both perspectives are useful in dealing with certain aspects of social structure and social change; they shed light on different dimensions of large-scale social patterns. For this reason, both traditions, as they evolve and adapt to answer criticism, are likely to continue in sociology.

Bibliography

Buckley, Walter. "Structural-Functional Analysis in Modern Society." In *Modern Sociological Theory in Continuity and Change*, edited by Howard Becker and Alvin Boskoff. New York: Dryden, 1957. An early attempt during a heated period of functional analysis to assess the role of the functional perspective for the second half of the twentieth century.

Merton, Robert. *Social Theory and Social Structure*. Rev. ed. Glencoe, Ill.: Free Press, 1957. Merton introduces the key distinction of manifest and latent functions in a chapter of the same name.

Sorokin, Pitirim. *The Sociology of Revolution*. New York: Howard Fertig, 1967. Sorokin acknowledges the economic conflict thesis but goes beyond this to show how social institutions are interrelated and to argue that revolution is a necessary and recurring step in maintaining societal equilibrium.

Szacki, Jerzy. *History of Sociological Thought*. Westport, Conn.: Greenwood Press, 1979. A particularly interesting chapter, "Sociological Functionalism and Its Critics," examines how other theorists see the functionalist perspective.

Timasheff, Nicholas. *Sociological Theory: Its Nature and Growth*. New York: Random House, 1967. A good critique of early functionalists, including Comte, Spencer, and the social Darwinists, plus a chapter on modern functionalism.

Turner, Jonathan. *The Structure of Sociological Theory*. 5th ed. Belmont, Calif.: Wadsworth, 1991. The best and most detailed analysis in overview format of the difficult theories of Talcott Parsons (chapter 3) and Robert Merton (chapter 4). Turner also assesses the functionalist aspect of other perspectives: neofunctionalism (chapter 5), general systems functionalism (chapter 6), ecological functionalism (chapter 7), and biological functionalism (chapter 8).

White, Harrison, and Cynthia White. *Canvases and Careers: Institutional Change in the French Painting World*. Chicago: University of Chicago Press, 1993. The Whites examine the rise of Impressionism as a dominant art form during the nineteenth century. Though not specifically labeled as a functionalist analysis, their work clearly shows the interconnection of social institutions and how the shift from one school (the Royal Academy) was beneficial for the artists and art patrons.

John Markert

Cross-References

Age Inequality: Functionalist versus Conflict Theory Views, 34; Conflict Theory, 340; Deviance: Functions and Dysfunctions, 540; Education: Functionalist Perspectives, 586; The Family: Functionalist versus Conflict Theory Views, 739; Interactionism, 1009; Religion: Functionalist Analyses, 1603; Social Change: Functionalism versus Historical Materialism, 1779; Social Stratification: Functionalist Perspectives, 1845; The History of Sociology, 1926; Sociology Defined, 1932.

GANGS

Type of sociology: Deviance and social control
Field of study: Forms of deviance

There is no common definition of the term "gang" that is universally accepted or is useful to all those who study or investigate street gangs. The contemporary definition of street gang, from a sociological perspective, comes from gang research pioneer Malcolm Klein. Klein defines gangs in terms of three criteria: first, recognition by the community that the group exists; second, that the group itself recognizes itself as a group, usually with a group name; and third, that the group engages in sufficient illegal activities to receive a consistently negative response from law enforcement personnel and/or neighborhood residents.

Principal terms

ANOMIE: a social condition that results in society's inability to control behavior because of natural or human-caused catastrophe

CULTURAL CONFLICT: a clash between different societal norms that can lead to criminal behavior

CULTURAL DEVIANCE: the manner in which an individual in society departs from dominant norms

DIFFERENTIAL ASSOCIATION THEORY: the view that criminal behavior is learned through social contacts

ECOLOGY OF CRIME: a phrase that indicates that crime is a product of transitional neighborhoods, which result in social disorganization

SOCIAL LEARNING: the way in which people learn to be criminals, which is the same way that people learn any behavior

SOCIAL NORMS: a set of accepted forms of behavior

Overview

Pioneer gang sociologist Malcolm Klein asserts in the introduction to *An Introduction to Gangs* (1991) that, with very few exceptions, the United States is alone in the development of urban street gangs. Sociologists theorize that a number of factors contribute to the formation of modern street gangs in the United States. A number of sociologists point to the extreme poverty suffered by inner city youth as the primary cause of gangs. The demise of lucrative unskilled industrial jobs resulted in the destabilization of the social and economic structure of America's inner cities. That structural catastrophe, they theorize, led to various forms of social dysfunction, such as the breakdown of the traditional family, with its internal control mechanism, and a rejection of conventional norms, such as a commitment to hard work, parental responsibility, education, and other values held by the dominant society.

Although government has attempted to address these problems by creating a welfare system to serve as a "safety net," its programs have not reached those who have adopted the value system known as the "culture of poverty."

In some areas, social dysfunction is so prevalent that even with social welfare and other institutions of government designed to assist the inner city resident, a condition of anomie exists. Anomie occurs when the existing social structure can no longer maintain control over an individual's wants and desires. In such a situation, gangs form to satisfy their own uncontrollable needs and to establish their own power structures.

Crimes such as drive-by shootings in crowded areas and murders committed because of the wearing of gang colors or other articles of fashion are examples of gang crimes that are based on the normlessness of anomie.

The United States is unique among industrial nations. Its diversity of ethnic and racial populations has produced a highly stratified society unlike those of other industrial giants such as Japan or Germany, which are relatively homogeneous. Some sociologists theorize that this stratified structure of society has resulted in a socioeconomic class system in which the dominant white population has assumed the top tier of the structure and other racial minorities have been relegated to lower levels. They believe that groups that occupy the lower rungs of the structure are effectively denied access to the rewards of the white top tier of the structure because of built-in inhibitors such as institutional racism. Therefore, members of the lower classes become so frustrated that they choose their own methods of seeking success outside the legally accepted method of the dominant society. Drug dealing, home invasions, and auto theft are examples of gang crimes that are based on frustration and rage against America's class structure.

Finally, a number of scholars believe that gangs are merely a reflection of society's move away from traditional ethical and religious values toward an acceptance of a lower standard of moral responsibility and behavior. These theorists point to statistics that show the dramatic increase in seemingly senseless gang violence among younger juveniles who exhibit a relative lack of remorse for their acts or for their victims as evidence of such moral decay.

The first U.S. gangs formed in New York City during the 1820's and 1830's. These original gangs sprang up in the Five Point section of New York's lower east side and were made up primarily of young males of ethnic and racial minorities who occupied the lowest rung on the socioeconomic ladder of society. In 1820's New York City, the gangs were Irish. As is true of gangs today, these early gang members were poorly educated, came from relatively unstable families, were recent immigrants to the United States or migrants from other areas in America, and tended to be outside the mainstream of society.

Like gangs today, they identified their groups by name. The first documented name of a street gang was The Forty Thieves. Other gangs of that era were the Roach Guards, the Dead Rabbits, and the Plug Uglies, to name a few. Most of the nineteenth century gangs were territorial and claimed a certain section of the city as their "turf," or territory. If any other group ventured on their territory, it would be attacked. Many of the early gangs were based on ethnic identity. In the 1840's, New York City had a gang known as the Kerryonian Gang. All its members were from County Kerr, Ireland. Their purpose was to mug their traditional adversaries: Englishmen.

Today, the same phenomena occur in gang crime activity. For example, some immigrant Asians form U.S. gang associations based on their homeland regional or ethnic identification. They war with other Asian Americans who originated from rival areas of their homeland.

There is evidence to support the theory that nineteenth century and early twentieth century street gang membership provided a vehicle for upward mobility. For those who happened to be fortunate enough to be in the right place and time in history, street gang experience served as a stepping stone to organized crime. Charles (Lucky) Luciano, Benjamin (Bugsy) Siegel, and Al (Scarface) Capone were but a few who came from urban street gang environments. For the most part, however, the transformation of common street gang members to organized criminal gangsters did not occur.

Most research indicates that although some gang members may seriously aspire to sophisticated organized criminal pursuits, most are juveniles who range in age from approximately ten to twenty. These gang members associate to fulfill a need of belonging, self-esteem, and a perceived obligation to defend their way of life and neighborhood from legitimate social institutions such as the police and other symbols of authority as well as rival gangs.

Many urban areas' street gangs are generational, going back five or six generations, and have been historically territorial. An excellent example of generational territorial gangs is the Mexican American street gangs of East Los Angeles, which date back to the turn of the century. Their primary reason for existence was to protect their neighborhoods (barrios) from anyone or anything that they perceived as a threat.

With the advent of widespread illicit drug use in the late 1960's, which was a form of deviance that was accepted by many people, street gangs in America began to change. The enormous profit that could be made by the easy activity of selling drugs influenced many inner city youths to form unsophisticated criminal street gangs to take advantage of a "get something for nothing" opportunity. The major African American street gangs of Los Angeles and Chicago in the early 1970's are an example of this phenomenon, which has now reached every urban community as well as many suburban and rural communities throughout the country.

Although most gangs do pay attention to territory, the main emphasis on territory has to do with the protection of criminal enterprises rather than with land (turf). Because they have easy access to automobiles, either legally or illegally, gangs have become extremely mobile. Many travel from one part of the city to another to conduct gang activities. Some gangs travel outside their own cities or even their own states to commit crimes. Asian street gang members who grew up in an environment of constant movement in southeast Asia that enabled them to escape political persecution are especially prone to travel.

Criminologists point to empirical evidence that supports the conclusion that as the number of street gangs has increased, primarily because of the illicit drug industry, so has the level of gang violence. In many areas of America's inner cities, gang crimes account for a significant percentage of all crimes—particularly acts of murder and mayhem.

Numerous local and national polls have indicated that citizens of urban areas, especially minority citizens, believe that street gang violence is one of the most serious problems facing urban America today.

Applications

Understanding why, how, and where street gangs evolve and what is the profile of the average street gang member will have significant impact on public policy decisions regarding law enforcement and the eradication of street gangs in the future.

Until the 1980's, not much attention was given to street gangs, except in areas where gang crimes were a problem, such as Chicago and Southern California. Since that time, a new awareness has developed regarding the composition of gangs, their growth, and the level of violence that has been associated with street gang activity.

With that new awareness, many observers believe, came a mythology of street gang "truths" that tended to inhibit effective gang responses. Examples of this phenomenon ranged from speculation that a number of street gangs in Los Angeles and Chicago franchised themselves to every state in the union, in a conspiracy of syndication à la La Cosa Nostra, to theories that street gangs were merely reflections of the poor job market. Research into the structure of gangs and the behavior of gang members found that both assumptions were incorrect. Although a few street gang names have gone nationwide, their original gang leadership and influence did not. Furthermore, gang crime research has found that the causes of this phenomenon are extremely varied and that policies that focused on only one problem, such as lack of jobs, did not significantly reduce gang crimes.

Although these and other theories have proved themselves to be incorrect and have led to a number of expensive and nonproductive gang abatement initiatives, they did establish a baseline from which future research and policy decisions can be made to reduce the number of street gangs and gang-related crime. Because the resources that are available to the government to address social problems are limited, policies that research has found will assist in that effort must be analyzed carefully and supported. A number of public policy approaches that have been used since the 1980's have been based on sociological research. Although most programs have been somewhat successful in retarding street gang activities, their efforts have not significantly reduced the level of violence associated with street gangs.

Three current approaches involve education, social programs, and law enforcement. Street gang education awareness programs in schools have been successful in exposing students and faculty to local gang identities, structures, and methods of operation. They have been less successful, however, in helping students to disassociate themselves from gangs.

Social programs that provide inner city youths with alternatives to gang life, such as recreational, social, and value-based partnership programs, have been relatively successful with younger adolescents and preadolescents but less successful with older teenagers and youngsters from extremely dysfunctional families and social environments.

Law enforcement's efforts to combat gang growth and violence have primarily resulted in the maintenance of the status quo. Given the dramatic rise in gang membership, the ability of law enforcement to prevent serious gang crimes and violence from rising in proportion to gang growth, with such programs as community policing, gang crime specialized training, and street gang investigation units, is a de facto success.

The successful application of sociological theory to public policy decisions is often not realized for a generation after implementation. Therefore, the hoped-for success of today's decisions addressing street gangs will probably not be totally evaluated until well into the next century.

Context

Sociological investigation into the causes of street gangs began as general research projects in the 1920's and 1930's to explain why urban areas had experienced a significantly higher degree of social dysfunction than suburban and rural areas had. A number of those studies focused on juvenile behaviors, and a few specifically concentrated on juvenile gangs, particularly in the Chicago area.

Whether the studies researched juvenile behavior in general or street gangs in particular, they all added to the general body of knowledge from which modern public policy is made.

These early studies have proved to be invaluable, since prior to that time criminal behavior was thought to be caused primarily by moral, biological, or psychological causations. Furthermore, the study of crime causation was primarily restricted to the behavior of the individual, not that of the group.

In 1927, Frederick Thrasher's *The Gang* found that gang behavior may be an evolutionary process by which children's play groups transform into adolescent street gangs in response to conflicts with other groups of peers and perceived common enemies, such as the police.

University of Chicago sociologists Clifford Shaw and Henry McCay's research on social urban dynamics of Chicago from approximately 1900 to 1930 concluded that increased incidents of delinquent behavior appeared in areas in which incidences of social disorganization were more likely to occur. Furthermore, the areas tended to pattern themselves in fairly uniform concentric zones emanating outward from the inner city (zone I) to the suburbs (zone V). The closer to the inner city, the higher the incidence of social dysfunction and street gang activity.

Sociologist Walter Miller concluded that many forms of criminal and antisocial behavior of residents of lower economic classes conflict with the conduct norms of those of the middle and upper classes. Miller argued that these norms do not necessarily represent rebellion or hostility toward the other classes; they are merely values that are accepted by the lower classes so that they can survive in their often hostile environment.

Robert Merton's research found that frustration and strain exist in a number of inner city residents, particularly juveniles who agree with the American dream of prosperity and wealth but do not believe they can accomplish that goal in a manner that conforms to society's norms. Merton's work is especially important in that he was responsible for identifying a particular gang structure and process by classifying gang member behaviors and values. Merton found that gang members adapt to their perception of reality in a number of ways, which he labeled innovation, ritualism, retreatism, and rebellion.

The adaptation that is of particular interest to law enforcement is innovation. Innovation occurs when a person invents an illegal way to obtain a goal such as wealth. Stealing cars rather than washing cars to earn money is an example of Merton's innovation theory.

Contemporary scholars have refined the theories of the earlier pioneers and have developed new bodies of research to explain the changes in composition and structure of gangs today and in the future.

Bibliography

Huff, C. Ronald, ed. *Gangs in America*. Newbury Park, Calif.: Sage Publications, 1990. *Gangs in America* focuses on post-World War II gang theory. This title will provide the student of gang behavior with a solid understanding of diverse gang typologies and activities.

Jacoby, Joseph E., ed. *Classics of Criminology*. Glencoe, Ill.: Moore, 1979. This series of articles provides a short walk through three hundred years of criminal causation theory. These articles are "fast reads" yet are mandatory for those who require a solid criminological grounding in current gang behavior.

Klein, Malcolm W. *Street Gangs and Street Workers*. Englewood Cliffs, N.J.: Prentice-Hall, 1971. Klein's book provides the student of gangs with ample evidence that most street gangs are not as structured and organized as they are held to be by some members of the media and law enforcement communities.

Knox, George W. *An Introduction to Gangs*. Berrien Springs, Mich.: Vande Vere, 1991. This is the most comprehensive work available on the theory, profile, and operations of contemporary urban street gangs in the United States. Knox provides the most extensive (forty-five pages) bibliography of gang research to be found in a single publication. The book provides an appendix that lists contemporary street gangs by state, along with examples of actual street gang constitutions and related paraphernalia.

Thrasher, Frederic M. *The Gang*. Chicago: University of Chicago Press, 1963. *The Gang* is the original sociological study of urban street gangs in the modern United States. Thrasher's account, first published in 1927, was instrumental in labeling developmental sequences of gang member behavior from childhood through adolescence. *The Gang* provides an excellent historical analysis of gang research in urban America in the 1920's. It also includes photographs of early twentieth century gang members.

Joseph George Andritzky

Cross-References

THE GAY LIBERATION MOVEMENT

Type of sociology: Collective behavior and social movements

The gay liberation movement refers broadly to the contemporary social movement—initiated by the Stonewall rebellion of June, 1969—which seeks an end to all forms of social control of homosexuals and for civil rights legislation to cover lesbians, bisexuals, and gay men.

Principal terms

COMING OUT: the psychological process of acquiring and acknowledging a gay or lesbian identity—first to oneself, then to friends and family, and then, some argue, to anyone with whom one has significant contact

DISCRIMINATION: the denial of the rights of, or social intolerance of, individuals on the basis of their perceived membership in a group

HETEROSEXISM: an excessive valuing of heterosexual persons, values, and behavior; an assumption that any behavior other than heterosexual behavior is abnormal

HOMOPHILE: literally "love of same," this term was employed by homosexual activists in the 1950's as a more positive one than "homosexual," which referred to sex acts

HOMOPHOBIA: a negative attitude toward homosexual persons and homosexuality; it refers to prejudice comparable to racism, sexism, and anti-Semitism, though it implies individual pathology, such as a hatred of or aversion to homosexual persons

SODOMY: an overarching term for sexual deviation, its legal definition specifies anal intercourse and oral-genital contact, either consensual or coerced

Overview

A relatively recent movement for social change, the gay liberation movement arose after the Stonewall rebellion (June, 1969) as a highly visible mass movement and as the most broadly organized effort to end legal and social intolerance of homosexuality. The Stonewall rebellion was a spontaneous resistance to police harassment by patrons of the Stonewall Inn, a gay bar on Christopher Street in New York's Greenwich Village, on the night of June 27. Such "raids" by Public Morals Section police had become routine in the preceding two decades, but that night and the following two nights the bar's clientele (largely composed of transvestites and street people) fought the police with stones and bottles.

From this resistance grew a mass movement, one made possible by the laborious work of the pioneers of the 1950's and 1960's homophile movement. The Stonewall rebellion marked a turning point in the move for homosexual rights: It signaled a victory for homophile militants, and it occurred within the culture of 1960's protest, a time when people were questioning traditional assumptions about power and authority.

The first group to arise, the Gay Liberation Front (GLF), formed on July 31, 1969, at New York's Alternative University, drew members from the ranks of the New Left and the student anti-Vietnam War movement and adopted a name reflecting their identification with national liberation movements in countries such as Vietnam and Algeria. They adopted a set of principles emphasizing building coalitions with other disfranchised groups—women, ethnic minorities, African Americans, people with disabilities, working class people, and Third World peoples—in order to dismantle oppressive socioeconomic structures. For the small group of rebels that chanted "gay power," gay liberation was not a civil rights movement but a revolutionary struggle to free the homosexual in everyone, challenging the social order that confined sexuality to marriage and that fostered compulsory heterosexuality. Carl Wittman spelled this out in *Refugees from Amerika: A Gay Manifesto* (1969): "Liberation for gay people is to define for ourselves how and with whom we live, instead of measuring our relationships by straight values . . . we must govern ourselves, set up our own institutions, defend ourselves."

Quickly GLF chapters formed on campuses and in many American cities, achieving visibility in antiwar marches, but all those drawn to a gay movement did not share their radical ideas or confrontational style, visible in the GLF newspaper *Come Out*, which carried photographs of the staff in the nude. Typical of the young, radical core of the GLF, the Berkeley chapter passed a resolution demanding that "all troops be brought home at once" and that all gays in the military be granted honorable discharges. The Chicago GLF invaded the 1970 convention of the American Medical Association (AMA) to protest the treatment of homosexuality as a mental disorder. The New York GLF occupied the offices of *Harper's* and *The Village Voice* to condemn articles hostile to gays. In June, 1970, between five and ten thousand marched to Central Park in New York to commemorate the Stonewall rebellion, as did hundreds in Los Angeles and Chicago; this June anniversary became the annual gay pride march observed worldwide today.

In November, 1969, Jim Owles and Marty Robinson left the GLF to found Gay Activists Alliance (GAA), rejecting the GLF as too "revolutionary" and as unable to address discrimination effectively. GAA elected their leadership, followed parliamentary procedure, and adopted a task-oriented committee structure. GAA organized petition drives to repeal laws against homosexual acts between consenting adults, demonstrated against media accounts that were derogatory of gays, and engaged in political "zaps" to confront elected officials and candidates over gay civil rights. Within two years gay and/or lesbian groups had emerged in every major city and campus in the United States, Canada, Australia, and Europe.

As a political force, the New Left declined soon after gay liberation appeared, and the GLF disbanded, leaving the political field dominated by the various reformist groups that mushroomed in the 1970's. Within four years there were more than eight hundred gay and lesbian organizations, the most visible of which was the National Gay and Lesbian Task Force founded in 1974 by Dr. Bruce Voeller, formerly president of GAA. Many activists entered electoral politics working with candidates sensitive to gay and lesbian issues. The first club, the Alice B. Toklas Gay Democratic Club of San Francisco, was founded in 1971. (Alice B. Toklas was the longtime lover of writer Gertrude Stein.) At the 1972 Democratic Party convention, Jim Foster, founder of the Toklas Club, presented the first gay rights address:

> We come to you affirming our pride . . . and . . . our right to participate in the life of this country on an equal basis with every citizen . . . there are millions of gay brothers and sisters . . . We will not go away until the ultimate goal of gay liberation is realized.

No openly gay speaker was permitted to address the 1976 Democratic convention, so Operation Gay Vote 1980 mobilized and sent seventy-seven delegates to the 1980 convention, formed a caucus, and pressed battles over "gay rights," making it a recurring presidential campaign issue. In San Francisco the movement rallied behind city supervisor Harvey Milk, who was elected to the city council. Milk was assassinated in 1978 along with Mayor George Moscone by an antigay city supervisor, Dan White. Milk became the movement's first martyr. Reinforcing the politics, especially in San Francisco and New York, was a thriving gay subculture with bars, bookstores, baths, guest houses, and services of all kinds and a gay press that discussed issues facing the community. In a few years, gay liberation achieved what homophile leaders had sought for two decades—the active involvement of masses of homosexuals in their own emancipation movement.

Applications

A modern social movement, gay and lesbian liberation has sought equality and an end to discrimination by applying the political strategies of the contemporary Civil Rights and women's movements. These strategies include: proclaiming identity as the basis of organizing; politicizing personal sexual relationships; using direct action to protest discriminatory laws and social beliefs; organizing lobbies to change laws; and forming community service organizations. From the beginning, gay radicals transformed the meaning of "coming out," making it both an end and a means. Previously it had signified the private decision to accept one's same-sex desires and to acknowledge this to other homosexuals. Gay liberationists recast coming out as a profoundly political act. The open avowel of one's sexual identity—at work, at school, even on television—symbolized the shedding of self-hatred that lesbians and gay men internalized. To "come out of the closet" succinctly expressed the fusion of the "personal and the political," a concept imported from the second-wave women's movement. Relinquishing invisibility made one vulnerable to attack, thereby creating an investment in the success of the movement. Examples of the difficulties caused by coming out range from writer Kate Millett, who came out in 1970 only to have *Time* magazine predict her career's demise, to Petty Officer Keith Meinhold, who, after coming out, was discharged from the U.S. Navy in 1992 (he was reinstated in 1993).

The best-known successful campaign of "out" gays and lesbians against a powerful social institution was the assault waged against American psychiatry, which resulted in the 1973 removal of homosexuality from the official diagnostic manual of the American Psychiatric Association (APA). Nearly a century of psychiatric labeling of homosexuality as a psychopathology had medically legitimized discrimination, excluding gays from a wide range of employment, barring them from entering the country, and suppressing their voices in the arts and literature. GLF "zaps," disrupting APA and AMA conventions in 1970 with cries of "barbarism" and "medieval torture" and demands for equal time, polarized the psychiatric community between hard-line conservatives and liberals who favored removing homosexuality as a mental disorder. At the 1972 APA convention a gay panel, with a gay psychiatrist wearing a mask, was permitted to testify; the issue reached a climax at the 1973 convention with the delivery of Ron Gold's paper, "Stop! You're Making Me Sick," representing the gay movement's position. Such direct-action politics hastened official changes underway in other professional organizations. The American Sociological Association passed a nondiscrimination resolution in 1969, the National Association for Mental Health called for decriminalization in 1970, and the National Association of Social Workers rejected the medical model of homosexuality in a 1972 resolution.

A second feature of post-Stonewall gay liberation was the appearance of a strong lesbian liberation movement. The nearly simultaneous birth of women's liberation and a gay liberation movement propelled large numbers of lesbians into radical sexual politics, gay and feminist. Angered by the male chauvinism they experienced in gay groups and the hostility they found in the women's movement, many lesbians founded separatist organizations (such as Radicalesbians in New York) and lesbian communes in rural communities. The feminist movement, however, did offer the psychic space for many women to define themselves as lesbian. Intense struggles over "lesbian rights" occurred in the women's movement, beginning in 1970 when Betty Friedan, president of the National Organization for Women (NOW), denounced an alleged "lavender menace" threatening the credibility of feminism. In response, twenty Radicalesbians "zapped" the second Congress to Unite Women wearing "Lavender Menace" T-shirts. In 1971 NOW reversed itself, acknowledging "the oppression of lesbians as a legitimate concern of feminism." Women's liberation served gay liberation as its ideas permeated the United States, especially through the Equal Rights Amendment (ERA) campaign and the affirmation of nonreproductive sexuality, implicit in demands for access to abortion.

Lesbians served as a bridge between the two movements, notably in the campaign to combat the first antigay backlash in the late 1970's. Two Christian fundamentalists, singer Anita Bryant and the Reverend Jerry Falwell, organized the Save Our Children campaign to repeal the Dade County, Florida, ordinance prohibiting discrimination because of "sexual orientation." Defeated there, the gay movement nevertheless thwarted the "new Christian right" on the 1978 Briggs Initiative in California, which would have banned gay teachers.

The proliferation of gay groups in the 1970's led to varied campaigns. The National Gay and Lesbian Task Force lobbied on nationwide issues, while many local organizations lobbied for statewide gay rights laws and municipal ordinances and executive orders. They also sought to block efforts to repeal gay rights ordinances. Portland, Oregon, and St. Paul, Minnesota, adopted rights ordinances in 1974. A number of other cities followed. In the 1980's and 1990's, however, antigay rights groups sought to have such ordinances repealed and gay organizations needed to work to block these actions. The struggle for decriminalization of homosexuality, especially the repeal of sodomy laws, continued to be fought on a state-by-state basis. By 1983, twenty-five states had fully eliminated their sodomy statutes. The U.S. Supreme Court, however, in its *Bowers v. Hardwick* (1986) ruling, upheld the constitutionality of Georgia's sodomy law on consensual sex. Sodomy laws have been used primarily against gay men. With political action came a new gay liberation press—*Advocate* (Los Angeles), *Come Out* (New York), *Gay Community News* (Boston), and *Body Politic* (Toronto)— connecting far-flung groups and carrying information about political initiatives. On three continents, gay movements developed along a similar course: parallel leftist gay liberation groups and liberal civil rights organizations.

Before the gains of the 1970's could be consolidated, the 1980's confronted the movement with new obstacles and challenges. The spread of acquired immune deficiency syndrome (AIDS)—the first cases appeared in 1981 among gay men—in the United States meant that large resources of time and money went into lobbying for research on the causes of AIDS as well as the financing of health care for patients. Gays and lesbians were in the forefront of a coordinated effort to provide care and support for people with AIDS. The prototype service organization, Gay Men's Health Crisis of New York City, opened in September, 1982. By 1987 the perceived lack of government action against the epidemic affecting predominantly gay men and poor people of color provoked a resurgence of radicalism, epitomized by ACT-UP (AIDS Coalition to Unleash Power), a direct-action group employing civil disobedience, and its offshoot, Queer Nation. Holding sit-ins and "die-ins," AIDS activists pressured the U.S. Food and Drug Administration to speed drug trials for new AIDS drugs and to consider a parallel track—an ACT-UP proposal that persons with AIDS be provided with drugs before official approval by the lengthy FDA testing process. The drug Zidovudine (also known as azidothymidine, or AZT), which prolongs the lives of AIDS patients but is extremely expensive, was reduced in price 200 percent as a result of ACT-UP protests. The AIDS epidemic served both to rekindle militant activism and to draw lesbians and gay men together in defense of the survival of their community, a self-conscious community largely constructed in the previous decade on a pride in a shared identity of sexual difference and social oppression.

Context

Before 1969, homosexuals were regarded as deviants by sociologists, psychologists, and the medical profession. Mainstream society drew upon a Western Christian tradition that looked upon homosexuality as immoral and as a "crime against nature."

The term "homosexual," first coined in 1869 by K. M. Kertbeny (a translator who opposed German sodomy laws) but not popularized until the 1880's, was adopted by people who wanted to make sense of their own experiences. Sigmund Freud, the founder of psychoanalysis, was more influential; he contributed the theory of arrested development, holding that homosexuals are perpetual adolescents. This concept gave rise to the medical model of homosexuality. American sociologists, Émile Durkheim's intellectual heirs, viewed homosexuality as "normal deviance," rare enough to affirm the sociomoral norm.

Beginning with the studies of Alfred C. Kinsey and his colleagues, *Sexual Behavior of the Human Male* (1948) and *Sexual Behavior of the Human Female* (1953), the incidence of homosexual behavior was revealed to be greater than previously acknowledged. Kinsey challenged the myth that homosexuality is rare or can be identified by obvious gender nonconformity, and he provided data indicating that 13 percent of the men and 7 percent of the women he and his associates surveyed had been homosexual for three years or more at some time in their lives. Kinsey's data, along with Laud Humphrey's study of homosexual activity in public rest rooms, *Tearoom Trade: Impersonal Sex in Public Places* (1970), discredited sociology's "labeling theory" in regard to homosexuality; homosexual conduct was shown to occur without labeling by others, and it was shown that homosexual identity could precede conduct. Social science discussions of the "homosexual community" have changed dramatically since the mid-1970's. They no longer view it as static and acknowledge it as a recently emerged (post World War II) community, rooted in the urban bar culture and homophile organizations, such as the Mattachine Society (begun in 1950) and the Daughters of Bilitis (1955). The homophile groups provided the positive self-image and a press, and the bar culture a critical mass of followers. The 1960's political movements provided models of organized protest and new recruits for gay liberation.

Gay liberation has secured formal "minority" status for homosexuals as well as contributing to identity politics and a new political vocabulary: "coming out," "homophobia," "heterosexism." With the inclusion of lesbians and gays in the Hate Crimes Statistics Act (1990), the first progay piece of federal legislation was achieved. Though disagreements over political strategies abound, there is nevertheless a gay and lesbian identity or, as sociologists refer to it, "consciousness of kind," and there is public acknowledgment of it. Finally, the fact that there are so many openly lesbian and gay organizations, political groups, and service agencies testifies not only to the success of the grass roots movement but also to a "culture" which expresses itself in myriad ways within the gay community.

Bibliography

Abbott, Sidney, and Barbara Love. *Sappho Was a Right-On Woman*. New York: Stein and Day, 1972. A chronicle of the heady days from 1969 to 1972 when new definitions of lesbianism arose from the turmoil of feminist and gay liberation activism.

Adam, Barry D. *The Rise of a Gay and Lesbian Movement*. Boston: Twayne, 1987. A concise social history, this book delineates the formation of gay and lesbian movements as a world phenomenon. Adam employs a political process model in this study in comparative-historical sociology.

Chauncey, George, Jr., Martin B. Duberman, and Martha Vicinus, eds. *Hidden from History: Reclaiming the Gay and Lesbian Past*. New York: New American Library, 1989. A readable, highly informative anthology of articles delineating the homosexual experience from ancient times to the present in various cultures. The work is especially helpful in detailing the current conflict over the concepts of "gay," "lesbian," and "homosexual" and in demonstrating the varied experiences of homosexuals worldwide.

Cruikshank, Margaret. *The Gay and Lesbian Liberation Movement*. New York: Routledge, 1992. This book examines the contemporary gay and lesbian movement from three different perspectives: as a sexual freedom movement, as a political movement, and as a movement of ideas. Linking the United States movement to other progressive movements Cruikshank analyzes its shortcomings and its sociopolitical impact.

D'Emilio, John. *Sexual Politics, Sexual Communities: The Making of a Homosexual Minority in the United States, 1940-1970*. Chicago: University of Chicago Press, 1983. The most complete account of the homophile movement of the 1950's and 1960's in the United States, contextualized in a social history of the era.

Marotta, Toby. *The Politics of Homosexuality*. Boston: Houghton Mifflin, 1981. A classic that examines the emergence of lesbian and gay politics in the decade of the 1970's, this study demonstrates that contemporary gay attitudes and beliefs were both extensions and syntheses of older ideologies and political forms: feminism and the women's movement; the New Left and the student movement; antiracism and the Civil Rights movement.

Teal, Donn. *The Gay Militants*. New York: Stein and Day, 1971. A rich documentary history of the Stonewall rebellion, this volume conveys the mood of the period like no other work.

Kathleen K. O'Mara

Cross-References

Acquired Immune Deficiency Syndrome, 8; The Civil Rights Movement, 265; Cultural Norms and Sanctions, 411; Individual Discrimination, 547; Discrimination Against Gays, 806; Prejudice and Stereotyping, 1505; Sex versus Gender, 1721; Social Movements, 1826; Subcultures and Countercultures, 2003; The Women's Movement, 2196.

DISCRIMINATION AGAINST GAYS

Type of sociology: Sex and gender

Discrimination against gays, as against other groups, has taken both individual and institutional forms, including legal prohibitions and social intolerance. It differs from discrimination against groups such as women or religious minorities, however, for the latter groups were not generally stigmatized as criminals or outcasts.

Principal terms

COMING OUT: the psychological process of acquiring and acknowledging a gay or lesbian identity—to oneself first, then to friends and family, and then, some argue, to anyone with whom one has significant contact

DISCRIMINATION: the denial of the rights of, or social intolerance of, individuals on the basis of their perceived membership in a group

HETEROSEXISM: an excessive valuing of heterosexual persons, values, and behavior; an assumption that any behavior other than heterosexual behavior is abnormal

HOMOPHOBIA: a negative attitude toward homosexual persons and homosexuality; it refers to prejudice comparable to racism, sexism, and anti-Semitism, though it implies individual pathology such as a hatred of or aversion to homosexual persons

MINORITY GROUP: any group that, on the basis of physical or cultural characteristics, is socially disadvantaged

PREJUDICE: arbitrary beliefs or feelings about an individual belonging to a certain group—racial, ethnic, sexual—or toward the group as a whole

SEXUAL ORIENTATION: refers to whether a person's dominant sexual or affectional desires are toward members of the same sex or the opposite sex

SODOMY: an overarching term for sexual deviation; its legal definition specifies anal intercourse and oral-genital contact, either consensual or coerced

Overview

Modern discrimination against gays and lesbians (homosexual men and women) is rooted in the Western Christian tradition of intolerance—especially from the late medieval period—toward those known to have engaged in homosexual activity. This traditional condemnation of homosexuality as a sin and a "crime against nature," along with social ostracism, drove homosexual men and women to desperate measures of deception and concealment in order to avoid the economic and social penalties that a hostile social environment inflicted on them. This is generally described as living "in the closet," a response to socially sanctioned discrimination. Most lesbian and gay theorists use the term "homophobia" to refer to the ideology that underpins antihomosexual prejudice and discrimination. The term homophobia appeared in the 1970's with the rise of a mass gay and lesbian political movement, and it has since gained public currency. While implying that antihomosexual prejudice is a phobia, an irrational fear and individual pathology, rather than an expression of cultural norms, it has been employed to describe prejudice comparable to racism. Like other "isms" it is manifested in individual and institutional forms. Gay bashing, assaulting a person believed to be homosexual, is an individual expression of it, whereas the legal enforcement of an antisodomy law is an institutional expression.

Until the post-World War II era, the rights of employers, landlords, and others to discriminate on the grounds of racial or ethnic origin largely went unchallenged. Then a mass movement—the Civil Rights movement—developed to make such forms of exclusion illegal, leading many states to enact laws prohibiting such practices. Ultimately the federal government passed the Civil Rights Act of 1964. Additional legislation has addressed discrimination based on sex, age, and disability. Discrimination based upon the sexual orientation of an individual was still legal as of the early 1990's, however, and many courts have upheld laws designed to remove "immoral" persons from the workplace or from housing.

In the 1940's, the United States federal government began maintaining that homosexuality was immoral and that homosexual conduct produced unfitness for employment. While federal appeals court decisions have limited the Civil Service Commission's ability to fire employees, the courts left open the possibility that homosexual conduct could justify dismissal wherever "interference with job efficiency" could be proved. Government agencies such as the Federal Bureau of Investigation (FBI) and Central Intelligence Agency (CIA) have and continue routinely to dismiss gay agents when they are discovered. The United States armed forces have been almost universally successful in defeating legal action brought against them by lesbian and gay male personnel challenging their discharges, both honorable and dishonorable. A 1992 campaign promise by Bill Clinton to end the antigay policies of the miiltary was met with considerable resistance. The result was the 1993 "Don't ask, don't tell" policy that restricts inquiries into "sexual orientation" but not discharges for homosexual activities.

Homosexual teachers and counselors face dismissal on the basis of substantive rules that disqualify such employees for "immoral or unprofessional conduct." Conviction of a homosexual offense generally leads to the revocation of the teaching credential of the person, regardless of the age of the sexual partner. Some state courts, however, have explicitly vindicated the rights of gay teachers. The Supreme Court of California, in *Morrison v. State Board of Education* (1969), held that the state could not revoke a teaching license on grounds of homosexual conduct unless it could demonstrate "unfitness to teach."

While certain forms of discrimination have not systematically affected gays and lesbians as they have ethnic or religious minorities in the past—for example, in housing or public accommodations such as restaurants, bars, and hotels—such discrimination does occur, usually directed against individuals perceived from their appearance to be homosexual. In another example, in occupations where a significant proportion of workers are gay, only those with a heterosexual appearance or demeanor may be chosen for advancement. Fearing discovery or dismissal from employment, many gay individuals live in fear or opt for self-employment. The economic aspect of discrimination against homosexuals is difficult to gauge because it may consist of denial of promotion, underemployment, or rejection for a position. The acquired immune deficiency syndrome (AIDS) epidemic beginning in the 1980's among the gay male population brought about the need for antidiscrimination measures regarding medical treatment and medical insurance. Efforts by insurance companies to identify gay men and exclude them from health insurance protection have in some cases been approved by courts and state legislatures.

The maintenance of antigay prejudice, like the other forms of prejudice, depends on the transmission of stereotypes. The restriction of societally sanctioned sexual expression to heterosexuality (and even further, to monogamous marriages) stands in contrast to the stereotypical heterosexual fantasy that homosexual people engage in unbridled sexual aggression and promiscuity. Opinion polls in the United States have found that 59 percent of those questioned, without supporting evidence, believed that "homosexuals have unusually strong sex drives," and 35 percent agreed that "frustrated homosexuals seek out children for sexual purposes."

Pressure from lesbian and gay organizations to include "sexual orientation" in the protected list of antidiscrimination laws began to succeed in the 1970's, resulting in the passage of fifty municipal and county ordinances. Portland, Oregon, and St. Paul, Minnesota, were the first to pass such laws in 1974, followed by San Francisco in 1978 and Los Angeles and Detroit in 1979. Wisconsin adopted the first statewide gay rights law in 1981. Organized opposition has, however, resulted in repeals of nondiscrimination laws; this occurred in St. Paul in 1977 and in Denver, Colorado, in 1992. Although most employers are legally free to discriminate against homosexuals, a number of corporations and universities (both public and private) in the 1980's adopted nondiscrimination policies and in the 1990's began to extend "spousal benefits" such as health insurance to gay and lesbian couples.

In Western society the tradition of ostracism and exclusion of gays and lesbians has only begun to decline with the efforts of an organized gay and lesbian movement. As elsewhere, lesbians and gay men in the United States remain largely outside the protective arm of the law. The campaign for antidiscrimination measures parallel to those protecting other minorities will continue to be a major focus of gay political activity for many decades.

Applications

Because of the efforts of the organized gay and lesbian movement since 1970, an increased recognition of discrimination against gays and lesbians as a violation of civil liberties has developed. There has also been a slowly growing inclusion of homophobia as an unacceptable prejudice in a democratic society. Knowledge acquired from the study of antigay discrimination and the effects of homophobia is applied in varied ways to eliminate institutional and individual prejudice. Among the varied approaches are legal efforts to overthrow existing laws, civil rights legislation, executive orders such as those prohibiting sexual orientation discrimination, and social science studies of gays, lesbians, and homophobia.

Attempts to include homosexuals within the legal protection afforded cultural, religious, and racial minorities failed before the 1960's. Only gradually did groups concerned with civil liberties come to agree with homosexuals that discrimination against them violated their civil rights. The American Civil Liberties Union (ACLU) frequently supported legal efforts to repeal consensual sodomy laws. By 1983 twenty-five states had eliminated their sodomy statutes. Yet the U.S. Supreme Court, in its *Bowers v. Hardwick* ruling (1986), upheld the constitutionality of Georgia's sodomy law.

The focus of the organized gay and lesbian political movement (such as the National Gay and Lesbian Task Force, Lamda Legal Defense Fund, and Human Rights Campaign Fund) has been to secure civil rights legislation, local and national, and recognition of gays and lesbians as a disadvantaged minority. Campaigns by lesbian and gay organizations to include "sexual orientation" in the protested list of antidiscrimination laws began to succeed in the 1970's, resulting in the passage of fifty municipal and county ordinances. Changes in law and legislation along with the growth of a politically conscious gay and lesbian "community" motivated social scientists to shift their focus from studying homosexuals as deviants to examining the experiences of gay men, lesbians, and bisexuals, their strategies of coping with social ostracism, and the causes and effects of homophobia.

Several psychodynamic explanations of extreme homophobia have been proposed: It may be a defense against the individual's own homosexual desires, it may be a strategy for making sense of past interaction with gays, and it may be a means for gaining social approval or affirming a particular self-concept. Lesbians and gay men, socialized into a culture with an antihomosexual norm, also acquire homophobic attitudes. This is termed "internalized homophobia" and is analogous to the self-contempt felt by some members of stigmatized ethnic groups. Internalized homophobia leads some individuals to reject their homosexuality and even to commit suicide. Studies by the U.S. Department of Health and Human Services and the Hetrick-Martin Institute, a New York City agency servicing lesbian and gay youth, have found suicides and suicide attempts among lesbian and gay youth occurring three times as frequently as among heterosexual youth. In a survey of 2,823 junior and senior high school students, the New York State Governor's Task Force on Bias-Related Violence (1988) found that respondents were not only overwhelmingly biased against gay persons but also sometimes acted toward them "viciously and with threats of violence."

National surveys and laboratory studies consistently have documented correlations between individual homophobic attitudes and particular demographic and psychological variables. Those with more homophobic attitudes are likely to subscribe to a conservative religious ideology, to have restrictive attitudes about sexuality and gender roles, and to manifest high levels of "authoritarianism." In addition, they are less likely to admit personal contact with openly gay people, to be older, and to have fewer years of formal education. They are more likely to live in areas where negative attitudes to gays are the norm. In many empirical studies, more antigay hostility was found among heterosexual men than heterosexual women. San Francisco's Community United Against Violence (CUAV) found that a typical "gay basher" is a young male, often acting together with other males; all are usually strangers to the victim.

Empirical research on homophobic behavior is sparse, but interest in "hate crimes" against perceived homosexuals is growing. The first national study on antigay violence conducted by the National Gay and Lesbian Task Force in 1984 found that among the lesbians and gays surveyed, 19 percent reported having been hit or beaten once in their lives because of their sexual orientation, 44 percent had been threatened with physical violence, and 94 percent had experienced some form of victimization (verbal abuse or being spat upon, chased, pelted with objects, abused by police, or assaulted). In this NGLTF study and others, gender differences surfaced: Males generally experienced greater levels of verbal harassment and physical violence from strangers, whereas lesbians experienced higher rates of verbal abuse from family members. In *Violence Against Lesbians and Gay Men* (1991), G. D. Comstock found lesbians and gay men of color to be at increased risk of violent attack because of their sexual orientation and found that gay men were more likely to be victimized in school or in publicly gay-identified areas (such as outside gay bars or in gay cruising areas). Federal government recognition of the consequences of discrimination was finally achieved with the inclusion of lesbians and gays in the *Hate Crimes Statistics Act* (1990), the first progay federal legislation ever passed.

Context

Studies of various forms of discrimination as well as efforts to combat it, have concentrated on economic discrimination—the denial to a group of access to opportunities and earnings commensurate with ability. Attention largely has focused on groups that are racial, ethnic, or religious minorities: African Americans and Jews in the United States; untouchables in India; and, though not a numerical minority, women in every country. In the early 1990's, no studies had yet examined the cost of antigay discrimination, but gay and lesbian political demands implicitly reveal some of the economic penalties; demands include recognition of lesbian and gay relationships as equivalent to marriage for purposes of "spousal" health insurance, pension rights, or transfer of apartment rental leases. Issues of child custody and rights of "next of kin" in cases of hospital visitations and medical decisions have also become important. This has led some municipalities (New York City, for example, in 1993) to begin registration of domestic partnerships, both homosexual and heterosexual. Such registrations provide evidence for claims to health benefits or housing in cases where employers provide them.

There is no body of sociological knowledge of institutional homophobia equivalent to that of institutional racism. From the perspective of sociologists studying the latter, consequences are viewed as evidence of discrimination, either unintentional or intentional. Institutional homophobia manifests itself in part through antigay laws, policies, and pronouncements from legislatures, courts, organized religion, and other groups. A forced discharge from the military or dismissal from employment results in economic penalties: lost income, lost health benefits, and lost pensions. The ultimate cost of homophobia—loss of life—gained national recognition in 1992 and 1993 with the highly publicized murder of Allen Schindler, a gay sailor beaten to death by shipmates in Japan in October, 1992, after he acknowledged his homosexuality to his commanding officer.

Institutional discrimination is also evident in the social processes that reinforce the general invisibility of lesbians and gay men in society (for example, in the mass media) and in societal definitions of "family" in exclusively heterosexual terms. Among the factors cited to explain institutional homophobia are society's presumed need to define strict gender roles and to connect sexuality with procreation. Both factors are presumed necessary for reproducing heterosexual family units and socializing children. Other explanations emphasize intergroup conflicts in which hostility to homosexuality has been used for one group's advantage (as in electoral politics).

Little empirical research has been conducted on ways to reduce individual homophobia. While not universally effective in countering prejudice, personal contact with openly gay people appears to be the most consistently influential factor in reducing heterosexuals' homophobia. In national opinion polls, persons who say they know an "openly" gay man or lesbian consistently report more positive attitudes towards gays. This pattern is consistent with the general social science finding that ongoing personal contact between members of majority and minority groups reduces prejudice among majority group members. Thus, "coming out" as a powerful means for challenging homophobia has been validated. This hypothesis underscores the importance of institutional changes (passing antidiscrimination laws, repealing sodomy laws, and outlawing hate crimes) that will allow lesbians and gay men to come out with fewer risks. The 1993 campaign to end discrimination against gays in the U.S. military, called Campaign Military Service, was not only part of a gay and lesbian struggle for equal rights but also an application of this hypothesis. That campaign, along with gay inclusion in the *Hate Crimes and Statistics Act* and social scientists' increasing attention to the gay vote (as in the 1992 presidential election campaign), signaled that formal minority status has been achieved by lesbians and gays in the United States. Thus, the gradual legal dismantling of institutional discrimination will probably continue, paralleling the process undergone by African Americans, Jews, women, and other minorities.

Bibliography

Altman, Dennis. *Homosexual Oppression and Liberation*. New York: Outerbridge & Dienstfrey, 1971. Written by a participant in New York's gay liberation struggles in 1969 and 1970, this book is regarded as the classic statement on liberation philosophy.

Blumenfeld, Warren J., and Diane Raymond. "Prejudice and Discrimination." In *Looking at Gay and Lesbian Life*. New York: Philosophical Library, 1988. A clear, concise discussion for the general reader on discrimination and its application to gays and lesbians.

Galloway, Bruce, ed. *Prejudice and Pride*. London: Routledge & Kegan Paul, 1984. An excellent overview of the concerns of the contemporary gay movement. This book's contributors draw a comprehensive portrait of being gay or lesbian in a homophobic society.

Herek, Gregory M., and Kevin T. Berrill. *Hate Crimes: Confronting Violence Against Lesbians and Gay Men*. Newbury Park, Calif.: Sage Publications, 1992. A pioneering anthology that covers what is known about antigay prejudice and violence in American Society.

Hunter, Nan O., Sherryl E. Michaelson, and Thomas B. Stoddard. *The Rights of Lesbians and Gay Men: The Basic ACLU Guide to a Gay Person's Rights*. 3d ed. Carbondale: Southern Illinois University Press, 1992. This informative volume provides a survey of the rights—and absence of rights—of lesbians and gay men under the law in regard to freedom of speech and association, employment, housing, the military, and family relationships.

Pharr, Suzanne. *Homophobia: A Weapon of Sexism*. Inverness, Calif.: Chardon Press, 1988. A lucid, well-constructed explication of homophobia, including its psychic, social, and institutional underpinnings. This is particularly directed toward helping gays and lesbians comprehend and cope with homophobic violence.

Kathleen K. O'Mara

Cross-References

Acquired Immune Deficiency Syndrome, 8; Individual Discrimination, 547; The Gay Liberation Movement, 799; The Medicalization of Deviance, 1178; Prejudice and Stereotyping, 1505; Theories of Sexual Orientation, 1735; Subcultures and Countercultures, 2003.

GENDER AND RELIGION

Type of sociology: Sex and gender
Fields of study: Dimensions of inequality; Religion

Religions are powerful social institutions that shape gender roles in society. They not only define how men and women participate in religious activities but also reinforce and legitimize the gender roles assigned to men and women in society.

Principal terms

ANDROCENTRISM: a point of view that emphasizes male-centeredness, the dominance of male interests, and the use of masculine traits to measure what is truly human

FEMINISM: a movement that attempts to institute social, economic, and political equality between men and women in society and end distortions in the relationships between men and women

GENDER: differences between males and females caused by the psychological and social development of individuals within a society

MISOGYNY: the devaluation or hatred of women

PATRIARCHY: the manifestation and institutionalization of male dominance over women and children in the family and in society

RELIGION: an organized system of beliefs and rituals about what is sacred

SACRED: pertains to values, symbols, and interpretations dealing with the belief in and worship of a divine being

SEX: biological differences between men and women; for example, visible sexual organs that distinguish men from women

TRANSCENDENT: pertaining to that which goes beyond sense perception, especially the infinite mystery of divine being

VALUES: socially shared beliefs about what is good or desirable, which are expressed in principles and rules that govern everyday life

Overview

Religion contributes to how a society understands relationships between men and women. Since the 1960's, feminists have raised the issue of the relationship of religion and gender. Feminists were the first to point out that it is not possible to study religious practice and religious symbols without taking into account the cultural experience of being male or female. All experience, including religious experience, is influenced by the gender of the person involved. In no society do men and women experience religion in the same way.

Feminists point out that religion generally serves to support society's patriarchal views about the roles of men and women in society. In so doing, religion supports and even endorses discrimination against women on the basis of gender. Therefore, to examine the relationship of gender and religion is largely to study the feminist critique of religion.

The feminist critique of religion is based on the earlier work of sociologists of religion, such as Émile Durkheim and Max Weber. Durkheim maintained that one of religion's main functions is to support the existing social arrangements in a given culture. Religion is a powerful social institution that justifies traditional social roles, including gender roles. To establish a fundamental distinction between what is sacred and what is worldly or profane, religion excludes the feminine from the sphere of the sacred. Through religion masculine identity is made sacred. Young men are initiated into the sacred by a culture's sacred society of men. Durkheim asserted that civilization depends on the suppression of the feminine through religion.

Max Weber's theory of religion also assumes the inequality of gender roles. He believed that religious development involved increasing degrees of reason. In his analysis of the Protestant work ethic, Weber contrasted rational masculine Protestant-ism with what is magical, sensual, and feminine. For Weber, religion serves to oppress the feminine in the interests of modern industrial civilization.

The nineteenth century social philosopher Karl Marx held that the dominant religion of a given society primarily reflects the interests of the powerful and privileged members of that society. Religion serves to divert the attention of the powerless from the misery of their earthly existence by focusing it on the promise of a future reward in a life after death. Since the power-holders in society are usually men, by extension it can be argued that religion serves the interests of men.

All religious traditions offer examples of the oppression of women in which religion is implicated if not directly to blame. More than 100,000 witches were burned in Christian Europe. In India, innumerable widows have died on their husbands' funeral pyres. The feet of Chinese women were bound for countless generations to please their menfolk. The genitals of African women were mutilated because it was believed that such mutilation would make them better wives and mothers.

The oppression of women through religion is one reflection of the main pattern of human history, in which most human societies have been ruled by men and have tended to denigrate the feminine. The vast majority of the world's religions are male-centered and male-dominated. In them, the highest earthly and heavenly values are identified with the masculine gender. Religion is perceived as a domain that is suitable for men only. With few exceptions, human societies exclude women from the most sacred religious functions.

Women are commonly characterized as the weaker sex, the sex less able to exercise religious authority. Women have not received much religious education, and they have seldom been the ones to develop the theology and ethics of their religious traditions. Nevertheless, the perception of women by the world's religions is not entirely negative. All the world's religions acknowledge the presence of saintly and wise women. Although in most religious traditions the principal deities are masculine, some religious traditions, such as the Roman, Greek, and Hindu traditions, have feminine images of divine being.

The relationship of gender and religion in human life is very complex. While religions frequently maintain official doctrines about feminine gender and the place of women in religion that are demeaning to women, these official views were created by men and do not necessarily reflect women's views and religious experience. Even when they have been relegated to second-class membership in their religious traditions, women have frequently disregarded official male definitions of their role and status in religion. While women are not immune to men's insistence that they are their religious inferiors, feminist scholars have discovered that women often have interpreted their religious traditions in their own way and have found means to affirm their religious experience and worth. For example, male and female religious writers in the European Middle Ages envisioned God as female. Julian of Norwich and other writers developed the notion of the motherhood of Jesus Christ.

Applications

At this point, it will be useful to examine the role of gender in the context of two major religious traditions: the Hindu tradition and the Judeo-Christian tradition.

The Hindu tradition provides examples of both the exaltation and the oppression of the feminine. From the times of the Vedas, the earliest scriptures of ancient India, Indians have worshiped divinity as male and female. The primordial female deity is Adi Shakti, the principle of passion and change who is responsible for creation and destruction. She is complemented by a primordial male deity who is sometimes identified as Shiva. Just as the Hindu tradition maintained that the energy of Adi Shakti would become excessive to the point of producing chaos if it were not for the control exercised over her by her male consort, Hindu society puts social constraints on women because women possess a vital energy that can destroy if it is not controlled.

In Hindu mythology, divinity explicitly embraces both female and male virtues and qualities. Divinity can exist only with both values present. The tales of goddesses and their divine consorts sometimes challenge official notions of the perfect Hindu wife, who is sweet, obedient, and totally submissive to her husband. In one legend, in which the god Shiva returns to his home only to be refused entrance by his son Ganesha, Shiva cuts off Ganesha's head, whereupon Shiva's consort Parvati denounces him and berates him for his neglect of their son. This example from Hindu mythology suggests how religious traditions can function on two levels: on one level that insists on the principle of the primacy of the male and on another level that affirms in practice the freedom of women to assert their right to vindication. Although the official tradition insists that women always be submissive to their husbands, the story of Shiva and Parvati illustrates that, in practice, women have the right to protest the conduct of their husbands and claim redress for their grievances.

Traditional Hindu society is patriarchal. Women are always under the control of a man or men: father, husband, or sons. Women are expected to obey and even worship their husbands. This notion is tempered in the ethical codes of the mythological lawgiver Manu, which demand that men honor women, treat them well, and make them happy. Nevertheless, women's dependence on men is dramatically illustrated by suttee, the practice in which widows burn themselves to death on their husbands' funeral pyres.

The Judeo-Christian religious tradition, to which Western civilization owes much of its heritage, has also served both to recognize women's dignity and to oppress women. Because the Hebrew scriptures were written about and for men, women's roles are not featured prominently. The Hebrew scriptures in some places honor women and in other places degrade them. The stories of Hagar in Genesis, of Tamar in II Samuel, and of the daughter of Jephthah and of the Levite's concubine, both in Judges, portray the degradation of women by means of exile, rape, and murder. Esther, however, was able to save the Hebrew people from destruction. Deborah was a great prophet. Naomi and Ruth display selfless friendship and loyalty to each other.

The two versions of the creation of humankind in Genesis exemplify contradictions in the Bible about the relative status of men and women. One version of creation simply states that God created men and women in the divine image. In the other version the first woman, Eve, is formed from the rib of the first man, Adam. This second version of the creation of human beings is interpreted by some religious thinkers to prove that women are subordinate to men. Some commentators have even asserted that the creation of the first woman from the rib of the first man indicates that only men are fully human and that women participate in full human nature only through their association with men. By themselves, women are not fully human. Jewish and Christian commentators who argue against the acceptance of women into the rabbinate and the priesthood cite the second version of creation as evidence for their position.

Christianity, which was an offshoot of the Jewish tradition, inherited and reaffirmed much of the Jewish bias against women. Although there is considerable evidence in Christian scripture that Jesus broke with Judaic tradition and law in his dealings with women, the Christian church adopted negative views toward women early in its history. The apostle Paul's comments about women, notably in the first letter to the Corinthians, where he asserts that women should remain silent in the assembly of believers, are often cited to justify misogynous attitudes and practices in Christianity.

In the Judeo-Christian tradition, God has been envisioned almost exclusively as male. Although feminine and nongender-related images can be found in the Hebrew and Christian scriptures, masculine language and symbolism dominate. If God is thought of almost exclusively in masculine terms, it is easy to surmise that men are more god-like and of greater worth than women. The use of exclusively male language and masculine images rather than neutral or feminine ones to address and talk about God in religious discourse reflects male dominance in both the Jewish and Christian traditions.

The controversies surrounding the ordination of women highlight the partriarchal features of Christianity. While some Christian denominations have recently begun to ordain women to the priesthood, the Roman Catholic church, for example, is not considering a change in its policy against ordaining women. It not only bases its position on the longstanding tradition of a male priesthood but also appeals to the notion that women cannot image Jesus Christ because they are not males. Behind this argument is the view that while men can fully image divine being, woman cannot do so because they are incomplete human beings. The Roman Catholic church asserts that it can affirm the dignity and equal personhood of women without allowing them to become priests.

Context

The first studies of the sociology of religion, such as those of Émile Durkheim and Max Weber, did not question the dominance of men in human religious activity. In the formulation of their theories about how the sacred became the exclusive domain of men, these scholars assume that the denial of female participation in the most sacred religious rituals of society was necessary for the advancement of civilization. The founder of psychoanalysis, Sigmund Freud, also developed theories of religion and society that predicated the survival and advancement of civilization on the dominance of masculine rationality.

In the nineteenth century, sociologists viewed gender-related behavior as an extension of biology. Biology determined the destiny of men and women. A woman's biology destined her for motherhood, while a man's biology made him aggressive and destined him to a life of accomplishment in society.

The rise of feminism in the 1960's led sociologists to examine social structure in order to understand and expose the nature of and reasons for the discrimination against women. In so doing, they came to distinguish sex from gender. Whereas sex refers to the biological characteristics of men and women, gender is learned through a person's interaction with social and cultural forces. Sociologists realized that the process of socialization, by which people learn what is expected of them from their parents, peers, and society at large, teaches men and women the norms of conduct for their gender.

In the conflict perspective of society that emerged in the 1960's among blacks, students, and women, gender plays an important role. Conflict theory maintained that society is composed of groups that compete for scarce resources. This theory has its roots in the social theories of Karl Marx. Sociologists who subscribe to conflict theory argue that traditional gender roles are among the most powerful social mechanisms by which men dominate women. Religion, because it is a powerful social institution that reinforces and sanctions traditional social roles, including traditional gender roles, lends support to the domination of women by men.

Feminist sociologists were the first to call attention to the importance of gender in shaping all human experience, including the experience of the sacred for both men and women. Since religious history and the texts of religious tradition were largely the creations of men and therefore reflected the religious experience of men, feminist students of religion sought to uncover the religious experience of women. They also sought to critique and expose the dominance of religion by men.

The elaboration of the ways in which religious traditions have devalued and repressed women's religious identity and experience have triggered reactions that suggest how the relationship of gender and religion might develop in the future. Radical feminist commentators on religion maintain that the women's movement constitutes the greatest single challenge to the religions of the world. Christianity and Judaism are singled out by Mary Daly and Naomi Goldenberg for the harshest criticism. These thinkers assert that feminists have to leave Christ and the Bible behind them because women cannot achieve liberation from male dominance through religious traditions that insist on imaging divine being as male. Women's groups are already cultivating new religious forms of expression that use feminine imagery to relate to the sacred. Some of these groups are fully segregated from men and are exclusively for women. This trend is likely to continue, because both the Jewish and Christian traditions have been unwilling to grant women equal standing with men and full access to leadership functions. In addition, their memberships resist the full incorporation of the feminine into all aspects of their group religious experience.

Other men and women see ways in which the Judeo-Christian tradition can serve to create justice between men and women. Some Jewish and Christian feminists assert that, when properly understood, scripture supports the liberation and affirmation of women. They propose to reconstruct the Jewish and Christian faiths by exposing their patriarchal bias and affirming the liberating possibilities of scripture and tradition. The Judeo-Christian tradition, in its utopian descriptions of the perfect society, does present the ideal of each person dwelling in peaceful relationships with God, with herself or himself, with others, and with nature.

Bibliography

Avis, Paul. *Eros and the Sacred*. Harrisburg, Pa.: Morehouse, 1989. The author is an Anglican vicar who takes to heart the feminist critique of Christianity and explores how Christianity might reform itself to answer the feminist challenge. Includes a bibliography and an index of subjects and names.

Bynum, Caroline, Stevan Harrell, and Paula Richman, eds. *Gender and Religion: On the Complexity of Symbols*. Boston: Beacon Press, 1986. A collection of scholarly studies on gender as a culturally constructed meaning, as a symbol with multiple meanings, and as a point of view in a variety of world religions. Includes an index.

Carmody, Denise Lardner. *Women and World Religions*. 2d ed. Englewood Cliffs, N.J.: Prentice-Hall, 1989. A textbook for university students that presents the experience of women in the major world religious traditions. Includes a glossary, a bibliography, and an index.

Doyle, James A. *Sex and Gender: The Human Experience*. Dubuque, Iowa: Wm. C. Brown, 1985. A university textbook with chapters on the sociological and anthropological aspects of gender as well as an extended discussion of religion and gender. Provides a bibliography of suggested readings at the end of each chapter, a bibliography of works cited, and name and subject indexes.

Erickson, Victoria Lee. *Where Silence Speaks: Feminism, Social Theory, and Religion*. Minneapolis: Fortress Press, 1993. Discusses how the theories of religion of sociologists such as Émile Durkheim and Max Weber shed light on the problem of gender in religion. A bibliography and an index of names and subjects are included.

Van Leeuwen, Mary Stewart, et al. *After Eden: Facing the Challenge of Gender*

Reconciliation. Grand Rapids, Mich.: W. B. Eerdmans, 1993. A comprehensive study that examines historical, cross-cultural, social, theological, and rhetorical perspectives on gender relations. Includes a bibliography and index of names.

Evelyn Toft

Cross-References

Christianity, 231; Gender Inequality: Analysis and Overview, 820; Gender Socialization, 833; Judaism, 1029; Legitimation of Inequality: Religion, 1068; Religion: Marxist and Conflict Theory Views, 1610; Socialization: Religion, 1894; The Sociology of Religion, 1952; The Women's Movement, 2196.

GENDER INEQUALITY: ANALYSIS AND OVERVIEW

Type of sociology: Sex and gender
Fields of study: Basic concepts of social stratification; Theoretical perspectives on stratification

Gender inequality refers to the distribution of resources within society by gender. This concept describes the relative advantages and disadvantages of men and women in society.

Principal terms
GENDER: the socially determined expectations for what it means to be male and female
GENDER ROLES: the socially determined sets of rights and obligations that are associated with being male and female
POWER: the ability to affect the behavior of others, with or without their willingness to comply
SEX: the biologically determined differences between men and women
STRATIFICATION: a system in which individuals or groups are ranked according to their differential access to valued resources in society

Overview

Gender inequality refers to the process by which resources are allocated differentially in society to men and women. Gender is one element in a larger stratification system in which individuals and groups are ranked according to their access to valued resources in society. Stratification occurs in many forms and can be based on social class, race/ethnicity, or age as well as on gender.

A major goal of social scientists has been to explain the nature of inequality between men and women. The types of questions asked and the answers proposed depend on the theoretical perspective that is used. Two major perspectives used to address this issue are the functionalist and conflict perspectives.

One of the major assumptions of functionalism is that society operates much like an organism in that it is composed of a system of interrelated parts, each of which operates in a unique way to contribute to the maintenance of the whole. Another assumption is that the ideal social system is one in which the parts function together to create a state of harmony and balance. An analysis using a functionalist perspective examines the various elements of society and the way in which each part fits into the working of the whole.

The functionalist perspective as it is used to understand gender roles comes from the work of sociologists Talcott Parsons and Robert F. Bales in *Family, Socialization and Interaction Process* (1955). Parsons and Bales wrote that men's and women's roles are complementary; both roles are necessary for the survival of society and the family. They drew upon their work on groups, in which they found that in all small groups two functional leaders emerge: instrumental (goal oriented) and expressive (integrative). Because of women's biological role in bearing children, it is they who specialize in nurturing and in providing for the emotional well-being of the family. Men, however, provide for their families' survival by serving as breadwinners and by representing their families to the outside world. According to the functionalist perspective, this specialization of tasks is adaptive not only for the family and society but also for men and women themselves.

The functionalist perspective has been criticized for not properly considering that the division of labor by gender leads to a disadvantage for women. Women become isolated in the home and lack access to valued societal resources that would give them power in the broader society and in family life. This type of arrangement has an inherent inequality of opportunity that is not addressed by functionalists.

Conflict theorists believe that conflict is an inevitable part of social life; they do not portray society as a harmonious system of interrelated parts. Society is composed of individuals and groups that have competing interests and varying amounts of power to promote those interests. The gender role system is one in which men benefit at the expense of women rather than a system of interdependence. A key question for conflict theorists, then, is how and why men maintain that advantage.

One of the earliest conflict theorists to address problems of inequality between men and women was the British social thinker Friedrich Engels. In his book *The Origin of the Family, Private Property, and the State* (1884), Engels drew upon the anthropological knowledge of his time to propose that monogamy came into existence with the advent of private property and that its motivation was to control that property. A primary concern for men was to ensure that property went to their own children by controlling women's reproductive capacity and their sexual activity. The origins of inequality between men and women are related to the emergence of private property.

Women's disadvantage is not confined exclusively to capitalist systems but exists in all types of economies. According to sociologist Rae Lesser Blumberg, it is necessary to examine the role of women in economic production to understand the relative advantages of men and women. If women's labor is strategically indispensable to society, if the kinship system allows women to control property, and if the goods are produced communally for the group rather than for the individual, women have more power in society. This power is expressed in the ability of women to control their own lives, including having control of reproduction and marriage and having power in the community.

According to sociologists Randall Collins and Scott Coltrane, in their book *Sociology of Marriage and the Family: Gender, Love, and Property* (1991), the key to explaining relative power between men and women is the degree to which men and women create their own organizations. Men's superior physical size and strength can be translated into political power in society, which allows them to play a primary role in protecting the community from outside threats. The greater the threat, the more likely men are to create all-male warrior groups that control the weapons in society and maintain political influence over women. In a society in which men also control the inheritance of property and women do not create their own all-female groups, there is little female power. Men's military power affects the type of work that men do and allows them greater control in family life, such as their involvement in marriage politics. The relative power of men and women in society can be predicted by the level of political power commanded by men in society.

Applications

Gender inequality exists in modern American society in several areas, especially in the economy. Overall, women earn lower wages than do men. For example, according to the U.S. Department of Labor, the median weekly wage in 1991 for families maintained by a sole male earner was $404, whereas it was $306 in families in which a female was the sole earner. The median yearly income for women in 1990 was $10,494; the median income for men was $21,147.

There are several reasons that women earn lower wages. Women are segregated in occupations that have lower wages. For example, within the medical field, men are more likely to be physicians and women registered nurses. In 1991, there were 198,000 male physicians and 72,000 female physicians, and 78,000 male nurses and 1,092,000 female nurses. Physicians earn higher wages: 1991 median weekly wages were $994 for physicians and $634 for nurses.

Women are paid lower wages within occupational categories. For physicians in 1991, the median weekly wages were $1,155 for men and $623 for women, and the median weekly wages for nurses were $703 for men and $630 for women. This discrepancy is partly explained by the fact that women often enter less-prestigious specialties. Women physicians are more likely to specialize in pediatrics and public health than are male physicians, who are more likely to be surgeons. Sociologist Christine Williams, in her book *Gender Differences and Work* (1989), showed that men who become nurses are less likely to specialize in hands-on care and more likely to move directly into more highly paid administrative positions.

Women also experience a disadvantage in work because of their primary responsibility for the well-being of the family. It is women who usually take time from work to take care of children or elderly relatives. According to the U.S. Department of Labor, married women with a spouse present were more than four times more likely to miss work time for reasons other than illness in 1991 than were married men with a spouse. Women also take time for pregnancy and maternity leave.

Women, at least until recent years, were less likely to have completed higher education. Even though women were more likely to receive college degrees than men in 1990, they were more likely to have taken degrees at lower levels. Doctorates and professional degrees were more likely to be awarded to men. Women also major in fields that pay less well. In 1990, only 8.5 percent of all mathematics degrees were awarded to women, while 72.7 percent of all education degrees were awarded to women. It should be noted that women have made significant gains in higher education. In 1950, 75.7 percent of all college degrees were awarded to men; in 1990, 47.3 percent of all college degrees were awarded to men.

One significant trend that reflects women's economic disadvantage is the feminization of poverty. This refers to one of the fastest growing segments of the poor population: female-headed households. This trend has an especially serious impact on children. In 1991, 57.5 percent of children of age six who lived in mother-only families lived below the poverty level, whereas only 39.5 percent of six-year-old children in married-couple families lived in poverty. The feminization of poverty reflects two separate trends. First, there has been an increase in the percentage of women who are having children outside of marriage. Second, there has been an increase in the divorce rate, along with a continuing trend of mothers maintaining primary custody of the children. Women are raising children without the benefit of a husband's income, and many women do not make enough to support a family on their own. The median income in 1991 of female-head-of-household families was $16,692, compared to a median income of $40,995 in married-couple families.

Economic disadvantages are especially severe for minority women. Minority women have even lower wages than do other women and are more likely to be in low-skill jobs and to be single parents. In 1991, African American families maintained by women had a median weekly wage of $339, compared to a median weekly wage of $401 in families maintained by African American men. The same pattern holds for Hispanic families. The median weekly wage for families maintained by men in 1991 was $462; for those maintained by women it was $343. The median yearly income in 1991 was $11,414 for African American female-headed households and $12,132 for Hispanic female-headed households. This is compared to a median income of $19,547 for white female-headed households. African American and Hispanic women are more likely to have low-birth-weight children and have higher infant mortality rates; they are less likely to receive prenatal care.

The gender system also has disadvantages for many men. For example, men do not live as long as women. Life expectancy at birth in 1990 was 71.8 years for males and 78.8 years for females. Men are more likely to die from risk-taking behavior. For example, the rates of alcohol-induced and drug-induced death are higher for men than they are for women. According to the Centers for Disease Control, in 1990, the rate of drug-induced death was 11.4 percent for men and 3.4 percent for women. The death rates for accidents and suicide are also higher for men than for women. This reflects the fact that in Western culture men are expected to take more risks and be more daring in their behavior, which has a serious effect on health.

Context

The conflict and functionalist perspectives are only two of several sociological approaches that have been used to examine the nature of gender inequality. Functionalism was popular in sociology in the 1950's and the 1960's but has since lost favor and is not as widely used in studying gender inequality as are other approaches. Sociologist Miriam Johnson contends that sociologists have many misconceptions about functionalism and that it can be useful for the study of gender inequality, especially with the addition of the element of conflict in social relations.

Most perspectives on gender inequality fall into the broad category of feminist theory. Feminist theory was first introduced in the 1970's, and in many ways it parallels the women's movement. Feminist theory refers to a general class of theories that are concerned with explaining the relative position of women in society. According to sociologist Janet Saltzman Chafetz in *Feminist Sociology: An Overview of Contemporary Theories* (1988), a feminist theory not only deals with women's issues but also deals with these issues in such a way that the findings have the potential to bring about change in societal gender roles. Chafetz states that a feminist theory has the following characteristics: Gender is the central concern, gender relations are considered to be problematic, and implied in the theory is the notion that gender relations in society can be changed. She also states that feminist theories often focus on the following issues: the causes of inequality, the manner in which gender systems are reproduced, the consequences of gender roles, and the ways in which gender systems are changed.

As is the case with most other sociological theories, feminist theories often focus on one of two basic levels of analysis. A theory may relate to the micro level of social life, which involves the one-on-one interactions that occur between men and women and the way in which gender is reproduced in those interactions. For example, a micro-level theory may examine the way in which verbal and nonverbal communication between men and women mirrors the broader structure of gender inequality in a society.

A macro-level approach examines gender roles at a larger societal level. One example of a macro-level feminist theory is one developed by sociologist Janet Saltzman Chafetz in her book *Gender Equity: An Integrated Theory of Stability and Change* (1990). In this book, Chafetz demonstrates the way in which societal-level variables such as major technological change create economic change, which increases the resources available to women. In combination with other societal conditions, such as the level of political conflict, sex ratio characteristics, and numbers in the working age population, such change can enable women to gain more power in society. Rather than focusing on individual-level variables, in this macro-level approach, the focus is on the characteristics of an entire society.

Bibliography

Chafetz, Janet Saltzman. *Feminist Sociology: An Overview of Contemporary Theories*. Itasca, Ill.: F. E. Peacock, 1988. Contains a brief summary of major feminist theories, organized by the type of question addressed. An excellent reference when a brief overview of the entire spectrum of feminist theories is needed.

_____ . *Gender Equity: An Integrated Theory of Stability and Change*. Newbury Park, Calif.: Sage Publications, 1990. Chafetz proposes a theoretical framework to explain the way in which gender inequality is maintained and reproduced and the levels of change in gender equality.

Collins, Randall, and Scott Coltrane. *Sociology of Marriage and the Family: Gender, Love, and Property*. 3d ed. Chicago: Nelson-Hall, 1991. A college textbook for courses in sociology of marriage and the family, this volume is rich in theoretical applications, especially for gender. Includes Collins' political theory of gender inequality.

Engels, Friedrich. *The Origin of the Family, Private Property, and the State*. Reprint. New York: International Publishers, 1972. Includes Engels' study of gender inequality and an introduction by anthropologist Eleanor Burke Leacock. The anthropological findings upon which Engels based his theory have changed, but his work is still relevant to the study of gender.

England, Paula, ed. *Theory on Gender, Feminism on Theory*. New York: Aldine de Gruyter, 1993. Contains essays applying mainstream sociological theory to the understanding of gender. Includes Miriam Johnson's essay "Functionalism and Feminism: Is Estrangement Necessary?" Also includes essays applying Marxism, rational-choice theory, and macrostructural perspectives to the understanding of gender.

Parsons, Talcott, and Robert F. Bales. *Family, Socialization, and Interaction Process*. Glencoe, Ill.: Free Press, 1955. Applies the perspective of functionalism to the understanding of gender and family roles. This influential book is useful for understanding the basic ideas of functionalist theory.

Williams, Christine L. *Gender Differences at Work: Women and Men in Nontraditional Occupations*. Berkeley: University of California Press, 1989. Reports of findings from a study of individuals in nontraditional occupations: men in nursing and women in the Marines. Focuses on how traditional gender roles are reproduced even in nontraditional settings.

Charlotte Chorn Dunham

Cross-References

The Feminization of Poverty, 754; Gender and Religion, 813; Gender Inequality: Biological Determinist Views, 826; Gender Socialization, 833; Health Care and Gender, 858; Legitimation of Inequality: The Mass Media, 1061; Sexism and Institutional Sexism, 1728; Social Stratification: Analysis and Overview, 1839; Women in the Labor Force, 2185; The Women's Movement, 2196.

GENDER INEQUALITY: BIOLOGICAL DETERMINIST VIEWS

Type of sociology: Sex and gender

Men and women undeniably have certain physical differences. It is a subject of debate whether these biological differences also cause behavioral differences and whether biology, therefore, is one of the causes of sex roles and gender-related social stratification. Biological determinism holds that biology does affect these things, but most sociologists argue against the idea.

Principal terms

BIOLOGICAL DETERMINISM: the belief that most human behavior is a result of genetic "programming" rather than learning

ENVIRONMENTAL DETERMINISM: the belief that most human behavior is shaped by learning and other postnatal, environmental influences rather than by hormones and genetics

GENDER: sometimes used as a synonym for the word "sex" in referring to male and female, but usually encompassing social and psychological as well as biological attributes

MISOGYNY: a belief that sex differences are based in biology and are therefore natural and also that women are lesser persons than men

SEX ROLES: social expectations and norms that are different for males than for females

SEX TYPING: the differential treatment of individuals based on stereotypes and beliefs about sex and gender differences

SEXISM: discriminatory attitudes or behavior exhibited toward an individual or group based upon stereotypes about sex and gender

SOCIOBIOLOGY: the study of the biological and evolutionary underpinnings of social behavior; controversial because its biological determinist assumptions sometimes have political implications, especially regarding gender relations

Overview

Sociologists and other scientists who study human behavior are ultimately engaged in an effort to understand human nature and the nature of human interactions. Biological determinists believe that "human nature" is based in human biology (genetics, evolution, hormones, and physiology) and that there are therefore some kinds of behaviors that are more "natural" than others. Environmental determinists, on the other hand, believe that the complexity and flexibility of the human mind and culture allow people to engage in a diversity of behaviors that have no relationship to biology. They argue that patterns of human behaviors and interactions must be explained by patterns in the environment, especially the human environment (including learning, socialization, discrimination, and oppression). Although almost everyone agrees that both biology and culture are important determinants of human behavior, when discussing particular behaviors, most people tend to agree with one side or the other in what has come to be called the "nature/nurture debate."

Explanation of the widespread existence of gender-related social roles is one of the most controversial issues in this debate. Biological determinists are convinced that the ubiquity of such roles across cultures strongly indicates that there must be a biological basis for them. After all, they would say, it seems to make sense that since women, but not men, can bear and nurse children, women must "naturally" be better than men at child rearing, and that that can explain why there are no societies in which child care is primarily the task of men. Using this logic, it is an easy next step to say that women are therefore probably more nurturant than men because of their biology rather than because they are taught to be, and that women are predominant in service roles and careers because they seek out such roles, not because they are relegated to them by prejudice and discrimination. Environmental determinists would counter that most gender differences are a result of the internalization of roles that people are taught through the process of sex typing—the differential treatment of boys and girls based on gender stereotypes—and that to continue teaching these gender roles is a form of sexism.

Generally speaking, biological determinists attempt to explain existing conditions rather than to make predictions or recommendations. The kinds of social conditions claimed to have biological underpinnings are many, including sex differences in aptitudes, interests, and performance; preferences for activities, lifestyles, and career; rates and types of criminal victimization and criminal activity; attitudes and behaviors related to sex, politics, and other social interactions; nurturance, empathy, and other emotions; cooperation, competition, and decision-making styles; and life expectancy and rates and types of mental and physical illness. In many cases , the arguments and data have been extrapolated from studies of nonhuman primates; in other cases, data come from cross-cultural comparisons.

Traditionally, most of the literature in this area attempted to provide proximate explanations for gender differences, that is, explanations about how social and psychological gender differences come about as a result of physical differences (such as hormone levels, body build, and brain chemistry). More recently, however, much of the literature has focused on ultimate explanations—that is, explanations about why sociological, psychological, and even physical gender differences exist in the first place. This newer approach is based on the successes of a field called "sociobiology" in explaining and predicting many attributes of the social organizations and interactions of nonhuman animals. Sociobiologists view every behavior as the result of an evolutionary process which selects only those behaviors that help the individual or species to survive and reproduce. According to this perspective, all behaviors have some adaptive function, and if some behaviors are differentially expressed by the two sexes, then there must be some adaptive, biologically functional reason for that difference. Thus, sociobiologists believe that gender differences exist because evolution designed humans that way.

This is the first time that biological determinists have had the benefit of a theory upon which to draw, and sociobiologists, unlike most biological determinists of the past, are beginning to make predictions about gender differences rather than only trying to explain already known conditions. If tests of these predictions prove to be correct, then biological determinism will gain a bigger following among sociologists. Until that happens, however, most sociologists will continue to believe sociobiology cannot be applied to humans to the extent that it can to nonhuman animals because of the role, neglected by sociobiologists, of cultural influences on behavior. In addition, a number of social scientists reject the sociobiological approach for political reasons.

Applications

The behavioral sex difference that has been most convincingly argued to be at least partly biologically determined is aggressiveness. The strength of this argument is based on the fact that research using many different approaches all converges on the same answer. Cross-cultural studies show that most crime, especially violent crime, is performed by males; most wars, as well as most personal (physical) battles, are fought by males; and boys are much more physically active and physically aggressive than girls across all ages. Studies of nonhuman primates show the same thing, leading scientists to believe that such differences are based in biology rather than in culture. Controlled experiments that manipulate prenatal and postnatal hormones in other animals consistently show that those which experience unusually high levels of masculinizing hormones while in the womb or during other critical periods of development show greater levels of aggressive behavior than normal. Likewise, although researchers cannot randomly assign children to different levels of hormones, data from so-called "experiments of nature" also suggest that it is biology, not rearing, that makes males more aggressive than females.

Unlike studies of aggression, which give fairly certain and consistent results, other studies of sex and gender differences in society are hard to interpret, because the variables involved preclude experimental manipulation and the behaviors and patterns of interest simply do not occur in nonhuman animals. An example of a biological determinist position that is more controversial is the claim that social stratification as it relates to gender is based on the fact that men and women choose different careers and lifestyles rather than on the concept that women are being discriminated against. In the United States, there are many stereotypes about the kinds of jobs that are acceptable for women versus men; women are more likely to be found in jobs that are considered service positions, jobs assisting someone else in a higher position, jobs related to child care or housework, and careers in the arts, while men are more often found engaging in entrepreneurial ventures, in positions associated with power and decision-making, in jobs relating to technology or machinery, and in careers in science and math. On the average, the jobs women are most likely to have are lower-paying and of lower status than the jobs men are most likely to have. The reasons behind this stratification are complicated.

Some biological determinists have argued that women are more skilled than men at jobs that involve nurturing (such as child care, elementary school teaching, and nursing) or fine motor skills (such as sewing and typing), and that this superiority explains their overabundance in certain jobs; men, on the other hand, are presumably more skilled at mathematics and jobs involving physical labor, and that is why they are overrepresented in those kinds of jobs. One of the arguments against this interpretation, however, is that it would predict that women would be more common than men in jobs such as surgeon and mechanic, whereas clearly they are not. The counterargument points out that women are selectively more common in low-status, low-paying jobs, no matter what kinds of skills are involved. Cross-cultural studies tend to support this latter view in that in cultures that put different values on jobs than is the case in the United States, women still tend to be found in the lower-status jobs and men in the higher-status jobs; where physicians are high in status, for example, they tend to be men, and where physicians are low in status, they tend to be women. This pattern would suggest that women are being denied access to higher status jobs solely because of discrimination.

This debate does not end there. Recent studies suggest that as women do break into traditionally male-dominated jobs in American society, those jobs start to lose their high status. The discrimination model would interpret this pattern by concluding either that because women started dominating a certain job, discrimination and the change in the job's status followed, or that when a job starts to decline in status, more women are allowed in. An alternative interpretation, however, consistent with biological determinism, is that women are by nature more cooperative and less competitive than men and that they therefore seek jobs that are less competitive. Thus, as a job started to lose status, it would become less competitive, less attractive to men, and more attractive to women; or, as women joined the ranks of men in a high-status job, the job would become less competitive, men would start to leave, and more women would start to apply. Most sociologists would tend to side with the environmental (discrimination) interpretation, but it could be argued that the two interpretations are equally logical.

Context

The idea that gender differences are based in biology is perhaps as old as humanity itself; it can be found expressed in religion, art, philosophy, and a variety of other areas. Most sociologists, however, prefer to distance themselves from this perspective. One reason for this is that many sociologists believe that biological determinism fosters misogyny; they argue that a commitment to the biological approach springs more from a political desire to "keep women in their place" than from a desire to seek scientific truth.

Misogyny is the belief that women are not only different from men but also somehow lesser than men in a social, spiritual, or political sense. Misogynistic attitudes can lead to discrimination, oppression, and male dominance. For some people, the belief that gender roles are caused by biology implies that no one should attempt to go against those roles or to improve the status of women. This illogical inference easily leads to consequences such as discrimination against women who choose not to have children or follow socially prescribed sex roles, lack of respect toward women in power, and violence toward women when they do not do what men want and expect of them. Most biological determinists argue that they are not condoning discrimination or misogyny; they are seeking only an explanation of current conditions, not a rationale or an ethic to determine what behavior is socially and ethically desirable.

Another argument made against the biological determinist position is based on the assumption that "biology is destiny"—the idea that, since biological sex differences cannot be changed, it is pessimistic to look for biological explanations of gender differences when there might be environmental explanations for those differences. The logic behind this criticism is based on two assumptions: that it is desirable to change some existing gender-based social stratification, and that environmentally caused phenomena are easier to change than those that are biologically caused. The latter assumption, however, is not universally correct; some biologically caused phenomena are easy to change, while some learned or encultured behaviors are quite difficult to modify. Thus, if the goal is to change gender roles and expectations, it is not necessarily more pessimistic to look for biological explanations and solutions than environmental or cultural ones.

A third argument against biological determinism is based on the fear that individuals in power will try to impose their own values on society through biological intervention such as involuntary drug treatment, psychosurgery, selective sterilization and breeding, or even infanticide. Fears of this type are not unfounded, given the many horrible examples of the past hundred years alone. On the other hand, totalitarian leaders who believe in environmental determinism give humankind just as much to fear, as they have implemented equally extreme environmental programs and sanctions, such as torture, brainwashing, and imprisonment. Neither biological determinism nor environmental determinism is, in and of itself, a danger; like any idea, each can be used as a tool or as a weapon.

Bibliography

Archer, John, and Barbara Lloyd. *Sex and Gender*. Rev. ed. New York: Cambridge University Press, 1985. Although more psychology than sociology, this is an excellent, balanced summary of gender differences using both the biological and environmental approaches. The book is research oriented but is nevertheless highly readable. Excellent introduction. Extensive bibliography, but not separated by chapters.

Birke, Lynda. *Women, Feminism, and Biology*. New York: Methuen, 1986. Birke's volume is an excellent example of a political (feminist) critique of biological determinism; it is very well-written, although it is activist, one-sided, and even angry.

Christen, Yves. *Sex Differences: Modern Biology and the Unisex Fallacy*, translated by Nicholas Davidson. New Brunswick, N.J.: Transaction, 1991. This easy-to-read presentation of the biological approach has twelve chapters, each subdivided into several brief essays summarizing issues related to gender differences. Occasionally a bit one-sided. Only 117 pages, it includes a bibliography for those seeking more of the original research. Originally published in French in 1987.

Durden-Smith, Jo, and Diane deSimone. *Sex and the Brain.* New York: Arbor House, 1983. Unlike the pattern established by the rest of the sources cited here, this example of biological determinism was written by women. For a lay audience, it presents a totally nontechnical synopsis of the research cited by Archer and Lloyd, Christen, and Mitchell, as well as a heavy dose of sociobiology.

Goldberg, Steven. *The Inevitability of Patriarchy.* New York: William Morrow, 1973. This book was extremely controversial when it was written, and although some of its "facts" are now out of date, it remains one of the best examples of a pure biological determinist approach to gender differences. (See following citation for a shorter, more recent version of this author's argument.)

Goldberg, Steven, and Cynthia Fuchs Epstein. "Is Patriarchy Universal and Genetically Determined?" In *Taking Sides: Clashing Views on Controversial Social Issues,* edited by Kurt Finsterbusch and George McKenna. 6th ed. Guilford, Conn.: Dushkin, 1990. This book reprints both sides of a debate published (under separate titles) in *Society* magazine in October, 1986. Goldberg argues that the near ubiquity of patriarchy and male dominance makes them, by definition, "natural"; Epstein argues that patriarchy is not inevitable. Both present an excellent case.

Mitchell, Gary. *Human Sex Differences: A Primatologist's Perspective.* New York: Van Nostrand Reinhold, 1981. Twenty-six short chapters, each covering some issue related to sex differences from a primatological viewpoint. Each chapter discusses nonhuman primates and then humans; topics for which there is no similar behavior in nonhumans do not get addressed. Separate reference sections for each chapter.

Montagu, Ashley. *The Natural Superiority of Women.* New rev. ed. New York: Collier Books, 1974. Montagu, an anthropologist, wrote this book (first published in 1952) as a counterargument to the prevailing notion of the times that men are the superior sex. Montagu mixes biological and sociocultural arguments in making his case.

Rhode, Deborah L., ed. *Theoretical Perspectives on Sexual Difference.* New Haven, Conn.: Yale University Press, 1990. Written at a more advanced level than the other works cited here, this edited text is more balanced than most books that attack biological determinism in that it includes several different types of arguments (scientific, philosophical, and political). Four chapters specifically address sociobiology. Contains extensive footnotes.

Ruse, Michael. *Is Science Sexist?* Boston: Reidel, 1981. This book takes its title from one of its ten essays. The author, a philosopher, has written many books on science, especially sociobiology, and has basically concluded that this approach is scientifically legitimate and not fundamentally sexist.

Linda Mealey

Cross-References

Gender Inequality: Analysis and Overview, 820; Gender Socialization, 833; Patriarchy versus Matriarchy, 1349; Sex versus Gender, 1721; Sexism and Institutional Sexism, 1728; Sociobiology and the Nature-Nurture Debate, 1913; Statuses and Roles, 1978; The Women's Movement, 2196.

GENDER SOCIALIZATION

Type of sociology: Sex and gender

Socialization, or the process of internalizing society's values in order to adapt to one's culture, influences how people behave as males and females in society. Gender roles are the specific behavior patterns and expectations that society holds for each gender; they vary among different societies and eras.

Principal terms

ANDROGYNY: the possession of both masculine and feminine social, emotional, or behavioral traits

GENDER: a term that refers to the culturally defined attributes of each sex or to the meaning people give to these biological differences

GENDER IDENTITY: the knowledge of being biologically male or female; it is usually achieved by age two

GENDER ROLES: specific patterns of behavior and expectations for each gender; learned through the socialization process

GENDER SOCIALIZATION: the adoption of gender roles through societal and parental expectations and the modeling of others in those roles

HOMOPHOBIA: an irrational fear of or aversion to people with a same-sex sexual orientation

SEX: a term that refers to the physical, biological differences between men and women

SEX-ROLE STEREOTYPING: notions that only certain pursuits or behaviors are appropriate for each gender; not based on individual ability or motivation for those pursuits

Overview

The social learning process that indoctrinates people (notably young people) into understanding the various aspects of their culture includes the process of gender socialization. Gender socialization encompasses the all-inclusive process of learning society's gender roles and their advantages and limitations. In most societies, including American society, there is a clear categorization of what it means to be male or female. This categorization process and the agents of socialization that transmit knowledge about gender roles influence how individuals define themselves and others in terms of gender and sex roles.

Gender roles—the expected or preferred ways for people of each sex to behave—are rigidly defined in many societies. In American society, although these roles have become less constrictive since the 1960's, men have traditionally been expected to be strong, aggressive, even domineering; the cliché that "big boys don't cry" typifies one aspect of the male role. Women have been expected to be nurturing, sensitive, emotional, and relatively passive. Children are taught these values, both consciously and unconsciously, from a very early age. Toys represent one example; unless and until children make other preferences known, boys traditionally tend to be given toys that emphasize activity, even violence; girls are often given what might be termed gentler toys. Increasingly, however, stereotypical ways of labeling the genders are recognized as too limiting and restrictive for both genders.

Agents of gender socialization include parents, siblings, peers, schools, society, formalized religion, and a variety of other institutions. For very young children, parents and family (including grandparents and other extended family members) play the central role in shaping gender socialization. They determine how the family interacts with a baby (this process is often unconscious) as well as the types of toys and clothes that the baby is given. Siblings also have a gender-specific influence; this influence is especially notable in certain situations, such as when some girls are reared with male siblings only. Some of these girls, although certainly not all, are described as being "tomboys," or more masculine in their interests and gender behavior than most girls are.

Gender identity itself is established by age two; its central component is the notion "I am male" or "I am female." Sigmund Freud theorized that identification and imitation of same-sex parents leads to effective gender-identity formation. In the latency period described by Freud (ages seven to twelve), males and females tend to segregate themselves from each other. This may be considered part of the socialization process and further solidifies gender identification and role-specific behavior. Schools and families continue to influence gender socialization throughout adolescence. During adolescence, however, peer influence becomes the strongest agent of gender socialization as teens bond together in small social groups to facilitate their transition into adulthood and into the larger society. The socializing effects of the mass media also become powerful in the teen years.

Gender identity and gender socialization can have serious ramifications for an individual's sense of self-esteem. The institution of education has been implicated by sociologists in the process of gender socialization and the stereotyping of the genders. For example, a 1990 study referred to as the Greenberg Lakes study showed the negative effects of the educational process on female self-esteem. Females in American schools were found to have significantly lower self-esteem than males by the end of high school. Such findings are undoubtedly related to the difficult and contradictory expectations that girls must face as they attempt to balance their academic, social, and career roles.

Personality and physical development is inextricably linked to the processes of socialization. Nancy Chodorow, a specialist in cross-cultural and psychoanalytic perspectives, has examined development in the light of the social and psychological oppression that can be perpetuated in the individual during personality development. Personality development is influenced heavily by gender socialization and the cultural valuation of the genders in society; research by Chodorow and others has examined how development is influenced by the societal devaluation of women.

Some researchers believe that very early patterns of influence strongly affect personality development and social roles, arguing that parental expectations about the gender of their yet-to-be-born child begin the gender socialization process. Even before a baby's birth, for example, the expectant parents start purchasing toys and clothes for the baby; in the process, they are already beginning to socialize the baby. (Early biological factors are also important; John Money, a leading sexologist, has noted the importance of the in utero environment, particularly the presence of masculinizing or feminizing hormones, to the development of the fetus.)

Sandra Bem, a social psychologist, developed a theory of androgyny suggesting that the healthiest, most flexible people are able to move back and forth between aspects of male and female sex roles. At times it is advantageous for men to be able to express their sensitive side and to be nurturing. Men have often missed out on the joy of rearing children because of rigid role restrictions involving their careers. Increasingly, however, fathers are likely to take a greater part in the parenting process than ever before. Likewise, there are times that women can profit from being outspoken and assertive and taking leadership roles. Women who are successful in their careers can bring economic and emotional strength to a family by being capable, independent role models for their children.

Both men and women have been constrained in American society by socialization into rigid, stereotypical gender roles. Cross-cultural studies have provided remarkable evidence that these gender roles vary across cultures. In some societies, for example, the majority of the women do the hard labor because they are considered better suited for it than the men. Another interesting fact is that in Russia, three-quarters of the physicians are women. Anthropologist Margaret Mead conducted a classic investigation in 1935 of the Tchambuli, an indigenous people of New Guinea. In that society, women were the aggressors, the power brokers, and the manufacturers. The Tchambuli men filled what Westerners consider the traditionally feminine role of being interested in jewelry, appearances, arts, and flirting. The fact that the genders behave differently in different cultures suggests that there is more flexibility in gender expression than was once believed.

Applications

There have been many forms of resistance to rigid gender socialization in the United States, most notably since the women's movement became a powerful force in the early 1970's. Educational activism and political activism have long been mechanisms for countering stereotypes and rigid gender-role assignment. The women's and men's movements, the gay liberation movement, and others have focused on educating society at large and "raising consciousness" about the capabilities of all of society's members as well as about the variety of behavioral expressions of gender that exist. The women's movement has focused attention on the prejudice and discrimination that has grown out of socialization into rigid gender roles. The notions of sexism (discrimination based on sex) and the economic inequality that it has produced continue to be a central focus of the women's movement.

Economic inequality based on gender expectations has led to some new terms. The term "glass ceiling," for example, refers to an invisible limit on the earnings of women in business and institutions. Economic limits are at least in part attributable to gender socialization. It has been common for male employers to believe that they did not have to pay their female employees as much as males because their husbands were thought to be supporting them. This type of rigid thinking has also been observed in academic and governmental structures. Very few top corporate positions or government posts are filled by women. Some people believe that the acceptance of a few women into high positions represents tokenism, or positive actions toward a few women to make it seem that an employer is "playing fair." As a result of becoming aware of the glass ceiling, some women have filed—and won—discrimination suits. Others have taken a different path and written extensively on the effects that gender bias has on women. A 1991 book by Susan Faludi entitled *Backlash: The Invisible War Against American Women* describes the cost of the progress that has been made for women in American society.

Other resistance to rigid male/female dichotomies has come from academic research. Sandra Bem's work on androgyny highlighted the benefits of being able to shift back and forth between masculine and feminine perspectives. In the 1970's, Bem developed the Bem Sex-Role Inventory to assess the presence of masculine and feminine characteristics in people of both genders. Bem found that many college students had a surprising degree of androgyny in their behavioral and emotional interactions.

Another significant approach in combating overly rigid gender socialization has been the creation of gender-neutral or nonbiased books and toys. Socialization starts at a very early age, and many manufacturers, educators, and parents are using gender-neutral books and toys to provide children with new ways of relating to the world that will not be as restrictive as those of the past.

Education plays a key role in gender socialization, and many experts hope that it will be an effective agent for transforming such socialization. Research has shown that teachers in elementary schools sometimes ignore girls and respond to boys in ways that may reflect their own unconscious gender biases. Such differential responses may have significant effects on students'—especially girls'—self-esteem. At the level of higher education, some colleges offer mentorships and scholarships for women with mathematical and science abilities in an effort to help overcome the effects of early sex-role typing and biased educational tracking. Beginning in the early 1990's, women were encouraged to set aside a day to "take your daughter to work" so that girls could be exposed early to options regarding economic security. Such efforts, it is hoped, will continue to help expand women's options and quest for economic parity.

Efforts are also underway to correct the extreme gender bias that is evident in unrealistic portrayals of women in the mass media, particularly on television and in motion pictures. It has been strongly argued that such portrayals are another source of low self-esteem for adolescent girls as they embark on an impossible attempt to emulate actresses, television personalities, and models with million-dollar salaries and appearances that society has deemed ideal. Assertiveness training, anger management therapy for male perpetrators of violence against women, and shelters for battered women are also widely considered to be parts of the solution to the problems brought about by rigid gender socialization and stereotyping.

Context

Virtually all societies use the biological assignment of sex to assign certain gender roles, although the degree of flexibility in these roles varies considerably among different cultures. These roles define the expectations for the behavior and activities of each sex. Sociologists have noted that, because there is such a varied expression of gender roles across cultures, social learning must be the basis for the transmission of gender roles.

In Western society, sexual differentiation, stereotyping, and cultural devaluation of the feminine gender led to a significant "wage gap" between the earning power of men and women. Sociologists Barbara Reskin and Heidi Hartman have argued that the primary reason for the wage gap was continued segregation of the genders into certain types of employment: The more females in a given profession, the lower the wages for that profession. When women began to move into male-dominated professions and demanded to earn equal wages, there was resistance from the men. In times of economic hardship, this gender friction becomes more intense. Considerable changes in American society's views of gender roles and of socialization into those roles have been underway since the late 1960's. Societal institutions have begun to incorporate various political and educational gains in this area, and children are being exposed to more flexible ways of behaving and relating to one another. There has clearly been a move away from strict gender stereotypes.

In the 1960's, birth control via oral contraception became available, creating new options for women. Some women chose to remain childless. Others limited their number of offspring or postponed childbearing until they completed their formal education. By the 1970's and 1980's, day care became more widely available, and more families—partly from economic necessity—had two breadwinners. Gender socialization patterns began to change.

One facet of traditional gender socialization that gained attention in the 1980's was that of male strength, leading to male domination. This aspect of the male role has been linked by some sociologists and psychologists to the prevalence of sexual assault and domestic violence. Some authors have referred to American culture as a "rape culture"—one that promotes the macho overtaking of women and sets the stage for abuse of women. The notion of "male entitlement," they note, has been used to justify men's forcing themselves on women even when women clearly do not want their attentions. Statistics have suggested that more than one-third of emergency room visits for women in the United States are attributable to violence against women, most of which occurs in the home.

Bibliography

Andersen, Margaret, and Patricia H. Collins, comps. *Race, Class, and Gender: An Anthology.* Belmont, Calif.: Wadsworth, 1992. An interdisciplinary collection of essays that integrate the intricate contributions of race, class, and gender into the overall framework of prejudice, oppression, and discrimination. Particularly excellent for its first-person accounts.

Bem, Sandra L. "Psychological Androgyny." In *Beyond Sex Roles*, edited by Alice G. Sargent. St. Paul, Minn.: West, 1977. Bem discusses androgyny as an ability to switch between facets of male and female attitudes and behaviors, arguing that it is valuable and healthy.

Chodorow, Nancy. "Being and Doing: A Cross-Cultural Examination of the Socialization of Males and Females." In *Woman in Sexist Society: Studies in Power and Powerlessness*, edited by Vivian Gornick and Barbara K. Moran. New York: Basic Books, 1971. Examines cross-cultural views of the socialization of males and females and the powerful influence that this socialization has on the future status of the genders.

Lips, Hilary M. *Sex and Gender: An Introduction*. Mountain View, Calif.: Mayfield, 1988. Presents a thorough review of myths, theories, and research regarding sex and gender. In addition, the author explores the behavior and experiences of males and females, comparing similarities and differences. Sex and gender is examined in social relationships, political life, and the workplace.

Mead, Margaret. *Sex and Temperament in Three Primitive Societies*. New York: William Morrow, 1963. A cross-cultural study that compares sex and temperament in primitive (that is, nonindustrial) cultures from an anthropological perspective.

Karen M. Wolford

Cross-References

Comparable Worth and Sex Segregation in the Workplace, 303; The Feminization of Poverty, 754; Gender and Religion, 813; Gender Inequality: Analysis and Overview, 820; Gender Inequality: Biological Determinist Views, 826; Patriarchy versus Matriarchy, 1349; Sex versus Gender, 1721; Women in the Labor Force, 2185; Women in the Medical Profession, 2191; The Women's Movement, 2196.

THE GERM THEORY OF MEDICINE

Type of sociology: Major social institutions
Field of study: Medicine

Introduced during the latter half of the nineteenth century, the germ theory of medicine held that contagious diseases are caused by microorganisms. This realization had profound effects on the institution of medicine and on society at large, as sanitation systems were improved and as vaccines, then antibiotics, were developed.

Principal terms

ASEPSIS: the ability to carry out a technique in the absence of microorganisms; the use of sterile techniques

BACILLUS: a rod-shaped bacterium, an example of which is the agent which causes the disease anthrax

CONTAGION: an unknown substance that caused disease while spreading through populations; the term was used prior to the discovery of microorganisms

FERMENTATION: any chemical reaction carried out by microorganisms in the absence of oxygen

KOCH'S POSTULATES: criteria for establishing that a particular disease is caused by a specific etiological agent

MICROORGANISM: any microscopic cell or organism capable of carrying out living processes; includes bacteria, fungi (mold), and viruses

PURE CULTURE: the growth of a specific microorganism in the laboratory, in the absence of any other type of microbe; of vital importance for associating that particular microorganism with a specific disease

Overview

Although the spread of human disease through populations has been recognized for thousands of years, the role played by microorganisms in this process has only been understood since the latter half of the nineteenth century. The impetus for this role was supplied by Dutch lensmaker Antoni van Leeuwenhoek. During the seventeenth century, Leewenhoek designed and built microscopes with which he was able to observe biological structures, including the larger microbes. Crude by today's standards, these instruments were nevertheless able to magnify some 300 diameters in size. Almost certainly, some of the organisms described by Leewenhoek were bacteria.

The role played by bacteria in disease remained ambiguous. By the early nineteenth century, the role of fungi in certain skin diseases had been established, but it remained for the French chemist Louis Pasteur to link the presence of microorganisms to specific diseases—first to disease of silkworms and to problems in the beer industry, then to disease in animals.

Concurrent with Pasteur's work in France were investigations being carried out by the German physician Robert Koch. Though bitter rivals, Pasteur and Koch are inextricably linked. During the 1870's, both men were performing research on anthrax, a highly contagious disease of animals that would sometimes infect humans. Koch demonstrated, as had others before him, that a particular rod-shaped bacillus was invariably present in the blood of an animal infected with anthrax. By passing the organism from animal to animal, Koch demonstrated that anthrax only developed in the presence of that organism; it was always present in animals with the disease, and was not present in animals without the disease. Further—and it was here that Koch made an additional critical contribution to associating bacteria with disease—Koch was able to grow these microorganisms in the laboratory in pure culture. In this manner, any bacterium could be studied independently, without concern over the influence of contaminants on the results of experiments.

Working independently of Koch, Pasteur was also able to grow the anthrax bacillus in pure culture. Reflecting his background as a chemist, Pasteur was able to attenuate the organism, creating an anthrax vaccine which effectively protected animals against the disease. Pasteur's most famous work is probably that involving rabies. Though never a major disease in terms of actual numbers, rabies was still a terrible disease that created justifiable fear. By passing the rabies virus through rabbit brains, Pasteur was able to create an attenuated form of the virus that could be used to immunize humans and other animals against the disease.

With the development of methods of pure culture, the 1880's and 1890's became the golden years of microbiology. The association of specific microorganisms with particular diseases became almost commonplace. Etiological agents for diseases such as tuberculosis, cholera, typhoid fever, diphtheria, plague, and tetanus were isolated. A high proportion of these discoveries were made by Koch and his students. In many cases, the isolation of these microorganisms led to treatments or preventive measures. The first vaccine against human disease was that against smallpox, developed in the 1890's. With the isolation of specific agents of disease, however, and with Pasteur's demonstration as to their attenuation, the 1890's also saw the use of vaccination as an effective measure against other common childhood scourges. Diphtheria was among the first; there would be others.

An important correlate to the establishment of the germ theory of medicine was that many forms of illness were clearly caused by ignorance of the presence of these organisms. For example, surgery could be a deadly process, even discounting the risk of surgical intervention itself. The risk of infection was high; as many patients died from the aftermath of surgery as from the process itself. This was also true of childbirth, as mortality rates in hospitals among postpartum women were often higher than if these women gave birth at home, in the presence of midwives.

Though the concept of "germs" as the cause of disease predated the work of Pasteur and Koch, it was these two individuals who most clearly linked bacteria with illnesses. Pasteur's early work on spontaneous generation proved that microorganisms are ubiquitous. Further, he was able to show that diseases in silkworms were attributable to infectious agents. It was then a short jump to establish a similar association of microorganisms with diseases in plants, animals, and humans. Koch's ability to grow these microbes in pure culture, and his methodologies which evolved into Koch's postulates, provided a firm ground for associating "germs" and disease.

Applications

The evolution of the germ theory of medicine had its most immediate applications in the area of surgery. The nineteenth century concept of infectious agents as cause of disease was particularly evident in the attempts to eliminate childbed fever (or as it was more commonly known, puerperal fever). The observations of two physicians, Oliver Wendell Holmes in the United States and Ignac Semmelweis of Austria, were instrumental in the elimination of this disease. Ironically, their theories were formed several decades before the work of Pasteur and Koch placed the germ theory on sound footing. As Sherwin Nuland expressed the situation in his book *Doctors: The Biography of Medicine* (1988), it was a case of "the germ theory before the germs."

During the first half of the nineteenth century, puerperal fever was a killer of young mothers. Women would deliver a child and then, days to weeks later, would succumb to overwhelming disease. In some hospitals in Vienna, reportedly a city in which the best medicine in the world was practiced, mortality rates among new mothers reached as high as 25 percent. The cause of the disease was unknown.

Independently, Holmes and Semmelweis formed similar perceptions. They observed that the high rates of mortality were only associated with deliveries aided by obstetricians; deliveries helped by midwives were generally uneventful. Further, these obstetricians often moved from patient to patient without having first washed. In some cases, the doctors had participated in autopsies. Holmes and Semmelweis came to the same conclusion: puerperal fever was being transmitted by the obstetricians themselves. Semmelweis argued that it was pus in particular that contained an infectious element. After he instructed the obstetricians under his authority to wash their hands in a chlorine solution between patients, puerperal fever disappeared. It was to remain years before the nature of the infectious pus was understood; nevertheless, the application of a "germ theory before germs" resulted in the virtual elimination of childbed fever.

Despite the studies of Pasteur on the role of microorganisms in fermentations, it was not immediately apparent that an analogous process was involved in human disease. Surgery remained a risky process. The introduction of anasthesia during the 1840's resulted in a dramatic increase in the number and types of surgical operations. Along with this increase, however, came the danger of sepsis, or infection. In these pre-antibiotic days, development of gangrene meant that amputation of limbs would often be necessary following even minor surgical procedures. Even with amputation, death from "blood poisoning" was often the result; in some hospitals, as many as 60 percent of surgical patients succumbed to gangrene.

The English surgeon Joseph Lister was the first to apply Pasteur's work to the area of aseptic surgery. Lister was aware that the fermentative organisms Pasteur found, which were causing problems in the French beer industry, originated in the air. He assumed that a similar process was at work in surgical patients; the microorganisms causing putrefaction in surgical openings were originating in the air of the hospital.

In order to eliminate the danger of infection, Lister introduced the concept of surgical sepsis. The air around the surgical patient was to be sprayed with a carbolic acid aerosol, and the surgeon washed thoroughly in a carbolic acid solution. The patient's skin was washed; surgical dressings were sterilized prior to their use. Postsurgical infections immediately decreased. It would be some time before Lister's application of antiseptic surgery became widely accepted. The process by which the hands were washed in carbolic acid was uncomfortable; nor were surgeons happy with the conclusion that they were themselves the cause of most hospital infections. Nevertheless, as the germ theory became established, physicians gradually became aware of the necessity of aseptic technique in their practices.

The most dramatic changes in the spread of infectious disease resulted from improvements in sanitation. As the studies of Koch had demonstrated, disease organisms were often passed through contaminated food or water. Epidemics of some diseases, such as cholera, were a direct result of sewage contamination of drinking water supplies. As governments became aware of the source of microorganisms, proper sewage disposal became increasingly imperative. The elimination of slums was as much a social problem as one of health, but the problems were now seen as interrelated. Not only were the slums breeding areas for crime, but they also represented reservoirs for disease.

It was within this context that the practice of preventive medicine evolved. Beginning in the mid-nineteenth century, a series of Public Health Acts in England established a Board of Health with the power to enforce rules of sanitation. Similar processes were carried out in other countries, including the United States. In 1912, following several reorganizations, the United States Public Health Service came into existence.

The creation of health departments had several immediate effects. The purity of water supplies was regulated; sewers were constructed under strict provisions. As is often the case with progress, these improvements were slow to appear in many places, particularly in the poorest areas of cities. In addition, the recognition that "filth" was the cause of many disease outbreaks often predated general acceptance of the fact that it was microbial contamination of that "filth" which was the ultimate cause of illness. Nevertheless, the eventual result was the building of storage areas for urban water supplies and filtration of that water prior to its use. Application of the germ theory of medicine was dramatic; by the beginning of the twentieth century, the incidence of large-scale epidemics was beginning to decrease. When outbreaks did occur, it was often possible to pinpoint and eliminate the source.

Historically, in theory, physicians treated the sick according to need and charged fees commensurate with the ability to pay. Too often, however, the patient was unable to pay. With the loss of income if the victim was the family breadwinner, both the doctor and the patient's family would ultimately suffer. Eventually, this problem was to give rise to forms of health insurance. The first national system of compulsory "sickness" insurance was established in Germany in 1887. By 1912, similar programs were found in most of Europe and England. Yet other than small local benevolent societies, such programs did not appear in the United States until the Depression years of the 1930's. Private companies, such as Blue Cross, formed during this period; by 1940, they had six million subscribers.

Health insurance was not included in Franklin Roosevelt's Social Security Act (1935); the act did provide matching funds for the states in the health area. It remained until the 1940's, and the Truman Administration, for even rudimentary insurance programs to be accepted. The major exception was the returning war veterans, who received extensive care through the Veterans Administration. Extensive government involvement in the health-care industry evolved only in the 1960's, in the years of the Lyndon Johnson Administration.

Context

The names of Pasteur and Koch are inextricably linked with the germ theory of medicine; however, they were not the first who attempted to link microorganisms with disease. Bacteria had been observed using crude microscopes as early as the seventeenth century. The theory that a "contagium animatum," an infectious germ of some unknown sort, was associated with disease dated back even further, to the sixteenth century Italian scholar Hieronymus Fracastorius.

Science itself had undergone a revolution during this period. Society was beginning to evolve from a church-mandated view of existence, and the implications for medicine were profound. William Harvey observed the circulation of blood, while Gasparo Aselli discovered the lymphatic system. Epidemics, however, continued to devastate Europe; European diseases also had disastrous effects on the American Indian population. Physicians could merely observe and compile effects. What treatments did exist were almost as deadly as the diseases themselves: the use of emetics, bleeding, and induction of vomiting. Such treatments were used for both kings and commoners. Antiplague measures consisted almost entirely of isolation, as victims were generally quarantined. Most European towns had their sanitary corps, whose function was to both treat the victims and enforce the isolation.

Beginning in the 1850's, Pasteur carried out an extensive series of experiments on putrefaction and fermentation. Ultimately, he demonstrated that the organisms that perform these processes do not originate within the tissue factors themselves (the concept known as "spontaneous generation") but must be introduced from the outside. Further, these organisms carry out specific types of chemical reactions, altering the nature of the substrate on which they react. Though Pasteur was not the first to suggest that fermentation reactions were caused by living organisms, it was his experiments that proved the theory. It was Pasteur who imparted this knowledge to colleagues often unwilling to accept such ideas. During the 1860's, Pasteur began his investigations of the silkworm disease pebrine. He was able to demonstrate the parasitic nature of the cause. In 1870, he carried out similar work on "diseases" affecting beer production, eventually confirming the bacterial nature of the contamination. The role of microorganisms in disease was being established.

In 1876, Robert Koch demonstrated for the first time that a specific microorganism is associated with a particular disease. Koch isolated the anthrax bacillus from the blood of a sick animal, cultured the organism in the laboratory, and confirmed that this organism was the cause of anthrax by inoculating the microbe into a healthy animal. Eventually, this process coalesced into what is known as Koch's postulates. Koch was also able to solve a problem that had bothered other researchers: Why did fresh outbreaks of anthrax suddenly appear in previously infected areas? Koch demonstrated that the anthrax bacillus formed a dormant state, a spore, which could remain in the ground until ingested by an animal. The spore was the source of the fresh outbreaks. In 1878, Koch linked a number of postsurgical infections to specific types of bacteria, essentially completing the earlier work of Joseph Lister. By doing so, Koch had confirmed the germ theory of medicine.

Bibliography

Bibel, Debra Jan, ed. *Milestones in Immunology*. Madison, Wis.: Science Tech, 1988. A historical discussion of classic papers on the subject. Though primarily dealing with immunology, as the title implies, some of the historical works of early bacteriologists are included. Along with reprinting classical works, the author provides discussion on the significance of the research.

Brock Thomas, ed. *Milestones in Microbiology*. Washington, D.C.: American Society for Microbiology, 1975. A collection of articles written by Koch, Pasteur, and others from the early years of bacteriology. The editor (Brock also translated the works) includes extensive discussion of the historical significance of the works. An excellent source for the early history of the subject as described by the subjects themselves.

_____ . *Robert Koch: A Life in Medicine and Bacteriology*. Madison, Wis.: Science Tech, 1988. The definitive biography of the man instrumental in development of the germ theory. The author provides a detailed description of Koch's life and a vivid depiction of the process of experimentation. Events leading to the formation of Koch's postulates are described in a manner appropriate for nonscientists and biologists alike.

Bulloch, William. *The History of Bacteriology*. New York: Oxford University Press, 1938. Though decades old, this book remains a classic on the subject. It contains an outstanding history of the early years of bacteriology. Numerous illustrations are provided. An extensive bibliography is included.

Nuland, Sherwin. *Doctors: The Biography of Medicine*. New York: Alfred A. Knopf, 1988. An excellent history of the development of medicine. The author provides a mix of anecdotal information with in-depth discussion of numerous historical characters. An extensive biography of historic persona is the basis for each chapter. The section on Lister is a particularly good description of his trials and contributions.

Singer, Charles, and E. Ashworth Underwood. *A Short History of Medicine*. 2d ed. New York: Oxford University Press, 1962. A thorough study of the development of medicine from the scientific standpoint. Little is found in the way of specific biography, but the evolution of science and scientific study is covered in depth. The scientific history of the Middle Ages is given extensive play, as is the later development of the cell theory, culminating in the germ theory of medicine.

Starr, Paul. *The Social Transformation of American Medicine*. New York: Basic Books, 1982. A sociological look at the medical industry in the United States. Medical practice is observed from its eighteenth century roots with the independent practitioner through the government-regulated corporate practice of the twentieth.

Richard Adler

Cross-References

Endemic and Epidemic Diseases, 640; Health and Society, 852; The Hippocratic Theory of Medicine, 890; Medical Sociology, 1166; Medical versus Social Models of Illness, 1172; The Institution of Medicine, 1185; Sexually Transmitted Diseases, 1742; Social Epidemiology, 1793.

THE GRAYING OF AMERICA

Type of sociology: Aging and ageism

The graying of America refers to the process by which the age distribution of the United States population is becoming increasingly older. The trend is demonstrated by an increase in the median age as well as an increase in the proportion of the population over the age of sixty-five.

Principal terms

AGE COHORT: a group of people born within the same time period

AGE DEPENDENCY RATIO: the ratio of the number of people sixty-five and over to those who are of working age (eighteen to sixty-four)

AGE STRATIFICATION: the distribution of statuses, roles, and resources in society according to position in the age structure

BABY BOOM: an unusually large cohort of individuals who were born between 1945 and 1962

GENERATIONAL EQUITY: the distribution of societal resources equally between all age groups

POPULATION PYRAMID: a graphic representation of the age structure of a society

Overview

The "graying of America" is a phrase used to refer to the phenomenon in which the age structure of the United States is becoming increasingly older. According to United States Census Bureau statistics, the median age of the United States population changed from 22.9 in 1900 to 33.1 in 1991 and is projected to be 40.8 by the year 2030. There has also been a corresponding change in the percentage of the United States population that is 65 and over. In 1900, 4.1 percent of the population was over 65. In 1960, 9.2 percent was over 65. By 1991, 12.5 percent was over 65, and it is projected that in the year 2030, 21.2 percent will be over 65.

There are two major reasons for the graying of America. The first is that people are living longer than before. According to the Census Bureau, at birth, an American born in 1900 could be expected to live to an average age of 47.3. By 1950, average life expectancy had increased to 68.2, and by 1985 it had increased to 74.9. In 1992, life expectancy was 75.4 and was as high as 79.3 for white women.

Most of the life expectancy increases over the twentieth century have occurred because people are less likely to die at young ages. For example, the invention of antibiotics has reduced the number of infants who die from infectious diseases such as pneumonia and influenza, as well as the number of mothers who die in childbirth. There has also been an increase in life expectancy of the old. In 1900, a person who lived to age 65 could expect to live 11.9 more years, to the age of 76.9. In 1950, 65-year-olds lived, on average, 13.9 more years. In 1989, 65-year-old men would be expected to live 15.2 more years, and 65-year-old women 18.8 more years. It is projected that by the year 2020, at 65, men will live 16.4 more years and women will live 20.7 more years. Medical science has also slowed the rate of death from diseases that kill the elderly. For example, there are more successful techniques for treating, if not curing, several forms of cancer as well as improvements in the treatment of heart disease. (Nevertheless, both these diseases are still among the leading causes of death for both men and women.)

The second factor that accounts for the graying of America is that women are having fewer children. The average number of children born to a woman in 1960 changed from 3.449 to an average of 2.480 children in 1970; the number went from 1.840 children in 1980 to 2.014 children in 1989. Replacement fertility is 2.110, which means that without migration the United States' population would decline. Replacement fertility is the average number of children necessary for the population to remain stable.

The reasons for the decline in the birthrate are complex, but they are related to the changing structure of the economy and an accompanying increase in female participation in the labor force. Changes in the ways Americans are making their living changed the meaning and value of children over the course of the twentieth century. When the United States was primarily an agricultural country, large families were an economic asset. The more children there were in a family, the more workers who were available for farming. With industrialization, however, children have become an economic liability. Children are not necessary for their economic contributions to the family, as they were in the past. It is to a family's advantage to have fewer children and to invest more resources in each one. Also, with more women working rather than staying home, the expense of having children is greater. For example, women who take time out of the labor force to bear children often lose wages and opportunities for promotion. Working women also must pay for child care, which increases the economic costs of children.

In his chapter "Demography of Aging," in the *Handbook of Social Gerontology* (edited by Clark Tibbitts, 1960), sociologist George Maddox demonstrates that there is a worldwide trend toward population aging in many industrialized countries. Even though there has been an increase in life expectancy in most parts of the world, only Western industrialized countries have had the accompanying declines in fertility rates that affect the age structure. Six percent of the world's population was over the age of 65 in 1985, with a projected increase to 9.7 percent of the world's population in 2025. In Europe the increase in proportion of elderly will change from 12.7 percent in 1985 to 20.1 in 2025. In Africa the increase will be only from 3.1 percent in 1985 to 4.1 percent of the population in 2025. This is predicted even though Africa has had one of the highest rates of growth in absolute numbers in the elderly population. African nations also have high birthrates, which will keep the proportion of elderly low.

The trend of an aging population is expected to continue well into the twenty-first century when the baby boom cohort reaches old age. The period after World War II experienced an increase in fertility because women married younger and were more likely to have three or more children. It was also a time of postwar growth in the economy that made it possible for Americans to afford larger families than those of previous generations. This large cohort has progressively affected the age distribution of the United States as it has moved through the life course. The oldest members of the baby boom will be in their eighties in the decade of 2030 and will reflect an increase in the elderly population. At that time more than 20 percent of the United States population will be over the age of 65.

Applications

The change in the age structure of American society will have serious effects on many societal institutions, including the economy and the family. The increased numbers of elderly will affect the age dependency ratio—the numbers of people over 65 compared with those between the ages of 18 and 64. This number is important because it is an indicator of the number of workers available in the economy to support the number of dependent elders. The age dependency ratio has increased steadily since the beginning of the twentieth century, reflecting the increased age of the American population. In 1960, the ratio was 16.8 (that is, there were 16.8 elders for every 100 adults of working age). This number increased to 19.3 in 1985 and is projected to reach a high of 38.0 in the year 2050.

It should also be noted, however, that even though the age dependency ratio has increased, the total dependency ratio has remained approximately the same. In an aging population, the number of elderly increases as the number of children declines. The total number of dependents in society remains the same although the dependents themselves change from the very young to the very old.

Old age dependency can manifest itself in many ways. One important way is the strain that large numbers of elderly place on the Social Security system. Fernando M. Torres-Gil, gerontologist and assistant secretary of aging under President Clinton, states in his book *The New Aging: Politics and Change in America* (1992), that traditional old-age security funding is like a four-legged stool. Elders depend on private and public pensions, private assets and savings, public insurance plans such as Social Security, and other public aid programs such as Medicare. More and more elders are depending primarily on Social Security as their primary means of support.

Social Security had a surplus in the late 1980's, but that surplus has been used to offset the federal deficit rather than remaining safely earmarked for future retirees. Eventually the money will have to be returned to the system to finance the retirement of the baby boom. It is likely that this will be done by taxing younger workers at a higher rate. Phillip Longman, in his book *Born to Pay: The New Politics of Aging in America* (1987), demonstrates that at the current rate of usage, younger workers will pay more money into the system than they will receive in benefits. Social Security was the single largest item on the federal budget in 1989. Federal expenditures for Social Security (and federal retirement plans such as railroad retirement) totalled $387 billion.

One solution undertaken to help avert the future crisis in Social Security was to change retirement laws. In an effort to prevent age discrimination as well as to reduce the load on the retirement system, mandatory retirement was eliminated in 1986. Workers will be working longer in the future and therefore will be collecting fewer lifetime benefits.

The costs of other programs, such as Medicare, will also increase as more and more people use those programs for medical care after the age of 65. According to physician William Fries, there is a period of morbidity in the life of elderly people in which they are more vulnerable to chronic conditions that require medical care and hospitalization. According to the U.S. Bureau of the Census, in 1988, people 65 to 74 had an average of 2,116 days of hospital care per 1,000 people; there was an average of 4,087 for those over 75 years old (compared with an average of 502 days for those 35 to 44). More than 90 percent of persons over 65 used Medicare and Medicaid as the primary sources of payment for those hospital stays. In 1988, $34 billion of the federal budget was for Medicaid payments. Even though some people expect the period of morbidity to grow shorter and for elders to live longer and healthier lives, there will be an increased demand on the medical system because of the increase in sheer numbers of elderly.

The changing age structure will reflect a change in the family structure as well. The generational structure of the family will change so that there are more elderly and fewer children in what sociologist Vern L. Bengtson has called the "beanpole" family structure. In this type of family structure, there will be more generations surviving and therefore coexisting at the same time, but each generation will have fewer members. One consequence of this type of family structure is that there will be fewer family members available to care for more dependent elders. According to sociologists Beth Soldo and Emily Agree, for the noninstitutionalized elderly, 90 percent of care is provided by family members—if not by a spouse, then by an adult child. Because generations are having smaller families, there will be fewer adult children available to provide care for frail elders. As a result, elders will have to find alternative forms of care, placing an even greater demand on the public sector. There will also be fewer children available to provide an intergenerational transfer of funds to needy elders. In theory, if families spend less money rearing children, they should have more disposable income for older age. Unfortunately, neither most elderly nor their baby boom children have high rates of savings.

Context

One point of controversy concerns whether the elderly have an unfair advantage over other age groups in society. This is called the debate over generational equity. In some respects, the introduction of social programs designed to aid the elderly, including Social Security and Medicaid, have helped to improve their economic well-being. In 1989, the elderly had a lower percentage of their population with an income level below the poverty line than did the general population. During that year, 11.9 percent of individuals over the age of 65 had income below the poverty line, compared with 12.8 percent of individuals younger than 65. Social Security benefits, unlike other social programs, have been granted cost-of-living increases that protect fixed incomes from the effects of inflation. Nevertheless, there are still segments of the elderly population that are quite vulnerable to poverty. In 1989, 30.8 percent of black elderly, 20.6 percent of Hispanic elderly, and 9.6 percent of white elderly had incomes below the poverty line.

At the same time that the well-being of many of the elderly has improved, the well-being of American children has declined. The fastest-growing group living in poverty in the United States is children under the age of 18. In 1989, 19.0 percent of children lived in households with incomes below the poverty line. Sociologist and demographer Samuel Preston has argued that the well-being of children has also declined as measured by standardized scholastic tests, rates of suicide and delinquency, and other measures of social well-being.

One reason for the elderly's advantage in social program funding is that the elderly have relatively more political power than do younger age groups. For example, the elderly have high rates of voter participation and are willing to support issues that benefit them directly. Younger and middle-aged adults with children in the household traditionally have low voter turnout rates. There are some, such as Longman, who say that there is evidence that the elderly are getting more than their fair share and that they are not investing in the United States' future. There is a call for rethinking national priorities, giving more resources to children and other age groups. Those on the other side of the generational equity debate, however, have pointed out that the elderly have earned their advantages through a lifetime of hard work and contributions to society.

Bibliography

Bouvier, Leon F., and Carol J. De Vita. *The Baby Boom—Entering Middle Life*. Washington, D.C.: Population Reference Bureau, 1991. This pamphlet produced by the Population Reference Bureau shows what has come of the baby boom in midlife. Includes charts, graphs, and figures to supplement the text.

Easterlin, Richard. *Birth and Fortune: The Impact of Numbers on Personal Welfare*. 2d ed. Chicago: University of Chicago Press, 1987. This book provides a theoretical framework for understanding the role of cohort size on well-being. The second edition includes an update on the fate of the baby boom in midlife.

Longman, Phillip. *Born to Pay: The New Politics of Aging in America*. Boston: Houghton Mifflin, 1987. This somewhat controversial book outlines many of the arguments from the perspective of those arguing for generational equity.

Soldo, Beth, and Emily M. Agree. *America's Elderly*. Washington, D.C.: Population Reference Bureau, 1988. A pamphlet in the Population Bulletin series produced by the Population References Bureau in Washington. It provides a good overview of status of the elderly in society using figures, charts, and graphs to supplement the text.

Torres-Gil, Fernando M. *The New Aging: Politics and Change in America*. New York: Auburn House, 1992. Provides a discussion of relevant political issues concerning aging in society. Contains a clear and well-written explication of the various programs designed for the elderly as well as the impact in changes in aging in the United States on these programs.

Charlotte Chorn Dunham

Cross-References

Age Grading and Age Stratification, 27; Ageism and the Ideology of Ageism, 41; Aging and Retirement, 47; The Aging Process, 53; The Elderly and Institutional Care, 621; The Elderly and the Family, 627; Life Expectancy, 1087; Social Gerontology, 1799; Social Security and Issues of the Elderly, 1832.

HEALTH AND SOCIETY

Type of sociology: Major social institutions
Field of study: Medicine

Health is an integral part of any society. Without adequate levels of health, society's members cannot productively contribute to its growth and development. Different societies emphasize health and health care in different ways. Lesser-developed societies tend to have lower levels of health and less advanced health care systems than more developed societies.

Principal terms
ACCESS: the dimensions that describe a population group's entry and passage through the health care delivery system
GROSS NATIONAL PRODUCT (GNP): the measure of a society's total economic output
INFANT MORTALITY RATE: the rate of death among infants under one year of age
MORBIDITY RATE: the rate of illness in a population
MORTALITY RATE: the rate of death in a population

Overview

The issue of health is central to all societies. Without adequate levels of health in a population, society cannot function. Its members must be healthy in order to be productive and to contribute to society's growth. Different societies, however, place different emphases on health's importance. In large part, a society's emphasis on and philosophy toward its members' level of health is reflected in the ways it provides health and medical care to those members. As economist Victor Fuchs notes in *Who Shall Live?: Health, Economics, and Social Change* (1974), "No country is as healthy as it could be; no country does as much for the sick as it is technically capable of doing." Without adequate health care, an acceptable societal health level is virtually impossible to achieve.

Health is interrelated with other social institutions in a number of ways. If the health level of a society is low, technological development may be thwarted, the economy will be negatively affected, the family structure may undergo tremendous crises, and so on. Similarly, technological growth may produce low health levels as an unwanted and unanticipated side effect. For example, rapid industrial growth may stimulate the economy, but the pollution caused by the industry will have short-term and long-term effects on the health of the population.

Sociologist Otis Dudley Duncan illuminated these interrelationships through his POET model. POET is an acronym for population (including its level of health), organization, environment, and technology. He maintained that a change in any one of the four components has major implications for the other three components. Thus, a change in technology may have an impact on the environment, as in the case of increased air pollution. This negative environmental change will, in turn, affect the population's health by increasing respiratory problems among the population. That change in health status should stimulate a change in the social organization of the society. That is, new organizational arrangements may be developed to counteract the negative effects of the technology on health. Further, new technology may be developed to help improve the society's health levels. A good example of such a development is the invention of automotive catalytic converters.

A society's economic structure and level of development has considerable influence on its health. In general, societies that are underdeveloped (by Western standards) tend to have lower levels of health than more developed societies. Lesser-developed societies also tend to have higher mortality rates among all age groups especially among infants, higher morbidity rates for acute diseases, and a lower level of technological development within their health care systems.

The technological level and the organization of the health care delivery system is also related to a society's emphasis on and philosophy toward health. From a philosophical perspective, how a society develops its health care system is heavily dependent on whether it views health and health care as a right or as a privilege. Medical sociologist William Cockerham, in his book *Medical Sociology* (1989), discusses these two divergent views. Proponents of the "health as privilege" viewpoint maintain that people requiring or desiring health care should have to pay for that care. Those who believe that good health is a right suggest that it is society's responsibility and duty to provide quality health care for any of its members who require treatment. A few have tried to find a middle ground, arguing that good health is a right but good health care is a privilege. The separation of the two concepts, however, is neither logical nor practical.

In addition to society's responsibility, individual responsibility must also be considered. In the long run, it is everyone's responsibility to do their best to maintain their own health. Some have argued that, to the extent that individuals engage in unhealthy behaviors such as smoking, eating high-fat diets, or engaging in unsafe sexual activities, society's responsibilities may be diminished. Such behaviors are very costly to society and to the health care system.

Applications

One application of the relationship between health and society is in the area of comparative health systems. Medical sociologists interested in making cross-cultural comparisons typically analyze and compare the ways different societies view the role of health and how they organize their health care delivery systems to coincide with those views.

Between the 1960's and the mid-1990's, American sociologists and health care experts most often drew comparisons between the American health care system and the system developed in the United Kingdom after World War II. The British system covers the fifty-five million people living in England, Northern Ireland, Scotland, and

Wales. British society and American society have traditionally held differing views of the roles of health and health care. In Great Britain, good health and good health care are treated as rights. In the United States, there has been ongoing debate concerning whether health and health care are rights or privileges, but they have generally been considered privileges.

The health care delivery systems of the United States and the United Kingdom in the mid-twentieth century were organized in very different ways. In the United States, the system revolved around a general capitalistic philosophy consistent with the view of health and health care as privileges. Private insurance companies offered health insurance to those who could afford it or whose employers provided it; people without insurance coverage had to pay medical expenses themselves. The British system, based on a socialistic perspective, provided universal health care to members of its society through the National Health Service (NHS), which dictates the types and quantity of care patients receive. Problems with the American system led to adamant calls for reform in the system by the late 1980's. Among the problems was the fact that some thirty million Americans were uninsured and, since medical costs were continuing to escalate dramatically, could not afford adequate health care. In addition, the United States was devoting roughly 12 percent of its gross national product (GNP) to health care, compared with the 9 percent of the British GNP devoted to health care.

Universal coverage in the British system does not come without costs. In fact, because of the high economic costs of providing health care to a large population, society has made decisions about what types of care will be provided and to whom they will be provided. That is, although all members of society have access to health care under the British system, not everyone has access to the same types of care. To help contain costs, a system of rationing was put into place. For example, the NHS has determined that kidney dialysis will not be provided to patients over fifty-five years of age. In addition, patient choices of physicians and hospitals have been reduced. These restrictions represent a societal consensus on the priority that health has in Great Britain. That consensus, reflective of an underlying social philosophy, has been transformed into a widely supported health policy. The American system, in contrast, maximized patient choice of physician and hospital. Cost containment, however, was approached only through competition, which in practice did little or nothing to control costs.

As physician Steven Jonas points out in *An Introduction to the U.S. Health Care System* (1992), attempts to bring a nationalized system of health care to the United States go back to the late nineteenth century. Each time proposals were offered, however, they were defeated. A major reason for these defeats was that a socialistic, nationalized system seemed contrary to the basic tenets of the United States' capitalistic, laissez-faire philosophy. Constantly increasing costs, however, continued to bring health care reform proposals designed to improve access to the health care system to the forefront of public policy debate. The ideal goal of a health care system would be to maximize the health of the population, maximize people's choice of providers, and maximize quality, while controlling and minimizing costs. In 1992,

Americans elected Bill Clinton president, signaling that public opinion supported broad health care reforms; a central aspect of his campaign was the promise to reform the American health care system to provide coverage for all Americans. In 1993, the Clinton Administration presented its plan to Congress, and congressional debate began on how to revise and implement the plan. Analysis and comparison of the advantages and drawbacks of the health care plans of other countries, notably the United Kingdom and Canada, figured in the formulation of the administration's plan.

Context

Historically, the societal view of health and subsequently of the health care system developed very differently in the United States and in Great Britain. Although many of the United States' social values were derived from Great Britain, the two societies view the role of health differently. In the United States, health's role, and the development of a health care system to maintain an acceptable level of health, unfolded in an unplanned manner. Rooted in the American value system of freedom and equality, a capitalistic economic system based on competition evolved. This competitive philosophy carried over into the health care system. In general, Americans have never been particularly fond of government control. Physicians were not required to undergo a licensing process until the mid 1920's, for example. As a result, health care in the United States grew as a primarily private system without a well-defined public policy to direct it. Even though the degree of government regulation increased dramatically since the 1960's, the system remained in large part a private enterprise.

In the 1980's, the concept of competition was revitalized and more strongly introduced as a means of improving quality and controlling spiraling costs. This was the result of a general societal policy of government nonintervention and increased private sector development. In theory, what works for for-profit corporations such as General Motors should also work for health care. Nearly all experts agree, however, that health care is unlike any other industry. In fact, it has been demonstrated that competition in the health care industry actually increases rather than decreases costs. In 1992, however, American society may have made a major shift in its view of the priority of health and health care by electing a president whose platform included health care reform as a major component.

In the United Kingdom, a societal decision was made in the late 1940's to nationalize the health care system. Prior to the establishment of the NHS, the British system was very similar to the private American system. The NHS was established in 1948 to administer a national system under which medical care is provided without charge to the patient and services are readily available. This step was deemed necessary to broaden societal access to health care and to contain health care costs. Unlike the American approach, physicians are government employees and the hospitals are state institutions.

The nationalized system employed by Great Britain, to maintain cost efficiency, utilizes the general practitioner as the patient's first point of contact. The general practitioner serves a "gatekeeper" function by controlling the patient's further access to more expensive and specialized care. This procedure ensures that patients demonstrate a need for secondary care and that services will not be used frivolously. It also emphasizes less expensive and perhaps more effective preventive care rather than curative care.

In the early 1990's, the United States and South Africa were the only westernized societies lacking some form of universal health care coverage. As Jonas noted in 1992:

> The problems are not those of lack of resources but their misuse and misallocation. Neither providing more money nor artificially capping the amount of money spent is the solution. Rather, the *causes* of the misuse and misallocation must be identified and dealt with.

In other words, to make health care more accessible, society must reprioritize its goals and move health to the forefront. This process took its first steps with the reform plan of the Clinton Administration in 1993.

Bibliography

Aaron, Henry J., and William B. Schwartz. *The Painful Prescription: Rationing Hospital Care*. Washington, D.C.: Brookings Institution, 1984. An excellent examination of the British rationing policy and the possibility of rationing health care in the United States. Aaron and Schwartz tackle a difficult and sensitive social policy question. This book has a good bibliography and is well indexed.

Brown, Phil, ed. *Perspectives in Medical Sociology*. Belmont, Calif.: Wadsworth, 1989. Brown presents forty-five articles on a variety of topics central to the field of medical sociology. The book is broken into five parts and thirteen sections. Not only are most of the traditional aspects of the field covered, but several newer areas of interest are also highlighted. The chapter by Lee comparing the U.S. and Canadian health care systems of the 1980's is relevant, as is the chapter on the Swedish system.

Cockerham, William C. *Medical Sociology*. 4th ed. Englewood Cliffs, N.J.: Prentice-Hall, 1989. A good introductory text overviewing the field of medical sociology. What differentiates this book from other generic medical sociology texts is its public health approach. It has a good chapter on comparative health care systems, although the section on the Soviet Union is no longer relevant. Extensive bibliography.

Fuchs, Victor R. *Who Shall Live?: Health, Economics, and Social Change*. New York: Basic Books, 1974. This is one of the best books available that discusses the choices any society must make in order to provide its members with adequate health levels. Although the work is somewhat dated, American society is still confronted by the dilemmas detailed by Fuchs.

Jonas, Steven. *An Introduction to the U.S. Health Care System*. 3d ed. New York: Springer, 1992. A useful introduction to the way health care was delivered in the United States through the early 1990's. Each chapter ends with two to three pages of relevant references. This book is well indexed and is useful for gaining a better understanding of how the health care system works. The chapter "National Health Insurance" is an interesting examination of the often overlooked history of attempts to introduce a nationalized health plan to the United States.

Raffel, Marshall W., and Norma K. Raffel. *The U.S. Health System: Origins and Functions*. 3d ed. New York: John Wiley & Sons, 1989. This book provides a concise history of the development of health care in the United States. It has no bibliography, but there is a useful appendix that lists the acronyms commonly used in the field.

Starr, Paul. *The Social Transformation of American Medicine*. New York: Basic Books, 1982. Paul Starr's book won the Pulitzer Prize and the C. Wright Mills award for the best book in the field of sociology. It presents a detailed and exhaustive analysis of the historical development of medicine in the United States. It is long and is sometimes a bit difficult to read, but it is an interesting account of the rise of physicians and hospitals in American society.

Ralph Bell

Cross-References

Endemic and Epidemic Diseases, 640; The Environment and Health, 647; The Germ Theory of Medicine, 839; Health Care and Gender, 858; Health Maintenance Organizations, 864; Inequalities in Health, 966; The Medical Profession and the Medicalization of Society, 1159; Medical versus Social Models of Illness, 1172; The Medicalization of Deviance, 1178; National Health Insurance, 1289; Social Epidemiology, 1793.

HEALTH CARE AND GENDER

Type of sociology: Major social institutions
Field of study: Medicine

Sex and gender are determining factors in the ways in which male and female patients are treated by health care providers and in the ways in which they respond to treatment.

Principal terms
DISCRIMINATION: the denial of opportunities and rights to people on the basis of their membership in certain groups
GENDER ROLE: a set of behavioral expectations for males or females
MORBIDITY: illness, injury, or disability; any detectable departure from well-being
MORTALITY: death, generally on a large scale
SEXISM: individuals' prejudicial attitudes and discriminatory behavior toward persons of a particular sex; institutional practices that subordinate persons of a particular sex
SOCIAL SUPPORT: instrumental, informational, and emotional support that a person receives from others

Overview

The issue of health care and gender is interesting for various reasons: Women and men differ in their rates of morbidity and mortality; health risks and enhancement may affect men and women differently; men and women differ psychosocially, in their control beliefs and in their social support, and these differences affect health outcomes; and there are definite differences in the ways in which men and women are treated by health care providers.

Psychologists Judith Rodin and Jeannette R. Ickovics have given an excellent overview of sex differences in mortality rates in their article "Women's Health: Review and Research Agenda as We Approach the Twenty-first Century" (1990). According to their research, for every 100 female fetuses that are conceived, approximately 127 male fetuses are conceived, yet more men than women die at every age level between birth and death. For this reason, among those individuals who live to age 100, there are five women for every man. Some researchers explain this difference biologically, by pointing to either genetic differences or the beneficial effects of certain hormones. Others argue that this sex difference in mortality is caused by gender differences in lifestyle, such as differences in the levels of smoking and the drinking of alcohol.

Despite this advantage in mortality for women, women have a morbidity rate that is higher than that of men, according to epidemiologist David L. Wingard (1984). Most categories of self-reported chronic and acute conditions are more common for women than for men, except for the category of injuries. Hypertension is more common among men before age sixty and among women after age sixty. Women are more likely than men to be obese and to have diabetes, anemia, respiratory problems, gastrointestinal problems, rheumatoid arthritis, lupus, poor vision, and dental problems. Women have higher rates of restricted activity (such as days of disability, lost work days, and days spent in the hospital) and more physician visits than men have. There are several explanations for these sex differences in morbidity. One explanation is that women have higher poverty rates than do men and therefore have poorer health because of their poorer socioeconomic status. Women also tend to live longer than men do, which may contribute to women's higher morbidity rate. Furthermore, women tend to experience more stress than men do, which may also have a negative effect on their health.

It is interesting that the mortality advantage for women has decreased in recent years. This development may be linked to the fact that women's substance abuse rates increased during these years. The smoking rates for men and women are converging (the rate for women was once much lower than that for men), which explains the narrowing gap between men's and women's lung cancer rates. Furthermore, alcohol abuse has increased dramatically in women in recent years. Another factor that contributes to increased mortality rates for women is women's increased participation in the workforce. It should be understood that women's employment per se is not an indicator of impaired health. On the contrary, epidemiologist Lois M. Verbrugge has shown that women with less or no employment have greater rates of health problems than do employed women. It is difficult to determine whether unemployment causes bad health or whether persons with bad health are less likely to seek or keep employment. In any case, it is clear that employment has definite advantages for women, such as financial remuneration and increased self-esteem, control, and social support. Health problems occur in employed women when they believe that their jobs fail to utilize them fully (in terms of hours worked, wages paid, or utilization of skills) or when they have a negative attitude toward the work that they perform.

Gender differences in psychosocial factors such as control beliefs and social support are also related to women's health. The fact that women tend to believe that they have less control over their lives than men do has a negative effect on women's health. Sociologists Ronald Kessler, Jane McLeod, and Elaine Wethington have suggested that the reason that women's rate of depression is twice that of men may be that women are part of a larger social support network and thus are more likely to be burned out by caring for and sharing with others.

Gender differences in health treatment are also striking. Rodin and Ickovics report, for example, that 70 percent of all psychoactive medications (such as antidepressants and tranquilizers) are prescribed to women and that two-thirds of all surgical procedures performed in the United States are performed on women. The most frequent kinds of surgery for women are obstetrical and gynecological surgeries, with cesarean sections being performed most frequently and hysterectomies being performed second most frequently. Every day in the United States, 1,700 hysterectomies are performed.

Physicians Karen J. Carlson, David H. Nichols, and Isaac Schiff point to the fact that by age sixty, more than one-third of the women in the United States have undergone hysterectomies. Hospital costs for this procedure exceed $5 billion annually. It is interesting to note that hysterectomy rates differ by country (the United States has the highest rate, which is about six times as high as those of such countries as Norway, Sweden, and England) and by region (the highest rates in the United States are in the South and the Midwest). In addition, these rates are a function of a physician's gender (male gynecologists perform more hysterectomies than female gynecologists do) and the patient's ethnic and racial background (African American women are more likely than European American women to have hysterectomies). Research shows that alternative treatments exist for most problems that are treated by means of hysterectomies.

Interestingly enough, women and minorities seem to receive fewer diagnostic tests and surgeries than men do when it comes to technological interventions for coronary artery disease or transplants. A survey conducted by the American Medical Association Council on Ethical and Judicial Affairs in 1993 found that women between the ages of forty-six and sixty who undergo dialysis are half as likely as men to receive a kidney transplant. For patients with smoking habits, physicians were twice as likely to order lung cancer tests for men. Men are 6.5 times more likely to be referred for cardiac catheterization, although men are only three times more likely than women to have heart disease. Women are also more likely to have their heart pains attributed to emotional problems. The fact that women are treated differently from European American males might be because most physicians are European American males. Stereotypes of women may be preventing women from receiving optimal health care.

The underrepresentation of women in the medical profession—especially in some of the more prestigious specialties such as surgery—needs to be rectified because it definitely affects the quality of treatment that women receive. The gender of the physician clearly affects the physician-patient relationship. Research has shown that female physicians spend more time than male physicians do with each patient and are more likely to be informed about the emotional and social aspects of their patients' lives that may affect their patients' health. Furthermore, a patient's willingness to comply with treatment recommendations is a function of the quality of the physician-patient relationship. This fact has been discussed extensively in the literature on the issues of health care and gender. Health psychologist Robin DiMatteo explores these issues in detail in *The Psychology of Health, Illness, and Medical Care* (1991).

Applications

Understanding the issues of health care and gender can be crucial in coping with new trends in medicine in general and with women's health issues specifically. According to DiMatteo, there are three general trends in medicine that must be considered in any discussion of the issues of health care and gender. The first trend is the rising costs of health care, which must be curbed. In this context, it seems significant to conduct sound health services research that will show where costs can be cut (for example, by avoiding unnecessary hysterectomies and cesarean sections) and where preventive treatment for women can be more cost effective. The second trend is that the pattern of diseases is shifting away from infectious diseases toward lifestyle-related diseases such as coronary artery disease and strokes. Educating women about the negative effects of smoking, alcohol abuse, and high-fat/low-fiber diets is a key preventive measure that will make it possible to reduce the rate of lifestyle-related diseases in women. Such education might have a great impact not only on women's health but also on family health, because data show that women are still the primary socializing agents for children and do most of the cooking in households. The third trend is that there is a growing aging population in the United States. By the year 2050, one-fifth of the U.S. population will be more than sixty-five years old, and because of the gender differences in mortality rates, a large percentage of these people will be women. Rodin and Ickovics point to the fact that it is important to understand the special issues that concern older women, such as the increased rate of Alzheimer's disease in women and the high rate at which older women take many kinds of medications. Furthermore, ageist and sexist attitudes are likely to affect the well-being of these women and the way in which they are treated in the health care system. The changing pattern of disease away from infectious diseases toward life-style-related diseases and the changing technology of the medical field must also be considered in discussions of the health care issues of older women.

It is also important to understand gender differences in psychosocial factors such as social status, control beliefs, and social support networks. On the average, women tend to have a lower social status than men, which might be related to their insufficient financial resources. Women also tend to have a lower sense of control over their lives than men have, which seems to decrease their ability to cope with stress. Women also have larger social support networks, which may drain their energies and burn them out more easily. Research shows that these psychosocial factors tend to affect a person's health because they are related to a person's lifestyle, which affects lifestyle-related diseases such as coronary artery disease and strokes.

Among the specific issues concerning women and health are the growing percentage of women who are diagnosed as having AIDS; the effects of specific health treatments of women, such as estrogen replacement therapy; and the use of new reproductive technologies. Rodin and Ickovics point out that the growth rate of AIDS is 2.5 higher among women than among men and that women die more quickly than men after they are diagnosed as having AIDS. It seems that research designed to study the specific issues of women who have AIDS has been neglected. Another interesting area of women's health care is that of reproductive technologies. Legal, moral, and ethical questions are being raised concerning such new technologies as in vitro fertilization, embryo transfer, artificial donor insemination, and the genetic testing of fetuses. As further progress is made in technology and in the basic and applied sciences, new ethical issues will certainly arise.

Research on gender differences in morbidity, the degree to which drugs are prescribed, and the degree to which diagnostic tests are ordered and surgical procedures are performed clearly indicates the importance of understanding the issues of gender and health in more detail.

Context

Health care and gender can be discussed in the context of the interconnectedness of mind, body, and health. Despite progress in medical research, it seems obvious that the close interaction between body and mind needs to be considered in discussions of health issues. In *Reactions to Critical Life Events: A Social Psychological Analysis* (1991), Marita Inglehart points to the significance of understanding how human beings react to stressful events in their lives and what determines the way in which they react to these events. Stress and the way in which it is handled can be a critical factor in a person's health. Furthermore, being sick and being treated is in itself stressful. It is accepted in stress research that stress is not only a function of objective circumstances but also a function of the way in which people think about a stressful event. There are clear gender differences both in the objective circumstances in which men and women live (such as income levels and levels of poverty) and in the beliefs and values that men and women are socialized to hold. Women's self-esteem tends to be lower than that of men, and women on the whole seem to have more external and fewer internal control beliefs. These beliefs and values determine the way in which people approach their lives in general and stressful life events in particular; they are thus significant determinants of a person's psychological health as well as physical health.

Providing health care to men and women is clearly dependent on the relationship between health care providers and patients. Health care providers cannot treat a medical problem alone—they must consider the fact that the problem is part of a person's life. Unless this fact is accepted, serious problems such as increasing rates of malpractice suits and a high rate of patient noncompliance (for example, missing appointments, not taking prescribed medications, not following medical advice) are likely to arise.

Furthermore, health care and gender is also a topic that can easily be related to sexism and gender discrimination in general. Women are still a minority in the medical profession, especially in such prestigious specialties as that of surgery. Female health care providers still face significant individual and institutional sexism. For patients, it is important to relate health issues to discrimination at the workplace and in families, and to the stress that women experience. It is also important to understand that there are biases against women in the health care system that stand in the way of the provision of optimal medical care for women.

Bibliography

Carlson, Karen J., David H. Nichols, and Isaac Schiff. "Indications for Hysterectomy." *The New England Journal of Medicine* 328 (March 25, 1993): 856-860. This review article provides an excellent overview of research into the reasons for and the effectiveness of hysterectomies.

DiMatteo, M. Robin. *The Psychology of Health, Illness, and Medical Care.* Pacific

Grove, Calif.: Brooks/Cole, 1991. This book provides an excellent overview of health psychology and gives a clear impression of the issues that face medical practitioners.

Kessler, Ronald C., Jane D. McLeod, and Elaine Wethington. "The Costs of Caring." In *Social Support: Theory, Research, and Applications*, edited by Irwin G. Sarason and Barbara R. Sarason. Boston: Martinus Nijhof, 1985. Describes very carefully the costs of giving social support for women.

Koblinsky, Marge, Judith Timyan, and Jill Gay, eds. *The Health of Women: A Global Perspective*. Boulder, Colo.: Westview Press, 1993. This book is useful because of its international approach to issues related to women's health care.

Muller, Charlotte Feldman. *Health Care and Gender*. New York: Russell Sage Foundation, 1990. An in-depth study of the ways in which women are treated by the medical community.

Rodin, Judith, and Jeannette R. Ickovics. "Women's Health: Review and Research Agenda as We Approach the Twenty-first Century." *American Psychologist* 45 (September, 1990): 1018-1034. An excellent review article about women's health issues.

Verbrugge, Lois M. "The Twain Meet: Empirical Explanations of Sex Differences in Health and Mortality." *Journal of Health and Social Behavior* 30 (September, 1989): 282-304. An excellent, updated explanation of gender differences in health and mortality.

Wingard, David L. "The Sex Differential in Morbidity, Mortality, and Life Style." *Annual Review of Public Health* 5 (1984): 433-458. A fine review article about mortality, morbidity, and lifestyle factors as they relate to gender.

Marita Inglehart

Cross-References

Gender and Religion, 813; Gender Inequality: Analysis and Overview, 820; Gender Inequality: Biological Determinist Views, 826; Health and Society, 852; Medical Sociology, 1166; Medical versus Social Models of Illness, 1172; Women in the Medical Profession, 2191; The Women's Movement, 2196.

HEALTH MAINTENANCE ORGANIZATIONS

Type of sociology: Major social institutions
Field of study: Medicine

Changes in modern medicine have led to the development of several types of health maintenance organizations (HMOs), all of which are prepaid, comprehensive coverage, group medical plans. HMOs became popular because they are less expensive than traditional health insurance plans, but they have raised concerns that they provide depersonalized care.

Principal terms

CAPITATION: actuarially based payments to caregivers based on projected numbers of patients rather than on actual numbers or services rendered

COINSURANCE: extra costs paid by patients according to predetermined schedules; often included are costs of care outside HMO service areas and mental health care costs

COMPREHENSIVE CARE: health coverage that includes almost all health problems likely to be encountered by patients

COPAYMENT: a small payment charged to offset paperwork and other special costs (such as for prescriptions)

FEE-FOR-REIMBURSEMENT BILLING: a payment method in which a physician is paid by an HMO for services at a date after the services were rendered

FEE-FOR-SERVICE BILLING: traditional billing for medical service at the time when it is rendered

GATEKEEPER: a physician who refers patients to specialists, usually in an individual practice association, lowering HMO costs by preventing unneeded visits to specialists

HEALTH MAINTENANCE ORGANIZATION (HMO): a type of prepaid, comprehensive, coordinated coverage group medical plan

NEGOTIATED FEE: a physician payment in which health care providers work for a discounted portion of their usual fees in exchange for an HMO-guaranteed patient base

PRIMARY CARE PHYSICIAN: a physician seen when medical care is first sought; such physicians serve as gatekeepers, sending patients on to specialists only when necessary

Overview

The rising cost of medical care since the 1960's has led to significant alterations of the methodology of health care delivery. Prime among these is the development of the health maintenance organization (HMO), which has generated several topics that merit discussion: changing philosophies of patient treatment and the patient-caregiver relationship, altered delivery of treatment and means of billing/payment of medical costs, and variations in the ownership and staffing of caregiver organizations. The first thing to consider is the definition of the health maintenance organization. Defining the HMO is difficult because numerous different health care entities now fit under this umbrella term. Because of the resultant uncertainty, HMO has come to refer to any prepaid group medical plan that offers comprehensive coverage. Hence, there are many types of HMOs, including staff-based HMOs, group practice HMOs, individual practice association HMOs, and preferred provider organization HMOs. Many HMOs are owned by large corporations (such as insurance companies) whose main interest is not medicine and whose executive staff is not composed of physicians.

The origin of the HMO is stated by some to be in the English health insurance clubs formed during the eighteenth century by workers who wanted health care for their families. Such plans also arose in the United States during the Great Depression; they acted as "banks" in which money for medical costs was saved up. The monthly fees of such organizations were reasonable and reflected the low medical costs of the times.

Since the 1960's, however, a number of factors have driven the cost of health care, including membership in HMOs, sharply and continuously upward. One of the factors is the expensive advanced technology now used to save or prolong lives. As in any business or service, such costs are passed on to the consumer. Data indicate that the average amount each American spends (or has spent by others in his or her behalf) was about two thousand dollars in the early 1990's. Much debate has ensued regarding the sociological and political ramifications of high health care costs; no one had been able to find a realistic way to halt the spiraling costs. The problem eventually led to the call for national health care mandated by the federal government.

The evolution of these changes can also be related to changing personnel composition. For example, in the initial decade of the twentieth century, the first modern HMO-like organizations were modest in cost. Part of the reason was technological, but another important aspect was the fact that hospitals were subsidized by charitable donations and did not rely only on patient fees to meet expenses. The Great Depression changed that, as donations slowed to a trickle. Hospital costs rose quickly, a matter of the institutions' survival.

At that time, HMO-like organizations arose in Texas and California. In the mid-1930's the Kaiser Permanente network became the forerunner of today's HMO; then the American Medical Association helped to establish Blue Cross plans. By the late 1950's, a number of established HMOs were giving to patients quality service at low cost. In 1973, the federal government passed an HMO act that standardized the quality of HMOs. Its consequences also included higher costs.

HMOs grew in size and complexity; they required more staff and many new kinds of staff. By the mid-1980's, more than 10 percent of Americans belonged to HMOs, making large nonmedical companies eager to become involved with HMOs. Their entry and the increasing numbers of Americans in HMOs has raised the price of health care/HMOs still further, because still more layers of personnel, unrelated to the providing of health care, are employed. Furthermore, such corporations seek to obtain the largest profit possible for their stockholders. That fact further diminishes the cost effectiveness of HMOs, in their many forms, and raises social issues including the questions of how to ensure fair pricing and good consumer treatment, and how to avoid impersonal health care. A related problem is that the high cost of group health plans adds to layoffs of permanent and full-time employees. The high cost of health care is thus a factor in the trimming of the labor force that occurs in an unfavorable economic environment. This unemployment causes further upheaval in the lives of people who must then meet their own high health care costs. Such problems have led to the question of the role that government will play in health insurance, including discussions of the need to provide universal care for the poor and the unemployed as well as the merits of socializing medicine.

Applications

A health maintenance organization is a managed health care plan that provides prepaid, comprehensive, coordinated medical services to members enrolled voluntarily. There are a number of different types of HMO. One is the simple, staff-based HMO. Such an HMO is a fair-sized health center that provides its subscribers with most of their health care under one roof. The first HMOs of this sort were modest in size and were nonprofit organizations (after operating costs and salaries were paid). All aspects of the operation of such an HMO—diagnosis, testing, treatment, administration, billing, and payment—are carried out at that one site. The members of the HMO staff are constant, and all operate out of that site. Almost all staff members work full time, and the staff network is both tight and carefully organized in order to keep within the budget that accrues from patient payments. No outside patients are normally seen.

In a few cases, special services unavailable at the HMO must be obtained. The HMO contracts with outside providers to perform the services. Such services are rendered at no extra immediate cost to the patient, within a ceiling built into the monthly cost of membership. Within the framework of such an HMO, any member—but no outsiders—can call for a routine appointment and obtain one quickly. Each member has a regular physician, and the only fee charged for a visit is a copayment of a few dollars to cover the cost of the paperwork it engenders.

One disadvantage, according to some observers, is the fact that an office visit typically begins with a physician's assistant, who can handle routine tasks, followed by a visit with the primary care physician (the patient's usual HMO physician) if needed. After that, some patients are routed to the HMO's specialists; from there, a few go to external providers of services unavailable at the HMO. This managed handling, often called screening, is necessary so that the HMO, designed to be a very efficient organization, can operate within its budget. In some cases a patient must pay a portion of expenses incurred for special treatments, an expenditure that is called coinsurance. This is unusual, occurring only after the treatment limits outlined to patients before they join the HMO are reached. All in all, the staff-based HMO is very efficient, and this efficiency makes its costs relatively modest. Costs in staff-based HMOs are rising, however, because the need for a sound economic base has made many of them seek outside investors and for-profit status.

A second type of managed prepaid comprehensive health care service, thus also an HMO, is the individual practice association (IPA). These associations, larger than staff-based HMOs, are composed of physicians who are not willing to relinquish their private practices. Often, an IPA is composed of all the physicians in a given city or another geographic area. Physicians joining this type of HMO gain a guaranteed patient base beyond their private practices because all patients belonging to an IPA must use member physicians. In addition, the physicians involved obtain a solid referral network of associated colleagues. The IPA also handles all the billing paperwork of associated physicians.

Additional costs for patients may arise because IPA members must maintain their own malpractice insurance and place a percentage of all medical fees into a risk pool that helps the IPA to be sure of covering the costs of all insured patients. When unneeded, this money is returned to the physicians at a later date. In addition, paperwork must be sent to the IPA for reimbursement, a process called fee-for-reimbursement billing. Sometimes, to avoid this process and to simplify the work of the physician's office staff, capitation is used. Here, a member physician receives an overall monthly fee that is based on expected patient number rather than on the number of patients actually seen. Aside from slightly increased monthly payments to IPAs, patients rarely see differences between them and staff-based HMOs.

Many patients enjoy IPAs because they visit the office of an individual physician and feel that these physicians are less impersonal than those at a staff-based facility. No central facility is involved for patient treatment; patients also go to area hospitals. Generally, the primary care physicians in IPAs act as gatekeepers, determining needs for specialists and deciding to whom to send patients. This increases the efficiency of an IPA. The most clearly organized central aspect of the IPA is the administrative staff, which handles claims, billing, and all other management functions. The costs of this entity are reported to be offset by the lack of need for the medical center complex used by staff-based HMOs.

A third important type of HMO is the preferred provider organization (PPO). It differs from an IPA in allowing subscribers to use nonmember physicians if they are willing to pay a portion of the physician's fees. This portion is based on a sliding scale determined by the PPO. PPOs are large entities that are not often physician-owned. One characteristic that clearly differentiates them is their use of negotiated fees for nonmember physicians: The physician agrees to a fee that is somewhat lower than usual and bills the difference to the patient. This method, balance billing, costs the patient more but allows freedom to choose nonmember physicians.

Another aspect of PPOs is that fees delivered to physicians are only 80 percent to 90 percent of billings and, unlike IPAs, the fee pool is not returned to them. Rather, it goes to the PPO management. Advantages of PPOs to physicians include simplification of their bookkeeping. A second characteristic of PPOs is very strict claims monitoring to assure that medical treatment is justified. PPOs are now successful parts of many insurance companies. The large size of PPOs and their ability to decide retroactively whether to pay a bill (and how much of it to pay) are viewed as drawbacks by some consumers. Companies often deem PPOs their best option, however, because group health care costs are often much lower than those associated with staff-based HMOs or IPAs.

A final aspect of HMOs that should be noted here is that big business is continuing to buy or take over HMOs and to develop them into multiservice systems that embrace aspects of a number of HMO types as well as other types of health insurance plans. Such organizations are changing the shape of health care; they may, for example, vary their operations from locale to locale in order to market their services to the largest possible number of medical consumers. They are also purchasing medical supply companies and other components of the medical industry.

Context

Both the rising cost of medical care and the increased impersonality of today's caregivers in both traditional practice and HMOs are seen by health care consumers as important social problems. This problem could, at least in theory, be addressed relatively easily were physicians simply to decide to give more thought to patients' emotional and psychological needs and improve caregiver-patient rapport. Some observers believe that, as times change and competition increases, physicians—including HMO physicians—will move to revive some aspects of the 1950's model of the physician, the family doctor who offers advice and acts as a health mentor.

Much more difficult to solve, and fundamentally much more worrisome, is the issue of spiraling medical costs. Sharply rising medical costs have not been held down by health maintenance organizations, which were first conceived as nonprofit organizations that could provide good patient care at a modest cost. A major part of the problem has been the growth and amalgamation of HMOs, their widespread switch to for-profit status, and their purchase by large corporations whose main interest is profitability, not medicine.

In addition, the cost of HMO memberships has risen because of advanced medical technology. Despite the fact that more lives are saved by, and prolonged by, modern medical practices, high medical costs have caused serious social problems. For example, they add to the list of reasons that employers lay off permanent employees and hire more temporary workers, for whom they do not feel obligated to provide health care. Serious economic dislocation results, including the added problem that the employees who have been let go must suddenly attempt to pay for health care for themselves and their families. More optimistic observers believe that these problems, too, will be solved, either as the result of competition among providers for a patient base or as the government steps in with mandated health care for all Americans. The role of the government in the provision of health care became a major policy debate in the early 1990's; the extent to which the government should be involved and the type of program it should implement were heatedly discussed. All sides expressed the desire that any program would include codes ensuring fair medical pricing and fair coverage for the poor, the elderly, and the unemployed.

Bibliography

Bloom, Jill. *HMOs: What They Are, How They Work, and Which Is Best for You.* Tucson, Ariz.: Body Press, 1987. This book covers the main types of HMOs in detail, including costs, memberships, similarities, differences, and advantages/disadvantages. A glossary, a guide to HMO shopping, a resource directory, and a national HMO directory are added useful features.

Leutz, Walter N., et al. *Changing Health Care for an Aging Society: Planning for the Social Health Maintenance Organization.* Lexington, Mass.: Lexington Books, 1985. This book deals with an emerging topic, the development of a social HMO to deal with an aging society. This issue includes a number of important facets related to health care as it is handled by the government, HMOs, and other parts of the biomedical infrastructure.

McCuen, Gary E., ed. *Health Care and Human Values: Ideas in Conflict.* Hudson, Wis.: G. E. McCuen, 1993. Addresses many topics associated with modern health care. Coverage includes a health care overview, medical care and social justice, health care options, the rationing of health care, and global health care. Numerous important issues, including those related to HMOs, are covered.

Mayer, Thomas R., and Gloria G. Mayer. *The Health Insurance Alternative: A Complete Guide to Health Maintenance Organizations.* New York: Perigee Books, 1984. This book addresses the definition of an HMO, HMOs versus standard health insurance, costs and charges, what HMOs offer, choosing and using an HMO, HMO supplemental features, PPOs, and the future of HMOs. A glossary and a bibliography are included.

Williams, Stephen J., and Sandra J. Guerra. *Health Care Services in the 1990's: A Consumers Guide.* New York: Praeger, 1991. This comprehensive book addresses the topics indicated in its title. HMOs are not the main thrust, but they are covered usefully, compared with competitive systems, and evaluated. Useful information sources appear in the appendices.

Sanford S. Singer

Cross-References

The Graying of America, 846; Health and Society, 852; Health Care and Gender, 858; Inequalities in Health, 966; Medical Sociology, 1166; The Institution of Medicine, 1185; National Health Insurance, 1289.

HIGH CULTURE VERSUS POPULAR CULTURE

Type of sociology: Culture
Field of study: Components of culture

Social scientists debate the distinction between culture for the elites and culture for the masses. Some sociologists argue that social class determines cultural preferences, while others argue that the media dissolve class-based distinctions between high and popular culture and create "media cultures" instead. Another point of debate among sociologists is the extent to which mass culture is detrimental to the public that consumes it and to society as a whole.

Principal terms
> FOLK CULTURE: art, literature, and other symbolic products created by and primarily consumed by the common people or working class
> FRANKFURT SCHOOL: a group of 1930's German theorists and critics who developed the Marxist mass culture critique
> HIGH CULTURE: the symbolic products preferred by and designed for the well-educated elite; also refers to the style and feelings of the elite who choose these products
> KITSCH: a pejorative term for mass culture
> MASS CULTURE: a pejorative term for the cultural products designed solely for mass consumption
> POPULAR CULTURE: a positive term for mass-produced or mass-disseminated cultural products
> RECORDED CULTURE: the products of a culture that exist either as artifacts (such as films, television shows, and diaries) or acts (such as musical performances and exhibitions)
> TASTE CULTURE: the values of a given segment of society and the products and media that express these values
> TASTE PUBLICS: the creators or users of various cultural products who make similar choices in culture products and share similar aesthetic values

Overview

Since the 1930's, most discussions of recorded culture have distinguished between culture for the elites, often termed "high" culture, and culture for the mass public, called "popular" or "mass" culture. By and large, sociologists have contended that the characteristics of different social classes determine their cultural preferences. Things such as wealth, education, and upbringing are associated with preference for high culture—cultural products designed for, patronized by, and often controlled by a small number of society's elite. Those who possess little or no education and wealth typically consume popular culture, culture created by the economic elite—for example, the American film, television, and recording industries—for the mass public. Neither high nor popular culture, however, should be confused with folk culture, a type of symbolic expression created by and designed for a particular taste culture. Appalachian folk music and American Indian pottery are two examples of folk culture.

American sociologists Herbert Gans, Ian Angus, and Suht Jhally and French sociologist Pierre Bourdieu have asserted that high culture and popular culture express different values and represent different aesthetic standards. Angus and Jhally claim that there is a distinct separation between high and popular culture, that the two are consumed by different classes, and that the prestige of each class is attached to its culture. Bourdieu also views cultural preferences as being determined by social class background. He argues that cultural knowledge, which he calls cultural "capital," enhances and reinforces social class status. Gans contends that each social class constitutes a different taste public whose members have similar values or preferences for cultural content, but he argues that the distinctions between high and popular culture have been exaggerated and that, in fact, American society is made up of five different "taste publics," each with its own aesthetic standards and cultural products.

Although sociologists have tended to agree that distinctions between high and popular taste cultures are class-based, they have often disagreed on the impact of mass culture on its audience, on high cultural production, and upon society as a whole. Some conservative critics claim that mass culture is profane and dehumanizing and that it encroaches upon high cultural production. Such critics call for the reestablishment and protection of high culture for elite consumption. Other conservative critics maintain that high culture, supported primarily by such organizations as the National Endowment for the Arts (NEA), is controlled by special-interest groups who impose their own ideology on cultural production. These critics assert that government should not be the primary support for art production in the United States. By contrast, such radical critics as Dwight MacDonald and Clement Greenberg agree with the conservative assessment of mass culture as destructive and dehumanizing, but they focus on mass culture's negative impact on those who consume it and upon society as a whole rather than on the high culture upon which it encroaches.

Radical critics who share this orientation often call for what Gans terms "cultural mobility": raising the masses' tastes through education, opportunity, and economic redistribution. Cultural mobility, it is argued, would free the public from the demagoguery of the economic elite and provide them the opportunity to appreciate high culture fare. In the middle of the debate stand moderate or liberal critics such as American sociologists David Riesman and Gans, who take the position that popular culture (a less pejorative term than "mass culture") is harmful neither to the people who consume it nor to society as a whole. They declare that all taste cultures are of equal worth if they meet the needs of taste publics. These liberal sociologists therefore call for the reinvigoration of various taste cultures or subcultures.

In the late 1980's, many sociologists and communication scholars began challenging the validity of the class-based distinction between high culture and popular culture. Viewing this classification as increasingly arbitrary, some critics claim that modern mass media, particularly television, create "media cultures" accessible to multiple taste publics. In other words, mass media break down the traditional class and education barriers among taste cultures. Some theorists even suggest that "lifestyles," indicated by media consumption patterns, might be a more reliable indicator than social class of American tastes.

Most sociologists and media critics agree that high culture has not disappeared. Many, however, claim that high culture has become relegated to a shrinking avant-garde and academic elite who produce art more often for themselves than for a tangible and well-defined taste public.

Applications

Numerous public policy alternatives are suggested by the high culture-popular culture debate, but attempts to set policy in the area of cultural programming are often problematic. As Gans points out, "The mere attempt to decide what culture is or is not in the public interest raises the possibility of cultural dictatorship." With this in mind, it should be noted that the policy a critic advocates depends almost entirely on whether the critic accepts the high culture-popular culture distinction and on whether the critic views popular culture as detrimental to society. For those who accept the distinction between high culture and popular culture, there are two primary policy alternatives, cultural mobility and subcultural programming.

Cultural mobility advocates increasing the availability of high culture to the general public and raising the public's taste level. This approach, Gans has written, "assumes that if every American had access to income, education, and other background characteristics of the upper-middle class, many although not all would choose upper-middle or even high culture content." Although mass culture critics such as Dwight MacDonald prefer the reinvigoration of folk art and avant-garde art, most mass culture critics tend to advocate a policy of cultural mobility. They acknowledge, however, that cultural mobility would require considerable redistribution of income and educational opportunity and that this approach assumes that people can and should change their cultural tastes.

Advocates of popular culture such as Gans prefer subcultural programming over cultural mobility. Although Gans acknowledges that high cultures may be more comprehensive, may provide more information, and may draw upon more complex understandings of, for example, aesthetics, philosophy, and social reality, this alone is not a sufficient basis for policy decisions.

Gans, like many liberal or moderate critics, advocates subcultural programming as an alternative to cultural mobility. Subcultural programming involves "providing cultural content to express and satisfy the specific standards of every taste public"; Gans argues that this approach would encourage all taste cultures. The benefit of subcultural programming is that it allows taste publics to find cultural products that speak to their needs and desires. This increases their aesthetic satisfaction, makes culture more relevant to their lives, and adds to cultural diversity and an enriched society.

Critics of subcultural programming point out that it supports the mass media's insistence that they are "giving the people what they want" and thus justifies inferior culture. Others argue that subcultural programming is still mass-produced and mass-disseminated and is the expression neither of the individual artist nor of the people themselves. Finally, a major argument against subcultural programming is that it would further stratify society and "ghettoize" various taste publics.

Those critics who do not accept the class-based distinction between high and popular culture suggest other policy alternatives. Sociologist and media critic Diana Crane, for example, argues that, instead of using the terms "high" and "popular" culture, "It is more useful to think in terms of culture produced by national culture industries and culture produced in urban subcultures, including various art worlds and ethnic subcultures." Crane distinguishes among core cultural industries, peripheral cultural industries, and urban cultures. Core cultural industries, such as television, film, and major newspapers, attract taste publics that cut across class lines. Peripheral culture industries, including books, magazines, radio, music, and other newspapers, also cut across class lines and are best defined in terms of "lifestyles" rather than social class. Urban cultures, such as concerts, exhibits, fairs, and parades, are the only cultures still definable and stratified in terms of social class.

Crane argues that with the exception of urban culture, the mass media is the driving force behind taste cultures. An implicit public policy alternative, therefore, is governmental encouragement of mass media industries to provide diverse cultural fare. Sociologist have argued that there are four possible ways government can assist culture: as "patron," as "market manipulator," as "regulator," or as "impresario." With the exception of 1930's New Deal policies that focused on government as impresario and patron, the U.S. government has historically preferred the roles of market manipulator and regulator. Although many European countries, such as Great Britain and France, have often acted in all four capacities, there is evidence that they are also embracing a more market-driven approach to cultural policy.

Context

The nature of mass culture and its impact on those who consume it has been the subject of continued debate among social scientists. The subject was the focus of extensive discussion in the 1930's by sociologists of the "Frankfurt school" in Germany. Neo-Marxist members of the Frankfurt school such as Theodore Adorno, Max Horkheimer, and Herbert Marcuse argued for the superiority of high culture and against the decadence of mass culture. Mass culture, they claimed, reflected the values of the economic elite by providing undifferentiated standardized products that offered the illusion of novelty while keeping the masses indulged, ignorant, and pacified. Mass culture was accepted by the public because the dehumanizing nature of a technologically saturated society made them unable to appreciate more sophisticated forms of culture.

These ideas, which came to be known as the mass culture critique, had their origins in the changing structure of Western society after the Industrial Revolution. The rise of a middle class with disposable income and an increasing amount of leisure time allowed for wide-scale consumption of the arts. This demand for art created a mass culture market, weakened the importance of high cultural production, diminished the role of the individual artist and original art, and invited a critical exploration of the impact and effect of mass culture in society.

The German mass culture critique strongly influenced American sociology in the 1950's. After World War II, many Frankfurt school theorists emigrated to the United States, where their ideas continued to influence the American high culture-mass culture debate, particularly the ideas of American writers such as Clement Greenberg, Irving Howe, Dwight MacDonald, and Bernard Rosenberg.

American mass cultural theorists in the 1950's continued to assume that mass culture was detrimental to the public, was homogeneous, and expressed a monolithic ideology marketed to an undifferentiated audience. The critique argued that culture was ideological and that cultural products shaped social and political consciousness and behavior. Mass culture, according to MacDonald, "is imposed from above. It is fabricated by technicians hired by businessmen; its audiences are passive consumers, their participation limited to the choice between buying and not buying. The Lords of *kitsch*, in short, exploit the cultural needs of the masses in order to make a profit and/or to maintain their class rule."

After World War II, a number of events in American society occurred that changed both the nature of cultural consumption and the validity of the mass culture critique. In 1992, American sociologist Diana Crane suggested that in the second half of the twentieth century, the prestige of high culture continued to diminish, while the impact of popular culture increased. Additionally, the boundaries between high and popular culture began to disappear. After World War II, as elites lost control over the production of high culture, they were replaced by government and corporate sponsors who programmed for a wider and more diverse audience. Additionally, the increased education level of the "baby boom" generation expanded the potential taste range of the middle class, while the growing number of cultural products available from expanded mass-media markets added to the potential diversity of taste publics. As a result, class-based taste publics have become harder to discern. Crane claims that "lifestyle" identification, exhibited by product and mass-media consumption patterns, has become a better characterization of American tastes than social class.

Beginning in the mid-1950's, a new understanding of mass culture and the high culture-popular culture distinction also emerged. In 1964, Marshal McLuhan, recognizing the enormous importance and impact of television as a relatively new form of cultural expression, argued that the medium of television affected the viewer more than the actual content of the transmission. The "medium," according to McLuhan, was "the message." Others have extended McLuhan's ideas to explain why television, unlike print, does not require high levels of education or specialized linguistic and aesthetic codes and is therefore accessible to greater numbers of people. Mass media's impact on culture, therefore, has assumed a central place in sociological theories concerning taste publics and taste cultures. Many sociologists and communication scholars now argue that media culture, rather than high culture, sets the standards for culture and shapes popular taste. Despite this, the view of cultural consumption in terms of class remains a dominant theme in sociological literature.

Bibliography

Angus, Ian, and Suht Jhally, eds. *Cultural Politics in Contemporary America*. New York: Routledge & Kegan Paul, 1989. The authors and their contributors argue that there is a distinct separation between high and popular culture and that the prestige of each social class is attached to the culture it consumes.

Benjamin, Walter. "The Work of Art in the Age of Mechanical Reproduction." In *Illuminations*, edited by Hannah Arendt. Translated by Harry Zon. New York: Schocken Books, 1969. According to Benjamin, a major effect of the mass dissemination of culture is that content is decontexualized and loses its "aura." In other words, specific types of cultural symbols, as they are reproduced and disseminated, lose their original significance and social status while taking on other meanings. Decontextualization leads to a vast increase in a culture's symbolic repertoire while diluting the effectiveness of each item by continual reproduction. Seminal article in the mass culture critique.

Bourdieu, Pierre. *Distinction: A Social Critique of the Judgement of Taste*. Translated by Richard Nice. Cambridge, Mass.: Harvard University Press, 1984. Basing his analysis on French culture of the 1960's and 1970's, the author explores the idea that taste publics are defined by social class. He argues that cultural knowledge, or "capital," enriches and reinforces social class status. Bourdieu's insights, although significant, are somewhat dated.

Crane, Diana. *The Production of Culture: Media and the Urban Arts*. Newbury Park, Calif.: Sage Publications, 1992. The author explores changes in culture production and consumption in America from 1945 to 1990. Tracing the increasingly complex ways that types of social differentiation affect cultural consumption, she discards the traditional distinction between high culture and popular culture to offer a mass-media-driven classification of taste publics.

Gans, Herbert. *Popular Culture and High Culture*. New York: Basic Books, 1974. The author explores the similarities and differences between popular and high culture to argue that the similarities between the two have been undervalued and the differences exaggerated. He posits the existence of five different "taste cultures" in America, all of which have their own preferences in art, literature, and music. He provides an extensive critique of the Marxist or mass culture critique to conclude that popular culture is harmful neither to the people who consume it nor to society as a whole.

MacDonald, Dwight. "A Theory of Mass Culture." In *Mass Culture: The Popular Arts in America*, edited by Bernard Rosenberg and David Manning White. Glencoe, Ill.: Free Press, 1957. Extremely readable and often quoted, MacDonald's article best represents the bases of the American sociological mass culture critique in the 1950's and early 1960's.

Susan Mackey-Kallis

Cross-References

Culture: Material and Expressive Culture, 430; Culture and Language, 436; Culture and Technology, 443; Leisure, 1075; Social Stratification: Analysis and Overview, 1839; Socialization: The Mass Media, 1887; Subcultures and Countercultures, 2003.

HIGHER EDUCATION: COLLEGES AND UNIVERSITIES

Type of sociology: Major social institutions
Field of study: Education

Higher education is a system of organizations providing education and training beyond high school. While elementary and secondary school attendance is required by law in many countries, colleges and universities confer academic degrees or certification to individuals who are voluntarily pursuing further education.

Principal terms

CREDENTIALISM: the tendency in modern societies to require credentials for entry into certain occupations even though the educational qualifications may have very little to do with the skills actually used in the job

INSTITUTION: continuously repeated social practices developing around a basic social need that over time become established patterns of behavior; examples include education, family, religion, and the economic system

SOCIAL CLASS: those members of society that have a relatively similar share of wealth and who share attitudes, values, and an identifiable lifestyle

SOCIAL MOBILITY: the movement of individuals from one social status to another, usually defined occupationally

SOCIAL STRATIFICATION: the separation of society into levels based on wealth, age, race, or other characteristics; it is maintained by the educational, economic, religious, and familial institutions of society

SOCIOECONOMIC STATUS: a combination of factors such as income, occupation, and education that determine an individual's position in society

STATUS: any socially defined position occupied by an individual; for example, child, student, or parent

Overview

Higher education is a system of educational organizations offering some academic degree or certification after high school. In the early 1990's, almost thirteen million students were enrolled in more than three thousand colleges and universities in the United States. Unlike elementary and secondary school attendance, which is required by law, students choose to attend a college or university. There are multiple systems of higher education in the United States. This network of educational institutions consists of two-year colleges, four-year colleges, and universities.

Two other characteristics can also be used to differentiate the systems of higher education: control and types of degrees and programs. First, colleges and universities can be characterized by two types of control—public and private. Most public four-year colleges and universities are state funded. Two-year colleges are often publicly supported through both state and local financing. Privately funded institutions include religiously affiliated and independent secular colleges and universities. Second, the types of degrees and programs offered by institutions further categorize systems of higher education. Two-year colleges tend to specialize in vocational education and preparation for transfer to a four-year institution. Most four-year colleges offer both baccalaureate and master's level degrees. Universities typically grant the baccalaureate and master's degree, PhD, and such professional degrees as law and medicine degrees.

Sociologists have examined how important higher education credentials are to future occupational status and higher earnings. Sociologist Randall Collins, in *The Credential Society* (1979), suggests that new credentials evolve and educational requirements for jobs rise not as a result of necessary educational knowledge but because of the increased number of people seeking higher-level jobs. Students seek credentials to obtain an advantage in the pursuit of higher occupational status.

Sociologist Jeanne H. Ballantine notes that colleges and universities have proliferated rapidly in the United States and throughout the world since World War II. Advanced industrialization and the changing needs of capitalism are often used to explain the expansion. Explanations of the growth of higher education continue to be debated, but the importance of a college education as a predictor of future success is well established.

Obtaining a college education results in higher annual income regardless of race or sex. Research from the late 1980's reveals that males who complete college report average incomes more than double the average income of high school dropouts. White male college graduates earn 40 percent more than white male high school graduates. The incomes of African American male college graduates are 38 percent higher than those of high school graduates. Among females, financial effects of a college education are even more substantial. African American college graduates earn annually almost four times the amount of African American high school female dropouts; for white females, income is tripled.

Inequities in the effects of a higher education on income appear when comparing race and gender groups. African Americans and females benefit from a college education, but they earn substantially less than white males with identical educational credentials. Although African Americans and women suffer in comparison with white males, the relationship between income and higher education remains substantial.

A higher education may not produce the same rewards for all individuals, but possessing a college degree, nevertheless has a significant impact on future economic and occupational status. Consequently, sociologists are interested in determining which applicants are admitted to a college or university and why they are. In the United States, several criteria determine admission to higher education; these include high school grades, extracurricular activities, letters of recommendation, and standardized test scores.

There is considerable controversy concerning the use of national achievement tests for college entrance. Those in favor of using test scores in the admissions process argue that they help screen out students who cannot succeed in higher education. Critics of national achievement tests such as the Scholastic Achievement Test (SAT) believe that the tests neither measure what they say they do nor give an accurate representation of what students have learned; they also argue that the tests are unfair to minority students.

Gatekeeping is a term used to refer to the process that determines who has access to the best colleges. Student access to higher education is influenced not only by test scores but also by social class, race, sex, and tracking. Placement into either college preparatory or vocational courses begins early in the students' school years. Difficulties arise for students who have high aspirations but little support in the form of teacher recommendations, counselor evaluations, and parental encouragement.

Sociologist Burton R. Clark reports that just as elementary and secondary schools channel students into vocational or academic tracks, so the higher educational system can be viewed as a series of tracks. In his book *The Open Door College: A Case Study* (1960), Clark describes a "cooling-out function" in which students entering a two-year college with aspirations to transfer to four-year colleges or universities are encouraged to define success as a two-year degree. The consequences of this process affect future life chances, because the potential occupational status of a two-year college graduate is less than that of a university graduate.

Colleges and universities vary in enrollment, resources, programs, and student characteristics. Variations among the systems of higher education are noteworthy. What they share is service to individuals who are voluntarily furthering their education. To understand access to higher education, sociologists examine several parts of the system: the people who make admissions decisions, the criteria used, and the mission of the institution. The admissions process reflects the college's or university's position in the larger society, and individual struggles or access to social mobility is reflected in the admissions process. While higher education graduates continue to earn more than high school graduates, differences remain between race and gender groups as well as between types of colleges and universities attended.

Applications

Sociological research on colleges and universities is extensive. Two important topics in the sociology of higher education are access and attainment. Access refers to the requirements needed to enter an institution of higher learning. Studies of educational attainment generally involve examining the factors that lead to graduation from college. Knowledge gained from the study of college enrollment and completion rates have a number of policy implications for higher education.

A major debate in the United States centers on access to higher education—whether some groups have greater opportunity than others. Among the earliest evidence of a social class gap in college attendance is research from the 1960's showing that qualified students from lower socioeconomic backgrounds are less likely to enter college after high school graduation. Race and ethnic differences in enrollment rates have also been reported. Although minorities make up more than 25 percent of the American population, only 17 percent are enrolled in higher education.

Some colleges and universities have initiated "open door" admissions policies, meaning that any high school graduate will be admitted. These policies were created in large part as a result of demands for greater access to higher education. Critics argue that such a policy threatens academic standards. Supporters claim it increases minority opportunities and reduces social inequality.

Sociologist David E. Lavin and associates, in *Right Versus Privilege: The Open-Admissions Experiment at the City University of New York* (1981), examine the consequences of an open admissions policy in a New York system of higher education. In 1970, responding in large part to community demands for improved access to college, City University of New York (CUNY) began admitting any high school graduate in New York City. The university traditionally competed with the most prestigious colleges and universities for the best students. Consequently, the policy represented one of the most ambitious efforts to expand educational opportunity ever attempted in a university system.

Though open access policies have a long history, the City University of New York program contains elements not used in other systems. The goal was not simply to broaden access to higher education but also to create wider opportunity for baccalaureate degree completion. Consequently, a larger proportion of minority students entered four-year colleges directly from high school, instead of enrolling in a two-year college transfer program. City University of New York also developed extensive programs of compensatory education and supportive counseling in an effort to improve students' chances for academic success.

Lavin and his colleagues report that many students attended the university who previously would not have been admitted. The first class after the policy change was 75 percent larger than the previous year's entering class. The program's concept of opportunity embraced not only access but also graduation. The results reveal both the contribution and limitation of policies designed to decrease inequities in educational access. City University of New York's open access program helped to expand the ranks of college-educated men and women in minority communities. The past disadvantages of minority students, however, continued to hinder their efforts to earn advanced degrees. Although the policy has critics, the university is serving a wide variety of students representative of the diverse population of New York City.

Alexander Astin, in *What Matters in College?* (1993), examines how undergraduates are affected by their college experiences. One purpose of this research is to enhance understanding of educational attainment, particularly completing a bachelor's degree. Astin identifies a number of factors related to degree completion. Astin's work concentrates on the relative importance of student input and college environmental influence on educational attainment. Inputs refer to characteristics of students at the time of enrollment in college. Most common among these are race, sex, socioeconomic status, high school achievement, and standardized test scores. Environmental factors include the various programs, policies, faculty, peers, and educational experiences to which students are exposed.

Astin reports that students who are most likely to complete a bachelor's degree within four years have high grades in high school and high scores on college admissions tests. Educational attainment is also increased for students from high socioeconomic backgrounds. The single strongest input predictor of degree completion is the student's high school grade point average.

Environmental factors also exert an important influence on graduation from college. Astin reports that living in a campus residence hall enhances degree completion. The number of students attending an institution, however, reduces students' chances of completing the degree. In other words, all things being equal, the larger the size of a college, the more difficult it is to earn a baccalaureate degree in four years.

Degree completion is facilitated by both student-student and student-faculty interaction, hours per week spent socializing with friends, and talking to faculty outside of class. The single largest negative effect on retention is associated with working full-time while being a student. Other negative factors involved working off-campus at a part-time job and commuting. The pattern of results reported by Astin indicate that student academic development can be enhanced by heavy involvement in college life. Learning, academic performance, and retention are positively associated with involvement with faculty and student peer groups.

The issues of access to and graduation from institutions of higher education are of major concern to educational policy makers. Despite some inconsistency in results, open admissions programs such as that of City University of New York help increase the ranks of minority college graduates. Finally, colleges that create a climate that promotes involvement in campus life appear to enhance student opportunities for graduation.

Context

Higher education dates back to the twelfth and thirteenth centuries in Europe. The primary mission of the earliest universities was the transmission of knowledge. Over time, the structure and functions of higher education have changed considerably. In the nineteenth and twentieth centuries, research became an important function. In *Perspectives on Higher Education: Eight Disciplinary and Comparative Views* (1984), Burton R. Clark notes that since the last half of the twentieth century, higher education has become a vital institution in societies around the world. Nearly everywhere, national systems of higher education have grown tremendously in size and scope in response to increased demand for access.

Research examining colleges and universities increased substantially in the 1950's and 1960's. This literature examines stratification in higher education and the related problems of mobility and inequality in society. The role of higher education in relation to social mobility and social reproduction has long been debated between sociologists who emphasize its contribution to mobility and those who focus on its contribution to social reproduction (maintaining the status quo). Research on the role of higher education in the process of social mobility or reproduction has produced conflicting evidence.

The opposing positions are formalized in the functionalist and conflict theories of social stratification. Functionalists view higher education as both developing and reflecting individual skills and abilities, and therefore they see it being used as a means of social selection. Thus, colleges and universities enhance social mobility by allowing for social selection based on the merit of individuals.

Most conflict theorists argue that higher education helps to reproduce and legitimize the stratification system by portraying attainment as an individual achievement whereas in fact higher education selects and processes individuals based on ascribed characteristics such as socioeconomic status. Students from higher social classes are more likely to be able to afford a university education and therefore have a better chance for occupational and financial success after graduation. Consequently, universities tend to preserve society's existing stratification system.

Despite the participation of relatively few citizens (in proportion to the total population), higher education influences the structure and development of the United States' economic, political, and social life. In 1989, 31.9 percent of all adults had completed one to three years of college, and 16.2 percent had completed at least four years. Even people who do not attend college are affected by higher education's influence on the nation's institutions.

Helen Horowitz notes that as the United States has changed since the eighteenth century, so too have colleges and universities been changing. A central sociological insight into higher education is that colleges and universities are both products and shapers of society. Knowledge of the role of higher education is essential to an understanding of modern society. As agents of socialization and certification, colleges and universities continue to exert power over individual life chances.

Bibliography

Astin, Alexander. *What Matters in College?* San Francisco: Jossey-Bass, 1993. A comprehensive discussion of how undergraduates are affected by their college experiences. Topics include the impact of higher education on attitudes, behaviors, and achievement. Written in a style appropriate for both high school and college audiences. Several chapters can be read independently of others. Includes a bibliography and subject indexes.

Ballantine, Jeanne H. *The Sociology of Education: A Systematic Analysis.* 2d ed. Englewood Cliffs, N.J.: Prentice-Hall, 1989. An introduction to the sociology of education that covers a variety of theoretical issues using topics of high interest to students. The chapter on higher education is very comprehensive. Each chapter offers several exercises that enable students to approach education. Contains footnotes and a combined subject and name index.

Clark, Burton R. *The Open Door College: A Case Study.* New York: McGraw-Hill, 1960. An excellently written analysis of the process used within higher education to place individual students in educational programs consistent with the college's expectations of a student's eventual occupation. Accessible to both high school and college audiences. Contains footnotes, a combined name and subject index, and a bibliography.

_____ , ed. *Perspectives on Higher Education: Eight Disciplinary and Comparative Views.* Berkeley: University of California Press, 1984. A collection of essays that offer eight international perspectives on higher education: the historical, the political, the economic, the organizational, the sociological, the cultural, the scientific, and the policy-centered. Contains footnotes, index, and a separate bibliography for each essay.

Collins, Randall. *The Credential Society.* New York: Academic Press, 1979. An interesting and provocative analysis of the reasons for the importance attached to educational credentials. The book proposes that the educational requirements for jobs are raised not because of demands for high levels of skills but because of the increased number of people seeking higher-status jobs.

Horowitz, Helen Lefkowitz. *Campus Life: Undergraduate Cultures from the End of the Eighteenth Century to the Present.* Chicago: University of Chicago Press, 1988. A superbly written historical account of the nature and meaning of the undergraduate experience in the United States. The discussion of the development of student cultures in higher education is especially interesting. Accessible to both high school and college audiences. Contains footnotes and an index.

Lavin, David E., Richard D. Alba, and Richard A. Silberstein. *Right Versus Privilege: The Open-Admissions Experiment at the City University of New York.* New York: Free Press, 1981. An excellent review of the results of City University of New York's open admission policy. Accessible to college students or high school students enrolled in an introductory sociology course.

Michael Delucchi

Cross-References

Education: Conflict Theory Views, 579; Education: Functionalist Perspectives, 586; Educational Credentials and Social Mobility, 600; Equal Educational Opportunity, 661; Higher Education: Community Colleges, 884; Standardized Testing and IQ Testing Controversies, 1966; Tracking and Inequality in Education, 2057.

HIGHER EDUCATION: COMMUNITY COLLEGES

Type of sociology: Major social institutions
Field of study: Education

Community colleges both train high school graduates for the job market and offer the first two years of college for students planning to transfer to a four-year institution. Whether these two-year colleges effectively help students achieve their life goals or primarily serve to maintain class distinctions has been the subject of debate.

Principal terms

CLASS REPRODUCTION: the concept that the number of people in each social class is about the same from one generation to the next; social mobility is seen as a relatively rare exception

LIFE CHANCES: the chances (education and career opportunities) available to an individual based on rank in society

MATRICULATION: enrollment in college

OPEN-DOOR COLLEGE: a college that has few admissions requirements

STANDARDIZED TEST: a test devised so that certain percentages of the test-takers have below-average, average, and above-average scores

SUBORDINATE GROUPS: society's "have-nots" who are disadvantaged compared with other groups

TERMINAL DEGREE: a degree that is not intended to lead to a more advanced degree; it is seen as an end in itself

WORKING CLASS: a large group in society that is not poor but is below the middle class

Overview

The American public higher education system is three-tiered, being composed of state universities, senior colleges, and junior or community colleges. (Vocational-technical schools that offer job training are a fourth option, but they are not considered colleges.) State universities offer, in addition to four-year degrees, advanced and professional degrees not available on other campuses. They often have the highest entrance requirements and the most expensive tuition rates in the state. Typically, senior colleges offer four-year baccalaureate degrees. Some offer two-year or five-year programs as well. Community colleges generally both offer two-year degrees and prepare students (those who wish to and are able to) for continuing their education at a four-year institution. Community colleges vary by curriculum, prestige, tuition, enrollment, athletic departments, physical plants, cultural offerings, and availability of community-interest programs.

An increase in the percentage of people in the United States attending college has been a general trend; however, the overall enrollment of students in four-year institutions has not been where the increase has been felt. Rather, it has been the growth of two-year colleges since the 1960's that has been remarkable. Because of this growth, most states now have postsecondary education within commuting distance of nearly all prospective students.

Junior or community colleges vary widely within and among states. Comparatively few offer a campus residential experience; most students' primary identity involves off-campus work or family. Some states divide vocational-technical training institutions from those that offer the first two years of college, but others combine them on the same campus. Junior colleges have an open admissions policy; that is, unlike other institutions of higher education, they enroll anyone who has been graduated from high school or who has obtained a general equivalency diploma (GED).

Many students attend junior college primarily for economic reasons: They believe that attending will help them earn more money in their careers. These students are more interested in subjects that relate to jobs than in liberal arts or education pertaining to leisure pursuits. They tend to be task-oriented, practical, and impatient. These characteristics are especially common in students who select a two-year degree designed for a specific occupation such as nursing or working as a laboratory technician. The relatively low tuition attracts many first-generation college students, including minority students, who might otherwise be unable to attend college. The families and spouses of these students may see the students' desire for education as both laudable and threatening.

Another factor that influences students to choose a community college is geographical proximity combined with family considerations. Children, ailing parents, or employed spouses may narrow a person's educational choices, especially in rural areas, making it impractical to seek education far from home. Some students simply prefer to live at home as they begin their higher education. Poor performance on college entrance exams is another factor that leads some students to attend a two-year college. Attending a community college with the intent to transfer to a four-year college allows the student to prove that he or she can perform academically and then gain admittance to a senior college or university.

Psychological attitudes may also play a part in enrollment decisions. Students may feel poorly prepared for college and thus fear failure; such students may prefer a smaller community school, with its higher degree of attention from teachers and advisers, to a less personal four-year institution. Junior colleges traditionally have low student-teacher ratios and stress teaching over research. Faculty members are encouraged to be available to students for more hours than their colleagues at senior institutions.

Community colleges have diverse student bodies with regard to both age and ethnicity. Students of different ages have different problems and needs; older students—mostly adults who are also working, many full-time—must juggle the responsibilities of work, marriage, family, and school. Younger students are often first-generation college students experiencing pressure from family and friends to succeed. Members of minorities face additional challenges; some, for example, have come to college from schools with inadequate college-preparation programs and must overcome the psychological and academic disadvantages caused by this situation.

Community colleges meet the diverse education needs of a large segment of society that might otherwise think it impossible or even absurd to consider postsecondary education. Further, community colleges are structurally designed to offer opportunities for social mobility. For example, in many cases students may enter through remedial or "second-chance" programs. Junior colleges attract both students who have the promise to go on to become productive, creative scholars and professionals and those who have below average verbal ability but might become responsible and efficient paraprofessionals.

Applications

It has often been argued in the sociological literature that community colleges have contradictory missions. Community colleges proclaim an aim of open access and equality of opportunity regardless of ethnicity, social class, or gender. Yet the hidden agenda, some have said, is that they serve as "cooling-out" institutions that take pressure off four-year colleges and universities. This concept suggests that senior institutions want to reserve their resources for middle- and upper-class students. Social forces encourage working-class students to choose local community or junior colleges, with their far lower tuition, where they receive an introduction to—and credentials for—jobs of lower status than those they could obtain with degrees from more prestigious schools.

The community college is the dominant point of entry into higher education for many working-class and minority students. Students who enter junior colleges with a four-year degree as a goal less frequently achieve this aim than do students who enter senior institutions with the same goal. Class-reproduction theorists claim that education sorts students according to social class. The entrance requirements for universities close them to most members of the working class or minorities. (It has been strongly argued, for example, that college aptitude tests, by their nature, discriminate against minorities.) The development of community colleges became both a compensation and payoff for such groups. Early developmental trends such as "open-door" policies gave the illusion of equal access and opportunity, but two-year colleges soon began moving away from the goal of being transfer institutions by starting an increasing number of two-year terminal degrees and vocational programs.

Given the existing choices in higher education, a generalized schema can be drawn. A majority of wealthier families will send their children to expensive private schools or to the most prestigious state universities. Sons and daughters of upper-middle-class parents will enroll in state universities; members of the middle and lower middle class will attend senior colleges. Prospective students from the working class will seek the junior colleges and vocational-technical schools. The prestige of the degree-granting institution greatly affects what the student's first job after graduation will be. Therefore, with crucial exceptions, higher education becomes the sorting agent to uphold class rank through succeeding generations of families.

Another serious concern is that most students who desire four-year degrees do not complete them if they begin higher education at a two-year school. This pattern is apparently weaker in some community college systems than others. For example, the systems in Washington and Florida have higher-than-average transfer rates when compared with the community colleges in many other states. In some states, transfer students do perform as well at universities as do students who begin higher education at senior institutions. In many states, transfer networks have been adopted by senior institutions to facilitate the transfer process. These states come much closer than others to delivering on the promise of equal access and opportunity.

Critics have charged that community and junior colleges act as devices to reduce, not fulfill, the aspirations of the American working class. Critics have a tendency, however, to discuss two-year institutions as though they were all nearly identical. Not enough is known about the differences between those schools that act to fulfill student aspirations and those that thwart them. Few researchers have conducted studies on specific community colleges and their responses to the needs and desires of their students; most research has involved multicollege quantitative studies. Nationwide surveys are conducted far more often than case studies of single colleges. Analysts have repeatedly assumed that junior college students are alike—primarily that they all want, or should want, eventually to attain a four-year degree. Another variable that is difficult to determine is whether community college systems may be providing equal access and opportunity but that students, for whatever reasons, may have chosen paths that limited their attainment before they arrive at the college. The question then would become one of how extensive the remedial and counseling functions of the community college should be or can be expected to be.

Because of the diversity (especially the age diversity) of community college students, their goals at the time of enrollment differ widely from student to student. For an older female single-parent student, for example, who must balance her choices based on family and financial responsibilities, a two-year nursing degree may enhance her life chances compared with other available options. Because older students are often uncertain of their ability to do entry-level college work, they frequently select the terminal (two-year) program at registration. By the winter of their sophomore year, however, many have gained the necessary confidence to shift to college-transfer programs. Community colleges can also be a tool for implementing older students' plans for a new future. For a newly divorced woman, a couple seeking dual-career status, people considering midlife career moves, or laid-off factory workers, affordable college education within commuting distance provides important possibilities for creating new life patterns or for escaping poverty and despair.

General assumptions that most high school students aspire to or need bachelor's degrees from four-year institutions have fueled the charges that community colleges block the dreams of the less privileged. By the early 1990's, however, such assumptions were being questioned in many quarters. Increasing numbers of recent college graduates were reporting having difficulty finding the good jobs that they had hoped a college degree would make possible. There was a larger number of students with business degrees, in particular, than there were companies ready to hire them. It was also being questioned whether a college degree was really necessary for many jobs that had begun to require them. In this context, certain two-year degrees and vocational programs began to seem more relevant. A degree in automobile mechanics, for example, although it might seem limited and restrictive to upper-middle-class critics of the two-year system (many of whom themselves hold degrees higher than a bachelor's degree), offers a good chance of employment upon completion.

An assumption in the philosophy of the two-year system is that the junior college should pay dividends (in the tangible sense of employment opportunities or advancement) to students. Increasingly, jobs require technical training beyond high school. An additional benefit may be the ability to remain employed longer once a job has been found. One study has shown that people with vocational training are less vulnerable to layoffs for approximately twelve years longer than are people without it.

Tuition is a crucial factor in students' choice of a community college. Although tuition varies among different states' systems, tuition at junior colleges is comparatively low; it is usually a fraction of the cost of attending a public four-year college and is a tiny percentage of the cost of private schools. Junior colleges face the same budget problems and challenges facing all public education, however, and a consistent debate has concerned the effects of tuition increases on the ability of poorer students to attend classes at junior colleges. In California, for example, significant tuition increases in the 1993-1994 school year caused a marked decrease in the number of students enrolling in junior colleges.

When prospective students are choosing between attendance at a community college and at a vocational institution, the types of financial aid available to them is frequently a factor in their decision. The federally funded Job Training Partnership Act (JTPA) pays tuition for an Associate of Science degree, a terminal two-year degree that does not include meeting the general education requirements for transfer to four-year schools. In some states JTPA will not provide assistance for an Associate of Arts degree (another two-year degree) or for a program aimed at transfer to a four-year college. Students' knowledge of such situations undoubtedly influences their choices, and such restrictions on aid may well discourage a student's long-held educational goals or professional aspirations.

Context

Among the early junior colleges in the United States were both public and private institutions. The community college system developed from the junior college movement. Depending on who is describing the beginnings of the community college system, the movement is attributed to a conspiracy of the elite (to keep "undesirable" students out of the existing higher education system), a populist alliance, or the efforts of a group of professional educators.

More than half of all college students in the United States attend, and nearly half of all college faculty teach at, two-year colleges. The rapid increase of students at these schools reflects the American notion that society should provide education for the social and individual good, exhibits the economy's ability to support more college students, indicates a need for better-educated workers, and reveals the value to students of an institution dedicated to teaching rather than research.

One of society's views of college is as a vehicle that members of less-fortunate groups can use to escape their environment and achieve success. Since the Civil Rights movement, the community colleges have sometimes been perceived as a great equalizer for those students not formerly considered "college material." The success of the community college in the United States is linked directly to demands for further education among previously excluded groups. The development of junior colleges can be viewed either as an attempt by government to provide disadvantaged groups with the means to improve themselves or as a means of controlling those same groups by giving their members the illusion that they can enjoy the same advantages that the upper classes enjoy from birth.

Bibliography

Astin, Alexander W. *What Matters in College?: Four Critical Years Revisited.* San Francisco: Jossey-Bass, 1993. Astin's earlier *Four Critical Years* became one of the most often cited books about higher education. This volume is also filled with findings about every aspect of higher education, including junior colleges.

Bourdieu, Pierre, and Jean-Claude Passeron. *Reproduction in Education, Society, and Culture.* Translated by Richard Nice. London: Sage Publications, 1990. A respected book in the area of class reproduction. The authors argue that education as an institution is not intended to provide equal opportunity or liberation but to maintain class divisions.

Bowles, Samuel, and Herbert Gintis. *Schooling in Capitalist America.* New York: Basic Books, 1976. A classic book in class reproduction theory that (unlike Bourdieu and Passeron's work) focuses exclusively on the effects of education on class reproduction.

Robertson, Ian. *Sociology.* 3d ed. New York: Worth, 1987. A popular standard introduction to sociology text for college students. The chapter on education contains a clear discussion of most of the field's basic concepts.

Weis, Lois. *Between Two Worlds: Black Students in an Urban Community College.* Boston: Routledge & Kegan Paul, 1985. A highly recommended study that illuminates the social forces that cause poor students to drop out of college.

Willis, Paul. *Learning to Labor: How Working Class Kids Get Working Class Jobs.* New York: Columbia University Press, 1981. A well-established and widely cited study of how education works to maintain social class and steers students toward rather than away from jobs in their own class.

Sue Hammons-Bryner

Cross-References

THE HIPPOCRATIC THEORY OF MEDICINE

Type of sociology: Major social institutions
Field of study: Medicine

Born during the fifth century B.C.E., the Greek physician Hippocrates combined centuries of observations by philosopher-scientists with his own studies to produce the first major body of work on the rational basis of medicine. Hippocrates correlated the presence of disease with such factors as diet, race, and environmental influences. The Hippocratic Oath, written by Hippocrates' followers, has remained influential in the modern practice of medicine.

Principal terms

CORPUS HIPPOCRATICUM: the "Hippocratic Collection"; the collection of writings by Hippocrates (and others) assembled in fourth century B.C.E. Alexandria at the great library

HIPPOCRATIC METHOD: the rational use of observation and study in the evaluation of disease rather than reliance upon superstition or supernatural explanations

HIPPOCRATIC OATH: the pledge, attributed to Hippocrates but probably composed later, that serves as an ethical guide for medicine; traditionally spoken during graduation ceremonies at medical colleges

HUMOR: in its original ancient meaning, any of the four major body fluids: blood, phlegm, choler (yellow bile), and melancholy (black bile)

TREPANNING: surgical opening of the skull to relieve pressure on the brain; a technique utilized with success by the Hippocratic physicians

Overview

The development of the Hippocratic theory of medicine represented a revolution in human thinking about people's relationship to health and disease. Prior to the period in which Hippocrates lived, about 460 B.C.E., disease was often considered a supernatural occurrence, a punishment from the gods. The Greeks had their own gods, notably Apollo, Artemis, and Athena, in which they believed the healing arts could be found. The Greek tradition also taught, however, that the universe was governed by a set of rules and that all effects had a specific cause. It was this tradition which was drawn upon by the Hippocratic school.

The writings of Hippocrates, the *Corpus Hippocraticum* (or simply "Hippocratic Collection") were believed first assembled in the fourth century B.C.E. by the Greek ruler Ptolemy at the great library of Alexandria, Egypt. Though these works, some seventy-two books and fifty-nine treatises, are attributed to Hippocrates, they most likely include writings by many authors. The Hippocratic Collection is written in a variety of styles and contains some contradictory statements. It is difficult to categorize the subject matter in any one specific format, since various clinical conditions were often grouped under one heading because of similar symptoms, such as pocks (pustules) or fever. In a sense, this was what made the Hippocratic school unique in its time. Disease was not viewed as originating with the gods but was rather seen as the result of what could be considered "nature." Disease resulted within the context of the patient—a person's diet, environment, and even race. Treatment, holistic in nature, consisted of attempting to restore the natural balance of defenses.

For example, the general pathology of disease was believed caused either by internal influences (the four "humors") or by external factors: climate, diet, or hygiene. The concept of the humors—blood, phlegm, black bile, and yellow bile—did not originate with the Hippocratic school, but their visibility was used in the attempt to understand the disease. The humors were moved and mixed within the body by "innate heat," generated from the "pneuma" of the air taken in by the lungs and the food eaten. When the humors were no longer in equilibrium, disease was thought to result. The prevalence of certain humors was a function of the season, with yellow bile being more prominent in the summer, black bile in the autumn, and so on. In this manner, the seasonal prevalence of disease was related to the internal constitution of the patient. If the water supply in certain areas differed, this could also be reflected in alterations of the humors, as could the eating of different foods. Thus, nature itself could upset the body's constitution.

Just as nature could cause disease, the Hippocratic physician believed that nature could be used to cure disease. The role of the physician was to help the body to cure itself: "To help, or at least do no harm." Unfortunately, at times the Hippocratic physicians carried the logic of an imbalance of humors to its next step: If an imbalance was the cause of the disease, then removal of the excess humor could restore the balance, and hence the health of the individual. The production of pus, phlegm, and mucus was thought a natural process of the coction, or cooking process by the innate heat to expel the unwanted material. Consequently, the use of baths, emetics, and purgatives became standard methods of treatment for certain illnesses. The use of bleeding for removal of "excess" blood may also have been practiced.

The study of surgical methods for treatment of traumas was among the highlights of the Hippocratic Collection. Surgical procedures formed a significant portion of the treatises. The Hippocratic physicians were experts at setting fractures; much attention in the writings was given to wounds of the skull. It was in the treatment of such head wounds that the Greeks were particularly adept, even recognizing the importance of early intervention (trepanning) to relieve pressure on the brain. Detailed observations by the physicians allowed them to present an accurate prognosis. The extensive coverage of the writings dealing with surgery has led many historians to believe that these sections were composed by Hippocrates himself. Injuries associated with fighting were given extensive coverage. In addition, procedures for the drainage of chest or abdominal fluids (blood or pus) were detailed. Extensive descriptions of operative techniques and of preparation of the patient and the surgical room are found in the writings. The clarity and detail of the writings attest the skill of the physicians.

The question of ethics played an important role in the Hippocratic school. The writings deal with the question of who should become a physician. Since there was no licensing, students were trained by observing others, including their peers. Emphasis was placed on observation and understanding the relationship between symptoms. In this manner, a proper prognosis could be made, which was especially important during a time when there was little a physician could actively do to treat many forms of disease. Since physicians rarely remained in one place for long periods, they were expected to comport themselves properly. They were also expected to maintain a healthy and clean appearance.

Applications

The Hippocratic tradition is applied most clearly in the Hippocratic Oath, the ethical guide for physicians which is still sworn upon graduation from medical colleges. The origin of the oath is unclear. Whether it predated or postdated Hippocrates is unknown, but it does not appear to have been among the teachings of Hippocrates or his followers. The earliest references to the oath are found some five hundred years after Hippocrates, and its use may have evolved with the religious changes in the Greek and Roman worlds of that period.

The oath begins with a pledge to the gods: "I swear by Apollo the physician, by Aesculapius, Hygeia, and Panacea . . . to keep the following oath." The oath itself can be divided into two sections. It starts with a promise to continue the tradition, with the imparting of knowledge to future generations of physicians "without fee or stipulation"). The teaching of medical arts was as important as their practice.

The remainder of the oath is a collection of obligations and prohibitions. Some obligations continue to this day: to refrain from the use of deadly drugs, to refrain from seduction of the patient, and to use one's judgement for the benefit of the patient. Some portions of the oath actually differ from the known practices of the Hippocratic physicians. For example, a line in the oath prohibits the physician from inducing an abortion, a practice known to be carried out during the time of Hippocrates. The reason for the inclusion of this prohibition is not clear. One possible reason is that the oath was developed in the first century C.E., a time when the Christian church was in its ascendancy. Prohibition of abortion, or any form of contraception, may have fit the teachings of the early church. Sherwin Nuland, however, in his discussion of Hippocrates, argued the dichotomy in a different manner. Nuland pointed out that the Hippocratic physicians were not interventionists. Their philosophy was to aid nature in running its course. To abort was to open the way for numerous complications, not least of which was sepsis and a high rate of death. Abortion might be practiced, but not at the risk to the woman's life.

In a similar manner, discussion of the obligation inherent within this portion of the oath has plagued modern physicians. The questions of when, or whether, a fetus is to be considered a human being has been argued not only in the scientific arena but also in the realms of theology, morality, and law. The modern physician is no longer constrained by dangers of infection resulting from properly performed abortions; the process carries less risk than childbirth itself. The question of whether an induced abortion, used solely as a means of preventing childbirth, is a violation of the Hippocratic Oath bears no simple answer, and the decision must rest within the physician.

Likewise, the question of physician-aided suicides has no easy answer. The oath clearly proscribes the practice (the physician will "give no deadly drug, nor give advice which may cause [the patient's] death"). Yet suicide, in the time of Hippocrates, was an acceptable form of death. The difference between promise and practice may be similar to the situation with abortion. To aid in a suicide was to interdict the forces of nature. Nature must run its course, aided, but not overtly hastened, by the physician.

Catalyzed by the actions of physician Jack Kevorkian, the question of physician-aided suicides became an issue in the early 1990's. Kevorkian believed that if, in the absence of any hope of improvement, a terminally ill patient wishes to end his or her life, then the patient should be allowed to do so in a quick and humane manner. Acting on this belief, Kevorkian began the practice of assisting in such suicides. In addition to presenting the medical profession with a significant moral dilemma, this practice poses the question of whether it violates the Hippocratic oath. The debate centers on whether it is better to allow a patient to suffer to a degree beyond that which can be controlled by medication or better to aid the patient in ending such suffering. Most physicians, drawing upon their individual consciences, are able to reach a compromise in cases in which terminally ill patients are suffering; one approach is to withhold additional support that may prolong life, thus allowing nature to come to its conclusion. In a sense, this approach may be closer to the Hippocratic tradition than is the attitude that death must be delayed in all situations, even to the extent of using extreme (sometimes called "heroic") measures.

The physicians of Hippocrates' time recognized the role of the brain in determining emotions or thoughts. They also understood the role of the brain in mental illness, recognizing this form of disease as being unique in its origin. Brain dysfunction associated with epilepsy was also described.

In modern industrial societies, application of the Hippocratic theory of medicine retains its emphasis on a holistic approach. The object of the physician is to assist nature—to assist the body in restoring itself. The most common medical problems in the United States are related to lifestyle; middle-class Americans tend to eat, drink, or smoke too much and to exercise too little, and they suffer the effects of various forms of stress. The most common injunctions from physicians relate to one or more of these behaviors. Injunctions relating to diet and behavior were also given by Hippocrates and his followers to their patients.

Context

Hippocrates was born on the island of Cos about 460 B.C.E. and practiced medicine well into old age. Little is known for certain about him beyond what was written by Plato. Much of what is attributed to him is probably myth, originating in the biography written by Soranus of Ephesus more than five hundred years later. Nevertheless, the Hippocratic theory of medicine, whether written entirely by Hippocrates or by his followers, was a direct result of Hippocrates' teachings.

Hippocrates and the school that developed as an offshoot of his teachings represented a victory of rationalism over superstition. In the centuries prior to development of Hippocratic theory, the power of healing was attributed to the gods. Originally ascribed to Apollo, Artemis, and Athena, the powers of healing were eventually transferred to Apollo's son, Aesculapius. (One myth suggested that Hippocrates was a lineal descendent of Aesculapius.) The tradition of these gods as healers remains reflected in the opening sentences of the Hippocratic oath. Worship of the gods was reflected in the belief that the cause of illness was supernatural, a punishment from these gods. The cure of disease was attributed to these same forces.

Building on an evolving Greek tradition of observation, Hippocrates stressed the major principles of observation, study, and evaluation. Disease was not supernatural; it followed the laws of nature. Though the cause might be nebulous, it was still within the realm of human understanding to determine what that cause might be. The Hippocratic school taught and practiced that by careful observation and study, an explanation was possible. Equally important, with the emphasis on the patient, the physician could aid patients in their own recovery.

Much of the Hippocratic tradition was later reflected in the writings of Galen. Born in Asia Minor around the year 130, Galen became the preeminent physician of his day. A voluminous writer, Galen incorporated Hippocrates' views of observation and study into his own teachings. Equally important, though Galen was a pious theist in his beliefs, he emphasized the natural causes of disease. His belief was that one can best serve God through study and understanding rather than by invoking God's will as the cause of human problems. Such beliefs were often in conflict with the church during that period. Galen's observations were so detailed in their descriptions that his teachings on anatomy were considered infallible for more than twelve hundred years. (In one respect this was unfortunate, since a number of significant errors were incorporated into these teachings.)

Modern interpretation of Hippocrates owes much to the work of the French physician Maximilien-Paul-Émile Littré. Littré spent much of the period between 1840 and 1860 translating and interpreting Hippocrates' work, applying it to medicine as it was being practiced during that period. In particular, Littré emphasized the observation of symptoms for understanding the cause of illness. Though a trained physician, Littré did not practice the craft. Although his interpretations of Hippocratic theses could be justly criticized, he provided a stimulus for the study and application of these ancient works.

Modern science and technology have developed more rapidly than society's abilities to deal with the problems and moral dilemmas that the advances have created. Life can be prolonged for longer than ever before, but the cost is high and the patient's quality of life may deteriorate so much that prolonging life seems pointless. The interest of the patient can be lost, overshadowed by the technology used in treating the patient's problem. With regard to such issues, the Hippocratic theory of medicine is as relevant today as it was twenty-four hundred years ago.

Bibliography

Edelstein, Ludwig. *Ancient Medicine*. Edited by Owsei Temkin and C. Lilian Temkin. Translated by C. Lilian Temkin. Baltimore: The Johns Hopkins University Press, 1967. An older source on the subject, but nevertheless an interesting account of medical practice as carried out during the time of Hippocrates and others. Provides an interesting sense of history.

Lyons, Albert, and R. Joseph Petrucelli. *Medicine: An Illustrated History*. New York: Harry N. Abrams, 1978. A well-written and profusely illustrated history of medicine. An excellent overview of Hippocrates is provided. Of particular historical interest are the photographs, diagrams, and drawings found through the book. These include photographs of ancient Greek statues relevant to the history of medicine.

Nuland, Sherwin B. *Doctors: The Biography of Medicine*. New York: Knopf, 1988. The story of the development of medicine. A highly recommended book on the subject, which with its mixture of numerous anecdotes and historical accounts provides pleasurable reading. A chapter on Hippocrates contains an excellent analysis of his teachings and their modern application. The discussion of medicine is at times detailed but should be easily followed by the reader with basic knowledge of science.

Singer, Charles, and E. Ashworth Underwood. *A Short History of Medicine*. 2d ed. New York: Oxford University Press, 1962. Though several decades old, the book remains an excellent source for following the early evolution of medicine. The role of Greek physicians and philosophers is discussed in the early portion of the text. Included are extensive discussions of the Hippocratic school, and examples of their observations and writings.

Smith, Wesley D. *The Hippocratic Tradition*. Ithaca, N.Y.: Cornell University Press, 1979. The author provides an in-depth analysis of the Hippocratic tradition and its evolution through history. Interpretation of Galen's writings on the subject comprises much of the book. Though little of the subject matter is modern (twentieth century), Smith nevertheless presents the reader with an excellent evaluation of the manner by which various writers understood Hippocrates. Included are extensive portions of these writings.

Thorwald, Jurgen. *Science and Secrets of Early Medicine*. Translated by Richard Winston and Clara Winston. London: Thames & Hudson, 1962. A discussion of the development of medical practices in ancient China, Egypt, India, and Mexico. Reliefs and paintings on the subject from these cultures are pictured. Little is included that deals specifically with Hippocrates, but the book provides an interesting perspective on how medicine was practiced among various peoples.

Richard Adler

Cross-References

HOMELESSNESS

Type of sociology: Social stratification
Fields of study: Dimensions of inequality; Poverty

Homelessness refers to a marginalized condition of detachment from society and to the lack of bonds that connect settled persons to a network of institutions and social orders. The presence or absence of homelessness in a world without physical and technological shortages reveals the varying degrees to which societies have eradicated exploitation and oppression and/or have established social justice and liberty.

Principal terms
AFFORDABLE HOUSING: local, state, and national policies aimed at providing long-term, low-income housing
CRIMES OF OMISSION: the lack of public and private policies that could eliminate both homelessness and the criminogenic acts that accompany the homeless condition
EXPLOITATION: the creation of a surplus profit by one section of the population that is controlled by another section, resulting in a grossly unequal exchange of goods and services
HOMELESS: those persons who lack the necessary resources and community ties to provide for their own shelter
INEQUALITY: the deprivation and privilege resulting from the unequal sharing of political, economic, and social power in society
SOCIAL JUSTICE: social orders that are based on principles of feminist, antiracist, and ecologist communitarianism that emphasize qualitative living for all rather than quantitative consuming for a majority

Overview

By the late 1980's, the homeless population in the United States, according to both governmental and advocacy reports, was estimated to be between 600,000 and 3 million. Included among these casualties were men, women, and children of all racial and ethnic backgrounds; urban and rural workers; displaced and deinstitutionalized persons; alcoholics, drug addicts, AIDS victims, and the mentally ill; physically abused mothers and their babies, sexually abused teenagers and preadolescents, neglected elderly people; and migrants, refugees, and veterans.

Like other social problems, the problem of homelessness has historically revolved around the way in which specific societal groups and class interests have defined the social issue in the first place. Generally, public policies in the United States regarding homelessness, the homeless, and the shortage of low-income or subsidized housing in America are influenced by and inseparable from local and national politics. Moreover, economic crises and considerations, grounded in the ideological perspectives of laissez-faire, free-market capitalism and liberal social reformism, are also at work. At the same time, while most people do not blame individual homeless people per se for their predicament, they still support a public policy ideology that essentially does nothing to alter the victimizing conditions of homelessness.

In part, this has to do with a legacy of viewing homeless people primarily as white middle-aged men and elderly eccentric "shopping-bag ladies" rather than primarily as children, mothers, and families. When most people think about the homeless, rarely do images come to mind of teenage runaways, lacking marketable skills and financial resources, selling their bodies to the highest urban bidders. Typically, people do not think about homeless children, most of them abused or neglected, sleeping in abandoned buildings without heat, electricity, and running water. Most people do not think about homeless mothers who believe that it is better to exchange sexual services for shelter than to avail themselves of shelter opportunities that may entail the risk of losing their children to foster care or an adoption agency.

As a group of people, today's homeless may be though of as a new subclass of people at the bottom of the U.S. stratification system. The homeless may also be thought of as a group of people whose human potential is constantly suppressed and under attack and whose misery is the product of a society characterized by gross political and economic inequality and social injustice. In different terms, the experience of the homeless in the United States should be viewed in relationship not only to the debilitating social formations of a political economy in transition but also to an inadequately developed public policy on low-income housing, community health, and violence reduction.

The growing size of the homeless population over the past two decades is not a temporary aberration of an otherwise healthy political economy and domestic policy. On the contrary, the plight of the homeless is a permanent and fixed expression of contemporary U.S. public policy that has yet to address seriously the problems of a postindustrial society in a changing global economy. Therefore, solutions to the homelessness crisis in America require not only the development of permanent low-income housing alternatives and the consolidation and improvement of temporary or transitional housing, but also the development of a radically different and comprehensive domestic policy that simultaneously addresses public housing, health care, education, and crime prevention.

Discourse on both the phenomenon of U.S. homelessness during the era of a postindustrial service economy and the new homeless have-nots of an affluent American society should not be confined merely to the lack of material possessions or deprivations, but should also refer to the psychological, physical, and social condition of the homeless. As a group, homeless people, regardless of their personal traumas, find themselves struggling to cope with numerous indecencies and indignities that characterize their daily existence. On top of these burdens, homeless people are in the position of having to resist further victimization by other homeless people, traditional street criminals, and the forces of alienation and detachment.

Applications

Knowledge gained from studying homelessness and societies' responses to the homeless indicates that it is possible to create progressive, humanistic alternatives to the existing public and private practices of an uncaring capitalist welfare system in crisis. During the 1980's and 1990's, there have been public and private, individual and community, statewide and national responses to the homeless and the homelessness condition that reveal both compassionate and selfish feelings. In short, responses to homelessness have represented disparate ideological and political pressures, ranging from extreme cruelty and inhumanity to extreme kindness and compassion.

The two homelessness scenarios that follow provide a sense of the extremes on a response continuum. In the first, a "repressive" Social Darwinist scenario, the homeless are viewed as undeserving vagrants/criminals who received punitive forms of intervention from people who are trying to rid themselves and their environs of spoiled goods. In the second, a "nonrepressive" Judeo-Christian scenario, the homeless are viewed as deserving, unfortunate people in need of human services who receive caring intervention by concerned citizens who are attempting to address the problem of the homeless condition.

In perhaps fewer and fewer "repressive" communities, but generally in the smaller and larger towns across the nation, the homeless are looked upon as being fully responsible, and therefore they are regarded with less empathy and more scorn. In these rural areas of the country, if friends and family have abandoned the homeless, then it is time for these people to disappear, literally and figuratively. The homeless in these communities can become victims of citizens' beatings and bashings or objects of law enforcement, subject to criminalization and incarceration. In these typically poor communities, where emergency assistance is not usually available, where few if any shelter beds or soup kitchens exist, and where official and unofficial policies are to run the homeless out of town, these vagrant people have been verbally harassed and physically abused.

Thus, far away from the more conspicuous sights of the urban homeless, on the rural roads of the corporate agrieconomy of the United States, there are thousands of hidden homeless who are doing their best to stay out of the way of local citizens and police, who may arrest and charge them for criminal trespassing, squatting, panhandling, or littering. In more than a few cases, these homeless person has been arrested for merely trying to feed themselves. In the sparsely populated regions of the Midwest and the South, it is quite common to find recently bankrupted and marginal farmers who have been forced off the land joining the ranks of other migrant workers in search of unskilled work. Criss-crossing the country, these members of a new migrant class, with and without their families, spend varying periods of time traveling the state highways and byways. If they are fortunate, they sleep in cars and trucks; if they are not, they sleep at rest stops, all-night truck stops, in plowed fields, or on the side of the road.

In many more communities, including medium-sized cities as well as urbanized metropolitan areas, a sizable majority of the homeless population remain, if not hidden, at least relatively invisible. That is to say, most of the urban homeless populations are warehoused out of sight in abandoned armories, terminals, or motels. In part, this situation is a result of governmental assistance and programs; it is also a result, in part, of the private efforts of concerned citizens and groups, especially of church-related assistance.

In these "nonrepressive" communities, temporary or emergency assistance is available through bureaucracies that operate at all levels of government. At the same time, public and private armories and shelters—some for whole families, some for couples only, some for single women, and some for battered women and their infants—protect these homeless groups from physical elements, at least during the night. There are also various secular and religious efforts to provide the homeless, hungry, and the nearly destitute with day shelters, soup kitchens, clothes closets, and food pantries. A few notable private nonprofit secular programs out of literally hundreds of programs nationwide are the Atlanta Day Shelter for Women, the Birmingham Partnership Assistance to the Homeless, and Cincinnati's Alcoholic Drop Inn Center Shelterhouse.

Without this array of programs to regulate the behavior of the new poor and homeless, these members of society would quickly become a threatening element that would call into question established political and economic arrangements. The sheer numbers of tens of thousands of homeless people roaming the urban streets in search of food and shelter would contribute to the widespread victimization of both the homeless and others. In turn, this would contribute to the further deterioration of the urban United States and to growing social disorder.

Despite these programs and other services, such as city policies that require the police to pick up homeless individuals and drive them to one of the nearby community shelters on cold nights when the temperatures drop below zero, hundreds of Americans still freeze to death every winter. As for the homeless of communities that do not or cannot provide forms of social welfare, most do not quickly perish. Even in the most caring and compassionate urban communities, where people do not necessarily look away as they step over or around homeless persons, after a while even those unfortunate souls who can be found sleeping in doorways, in metal trash receptacles, and in homemade cardboard shelters become invisible.

The social problem of inadequate low-income housing and homelessness could be addressed by public policies. So far, however, the legislation or judicial rulings necessary for developing proactive housing policies capable of providing an adequate stock of low-income housing and of reversing current trends in U.S. homelessness have not been backed by those who have political or legal power to institute them and make them work. There is no shortage of workable ideas to rid America of homelessness; there is only a shortage of political ingenuity and political funding.

Context
In the wake of the depression of 1873 to 1875, there were some three million unemployed persons and many more poor people. At an address before the Conference

on State Charities in 1877, the poor were divided into three categories: those who had been reduced to poverty by physical or medical infirmities, the permanent paupers; people who were entitled to emergency relief because of temporary difficulties—war, famine, and natural disasters; and able-bodied persons without homes who were either unable or unwilling to work. What was missing from this categorization was a category that identified the poor as victims of structural underemployment.

A classic sociological study of Chicago's homeless population, Nels Anderson's *The Hobo* (1923,1961), listed some six reasons why people became homeless: seasonal work and unemployment, an inability to work because of physical handicaps, defects of personality, crises in the life of the person, racial or national discrimination, and wanderlust. Later, during the Great Depression, the themes of disaffiliation and nonconformity were again used to describe the homeless majority of men. One radically different theme was that articulated by Edwin Sutherland and Harvey Lock in another classic study of Chicago's homeless, *Twenty Thousand Homeless Men: A Study of Unemployed Men in the Chicago Shelters* (1936). What set their analysis apart from those earlier turn-of-the-century analyses and 1950's and 1960's studies of the homeless that were grounded in "functionalist" perspectives was Sutherland and Locke's ability to draw out the historical relationships and social experiences that differentiated the homeless from the nonhomeless, such as the dislocation of the former from the agricultural and industrial economies.

By the 1980's, the proliferation of writing on or about the homeless came to be dominated by three types of advocacy studies: those that rejected personal deficiency models of the homeless, favoring models that asserted instead that there was simply not enough low-income housing to go around, especially in urban America, thus forcing people into an involuntary state of homelessness; those that examined public policies, the shelterization process, and political responses to homelessness; and those that examined one of the several subgroups within the homeless population, such as the mentally ill, single mothers with children, or victims of AIDS.

When one examines the significant increase in homelessness from some 10,000 to more than a million in only two decades—within the context of an expanding base of poor persons in the United States, one finds that more and more people not only slipped down the socioeconomic ladder but also became part of a permanent group of have-nots. These people, many of whom had become members of the new homeless groups consisting of women and children, could therefore be regarded as marginal victims of a changing global political economy that has reduced the size of the unskilled and semiskilled industrial work force in North America. These fundamental changes in the domestic economy must be reflected in the development of social housing for the nonaffluent. Until the United States adopts a public policy grounded in both a commitment to social and economic justice and a recognition of the need for the development of an alternative approach to homelessness and inexpensive housing, the delivery of adequate and permanent housing for all persons living in the United States will remain a utopian dream of the thousands of homeless advocates and volunteers found nationwide.

Bibliography

Barak, Gregg. *Gimme Shelter: A Social History of Homelessness in Contemporary America.* New York: Praeger, 1991. The most comprehensive overview of the history and contemporary development of homelessness in America. This award-winning book goes beyond the insistence that homelessness is fundamentally a housing problem. It explains not only the root causes of homelessness but also why it is not going to "go away" unless a radically different social policy is introduced.

Golden, Stephanie. *The Women Outside: Meanings and Myths of Homelessness.* Berkeley: University of California Press, 1992. This book tells the story of homeless women throughout history. Golden brings together objective history and cultural critique with both first- and third-person writing, a technique seldom employed by authors of books on social problems. This book is both a history and an analysis of images and perceptions of homelessness as well as an examination of the socioeconomic context and psychology of homeless women.

Polakow, Valerie. *Lives on the Edge: Single Mothers and Their Children in the Other America.* Chicago: University of Chicago Press, 1993. Drawing upon historical, feminist, and public policy perspectives, Polakow develops a rich cultural critique of the femininization of poverty and the increase in child poverty. While presenting the lives of today's poor homeless children, this book locates the current crises in U.S. social and domestic policies in the history of American institutions and the history of childhood itself.

Rossi, Peter H. *Down and Out in America: The Origins of Homelessness.* Chicago: University of Chicago Press, 1989. A carefully researched and skillfully analyzed presentation of homelessness in America. This book explores the incidence of homelessness in relation to such correlates as disabilities, addictions, illnesses, lack of relatives, unemployment rates, and housing costs. Rossi, like the authors of the other books in this bibliography, highlights bold new public policies capable of addressing this increasingly serious social problem.

Snow, David A., and Leon Anderson. *Down on Their Luck: A Study of Homeless Street People.* Berkeley: University of California Press, 1993. Provides the best description available of the social order of homeless society and of the varieties of resourcefulness employed by the homeless to cope with their situations. Snow and Anderson, through interviews, participant observations, and the tracking of homeless people through social service agencies, reveal who the homeless are, how they live, and how they ended up on the streets.

Gregg Barak

Cross-References

Deinstitutionalization of Mental Patients, 469; The Feminization of Poverty, 754; Poverty: Analysis and Overview, 1453; Poverty: Women and Children, 1466; The Poverty Line and Counting the Poor, 1478; Racial and Ethnic Stratification, 1579; Social Stratification: Marxist Perspectives, 1852; Unemployment and Poverty, 2083; The Urban Underclass and the Rural Poor, 2122.

ALPHABETICAL LIST

XV

CATEGORY LIST